NEVER AGAIN

by the same author

STATES OF EMERGENCY (WITH KEITH JEFFERY)

SOURCES CLOSE TO THE PRIME MINISTER
(WITH MICHAEL COCKERELL AND DAVID WALKER)

WHAT THE PAPERS NEVER SAID

CABINET

RULING PERFORMANCE (CO-EDITOR WITH ANTHONY SELDON)

WHITEHALL

NEVER AGAIN
Britain, 1945-1951

Peter Hennessy

PANTHEON BOOKS
NEW YORK

Library of Congress Cataloging-in-Publication Data

Hennessy, Peter, 1947–
Never again : Britain, 1945–1951 / Peter Hennessy.
p.   cm.
Includes bibliographical references and index.
ISBN 0-679-43363-5
1. Great Britain—History—George VI, 1936–1952.   2. World War,
1939–1945—Great Britain—Influence.   I. Title.
DA588.H46   1994
941.085′4—dc20   93-48430
CIP

Manufactured in the United States of America
First American Edition
2 4 6 8 9 7 5 3 1

For a sextet of teachers at Marling School
who had a big influence on my personal history –
Cyril Campbell, Michael Gray, Eric Pankhurst,
Peter Young, Oliver Wicks and L.E. Godfrey-Jones

Contents

Illustrations

The author and publishers are grateful to the following for permission to reproduce illustrations: Associated Press, pls 14, 44, 48, 53; *Evening Standard/Solo Syndication*, pl. 31; Hulton Picture Co., pls 2, 3, 4, 5, 9, 10, 11, 13, 17, 18, 19, 20, 22, 25, 27, 29, 32, 35, 40, 41, 52, 57, 59, 60, 62; Imperial War Museum, London, pl. 7; Popperfoto, pls 6, 38, 54; Syndication International pl. 43; Sergeant Ernie Teal, pl. 12; Times Newspapers, pls 15, 16, 42, 45, 49, 50, 51, 55, 56; Topham Picture Source, pls 1, 8, 21, 23, 24, 26, 28, 30, 33, 34, 36, 37, 39, 46, 58, 61.

Preface

A cultivation of trained, shared remembrance sets a society in natural touch with its own past. What matters even more, it safeguards the core of individuality. What is committed to memory and susceptible of recall constitutes the ballast of the self. The pressures of political exaction, the detergent tide of social conformity, cannot tear it from us.
George Steiner, 1989[1]

Every generation is unjust to the preceding generation: it respects its distant ancestors but thinks its fathers were 'quite wrong'.
Walter Bagehot, 1868[2]

My experience of other countries stems not from reading about them or visiting them: I have lived in several, and while I lived there had no inkling that I might come to live here. Let me therefore say quite simply this: England is, perhaps was, different from any other country I know at first or second hand. As a society and a body politic it is unique in ways which are exceptionally instructive and, considering the nature of man and of the world he has built for himself, exceptionally consoling . . . I know very well that this is not a realm of unfailing virtue and goodness. That does not alter the fact that it managed to produce a form of existence which is freer of sin against one's neighbour than any other community has attained. I know as well as anyone that its managements, its unions, its weather and its restaurants stand a long way behind qualities easily attained elsewhere. But it excels in having come to terms with the fact that people in large numbers need both to be conscious of one another and leave one another alone. Its people have contributed disproportionately to the stock of human invention and achievement . . . Since it is obviously desirable to understand how an organism so untypical and yet so generally successful actually worked, the history of England retains its special claim to attention.
Professor Sir Geoffrey Elton, 1984[3]

The history of one's own country always has a 'special claim' to one's personal attention whatever its place in the spectrum of world power. It was Enoch Powell, who said, significantly enough, on a visit to Russia in 1989, that 'What an important thing memory is, collective memory. It's really collective memory that makes a nation, its memory of what its past was, what it has done, what it has suffered and what it has endured.'[4]

It was Mr Powell, too, who made me realise just how much personal passion I had put into the pages of this book shortly after I had completed the main draft. The occasion was the Institute of Contemporary British History's Summer School at the London School of Economics in July 1991. After reprising the themes of the book, I suggested that soon the historical torch would have to pass to a younger generation than mine (I was forty-four at the time), 'people who are free of nostalgia; who are not susceptible to the old drumbeat; people who don't get a spasm of one kind or another when the word "Suez" is mentioned.'[5]

This, I recorded in my diary that evening, 'stimulated the first discussant, Enoch Powell, to a tremendous outpouring of emotion'.[6] I shall never forget the effect upon his audience, their eyes widening with, I suspect, a mixture of amazement and incredulity, as that air-raid siren of a voice, its West Midlands cadences adding, as always, to the effect, rose higher with increasing intensity.

Turning to Paul Addison, Mr Powell said:

> Mr Chairman, I found myself in far-reaching sympathy with the cry from the heart with which Dr Hennessy ended his lecture. I think he is right to put his finger upon a factor which the historian chronically neglects – the emotional factor. One, of course, understands why the historian neglects it. It is unquantifiable. It is rather shameful and it is difficult to handle. But without the emotional factor, I do not think one can understand the turnaround which occurred in this country or some of the most surprising things which this country did in the second half of the twentieth century.[7]

The remarkable seventy-nine-year-old, who, alone among the postwar British political elite made the link between nation, race and patriotism in explicit terms with his notorious 'River Tiber' speech in 1968,[8] dipped into his own past to illustrate his theme. He told his ICBH audience:

> When I resigned my chair in Australia in 1939 [he had been appointed Professor of Classics at Sydney University at the age of twenty-five[9]] in order to come home to enlist, had I been asked 'What is the State whose uniform you wish to wear and in whose service you expect to perish?' I would have said 'The British Empire' . . . I also know that, on my deathbed, I shall still be believing with one part of my brain that somewhere on every ocean of the world there is a great, grey ship with three funnels and sixteen-inch guns which can blow out of the water any other navy which is likely to face it. I know it is not so. Indeed, I realised at a relatively early age

that it is not so. But that factor – that emotional factor . . . will not die until I, the carrier of it, am dead.[10]

I am not a 'grey-funnels-on-the-horizon' man, nor am I a 'River-Tiber-foaming-with-much-blood' man. But I know what Mr Powell means and I know there is a great deal of my own equivalent emotion in these pages. As a child of the late 1940s, a grammar school boy and a product of the 1944 Education Act, I could not have written without a degree of personal passion.

I have, however, been carried along by other streams than the mere emotional. I have tried very hard to ensure that solid historical evidence has been the main determinant of what moves through the coming chapters. Above all, there has been deep fascination in telling the story of the world in which my generation, the postwar baby boomers, was born and grew up.

In that same inaugural lecture in Cambridge from which I quoted at the head of this Preface, Sir Geoffrey Elton said that 'the long-term history of England continues to merit attention even though the Empire is gone and we no longer wish to show off the Westminster Parliament as the last word in political wisdom'. He went on to declare his conviction that 'we shall never properly understand the history of the last millennium unless we preserve and improve our understanding of the way in which over that long span of time the people and rulers of England – for most of that time a small and seemingly insignificant realm – managed their existence between those two inescapable reference points: the misery of birth and the certainty of death'.[11]

My postwar history will cover a mere fifty-five years – from 1945 to the turn of the twentieth and twenty-first centuries – a far cry from the long stretches of history Sir Geoffrey believes a reader needs to absorb the essence of his or her nation, and it will cover the whole of the UK not just England. Its volumes will, however, be written in the knowledge that five-and-a-half decades in the life of a country, especially an ancient, sovereign entity like the United Kingdom, is but the blinking of an eye. Yet I hope they will contribute to the creation of that historical 'continuum' Sir Geoffrey rightly regards as vital for a nation to possess, and not fall into the error of treating the people and episodes of the postwar years as 'portions or sections' of a truncated whole.

In the course of preparing Volume One I have accumulated heavy debts of gratitude to individuals and institutions. Three clusters deserve special mention: my fellow historians in the Institute of Contemporary British History, the members of the Twentieth Century British Policy and Administration Seminar at the Institute of Historical Research and the remarkable team which produces the BBC Radio 4 *Analysis* programme. Not only have they provided me with a second home, but several productions, especially *Moneybags and Brains*, a study of the US–UK 'special relationship', and *From Clogs to Clogs?*, an appraisal of Britain's relative economic decline (both made with Dr Caroline Anstey), had a crucial, shaping influence on this volume.

Once more I owe a huge bundle of gratitude to that energising duo of Giles Gordon, my agent, and David Godwin, my publisher, to Anne Newman, my editor, Tony Raven, my indexer, Cathie Arrington, my picture researcher and to my friend Mrs Sheila McNeil who types my chapters and has the feel of the Attlee years in her bones. Thanks, as always, to those superb document grubbers, the staff of the Public Record Office, and to my researchers Brett Arends, Sarah Smith and Rebecca Farr. I am grateful, too, to Lady Clarke for allowing me to make use of the diaries of the late Sir Richard Clarke and to Lady Younger for permission (via Professor Geoffrey Warner) to quote from the diaries of the late Sir Kenneth Younger.

Finally I must thank a fistful of schoolteachers. First John Douglas, Mike Brown and Beverley Wilson of the Sir George Monoux Sixth Form College in Walthamstow who, once a year, allow me to try out my thoughts on the coming generation at a one-day Postwar British History Workshop. Each year they remind me both how central history is to any properly balanced school curriculum and just how gifted teachers can be, as I know only too well from my thirty-year-old memories from Marling School in Stroud when Cyril Campbell, Michael Gray, Eric Pankhurst, Peter Young, Oliver Wicks and L.E. Godfrey-Jones played such a critical role in shaping my own youthful mind. This book is dedicated to them with affection and gratitude.

Peter Hennessy
Walthamstow, April 1992

Introduction

There *is* something distinctive and recognisable in English civilization . . . It is somehow bound up with solid breakfasts and gloomy Sundays, smoky towns and winding roads, green fields and red pillar boxes. It has a flavour of its own. Moreover it is continuous, it stretches into the future and the past, there is something in it that persists, as in a living creature . . . And above all, it is *your* civilisation, it is *you*. However much you hate it or laugh at it, you will never be happy away from it for any length of time.
George Orwell, *The Lion and the Unicorn*, 1940[1]

The politician has to simplify in order to do his business with his public: but the historian can be so obsessed with the falsity of simplification as to qualify his subject out of recognisability.
Enoch Powell, 1988[2]

I first read George Orwell's *The Lion and the Unicorn* in the autumn of 1973 shortly after I returned with my wife Enid from a year spent in the United States. Its patriotism, its adoring yet critical appraisal of the English character and tradition, its loving embellishment of the decencies of everyday life, its appalled recognition of its accepted brutalities, left a mark that has never been erased. I suspect it helped germinate the seed of a desire that has grown intense with the passage of time – to write a history of Britain which can encompass my own lifetime (I was born in 1947, trace my first memory to 1950 and my sustained interest in current affairs to the Suez autumn of 1956) and be written, like Orwell's incomparable essay, with his mixture of affection, irritation and candour. In the autumn of 1988, sixteen years after getting off the overnight TWA flight from Boston to Heathrow, liking America but longing for home, I picked up my fountain pen and started writing it in earnest.

The plan was to spread the project over twelve years to cover the fifty-five years from the end of the Second World War to the end of the twentieth century. The aim was to create a picture of British life – embracing high politics and everyday experience – from Court and Cabinet Room to kitchen and queue. The technique was to pitch the narrative somewhere between the meticulousness of the historian's fine print and the word-pictures and simplifications of the politician. There is a profession which trains you to do this. It's called journalism, a craft I practised full-time from 1972 to 1984 and part-time thereafter. I even used to regard my job on *The Times* in its old, paper-of-record incarnation, as helping provide the first rough draft of history.[3]

Each volume is watertight in the sense of being a self-contained read and not requiring vast amounts of prior knowledge of the preceding period or hindsight about what is to come after. But I hope the series when complete will be much more than the sum of its parts and, above all, that it will be readable. History for me is the Queen of the Arts. The moment it ceases to be fun to write and a pleasure to read it has abdicated its throne.

Postwar Britain cannot be understood at all without a proper appreciation of *the* great formative experience which shaped it and dominated its economics, its politics and its ethos for at least three decades – the war itself. This first volume, though the date on its title page is 1945, really begins, therefore, in September 1938 with the Munich Crisis, and a substantial chapter on the British at war marks its prologue. It ends in October 1951, when the first postwar Labour Government of Clement Attlee falls and is replaced by Winston Churchill's Conservatives.

I've called the first volume *Never Again* as, for me, the phrase captures the motivating impulse of the first half-dozen years after the war – never again would there be war; never again would the British people be housed in slums, living off a meagre diet thanks to low wages or no wages at all; never again would mass unemployment blight the lives of millions; never again would natural abilities remain dormant in the absence of educational stimulus.

Of course there were setbacks. The economy was a near-constant disappointment. The bundle of social and economic problems the welfare state was designed to break open and solve proved tough to crack. But real progress there was; progress on a scale and a duration never surpassed in the nation's history.

Of course greed and selfishness and sectional interest remained. No state, short of a seventeenth-century puritan's ideal of 'rule of the saints', could curb that (and not even then). Altruism could not be spread across the land courtesy of Beveridge and Attlee. Yet the period was lived, in public and political life at least, on a higher plane than certainly the interwar decades.

It was an age dominated by the shadow of war, its accomplishments and shortcomings constantly measured against the hopes and expectations of 1945 when, this time, Britain really was going to be a land fit for returning war heroes to live, work and raise a family in. Virtually every serious politician, certainly every senior one, acted and calculated within the boundaries of what became known as 'the postwar settlement' built around an understanding that Britain would remain a great power abroad while operating a mixed economy and building a welfare state at home, a presupposition that a change of government from Labour to Conservative in 1951 did little to alter.

By the late 1970s the legacy of this 'consensus', the accumulated inheritance of the 1940s, was the very stuff of political dispute. The understanding had broken down and with it came a revived partisanship whose stridency spilled over into retrospective writings about the period which brought heat but not always light to its events and to the personalities who sought to shape them. All too often passion meant parody. In crossing any battlefield, care over small matters is essential as is an appreciation of the bigger strategic picture, the wider context in which individual happenings occurred. And in order to meet the need for perspective, the story of Britain's road to war has to begin in the summer of 1938 before a shot had been fired in anger between the British Empire and the German Reich.

The war chapter, 'Who Do You Think You Are Kidding?', is a big one as are several of those which follow it. The reason the volume is 'front heavy' is the need to bring the reader up to speed on each theme as it's first tackled, explaining, for example, the several stages through which the early welfare state and its precursors passed before the great burst of creative activity in the postwar period. Once the historical background has been covered, the pace will quicken and the style will become more narrative. I hope the reader will bear with me in the scene-setting sections. For without them, perspective would be lacking.

CHAPTER 1

Who Do You Think
You Are Kidding?

Who do you think you're kidding, Mr Hitler,
If you think Old England's done?
We are the boys who will stop your little game,
We are the boys who will make you think again.
Bud Flanagan, 1969[1]

In the Second World War the British people came of age. This was a people's war . . . Few now sang *Land of Hope and Glory*. Few even sang *England Arise*. England had risen all the same.
A.J.P. Taylor, 1965[2]

England is the most class-ridden country under the sun. It is a land of snobbery and privilege, ruled largely by the old and silly. But in any calculation about it one has got to take into account its emotional unity, the tendency of nearly all its inhabitants to feel alike and act together in moments of supreme crisis.
George Orwell, 1941[3]

There is a total gulf in politics today, among Cabinet colleagues, between those who were brought up in the 1930s and served in the war, and those who didn't. It's a very strange and almost indefinable difference.
Lord Whitelaw, 1988[4]

The Second World War and Britain's part in it is one of the most heavily ploughed patches of our history. It would be impossible and pointless for me to crawl over every square foot of a vast field. I shall concentrate, therefore, on a few themes and occasional episodes which are essential to understanding the condition of Britain, its people and its politics, when the postwar period begins. Such a crowded seven-year stretch from Munich to Lüneberg Heath (where Montgomery took the German surrender) cannot be tackled in a single dash. I have divided it into three sections – 'The Beginning', from Munich to the fall of Neville Chamberlain; 'The Shock-Absorber', covering the Battle of Britain and the Blitz, the critical year when Britain stood alone between Germany and Hitler's aim of a Nazi-dominated Europe; and 'The Long Haul', the endless slog on the battlefields, the oceans, in the air and in the factories of the Home Front until the white flags appeared along the Wehrmacht's front-line.

PART ONE: *The Beginning, 1938–40*

My son would stay at school and go to Oxford in the autumn. My home and children, like all the other homes throughout the country, would be spared . . . It was as if we had come to the edge of a precipice and then – by some miracle – had been pulled back to safety. Yet when we met to discuss the true situation and to hear the reflections of those whose judgment we trusted, we began to see beyond the fragile screen of complacency and self-deception, skilfully designed to delude a whole people and lull them into a fictitious sense of security.
Harold Macmillan on Munich, September 1938[1]

I was at home, having just returned from camp, and was eating a late breakfast of bacon and fried bread. I was alone, the rest of the family having gone to Church, but I had the radio and the cat for company. As I listened to the sepulchral tones of Mr Neville Chamberlain . . . I realized things had gone from bad to worse in my absence, and when he finished, the ominous wail of the air-raid sirens began, I put down my knife and fork and went over to the window, I could see the balloons all going up into the sky like lifts, until hundreds of these silver sausages floated over London. 'This is it,' I told the cat, and realizing that I could do nothing about it, we both sat down to breakfast again, I to my bacon, he to his rinds.
Captain E.G.M. Roe, recalling 3 September 1939[2]

All you could hear was the feet of the children and a kind of murmur because the children were too afraid to talk. We had a big banner with our number in front . . . Mothers weren't allowed with us but they came along behind. When we got to the station we knew which platform to go to, the train was ready, we hadn't the slightest idea where we were going and we put the children on the train and the gates closed behind us. The mothers pressed against the iron gates calling, 'Goodbye darling'. I never see those gates at Waterloo that I don't get a lump in my throat.
A schoolteacher recalling the Great Evacuation of September 1939[3]

The PM has come back from the Palace . . . The King has sent for Winston . . . Alec [Home] and I went over to the FO to explain the position to Rab [Butler], and there, with Chips [Channon], we drank in champagne the health of the 'King over the Water' [Chamberlain]. Rab said he thought that

the good clean tradition of English politics, that of Pitt as opposed to Fox, had been sold to the greatest adventurer of modern political history.
Sir John Colville, diary entry for 10 May 1940[4]

It was the gas masks that did it, that and the trenches which appeared over-night in the public parks and private gardens in the last days of September 1938, crude pits dug as primitive air-raid shelters, when for many in Britain war with Germany seemed inevitable before the month was out. During the Munich crisis the country went over to a war mentality, if not to a proper war footing (our lack of readiness remains a legend even in a notoriously 'eleventh hour' nation). The surge of relief, when Neville Chamberlain returned from Bavaria with his scrap of paper signed by Hitler, was but a temporary abeyance in a state of mind that was to endure for nearly seven years.

The rights and wrongs of Hitler's claim to the Sudetenland, the German-speaking part of Czechoslovakia, the comings and goings of what is now a familiar pattern of shuttle diplomacy (but was then a novel use of air travel by a sixty-nine-year-old Victorian gentleman in a wing collar) created a sense of apprehension among the people at large. Saturation coverage in the popular papers and on the wireless, *the* great medium of mass communication in the 1930s, saw to that. But it took the fitting of those tight, smelly, H.G. Wellsian science-fantasy contraptions – the gas masks – to turn apprehension into fear and sometimes panic.

It was on 27 September 1938, between Chamberlain's second and third flights to Germany, that Air Raid Precautions (ARP), the fledgling nationwide civil defence organisation pieced together by the Home Office, distributed the masks – 38 million of them for a population of some 45 million.[5] Mass Obser-vation (MO), the pioneering and independent opinion-polling organisation, with three regularly manned posts in 'Metrop' (Fulham, West London), 'Worktown' (Bolton in Central Lancashire) and Blackpool, watched and lis-tened as the unemployed, temporarily recruited by councils, dug up the green-swards of municipal life and thousands, including herdsmen on the Lancashire moors,[6] prepared for mustard gas from the skies. 'With distribution of gas masks', one MO observer reported, 'began real fear. All over the place one heard: "To think that one man [Hitler] is responsible for all this!" "War! It doesn't bear thinking of."[7]'

Tom Harrisson and Charles Madge, the young pioneers of MO, writing to a 'Penguin Special' deadline within days of Munich, noted that 'Gas masks brought the war danger home to everybody and to every home. It was demo-cracy inverted – everyone had the vote, now everyone had a mask. Especially among the women and the elderly, fear grew almost to a panic, as can be seen from these reports from all over the country:

'After lunch I went to be fitted . . . I was horribly sick after a half-minute, through the smell of the rubber, and have been feeling nauseated since during the afternoon. Two colleagues of mine were fitting masks, and they said they had a dreadful morning, with babies and toddlers crying and screaming. Quite a number of elderly folk looked ill, an expectant mother fainted, an old lady had a heart attack.'

'A neighbour who lives alone and is rather timid opened the door last night to a man with a gas mask. She was so frightened that her knees shook for half an hour after his visit.'

'Some children thought the gas was in the defence valve and said they could smell it. Actually it was the Izal used for disinfectant.'[8]

At such times, as the mass observers constantly found, ordinary people felt left in the dark by the authorities. Rumour reigned. The sale of wills soared. Marriages shot up by 500 per cent.[9] On this occasion those in charge scarcely knew better. On his own initiative Chamberlain mobilised the Fleet.[10] The reservists swung into Chatham Naval Base singing 'The Lambeth Walk', the hit tune from the West End show *Me and My Girl* then sweeping everyone off their feet, whatever their station in life.

At the Chelsea Barracks, crack troops of the Brigade of Guards were told by their officers that they 'were going to fly to Czechoslovakia from Croydon to stop that feller Hitler'. The guardsmen were confined to barracks, their kit and weapons prepared.[11]

What few anti-aircraft guns there were – forty-four of them to be precise – were trundled out to protect London from the Luftwaffe. A flurry of fat, silver-grey cigars, the barrage balloons, wallowed in the skies above the capital which only served to unnerve the citizenry even more.[12] The King fretted about 'this awful waiting for the worst to happen' and did what he could by giving retrospective authority to Chamberlain's activities by calling a Privy Council and issuing a Royal Proclamation to cover the mobilisation of the reserves and declaring a State of Emergency.[13] Meanwhile, the head of the Secret Intelligence Service, Sir Stewart Menzies, arguably the best-informed man in the Kingdom, put his organisation on a war footing and despatched his code-breakers to Station X, Bletchley Park in Buckinghamshire, where, when war came, they were to perform herculean feats of brainpower and technical innovation.[14]

All in all, the general public was gripped in a way it had not been since that first great wireless-enhanced event, the Abdication, in December 1936, had despatched King Edward VIII into oblivion and propelled his reluctant, retiring, stammering brother, 'Bertie', into Buckingham Palace as King George VI. Unlike the crisis in the monarchy, uncertainty in Europe could not be ended by the near singlehanded actions of a British Prime Minister. Wallis Simpson's determination may have matched that of Hitler (as her grip on the British Sunday newspaper-reading public was to continue to do after 1945), but the wilful only matter, in global terms, when they are in control of a country positioned, like Germany, at a strategic crossroads and backed by a sophisti-cated war machine.

After Munich, Britain set about acquiring one of its own with a vengeance in the first of several organisational improvements and production surges which by 1944 made it the most thoroughly mobilised of any of the combatant nations on either side, Allied or Axis.[15] Much of the preoccupation had to do with the air where pretty well every expert, from the top brass around the Chiefs of Staff Committee table to the 'experts' in the pub tap-room, thought the next war would be decided, in contrast to the mud of the Franco-Belgian border of the Great War. In September 1938 the Royal Air Force had six efficient squad-rons. When war came a year later it had twenty-six. Radar cover, confined to the Thames estuary during the Munich crisis, was in action as a defensive shield from Orkney to the Isle of Wight by the time the first air-raid warning wailed across the land on Sunday 3 September 1939.[16]

Two months after Munich, probably the greatest administrative genius ever produced by the British Civil Service, Sir John Anderson, was appointed Lord Privy Seal by Chamberlain with a brief to bring civil defence to the centre of civilian life. The funding of ARP soon rose fivefold. And the Anderson shelter, a primitive but effective device of folded corrugated iron covered by earth, carried its begetter's name into countless back gardens, though it was, in fact, designed by an engineer friend of Anderson's, William Patterson. The first 'Anderson' came off the production line in February 1939. By the time war came, 1.5 million of them had been installed, capable of sheltering 6 million people, and production was running at 50,000 a week.[17] Patterson, together with the designer of the 'pill box' gun emplacement for taking on the invading Germans, had more influence on the mid-century British landscape than anyone else, apart from the Luftwaffe itself, of course, the first and worst unwanted developer of our city centres.

Casualty forecasts were grimly immense and, mercifully, were to prove hugely exaggerated. In 1937 the Committee of Imperial Defence had calculated that if aerial bombardment of Britain lasted sixty days there could be as many as 1,200,000 casualties. In April 1939 a Cabinet committee decided 300,000 hospital beds were all that could be provided and the Ministry of Health was instructed to proceed accordingly.[18] A month after Munich the Cabinet were informed that 5 per cent of all property in Britain would be destroyed in the first three weeks of war. The Home Office calculated that 20 million square feet of timber per month would be required for coffins.[19]

With every month the arrival of the bomber seemed more likely. Hitler demonstrated beyond question his lie at Munich, when he said Germany's territorial claims were sated by the absorption of the Sudetenland into the Reich, by seizing the rest of Czechoslovakia on 15 March 1939. Poland was plainly to be the next victim on the list of conquests. By the end of March the British Government had pledged support to the Poles should they be threatened. On 25 August the pledge was converted into a formal alliance. Six days later Germany invaded Poland.

Sunday 3 September 1939, the day war broke out, is one of the most heavily chronicled days in British history. Anyone who was anyone, and anybody with anything interesting to relate, had their say about that singular day in British life. But for anyone with the slightest understanding of current affairs or the most fleeting concern with the doings of Adolf Hitler (which, thanks to the mind-concentrating days of the Munich Crisis meant practically everybody), the day that war became inevitable was the Friday before – 1 September – when German troops invaded Poland. The War Minister, Leslie Hore-Belisha (immortalised by the flashing yellow beacons he had installed by every pedestrian crossing in the land as Transport Minister) was awakened at his country home at 5.30 a.m. by a phone call from the Chief of the Imperial General Staff, Lord Gort, giving him the news. He returned to Whitehall to mobilise the army.[20]

Fifty miles away in Oxford, the man whose biography of Hitler was to win him an international reputation after the war,[21] was at work on his doctoral thesis devoted to Elizabeth I's policy towards France after another invasion threat, that of the Spanish Armada, had been averted. 'On September 1 1939', Alan Bullock told me years later, 'I was sitting at home taking notes on France in the 1590s. The wireless was on and it announced there were bombs on Poland. I closed the book and thought that was the end of that.'[22] It was. The thesis was never finished. Alan Bullock went on to help set up the BBC's wartime broadcasts to Europe, to a career as a twentieth- as opposed to a sixteenth-century British historian, a college and university administrator of distinction and the chairmanship of several Government-appointed committees of the 'good and the great'.

In different ways and to varying degrees Hitler had that kind of effect on most of the 46 million lives still being lived in relative tranquillity in Britain that September Friday in 1939. 'Wars', as the 'Home Front' historian Arthur Marwick likes to remark, 'are like weddings: essentially extravagant and unnecessary but a great stimulant in a convention-bound society.'[23] And few advanced societies come more convention-bound than Britain's in the late 1930s. But for all that, the shock of Poland was less than that of the Czech crisis a year earlier. Once Hitler had marched into Prague in March 1939 for most people it became a question of when war came rather than whether. As the historian of the Home Front, Norman Longmate, wrote, 'the war which began on that sunny autumn morning, the 3 September 1939, was the least unexpected war in history'.[24]

But the outcome of that war was far from certain for a very long time, not, in fact, until another Sunday – 7 December 1941 – when the Japanese attacked the American Fleet in Hawaii at their base in Pearl Harbor. Churchill, who heard the news on his 'small wireless set' at Chequers, was overcome with relief. 'So we had won after all! . . . We should not be wiped out. Our history would not come to an end . . . Being saturated and satiated with emotion and sensation, I went to bed and slept the sleep of the saved and thankful.'[25]

Within days Hitler had declared war on the United States in the most beneficial, if longest delayed, suicide note ever written. Victory was only a matter of time though it took nearly three and a half punishing years to achieve and the expenditure of much blood and treasure in payment for it. By the time peace came, the abrasions of war had scoured every avenue of life, every channel of activity in Britain. New assumptions gleamed where old certainties had been whisked away under the pressure and motion uniquely applied by total war. Everything – the parameters of politics, the organisation of industry, the place of labour, the status of women, the philosophy of economics, the power and reach of the State – had altered visibly. It was as if all the historical processes at work in Britain had been speeded up when one man, Adolf Hitler, pressed the button for the invasion of Poland in September 1939.

In the early months of the conflict, however, such an assertion would have been greeted with incredulity and derision. The period of the Phoney War – from September 1939 to May 1940 – was surreal, as if a people was living on borrowed time in the knowledge that at any moment, literally out of the blue, could come death and destruction on a scale that could only be imagined.

Though the twenty-four hours in which war came were not without drama. As the Cabinet broke up at midnight, having met after the heated Saturday debate in the House of Commons which convinced even the most determined appeasers that the country would stand for no more vacillation, a thunder storm broke over London as if the whole event was being orchestrated by some celestial Richard Wagner. With the Cabinet's approval a telegram was drafted and encoded for transmission to Sir Nevile Henderson, the British Ambassador in Berlin. Hitler was to withdraw his troops from Poland or a state of war would exist between Britain and Germany. At eleven that Sunday morning the deadline expired. No reply had been received from Berlin. At eleven-fifteen Neville Chamberlain's mournful voice came through just about every wireless set in the land.

He returned to the Cabinet Room from his study where his ministers were waiting. The drollest if most fervent of the appeasers, R.A. Butler, then the junior minister to Lord Halifax, the Foreign Secretary, recalled:

He had hardly asked his colleagues how we liked it [the broadcast], when the air was rent by a terrible wailing which no wartime Londoner will ever forget. 'That is an air-raid warning,' announced Chamberlain quite calmly. We all laughed, and someone said, 'It would be funny if it were.' He repeated several times, like a schoolteacher dinning a lesson into a class of late developers, 'That is an air-raid warning!' Then Mrs Chamberlain appeared in the doorway with a large basket containing books, thermos flasks, gas masks and other aids to waiting, and everybody began to make their way to the War Room through the basement of No. 10. I found myself alone in the Cabinet Room. A few people were scurrying across Horse Guards to try to take shelter. I decided that I had better die in the Foreign

Office and so walked slowly across Downing Street, which was by then deserted.[26]

But 'Rab' didn't die. Nobody did on this occasion. The sirens had wailed across southern England because an RAF pilot, flying home unexpectedly from France, had appeared on the radar screens and been mistaken for a Luftwaffe aircraft. 'That phase', wrote Rab, 'which was later to be called the Phoney War (and by some humorists the 'bore war') had started with a phoney alarm.'[27]

The 'phoniness' of that peculiar period, between the declaration of war and the fall of the Low Countries and France in the Spring of 1940, which placed Hitler literally on Britain's doorstep as he danced a jig on the cliffs of northern France in sight of the White Cliffs of Dover, can be overdone, however. There were serious military engagements, the most spectacular being at sea. The *Graf Spee*, a German pocket battleship which had caused havoc raiding British shipping in the Atlantic, was driven up the River Plate in Uruguay by relatively lightly armed ships of the Royal Navy where her captain scuttled her on Hitler's orders in December 1939. A chill had gone through the nation in October when a German U-Boat penetrated the Navy's supposed safe haven in northern waters – Scapa Flow – and sunk the great battleship, *Royal Oak*, one of the huge floating gun platforms kept up by the Fleet since the First World War. It sank within thirteen minutes of U 47's two torpedoes striking home with the loss of 833 men out of a ship's company of 1,400. The shore was a mere mile-and-a-half away. But swimming at night in the thick furnace oil which clogged the Flow was near impossible.[28]

The Royal Navy was the symbol of British strength. Ours was, after all, *the* classic seaborne Empire. Remember what Enoch Powell said about the image that would haunt his deathbed.

The Fleet and most potently its great capital ships like the *Royal Oak* were the steely manifestations of our supposed impregnability and never more so in the autumn of 1939 when it was Britain's naval might that people expected to trump the superiority of Germany's forces on land by enforcing a shipping blockade which would starve its civilian population and deprive Hitler's war machine of the raw materials needed for protracted conflict.

The concentrated human cost of over 800 lives lost in one night was a deep shock at that stage of the war before people had become hardened to big body counts. The young Frank Cooper, just finishing at grammar school in Manchester (he later became a Spitfire pilot and ultimately the top civil servant at the Ministry of Defence in the mid-1970s) can still remember hearing the news of his sixteen-year-old schoolfriend, Kenneth England, who went down in the *Royal Oak*. 'It was a very personal thing. It brought the war home to you in a very personal way.'[29] Nearly fifty years after the *Royal Oak* was sunk I witnessed the eeriness that surrounds a war grave at sea from the coast road just south of Kirkwall (the Flow is a mecca for divers, given the clarity of its water and the wrecks which lie there from the interred and scuttled German High Seas Fleet of the Kaiser's War; but they keep away from *Royal Oak* which, occasionally, still emits pools of oil from its corroded tanks). The Royal Naval Cemetery at Lyness on the bleak Orkney Island of Hoy on the other side of the Flow contains the beautifully tended graves of many of the men who died that night – probably the most moving Second World War monument I have experienced.

Phoney or not it was already plain that this war was going to be like no other war. It would not just be a battle conducted at sea or on distant land wherever a British garrison or a naval squadron commanded palm or pine (to use the phrase beloved of old Empire hands). The front line was here, in everybody's front room and back garden. The bomber, as everyone knew, would see to that. In this sense it was a 'People's War' long before the solidarity and the enforced collectivism of the Home Front began to change the nature of individual relationships and the wider configurations of British society and politics.

Just as the fitting of the gas mask is, with Chamberlain's scrap of paper at Heston Aerodrome, the symbolic photographic memory of Munich, the visual image of the first weekend of the war is waves of children, address labels round their necks, gas-mask bags hanging from their shoulders, satchels on their backs, scraps of luggage in their hands, trudging to the city and suburban railway stations to get on the evacuation specials. Just about every steam locomotive and railway carriage was pressed into service that weekend. Kids from London's East End boroughs which lined the Thames left by riverboat for the calm of East Anglia. Ironically, they were going closer to Hitler than the parents they left behind. In Sheffield fear of Adolf's long arm caused many parents to keep their children at home rather than send them to the designated area in Lincolnshire.[30]

During the last two months of peace and the first week of war nearly 3.75 million people moved from 'evacuation' areas to 'reception' areas (these were usually separated by what the civil defence planners called 'neutral' areas), a mixture of mothers, children and their teachers. Each had a very personal story to tell, a veritable ratatouille of excitement, fear, pain of separation, joy of discovering another and wonderful rural England for an urban generation which very often didn't travel to a British, let alone a foreign coast, if they took a holiday at all. It was, too, a story of the underclass and the middle (sometimes even the upper) classes discovering each other and their variations in diet, clothing, hygiene and the use of English. Never before had Disraeli's 'two nations' been forced into such intimate and enduring proximity.

The folk tales which emerged have all too often the air of a black Ealing Comedy. These two could be reproduced a thousand times. Ben Wicks' compilation preserves the memory of Joan Tyson who was twenty-one years old when her parents took a group of evacuees from industrial Manchester into their rural home:

Each night was spent in de-lousing these two little boys, as they were infested with lice. With newspapers spread out on the table, a small tooth comb and a good light, it was the case of who could collect the most lice between my sister and me. They did not appear to know the use for a knife and fork as they never sat down to a meal at a table and lived on sandwiches. When [they were] out playing, their mother lowered their food down on a rope, as they lived in a flat . . .

When their parents came from Manchester to see them, arriving by train after lunch, their first call was the public house, so they were always merry when they reached us late in the afternoon. Their father would always sing for us, standing before the fireplace . . . My mother found this embarrassing but my sister and I would be stifling our laughter till we ached with the effort.[31]

Sometimes the strain of criminality was added to less important, if personally disturbing differences. Bryan Coleman lived with his parents in Dunstable, a small town in Bedfordshire. Their evacuee family, the 'Bates', arrived from London:

The children would make wild animals' behaviour look like angels. Their toilet training – they were ten, seven and five – was non-existent, absolutely appalling. Mrs 'Bates', their mother, went out every night to the local [public house] with her friend Mrs 'Davies', who was taken in by my grandmother. Mrs 'Bates' brewed tansy tea the following morning which she took as a 'get rid' potion. Mr 'Bates' appeared suddenly one weekend, he had apparently just been released from a long prison sentence. Mrs 'Davies' disappeared, taking my grandmother's best fur coat with her.[32]

One of the evacuation stories is beyond Ealing Comedy and fit only for one of those cock-eyed Will Hay film comedies of the war years. It was sent in by Frederick Partridge who showed himself the kind of promising child MI5 could have made use of in later life:

We were forty-eight children and they only had billets for forty-six. The rich man of the village said he didn't want any evacuees and his son lived next door. When the vicar explained they had two boys he agreed to take one and the son took the other boy.

So I spent two and a half years living in his big house. We were driven up by the vicar the next day and I'd never been in a car before. On the gear-lever was a diagram that I thought was a swastika. So when we got to the house we told him that the man who drove us had a swastika in his car. So the local bobby was alerted and went round to interrogate the vicar.[33]

Many evacuee stories are heart-rending, ranging from homesickness, protracted coldness or indifference towards vulnerable little children by those who reluctantly took them in, to downright physical or mental cruelty and even child-abuse. Some experiences, however, were idyllic by any standards. Brian Cleminson lived in Leyton close to The Bakers' Arms on the Leyton-Walthamstow boundary in the inner suburbs of north-east London. His family kept a fruit stall on the cobbles in front of The Bakers' Arms pub.

He can't remember his first evacuation billet as he was not quite four when war broke out. When he was five he was moved to Gerrards Cross in Buckinghamshire. And, though separated from his sister, he remembers his five years there with nothing but pleasure:

> I stayed with Richard and Harriet Harman. He was a publisher, the Blandford Press – lots of books on birds and plants – she wrote children's books. They had a daughter, Hilary, who was seven years older than me. We got on well.
>
> They were very religious people and lived life as truly religious people. He wouldn't tell a lie, wouldn't do anything that was wrong. They just took me into the family. He always treated me as a son. They sent me to a private school. As far as I know they paid. They taught me to be fair, not to cheat. I've got a Bible she gave me.

When Brian Cleminson returned to Leyton at the end of the war he didn't miss the Harmans – 'I started roaming the streets with all the other lads; it was a whole different life'. But they kept in touch. Brian would go to Mr Harman's office in the city as a teenager. He sat in at board meetings sometimes and they would lunch together afterwards. The Harmans would visit the Cleminsons' stall in Leyton. They came to Brian's wedding in 1957 and, when he bought his own shop shortly after, Mr Harman helped him with a loan. They kept in touch until Mr Harman died in 1969.[34]

Evacuation left a mark on a large chunk of the country's urban children in the 1940s which endured, not just in the kind of friendship which meant a great deal to Brian Cleminson, but in a variety of ways. One of the most fascinating passages in Wicks' book is the recollection of Freda Risley (now Mrs Costa). She was an evacuee in Cornwall. Despite the kindness shown to her by 'Mrs S',

> the whole experience marked me for life. Until fairly recent years I suffered bad bouts of homesickness if I was away from home for any time; I find it exceptionally difficult to trust anyone other than my husband; for a large part of my young adult life I suffered badly from depression and feelings of rejection – I am angry that the whole scheme was so ill thought-out and put into operation – they were messing about with children's lives, for God's sake, how dare they give it so little thought!
>
> I thought at the time, and I still think, that because they needed our mothers to work long hours in munitions, evacuation served a dual purpose – it got us away from the big towns and it also provided cheap child care.
>
> The war – and the war effort – was paramount and I think this is why we

only hear good experiences. I don't deny these experiences; anyone lucky enough to have been billeted with Mrs S. in Wadebridge and people like her has only good experiences to relate. But there was another, darker side, and I think it has been covered up and I'm bitter about it. I still get upset – old newsreels showing evacuees with those damned luggage labels round their neck still make me weep.

On the positive side, since I work with children, I've learned invaluable lessons. I never take an adult's word against a child's at face value; I respect what kids have to say. I credit them with more understanding and awareness than is general. I know why battered children never tell, and I'm pretty good at spotting when something is wrong. Children trust me – it helps in my work. But was the evacuation experience worth it to have gained understanding? On balance – no. It brought too much misery at the time and its effects ruined large parts of my life for too long.[35]

As for the areas the children left to whatever fate the gods of war had in store for them, civil defence planners devoted frantic attention in the autumn of 1939. ARP became the most familiar acronym of the day.

The nationwide network, put together with remarkable speed after Munich, was put at battle stations on 23 August with the arrival of a single code-worded telegram – 'WOW' – sent to Regional Commissioners who, like Oliver Cromwell's major-generals 300 years before, parcelled out the country between them with, as it happened, near identical boundaries. The Regional Commissioner for the Metropolis, Sir Harold Scott, a senior but remarkably unstuffy Home Office civil servant, installed himself, with defiant perversity, in one of the few all-glass buildings in Thirties London – the Geological Survey Office and Museum in South Kensington (in fact it was a steel-framed construction and scarcely a pane of glass was lost throughout the whole war).[36]

In short, it was Scott's job to cover greater London and the adjacent parts of Essex, Middlesex, Kent and Surrey not just with Anderson shelters but with sandbags, too, to protect people and buildings from blast. The exercise illustrated to perfection the way the demands of war changed every part of the traditional British landscape, the bureaucratic as much as the physical. 'I myself', Scott wrote later,

could not afford too strict a respect for orthodox Civil Service procedure: this was not the time to apply the lessons of precedent learned in my apprenticeship at the Home Office. Thus, towards the end of August I had to organise the filling of hundreds of thousands of sandbags to protect buildings of every kind and description. It was obvious that vast quantities of sand would be needed beyond the normal limits of the market, and to buy it at the current commercial price of about fifteen shillings a yard [75p; the 1989 price was £17 for a yard] would run up an enormous bill; so I asked the Geological Survey (our involuntary hosts in Exhibition Road) to select some twenty sites, well distributed throughout the Region, where sand could be readily excavated . . .

Meanwhile I arranged for the hiring of every available mechanical excavator within fifty miles of London, dividing this task force between the sites selected by the Survey, and the public was told that it could take away as much sand as it could carry. There was an overwhelming response from both public bodies and private citizens; a special corps of telephonists was on duty day and night giving advice and information on Operation Sand, as it would no doubt have been called in the later jargon of the war; and millions of yards of sand were distributed at a cost which worked out at less than a shilling [5p] a yard.

Nowhere was sacred, not even one of the most elegant and green patches of central London:

In Hyde Park the site of the 1851 Exhibition was excavated to a depth of some forty feet, uncovering the concrete foundations of the original Crystal Palace, and leaving an enormous crater. This was later filled by rubble from London's bombed buildings, which rose to a mound forty-feet high; and this in turn vanished, for it was carried away to East Anglia to make the foundations for those runways from which the American Superfortresses carried even greater destruction to the cities of Germany.[37]

The choicest beauty spots of the capital fared no better than Hyde Park. During one of the last days of peace, the 'Dictator of London', as Scott, to his chagrin, was described in the press,[38] journeyed through the northern suburbs to the rim of sandy hills which surround the capital where,

on Hampstead Heath the sand-diggers created a miniature Cheddar Gorge, which glowed in the sunshine of that wonderful autumn in warm lines of ochre, orange and red . . . Up from the Vale of Health roared and rocked a continuous stream of three-, five- and ten-ton lorries, and then amongst them appeared a small Austin car with a tiny trailer attached. Beside the driver sat his small daughter. When their turn came they drew up beside the giant grab, received a great dollop of sand on their trailer, and drove happily away to fortify their home against the wrath to come.[39]

But wrath of the high explosive variety didn't come for another eight months. The destructive powers of Nazism were directed first at Scandinavia (neutral Sweden apart), the Low Countries and France. The indirect effect of the fall of Norway, however, was to sweep away the Chamberlain Government in May 1940 through an upsurge of political wrath of a kind not seen before or since, given the usual capacity of a three-figure majority to insulate a British Prime Minister from pretty well anybody or anything.

There was nothing of business as usual about the political crisis brought about by the dramatic finish to the Phoney War. It had its origins in an ill-conceived plan to send British troops to aid the Finns fighting a brave if doomed border war with Germany's ally since the Molotov-Ribbentrop Pact, the Soviet Union. The idea was to land British troops in the far northern port of Narvik in the Norwegian Arctic and move them overland across neutral Sweden to Finland. In the first days of March 1940 the War Cabinet finally gave the expedition its approval. The Finns promptly sued for peace with the Russians.

The Finnish expedition-that-never-was was something of a shambles and an embarrassment and public concern was agitated accordingly. It prompted Chamberlain into a penultimate outburst of hubris (his final one was to come in the Commons a few weeks later). It's one thing for the ordinary citizen to be deceived by the apparent calm of external events, quite another if it's a Prime Minister practising self-delusion on the grand scale. 'Hitler', announced Chamberlain on 4 April, 'has missed the bus.' Four days later, Hitler, surmising correctly that the British might still put a force ashore in Scandinavia to protect Norway and deny the Germans greatly improved access to the shipping lanes of the North Atlantic, invaded Denmark and Norway.

Churchill, confined to the Admiralty but still the best hope of those in all political parties who craved a resolute war policy, put a brave face on the disaster and promised that thanks to the might of the Royal Navy – vainly as it turned out – every enemy ship using the stretch of water between Denmark and Norway would be sent to the bottom. The deployment of British forces in Norway itself was chaotic in conception, confused in execution and humiliating in its outcome. Two fishing ports in the south, Namsos and Andalsnes, were taken, as was Narvik in the north. The Navy and the Army were at cross-purposes much of the time, the troops ill-trained for this kind of terrain. Most important of all, the Germans had near-complete superiority in the air once they had seized the bulk of the Norwegian airfields.

Five days after the evacuation from Namsos and Andalsnes (Narvik did not fall to the Nazis for another month) Chamberlain faced his critics in the House of Commons in a two-day debate on the Norwegian operation. The Norway Debate of 7–8 May 1940 is celebrated not merely as a turning-point in the command and control of Britain's war effort between 1939 and 1945, but as one of *the* classic parliamentary occasions of the twentieth century when the House of Commons had the power to break a man and an administration and, effectively, to make a new premier and a new Cabinet.

At the outset, nobody could have predicted the outcome. There was nothing artificial or choreographed about the pattern the debate took. Lord Lloyd, a ferocious Empire man and formidable imperial civil servant, wrote to his son a few hours before the debate opened, in a manner which summed up the mood of anger and urgency of all those who loathed the appeasers and feared the consequences of their half-hearted prosecution of the war:

I am much afraid that the weakness of the Opposition and subservience of the Commons majority will leave Chamberlain at the head of affairs until some further blunder brings fresh humiliation and disaster to our armies. It is the terrible complacency of Neville [Chamberlain], [Sir John] Simon and Sam Hoare that alarms me so much. We all behave as if we had three years or more in which to win the war, whereas it is certain that it is in the next 4 or at latest 5 months that Hitler will stake his all in his attempt to administer a knock-out blow . . .[40]

There was every reason, too, to believe that even if a miraculous uprising by an apparently supine Parliament did shake Chamberlain to his roots, there was no guarantee that his huge majority would fail to cushion his fall or, if it did, the King would be able to send for Churchill. (It's widely forgotten that sending for a new premier is the *personal* prerogative of the monarch and not one of those powers transferred to Parliament by the 'Glorious Revolution of 1688'.)[41] The former diplomat, Harold Nicolson (by this time a National Labour MP and a determined anti-appeaser) was one of the few politicians to appreciate the precarious nature of our informal, unwritten constitution at moments of national peril and uncertainty.

Another was the Liberal, Clem Davies, with whom Nicolson discussed the matter as they waited for the debate to begin: 'He [Davies] makes the point that we all forget the constitutional position, which is extremely difficult. If there is not to be a Coalition, the King would have to send for Attlee [Leader of the Labour Party] and it would be extremely difficult for him to send for Lloyd George [the great war leader of 1916–1918].'[42] Davies and Nicolson were plumb right to anticipate confusion and vacillation if – and it was a big if – Chamberlain's position became untenable.

The Norway Debate is worth savouring not only for the dramatic reversal of fortunes it produced, but as an event in its own right. For one of the greatest claims made for the British people in the country's direst moment of peril, certainly this century, is that the great institutions of national life were not diminished or contaminated even though the pressure to take short cuts with democratic procedure must have been intense. The most eloquent expression of this thesis came, for example, in the first year of peace from that most influential Anglophile among the American press corps in London, Ed Murrow of CBS.[43] In a radio broadcast on the BBC, Murrow confessed he had not been wildly impressed by Britain when he first came to know it in the 1930s:

I knew something of your history and more of your literature. But, to me, England was a small, pleasant, historical, but relatively unimportant island off the coast of Europe. It was different and therefore interesting. Your country was a sort of museum piece . . . You seemed slow, indifferent and exceedingly complacent . . . I thought your streets narrow and mean; your tailors over-advertised; your climate unbearable; your class-consciousness offensive. You could not cook; your young men seemed without vigour or purpose. I admired your history, doubted your future . . .

Seeing us under bombardment, under threat of invasion and mobilised to the limit between 1939 and 1945 led Murrow to believe

that I have learned the most important thing that has happened in Britain during the last six years. It was not, I think, the demonstration of physical courage. That has been a cheap commodity in this war. Many people of many nations were brave under the bombs. I doubt that the most important thing was Dunkirk or the Battle of Britain, El Alamein or Stalingrad. Not even the landings in Normandy or the great blows struck by British and American bombers.

Historians may decide that any one of these events was decisive, but I am persuaded that the most important thing that happened in Britain was that this nation chose to win or lose this war under the established rules of parliamentary procedure. It feared Nazism, but it did not choose to imitate it . . . Representative government, equality before the law, survived. Future generations who bother to read the official record of proceedings in the House of Commons will discover that British armies retreated from many places, but that there was no retreat from the principles for which your ancestors fought.[44]

The Norway Debate, which was to demonstrate that pressure from its elected representatives *could* change the people at the top of its war machine in mid-conflict without fatal consequences (the reverse in fact), began tepidly enough with 'a feeble speech'[45] from the Leader of the Opposition, Clem Attlee, who, despite his many virtues, was not an orator for any occasion, great or small. But the chemistry of the House of Commons, all important at such times, is unpredictable in its volatility.

Harold Nicolson, who saw it fizzle then fizz, described it brilliantly on paper that same night:

The House is crowded, and when Chamberlain comes in, he is greeted with shouts of 'Missed the bus!' He makes a very feeble speech and is only applauded by the yes-men. He makes some reference to the complacency of the country, at which the whole House cheers vociferously and ironically, inducing him to make a little, rather feminine, gesture of irritation.[46]

Attlee is called next and underwhelms. Sir Archibald Sinclair, the Liberal leader, does rather better. A Conservative nonentity follows. He is succeeded by a Labour veteran, Josiah Wedgwood, whose slightly dotty speech, suggesting that the Fleet has fled to its Egyptian base in Alexandria for fear of being

bombed by the Germans, is the match which lights the fuse of the first explo-
sion which rattles the Government front bench. The MP in question was Sir
Roger Keyes, a great naval figure and hero of the Zeebrugge action in the First
World War. Nicolson captured the scene:

> A few minutes afterwards Roger Keyes comes in, dressed in full uniform
> with six rows of medals. I scribble him a note telling him what Wedgwood
> has just said, and he immediately rises and goes to the Speaker's chair
> (pressing his right to intervene in the debate after such an attack on his old
> service). When Wedgwood sits down, Keyes gets up and begins his speech
> by referring to Wedgwood's remark and calling it a damned insult. The
> Speaker does not call him to order for his unparliamentary language and the
> whole House roars with laughter, especially Lloyd George who rocks back-
> wards and forwards in boyish delight with his mouth wide open.
>
> Keyes then returns to his manuscript and makes an absolutely devastating
> attack upon the naval conduct of the Narvik episode and the Naval General
> Staff. The House listens in breathless silence when he tells us how the Naval
> General Staff had assured him that a naval action at Trondheim was easy but
> unnecessary owing to the success of the military. There is a great gasp of
> astonishment. It is by far the most dramatic speech I have ever heard, and
> when Keyes sits down there is thunderous applause.
>
> Thereafter the weakness of the Margesson system [Captain David Mar-
> gesson was Chamberlain's Chief Whip and scourge of the anti-appeasers] is
> displayed by the fact that none of the yes-men are of any value whatsoever,
> whereas all the more able Conservatives have been driven into the ranks of
> the rebels.[47]

As so often happens on these occasions, it was a man not normally found
among the regular rebels (whose predictability, then as now, leads them to be
discounted) who delivered the truly crippling blow. In this instance it was the
pint-sized former Colonial Secretary, Leo Amery, a man whose love of country
and Empire was in reverse proportion to his diminutive stature. It was he who,
on the Saturday debate on the eve of war, had urged Greenwood, Labour's
deputy leader, to 'Speak for England, Arthur'. Following on from Lloyd
George, who urged Chamberlain to 'give an example of sacrifice because there
is nothing which can contribute more to victory than that he should sacrifice
the seals of office', Amery reached deep into the history of the Commons itself
for his lethal weapon. For the climax to his verbal assault he chose the words
Oliver Cromwell had used to the Long Parliament – 'You have sat here too
long for any good you have been doing. Depart, I say, and let us have done with
you. In the name of God, go!'

With so many of his own ranks speaking out against him and the mood of the
House so hostile, Chamberlain, an intelligent man though vain and stubborn,
knew by the evening of 7 May that he was in trouble but he did not believe it

was necessarily terminal. He appeared quite chipper when he turned up at the Palace to brief the King about his hopes for a reconstructed Government which would include Labour politicians. And for those who think that royal influence in matters of high politics died with the nineteenth century, George VI's diary entries for those crisis days of May 1940 are very revealing, starting with his note of the conversation between sovereign and premier on 7 May.

I said to the P.M. would it help him if I spoke to Attlee about the national standpoint of the Labour Party, and say that I hoped that they would realize that they must pull their weight and join the National Government.[48]

Chamberlain advised the Monarch to postpone any approach to the Labour leaders until their annual party conference, due to be held in Bournemouth that weekend, was over. There is no doubt where the Monarch's sympathy lay. His diary entry continued: 'I told the P.M. that I did not like the way in which, with all the worries and responsibilities he had to bear in the conduct of the war, he was always subject to a stab in the back from both the H. of C. [House of Commons] and the Press.'[49]

The depth of division within the 'political class' (by which I mean those sufficiently close to events to be playing some personal role in the drama) can be appreciated by contrasting the King's reflections on that fraught evening with those of a confirmed anti-Chamberlainite. 'The general impression left by the debate', Harold Nicolson wrote, 'is that we are unprepared to meet the appalling attack which we know is about to be delivered against us. The atmosphere is something more than anxiety: it is one of actual fear, but it is a very resolute fear and not hysteria or cowardice in the least. In fact I have seldom admired the spirit of the House so much as I did today.'[50]

It was partly to do with the fact that, unlike most moments in the life of a Parliamentary Opposition with a three-figure majority against it, the Labour Party found itself in a position to determine the fate of the Government. As the second day of the Norway Debate began this had not really dawned on the Labour leadership. There was a genuine reluctance, at such a moment of national peril, to divide the House on party lines. It was Chamberlain himself, in an outburst of vanity, arrogance and stupidity who finally fashioned the instrument of his own destruction. Before he spoke it seemed possible there would be a vote on the technical issue of the adjournment (i.e. a division taking place on the motion 'That this House do adjourn'). Chamberlain turned it into a personal vote of confidence in himself when he intervened at the end of a combative speech from the Labour frontbencher Herbert Morrison. 'To say that the situation is grave and that the attack which Morrison has made upon the Government "and upon me in particular" makes it graver still ... This really horrifies the House,' Nicolson recorded, 'since it shows that he always takes the personal point of view. He goes on to say that he accepts the challenge of a division, since it will show who is with him and who is against him. "I have", he says with a leer of triumph, "friends in this House". Until that moment the House had not really foreseen that the Opposition were to press for a division.'[51]

Attlee, who thought as a war leader Chamberlain 'was quite unsuited for it – he knew nothing about defence; he knew nothing about foreign affairs and he couldn't enthuse the people,'[52] was surprised by the degree of discontent the first day of the debate had revealed. At a meeting of Labour's Parliamentary Party on the morning of the eighth, he proposed that Labour should divide the House against the advice of Hugh Dalton who thought it might unite the Conservative ranks behind the Prime Minister, as well it might if Chamberlain had not referred so dismissively to his 'friends'.[53]

When the division came, substantial numbers of Conservatives (some formerly fervent admirers of Chamberlain, some in tears) voted with the Opposition. Leo Amery, who had made the speech of his life the day before, caught the moment when the Parliamentary system, so often the subject of derision before and since, lived up to its job specification by dislodging a man whose time was past (though whether it would get Churchill, the man whose time had come, was another matter):

> So unexpectedly large was the number of Conservatives voting against the Government – we were forty-four in all – and so many remained ostentatiously in their seats determined not to vote, that, for a moment, we half thought we might have an actual majority. We streamed back into the House. But as the Whips marched up to the table, making their well-drilled three bows, the Government Whips were on the right.
>
> We strained our ears to hear David Margesson read out the figures: 281 to 200. A gasp, and shouts of 'resign, resign'. The drop from the normal majority of over 200 was enough to show that the confidence was no longer there, that the Government, as it stood, was doomed. Chamberlain stood up, erect, unyielding, sardonic, and walked out past the Speaker's Chair and over the feet of his colleagues, who then followed. The Government benches cheered, while the Socialists shouted: 'Go, in God's name, go!'[54]

Chamberlain seems to have deluded himself that he could still put together a National Government, an illusion fostered by the 'number of those who voted against the Government [who] have since either told me, or written to me to say, that they had nothing against me except that I had the wrong people in my team'.[55] If it could not be him at the head of it, Chamberlain was determined, as was the King, that it would be the Foreign Secretary, the devout, aristocratic Lord Halifax, like Chamberlain a convinced appeaser. The Labour leaders, Attlee and Greenwood, made it plain that their condition for entering a coalition was the removal of Chamberlain from the premiership. Attlee preferred Churchill, but there is every indication that Labour would have served under Halifax, whom Attlee captured perfectly in a wonderfully pithy aside – 'Queer bird, Halifax. Very humorous, all hunting and Holy Communion.'[56]

Leo Amery, whose name will always be associated with the destruction of Chamberlain in the House of Commons, was undoubtedly right when he said in 1947 that 'the change of Government in 1940 was, indeed, the direct result of a parliamentary demonstration of dissatisfaction with Mr Neville Chamberlain's war leadership . . . All the same, if the matter had been left to a parliamentary vote, a majority vote both of Conservatives and of Socialists would have favoured Lord Halifax.'[57]

It was, in fact, Halifax himself who ensured the country got the leader it needed at a meeting with Chamberlain and Churchill at No. 10 on Thursday 9 May. Attlee and Greenwood were present at the outset to make it plain that Labour would not serve under Chamberlain and that consultation with their colleagues would be required before they could commit themselves to the idea of a Coalition. They left for Bournemouth to take soundings at their party conference leaving the doomed premier and his two potential successors. For once Churchill used silence as his ultimate weapon. Chamberlain by implication expressed his preference for Halifax. 'As I remained silent,' Churchill later wrote,

> a very long pause ensued. It certainly seemed longer than the two minutes which one observes in the commemorations of Armistice Day. Then at length Halifax spoke. He said he felt that his position as a Peer, out of the House of Commons, would make it very difficult for him to discharge the duties of Prime Minister in a war like this. He would be held responsible for everything, but would not have the power to guide the assembly upon whose confidence the life of every Government depended. He spoke for some minutes in this sense, and by the time he had finished it was clear that the duty would fall upon me – had in fact fallen upon me.[58]

In the small hours of Friday 10 May the Germans invaded Holland and Belgium. Never have the British changed prime ministers in such fraught circumstances. The actual change-over took place 'after tea', as the King put it. Chamberlain came to resign. The King told him 'how grossly and unfairly I thought he had been treated', suggested Halifax 'of course' should succeed him, reluctantly accepted Chamberlain's advice that this could not be and sent for Churchill who 'was full of fire and determination'.[59] Thus began one of the greatest P.M.–Monarch partnerships in British history.

Churchill returned to the Admiralty, summoned Attlee and Greenwood, offered Labour 'rather more than a third of the places' in a new National Government and 'two seats in the War Cabinet of five'[60] (thus, albeit unwillingly, setting Labour on the road to untrammelled power five years later brimming, thanks to their Coalition service, with both ministerial experience and popular support). At 3 a.m. on the Saturday morning he finally eased his vast frame into bed 'conscious of a profound sense of relief. At last I had the authority to give directions over the whole scene. I felt as if I were walking with destiny, and that all my past life had been but a preparation for this hour and this trial.'[61] For once the hyperbole was justified. In personal terms, he really was a war-winner. For once the political system had thrown up exactly the right individual at the right moment. The normally anti-heroic A.J.P. Taylor ended his short biographical note on Churchill in his *English History 1914–1945* with the words 'the saviour of his country'[62] and he was right.

PART TWO: *The Shock-Absorber, 1940–41*

The sloping, sunny field in the south of England is the graveyard of German aircraft shot down along a part of the south coast. Ninety have been brought to this field alone in the past week or so. And for every one here, probably half a dozen more are in the sea. Clambering among this mass of wreckage is not pleasant. The smell of burnt metal and paint still hangs about; here and there a wreck smells like an operating theatre.
J.L. Hodson, diary entry, 24th August 1940[1]

We had somehow to form a body for burial so that the relatives (without seeing it) could imagine that their loved one was more or less intact for that purpose. But it was a very difficult task – there were so many pieces missing and, as one of the mortuary attendants said, 'Proper jigsaw puzzle, ain't it, Miss?' The stench was the worst thing about it . . . It became a grim and ghastly satisfaction when a body was fairly constructed – but if one was too lavish in making one body almost whole, then another would have sad gaps.
Frances Faviell recalling the London Blitz, autumn 1940[2]

Thirty years after the Second World War had ended, an especially thoughtful airman said to me, 'Never forget war is about destroying things and killing people.'[3] The triumph of 1940, the heroism of the Royal Air Force pilots, the bravery of the civilian population beneath the bombers of the Luftwaffe was real, remarkable and should never be forgotten. The images that keep the memory alive are from the celluloid of contemporary newsreel and retrospective reconstruction for the cinema – the exquisite shape of a Spitfire coming, as if out of the sun, to destroy wave after wave of German aircraft with its Browning guns ablaze; of old ladies being hauled out of a ruined street in the East End peering at the camera and declaring in perfect Cockney that 'One day, that 'itler, 'e'll go too far.'

But the image that haunts me most is that of the basket of 'unidentified flesh' the wardens were instructed to gather from the rubble after a raid for use in the mortuaries where attendants spent long hours putting together something resembling a body for distraught relatives to bury.[4] It's an image which anyone of a later generation that did not live through the Blitz needs to keep vivid, not for ghoulish, morbid reasons, but because the fear, the shock and the suffering of ordinary people in the periods when Britain came under aerial bombardment have tended to be diminished as the years have passed for three reasons: the healing, erasing effect of the passage of time itself; the retrospective knowledge of other combatants who suffered on an almost unimaginable scale – the Russians, the Poles, the victims of the Holocaust; and the post-atomic bomb appreciation that if war came again the Blitz would be surpassed a hundred times and more in devastation. None of this was knowable in 1940.

And the prospect of untold horrors – fifth columnists dropping from the air, sabotage by British-born German sympathisers, invasion itself – seemed dramatically closer the day Churchill took power and the Wehrmacht took the Low Countries. Churchill himself certainly felt it and admitted as much to his personal detective, W.H. Thompson, as they drove back from the Palace after his appointment as P.M.

'You know why I have been to Buckingham Palace, Thompson?'

'Yes, Sir. I only wish that the position had come your way in better times, for you have an enormous task.'

'God alone knows how great it is,' said Churchill with tears in his eyes. 'I hope that it is not too late. I am very much afraid that it is. We can only do our best.'[5]

Such sentiments, however, were for intimates on private occasions. In public it was all the lion's roar. Years later he was to say, 'It was the nation and the race dwelling all round the globe that had the lion's heart. I had the luck to be called upon to give the roar.'[6] He quickly mobilised that force over which he had always exercised a supreme command – the power of language. On 13 May, addressing the Commons for the first time as premier, he delivered himself of one of his best-remembered orations. As was his habit, he built morale, paradoxically enough, by sparing his listeners nothing.

> I would say to the House, as I said to those who have joined this Government: 'I have nothing to offer but blood, toil, tears and sweat.'
>
> We have before us an ordeal of the most grievous kind. We have before us many, many long months of struggle and of suffering. You ask what is our policy? I will say: it is to wage war, by sea, land and air, with all our might and with all the strength that God can give us; to wage war against a monstrous tyranny, never surpassed in the dark, lamentable catalogue of human crime. That is our policy.
>
> You ask, what is our aim? I can answer in one word: It is victory, victory at all costs, victory in spite of all terror, victory, however long and hard the road may be; for without victory there is no survival.[7]

As with Lloyd George, that other great mobiliser of words for the purpose of waging total war, cold print cannot convey more than a fraction of the force. The pregnant pauses, the sibilant delivery, the grand gesture, the rising and falling of his voice – all made him instantly recognisable and permanently unforgettable. Part of his secret as a mover of hearts and minds was that he had been practising his more effective word patterns for decades, a trick he could get away with in an era when it was rare indeed for a political speech to be recorded on celluloid or gramophone record (video and tapes were still a generation away). The longevity of his political career (he was sixty-five when he became premier), the width of his ministerial experience (Colonial Office, Board of Trade, Home Office, Admiralty, War Office and Treasury) as well as his love for the flowing phrase, produced by 1940 as rich a rhetorical compost as any politician had had to nurture his words.

The Cambridge historian, Ronald Hyam, told us a great deal about Churchill when he traced the genesis of his most famous wartime speech in praise of the pilots of RAF Fighter Command when the Battle of Britain was at its height.

Take the origins of perhaps Churchill's most famous phrase delivered on 20 August 1940 that 'Never again in the field of human conflict was so much owed by so many to so few.' This had been perfected over several trial runs:

Never before were there so many people in England, and never before have they had so much to eat. (1899, during Oldham by-election.)

I do not think it is very encouraging that we should have spent so much money upon the settlement of so few. (April 1906, on land settlement in South Africa.)

Never before in Colonial experience has a Council been granted where the number of settlers is so few. (November 1907, on the Legislative Council for Kenya.)

. . . nowhere else in the world could so enormous a mass of water be held up by so little masonry. (1908, on a dam at Ripon Falls across the Victoria Nile.)

Never before has so little been asked and never before have so many people asked for it. (1910, on Irish demands for Home Rule.)[8]

However recycled his material, Churchill refashioned it into a remarkable weapon. In 1940 he commandeered the English language for war. His words stood up and fought. It was worth, I reckon, ten divisions and as many squadrons of fighters the Army and the RAF did not have but desperately needed.

No British Government has ever taken office at such a testing time. A big mistake in 1940 and there simply would be no 1941. The worst case – invasion – was contemplated, as it had to be, at all levels. The Home Guard, the redoubtable 'Dad's Army', prepared to leave its more robust members behind the lines if the Germans came ashore and moved across the southern English countryside on their way to London and Hitler's victory parade down Whitehall.[9] Aesthetes like Harold Nicolson and his wife, Vita Sackville-West, had poison ready to take should the Wehrmacht approach their Kent home at

Sissinghurst a few hours fighting away from the coast.[10] If invasion came and was not repelled Churchill planned to lead a resistance movement from some unspecified location outside London with the aid of a 'Committee of Public Safety' consisting of himself, Lord Beaverbrook (presumably to handle propaganda) and Ernest Bevin, the new Minister of Labour and the incarnation of working-class solidarity and commitment to the war.[11]

Despite the Lion's roar from No. 10 and the spirit of defiance among ordinary people (even an old cynic like A.J.P. Taylor had no doubt that in the summer of 1940, the Phoney War was over, 'We were a united nation. Despite our fears we were convinced that we should win in the end. Strangers stopped me in the street and said, "Poor old Hitler. He's done for himself this time now that he has taken us on"'[12]), the position looked utterly desperate after the fall of France, despite the heroic evacuation of 338,226 troops, 225,000 of whom were British, from the beaches of Dunkirk in the last days of May and the first days of June.

However many generations of historians in the future rearrange the particles of the years 1939–45, none of them, without gross distortion, can deny the absolutely pivotal role of Britain in the twelve months from the fall of France to Hitler's invasion of the Soviet Union. If Britain hadn't stood alone and had gone down at any point in that year, it's difficult to see how the Nazis could have been prevented from dominating Europe for generations to come. With existing levels of air, naval and military technology, it would have been impossible in the early 1940s even for the mighty United States to have mounted a successful attack on Hitler's 'Fortress Europe' from across the Atlantic Ocean. However hyperbolic Churchill's rhetoric may sound to the ears of later generations, this period really was Britain's 'Finest Hour'. If it had not been, it would have assuredly been her 'final hour'.

It's intriguing to reflect on reason in the pursuit of politics in the context of 1940. Any reasonable policy analyst, surveying dispassionately the options before the British Government in the summer of 1940, could have reached only one conclusion: it's White Flag time. On this occasion, every reasonable policy analyst would have been wrong. The War Cabinet, in fact, did subject itself to just such an exercise on 28 May as the news from France grew grimmer and grimmer, at the one meeting Churchill's official biographer, Martin Gilbert, wishes he could have witnessed as a fly-on-the-wall.[13]

It took place in the Prime Minister's room in the Palace of Westminster just along from Big Ben at four in the afternoon after Churchill had told the Commons that the news from Dunkirk should not 'destroy our confidence in our power to make our way, as in former occasions in our history, through disaster and through grief to the ultimate defeat of our enemies'. Present at the meeting was at least one member of the War Cabinet who thought that disaster and grief might be avoided if the British Government took up the Italians' offer to mediate as a step towards a negotiated peace. He was Lord Halifax. 'We must not ignore the fact', Halifax told his colleagues, 'that we might get better terms before France went out of the war and our aircraft factories were bombed, than we might get in three months' time.'[14]

Churchill would have none of it: 'It was impossible to imagine that Herr Hitler would be so foolish as to let us continue our rearmament. In effect, his terms would put us completely at his mercy. We should get no worse terms if we went on fighting, even if we were beaten, than were open to us now.' Halifax persisted. He couldn't see what was 'so wrong' in the idea of the Italians mediating. Chamberlain, a sick man but still a member of the War Cabinet as Lord President of the Council, kept the old appeasement duo in business by saying he didn't see 'what we should lose if we said openly that, while we would fight to the end to preserve our independence, we were ready to consider decent terms if such were offered to us'.[15] Churchill countered with the view that the chances of being offered 'decent terms' were about a thousand to one against and 'nations which went down fighting rose again, but those which surrendered tamely were finished'.[16]

At this stage it was two for mediation, one against. Everything would turn on the Labour members of the War Cabinet, Attlee and Greenwood. They did not hesitate. Attlee backed Churchill unequivocally. If negotiations began 'we should find it impossible to rally the morale of the people'. Greenwood said the industrial areas of Britain (which returned a preponderance of Labour MPs) 'would regard anything like weakening on the part of the Government as a disaster'.[17]

All in all, it took two hours to reach the decision to fight on; the most crucial two hours in modern Cabinet history. At 6 p.m., twenty-five senior ministers not in the War Cabinet came in to be briefed by the old man. 'I have thought carefully in these last days', he told them, 'whether it was part of my duty to consider entering into negotiations with That Man.' Hugh Dalton took up the story in his diary. It was idle to think, Churchill continued,

'that if we tried to make peace now, we should get better terms than if we fought it out. The Germans would demand our Fleet – that would be called "disarmament" – our naval bases and much else. We should become a slave state, though a British Government which would be Hitler's puppet would be set up – "under Mosley [Leader of the banned British Union of Fascists] or some such person". And where should we be at the end of all that? On the other hand we had immense reserves and advantages.

'And I am convinced', he concluded, 'that every man of you would rise up and tear me down from my place if I were for one moment to contemplate parley or surrender. If this long island story of ours is to end at last, let it end only when each of us lies choking in his own blood upon the ground.'[18]

His reception was tumultuous. Ministers shouted, rushed forward, patted him on the back. The War Cabinet resumed at seven. Chamberlain, to his credit, swung into line behind Churchill adding that the French premier, Reynaud, should be told 'it was worth his while to go on fighting'.[19] Inside three weeks, however, France had capitulated and Britain was alone.

It seemed only a matter of time before Hitler tried to leap the 22 miles of English Channel separating the two countries. The cryptographers at Bletchley had cracked the Luftwaffe codes on 22 May and a thin stream of precious signals intelligence became available to Churchill and a tiny group of insiders privy to the most sensitive secret of the war. Ironically, its first effect was to mislead. A German Air Force request, four days after France surrendered, for maps of England and Ireland contained in a message broken by Bletchley, led Churchill to think invasion was imminent when, in fact, Hitler did not issue his order to prepare for it until 2 July.[20]

You didn't have to be an insider, however, to realise that command of the air was to be the key to Britain's survival or demise in the coming weeks. No invasion fleet of slow, flat-bottomed barges would set out from northern France and Belgium until the Royal Air Force had been destroyed. The scene was set for the weeks and months when the front line of virtually the entire war curled its way from the chalk cliffs on the south coast, across the woods of the Weald of Kent and Sussex and the North Downs, around every RAF station placed in a protective ring around London and through the high streets and back streets of the capital itself. The Battle of Britain and the Blitz tend to be remembered as separate occasions. They weren't. In the opening stages of the Blitz, they were intertwined.

It's difficult to date the opening of either of them. The official marker for the start of what Angus Calder described as 'the first battle fought over British soil since Culloden',[21] is 10 July 1940.[22] But as London's civil defence supremo, Sir Harold Scott recalled, 'Soon after the fall of France, in mid-June, odd German raiders began to be signalled; airfields and industrial areas were attacked, and although the raids were on a small scale they were persistent and widespread.'[23]

Six days after the air battle around Hellfire Corner (the popular name for the Dover area) which resulted in a memorable live broadcast on BBC Radio ('There's one coming down in flames – there somebody's hit a German . . . he's a Junkers 87 and he's going slap into the sea and there he goes – sm-a-sh!'),[24] and which gave the official historian his starting date, Hitler issued his directive for the invasion of Britain. Yet three days later on 19 July, he called on an empire with which he had no quarrel, the British Empire, to make peace. Its text was dropped over Hampshire and Dorset by German bombers on the night of 1 August as 'The Last Appeal to Reason'. Local people scooped them up and they were auctioned off to raise funds for the Red Cross.[25] On 2 August Hermann Goering ordered the Luftwaffe to destroy the RAF. The moment of their final destruction was fixed – 13 August, Eagle Day. One month later the invasion, Operation Sea Lion, was to take place. On 8 August, the aerial attack began in earnest. The RAF shot down thirty-one German aircraft, the Luftwaffe destroyed twenty British planes. To the public in general, some of whom in the south-east witnessed the battle as a criss-cross of vapour trails against a blue summer sky, the sun occasionally catching an aircraft in its shafts, the battle was reflected as if it were a Test Match with each side accumulating a total of runs.

With the passage of time it is, again, all too easy to invest the Battle of Britain with a false glow reflecting the gleam of gilded youth in the sky twisting and turning in their beautiful Spitfire and Hurricane flying machines as if they were driving shiny new MG sports cars through the leafy lanes of Kent and Sussex. The studied insouciance and understatement of the young men themselves has encouraged this.[26] But, as Angus Calder wrote of those knife-edge days of mid-August 1940, 'It was now that the life of its [Fighter Command's] pilots became a hectic blur of fear, fatigue and fear again, and that the ordinary citizens of southern England began to realize how much depended on this struggle which they glimpsed overhead.'[27]

Mercifully, Goering made several important tactical errors as the air battle was joined in earnest, failing to persist in his attacks on the chain of south coast radar stations, directing his bombers to less crucial airfields, underestimating by almost half the planes his opposite number, Air Chief Marshal Sir Hugh Dowding, had at his disposal. 'Eagle Day' came and went without the knock-out blow. Two days later, on 15 August, the Luftwaffe mounted its maximum effort with almost 1,800 sorties. The RAF brought down seventy-five German aircraft for the loss of thirty-four of its own fighters. The London area had its first experience of the Blitz that day with sixty-two people killed and nearly 200 more made homeless.[28] Five days later, Churchill delivered his famous tribute to 'The Few'. In keeping with Fighter Command's spirit of youthful irreverence, 'one pilot, hearing about that famous phrase . . . "Never was so much owed by so many to so few," said: "That must refer to mess bills."'[29]

If there was a single day when the reality of total war, the danger, the fear, the pain, the horror of it, came home to truly large numbers of the British people it was Saturday 7 September 1940 as the Battle of Britain moved towards its intense climax and the London Blitz began in earnest. 'Even in that splendid summer,' wrote Angus Calder,

[it] stood out as a beautiful day. In spite of everything, tea cups clinked in suburban gardens and tired workers dozed in the sun. The Luftwaffe's change of tactics took Fighter Command by surprise. A force of hundreds of bombers broke through the defences, arranged to protect the sector stations, and streamed with its fighter escort towards London. Arriving about five o'clock, the first bombers set the docks alight with their incendiaries. Guided by those flames, others followed in a shuttle service until four-thirty next morning, pouring high explosive into the blazing East End.[30]

Harold Scott, London's 'Mr Civil Defence', was enjoying his first weekend in the country when the phone rang. 'It's come at last,' his staff told him. 'They've launched a full-scale raid on the docks and the river front is ablaze for miles below Tower Bridge.'[31] Attlee, enjoying a few days rest in the Cotswold village of Bibury, rushed back to London with his daughter, Felicity. From their home in the hilly north side of the city father and daughter looked at the 'livid orange sky' over the city before going to his East-End constituency 'watching while the digging went on among the rubble and talking to the pathetic queue of people waiting for news of their next of kin'.[32]

Of crucial importance to the state of public opinion in the United States, that 'arsenal of democracy' as Jean Monnet called it, a clutch of American correspondents had *the* grandstand view that day and reported what they saw in appropriately vivid terms. Ed Murrow had driven a carload of colleagues through the East End to the Thames estuary.

Quietly munching apples on the edge of a turnip field, their reverie was ruined as wave after wave of German bombers appeared on their way up river with the RAF coming up to meet them in a vain attempt to halt the flow. The Americans spent the night in a ditch as the glare over London grew brighter and the smoke spread a pall of black as far as the North Sea. That Sunday night Murrow described in graphic terms for his mass radio audience what he saw as he drove back through the shattered East End to his studio in BBC Broadcasting House: 'A row of automobiles, with stretchers racked on the roofs like skis, standing outside bombed buildings. A man pinned under the wreckage where a broken gas main sears his arms and face . . . the courage of the people; the flash and roar of the guns rolling down streets . . . the stench of air-raid shelters in the poor districts.'[33]

The writer and politician, A.P. Herbert, witnessed the conflagration from his Royal Naval Auxiliary vessel on the Thames, the Pool of London 'a lake of light', to the south of the river 'a stupendous spectacle. Half a mile or more of the Surrey shore was burning . . .' On the river itself, 'the scene was like a lake in Hell. Burning barges were drifting everywhere . . . We could hear the hiss and roar of the conflagration, a formidable noise, but we could not see it, so dense was the smoke.'[34]

As the German bombers left their airfields that afternoon, the Joint Intelligence Committee in Whitehall was about to brief the Chiefs of Staff on the conclusions of the latest signals and photographic intelligence. All sources pointed to an imminent invasion – dive-bombers transferred from Norway to France, a dramatic build up of barges on the Belgian coast, all leave stopped in the Wehrmacht from the following day. Just after eight o'clock, as the East End burned a mile and a half away, the Chiefs signed the code-word CROMWELL – invasion imminent.[35]

In the week ending 11 September the bombing claimed the lives of 1,211 civilians, 976 of them in the London area.[36] Such a civilian body count was unprecedented in British history. Though nothing can compensate for such losses in human terms, in strategic terms the Luftwaffe's attempt to break the spirit of the capital saved the airfields from which the following Sunday, 15 September, every aircraft that could fly went up, and fought. That was the afternoon which turned the Battle of Britain, saving the United Kingdom from invasion and with it preserving the possibility, one day, of a Nazi-free Europe.

Churchill witnessed the battle from Fighter Command's No. 11 Fighter Group's Headquarters in an underground bunker at Uxbridge in the west London suburbs, a riot of maps, WAAFs, communications equipment and bulbs indicating what was airborne and where. The Prime Minister watched as the New Zealander Air Vice-Marshal Keith Park

> walked up and down behind, watching with vigilant eye every move in the game . . . In a little while all our squadrons were fighting, and some had already begun to return for fuel. All were in the air. The lower line of bulbs was out. There was not one squadron left in reserve.
>
> At this moment Park spoke to Dowding at Stanmore, asking for three squadrons from No. 12 Group to be put at his disposal in case of another major attack while his squadrons were rearming and refuelling. This was done. They were specially needed to cover London and our fighter aerodromes, because No. 11 Group had already shot their bolt.

At this point, Churchill became aware of anxiety on the part of the heretofore calm Group Commander.

> Hitherto I had watched in silence. I now asked: 'What other reserves have we?' 'There are none,' said Air Vice-Marshal Park. In an account he wrote about it afterwards he said that at this I 'looked grave'! Well I might. What losses should we not suffer if our refuelling planes were caught on the ground by further raids . . . The odds were great; our margins small; the stakes infinite.[37]

This was far from Churchillian hyperbole. It was true. The war could have been lost that afternoon when the RAF downed fifty-two Luftwaffe aircraft taking losses exactly half that size itself. A small advantage in superb aircraft, piloted by a small number of brave young men backed up by the latest electronic high-tech in the shape of radar and a war production machine working flat out, was all that stood between Britain and a catastrophic loss of its very existence as an independent democratic nation. Two days later on 17 September Hitler postponed the invasion. On 28 September he ordered *his* war economy to be redirected to a new objective – an assault on the Soviet Union.

It was a superb, life-saving collective operation. Nothing can detract from that simple, abiding truth. The historian Correlli Barnett won fame in the 1980s among a section of the British intelligentsia which had never been reconciled to the collectivism of the 1940s Home Front by pointing out Britain's dependence on American machine tools during the frantic rearmament of 1939–40.[38] He claimed that 'the rise in British aircraft production from 1939 to the end of 1942 (though never up to target) was achieved not by a revolution in productivity, but by simply deploying 111,500 extra machine tools and over 1 million extra workers'.[39]

A sense of proportion is needed here. As somebody born just north of London into a free society in 1947, my overwhelming reflection on 1940 is one of relief that there were enough Spitfires and Hurricanes airborne on that crucial September Sunday. The fact that their power plant, the Merlin engines pouring off the production lines at Rolls Royce's factory in Derby, were or were not fashioned by British or American lathes, is an intriguing but a second-order question. As is the overall size of the workforce. It matters to me that individual workers drove themselves to exhaustion and beyond to deliver enough in time. If a great nation is engaged in what might be its, and democratic Europe's, last throw, the manufacturing process, chemical composition and countries of origin of the dice's raw materials are not the main issue. Survival is.

It was a moment which mattered at the time and for decades after to those with the slightest sense of history or nationhood. A man with an acute sense of both, Phillip Whitehead grew up a few miles north of that Derby factory. His dad worked there. Writing forty-three years later of the Derby generation which endured the dislocations and setbacks of the 1970s, Whitehead said:

> They do not remember the seventies as 'the devil's decade', but their memories hold little enthusiasm. They have an uneasy sense that changes outside their personal world will not match the comforts within it. Will they be able to cope when the bill comes in? I am as sure that they can as my father was that he could build the Merlin engine in time, when a different danger threatened.[40]

August–September 1940 on the Derby shopfloor is Phillip Whitehead's comforting talisman for troubled times.

In 1976 I found I possessed one of my own. It was the legacy of the British people and their conduct under aerial attack from August 1940 to May 1941, the period that will be known forever as the Blitz. It was the collapse of the pound in September 1976 which caused me to make this discovery. A month earlier my first child had been born. And as I observed the panic, the sheer lack of any convincing plan of action on the part of the politicians and civil servants in Whitehall, from my observation post in Westminster (I was the *Financial Times* political correspondent at the time), I began to fear for my country's long-term future with an intensity I had never felt before in what were then my twenty-nine years of citizenship.

Naturally enough much of it had to do with the novel responsibilities of parenthood. But on that grim weekend after the Chancellor of the Exchequer, Denis Healey, had been forced to turn round at Heathrow Airport to defend his currency, I found myself re-reading Tom Harrisson's masterpiece, *Living Through the Blitz*. By the Saturday evening I had come to the simple but comforting conclusion that no people changed beyond recognition in thirty-six years and that if the British people could endure what Hitler threw at them in 1940–1 they could endure anything the international financial community and a faltering economy might inflict.

The beauty of Harrisson's book was that it did not embalm the Blitz experience in the soothing ointment of sentiment. Based on the reports of M-O observers drawn up at the time, it did not conceal the many examples of panic and desperation which the authorities, understandably enough, kept out of the papers at the time. There were graphic accounts of the effect of sustained bombing on the southern harbours of Portsmouth and Southampton, including 'the inadequacy of the civic leadership in the face of these vast new experiences' in the latter city.[41] When official files were declassified in the early 1970s it was found that 'the city's leading trekker' (the name given to those who forsook target areas for the surrounding countryside each night) was 'the highest political local, the Mayor [who] . . . left his key post around 3 p.m. each afternoon to trek to his rural hideout'.[42]

The incessant bombing in late November and early December 1940 left Southampton 'broken in spirit' in the words of Dr Cyril Garbett, the Bishop of Winchester. On 2 December he noted that 'For the time, morale has collapsed. I went from parish to parish and everywhere there was fear.'[43] And yet what is remembered as the spirit of the Blitz could and did prevail even in the most shattered circumstances. In its section on Southampton in a report for the Home Intelligence division of the Ministry of Information, M-O concluded on 9 December that:

> The strongest feeling in Southampton today is the feeling that Southampton is finished. Many will not say this openly, but it is a deep-seated feeling that has grown in the past fortnight. Yet many householders continue to come in every day, and quite a number of women spend the day in their homes and the night in outlying billets. No special bus service has been organised to transport workers to and from outlying areas, even as far as Salisbury (72 miles). The 'instinct' for home and local associations remains, and the feeling of despair about Southampton could surely be much reduced by local leadership, propaganda and some brighter touches.[44]

As Tom Harrisson commented aptly more than thirty years after that report was filed, 'the feeling that Southampton was, for the time being, finished did not in itself mean that Sotonians – let alone Britons – were finished. Maybe they could no longer be so fully Sotonian. But they could and did carry on being people, *homo sapiens*, albeit in varying degrees displaced.'[45]

That could equally have been written of Coventry in the Midlands, subjected to an especially intense ten-hour attack on 14 November 1940 which destroyed a third of its homes and devastated 100 acres of the city centre killing 554 and seriously injuring a further 865 people; or of Clydebank in Scotland on

13–14 March 1941 after raids spread over two nights which damaged all but seven of its 12,000 houses which gave the small shipbuilding community 'the honour of suffering the most nearly universal damage of any British town'.[46]

The statistics of the Blitz tell a story of suffering in a spartan, economical fashion. By mid-June 1941, over two million houses had been damaged or destroyed, 60 per cent of them in London.[47] Some 43,000 civilians were killed through enemy bombing in 1940–1 (a further 17,000 were to die in later attacks by aircraft, flying bombs or rockets).[48] As Richard Titmuss, the official historian of wartime social policy noted, 'not until over three years had passed was it possible to say that the enemy had killed more soldiers than women and children.'[49] To put it in still more human terms, when the War Graves Commission released figures of the victims of the Blitz, it became known that the age-span of the dead embraced an eleven-hour-old baby and a hundred-year-old Chelsea pensioner. One man in the East End of London had lost no fewer than twenty-three relatives.[50]

As usual, the most plentiful contemporary evidence about the reality of an air raid and its ruinous aftermath to survive comes from the pens of the literary, the political, the influential; the kind of people, in short, who keep diaries or write books. But you didn't have to be skilled with the pen to move the non-participant generations after the event. Take this quartet of descriptions of life at its worst in 1940–1. The first is about the smell left behind by a raid:

> Its basis certainly came from the torn, wounded, dismembered houses; from the gritty dust of dissolved brickwork, masonry and joinery. But there was more to it than that. For several hours there was an acrid overtone from the high explosive which the bomb itself had contained; a fiery constituent of the smell. Almost invariably, too, there was the mean little stink of domestic gas, seeping up from broken pipes and leads. But the whole of the smell was greater than the sum of its parts. It was the smell of violent death itself.[51]

That was the author, left-wing politician and future War Minister, John Strachey. Next, a letter from a Hull schoolgirl to her rescuers in the Civil Defence Corps: 'Just a few lines thanking you for what you did for us on July 14th . . . How you helped to get my mother out, and to get my two brothers which was dead, how you help me to get to shelter when I hadn't any shoes on my feet.'[52]

The poet John Lehmann was able, despite being evicted from his home in the elegant Bloomsbury Square in which he lived, just off the Grays Inn Road, to describe the scene like a dispassionate travel writer:

> Mecklenburgh Square was a pretty sight when I left it. Broken glass everywhere, half the garden scorched with incendiary bombs, and two houses of Byron Court on the east side nothing but a pile of rubble. Clouds of steam were pouring out of one side, firemen still clambering over it and ambu-

lances and blood transfusion units standing by with ARP workers and police. The road was filled with a mass of rubble muddied by the firemen's hoses, but the light grey powder that had covered the bushes at dawn had been washed off by the drizzle. The time bomb in the Square garden sat in its earth crater coyly waiting. The tabby Persian cat from No. 40 picked her way daintily and dishevelledly among the splinters of glass on her favourite porch.[53]

Finally, perhaps the most moving passage of narrative to survive from the Blitz which, as Angus Calder put it, 'speaks for many men in many countries'.[54] The man in question was an elderly air-raid warden in Hull which suffered terribly in the last few weeks of the Blitz in May 1941 before Hitler's aerial assault turned eastwards against Russia the following month. Returning to his own street after the raid he found it

> was as flat as this 'ere wharfside – there was just my 'ouse like – well, part of my 'ouse. My missus were just making me a cup of tea for when I came 'ome. She were in the passage between the kitchen and the wash'ouse, where it blowed 'er. She were burnt right up to 'er waist. 'Er legs were just two cinders. And 'er face – the only thing I could recognize 'er by was one of 'er boots – I'd 'ave lost fifteen 'omes if I could 'ave kept my missus. We used to read together. I can't read mesen. She used to read to me like. We'd 'ave our armchairs on either side o' the fire, and she read me bits out o' the paper. We 'ad a paper every evening. Every evening.[55]

An observer like George Orwell, whose gifts verged on genius, didn't need a gap of fifty years to distil the essence of the Blitz. He captured it at the time in his magical, unsurpassed evocation of England and the English spirit, *The Lion and the Unicorn*. His essay, subtitled 'Socialism and the English Genius', was published in book form early in 1941, but it was written at great speed in London at the height of the 1940 bombardment[56] and began with the stark sentence: 'As I write, highly civilized human beings are flying overhead trying to kill me.'[57]

But the book was not about the young Germans opening the bomb-bays of their Heinkels and Dorniers thousands of feet above London. It was about *us*, the British people whom, as a collectivity, Orwell adored despite his burning hatred of 'Blimps', the myopic, old-style military class and the sneering intellectuals of the Left who 'take their cookery from Paris and their opinions from Moscow . . . The Bloomsbury highbrow, with his mechanical snigger, is as out of date as the cavalry colonel. A modern nation cannot afford either of them. Patriotism and intelligence will have to come together again.'[58]

One of the many remarkable features of Orwell's *tour de force* is the degree to which he anticipated the thesis, made much of subsequently by scholars such as Arthur Marwick,[59] that total war is a great accelerator of historical processes. Orwell's thesis at the time was that:

The English revolution started several years ago, and it began to gather momentum when the troops came back from Dunkirk. Like all else in England, it happens in a sleepy unwilling way, but it is happening. The war has speeded it up, but it has also increased, and desperately, the necessity for speed.[60]

But 'we have moved with glacier-like slowness, and we have learned only from disasters'.[61] For Orwell only a democratic revolution which made a Socialist Britain would give us a chance of holding out and, eventually, winning the war. For him it was crucial 'to break the grip of the monied class as a whole. England has got to assume its real shape. The England that is only just beneath the surface, in the factories and the newspaper offices, in the aeroplanes and the submarines, has got to take charge of its own destiny',[62] or the country would remain, what Orwell called in one of his most brilliant phrases, 'a family with the wrong members in control'. A 'rather stuffy Victorian family', he explained,

with not many black sheep in it but with all its cupboards bursting with skeletons. It has rich relations who have to be kowtowed to and poor relations who are horribly sat upon, and there is a deep conspiracy of silence about the source of the family income [the British Empire]. It is a family in which the young are generally thwarted and most of the power is in the hands of irresponsible uncles and bedridden aunts. Still, it is a family. It has its private language and its common memories, and at the approach of an enemy it closes its ranks.[63]

Orwell's singular sensitivity towards the English character, his view of the nation as 'an everlasting animal stretching into the future and the past, and like all living things, having the power to change out of recognition and yet remain the same',[64] led him to predict, with great accuracy, that though 'the English are in process of being numbered, labelled, conscripted, "co-ordinated" . . . the pull of their impulses is in the other direction, and the kind of regimentation that can be imposed on them will be modified in consequence.'[65]

Like most of his fellow countrymen in 1940, Orwell felt Britain would prevail in the end but, like everyone else, he had no idea how. 'We have got to face bombing, hunger, overwork, influenza and treacherous peace offers,' he wrote. 'For a long time, a year, two years, possibly three years, England has got to be the shock-absorber of the world',[66] which is exactly what we were from the fall of France to the second half of 1941 when Hitler invaded the Soviet Union and the Japanese attacked Pearl Harbor. If we hadn't been, the history of postwar Britain, and the world, would have been entirely different.

PART THREE: *The Long Haul, 1941–45*

We threw good housekeeping to the winds. But we saved ourselves and helped save the world.
John Maynard Keynes, undated[1]

By 1945 net overseas assets were a minus quantity. In the First World War 15 per cent of the country's wealth had been wiped out by disinvestment in foreign assets and increased foreign indebtedness; in the Second World War the loss was 28 per cent – nearly twice as great proportionately . . . No other major country suffered such a setback.
Sir Alec Cairncross, 1985[2]

However ingeniously and wisely the civil and industrial controls and rationing schemes may have been devised, they would not have achieved that full success but for the good will with which, amid the strain and stress of war, they were accepted by industry and by the community as a whole, [a goodwill, which] went beyond – in my judgment much beyond – any forecast which could reasonably have been made before hostilities began.
Sir Richard Hopkins, Head of the Civil Service (1942–5), 1951[3]

It seems to me that the most remarkable of the many remarkable things about the Second World War is that it really was our 'Finest Hour'. There were, of course, some who were 'private-spirited' . . . but they were never a large number . . . There was a sense of comradeship that spread right across the old class distinctions. I got a thrill of pleasure from the first time one of our office cleaners handed me my blanket and pillow for fire-watching duty with the words: 'Here you are dearie.'
Dame Alix Meynell, senior civil servant, Board of Trade (1925–55), 1988[4]

Detonators (known as Dets), are especially dangerous to handle. The young male manager of this branch said: 'We've had an accident this morning, but the injured girl, with her arm in a sling, has been back asking if she can start again right away. But she's got to rest a bit. The girls are braver than the men – never worry about danger.'
J.L. Hodson, on a visit to a Royal Ordnance Factory in the North-West, 1942[5]

The Second World War, naturally enough, is chiefly remembered for the great military, naval and air battles on which the outcome turned. Folk-memory, insofar as it is sustained fifty years after the event in war movies, old and new, or pub quiz questions settles on the Battle of Britain, El Alamein, the sinking of *The Bismarck*, Anzio, Monte Cassino, Operation Overlord (D-Day), a 'Bridge Too Far' (Arnhem) or the final surrender to 'Monty' on Lüneberg Heath. That strand of the story will always be familiar, is extensively chronicled and does not need reprising in detail in these pages, though it is a constant and essential part of the backdrop to everything that happened within the British Isles in the long slog to victory.

But the total nature of the 1939–45 conflict made it a people's war, not merely in the sense that, thanks to the bomber, the front line was everywhere; and not simply because shared danger and privation temporarily dissolved social and financial distinctions. From the historian's perspective, the Second World War was different in kind and degree even when compared to the Great War of 1914–18. This, remarkably enough, was appreciated at the highest levels in the land, even on the part of someone, Sir Edward Bridges, Secretary of the War Cabinet, whom Orwell certainly would have regarded as one of the 'wrong' members of the family occupying a position of authority.

In late 1941, long before the tide of the war had turned in the allies' favour, Bridges summoned Professor Sir Keith Hancock to the Cabinet Office for a chat about recording it for posterity. 'Was there any use or point', Sir Keith recalled asking Bridges, 'in starting to write the history of the war before we had won it?'

> He replied that I would find ways of making myself useful in the short-term but I must also think in long term of the continuity of the State and the advantage of funding our wartime experience for future use . . . He told me about the [Cabinet Office's Historical Section] which hitherto had confined itself to military history; but the armed forces nowadays were no more than the cutting edge of the nation at war and their history had no higher importance than that of munition making and agriculture, of shipping, land, transport, mining and all the other civilian activities.[6]

There was a great deal of truth in Bridges' assessment which does not detract one iota from the skill and bravery of the wielder of the weapon in the armed services who would be the first to recognise that in warfare valour is not enough. Superiority of force effectively applied is what determines who wins and who loses. And in providing that, the munitions worker at the lathe is absolutely crucial. In fact, the most vivid image of modern warfare I have come across was depicted in November 1984 at Templeton College, Oxford, when Professor Norman Dixon[7] told a group of businessmen that in the end, it came down to each combatant nation converting as high a proportion of its human and material resources as it could into energy which it then hurled against its opponent.[8]

Dixon's is a good metaphor, conveying as it does the impression of a whole country's involvement from the most minor munitions worker on piecework at home, to the first 'Tommy' ashore on D-Day. It is valuable for another reason: it hints at the nature of energy consumption in war and, particularly, at its non-renewable nature. The shell once fired is redundant. The expensively trained pilot's body is useless once his Lancaster bomber has disintegrated in mid-air. It is totally different from the accumulation of human and physical resources in peacetime where the growth of assets, if well managed, leads to the creation of still more assets and so on in a dynamic process of production. War is a uniquely wasteful activity in economic terms, even though it can hasten the development of new technologies on which great postwar industries can be based.

After the shock of Dunkirk and the disappearance for once and for all of the phoniness of the war, it was an understandable necessity for Britain to create as fully-fledged a war economy as it could, whatever the consequences for its postwar economic prospects. There is always a degree of aphasia in economic transformations and the siege economy of the 1940s was no exception. It came in stages. Only in 1941, up to a year after Britain's world-saving confrontations with the German war machine, did it get into its stride and it lasted late into the 1940s long after the firing had stopped in central Europe.

Never before and never since has a British Government taken so great and so intrusive a range of powers over the lives of its citizens – where they worked, what they did in uniform or in 'civvies', what they ate, what they wore, what they could read in their newspapers, what they could hear on their wireless sets. It was, however, done with complete legality under the Emergency Powers (Defence) Act passed by Parliament in the last days of peace in August 1939 (with a bit of refinement and tightening-up during the perilous summer of 1940). This statute gave the Government power to make regulations and to issue orders. For example, Regulation 55 was the basis for its construction of a command, state-directed siege economy and Order 1305 was the locus of its power to ban strikes. Parliament, however, 'showed a steady disposition to criticise and, where necessary, to curb governmental interferences with individual liberties' throughout.[9]

Statutory powers are one thing, using them to make things happen in the factories, down the mines, on the farms and along the waterfronts is another. The key to the creation and operation of a successful war economy depended, as its official historians Keith Hancock and Margaret Gowing put it, on 'the United Kingdom's capacity to procure and transport overseas supplies, the mobilisation of its military and industrial manpower, the condition of its basic industries, the suction of resources out of the sector of civilian industry, the efforts to ensure "fair shares" of what remained, the efforts to curb the inflationary tendencies of the whole process.'[10]

Britain, quite apart from her military unpreparedness, had to compensate for a numerical inferiority *vis-à-vis* her Axis enemies once France had fallen. The key to this was mobilising a greater proportion of her smaller population for war purposes. As Professor Paul Kennedy, calibrator of the rise and fall of great powers, put it, 'The triumph of any one Great Power in this period [since 1500], or the collapse of another, has usually been the consequence of lengthy fighting by its armed forces; but it has also been the consequence of the more or less efficient utilization of the state's productive economic resources in war-time . . .'[11] In mid-1939 'Greater Germany' [Hitler's Germany plus his Reich's accretions in Austria and Czechoslovakia] had

> a population of nearly 79½ millions with a total military and working force of about 40½ millions: Great Britain's population was nearly 45½ millions, of whom nearly 20 millions were gainfully employed. But this formidable contrast in human resources shrinks sensationally when the distribution of the two labour forces is examined. Great Britain, for example, employed on the land less than a million people or not quite five per cent of her labour force; whereas Germany, to provide her people with food, was employing on the land 11 millions, or twenty-seven per cent of her labour force.[12]

As Hitler's conquests continued, seemingly irresistibly, in 1940–1 his empire embraced the productive resources of Norway, Denmark, France, Eastern Europe, the Balkans, the Ukraine and parts of the Russian homeland. Hancock and Gowing took this fully into account in their assessment of relative economic advantage, concluding that

> the productive resources that Germany's land neighbours could make available to the German war economy were immensely inferior to Britain's potential gain from her oceanic neighbours. The agricultural countries of the tropics, although their average economic efficiency was low, could contribute specific commodities of great value, such as rubber and oilseeds, cotton and sisal and cocoa: some of them could contribute valuable minerals as well. The agricultural countries of the temperate zone, such as Australia and New Zealand and the Argentine, had an immensely higher output per man than any of the peasant countries of Europe; they had besides a respectable and increasing manufacturing productivity. And on the continent of North America there was established, both in agriculture and industry, the most formidable concentration of productive power in the whole world.[13]

This global economic strategy – of treating the whole non-Axis world, not just the British Empire – as your supplier was, however, immensely risky in terms of military strategy: 'Whereas the Germans held on secure tenure – until the liberating armies at last drew near – their modest profits from Polish or Bulgarian economic effort, the British held on precarious and conditional tenure their much greater benefit from Argentinian or American production. If the Axis powers had been able to break British naval strength they would have turned the tables indeed: the United Kingdom would then have been compelled to struggle for economic self-sufficiency, at so pitiable a level that she could neither have made effective war nor even maintained her civilian population.'[14]

This is why had the Battle of the Atlantic been lost (and it was won by skilled airmen, brave sailors and code-breakers in Buckinghamshire making crucial breakthroughs into U-boat communications[15]) in 1942–3, *all* could have been lost. After the Spitfire September of 1940, the second occasion when the United Kingdom stared defeat in the face were the long months when the convoys carrying weapons, raw materials and food struggled across the high seas to British ports taking immense losses from submarine attack.

There was, too, an indispensable financial lifeline winding its way across the North Atlantic which made all else possible. The British Chiefs of Staff never contemplated the raising of the white flag of surrender but, as they faced up to the consequences of their country standing alone, they had no illusions either about what holding out and, eventually, defeating the enemy would require. In a study prepared in early May 1940 with the marvellously understated title of 'British Strategy in a Certain Eventuality', 'they ruled out submission but saw no chance of final victory unless full economic support was forthcoming from the United States'.[16] From early 1941 it came, in the shape of 'Lend-Lease'.

Churchill timed his approach to perfection, waiting until President Roosevelt had won re-election for an unprecedented third term in November 1940. In what he called 'one of the most important [letters] I ever wrote',[17] the Prime Minister informed the President that without American goods carried in American shipping with American naval escorts, Britain could be starved into surrender. Churchill added for good measure that the time was approaching when Britain's financial reserves would be too drained to pay for American help. He concluded by asking his friend 'to regard this letter not as an appeal for aid, but as a statement of the minimum action necessary to the achievement of our common purpose'.[18]

Roosevelt promptly put a Lend-Lease Bill to Congress. After a stormy passage it became law in March 1941. There was an immediate price to be paid. Fifty million dollars' worth of British gold was shipped from South Africa to the United States and a profitable American subsidiary of the chemical and textile company, Courtaulds, had to be sold off, a symbol demanded by the US Treasury to ease the necessary legislation through Congress.[19] Britain, as the price of survival, became in effect an economic subsidiary of the United States for the duration of the war and for many years afterwards.

It was, however, a generous transaction by any standards on the part of the United States. By the time Lend-Lease was suspended in August 1945, over £5 billion worth of goods had been 'borrowed' and Britain had spent some £1.2 billion on 'Reverse Lend-Lease' transactions with the United States. Of the balance Britain, in the end, was only required to repay £162 million, an exchange well over £3.6 billion in our favour.[20] Without it I shudder to think what our troops would have done for weapons, our factories for materials, our tables for food. Without Lend-Lease, good housekeeping could not have been thrown to the winds.

Running this global resources strategy and mobilising the Home Front to extract every last ounce of energy and pound of output, required a feat of organisation to match. At the summit of the political and administrative system, the Cabinet went instantly on to a war footing as it had done in the Great War, though only after 1916 when Lloyd George became Prime Minister. Chamberlain presided over a small War Cabinet but, as in so many other areas, it took the arrival of Churchill to extend and streamline arrangements in a truly effective fashion.

In essence the Churchillian War Cabinet system was split into two parts beneath the small group of ministers who comprised its full members: Churchill, with the Chiefs of Staff, got on with the prosecution of the war in its Defence Committee, while the Lord President's Committee became, in effect, the Cabinet for domestic and economic matters – the Cabinet, in short, for the Home Front. Its very real power was exerted through three instruments: control of manpower; control of raw materials and the means of transporting them.

Whitehall was rearranged accordingly. Bevin at the Ministry of Labour was more powerful than Kingsley Wood or, later, John Anderson at the Treasury. Power over people, the scarcest resource, eclipsed the power of the purse between 1940 and 1945. The Ministry of Supply was the supplier of factories (often their builder as well); the Ministry of War Transport was the nation's carrier on sea and land; the Ministry of Agriculture its grower; the Ministry of Food its distributor. A variety of devices – boards, supervising departments such as the Ministry of Production – were tried in the perpetual struggle to reconcile urgent, often strident demands which always threatened to get out of hand and sometimes did when Lord Beaverbrook was at the Ministry of Aircraft Production in 1940–1.[21]

Whitehall people, too, became a special breed in wartime with gifted individuals from industry, the City, the universities and the professions mingling with career officials to make a Civil Service of a kind and effectiveness we have not seen since.[22] Often it was not so much a mingling of regulars and irregulars, more a reverse takeover. The Ministry of Food simply recruited the people who had run the food industry in peacetime and turned them into temporary civil servants for the duration. Responsibility for the fish and potato industries, for example, passed to divisions led respectively by a prominent fish merchant and the chairman of the Potato Marketing Board. Both were housed in St John's College, Oxford, which became the biggest fish and chip shop in the world.[23]

In reality, the neat organograms and precise boundaries between one department and another meant very little in terms of the efficient working of the whole as, very often, did the division between ministers and civil servants especially as the cruder kinds of political divisions in Parliament and the country were temporarily suspended. Very often it was people that mattered – individuals or small groups that really counted in shifting a policy blockage, despite the size of the greatly expanded leviathan of Whitehall at war.

Norman Chester (a great figure in postwar Oxford who towered over the study of public administration from his Warden's eyrie at Nuffield College),[24] was one of the gifted temporaries recruited into wartime Whitehall whose atmosphere and *modus operandi* he captured in a primer on the war economy:

> The formal apparatus of communication was the minutes of committee meetings from the War Cabinet downwards; and in addition when Mr Churchill was Prime Minister, a series of directives. But the most effective method was the close personal contact which existed between a comparatively small number of Ministers and civil servants – permanents and temporaries. From their daily attendance at this or that committee they took back to their departments the current attitude. By lunching, dining or even breakfasting together, during the long days worked during the war they not merely kept in touch with what was happening . . . but also developed a corporate thought which was more effective than any series of minuted decisions . . . Notwithstanding the vastness of the machine and the many stages which might have to be gone through before a decision could be reached, it could be galvanized into sudden action or the course of policy dramatically changed by the actions of a comparatively small number of people. In the sphere of general economic policy there were probably twenty to fifty people in Whitehall who, if their views coincided, could do almost anything.[25]

However efficiently Government business was transacted in the Whitehall committee rooms or over luncheon in the Cabinet Office Mess, all the enterprise of the hugely enlarged wartime state would have come to very little without the means of transmitting decisions and targets downwards through a myriad of local 'War Ags' (County War Agricultural Executive Committees), Pit Production Committees, Joint Production Committees in the war factories and Food Control Committees in every area. These bureaucratic sinews of the war economy would, in their turn, have been little use without the application of real, human sinew in the factories, on the farms and down the mines, or the application of sustained human ingenuity on what the Ministry of Food liked to call the 'Kitchen Front'.

As the grim experiences of eastern Europe and the Soviet Union showed for four decades after the war, a siege economy can only run efficiently and effectively if the people whom it is intended to benefit perceive it as necessary and fair. Without Home Front solidarity of a remarkable kind – the widespread, if not wholesale, usurpation of individual greed by collective good – the best-laid schemes of the technocrats of the war economy would have foundered as that supreme Treasury mandarin, Sir Richard Hopkins, recognised. Real life at the producing end of the war economy proved just as potent a formative experience for the men and women of its labour force as did active service for the men and women of the Armed Forces – an experience which was to shape expectations and attitudes into the 1945 general election and far beyond.

There are twin dangers in writing about wartime Britain and they are poles apart. For too long the image fostered by Ministry of Information Films of a nation of Bernard Miles-style character actors working their fingers cheerfully to the bone in uncomplaining submission to a noble cause, obscured the picture of traditional inefficiencies, class warfare between master and man and even the now technically illegal strike continuing to disfigure the British industrial scene.

It would, indeed, have needed a miracle of biblical proportions for the aches and pains of the interwar slump to have been wholly spirited away even in the Dunkirk summer of 1940. And, of course, they weren't. Equally misleading, however, are those who have absorbed their Correlli Barnett whole and see nothing but lack of change and continuation of decay in overmanned, under-productive wartime engineering shops dependent on America for their equip-ment and ultimate funding and on the whips and scorpions of Bevin's Essential Work Orders for even those achievements they could claim. By the standards of what had gone before, especially in the 1920s and 1930s, the factory floors, the shipyards and the mines *were* different and better and more productive places. As so often, the picture was mixed.

Take J.L. Hodson's diary of a visit to shipyards in the north-east in 1942.

This is Whitsun; shipyards close at twelve noon today [Saturday] till Tues-day morning. I'm sure the men deserve their rest . . . Absenteeism is six or seven or eight per cent; in peacetime it was four or five per cent . . . But it must be remembered that they are normally working a fifty-six hour week – on three days a week they start at seven-thirty a.m. and work till eight-thirty p.m. (three hours overtime in that) with only an hour off for lunch and half an hour for tea. That's a gruelling day.

Moreover, a proportion of the labour is that of men who've come back to the yards after being away ten or fifteen years . . . the men on the whole are working well – no doubt about that. A lot of them do that hard work on sandwiches. True, there's a canteen, but it won't seat them all, nor would all use it if they could.[26]

It must be remembered, too, that even in longstanding areas of heavy engin-eering such as Tyneside, the war threw together a dramatically new workforce bringing back those who had been on the dole for years and bringing in women for the first time:

The young manager I talked with started this war on a minesweeper but was brought back. Now he runs a company of 300 men in the Home Guard, and companies of Sea Scouts too. In the slack times, men who were riveters or platers often went back to labouring, or became platers' helpers. Now they've been upgraded again. Others left the yards and became chicken farmers, salesmen, shopkeepers, etc. Some were hand riveters and now find themselves using – or trying to use – machines. Some can't get used to it, or are too old, and have to give it up. Hands had got too soft, muscles stiff. It's been a hard job coming back.

The 120 women employed (out of a workforce of 1,800) are doing various jobs – some drive the lighter trucks. He [the young manager] said, smiling: 'The yard isn't so safe as it was, because the women drive too fast!' Women are using pneumatic hammers (driven by compressed air), they're driving the smaller cranes and mono-rail cranes – he said they've got a 'nice touch'. 'We've had to persuade them not to wear high heels', he said . . .

I inquired what it is that causes labour troubles. (There are not many of them.) Arguments, it appears, arise over different pay for different jobs. If an oil tanker comes in for repair or alterations, there's extra pay because she's a dirty ship – men need to spend more on soap, clothes get spoiled quicker. Arguments arise – 'What ruling does this ship come under?'[27]

Just about everywhere a shrewd observer like Hodson travelled in Britain after the closing months of 1941, by which time 'the tasks of economic mobilisation had been very largely mastered . . . thereafter, the main economic story is of a tighter turning of the screw',[28] he or she would have found an economy and a society stretched to the limit. Angus Calder created the perfect image when he described Britain as 'the India-Rubber Island'[29], an image which grew out of a passage in the Official History of *Civil Industry and Trade*: 'As one Controller-General put it, the dream of the Factory Control was "an india-rubber Britain with india-rubber buildings which can be stretched vertically and horizontally and still carry a minimum of five cwt [hundredweight] per square foot." '[30]

The 'india-rubber' phenomenon stretched far beyond the factory gate into every shop and larder in the land. Rationing probably constitutes the most vivid single folk memory of the war years. In the First World War it had lasted a mere four months until the Armistice brought relief in November 1918. Even this brief experience proved invaluable when Whitehall began to plan the rudiments of another siege economy in 1936 in case war came once more.

William Beveridge, the prickly, brilliant social scientist then directing the London School of Economics, was brought in to chair a committee on rationing (he had been a precocious permanent secretary at the Ministry of Food at the end of the Great War). The Beveridge Committee recommended that, if war came, the Ministry of Food should swiftly be reconstituted; that a system of national registration should be established based on identity cards; that local authorities should construct a shadow network of food offices and that the paperwork of rationing (books for the citizen, permits for the retailers) should be ready to roll off the presses of His Majesty's Stationery Office.[31] Within four months of the war starting, the scheme was in operation. The 'National Registration Identity Card' and the 'Ministry of Food Ration Card' became two of the most familiar artefacts of the war and lasted deep into the peace – identity cards until 1952, ration books till 1954.

By the closing days of 1939 millions of ration books had gone out through the post. Food Offices were ready for business in every town, city and borough. Sub-schemes for factories, military bases and restaurants were in place. Each citizen registered with a grocer and a butcher who, henceforth, became their regular authorised supplier to avoid the chaos of a free-for-all. Shopkeepers gave Food Offices estimates of their needs. Food Offices added up the totals and sent them on to the commodity divisions of the Ministry of Food. The coupon from the ration book became as reliable and as vital as currency once the scheme started on 8 January 1940 with sugar, butter and bacon as the first items to be put 'on the ration'. A grim trail of additions followed, starting with meat in March, tea, margarine and cooking-fats in July (bread was never rationed while the war was on, though the Attlee Government suffered a great deal of public opprobrium when it felt forced to do so in 1946).

Selling rationing to the people during the war was the most successful Government public relations exercise I have ever encountered (either in the history books or in personal experience). It succeeded in giving its huge apparatus, which forcibly pre-empted the usual laws of supply and demand, a human face, flooding the country with suggestions on the brilliant dishes that could be created from reconstituted egg or how best to serve Woolton Pies (meat pies without meat, named in honour of the most successful of the Ministers of Food who, as Fred Marquis, had been a great figure in pre-war retailing with the Boot Manufacturers Federation and Lewis's stores).[32]

Woolton used the Press to great effect and showed flair in recruiting irregulars to his cause like the great comedy duo 'Gert and Daisy' who did what Woolton called 'a little "turn"' at food shows organised by Mayors up and down the land.[33] Private publishers found they had best-sellers on their hands with booklets such as Ambrose Heath's *From the Kitchen Front. Two Hundred War-time Recipes* published by Eyre and Spottiswoode in 1941.[34] In a neat touch, Unilever, the peacetime makers of Stork Margarine, placed a clever advertisement just inside the back-cover of Ambrose's work. Entitled 'At your Service', it inquired, with great public spirit,

What's a nourishing dinner when you've no meat? What's a good breakfast without this or that? The Stork Cookery Service will answer these questions for you – and a hundred and one others . . .

This service is sponsored by the makers of Stork Margarine in the confident belief that when Victory has been finally achieved, Stork Margarine will once again be available to the discerning housewife.

It was the Ministry of Food's twin department, the Ministry of Agriculture, desperate to turn every possible square foot of land to food production (even the verges of trunk roads were ploughed up),[35] which launched one of the most famous Government-sponsored slogans of the war – 'Dig for Victory' – yellow letters on a black background beneath a gardener's basket bursting with vegetables.[36] Not a scrap could be wasted either. People were to form 'Pig Clubs', to buy a porker into whose swill just about anything could go to be converted, eventually, into a rare plate of white meat on the members' tables. The King, as exemplary as ever, formed one and posed, in immaculate country attire, smiling at an inquisitive hog in a sty, for a propaganda photo.[37]

Again, there is a danger of compiling an over-rosy picture of genius and solidarity at the store and in the queue. There were breakdowns in the rationing system as in meat supplies early in 1941. Inevitably there were grumbles. The sheer time and effort required to keep the table supplied and the family clothed can be judged from an evocative diary kept by housewife Doris Brewin in 1941:

Friday 3rd January. Found old suitcase in attic. Packed our shelter things . . . Mother bought pig's foot from Parrs. Made pea soup from it; quite a banquet. Sirens at 7.40. Down we went, I carrying suitcase which was very heavy. Harold with Denise in her drawer . . . All clear, about 9 p.m. Came back hoping for soup supper, but Wailing Winnie again at 9.40. So back. Returned at 10.30 to find our supper eaten by mother and father, who had not heard the sirens. Felt extremely disgruntled. Bread and cheese after all. Denise needed a feed, during which Jerry floating dismally overhead. Sirens again. Out into the snow once more. Returned at 1 a.m. and slept like hell . . .
10th January. Mother dropped the pudding mixture (treacle, made by me). Insisted on wasting-not, wanting-not, and scooped it up, despite protests from me about broken basin. I made another for H. and me. True enough, mother found a lump of pot in her pud and none of them enjoyed it . . . Managed to scrounge extra bird seed for Mickey (a budgie) by wrongfully declaring that we had two birds . . .
26th January. Brought home nice big basinful of beef dripping from Clarice's in exchange for the sausage we took there to cover our meat ration for dinner . . .
28th January. Morning shopping in town. Knitting wool; 1 lb pork. Go to Food Office and wait in queue to change retailer. Milkman tells me he needs another coupon for first quarter. I've forgotten it. Go again to Food Office to obtain form . . . Go to every fruit shop in town searching for oranges for Denise. Draw blank . . . I fill in milk form. H. and I go out to post it and we call at corner house with their fowl bits. Fish and chip shop open. We get some for supper. Cold, dark night. No sirens . . .[38]

Doris Brewin, like everyone else, became an expert on 'points', one of the Whitehall inventions which made the system bearable. The concept was to create a mixed-economy-writ-small. Rationed items were given a points value: the scarcer they were, the greater the number of points needed to buy them (you needed money, too, of course), and each citizen had a number of points surplus to basic requirements which he or she could dispose of according to choice and availability.

I can remember the last four years of rationing in the early 1950s. But shortages were easing fast between my third and seventh birthdays. So, in an attempt to get closer to universal experience, I lived for a week in the summer of 1988 on the rations for the last week of the war:

RATION FOR THE FIRST WEEK OF MAY 1945

Sugar	8 ounces
Preserves	4 ounces
Fats	8 ounces
Cheese	2 ounces
Bacon	4 ounces
Tea	2 ounces
Milk	2 pints
Eggs	1

In addition I was allowed 6 points worth of extra nourishment from the following list:

PRODUCT	POINTS PER POUND WEIGHT
Meat and meat products	16
Tinned soup	4
Tinned fish	16
Tinned or bottled fruit	4
Tinned or bottled vegetables	4
Condensed milk (per pint)	2
Dried fruits	16
Nuts	12
Biscuits	4
Cereals	8
Oatmeal	4
Dried peas or beans	4
Rice, sago, tapioca or semolina	2
Macaroni or spaghetti	4
Salad oil, salad cream or olive oil (per fluid ounce)	1
Table jellies, cornflour, custard or blancmange, cake, pastry, pudding mixtures or dried egg	8
Tinned peas or beans	3
Tinned stewed steak	20

On a separate system, chocolates and sweets were worth sixteen personal points per pound and a week's allowance was three points, i.e. 3 ounces.[39]

I kept to this regime with only one lapse (a slice of banana cake) which, given the unavailability of the fruit concerned between 1939 and the late 1940s, would have been impossible at the time. Overall I lost two pounds in weight though rarely did I feel hungry as bread and potatoes provided ample filling. It was an unrealistic experiment of course. Unlike those who lived through May 1945 I was not run down by five years of shortages and overwork. For at least thirty years I had had as much meat as I wanted for example. And it was twenty years since I had done a week's manual work. It was simply a very very boring diet for seven days. I could understand though the pleasure that an occasional 'off-ration' treat must have brought and how an entire nation could become obsessed with food.

Though not an exciting one the ration diet was healthy, not just compared to the rich spread of the 1980s that I forwent for seven days, but greatly improved when set beside the staple fare of working people and their families in the 1930s. War brought a rough and crude if temporary equality to the British people. The rich, of course, continued to fare better than the poor. Rationing was a question of price as well as coupon. But when the schemes which brought free school milk and vitamins to children[40] are placed alongside the basic minimum accorded to all via Food Office and ration book it becomes clear that 'war socialism' brought everybody up to somewhere around the consumption levels of the employed artisan (the old-fashioned word for skilled worker).

This represented a dramatic improvement by any standard. It meant that 'the families in that third of the population of Britain who in 1938 were chronically undernourished had their first adequate diet in 1940 and 1941 . . . [after which] the incidence of deficiency diseases, and notably infant mortality, dropped dramatically'.[41] Woolton was not exaggerating when he said in September 1941 that the nation had 'never been in better health for years'.[42]

The keys to the success of wartime rationing were simplicity and fairness. Woolton had the bright idea of seconding the Board of Education's maths inspector, Sir Martin Roseveare, whom he later described as 'little short of a genius'[43] when it came to tackling the intellectual and practical problems of rationing schemes. Roseveare tested his dummy books on his wife and her friends[44] and, as his *Times* obituarist noted, 'was wont to take a little pride in the fact that from being an apparently repressive document at the war's outset the ration book came through successive editions to be seen as a guide to a balanced and healthy diet given the siege conditions of life in Britain at war'.[45]

Conspicuous fairness, the Government swiftly realised, was indispensable to general public acceptance of institutionalised privation. It was not just commonsense that persuaded ministers and officials of this. So did their own social surveys conducted by the Ministry of Information. 'People are willing', a report in March 1942 concluded, 'to bear any sacrifice if a 100 per cent effort can be reached and the burden fairly borne by all.'[46] Two months later another

MOI report noted that 'the heavier penalties for black marketeers, the promise of restrictions on luxury meals, the extension of points rationing, the abolition of basic petrol . . . have been welcomed as real evidence that the Government is in earnest'.[47]

Corroboration for the MOI's findings can be found in the complaints files of the Ministry of Food itself. As the official historian, R.J. Hammond, recorded:

> The success of food rationing was something that the British people came to take for granted. Their satisfaction with control, speaking generally, varied directly with its completeness – it was the things amenable only partly, or not at all, to rationing techniques, like fish, oranges or milk, that evoked complaint. There could be no more powerful tribute to rationing than the demands that, say, cake should be rationed.
>
> They acknowledged the fairness of the system; but they also showed how well its limitations had been concealed not only from the public in general, but even from many in Whitehall and within the Ministry of Food itself. For it was from these latter enthusiasts – who would have rationed coffee and cocoa, for instance, in the name of equality – that those actually running the scheme had the hardest task to defend themselves.[48]

But the best appraisal of wartime rationing I have read was penned by Susan Briggs thirty years after the war ended. 'Rationing', she wrote, 'was thought of as a *necessary* restriction during the war, and people happily turned the queue into a national institution. Memories of wartime shortages during the First World War were associated with unfair distribution and with profiteering. The Second World War was not to be a war like that. There were black markets – and country folk in Cumberland could fare better than town-dwellers in the Midlands – but the Ministry of Food, as much an innovation as the Ministry of Information, was the biggest (and fairest) shop in the world.'[49]

For me, the ultimate test of Home-Front solidarity was the degree to which it was shared – and lived – in the grandest tied-cottage in the land. The wife of the American President, Mrs Eleanor Roosevelt, never got over her visit to Buckingham Palace in October 1942. Writing almost twenty years later she remembered:

> When we arrived at the Palace they [the King and Queen] took me to my rooms, explaining that I could only have a small fire in my sitting room and one in the outer waiting room, and saying they hoped I would not be too cold. Through the windows they pointed out the shell holes. The window-panes in my room had all been broken and replaced by wood and isinglass and one or two small panes of glass. Later the Queen showed me where a bomb had dropped right through the King's rooms, destroying both his rooms and hers. They explained the various layers of curtains [the blackout] which had to be kept closed when the lights were on . . .

Everything in Great Britain was done as one would expect it to be. The restrictions on heat and water were observed as carefully in the royal household as in any other home in England. There was a plainly marked black line in my bathtub above which I was not supposed to run the water. We were served on gold and silver plates, but our bread was the same kind of war bread [high extraction levels had made it grey-brown] every other family had to eat and, except for the fact that occasionally game from one of the royal preserves appeared on the table, nothing was served in the way of food that was not served in any of the war canteens.[50]

George VI exercised a divine, or at least a Kingly, right to live like his people for the duration. He was issued with his own ration book number CA 570011 on 16 January 1940. It reads as follows:

> Consumer's name (Block letters).
> HIS MAJESTY THE KING
>
> Address (Block letters).
> BUCKINGHAM PALACE
> LONDON S.W.1.[51]

He refused to send his daughters, Elizabeth and Margaret, to the safety of a Commonwealth Dominion. The Queen summed it up by saying: 'The children won't leave without me; I won't leave without the King; and the King will never leave.'[52] The King himself 'longed to fight . . . arms in hand, himself,' Churchill later revealed.[53] And the symbol of solidarity between constitutional ruler and the constitutionally ruled was never stronger than the day Buckingham Palace was struck by the Luftwaffe on 13 September 1940. 'I'm glad we've been bombed,' said the Queen. 'It makes me feel I can look the East End [of London] in the face.'[54] A few days before, George VI had taken one of his customary trips to the East End where he would suddenly appear, small, frail and in uniform, among the smoking rubble. 'Thank God for a good King,' someone cried. Quick as a flash the King called back: 'Thank God for a good people.'[55] In September 1940, both were right.

Any society at any time is a thing of paradoxes. Wartime Britain illustrates this truism vividly. It was, certainly after May 1940, a more politically united nation than at any other time in the twentieth century. It was better fed, more productive and less embittered between its social gradations. Yet it must never be forgotten that it was, at the same time, a society in great danger, certainly until the Battle of the Atlantic was won in 1943. It was, too, a society under near-constant mental stress from the first sounding of the air-raid sirens on 3 September 1939 until the explosion of the last V1 and V2 flying bombs and rockets at the end of March 1945. (The last V2 fell on 27 March; the last V1 two days later.)[56]

Fear and stress cannot be measured. Calculating that real but elusive concept, 'morale', proved difficult enough. The drolly serious Tom Harrisson recalled from *The Good Soldier Sveik* that the (fictional) Austrian Ministry of the Interior invented no fewer than twelve grades for measuring 'unshakeable loyalty to the [Habsburg] monarchy', commenting that 'No one did anything so refined this side of the channel in World War II . . . The stereotype of a good patriotic citizen was supposed to laugh, to make the V-sign when he saw a Cabinet minister, and so on. A lot of them didn't do much cheering even at the best of times. But they could cry and carry on, all the same.'[57]

As was so often the case, it was Richard Titmuss (who acquired, so it was said, his uncanny sensitivity about the intimacies of domestic life while collecting insurance in pre-war Bedfordshire[58]), who put the flesh of humanity on the bones of wartime statistics:

There was seldom a day in five years when enemy aeroplanes or flying-bombs or rockets were not over some part of Britain. Even if raiders were not signalled, there was always the threat of attack – a threat which touched not only the nerve-centre of Government, but many towns and villages throughout the country. A state of readiness became almost a permanent feature of life for those who manned the civil defence and post-raid services. A state of relaxation was not fully experienced until April 1945. Between the first bomb on Britain and the last, 2,019 days elapsed – a long and wearisome period during which, for the most part and for most people, nothing happened. But all the time there were threats; of bombs, of gas, of sabotage, of invasion and, at the end, of new and unsuspected horrors.[59]

Titmuss was right to emphasise the potential vulnerability of every square foot of Britain, a danger which distinguished it totally from its great ally, the United States, a country beyond the reach (if Hawaii and a tiny part of Oregon are excluded) of either German or Japanese bombers. Within the United Kingdom, however, the capital was *the* vulnerable point:

London was on duty for most of the war. Between the first and last incident, the alert was sounded on 1,224 occasions. If these are averaged it may be said that Londoners were threatened once every thirty-six hours for over five years, threatened at their work, having their meals, putting their children to bed, and going about the ordinary business of their lives.[60]

Titmuss made a brilliant attempt to compile an 'arithmetic of stress'.[61] For example, he compiled a tragic assessment of 'excess mortality' among babies and young children suffocated because 'Families had to sleep on basement floors, in domestic shelters and other crowded places. Improvised bedding and bulky pillows were used and people slept partly or fully dressed; often they were overtired and insensible to the cries of young children.' Titmuss reckoned that in '1940–43 an additional 426 children lost their lives this way – a number larger than the total deaths caused by war operations among all women in the

Armed Forces to (at least) the end of 1943'.[62] Another 880 children died in the war when they fell into the ubiquitous emergency water tanks, sewers or wells and drowned.[63]

The best way of recapturing the day-to-day reality of life in the Fighting Forties is to bring it down to a single locality, because even a Titmuss, for all his delicacy, is dealing with big numbers and a bigger picture. For example, in my own street – Merton Road in Walthamstow, north-east London – the scars of the Luftwaffe are still visible from the front window of the house.

The street was built in the Edwardian era for local tradesmen and City clerks by a single builder who constructed the homes around variations of a pair of designs. As a result the houses were of a uniform height and their fronts were of an identical, pale yellow brick. The Luftwaffe put a hole in this pleasing façade (now filled with council houses of Fifties and Sixties vintage) in the early hours of 19 April 1944, a night when Walthamstow 'was brilliantly lit with red-marker flares and we [the local Civil Defence authority] anticipated an overwhelming "cascade" raid'.[64] The raid, however, was not as bad as feared but between 1.10 and 1.30 a.m. 'four other H.E.'s [high-explosive bombs] were reported in Clarendon [where this book was written], Copeland, Fraser and Merton Roads . . . Fourteen people were killed that night and forty-two others suffered injury.'[65]

As I take the seven-minute walk from my home in Merton Road to my library in Clarendon Road each morning, I can trace the diagonal path of that stick of bombs not just through the relatively tiny council houses slotted in between the more spacious Edwardian villas but also by the rebuilding of houses near by, shattered but not destroyed. The Borough Council had to plug the holes with whatever material it had to hand there being no time or money to match existing design. The brick they used for patching was and remains bright yellow – like the road Dorothy trod in *The Wizard of Oz* – and serves as a daily reminder of Goering's attack.

Probably the most graphic location in Walthamstow for impressing upon subsequent generations the arbitrary horror of the Second World War is the intensively used shopping area around the Post Office where Hoe Street, the High Street and Church Hill meet. Hoe Street suddenly widens dramatically; the shops and banks and the flats above them are 1950s architecture where all around is 1890s. The reason – the V1 flying bomb which fell one summer morning on Hitchman's Distributing Centre. As Ross Wyld, the borough's civil defence historian (and pillar of the Civil Service trade unions) recorded prosaically:

The approach of the bomb was heard and people shopping in the vicinity took such shelter as was available; some dived into shops and doorways, others into an archway between two shops which led to a motor coach garage at the rear. By the worst of bad luck the bomb burst practically opposite to this archway collapsing the two floors above and burying people in the debris.

The incident was complicated by the fact that the bomb dropped just before 10 a.m. when shopping was in full swing, and it was not until after midnight that we were able to say just how many people were reported to be missing. The Rescue Service worked throughout the day and night and by 7 o'clock the next morning the last body had been recovered from the archway, the wall of one side of which was threatening all the time to collapse and bury the rescuers.

On the other side of this same wall a lad of 15 was trapped by debris to the waist, and at the risk of their lives the Rescue men, a doctor and the Casualty Staff Officer worked for some four hours before the lad was rescued at about 2.45 p.m., uninjured, but suffering from shock. The last body (that of an office cleaner) was recovered from the iron staircase buried under the debris at the back of some office buildings at the bottom of Church Hill. The casualty list at this incident was our worst for Fly Bombs, there being 19 dead bodies recovered in addition to three other deaths which occurred in hospital subsequent to rescue. The total of casualties recorded for this one Fly was 144.[66]

Over 2,300 of this kind of 'Fly' reached London in the 'second Blitz' of 1944–5.[67] Their menacing roar (and even more menacing cut-out just before they fell to earth) gave them the nickname of 'Buzz-Bombs'. Their technical successor the V2 rocket was a liquid-fuelled monster some 47 feet high (it towers over the Royal Navy's dummy Polaris missile at the Imperial War Museum by 16 feet). The V2 was the world's first ballistic missile. Unlike the V1, neither its trajectory nor the sound of the engine gave the slightest warning of its arrival. It really did bring death and destruction out of a cloudless sky.

The last V2 to strike Walthamstow fell 150 yards from my home in March 1945 a few weeks before the German surrender. 'Sixteen houses were wiped out. Among those killed was a soldier who had called round to one of the houses to say goodbye to some friends before returning to his unit and another tragedy in this incident was that of an RAF man returning home on leave knowing nothing of the death of his wife until he actually arrived at the incident where we were still searching for the body.'[68] Eight people were killed and 111 injured by that last V2 on the corner of Grove Road and College Road E17. The only sign of past destruction in the 1990s are the stretches of postwar housing. But I can never drive or walk past without remembering that RAF man coming home to find his world quite gone. It's only when tragedy is brought down to the particular, the personal and the local that the conglomerate horror of the Second World War can begin to be felt by those who did not feel it at the time.

CHAPTER 2

Buntings and Ballots

When we got to Holland we went to some of those houses in Nijmegen –
flush toilets, nice gardens, they were just ordinary people but so much better
off than we were. I was flabbergasted. And when we got to Germany I
thought 'these people have been living well even under Adolf and I don't like
Adolf'. I got ambitious. We owned two thirds of the world and we lived
worse off than them.
Sergeant Ernie Teal, Coldstream Guards, recalling 1944–5 in 1989[1]

He turned quite grey in his bath . . . I thought he would faint. Then he
turned to me and said: 'They are perfectly entitled to vote as they please.
This is democracy. This is what we've been fighting for.'
Captain Richard Pim on the night Churchill lost office, 26 July 1945[2]

Attlee: I've won the election.
George VI: I know. I heard it on the Six O'Clock News.
**First words (possibly apocryphal) exchanged between the King and
the new Prime Minister, 26 July 1945[3]**

Well the Prime Minister has had a very difficult time, I'm sure. What I say is
'Thank God for the Civil Service.'
King George VI, a few days later[4]

But this is terrible – *they've* elected a Labour Government, and *the country*
will never stand for that!
Lady diner in the Savoy Hotel, 26 July 1945[5]

Victory when it finally came arrived with more than a dash of anti-climax.
Partly it had to do with last-minute delay and confusion among the Allies.
George VI, for example, had returned to London from Windsor Castle on the
evening of Sunday 6 May 1945 expecting Monday to be *the* great day. But, as
he recorded in his diary for 7 May, things did not turn out as planned:

Came the news that the Unconditional Surrender document had been signed in the early hours of this morning. Preparations for the announcement of VE Day today were going on apace, outside Buckingham Palace and other places. Placing of loudspeakers and flood lighting lamps etc. The Press had worked everybody up that VE Day would be today as the news was already known. The P.M. wanted to announce it but President Truman and Marshal Stalin want it to be announced tomorrow at 3.0 p.m. as arranged. The time fixed for Unconditional Surrender is Midnight May 8th. This came to me as a terrible anti-climax, having made my broadcast speech for record purposes with cinema, photography and with no broadcast at 9.0 p.m. today![6]

The King was not alone in his sense of anti-climax as Victory in Europe had long been foreseen. In his 'London Diary' a month before, Kingsley Martin, editor of the *New Statesman*, predicted accurately enough that 'V-Day . . . will not be at all like Armistice Day, 1918. For one thing, very few people then had been expecting the war to end: one just couldn't believe it.' For all that, wrote Martin, 'When V-Day does come, it will be a day of wonderful release from tension. The killing in Europe will be over, or nearly over, and that to millions of mothers and sweethearts and friends, is the supreme thing. It will mean the end of rockets, and no more blackout; most important of all, it will mean family reunions and a rest and a holiday.'[7]

For the young men in the front line it meant quite simply survival. Ian Bancroft was a twenty-two-year-old Lieutenant in the Rifle Brigade when 'peace broke out on 5 May in North Germany. I found myself lying in the sun in an orchard near Hamburg, with early blossom dropping off the trees on to me, and thinking "I need never worry about anything ever again". I was wrong,' he added, with a laugh. On VE Day itself he found himself 'acting police chief of Hamburg for twenty-four hours',[8] with almost certainly more power than he was ever to wield again even though thirty-two years later he found himself Head of the Home Civil Service in Whitehall.[9]

Back in London on VE Day the atmosphere was not exactly heady, to start with at least. Even Churchill, the incarnation of Britain at war and a man with an acute sense of occasion and history, did not seem able immediately to stiffen the sinew or summon up the blood in the manner of Henry V before Agincourt. Captain Richard Pim, the Royal Naval reservist who ran the map room in Churchill's bomb-proof bunker beneath Whitehall where the Prime Minister also slept,[10] woke him on the morning of 7 May with news of the German surrender. 'For five years', the old man growled at Pim, 'you've brought me bad news, sometimes worse than others. Now you've redeemed yourself.'[11] In his diary Churchill's doctor, Lord Moran, noted, 'And yet the P.M. does not seem at all excited about the end of the war.'[12]

Like his Monarch, Churchill found Monday 7 May a day of intense frustration. He was determined it should be VE Day. Members of the War Cabinet and the Chiefs of Staff were instructed to be ready to go to Buckingham Palace at 6.30 where the King and Prime Minister would announce victory together. As Churchill lunched with the Chiefs, the plan began to unravel. Field Marshal Sir Alan Brooke, Chief of the Imperial General Staff, yet another diarist (has any country produced so many among its ruling circles?), recorded:

> It was a disturbed lunch. Winston was expecting a telephone call from the President which only came through after lunch. Meanwhile he received a telegram from Ike [General Dwight D. Eisenhower, Supreme Commander of the Allied Forces in Europe] stating that it was likely he would have to fly to Berlin for the required Russian negotiations. This necessitated a call being put through to Ike, which got through during the pudding period! In the intervals Winston discussed the pros and cons of elections in June. We stressed the cons from the military point of view, stating that it could lead only to dispersal of effort which would be better devoted to the [continuing] war [in the Far East – against Japan].[13]

As so often happens, great, long awaited moments, degenerate into farce. Churchill, striving to nudge the Americans along on the timing of victory, had considerable difficulty in understanding President Truman's top Chief of Staff, Admiral Leahy, on the transatlantic telephone – 'Will you let somebody with a younger ear listen to it? I am not quite sure I got it all down . . . My ears are a bit deaf, you know . . .'[14]

Amid the confusion Churchill, the sense of occasion now at work on his word bank, prepared a victory statement. His No. 10 secretaries, the famous 'Garden Girls' so-called because of their basement office overlooking the lawn, stood by. 'At half past five', Churchill's biographer records, 'he summoned Elizabeth Layton, and dictated to her three hundred words for a short broadcast. "They were stirring and purposeful to a degree," she wrote home that day. "At 5.55 we finished," she added, "then suddenly a phone call came through and it was decided not to broadcast." "It was an anti-climax to us," Marian Holmes noted, "especially with the crowds thronging the streets and Whitehall and already celebrating Victory."'[15]

Tuesday 8 May, official VE Day, is technically the beginning of the postwar period and the date usually adopted for the starting point of the contemporary history of Britain. But, in reality, the day will always be 7 May when everybody knew it was over, the word spreading fast across the world thanks to radio, the great transforming communications technology of the interwar years. Even the remotest positions of the British Armed Forces that day heard the news.

Three young Royal Air Force officers in Palestine, for example, decided to spend part of the 7th afloat on the Sea of Galilee in a sailing boat trying to pick out Capernaum along the shore. One of the men recorded in a letter home the events which transformed not only that day in the Holy Land but the disposition of power in the rest of the world. His name was Tony Benn and he was just twenty years old:

Coming in we entered a little Arab restaurant for refreshment. As we walked towards the place, a Jew hurried up with a smile and said 'the War is finished'. We didn't know whether to believe it or not, so we smiled back. It seemed to be confirmed by a special edition of the paper, so we solemnly celebrated with an orange squash and ice cream each hardly believing it could be true . . .[16]

There were celebrations that evening on the shores of the Sea of Galilee and beside and inside the fountains in Trafalgar Square. Tony Benn and his brother officers marked the fall of Nazism, appropriately enough, in a Kibbutz:

Outside on the grass an effigy of the swastika was burned and all the settlement crowded into the eating hall where a little wine and a lot of biscuits and nuts were laid along the tables. First came a short speech by the leader of the settlement and then the political organizer delivered a long tirade (which Eric translated to me as a description of the change-over in the world from Capitalism to Socialism). Actually this bored the workers as well as us. Then glasses were filled and we had our refreshment. I asked for an orange squash and was given one, however one old boy emptied about half a cupful of wine into it. I drank it up – it was practically communion wine and I thought rather an appropriate beverage to celebrate peace in.

No-one got drunk or even alcoholically merry and the tables were cleared away for the dancing . . . Then the national dances began – the Germans, Poles, Czechs, Turks and Yugoslavs all did their own national dances. Then there was a pause and an announcement in Hebrew. Everyone looked at us. We were mystified then it was explained that an announcement had just been made that the RAF officers would do an English national dance. We were dumbfounded. Hurriedly deciding to do boomps-a-daisy, two of us took the floor. It was an instantaneous success and everyone joined in . . .[17]

Shortly after midnight on 7–8 May, as Tony Benn and friends caroused in the Kibbutz, a particularly noisy thunderstorm broke over London. It sounded like the terrifying V1 rockets were coming once more. For the first time in five and a half years the inhabitants of the capital *knew* it wasn't yet another aerial attack. Acquired reactions and habits could, at last, be shed.

On the morning of VE Day proper, the Prime Minister, ever mindful of the creature comforts of his fellow citizens and conducting, as so often, the affairs of state from his bed, inquired of the Ministry of Food about the availability of beer in London. He was reassured that the pubs would not run dry.[18] The Board of Trade announced it would allow the public to buy red, white and blue bunting without coupons until the end of the month.[19]

Shortly after one o'clock, Churchill was driven to Buckingham Palace for lunch alone with the King. George VI, duty and concern oozing from every line, wrote in his diary: 'We congratulated each other on the end of the

European War. The day we have been longing for has arrived at last and we can look back with thankfulness to God that our tribulation is over. No more fear of being bombed at home and no more living in air raid shelters. But there is still Japan to be defeated and the restoration of our country to be dealt with, which will give us many headaches and hard work in the years to come.'[20]

Churchill returned to No. 10 to put the finishing touches to his broadcast as huge crowds gathered in Whitehall and Parliament Square in anticipation of the formal announcement that the war in Europe was over. Harold Nicolson, the MP, aesthete, former diplomat and polished socialite, lunched at his club, the Beefsteak, and, to his horror, had to force his way through the throng to the House of Commons, an experience he recorded in his inimitably precious style:

The whole of Trafalgar Square and Whitehall was packed with people. Somebody had made a corner in rosettes, flags, streamers, paper whisks and, above all, paper caps. The latter were horrible, being of the comic variety. I also regret to say that I observed three guardsmen in full uniform, wearing such hats: they were not Grenadiers; they belonged to the Coldstream. And through this cheerful, but not exuberant, crowd, I pushed my way to the House of Commons. The last few yards were very difficult, as the crowd was packed against the railings. I tore my trousers in trying to squeeze past a stranded car. But at length the police saw me and backed a horse into the crowd, making a gap through which, amid cheers, I was squirted into Palace Yard.

There I paused to recover myself, and seeing that it was approaching the hour of 3 p.m. I decided to remain there and hear Winston's speech which was to be relayed through loud-speakers. As Big Ben struck three, there was an extraordinary hush over the assembled multitude, and then came Winston's voice. He was short and effective, merely announcing that unconditional surrender had been signed, and naming the signatories . . . 'The evildoers', he intoned, 'now lie prostrate before us!' The crowd gasped at this phrase. 'Advance Britannia!' he shouted at the end, and there followed the Last Post and *God Save the King* which we all sang very loudly indeed. And then cheer upon cheer.[21]

Churchill's voice broke a little as he said 'Advance Britannia!' He left No. 10 via the Garden Gate through lines of cheering secretaries to Horse Guards Parade and an open car journey to Parliament. The cheering was deafening, the crowd pressing and it took an age to reach the sanctuary of the Palace of Westminster. Inside the MPs fretted as Sir Henry 'Chips' Channon noted:

. . . for a few embarrassed minutes we had nothing to do. Members, amused, asked desultory questions, keeping their eyes on the door behind the Speaker's chair. The Serjeant-at-Arms was in Court Dress, the Speaker wore his robes with gold braid etc . . . At last Winston, smiling and bent, appeared and had a tremendous reception. Everyone (except the recently elected cad for Chelmsford[22]) rose and cheered and waved handkerchiefs and Order Papers . . . Winston smiled and half bowed – as he often does, and turning towards the Speaker, read out the same short announcement of the surrender of Germany which he had already given over the wireless.

The House was profoundly moved, and gave him another great cheer . . . Then Winston, in a lower voice, added his personal thanks and praise for the House of Commons and the Democratic system: some Members wept, and the PM moved that we repair to St Margaret's to offer thanks to Almighty God using the identical phraseology employed by Lloyd George in 1918.

The Speaker headed the procession, followed by Winston, who walked with Arthur Greenwood [Deputy Leader of the Labour Party]. We walked through St Stephen's Hall and outside, where there was a terrific crowd, the sun shining. There were bells, police carved a way for us, and we must have looked like a picture by Giovanni Bellini as we filed, 500 strong, into St Margaret's for a short and impressive service.[23]

Churchill took the War Cabinet and the Chiefs of Staff to Buckingham Palace for the postponed meeting with the King. As they posed for the cameras and newsreels on the back steps, George VI remarked to Sir Edward Bridges, Secretary to the War Cabinet, and to General Sir Hastings 'Pug' Ismay, its Military Secretary and Churchill's personal Chief of Staff, that they were the only three men to have held the same jobs throughout the war.[24]

Next on the round of celebration was an appearance by Churchill and members of the War Cabinet on the balcony of what was then the Ministry of Health (and is now the Treasury) overlooking Parliament Street at the Westminster end of Whitehall. Churchill tried to bring Ernest Bevin, the incarnation of the Labour Movement and master of the manpower budget at the Ministry of Labour for five years, forward to share the waves of cheering and applause from the throng below. 'No Winston,' he said, 'this is your day.'[25] Churchill told the crowd it was *their* victory. 'No – it's yours!' they roared back.[26]

As Churchill took the applause thirty feet up in Whitehall, a few miles to the north in Whetstone my own family began a double celebration – Victory in Europe and my sister Kathleen's birthday. The day had started badly for Kath as she remembered for years afterwards:

I was looking forward with great excitement to having my name called out in school assembly and being applauded as a birthday girl. I also hoped to have cards, and possibly presents from my friends, and expected to be 'bumped' ten times.

Terry, Maureen [sisters] and I caught the trolleybus to Tally Ho [North Finchley], and I rushed them up Nether Street to get there as soon as possible, not noticing that there were not many pupils about. As soon as we got to the convent gates we realised that there was no one there at all. The nun on duty in the lodge seemed very surprised to see us and said that today was a national public holiday announced by Mr Churchill. Our parents must have been the only ones not to know! I was so disappointed. Very crestfallen, feeling rather foolish in our school uniform, we went home.

Later we had a family birthday tea and I had a special patriotic cake with a paper Union Jack stuck in it and 'Happy Birthday' written in red and blue icing. My mother had used a lot of cochineal to make bright red and, at a loss for blue colouring, had used ink – very dark ink. We weren't sure if it was safe to eat but, as all the ingredients had been saved from the rations, we couldn't waste it so we ate it anyway. We had blue tongues but no ill-effects that I can recall.[27]

After Kathleen's tea, my father and my Auntie Molly joined the thousands in Whitehall and the Mall. The sense of collective relief, the lifting of six years' worth of millions of individual anxieties – fear of invasion, bombing, the death of a father, son or boyfriend in the North African desert, the mountains of Italy or the fields of France – can only be guessed at, not measured.

For many, VE Day was bittersweet. The war with Japan was still raging and was expected to last well into 1946, if not 1947, with untold casualties the price for its eventual termination. For those in the Far East, the news of the German surrender was digested and pondered in the few moments allowed to men at 'action stations'. For example, a young petty officer and future Prime Minister, Jim Callaghan, 'was aboard the battleship *HMS Queen Elizabeth*, and in company with the French battleship, *Richelieu*, we spent the day in a fruitless chase of two much faster Japanese cruisers across the Indian Ocean'.[28] Churchill's broadcast, and its reference to 'Japan, with all her treachery and greed', was picked up by secret radios hidden under the floors and boilers of Changi Jail in Singapore and the word passed among the 7,000 prisoners living under a brutal Japanese regime.[29]

For the people of 'our dear Channel Islands', as the Prime Minister called them, the relief of VE Day was especially intense as they were the only part of the British Isles to endure actual occupation.[30] At the other extremity of the Kingdom, for the people of Orkney, who had suffered the first German bombing of the war in 1939[31] (the great naval anchorage of Scapa Flow was a prime target), the blackout remained in place 'for several days, or rather nights, until the Allies had occupied the Scandinavian airfields used by the Germans and also until all the U-boats had surrendered – just in case . . .'[32]

VE Day in Orkney was wet and somewhat subdued. As W.S. Hewison, the historian of Scapa, recalled, it was 'rather like a Sunday' for the troops still guarding the harbour. The soldiers were reported to be 'rather glum' as the civilians rejoiced, but even these celebrations seem to have been on rather a low key compared with the almost bacchanalian festivities in London and elsewhere.[33]

The revellers in London swelled up and down the great thoroughfares of the capital with Buckingham Palace a particular focus. The Royal Family made no fewer than eight appearances during the course of the afternoon and evening. George VI arranged for his daughters to join in the fun, chaperoned by a group of young officers, through the crowds in the Mall and Whitehall. 'Poor darlings,' he noted in his diary, 'they have never had any fun yet.'[34] High up on the roof of Admiralty Arch the First Sea Lord, Admiral Cunningham, gazed down over the crowds in Trafalgar Square with tears in his eyes.[35]

At the top end of society, the glitter of victory, in one case at least, was tarnished by bitterness. Harold Nicolson had gone

on to a party at Chips Channon's. Why did I go to that party? I should have been much happier seeing all the flood-lighting and the crowds outside Buckingham Palace. But I went and I loathed it. There in his room, copied from the Amalienburg, under the lights of many candles, were gathered the Nurembergers and Munichois celebrating *our* victory over *their* friend Herr von Ribbentrop. I left early and in haste leaving my coat behind me . . .

I . . . walked back through the happy but quite sober crowds to Trafalgar Square. The National Gallery was alive with every stone outlined in flood-lighting, and down there was Big Ben with a grin upon his illuminated face. The statue of Nelson was picked out by a searchlight, and there was the smell of distant bonfires in the air. I walked to the Temple and beyond. Looking down Fleet Street one saw the best sight of all – the dome of St Paul's rather dim-lit, and there above it a concentration of search-lights upon the huge golden cross.[36]

For all Nicolson's loathing of Channon and his appeaser friends, it was one of Chips' own close acquaintances who truly crushed the gushy Anglo-American in terms of the war's ending. His 'beloved'[37] Emerald Cunard, on hearing Chips, gazing across a crowded room of shimmering guests at a society wedding, declare that 'this is what we have been fighting for', turned on him with the devastating retort, 'What, are they all Poles?'[38]

Another guest at Chips Channon's on VE Night was Noël Coward. On the way from the Duchess Theatre where his *Blithe Spirit* was playing, the 'Master' 'walked down the Mall and stood outside Buckingham Palace, which was flood-lit. The crowd was stupendous. The King and Queen came out on the balcony, looking enchanting. We all roared ourselves hoarse. After that I went to Chips Channon's "open house" party which wasn't up to much. Walked home with Ivor [Novello, the composer, playwright and actor]. I suppose this is the greatest day in our history.'[39] It was, unquestionably.

By 8 May 1945 Hitler had been dead for over a week. The world can only be a better place when an especially, almost uniquely monstrous tyrant in an advanced and powerful nation is removed from the scene. Yet even without him, the world on that spring day remained a threatened and precarious place.

As the victorious Allies initialled the formal surrender document in Berlin, the cold war which was to dominate the world for the forty years between the fall of Adolf Hitler in Berlin and the rise of Mikhail Gorbachev in Moscow, was under way with a vengeance behind the scenery of Allied amity. After dinner on VE Day, Churchill despatched a telegram from his war bunker to the British Chargé d'Affaires in Moscow, the diplomat Frank Roberts. 'We are utterly indifferent to anything that the Soviets may say by way of propaganda. No one here believes a single word . . . It is no longer desired by us to maintain detailed arguments with the Soviet Government about their views and actions,' he said.[40]

This was *insider* talk. Popular admiration remained high for the Soviet people who, like the British themselves in 1940–1, had stood alone on the continent of Europe against Hitler's armies for two years until the invasion of Italy in 1943 and, more important still, the opening of a second front in France a year later. As Churchill confided his view to Roberts, his wife, Clemmie, was in Moscow on a goodwill visit arranged by the Soviet Red Cross to allow Mrs Churchill to inspect the use to which the goods garnered by her Aid to Russia Fund had been put.[41] And the first Embassy Churchill visited in London on his triumphant round on 8 May was Stalin's.[42]

Six thousand miles away in San Francisco, Anthony Eden, Churchill's Foreign Secretary, was leading the British delegation (which included Clement Attlee, Leader of the Labour Party and Deputy Prime Minister in the wartime Coalition) at a conference designed to construct a new world body, the United Nations Organisation, intended to sustain the amity of the wartime alliance. The idea was that, together, the victorious powers would prevent the rekindling of conflict. Eden and Attlee celebrated VE Day at a party atop a Californian skyscraper. Both would have preferred to be in London. As Attlee noted, 'In San Francisco the Japanese War was nearer and of greater concern to the citizens than the European contest and we were sorry not to be at home for the celebrations.'[43]

Eden, a far brittler character than Attlee, 'minded deeply' being in America on VE Day according to his official biographer Robert Rhodes James.[44] His morale and sense of purpose in the San Francisco talks would hardly have been enhanced by a telegram from Churchill full of forebodings only three days after the war in Europe was ended. 'Today', the Prime Minister reported to the Foreign Secretary,

there are announcements in the newspapers of the large withdrawals of American troops now to begin month by month. What are we to do? Great pressure will soon be put on us at home to demobilise partially. In a very short time our armies will have melted, but the Russians may remain with hundreds of divisions in possession of Europe from Lubeck to Trieste, and to the Greek frontier on the Adriatic. All these things are far more vital than the amendments to a World Constitution which may well never come into being till it is superseded after a period of appeasement by a third World War.[45]

This foreshadowed Churchill's famous 'Iron Curtain' speech a year later and, in its first part (though not, mercifully, in its second) what actually happened in Central Europe in the next five years. This grim appraisal was followed by a second cable briefing Eden on the options for a general election in Britain now the European War was finished.[46]

The electoral consequences of the Second World War have been heavily discussed and debated as are all turning-point elections, such as the Liberal landslide of 1906 and Mrs Thatcher's accession to power in 1979. Unlike the earlier and later contests, the result in 1945 startled virtually everybody, not least Attlee himself. When Attlee went to the Palace on the evening of 16 July (driven demonically and characteristically by his wife Vi in their modest family saloon) the King 'found he was very surprised his Party had won',[47] as 'indeed I certainly was at the extent of our success', Attlee later confirmed.[48] Vi went round for months telling people the Attlees 'expected Winston to win'.[49]

Whether Attlee, Churchill and their party managers should have been surprised is another matter. The men and women who compiled the Gallup Polls were not. Their forecast, published in the *News Chronicle*, 'continued to suggest as it had done for years, that an election would produce a Labour majority and that the Liberals and minor parties would fare badly'.[50] Nobody took any notice of opinion polls in 1945. Within a decade politicians, Nye Bevan apart ('they take the poetry out of politics,' he said),[51] took notice of little else once election fever had gripped them. Bevan and two other left-wingers, Manny Shinwell and George Strauss, were the only trio of senior politicians credited with having foreseen the outcome.[52] One of Bevan's most famous aphorisms – 'Why gaze into the crystal ball when you can read it in the book?' – fits to perfection the consistent evidence of the Gallup Polls. Though, significantly, William Beveridge himself, whose report was to have a profound influence on the election outcome, anticipated the result but not the aftermath. Beveridge travelled to a meeting in Reading in March 1944 to discuss his social insurance ideas. Afterwards he took tea with Ian Mikardo, Labour's prospective Parliamentary candidate, and his wife. As Mikardo recalls, Beveridge and his wife began to debate election prospects:

> I thought Janet [Lady Beveridge] won hands down, and at the end of it Beveridge made a confident forecast that in the postwar election, whenever it came, the Tories would suffer a slump like the one in 1906 – and he added that he thought the Labour Party wouldn't be as ready and able to cash in on it as were the Liberals in 1906.[53]

Rather lower down in the political firmament, Ian Mikardo (probably the most skilled Parliamentary tipster of the postwar period) identified 'a swashbuckling character named Lord Strabolgi, who before inheriting his title was Lieutenant-Commander Kenworthy and had a seat in the Commons as MP for Hull Central. He was offered 33–1 against Labour getting an overall majority of more than a hundred. He had a bet of £250 on it, and spent part of his £8,000 + winnings on a joyous victory celebration in the Savoy Hotel, no less.'[54]

Elections are highly vulnerable to folklore even in the 1990s when on average a national poll a day is published and their study rejoices in its own branch of political science – psephology.[55] However, I recognise the wisdom of the old pro when I come across it. Lord Fraser of Kilmorack, a party strategist at Conservative Central Office for thirty years after returning from the war, once declared that 'Elections are won and lost by a mood and everything that happens, the most unpolitical things that happen from one election to the next one, influence that mood.'[56] Some time before a benchmark election the political climate changes in a profound and enduring fashion. Political life thereafter is conducted within an entirely different weather system.

Another seasoned political pro, James Callaghan, recognised this in the last stages of the 1979 election campaign. As the Prime Ministerial limousine circumnavigated Parliament Square on its way back to Downing Street, Callaghan's aide, Dr Bernard Donoughue,

> drew Mr Callaghan's attention to the recent improvement in the opinion polls, remarking that with a little luck, and a few policy initiatives here and there, we might just squeeze through. He turned to me and said quietly: 'I should not be too sure. You know there are times, perhaps once every thirty years, when there is a sea-change in politics. It then does not matter what you say or do. There is a shift in what the public wants and what it approves of. I suspect there is now such a sea-change – and it is for Mrs Thatcher.[57]

Between 1940 and 1943 there was, I believe, another sea-change – and it was for Mr Attlee, though he knew it not. Usually it takes an election to demonstrate even the most fundamental change in the nature of the political sea. To mix aquatic metaphors, the psephologist David Butler is surely right to quote the historian Sir Lewis Namier so frequently to the effect that 'general elections are the locks on the stream of British democracy, controlling the flow of the river and its traffic'.[58] Elections are the point at which the flow of power and policies are finally diverted by forces in the making for some time. Quite often such forces are first appreciated at such moments as certainly happened in Attlee's and most other people's minds in July 1945. Walter Bagehot, the great mid-Victorian journalist and constitutional observer, recognised this as long ago as 1867 when Britain was still far from enjoying a mass electorate. 'All men', he wrote in his classic work *The English Constitution*,

> need great results, and a change of Government is a great result. It has a hundred ramifications; it runs through society; it gives hope to many, and it

takes away hope from many. It is one of those marked events which, by its magnitude and its melodrama, impress men even too much.[59]

The surprise result of the 1945 election impressed people at the time and has continued to do so ever since partly because, as Peter Clarke put it, 'there was not just a lot of explaining but a lot of explaining away to be done afterwards'.[60] It was and is right that it should. There was a widespread feeling, as William Beveridge put it in his celebrated report on social insurance in December 1942, that 'a revolutionary moment in the world's history is a time for revolutions, not for patching'.[61] Though Clem Attlee, the victor at the polls, was as far removed in appearance, style, background and rhetoric from being a revolutionary as could be imagined. It was said of him by a political opponent that 'If he had got up in the Commons and announced The Revolution . . . it would have sounded like a change in a regional railway timetable.'[62]

In old age Attlee would sometimes reflect on the factors which gave him his 146-seat victory, still the biggest postwar majority, surpassing Mrs Thatcher's 1983 total by two. In September 1965, two years before his death, he was asked 'Why do you think that the nation turned against Churchill?'

ATTLEE:	Well, they didn't turn against him; they turned against the Tories. They remembered what happened in the thirties.
INTERVIEWER:	Do you think that Munich had played a great part in this?
ATTLEE:	A good deal.
INTERVIEWER:	Or was it more a matter of unemployment?
ATTLEE:	I think the general feeling was that they wanted a new start. We were looking towards the future. The Tories were looking towards the past.[63]

As always, it is impossible to weigh precisely the factors behind a big shift in political thought and electoral preference. Certainly memories of the 1930s – of depression and appeasement in that dispiriting decade – played a big part in Labour's 'never again' rhetoric in 1945 and for many years afterwards. But would the Conservative-dominated National Government's 180–200 seat majority have melted away at a general election in 1939 or 1940 had peace been sustained? It is, at the very least, open to serious doubt.

The philosophical and political tide began to turn, I reckon, in May–June 1940 when Labour entered the wartime Coalition under Churchill as premier. And, insofar as a single person can ever symbolise a change, that figure was the looming presence of Ernest Bevin, General Secretary of the Transport and General Workers' Union, the incarnation of organised labour and the new Minister of Labour and National Service.

In personal and political terms it was, as Bevin once described himself, 'a turn up in a million'.[64] His biographer Alan Bullock took its full measure when he wrote:

> In May 1940 . . . Ernest Bevin had just passed the age of fifty-nine. Until his sixtieth year he had never held a ministerial post, never sat in Parliament nor even been a member of the National Executive of the Labour Party. From May 1940 until his death in April 1951, he was to remain in office, with only six weeks interruption, throughout one of the most eventful decades in British history, and to play a part in these events second only to that of the two Prime Ministers, Churchill and Attlee. It was as unexpected a climax as anyone could have devised to the career of a man who a short time before the war had been talking of retirement.[65]

Churchill brought Bevin into the Administration as the representative of the trade union movement in a Government of national unity encompassing, as it did, just about all the country's political leaders. But that didn't guarantee Bevin or the unions real influence in the inner councils of decision-making. The outcome could have been as modest as that created by George Barnes' presence in Lloyd George's First World War Coalition. It was Bevin's personality which, within a few months, projected him into the War Cabinet, led Churchill to pick him and Beaverbrook as his companions in a last-ditch Government should Hitler invade,[66] *and* achieved more real gains for working class people – 'my people' as Ernie invariably called them – in terms of welfare and life chances than had ever been won before in the space of a year.

From words (with which he was clumsy) and pictures (in which he looks grotesque) it is impossible to conjure up the force of Bevin. It is equally rare to find, even among those who knew him, a successful attempt to capture it on paper. But Douglas Jay has managed it. 'Late in 1939', he recalled in his memoir *Change and Fortune*,

> in the 'phoney war' period, at one of a number of so-called 'National Defence' lunches organized in Grosvenor House by Arthur Salter and Colonel Nathan, and laudably intended to support Churchill (then First Lord of the Admiralty in Neville Chamberlain's reconstructed Government), Bevin was addressing the polite company as prosaically as others (including John Simon) had done in the series.
>
> Suddenly, as he spoke of the Nazi persecution of Jews and trade unionists, his great head swung this way and that, his fist struck the air like a steam hammer and his voice rose to a roar. The words were no more than pedestrian: 'I'm not going to have my people treated like this.' But this highly respectable audience were astonished and enthralled, and sprang to their feet with unrestrained applause. Heavens, I said to myself, we shall win this war after all.[67]

When Churchill offered Bevin the Ministry of Labour he accepted enthusi-
astically. But, never forgetting where he came from, this towering figure who
began his working life carting mineral water around the suburbs of Bristol, told
the Prime Minister he must first seek the permission of the executive committee of the Transport and General and the TUC General Council as he would be
useless in the War Cabinet without the backing of 'his people'.[68] Needless to
say, their blessing was given. Bevin was not an easy man to say 'no' to even if
the labour movement had been minded to.

Bevin's philosophy which, thanks to war socialism, was translated very
largely into practice, was encapsulated a few months after he entered Whitehall
in the foreword to a volume on trade unions by John Price, one of his protégés
in the T and G. The trade unions, Bevin wrote,

> are tolerated so long as they keep their place and limit their activities to
> industrial disputes, industrial relationships and similar matters and are will-
> ing to bury all their memories and feelings and assist the nation or industry
> when in difficulties and go back to their place when the work is done.
>
> But there will have to be a great recasting of values. The conception that
> those who produce or manipulate are inferior and must accept a lower status
> than the speculator must go.[69]

Bevin, in short, wanted the trade unions to be recognised as a great and
permanent estate of the realm. This was no accidental shift of forces within the
land, appreciated only long after the event. Bevin knew exactly what he was
doing at the time as Francis Williams, his friend and former colleague on the
Daily Herald, appreciated. 'It was', wrote Williams,

> with the dual determination to mobilize national manpower – and woman-
> power – for war to a degree and with an efficiency far exceeding that of any
> dictatorship, and at the same time to recast values and permanently alter the
> status of the industrial worker, that he went to his new task. When I saw him
> at this time he made a joke which became a favourite with him. 'They say
> that Gladstone was at the Treasury from 1860 to 1930,' he said. 'I'm going to
> be Minister of Labour from 1940 to 1990.'[70]

And in a sense he was until 1979 at least, just eleven years short of his
forecast, when a Government was elected to kick away the trade union prong of
the three-legged stool on which the management of the British economy had
rested, albeit precariously, since the formation of the wartime Coalition. It was
a remarkable piece of self-awareness on Bevin's part at a crucial moment in the
life of what its critics called the 'corporate state'.

He had a remarkable empathy with 'his people', addressing factory meetings
as 'mates' in a way that would have sounded patronising from anyone else.
Radio enabled him to do on a national scale something of what Douglas Jay had

experienced in the flesh at the Grosvenor House, though, naturally, the steam hammer-like gestures could not be transmitted by wireless. 'It was characteristic of him', Francis Williams recalled, 'that when he needed to broadcast he scorned the "prestige position" after the nine o'clock news on Sunday evening [BBC radio only broadcast on two national wavelengths in those days, Home and Forces] to which most ministers aspired and asked the BBC to put him on instead after the one o'clock news on Sunday afternoon when "the family will be all together sitting down nice and comfortable to their Sunday dinner".'[71]

Throughout his ministerial career Bevin proved enormously creative in his use of power. The fuel of that creativity was provided by who he was, what he was and where he had come from. Like Churchill he embodied the species he represented, 'the other half of the English people', as the novelist and broadcaster J.B. Priestley put it after observing from the House of Commons gallery the enormous pair side-by-side on the Government front bench.[72]

Angus Calder captured the man, the motivation and the moment of opportunity when he wrote of Bevin:

> Towards the organized working classes . . . his attitude was that of an elder brother left to rear an enormous family. As Churchill conceived of a nation of Drakes and Nelsons, so Bevin embodied and spoke for and to a working class of, well, Bevins – sober, thick-sinewed men who had overcome their early abhorrence of their employers, had educated themselves, and would now show the bosses how to do the job properly . . .
>
> Bevin saw [in 1940] a chance to fulfil his work as a union organizer, which had lain largely amongst sweated or ill-organized trades, and those who worked in peculiarly bad conditions. Having acquired what seemed to him sufficient power over the fortunes of the working class, he clung jealously to it . . . He built his Ministry into a great office of state; more important at the time than the Exchequer itself.[73]

Bevin never lost sight of the reality that the war would be won on land, sea and in the air by brave young men equipped with the best kit 'his people' in the factories could provide. But he never accepted that improvements in conditions of work and welfare should wait upon Hitler's destruction. Such improvements were not only desirable in themselves, they were an essential precondition of a well armed fighting force.

This great shift in the balance of economic power in Britain, symbolised by Bevin's presence round the War Cabinet table and engineered by him from the Ministry of Labour across the park in St James's Square, was not widely appreciated in political terms at the time.

Yet, with hindsight, there is no mystery about the cause of this profound change from the do-nothing years of economic slump and high unemployment in the 1930s to the can-do, must-do 1940s. It was the combination of common experience shared by all classes under the stress of total war and the Coalition

Government's acceptance of responsibility for what, in Disraeli's time, was called the 'condition of England' which changed the social, economic and – once the lock-gates of the 1945 election were reached – the political direction of Britain.

'It would', wrote Richard Titmuss in his great summing-up of Home Front experience,

> in any relative sense be true to say that by the end of the Second World War the Government had, through the agency of newly established or existing services, assumed and developed a measure of direct concern for the health and well-being of the population which, by contrast with the role of Government in the nineteen-thirties, was little short of remarkable. No longer did concern rest on the belief that, in respect of many social needs, it was proper to intervene only to assist the poor and those who were unable to pay for services of one kind and another. Instead, it was increasingly regarded as a proper function or even obligation of Government to ward off distress and strain among not only the poor but almost all classes of society. And, because the area of responsibility had so perceptibly widened, it was no longer thought sufficient to provide through various branches of social assistance a standard of service hitherto considered appropriate for those in receipt of poor relief – a standard inflexible in administration and attuned to a philosophy which regarded individual distress as a mark of social incapacity.[74]

All were engaged in war where only a few were hit by poverty or disease, Titmuss explained. The Luftwaffe's bombs did not discriminate between the homes of the rich and poor. Government offered relief to both. The Emergency Hospital Service cared for all.

> The pooling of national resources and the sharing of risks were not always practicable nor always applied; but they were the guiding principles . . .
>
> These and other developments in the scope and character of the welfare services did not happen in any planned or ordered sequence; nor were they always a matter of deliberate intent.
>
> Some were pressed forward because of the needs of the war machine for more men and more work. Some took place almost by accident. Some were the result of a recognition of needs hitherto hidden by ignorance of social conditions. Some came about because 'war exposed weaknesses ruthlessly and brutally . . . which called for revolutionary changes in the economic and social life of the country' [here Titmuss was quoting the Conservative minister, Anthony Eden].
>
> Reports in 1939 about the condition of evacuated mothers and children aroused the conscience of the nation in the opening phase of the war . . . [and] . . . stimulated enquiry and proposals for reform long before victory was even thought possible. This was an important experience for it meant

that for five years of war the pressures for a higher standard of welfare and a deeper comprehension of social justice steadily gained in strength.[75]

The moment when this myriad of experiences and notions cohered is also without mystery – the weeks following publication of the Beveridge Report in the closing days of 1942. The flow of ideas and expectations had begun to change much earlier than that, however, in the summer of 1940[76] with the formation of the Coalition, the progressive mobilisation of the nation for war and its tangible manifestations in every factory with a production target and every home with a ration card during Britain's heroic period of standing alone. By the turn of 1942–3 when Beveridge produced his Five Giants it struck few as odd that he observed that revolutionary eras were a time for revolution not patching. Despite the rich compost of experience I have described, the document could so easily have offered all the excitement of a garden marrow rather than the striking bloom it turned out to be. Left to Beveridge the report would probably have been confined to the kitchen garden. The unsung heroine is that same lady who so impressed the Mikardos over tea in Reading a year later.

Janet Mair, or Jessy as she was known, was the wife of Beveridge's rather austere cousin, David Mair, the civil servant and mathematician. In the years before the First World War she and Beveridge became close personally and partners in what his biographer, José Harris, called Beveridge's 'dreams and ambitions'.[77] After David's death in 1942 they married within days of the publication of the great report. While Beveridge was piecing it together Mrs Mair was living with relations in Scotland.

His colleagues in London were civil servants drawn from the range of ministries concerned with social insurance. The Committee, which Beveridge chaired, had been set up with a brief to trim the existing, messy system of provision. Bevin was only too glad to transfer the difficult, wilful Beveridge from the Ministry of Labour, where he was a wartime temporary civil servant, to do what seemed a dry, marginal job which would keep the donnish Sir William out of everybody's hair. Never have such arid expectations been so thoroughly confounded.

It soon became plain, writes José Harris,

that Beveridge intended to place a very ambitious interpretation on the Committee's terms of reference – which were merely to make a survey of 'existing national schemes of social insurance and allied services, including workmen's compensation, and to make recommendations'. The official members themselves varied considerably in their expectation of what these rather vague words might be taken to mean. The Treasury representative, for example, expected merely 'a sort of tidying-up operation ...' The Home Office and Ministry of Health representatives were hoping for something more far reaching; but none of them was quite prepared for the panoramic review of national social policy which it soon became evident that Beveridge had in mind.[78]

Jessy Mair was crucial to both this grand design and its eventual, highly successful and lasting transmission into the national consciousness. Throughout the spring and summer of 1942 her encouragement and advice were constant. Beveridge's biographer could find 'no evidence to suggest that Mrs Mair was responsible for any substantive proposals;

> but much of his report was drafted after weekends with her in Edinburgh, and it was she who urged him to imbue his proposals with 'a Cromwellian spirit' and messianic tone. 'How I hope you are going to be able to preach against all *gangsters*', she wrote, 'who for their mutual gain support one another in upholding all the rest. For that is really what is happening still in England . . . the whole object of their spider web of interlocked big banks and big businessmen [is] a frantic effort to maintain their own caste.' And she urged Beveridge to concentrate on three main policy objectives – 'prevention rather than cure', 'education of those not yet accustomed to clean careful ways of life', and 'plotting the future as a gradual millennium taking step after step but not flinching on ultimate goals'.[79]

Without Mrs Mair and her pleadings for a Cromwellian tone, the Beveridge Report, almost certainly, would have been indistinguishable from the dry-as-dust, jargon-laden, statistics-ridden standard productions on social security and would have been treated accordingly with slim sales and downbeat if respectful coverage in the quality papers.

As it turned out, it was a call-to-arms to a better world, a talisman of the Government's intentions (however reluctant some ministers might be behind the scenes) to give a brave people its just postwar rewards *and* a best-seller to boot selling over 100,000 copies within a month of publication with, in addition, a special cheap edition for circulation among the British Armed Forces all over the world. In occupied Europe it was distributed clandestinely by the Resistance.[80] A Gallup survey in 1943 showed that nineteen out of twenty people knew about the Beveridge Plan.[81] There has never been an official report like it.

The genius of the Beveridge Report lay in its mixing of the profound and the populist. The bulk of its 200,000 words were highly technical treatises on the mechanics of social security. It was the 'Cromwellian' passages which made the report hum and projected it around the globe. They enabled the gist of the Beveridge Plan to be reported in an encapsulated form which informed without distorting and, in addition, Beveridge's Cromwell impressions turned into a headline-writer's dream.

Stripped to its core the Beveridge Report was targeted on 'Five Giants on the Road to Recovery' which he identified in bold, capital letters – '**WANT, DISEASE, IGNORANCE, SQUALOR and IDLENESS**'.[82] To defeat them

Beveridge designed a comprehensive welfare system (though, oddly, he never cared for the phrase 'the welfare state' preferring to call it 'the social service state')[83] based on three 'assumptions' – a free national health service, child allowances, full employment (which he defined as less than 8.5 per cent unemployment).[84]

That all this struck such a vibrant chord in the nation at war was, as Beveridge's biographer noted,

> a matter partly of luck and partly of careful calculation. The report was published a few days after the battle of Alamein, which to many people seemed like a turning-point in the war; and Beveridge was fortunate in that his mingled tone of optimism, patriotism, high principle and pragmatism exactly fitted the prevailing popular mood. It suited also the feeling of national solidarity that seems to have been engendered in all sections of the community by the Second World War.
>
> Nevertheless the groundwork for the reception of the report had been carefully and consciously prepared for many months before. Beveridge himself throughout 1942 had referred in numerous articles and broadcasts to the need for 'equality of sacrifice' and the possibility of abolishing poverty after the war. And without precisely 'leaking' advance information, he had contrived to create the expectation that his Report would be far-reaching in scope and radical in tone.[85]

Beveridge was no orator but he could fill a hall anywhere in the land and he could hold a radio audience with his prissy, Edwardian tones.

J.L. Hodson was one of the millions who heard him on the wireless the evening the Report was published:

> Sir William Beveridge has just been speaking on the radio about his history-making Report, which will be controversial for many a long day ahead. Sir William is one of our great men, full of brains, humorous, and can be devastating. He proposes that we should pay 4s 3d a week [22p] (those who are employed) and that in return we should all be insured against being sick or out of work and be provided with all the doctoring we need, either at home or in hospital. In due time, a man and a wife out of work would get £2 a week, and I (so far as I can see), would get £3 a week (being among the higher incomes).
>
> Some of the Big Business gentlemen are already calling it a scheme that puts us all on the Poor Law. Unless prices are to fall a good deal after the war, the scheme errs on the side of modesty of benefits paid. £2 a week won't go very far. T. Thompson writes me from Lancashire: 'Beveridge has put the ball in the scrum all right. I wonder what shape it will be when it comes out!'[86]

T. Thompson of Lancashire had finely tuned antennae. Much the same thoughts were occurring 200 miles down the A6 in the Whitehall committee-rooms where the imperious Beveridge was never a beloved figure among the 'permanent politicians' of the senior Civil Service. The Treasury in particular thought that, far from being mean, Beveridge's proposals would break the bank or, in the exciting language deployed by the Treasury (who could not in a thousand years have produced a White Paper capturing 'Five Giants'), 'experience shows that over-heavy public levies have a depressing effect upon the community and an adverse reaction upon industrial activity more especially in anxious times'.[87]

Meanwhile Beveridge was carrying his crusade to any in the country who would listen. His audience reached literally the highest in the land. George VI had long regarded social security as a subject close to his heart.[88] He asked to see Beveridge but rather bizarrely spent the interview asking questions about the 'queer people' said to inhabit the London School of Economics where Beveridge had been Director during the interwar years.[89] Beveridge was invited to dine at the Royal Family's least favourite Embassy in London (the murder of the Tsar and his family was not forgotten) and discovered that the Russian Ambassador, Maisky, 'was greatly impressed with his unemployment proposals – particularly with the prospect of "training camps" for those "suspected of malingering"'.[90]

More generally Beveridge's work was compared with the great Poor Law inquiries of 1834 and 1909. The towering figure on the latter, the formidable Beatrice Webb (whose minority report first proposed a free health service for all) commented how odd it was that Beveridge of all people should have 'risen suddenly into the limelight as an accepted designer of the New World Order'.[91]

For his biographer, José Harris,

how far Beveridge was genuinely seen in this light by the public at large, and how far it was an impression deliberately fostered by the media is difficult to say. Certainly the image of Beveridge as the embodiment of popular reforming ideals seems to have been carefully projected by the press and the BBC and pictures of Beveridge looking prophetically white-haired and benign, were flashed by Pathé News into every cinema in the country. [Television was stopped for the duration, cinema audiences were huge; and the newsreels with the characteristically 'gung-ho' commentaries were hugely influential.] But that Beveridge's impact was more than just a trick of wartime propaganda is suggested by the vast sales of his Report, by the apprehension it aroused in government circles and by his massive mail bag from members of the public – asking for his advice on social questions, urging him to press for immediate legislation, and assuring him that 'the spiritual forces of the Nation are on your side'.[92]

The Report continued to pour over the counters of His Majesty's Stationery Office. In the end 635,000 copies were sold which put Beveridge on a par with a best-selling author of fiction.[93] The authorities in Whitehall were chilled to the marrow. Distribution of a summary of its findings by the Army Bureau of Current Affairs was stopped shortly before Christmas 1942.[94]

In contrast to the private world of Whitehall, the public popularity of Beveridge soared. A survey carried out in early 1943 by the British Institute for Public Opinion showed 86 per cent in favour and a mere 6 per cent opposed. Three out of five thought, like J.L. Hodson, that pension rates were too low. The proposal for a free health service won 88 per cent support (the figure for the wealthier groups in society was 81 per cent).[95]

The pro-Beveridge sentiment had not abated by February 1943 when Parliamentary time was finally found to debate the Report. *Picture Post*, in one of the finest examples of popular journalism I have ever read, set the scene the week before by contrasting the evil days of depression, unemployment and despair with the new world Beveridge was promising.[96] For the Coalition, Sir John Anderson, Lord President of the Council, a dry old civil servant-turned-minister,[97] had the unenviable task of telling an impassioned House of Commons (especially the inflamed Labour benches) that 'there can be at present no binding commitment. Subject only to that . . . I have made it clear that the Government adopt the scheme in principle.'[98] Beveridge was booted into postwar touch and, I believe, the key battleground of the 1945 election was marked out some twenty-eight months before polling took place.

The lines were drawn, in fact, when the Beveridge debate ended in the ornate, gothic surroundings of the Lords' Chamber on the evening of 18 February 1943 (the Commons Chamber had been bombed out two years before and the peers made way for the MPs), when the House divided over Beveridge. Jim Griffiths, a future Minister of National Insurance and a key figure in the postwar building of the welfare state, put down a motion calling for an immediate commitment to the implementation of Beveridge in full.

A skilful speech from the Home Secretary, Herbert Morrison, who had fought hard against Treasury negativism on Beveridge in the privacy of the Cabinet's Committee on Reconstruction Priorities,[99] failed to sweeten the sour impression given earlier in the debate by Anderson and the Conservative Chancellor of the Exchequer, Sir Kingsley Wood. As a result, the Coalition suffered one of its biggest – certainly one of its most significant – backbench rebellions.

Some 121 MPs (out of a House of 650) voted against the Government and in favour of the Griffiths motion: 97 Labour; 3 Independent Labour Party; 1 Communist; 11 Independents and 9 Liberals including the great David Lloyd George, builder of the prototype welfare state just before the First World War, casting his last ever vote in the House of Commons. Only two Labour MPs supported the Government. Not a single Conservative voted with Griffiths. Lord Woolton, the Minister of Food and probably the greatest of the Conservative Party's postwar managers, watched the Beveridge debate from the peers' gallery. He observed shrewdly that while Anderson had 'made a complete 'mess' of the Government's case, the popular mood in favour of Beveridge was beyond dispute.[100] This was to be of cardinal importance in the weeks before the general election when, with both Labour and Conservatives pledging a comprehensive system of social insurance and a national health service along Beveridge lines, the issue turned on which party could best be trusted to convert fine words into reality.[101]

This strong tide of opinion and expectation which manifested itself so tangibly in popular support for the unlikely figure of the 'People's William', as Paul Addison called him,[102] is worth a moment of fairly precise measurement given the reshaping of British politics and the substantial extension of state power to which it led after 1945. And, for once, reasonably precise measurement is possible thanks to Mass Observation.[103]

In the middle of the Blitz, MO's panel of observers, including 'units of trained investigators . . . sent anonymously to make overall reports',[104] totted up the 'political and related change which people expected to emerge as a result of the new, "total" war'.[105]

MO's Top Six was as follows:

CHANGE	% EXPECTING THIS AS A MAJOR POSTWAR TREND.
Less class distinctions	29*
More state control	21
Education reforms	19
Levelling of incomes	15*
Increased social services	*14
Dictatorship, 'fascism'.	13

* An asterisk before the number means especially mentioned by men, after the number by women.[106]

As Tom Harrisson commented:

Of these six, all but the last came to pass! Other changes less often mentioned included religious revival (9% of women), revolution (5% of men) and better rural-urban understanding (8% of each sex). Only 6%, mostly women, foresaw higher taxation; none inflation.[107]

That last point is fascinating given it was double-digit inflation in the 1970s which brought much of the masonry of the postwar settlement crashing to the ground. 'The blitz', Harrisson continued,

played a part in realising some of these expectations mainly as one impetus towards equal sharing of war's burdens. But the big drive for change came later, influenced largely by the length of the war and the great numbers of people eventually involved in it. The war had to be made worthwhile to offset boredom not bombs. This mood was first crystallized in the Beveridge Report nearly two years after the blitz.[108]

A sub-theme of Mass Observation's findings is especially interesting in terms of the public's faith in the credibility of politicians as deliverers of a better world. The way the authorities coped or, in some cases, failed to cope, with the consequences of aerial bombardment did little, it seems, either to increase or decrease public cynicism about 'the system' and the people who ran it. 'The blitz', Tom Harrisson concluded, 'did not . . . arouse any wide or lasting antagonism to the leadership, although it occasionally accentuated existing local cynicism. Disillusion about the working of democracy was already well-established before the war.'[109]

In 1944 Mass Observation built on its previous work with a study of attitude changes stimulated by war, entitled *The Mood of Britain – 1938 and 1944*. Its most significant finding was that total war had dispelled the prewar combination of ignorance and fatalism overlain by the sense of guilt (two-fifths said they felt it) about the betrayal of Czechoslovakia at Munich. The experience of the 'Phoney War' had served to strengthen these attitudes.

It was the experience of 'total war' which changed the picture, according to Mass Observation. The 'selfish' set of attitudes revealed in prewar studies gave way to a sense of purpose which went beyond self and immediate convenience. MO found the Beveridge Report had focused the national mood powerfully. From 1943 people began to show a willingness to itemise what was wrong with British society and to suggest ways of putting it right. The same was true for foreign policy and the needs of the postwar world. By 1944, when the MO survey was conducted, job security and a place to live in had become major priorities. Britain, plainly, was going Keynes', Beveridge's (and Labour's) way.[110] Though not until the 'shock' result of July 1945 would this transformation become generally appreciated.

Yet democracy had not entirely been suspended since 1940 despite the party truce in by-elections whereby the party which had held the seat previously was not opposed by its Coalition partners. The Common Wealth Party, led by a utopian hereditary baronet, Sir Richard Acland (a secular saint who gave away his own personal fortune) came into being as a vehicle of protest. At its peak it never exceeded a membership of 10,000[111] (though by 1944 it had branches in no less than 321 constituencies).[112] Nevertheless it won three spectacular by-elections – defeating Conservative candidates at Eddisbury in April 1943, Skipton in January 1944 and Chelmsford in April 1945 – finishing the war with four MPs (Acland was the sitting member for Barnstaple when he underwent his conversion to Christian Socialism).

For all the tensions within the Coalition about reconstruction policy, the pace of postwar social change and the financing of it, Labour stuck loyally to the electoral truce which, to all intents and purposes, froze the House of Commons in its 1935 incarnation. In one respect, however, it differed from the Conservatives: it kept its Party agents and local organisations in better repair than its opponents. The Conservatives even abandoned their Party Conference until 1943.[113] And it was the vitality of Labour at the local level which gave the Party the second of its distinct policy themes at the 1945 election – the nationalisation of several basic industries for the purposes of both economic efficiency and social justice.

Public ownership had long been a pillar of Labour's economic philosophy entrenched in the famous Clause IV of its 1918 constitution emblazoned on the party's membership card (as it still was in the late 1980s) to the effect that policy should be 'to secure for the workers by hand or by brain the full fruits of their industry and the most equitable distribution thereof that may be possible upon the basis of the common ownership of the means of production, distribution and exchange and the best obtainable system of popular administration and control of each industry or service.'[114] To the disgust of many Labour activists, the document *Full Employment and Financial Policy* produced by the Party's National Executive Committee, struck a far from convincing note when it came to public ownership.

'Worse was to follow,' wrote Ian Mikardo, the constituency activist whose name will be for ever associated with the revolt which painted nationalisation boldly into the postwar picture.

> In the run-up to the [1944] Annual Conference the NEC published a revised statement for submission to the Conference as the centrepiece of the Party's manifesto for the postwar general election, whenever it came. The new text was much shorter than the policy paper on which it was based, and much more timid and conventional. It made no mention whatever of public ownership, and raised enhanced doubts about whether our leaders had the political will to carry out the radical reconstruction of the national economy which they themselves had asserted as being essential if we were to cope with the sharply changed conditions of the postwar world. Those leaders of ours, grossly miscalculating the mood of the Party members throughout the country, expected that they would have no difficulty in getting this new policy statement adopted at the Conference.[115]

Usually, history either ignores or cannot find the individual whose germ of an idea later develops into something of great substance. Thanks to Ian Mikardo we know the man who, in his own way, did for nationalisation in the late 1940s what Ralph Harris and Arthur Seldon of the Institute of Economic Affairs did for privatisation in the 1980s. The man was not Mikardo himself but another Party activist in wartime Reading, Wilf Cannon – 'a lean, vigorous, silver-haired, patrician-looking man, a good talker, a good listener and a discriminating reader, an intensely political animal'.[116]

Cannon was a Great Western man, a lifelong railwayman working beyond retirement age as his contribution to the war effort, in the Scurrs Lane marshalling yard just to the west of Reading General station. On his way home from the sidings one evening he attended a meeting of the Reading No. 1 Branch of the National Union of Railwaymen called to consider motions the constituency might submit to the next Party Conference. 'At that meeting of his branch', Mikardo recorded,

one of his fellow-members put up a resolution for Conference on the need to reorganise the railway system and argued that this was a natural and proper resolution for a railwaymen's branch to sponsor. But Wilf Cannon opposed him on the grounds that the railways were just one element in the national economy and that we should all aim, at the forthcoming Conference, to get policies adopted which would put the whole economy right: we would get an expanding and efficient railway system, he contended, only within a total economic system which was expanding and efficient. Accordingly he proposed a resolution which had the effect of correcting what he saw as the defects of the NEC statement, and in particular spelling out a programme for extending the public sector.[117]

Cannon's motion was chosen, forwarded by the Reading Party as a whole to the Conference in Westminster Central Hall in December 1944 as one of twenty-two motions from across the country urging a strong commitment to public ownership. After the usual compositing process, Reading's was chosen as the basis of the consolidated motion. Mikardo, his stomach flapping as if he 'had a whole flock of whacking great pterodactyls' in it, proposed the motion, declined Manny Shinwell's and Philip Noel-Baker's invitations (on behalf of the NEC) to withdraw it and carried the day by a huge majority on a show of hands. Herbert Morrison, the Home Secretary and Labour's Party manager-supreme, sought Mikardo after the vote, found him, placed a hand on his shoulder and said 'You realise, don't you, that you've lost us the general election.'[118]

The trail that wound from Central Hall via the Party's 1945 manifesto pledges to the great state concerns of the postwar period – coal, rail, gas, electricity, iron and steel (this last in and out of the public sector like a cuckoo clock) – changed the face of Britain's political economy. Not until 1979 did a Conservative Government truly reverse what Lord Joseph likes to call the 'ratchet effect' of socialism. In this sense, there has never been a pair of Party activists with quite the impact of Wilf Cannon and Ian Mikardo.

When their motion captured the hearts and minds of the delegates in Central Hall just across the square from Parliament, the Allied armies had just suffered an unexpected reverse in the forests of the Ardennes. The end of the war in Europe, however, was firmly in sight. In narrow electoral terms, though, it remained to be seen if Parliament was to be refreshed before the white flags flew above Tokyo as well as Berlin.

1 The horror to come? A gas mask for all in the Munich September of 1938

2   The Anderson shelters arrive, Islington, 1939

3   The Underground, 1940: every inch a bed

4　On the way to Blackhorse Road
　　Station, evacuation day,
　　Walthamstow, 1939

5　'Digging for Victory', even in the
　　moat at the Tower of London, 1940

6–7 The Blitz: what it meant. *Above* Forty-five children killed, Catford, 1943. *Below* A man and a dog come back from a Sunday walk to find . . .

8 Pixie-gunners in a people's army; straight from panto' to coastal action station, Christmas 1941

9 'I can look the East End in the face,' Buckingham Palace, September 1940

10 VE Day in London, 8 May 1945

11 Parliament on the way to give thanks on VJ Day, 15 August 1945: (left to right) Anthony Eden, Winston Churchill, Ernest Bevin and Clement Attlee

12 Politics by the tank: Sergeant
    Ernie Teal (second from left), and
    Sir William Anstruther-Grey
    (centre), Nijmegen, 1944

13 Barbara Betts, later Castle,
    Labour Party adoption meeting,
    Blackburn, 1945

14 *Left* Churchill leaves the war-bunker to resign, 26 July 1945

15 *Right* 'I've won the election.'
'I know, I heard it on the Six O'Clock News.'

16 The Labour Cabinet, 1945

Churchill began discussions with his party deputy, Anthony Eden, about the timing of the general election within days of the War in Europe ending. Churchill was torn between an early poll in June, generally regarded as the best prospect for the Conservatives, and October which might leave the Government 'paralysed'. But, on the other hand, as Churchill telegrammed to Eden, who was still in San Francisco helping piece together the United Nations, 'the Russian peril, which I regard as enormous, could be better faced if we remained united'.[119] Amid much conflicting advice, Churchill decided to try and prolong the life of the Coalition until Japan had been defeated. There was considerable support for this among senior Labour ministers including Attlee, Bevin and (so Churchill thought) Morrison. But to Churchill's surprise and chagrin, Attlee rang Churchill from the Labour Party Conference in Blackpool on 21 May with the view that 'My colleagues and I do not believe that it would be possible to lay aside political controversy now that the expectation of an election has engaged the attention of the country.'[120]

At the crucial Labour National Executive meeting in Blackpool Attlee, though his wish to sustain the Coalition was generally known, confined himself to 'a statement of the pros and cons'.[121] It was Morrison, Chairman of the Party's Campaign Committee, who swung the issue arguing forcefully that the mood was running strongly against continuing the Coalition.[122] Announcing the decision to the Conference in the Winter Gardens, Morrison was cheered to the echo, a factor which did nothing to discourage the plot he was hatching to displace Attlee as Leader.[123]

Two days after receiving Attlee's call from the seaside Churchill resigned, performing a fascinating little charade, in order to preserve the constitutional niceties, by returning briefly to the No. 10 Annexe for lunch in order that the King could decide whom he wished to invite to form a Caretaker Government to hold the fort until the election result was known (as if there would be the slightest doubt who it would be). At four he was back at the Palace and spent a disagreeable evening fitting names to jobs in what was obviously to be a very short-lived administration. His only consolation, he told his Chief Whip, was that unlike Mr Gladstone he could use the telephone instead of 'all those letters he had to write'.[124]

The decision to break up the Coalition was probably the correct one. The chemistry which bonded it began to alter as the danger which had created it began to recede. Oliver Lyttleton, the Minister of Production (a Conservative figure especially close to Churchill) was acutely aware of the decaying process. 'As soon as victory began to look assured', he recalled after the war,

the War Cabinet ceased to be a united or indeed an effective body. Disputes and disagreements began to paralyse action. Defeat knits together, victory opens the seams. The Labour ministers were preparing for a general election and would not let anything pass that had a bearing on their prospects.

The Prime Minister tried hard to keep the Coalition together and brought all his unique powers of persuasion to bear. His efforts were in vain; our Labour colleagues had decided to leave. I felt sad at the farewell party in the Cabinet Room at No. 10 Downing Street [on 28 May 1945]. The departing Labour members looked rather gloomy and sheepish and I could not help remembering all that we had been through together.[125]

It may not have been gloom or sheepishness. It could well have been emotion or, for the more hard-boiled, embarrassment because poor Churchill was overcome by the occasion. He stood behind the Cabinet table, tears pouring down his face, told them 'The light of history will shine on every helmet' and that whatever happened in the election, Britain would be a 'United Nation'.[126] It was, putting sentiment on one side, a considerable occasion – the ending of a brave, formidable and, by normal political standards, competent Government which had achieved more, far more, than cold reason might have suggested in the perilous moments of its formation five years before. Churchill never lost his high regard for the Labour people who had sat alongside him, Bevin in particular to whom he had written the day before the lachrymose farewell in the Cabinet Room, 'You know what it means to me not to have your aid in these terrible times.'[127]

Folklore remembers elections, if at all, by a single snatch of rhetoric. It's altogether surprising, therefore, given Churchill's respect for Attlee and Bevin that the one word 'Gestapo' should flash on to the visual display unit of memory each time the words '1945 general election' are keyed in. It was delivered during a party political broadcast on 4 June and couched in a passage intended to illuminate the dangers of excessive state power:

No Socialist Government conducting the entire life and industry of the country could afford to allow free, sharp or violently-worded expression of public discontent. They would have to fall back on some form of Gestapo, no doubt very humanely directed in the first instance. And this would nip opinion in the bud: it would stop criticism as it reared its head, and it would gather all the power to the supreme Party and the party leaders, rising like stately pinnacles about their vast bureaucracies of Civil Servants, no longer servants and no longer civil.[128]

That elaborate confection of rhetorical exaggeration did Churchill great harm. It made him sound ludicrous rather than eloquent, a crude partisan rather than the wise statesman above the fray.

It was a gift to Labour such as few, if any, Conservative leaders have presented in twentieth-century elections and Labour made effective use of it, starting with Attlee himself when he broadcast his reply. (Its dignity and bite were as apparent as ever when I listened to a BBC archive recording of it in 1989.) Anybody less like a member of the secret police of any nation, let alone Hitler's Germany, than the mild figure of Attlee would be hard to imagine. 'When I listened to the Prime Minister's speech last night', Attlee told the millions listening to the BBC Home Service in the evening of 5 June,

> in which he gave such a travesty of the policy of the Labour Party, I realised at once what was his object. He wanted the electors to understand how great was the difference between Winston Churchill the great leader in war of a united nation and Mr Churchill, the Party Leader of the Conservatives. He feared lest those who had accepted his leadership in war might be tempted out of gratitude for having followed him further. I thank him for having disillusioned them so thoroughly.[129]

Attlee, of course, wasn't deceived for a moment by the Churchillian hyperbole. Shortly before his death he recalled his feelings about the 'Gestapo' gibe.

ATTLEE: Nonsense. Just a kind of election cry that wouldn't be taken up.
INTERVIEWER: Didn't it hurt you that the man who had been your Prime Minister, to whom you had been deputy for such a long time, should suddenly turn on you in this way?
ATTLEE: I didn't mind. I knew my Winston.[130]

One aspect of Attlee's tart put-down of 'my Winston' was off-beam, however. He suggested in his broadcast that 'The voice we heard last night was that of Mr Churchill, but the mind was that of Lord Beaverbrook.'[131] In fact, neither Beaverbrook nor Churchill's other mercurial intimate from the world of the newspaper proprietors, Brendan Bracken, had anything to do with the 'Gestapo' speech. Of the few privy to its contents, Clemmie Churchill begged him to cut it out.[132] Beaverbrook and Bracken were simply not around or involved.

Churchill's private secretary, Jock Colville, who witnessed its preparation over the weekend at Chequers, recalled watching him deliver the speech from the Buckinghamshire countryside on the Monday evening and 'that his gestures to the microphone were as emphatic as those he uses in a political speech to a large audience and far more pronounced than those he employed in ordinary conversation. The speech, in which, contrary to general supposition, neither Brendan nor the Beaver had a hand, aroused widespread criticism and did not really go down well, at any rate with the educated classes.'[133]

Distaste was not confined to the 'educated classes' either. Over forty years later Tony Benn could still recall the widespread derision on his troopship returning from the Middle East when Churchill's 'Gestapo' party political was broadcast over the vessel's tannoy.[134] Churchill, I suspect, knew he was failing, in Enoch Powell's brilliant phrase, 'to give the people a tune to hum'.[135] Clemmie wrote to their daughter, Mary, just before the third of Churchill's four election broadcasts that 'He is very low, poor Darling. He thinks he has lost his "touch" and he grieves about it.'[136]

Labour, on the other hand, exulted about it though even at that late stage few sensed the victory to come. Ian Mikardo was not the only candidate to harp upon Churchill's 'monstrous blunder . . . For the remaining four weeks of the election campaign everybody who chaired one of my meetings was instructed (and was taught the correct pronunciation) to introduce me as Obergruppen-fuhrer Ian Mikardo, prospective Gauleiter of Berkshire, Buckinghamshire and Oxfordshire. That always got us off to a good start.'[137]

It is very doubtful, however, that the election was lost by Churchill's howler or the Conservatives' generally lacklustre campaign (despite a briefly vigorous attempt to portray Attlee as the feeble prisoner of a Labour NEC in the grip of its new Chairman, Professor Harold Laski, a political scientist from the LSE who, implausibly enough, became a bogey figure for the right). Though the size of Labour's majority may have been increased in consequence. In fact, it would be wrong to see Churchill as a minus for the Conservatives. It was the Party the electorate turned against – the Party of unemployment, the means test and appeasement – rather than the Party leader of 1945 whom the Conservatives had spurned throughout the 1930s. Tom Harrisson captured Churchill's electoral dilemma when he wrote that the old warrior 'himself received vast public and published acclaim as Britain's successful wartime leader. But the basic British distrust of strong leadership showed . . . Millions in fact thought of Churchill, specifically, as a mighty support in dire necessity, a sort of intel-lectual deep-shelter, intended for emergency protection only.'[138]

Another factor often misleadingly advanced as the critical downpour which engineered Labour's landslide is the servicemen's vote. Quite an elaborate conspiracy theory grew up in Conservative circles that left-inclined briefings disseminated worldwide to the troops by the Army Bureau of Current Affairs was responsible for such minor outrages as the short-lived Forces' Mock Parliament in Egypt in 1944 and the altogether greater one which put Mr Attlee into Downing Street. Kenneth O. Morgan has calculated that 'only 60 per cent of servicemen voted at all (1,701,000 in total) owing to difficulties in sending out and collecting voting forms. They were only a small fraction of those 25,000,000 who went to the polls, even though it was believed by Labour candidates such as Leah Manning at Epping and George Wigg at Dudley that those servicemen's votes that were recorded went overwhelmingly Labour's way.'[139]

Much has been made of the forces' radicalism and its more dramatic erupt-ions like the Forces' Parliament in Egypt.[140] In terms of sheer numbers the tide almost certainly moved towards Labour on the battlefronts in a less dramatic but equally powerful fashion. For Ernie Teal, a previously apolitical country-man from the East Riding of Yorkshire, it was, as we have seen, the experience of seeing first hand the living conditions of ordinary working people in Holland and Germany as the Guards Armoured Division moved across Europe. Like most of his tank squadron he voted Labour by proxy in July 1945.

Sergeant Teal had the near-unique experience of having a sitting Conservative MP as his commanding officer in the huge form of Sir William Anstruther-Grey:

> Anstruther-Grey would talk to our squadron about the political situation. We had a chap from Seaham Harbour and his MP was Manny Shinwell. Anstruther liked Manny Shinwell. He used to lecture us about the political situation. He was always keen to tell us that we were fighting for liberty and democracy.
>
> About May 1st 1945 (We were at Cuxhaven where we'd just knocked out a V2 station) Anstruther-Grey said 'We've fired our last shot in anger. I'm going back to be a pot-bellied politician. We [the Conservatives] shall get kicked out, but we'll be back.[141]

Sir William, who rose to be Chairman of his Party's 1922 Committee, was right on every count and joins the select band of politicians who predicted accurately the electoral tide as the war in Europe finished.

But the political water surging towards the lock-gate of the 1945 election, to borrow Lewis Namier's metaphor, was propelled by a tide already turned by Home-Front experience and a determination that, this time, peace would be more nearly synonymous with social justice. Labour rode in on its crest. Gallup's 'carefully constructed'[142] polls, appearing regularly in the Liberal-inclined *News Chronicle* from 1942 onwards, illustrated the electorate's preoccupations during the 1945 campaign: 'Housing' topped the list as the most important issue with 41 per cent followed by 'Full Employment' at 15 per cent, 'Social Security' at 7 per cent followed by 'Nationalisation of Industry' at 6 per cent[143] – findings replicated at the time by a British Institute of Public Opinion Survey.[144] Nationalisation apart, these were Beveridge's 'Giants on the Road to Recovery' translated into voters' preoccupations and, given Labour's greater emphasis upon them and the Conservatives' lack of credibility as giant-killers, translated into voting intentions as well.

Gallup's findings can be given a high degree of credence as its pollsters predicted simultaneously with near complete accuracy (to within 1 per cent) the outcome of the vote of 5 July when the results began to pour in three weeks later.

Gallup conducted inquiries in 195 constituencies between 24 and 27 June. They predicted a 47 per cent share of the poll for Labour (Labour took 47.8 per cent on the day); 41 per cent for the Conservatives (39.8 per cent); Liberals 10 per cent (9 per cent).[145] Still the electoral penny did not drop. Churchill told George VI on the day before the result was declared that he expected to win by between thirty and eighty seats.[146] For others, however, the truth began to dawn as canvass returns were totted up in the final days of the campaign. Three days before the poll Ian Mikardo's agent told him he was going to win. Mikardo did not believe him. The agent wrote out his prediction on a scrap of paper to be opened after the result. It read 'Labour majority 6,500'. Mikardo won by 6,390.[147]

Mikardo was far better informed than his leader. Attlee's daughter Felicity said, 'people find it extraordinary that before that election day in July 1945 we had never sat down as a family and discussed what we would do if my father should become Prime Minister'.[148] On 26 July, the greatest day in the history of the British Labour Party, the Attlees breakfasted together at their Stanmore home in the north London suburbs in utter ignorance of what was to come within a few hours. 'It was the early edition of the "Evening Standard", glimpsed over a fellow passenger's shoulder at Oxford Circus, which brought home to my sister Alison and me the full impact of what had happened. There was a picture of our father smiling [in his Limehouse constituency in London's East End] and wearing a rosette in his buttonhole, and a banner headline "The New Prime Minister". Alison and I joined hands and danced our way down Oxford Street.'[149]

By the time the family met for tea in the Great Western Hotel at Paddington, before the new premier set off for the Palace, Attlee, backed by the ever loyal Bevin, had beaten off a challenge to his leadership from Morrison: 'If the King asks you to form a Government you say "Yes" or "No", not "I'll let you know later!"'[150] A mile away Churchill's tea time in his war bunker was, naturally enough, a deeply gloomy affair. As the news of Conservative losses poured into the famous map room, Mary Churchill could stand it no longer:

[She] crossed the corridor to the small kitchen. There she found Mrs Landemare, Churchill's devoted cook housekeeper. She was making honey sandwiches. 'I don't know *what* the world's coming to', she exclaimed, 'but I thought I might make some tea.'[151]

CHAPTER 3

Songs in Their Hearts

What were your personal feelings about Sir Winston's defeat?
I was sorry for the Old Boy.

What were your own emotions at becoming Prime Minister?
Just to know that there were jobs that were to be done.

You didn't feel that destiny had overtaken you?
No. I had not much idea about destiny.
Lord Attlee, interviewed in 1965[1]

The transition to Attlee was . . . abrupt. Massive changes in the whole framework of politics took place within a fortnight . . . But this was by no means all. Britain's hour of perilous but spectacular glory was over. The inheritance was bleak. Our nominal membership of the triumvirate of world power [United States, Soviet Union, Great Britain] was guaranteed by our recent record. But it was as unsustainable as it was temporarily incontestable. The temporary reconciliation of these two facts was one of the most awkward processes in our history.
Roy Jenkins, 1988[2]

And so it was that, by the time they took the bunting down from the streets after VE Day and turned from the war to the future, the British in their dreams and illusions and in their flinching from reality had already written the broad scenario for Britain's postwar descent to the place of fifth in the free world as an industrial power, with manufacturing output only two-fifths of West Germany's, and the place of fourteenth in the whole non-communist world in terms of annual GNP. . . . As that descent took its course the illusions and the dreams of 1945 would fade one by one – the Imperial and Commonwealth role, the world-power role, British industrial genius, and, at the last, New Jerusalem itself, a dream turned to a dank reality of a segregated, subliterate, unskilled, unhealthy and institutionalized proletariat hanging on the nipple of state maternalism.
Correlli Barnett, 1986[3]

By today's standards the first majority Labour government ruled a poverty-stricken country exhausted by world war.
A.H. Halsey, 1988[4]

What, in the words of Churchill's housekeeper, *had* the world come to and what was Britain's place in it? The legendary lady diner in the Savoy was not alone in thinking her world had come to a close. Many people at different ends of the political spectrum were convinced that they really were on the brink of a new one. Sir Peregrine Worsthorne, for example, never forgot 'the panic that hit some of my rich fellow officers – Astors and Barings – when the news of Labour's victory reached our mess in Holland. They thought the game was up there and then, and blocked the 21st Army Group's headquarters' communications system telephoning anguished instructions to sell to their stockbrokers.'[5]

'As it was', Perry Worsthorne continued, 'for them the game wasn't up. The very rich managed to survive and do quite well under socialism. For short of forcible expropriation as in a revolution, it is exceedingly difficult to dispossess the very rich.'[6] There were other members of the British armed forces, however, who have never quite got over the fact that 1945 *wasn't* the moment which saw the end of the privilege of the rich.

The historian E.P. Thompson, warning of the dangers of reconstructing history from 'top level sources' in the Public Record Office, makes a distinction between high level impressions as captured in the files and 'how it was felt in the country'.

> As a soldier just returned from overseas service I had a walk-on part at several Labour election meetings in rural Buckinghamshire. Packed meetings of suddenly undeferential villagers applauded every expression of hope for a socialist Europe and every reference to the heroism of the European Resistance movements or the feats of the Red Army (which everyone knew had saved what small ration was left of British bacon).[7]

The debate about what 1945 *should* have meant and what it *actually* meant continued to rage forty years after Attlee accepted George VI's commission to form a Government. But before tackling the great, heavy-duty issues it continues to raise, the atmosphere of 1945 – the grain of everyday existence, the humdrum as well as the hopeful and the glorious – needs to be recaptured particularly for those whose experience of a rationed meal or a postwar train journey is mercifully second-hand.

If, by the good offices of a Dr Who-style time machine, you found yourself deposited in, say, 1945-Walthamstow, several phenomena would strike you simultaneously. It would smell different for a start. Instead of car exhaust, coal smoke would predominate. Coal was still king in the factory, around the hearth and on the railway. The clean air legislation which banished smogs from our inner cities was more than a decade away. As a result the buildings were a grimy black, especially the public ones – libraries, town halls and schools. The rich variety of British geology as reflected in our monumental masonry did not begin to be appreciated until the smog had gone and the high-pressure water hose had arrived in the 1960s.

Black buildings and poky, narrow streets went together. Most of the cities and their inner suburbs, like Walthamstow in north-east London, had been thrown up before the motor car began to change life, work and leisure. Given the shortage of petrol, however, the streets of 1945 were pretty empty; cars and lorries were tiny and low (and almost entirely British-made) though noisy. Crawling trams, running on rails down the middle of many a high street, were epic jam-makers. Street furniture was different, too. The road signs tiny and cluttered, the lamps short, feeble and still frequently gas-lit. To help motorist and pedestrian alike in the blackout, kerbstones were painted black and white, like mile after mile of liquorice allsorts. There were no noisy jets or helicopters in the sky. Police cars had tinkling bells rather than wailing sirens.

The appearance of ordinary people in the street would surprise you – pale faces, drab, often threadbare clothing with a sameness about it that came from rationing and standard Board of Trade-approved designs.[8] Men all seemed to be wearing the same suit of the classic demob type.[9] People looked poor, though, in reality, the population, as we have seen, was better nourished than it had ever been thanks to the minimum standards that accompanied rationing bringing many up and fewer down.

It wasn't merely the necessities of life which still caused the British to form the orderly lines with which so many foreigners continue to associate them. It was almost everything. In 1946 that acutest of observers of the British scene, the Hungarian humorist George Mikes, published his celebrated *How to Be an Alien*. Inevitably, it contained a section on the country's 'national passion' for queuing:

> At weekends an Englishman queues at the bus-stop, travels out to Richmond, queues up for a boat [on the Thames], then queues up for tea, then queues up for ice-cream, then joins a few more odd queues for the sake of the fun of it, then queues up at the bus-stop, and has the time of his life.[10]

The queue motif could be detected anywhere in the world that the British were in 1945. Wherever a defeated territory was occupied or a colony garrisoned, there were the members of what was, at this stage, a truly citizens' army in uniform queuing for tea (what else?) in NAAFI canteens around the globe. There was, too, the occasional mutiny in the Far East apart,[11] the same resignation to the monotony of life as men by the hundreds of thousands waited for the glorious moment of demobilisation with *its* great symbols, the trilby hat and the famous suit.

Never has a Government inherited a more disciplined nation than did the incoming Labour ministers in 1945, nor, almost certainly, a more united one.

The setbacks of the postwar period were all the more grimly felt because of the glory of its dawn, however phlegmatic and understated the British themselves may have been in their moment of triumphant survival. One of my greatest regrets is that I was not around or not old enough to savour and to share it. Certainly those Labour ministers who were, unlike Attlee, temperamentally capable of showing exuberance, were exalted by real power at last free of the constraints that minority or Coalition Government imposes. The ever-vibrant Dalton caught the mood when he introduced his first budget in November 1945 'with a song in my heart'[12] (the title of a popular song).

All politicians operate to some degree in the realms of delusion and wishful thinking. They have to. Without that trait, near despair would have afflicted the new Government in the late victory summer of 1945. A modern-day policy analyst, skilled in the ways of costs and benefits, would have offered a bleak prognosis. Some did, most notably the great economist, Maynard Keynes, who warned the Cabinet that Britain was facing 'a financial Dunkirk', a prospect all the more dire because 'the financial problems of the war have been surmounted so easily and silently that the average man sees no reason to suppose that the financial problems of the peace will be any more difficult'.[13]

Superficially Britain was still, with America and Russia, one of the world's three superpowers. Unlike the moment of victory in the First World War, supremacy could not be claimed in any of the constituent parts of super-powerdom. In November 1918, a tiny token force of American warships watched off the Firth of Forth as the great capital ships of the Royal Navy's Grand Fleet escorted the huge German High Seas Fleet to Scapa Flow and internment pending full surrender and a Peace Treaty.[14] In no single area of weaponry was the United States deficient to Great Britain in May 1945. And though the Red Army had travelled light and lived off the land as it crossed central Europe and the Balkans,[15] the strength, experience and combat-readiness of those famous '175 divisions' was already causing concern, occasionally approaching panic, among military planners in the West.

And yet there was almost no sense in Whitehall among the politicians, the diplomats, the civil servants or the military that the 'Great Game' of the pursuit of power on a world scale was soon to be over for ever. Bevin was not alone in basing his strategy on the premise that Britain's economic difficulties would prove temporary; that her domestic industrial base and international trading system based on the Empire would, with careful management and a degree of American help, soon recover to the point where the old roles would be financially sustainable. It was, perhaps inevitably, an hour for wishful thinking. The four corners of the earth had, after all, come – and Britain *had* shocked them as the cartoonist David Low's 'Tommy' had predicted as he stood on the White Cliffs of Dover in 1940, with wave upon wave of enemy bombers crossing the coast, and shook his fist across the English Channel and cried 'Very well, Alone'.[16]

Furthermore, it is all so crystal clear and so very simple for armchair Clausewitzes looking back and perceiving reality from the clutter of expectations, traditions and current experience forty and more years before. Even with the perspective of hindsight, the old chestnut of perception – is this glass half full or half empty? – can be seen to apply. It could be argued that Whitehall's postwar strategists had every reason *not* to think of Britain's future in terms of a slow, careful shift to the status of a Sweden or a Holland.

For example, the Royal Navy, *the* traditional symbol of national power, was bigger in 1945 than it had ever been with 929 capital ships, 137 submarines, 6,485 patrol boats, landing craft and auxiliary vessels, 70 Fleet Air Arm squadrons made up of 1,336 aircraft plus manpower and womanpower totalling more than 850,000.[17] While the Royal Air Force, reflecting the ever-rising importance of air power in the first half of the twentieth century, finished the war with 55,469 aircraft and over a million personnel.[18]

Within two years demobilisation, cuts in defence expenditure and the quite natural reluctance to replace the superabundance of weaponry purchased for the forces during the war, had produced a very different picture. That great national talisman, our blue-water navy, was a sorry spectacle by the end of the crisis year of 1947 with its Home Fleet, according to one American observer, 'reduced almost to the point of disintegration [when] for a short period at the end of 1947 it was down to a total active strength of one cruiser and four destroyers'.[19]

But even with such drastic retrenchment in the tangibles of military power, Britain's postwar duties as an imperial and an occupying power kept vast concentrations of khaki in a worldwide kaleidoscope. In addition to the thirty infantry battalions and seventeen armoured regiments stationed at home, the British Army's overseas billets in 1947 produced this impressive and costly tally:

EGYPT:	3 infantry battalions; 2 armoured regiments.
LIBYA:	3 infantry battalions; 2 armoured regiments.
CYPRUS:	1 infantry brigade.
SOMALILAND:	2 infantry battalions.
SUDAN:	1 infantry battalion.
FAR EAST:	13 infantry battalions.
JAMAICA:	1 infantry battalion.
WEST GERMANY:	18 infantry battalions; 8 armoured regiments.[20]

Britain was a superpower in 1945, as it had been in the nineteenth century, for a single simple reason: its possession of a global Empire. There was no other reason for 46 million people perched on a tiny island, even one 'almost made of coal and surrounded by fish', as Aneurin Bevan liked to describe it,[21] to hold sway over large stretches of the world and for their political representatives to fill key seats at any top table that might be constructed to cope with international issues large or small.

There have been more theories about the impulses of imperialism, of the rise and fall of the great empires, than about any other political or economic phenomenon. As a subject it attracts the crackpots and the conspiracists in small armies, each weaving an individual tapestry of fantasy which, at its most lunatic, can enfold not just international capitalists (especially the 'merchants of death', the arms manufacturers among them) but Jewish people (particularly those working in banks), Protestant missionaries, intellectuals like Alfred Milner, novelists such as John Buchan, poets of the Kipling sort, the Society of Jesus and assorted carpetbaggers and opportunists from Cecil Rhodes down.

I was brought up in the robust Cambridge school of imperial historians personified by those brilliantly cynical iconoclasts Jack Gallagher (whom I never knew) and Ronald Robinson (who taught me). I have never been tempted to jettison the belief, as Gallagher put it, that:

> All theories to explain the growth of imperialism have been failures. Here and there on the mountain of truth lie the frozen bodies of theorists, some still clutching their ice-picks. All perished; and most of them because they believed they could find some single cause or factor which could satisfactorily explain imperialism's efflorescence in the late nineteenth century. We may expect a similar fate for those who want a monocausal explanation of its fall. They may climb hopefully, but they will not arrive.[22]

India apart, nobody clutching or close to the levers of power in London in 1945 foresaw the imminence of the last chapter of the history of the British Empire, a crucial first point to be made in an area where, as Gallagher so vividly underlines, the temptations of historical determinism are so seductive.

James Morris, in the third volume of his alluring imperial trilogy, *Farewell the Trumpets*, captured the magical yet wishful thinking of the moment to perfection. 'The full meaning of the last War escaped the British at the time,' he wrote.

> They thought they were destroying a truly bestial enemy, but they were also destroying themselves and their heritage. Even their leaders, it seemed, seldom perceived this truth, and read in the story of the war only its heroic texts.[23]

Morris picks out one of the more poetic moments recorded in Harold Macmillan's war diaries to illustrate his observation – the day of the Victory Parade in Tunis on 20 May 1943 when 14,000 British troops overwhelmed Churchill's Minister Resident in North Africa with their confidence and pride, 'these brown faces, these brown bare arms and knees, these swinging striding out-stepping men'.[24] These men with their 'jolly honest, sunburnt, smiling English, Scottish or Irish' faces struck Macmillan 'on that day masters of the world and heirs of the future'.[25]

James Morris writes:

In one sense they were. Even when the war ended, when Russian and American power was vastly greater than British, they controlled more territory than they ever had before. Not only was the whole of the Empire restored to them, not only did they share with their allies the governance of Germany, Austria and Italy, but to an unprecedented degree the Mediterranean was a British lake. It was an imperialist's dream.

The whole of the North African littoral, the whole of the Levant was held by British arms, southern Persia was occupied and even Greece was more or less a British sphere of influence. With imperial armies deployed across the world, with a Royal Navy of 3,500 fighting ships and a Royal Air Force of unparalleled prestige, in theory the British Empire was a power as never before, and the ageing Churchill, intoxicated by the honour of it all, was determined to keep it so. Things had worked out pretty well, he told an exuberant London audience. The British Commonwealth and Empire stands more united and more effectively powerful than at any time in its long romantic history.[26]

Ernie Bevin, Labour's new Foreign Secretary, would not have dissented from a word of that, though the language in which he expressed it would have been homely rather than grandiloquent. Bevin was not one to relinquish voluntarily one ounce of British power. When the time came he could not bear to contemplate the 'scuttle' from India, 'without dignity or plan',[27] though the path to, at the very least, some kind of Dominion status for India was irreversible even before the Second World War speeded up the historical process.

But it was money, the stark lack of it, which led to the shift of influence in the Eastern Mediterranean from the old world policeman to the new. Not for nothing did Bevin tell the miners to give him another million tons of coal and he would give them a new foreign policy.[28] And, ironically, it was Dalton, the Chancellor with the song in his heart, who forced the issue over no more economic aid to Greece and Turkey, against the instincts of a breathless and exhausted Bevin, forced to walk up two flights of stairs to the crucial Cabinet committee meeting in mid-February 1947, as the Great George Street lifts were immobilised – symbolically enough – by a power cut.[29]

This may well have been a prospect foreseeable in the heady days of election victory eighteen months earlier, but foreseen it was not. The theory of economic power as it relates to diplomatic power has been much reworked since the late 1940s with a considerable debate about the size and duration of the gap that can be sustained between fading industrial force and the military equipment a once-great economic power can continue to deploy at sea, on land and in the air. But, as we've seen, Bevin understood it intuitively, hence his remark about coal and foreign policy. George Kennan, the brain behind the 'containment' policy, understood it too, in the Washington of the late 1940s when he continually pressed the view in official circles, buckling under the shock of the early cold war, 'that there were only five regions of the world – the United States, the

United Kingdom, the Rhine valley with adjacent industrial areas, the Soviet Union and Japan – where the sinews of modern military strength could be produced in quantity. I pointed out that only one of these was under Communist control; and I defined the main task of containment, accordingly, as one of seeing to it that none of the remaining ones fell under such control.'[30]

As Kennan's strategic assessment, and those garrisons, fleets and squadrons, testify, it would be a great error to allow historical retrospection to write down British power too far too fast. But the leading historian of rising and falling nations, Paul Kennedy, was undeniably justified in asserting

> the blunt . . . fact that in securing a victorious outcome to the war the British had severely overstrained themselves, running down their gold and dollar reserves, wearing out their domestic machinery, and (despite an extraordinary mobilization of their resources and population) becoming increasingly dependent upon American munitions, shipping, foodstuffs, and other supplies to stay in the fighting.[31]

We were, in short, morally magnificent but economically bankrupt, as became brutally apparent eight days after the ceasefire in the Far East when President Truman severed the economic lifeline of Lend-Lease without warning. Lend-Lease, 'the most unsordid act in the history of any nation' as Churchill called it,[32] was, as we have seen, negotiated in the early months of 1941 well before the United States entered the war. 'Unsordid' the beginning may have been, but the end of Lend-Lease was undeniably brutal. 'The British Food Mission, despatching tons of supplies from the United States, only learnt about it when one of their ships was refused permission to sail.'[33] Material already in transit would have to be paid for straight away and an audit was to be drawn up of all unconsumed Lend-Lease items in Britain. 'Thus,' as Sir Alec Cairncross starkly recalled, 'what had provided the United Kingdom with roughly two-thirds of the funds needed to finance a total external deficit of £10,000 million over six years of war was withdrawn unilaterally and without prior negotiation.'[34]

The news shattered the handmaidens of the special wartime relationship in the American Embassy in London. The Oxford economist, Sir Roy Harrod, who was personally involved in the story, has captured the panic of that second weekend of the peace as the US diplomatic corps took a breather in various parts of the Home Counties.

> On Sunday 19 August Mr E.G. Collado was having tea at a Cambridge teashop. He had come to Cambridge with some friends to do sightseeing. They were resting after an exhausting day. Their attention was attracted by news coming over the air . . . What was this? It was incredible. What could have happened? The US radio had carried the announcement that Lend-Lease had been completely stopped, and from now onwards Britain would have to pay for all supplies, including those in the pipeline.

Collado dashed for the next train to Liverpool Street and thence by tube to the American Embassy. On the platform of Bond Street station he ran into Harry Hawkins, who was looking extremely gloomy. Yes, he had seen the cable. The worst was true. Collado made for the Embassy; he was later joined by Mr Clayton [Will Clayton, a leading US economic negotiator on a visit to Britain], who had hastened up from the house of a friend, where he had been staying for the weekend. It was a sad occasion. Did Keynes know? They discovered that he had been informed earlier in the day. They suffered, these American friends of ours, perhaps more than the British, since it was their people who had done it. The British were inured to hard knocks.[35]

'Their people', in fact, was largely one person – Leo Crowley, Director of the Foreign Economic Administration, the Washington agency handling Lend-Lease. Accurately enough, he told the new and relatively inexperienced Harry Truman that Congress' authorisation of the aid did not extend beyond the cessation of hostilities. The seasoned economic diplomatists who were so astounded when the teleprinters tapped out the grim news, long maintained that some kind of extension would have been cobbled together if Roosevelt had been still around or some of the most skilled economic fixers, like Clayton, had not been out of town. As it was, Harrod recalled:

On Monday morning, Mr Clayton took up the transatlantic telephone and vented the vials of his wrath. It was good to see the whole six-foot-six of him reinforcing the vehemence of his rebukes. He was able to do some good. It was agreed that the question of payment for goods in the pipeline should remain over for negotiation. Mr Clayton and Mr Collado had the appalling task of conveying their intelligence to the British Ministers. They were received by Mr Bevin and Mr Dalton, who looked very downcast; but no words of recrimination were uttered.[36]

It was, however, a piece of news which, as Bevin's biographer put it, 'fell on Whitehall like a V2, without warning'.[37] Dalton, however, had feared it. Two days before Collado's Cambridge tea-party was disrupted, the Chancellor had noted how he and his colleagues were 'a bit tired and preoccupied' and that he himself was 'conscious of having some mountainous problems in front of me, especially with "overseas financial liabilities"; Lend-Lease may be stopping any time now and the resulting gap will be terrific.'[38]

At an official level, Whitehall had been pondering for a year or more how to cope with the consequences of good housekeeping thrown to the winds once the nation's grocer and armourer – the United States – closed down its line of indefinite credit. The fertile mind of Maynard Keynes had been especially active. Britain, Keynes knew, was to all intents and purposes, a bankrupt and could not borrow on strictly commercial terms to fund a deficit which he believed would be about £1 billion in the first year of peace. Gold and dollar reserves were about half that, not enough, even, to pay for military expenditure outside Europe (i.e. not connected with the war against Hitler).

Keynes, however, was optimistic about the chances of getting a loan on easy-repayment terms of between $5 billion and $8 billion from the US Government, the cost of the war to the United States for about a month.[39] He remained optimistic as he set sail across the Atlantic at the end of August to start negotiating it, his opening bid clear in his mind – £1.5 billion as a free gift or, at worst, an interest-free loan. The unintellectual but shrewd mind of the Foreign Secretary thought his Lordship was sailing under a delusion. 'When I listen to Lord Keynes talking', Bevin is reported to have said, 'I seem to hear those coins jingling in my pocket; but I am not so sure that they are really there.'[40]

If intellectual brilliance and verbal flair could have spun dollars from the air, the money would have been in the Bank of England within days of that precious Cambridge voice delivering the British case over three days within the marble halls of the Federal Reserve Building in Washington. 'It was', recalled the near-adoring Sir Roy Harrod,

> the pure gold of perfect English prose, describing a situation of vast complexity with the lucidity and good arrangement that only a master mind could have achieved. It was so easy and light and sparkling, that there was never a dull moment. The most sympathetic and those least sympathetic agreed on thinking that this was the finest exposition to which they had ever listened or were ever likely to listen.[41]

The 'least sympathetic', however, happened to be some of the more influential people in the Truman Administration whose instincts did not incline them, at the best of times, to offer condition-free largesse to other nations, especially one, for all its indispensability as an ally in the recent war, which seemed intent on siphoning-off American dollars to maintain a British Empire abroad, a welfare state and a nationalised economy at home. Keynes and his team were to endure three long months of rough, tough negotiations in Washington before any coins began to jingle.

Every night Attlee and his senior ministers would meet with Downing Street, Foreign Office and Treasury officials to await reports from the negotiating table in Washington five hours behind in terms of time. Bevin, who couldn't bear the prospect of Britain being anybody's pensioner, would waddle down the corridor to the Cabinet Room, his huge face breaking into a grin as he inquired 'Any danger of a settlement tonight?'[42]

Bevin and his colleagues knew, however, there was no alternative to accepting pretty well anything the Americans decided to offer. Their hearts were chilled rather than filled with song as crisis piled on crisis in Labour's first months as a majority Government. Douglas Jay, Attlee's economic adviser until winning a seat at a by-election in 1946, has captured the mood in Downing Street that autumn:

The realities in the ten months after September 1945 were three menacing and intractable economic strains: the dollar and balance of payments crisis, following the sharp ending of Lend-Lease in August; the world food scarcity caused by the war; and the coal and fuel shortage remorselessly building up in the UK itself. The country had voted for social reform. But the shortages of dollars, food and coal were no less stubborn because nobody had voted for them. My most vivid impression in all these months at No. 10 was the falsity of the illusion, harboured by journalists, academics and others that something called 'power' resides in the hands of a Prime Minister.

The picture drawn, or imagined, is of a great man, sitting down in his office, pulling great levers, issuing edicts, and shaping events. Nothing could be further from the truth in the real life of No. 10 as I knew it. So far from pulling great levers, the PM at this time found himself hemmed in by relentless economic or physical forces, and faced with problems which had to be solved, but which could not be solved.[43]

By the end of November, Keynes, close to exhaustion after weeks of negotiation, was within sight, if not of solving the external financial problems of the British economy, of at least buying a little time for domestic recovery to get under way. The British team by this stage were holding firm for $4 billion. The Americans were offering $3.5 billion. Eventually the difference was split – the deal was a loan of '$3.75 billion plus $650 million in final settlement of Lend-Lease obligations. The rate of interest was to be 2 per cent, beginning in five years, and repayment, also beginning in five years, was to stretch over the next fifty.'[44]

All this was manageable enough. But there was a snag – a potentially ruinous one. The Americans insisted that, as a quid pro quo, all holders of sterling (a tightly controlled currency since the beginning of the war) should be able to convert their pounds into dollars within a year of Congress ratifying the agreement. This was not the generosity of one victorious ally to another that Keynes had expected. The big figures in the Cabinet – Attlee, Bevin, Dalton, Cripps and Morrison – urged their colleagues to accept. Shinwell, Minister of Fuel, and Aneurin Bevan, Minister of Health, objected to the terms at the first of two Cabinet discussions on 29 November (Shinwell because they were incompatible with a planned socialist economy at home; Bevan because he disliked being a supplicant to the United States).[45] But at the second meeting on 5 December it went through without recorded dissent. Attlee maintained till his death that there was no alternative to accepting the terms Keynes had negotiated with Clayton and Vinson, the US Treasury Secretary: 'So far as possible nothing should be done to make them [the Americans] feel we were not grateful to them. They had to be humoured . . . our reserves were running out fast, we were as tough as we dared.'[46]

There were many in the House of Commons who had not entered Parliament to 'humour' the United States either because they mistrusted it as the citadel of capitalism or as Britain's great rival determined to increase its financial empire at the expense of our territorial one. When Parliament debated the loan on 12–13 December, twenty-three Labour left-wingers were joined in the 'No' lobby by more than seventy Conservatives, though Willie Gallacher, one of the two Communist members of Parliament, supported the loan as it would give the Government a four-year breathing space in which they could build socialism in Britain.[47] The American Congress finally approved the loan on 15 July 1946. In doing so they set a time-bomb ticking beneath the exhausted, depleted and overstretched British economy. 'We knew how much we risked when we accepted convertibility,' said Attlee.[48] Just how much, however, only became apparent in the days after 15 July 1947 when the pounds poured across the exchanges as the sterling holders took their money and ran for dollars. Lew Douglas, the American Ambassador to London, would later claim to have told Keynes (who was, literally, dying in front of everyone's eyes so acute was his heart trouble) to leave out the convertibility clauses of the agreement as no loan would be better than accepting such terms.[49] Lionel Robbins, Keynes' fellow negotiator, was much closer to hard economic reality than Ambassador Douglas when he wrote:

The American terms were onerous and the loan offered was not extensive. How much we should have all preferred to break off and come home. But there was no reserve position which gave any ground whatever for confidence. The alternative was a complete collapse of our international credit and a compression of the standard of life for the people at large to levels far below that of war-time with no hope of speedy alleviation. The idea that we could have come away empty-handed and carried on as before rested upon complete ignorance of the desperate nature of the situation.[50]

The contrast, said Robbins, between the opulence of postwar Washington and the austerity of 1946 London was constantly in the minds of the Whitehall team sitting opposite the unyielding Americans.

Just how fragile was the British economy in 1945? The 'great decline' debate, 'the leading problem of modern British history', as an influential American professor, Martin Wiener, put it,[51] took on a new lease of life in the mid-1980s when Correlli Barnett revisited the scene of the 1940s and found only ruination where, at the time, there had been so much hope.

The true picture, as so often, was fragmented and multi-coloured and susceptible to those who would impose a monochromatic tint – overly grey, or unduly rosy – only with a great deal of distortion. At any moment in the history of the British economy, as with any other, there are sunrise industries and services, those approaching their noontime, others entering their twilight or, in some cases, bathed in their final, irreversible sunsets.

What can be measured with precision, however, is the depletion of Britain's productive resources during the six years of war. It is possible to reduce the arithmetic of the country at war into a kind of ready-reckoner of national mobilisation.

POPULATION	46 MILLION
ARMED FORCES (PRE-1939, 0.5 M)	5 MILLION
CIVIL DEFENCE & MUNITIONS WORKERS	5 MILLION
DEATHS (MILITARY & MERCHANT NAVY)	380,000
DEATHS (CIVILIAN)	60,000
HOUSES DESTROYED	500,000
HOUSES SEVERELY DAMAGED	250,000
GOLD RESERVES DISPOSED OF	33 PER CENT
OVERSEAS ASSETS SOLD	33 PER CENT
DEBTS INCURRED	£3.5 BILLION
DIRECT TAXATION, 1939–45	+ 300 PER CENT
INDIRECT TAXATION, 1939–45	+ 160 PER CENT

Yet, the impact of war on industry was far from uniform, saving, temporarily, some old staples in poor shape, delaying the development of others, creating new capabilities where little or none had existed before. In *re*creating the industrial and economic picture of 1945 there is a greater danger of hindsight than in almost any other area of national life (the extent and durability of the country's imperial possessions being the other). Of course the ravages of later decades on cars, motorcycles, coal, steel, textiles, radios, televisions and aircraft cannot be expunged from anyone's consciousness. But it is hugely misleading to infer from what actually happened that it was bound to happen as if many of the major productive activities of postwar Britain were gripped by the ever-tauter webbing of economic determinism.

The economic historian Sidney Pollard was in greater touch with the reality of 1945 than any of the fatalists when he wrote:

At the end of the war . . . [Britain] was still among the richest nations of the world, ahead by far of the war-shattered economies of Europe. On the continent, only the neutrals Sweden and Switzerland, were better off than Britain, and elsewhere only the United States and Canada. Britain was among the technical leaders, especially in the promising high-technology industries of the future: aircraft, electronics, vehicles. The problem that exercised the statesmen of the day was whether the rest of Europe, even its industrialised parts, would ever be able to come within reach of, let alone catch up with, Britain.

Nor was that lead a temporary fluke, a result of the more destructive effects of the war on the Continent. On the contrary, the British lead in 1950 was fully in line with that of 1938: and even more so with that of earlier decades, when the British position had been firmly in the van of Europe. It had a solid and traditional foundation.[52]

Some of those solid and traditional foundations, however, had been terribly battered in the 1920s and 1930s once the short-lived boom after the First World War had dissipated.

Two of the staple industries which had given Britain much of its Victorian economic supremacy – cotton and shipbuilding – were saved then revived by the demands of renewed war after 1939. In the 1930s, the Bank of England had led a rescue of the Lancashire textile industry, reeling from recession and the rise of competitors in India and Japan. The introduction of tariffs after 1932, when the National Government engineered a strategic change of economic direction with a general shift from free trade to protection, had saved the home market for Lancashire but not the world market in which it had held sway overwhelmingly until 1914. By 1939 Lancashire had only half the spinning and weaving capacity in use in 1920 and the national workforce in cotton goods had shrivelled from 600,000 to 350,000 over the same period.[53]

The industry was saved by the fabric of war from the parachute to the ubiquitous battledress worn by squaddie and civil defence worker alike. So great were the demands of the military that civilian consumption of cotton and linen was cut by almost a third in the first year of the war.[54] Yet great gains in productivity were made by the thinning out of the workforce or 'dilution' as it was officially called. When the war finished the cotton industry had lost a further 150,000 workers.

So keen was the Attlee Government to revive cotton as an export that a substantial recruitment drive was mounted complete with its own advertising campaign (posters appeared with a ration book suspended from a mill by a fibre of cotton under the caption BRITAIN'S BREAD HANGS BY LANCA-SHIRE'S THREAD). Factories were made safer, the machinery laid out more rationally but, ominously, British mills still lagged far behind American in terms of automatic looms and the new ring-spinning techniques. When Britain had to be put in uniform, running ancient machines to the limit was a sensible, probably the only, policy. Competing successfully for the world's linen cupboards and wardrobes in peacetime required an entirely different approach. The war had given cotton a reprieve, not a pardon.

Much the same was true of shipbuilding whose cranes along the Clyde, the Tyne, the Wear and the Mersey are as much a symbol of Britain's industrial heyday as the great red-brick mills and chimneys on the Oldham, Bolton and Preston skylines. Its interwar history was directly comparable to that of cotton. Before the First World War, Britain built nearly two thirds of the world's vessels. Pre-1914 Clydeside was a kind of Caledonian Taiwan. In 1913 'Clyde yards set a record of 757,000 tons and 1,111,000 horse-power of marine engines . . . (respectively 33.4 per cent and 49 per cent of the UK total), when all Germany produced only 646,000 tons and 776,000 horse-power.'[55]

The Armistice brought more work than ever. The 1,700 British vessels sunk between 1914 and 1918 had to be replaced and overseas customers, starved of ships when the yards turned exclusively to war production, were there to be satisfied. In 1920 2 million tons slid down the slipways. Twelve years later, with a fifth of the world's merchant shipping idle because of the great slump, only 307 vessels were made worldwide and all but two of the seventy-two berths on the Tyne were empty.[56]

As with cotton, the Bank of England used its financial weaponry to achieve a rationalisation of capacity. Its instrument, National Shipbuilders Security, pursued a policy of closure and modernisation. The Jarrow Marchers, the most enduring symbol of interwar economic hardship, took to the A1 when their yard was shut down, a savage blow in a single-industry town doomed to stagnation even if demand picked up.[57] Gradual rearmament from the mid-Thirties revived the demand to such an extent that when war came again, every functional berth was filled. As with cotton, the siege economy protected British yards from foreign competition and guaranteed a market for every craft produced on contractual terms (the notorious 'cost-plus') which guaranteed the firm a profit however long they took, however expensive their materials and labour.

It would be churlish, however, not to recognise the sustained, back-breaking performance of the shipbuilding workforce year-in, year-out after 1939, getting naval vessel and life-saving merchantman to sea and coping with the perpetual flow of repairs caused by U-boat and Luftwaffe. As with so many other industries, the British war effort depended on what assets there were being run flat-out, and then a bit more, however ominously antiquated the techniques and technology in many yards. Riveting in the open air, for example, continued as if the infinitely more efficient welding under cover had not been pioneered in prewar Sweden and was not, even now, in America shoving Liberty ship after Victory ship into the North Atlantic on a production-line basis.

In return for the Admiralty and the Ministry of War Transport taking everything their members could make, the multiplicity of shipbuilding unions agreed to put aside their traditional demarcations as they would call them (an economist's phrase would be 'restrictive practices') for the duration. The Ministry of Labour, however, had to undertake to restore them in full when military hostilities ceased at the very moment when competitive hostilities would be resumed in the world markets. Immediate national survival demanded many such bargains, however Faustian they were in terms of the nation's ultimate economic well-being.

Until the mid- to late-1950s, the two great sinews of industrial strength remained the Victorian ones – coal and steel. Bevin was only exaggerating slightly when he told those miners' meetings that if they would give him a million more tons of coal, he could give them a new foreign policy.[58] The country couldn't have 'a completely independent policy' if we became 'a sort of financial colony of someone else'. If only they could dig more coal, he said, 'fifteen or twenty industries could be run at full blast' and the whole world position of Britain would be altered.[59]

Virtually all heavy manufacturing industry ran on coal in 1945 as did the railways. Yet fewer sectors were in worse shape when Labour inherited sole command of the siege economy. As one of its new MPs, the wartime civil servant Harold Wilson, wrote at the time:

> Almost the only black spot on the Home Front during the war has been the coal industry. From the beginning of 1941 onwards the country has constantly been in danger of having insufficient coal for military operations and home requirements, and the Government and the people have been confronted with one coal crisis after another.[60]

Despite a virtual state takeover of the pits (Churchill ruled out nationalisation but the new Ministry of Fuel and Power ensured its writ ran in every mine through a network of production directors) manpower, productivity and output fell as the war economy moved into an ever higher gear.[61] There were many reasons for this. Nowhere were labour relations worse than in the mines. This had long been the case. The scars of the 1926 General Strike, the eventual return to work for longer hours and lower wages, the unemployment brought on by increased foreign competition and world depression, the sheer awfulness and danger of the job – still largely reliant on muscle and pick with the owners' reluctance to mechanise – all linked recent with long-term memory in a manner that fuelled resentment.

Every man was put on a six-day week; absenteeism doubled. Conscripts were diverted from the forces, the famous 'Bevin Boys', and sent down the pits. They did not always make the most productive miners. The framework of compulsion generally, the Ministry of Labour's essential works orders in particular, kept men underground when munitions factories (many deliberately sited in areas of high unemployment such as the coalfields) paid higher wages in better conditions on the surface.

Strikes, though illegal under the emergency legislation, tripled the amount of coal lost between 1938 and 1944 (943,100 to 3,001,700 tons)[62] and at one stage in 1942 large numbers of striking Kent miners threatened to fill the jails of the south-east as a result of the Betteshanger dispute until the Government backed down.[63] Most disturbing of all for the industry's long-term prospects, 'the downward trend of production continued in face of an upward trend of mechanisation [when] from 1943 onwards more and more electrical equipment and machines for cutting, loading and conveying coal were going into the mines.'[64]

A major part of the problem was the fragmentation of the industry which still reflected its formative small-business phase in the pattern of ownership. The Reid Committee, commissioned by the Coalition to examine the technical efficiency of British coalmining, reported in the last days of the war that a much-needed change could not happen 'unless the conflicting interests of the individual colliery companies were merged together into one compact and unified command of manageable size'.[65] They did not recommend nationalisation. Indeed any mention of it had been effectively ruled out by Churchill on the grounds that such ideological questions had to be put on one side for the duration of the conflict.[66]

But coal never lost its symbolic, almost romantic, place in the Labour movement as *the* industry where the excesses of capitalism had left blood in the seams.[67] Its transition to public ownership had been Party policy since the 1920s when the saintly socialist and scholar, R.H. Tawney, had drawn up a scheme for nationalisation.[68] It was the first and most joyous of Labour's major transfers of ownership. None, except perhaps the National Health Service, was accompanied by such great expectations of what a clean break with a dark past would bring.

Coal and steel, in terms of the first industrial revolution, went together, to adapt the old song about love and marriage, like a horse and carriage. Where coal was dug, especially the good coking varieties, as processes improved, steel could be made in proximity. Where deepish water was added shipbuilding could make up a natural trio. The locations bequeathed to later generations by the miners, smelters and riveters of the world's first industrial take-off were among the mixed blessings of Britain's glory days as a pioneering manufacturer.

When size brought economies of scale with the growth of world markets in the late nineteenth century, a steelworks high up in a south Wales valley or a shipyard crammed into the narrow banks of the lower Tyne experienced increasing disadvantage. Take the great plant at Dowlais which was immortalised in 1936 when the soon to depart King Edward VIII gazed over the wreckage of what had been the world's greatest ironworks, and said 'These works brought all these people here. Something must be done to find them work.'[69] Tucked between the hills above Merthyr Tydfil almost into the uplands of the Brecon Beacons, its site was hopeless once local raw materials had been exhausted. Spanish ore had to be carried up by rail from the Cardiff docks. When it finally shut down in the 1930s local unemployment shot up to 73 per cent.[70]

Dowlais' fate was sealed by the acute technical redundancy of its equipment as much as its location. Compared to most other traditional British industries, steel had not fared too badly in the 1930s. When Britain turned again to import controls in 1932, steel was protected by an exceptionally high tariff – 33 per cent instead of the more general 20 per cent. Encouraged by the National Government, the steelmasters rationalised themselves into an Iron and Steel Federation led by Sir Andrew Duncan (destined to become an effective

Minister of Supply in the wartime Coalition) who sought even greater benefits from monopoly by taking his colleagues into the European Steel cartel.

The solution to steel's problems was half-hearted, however. New capacities were added to existing capability on traditional sites instead of investing in new integrated mills on greenfield sites close to the coast, with iron and coal going in at one end and finished steel emerging at the other fashioned in a continuous strip mill. As in other core industries, the Americans and the Germans were piling up an ever greater technological advantage. The effect of war, as in the shipyards and on the railways, was to operate what the industry had got flat out. 'Existing furnaces and mills, many of them already worn out in 1939, were run as hard as they could go, with little time to stop for maintenance.'[71] Seventy-two million tons of British steel were converted into tanks and guns for the front and girders to repair the damage wrought by the enemy at home. From the spring of 1940 the licensing and distribution of steel by the Board of Trade was one of the key controls exercised by the state over the war economy.

But by 1944 stretching existing resources, india-rubber fashion, had reached its limit. As the official historians of the war economy put it, in addition to the railways, 'repair and maintenance had also been purposely neglected in such important industries as iron and steel, chemicals, textiles and the generation of electricity. Indeed, much plant was already in a condition in which continued working depended on a substantially increased allocation of manpower to provide for proper overhaul and repair'.[72] As we have already seen, 1944 was also the year in which that peculiar British battleground – the ownership of 'commanding height' industries – saw its lines of engagement laid down at the Labour Party Conference, with iron and steel as its most disputed prize. The public ownership debate raged around the totem of coal, run-down industries such as rail and steel, and the old favourite utilities of early twentieth-century municipal socialism – gas and electricity. What of the great growth industries of that century like cars and chemicals, radio and television, aircraft and electronics? Here the picture in 1945 looked remarkably promising not least because the impact of war had speeded up the processes of technical advance rather than draining old technology of all it had.

To an export-minded figure like Attlee's President of the Board of Trade, Sir Stafford Cripps, vehicle manufacturing presented a paradox. It had a negligible track record in overseas markets prewar. It had flourished first as a pioneer industry propelled by enthusiast/autocrats like William Morris and Herbert Austin; then as a supplier of the needs of the growing middle-class market for family saloons in the 1920s and 1930s. Cripps, however, was determined to make cars the cutting edge of the country's postwar export drive upon which, as he never ceased reminding Parliament and the public, everything depended.

Cripps was virtually unique in the upper ranks of political life in having a scientific and industrial background which preceded the shining career as a barrister on which his public reputation rested. After driving a lorry in France for the Red Cross in the early phase of the First World War, his chemist's training was made use of when he helped build and run an explosives factory at Queensferry for the Ministry of Munitions.[73]

Within a few months of Labour's taking office, Cripps unveiled his plans to a sceptical trade dinner. 'We must provide', he told the Society of Motor Manufacturers and Traders in November 1945, 'a cheap, tough, good-looking car of decent size – not the sort of car we have hitherto produced for smooth roads and short journeys in this country – and we must produce them in sufficient quantities to get the benefits of mass production.' When the patrician President of the Board of Trade proceeded in his exquisitely cultivated voice and lawyer's delivery to tell the manufacturers that at least half of their output had to be sold overseas, he was greeted with cries of 'No' and 'Tripe', made all the more vocal by the car men's knowledge that, as the allocator of precious steel under still extant wartime controls, Sir Stafford was in the driving seat. 'I have often wondered', he continued, 'whether you thought that Great Britain was here to support the motor industry, or the industry was here to support Great Britain. I gather from your cries that you think it is the former.'[74]

Was the motor trade a plausible candidate for a leading role in the hoped-for export boom after the war? The answer is an almost unqualified 'Yes'. One of the first fruits of rearmament in the mid-1930s was the Shadow Factory Scheme whereby the big car companies, with Government money, built new plants beside their existing works which were tooled-up with equipment also paid for by the state ready to mass-produce aircraft, aero-engines, tanks and armoured cars if war came. When war did come civilian production ceased almost entirely and many of the industry's top managers and engineers, such as Standard's John Black and Ford's Patrick Hennessy, were seconded to one or other of Whitehall's supply and production departments.[75]

Rearmament and war brought the British motor industry the kind of infra-structural windfall that a manufacturer could normally only dream of by putting up modern, well laid-out production lines in new, million-square-foot plants such as Banner Lane in Coventry, which the now knighted Sir John Black took over when he returned to Standard after the war (companies could lease the factories from the Ministry of Supply before deciding whether to buy them outright). Virtually all sections of the motor trade benefited. The body-makers Fisher and Ludlow moved into the Castle Bromwich factory in the West Midlands from which the Morris workforce had turned out seven out of the ten Spitfires made; while the tyre manufacturers, Dunlop, took over the shadow factory at Speke on Merseyside run for the Government by Rootes during the war when it had built Blenheim bombers for the RAF. And that great symbol of the postwar motor trade the Land-rover (eventually exported everywhere except Albania and Vietnam) began its life in yet another former shadow plant at Solihull.[76]

In short, war had brought a boom to the motor industry, especially the West Midlands (the heart of the engineering industry in the twenty golden years after 1945). And conversion to a peacetime basis was probably easier here than in any other manufacturing sector. When the car industry was demobilised, the aircraft jigs were moved out. At the Standard works in Canley they carefully unpacked the conveyor systems and special tools they had dismantled in 1940, and started to produce the same models they had been making again. In 1943 only 1,650 cars had been made in Britain. By 1946 the figure was up to 200,000 once more.[77]

An encouraging recovery, but a flawed one because *pre-war* trading patterns were re-established along with rising *postwar* output. In the last full year of peace, an amazing 97 per cent of all cars produced on British lines went into protected markets, domestic or imperial.[78] It was this kind of softness that Cripps was so concerned about.

With it went an appalling smugness. As Andrew McLaughlin's researches have shown, the Board of Trade had been pressing the badly organised British motor manufacturers to prepare themselves for a much more bracing postwar export climate since 1941.[79] Cripps' was only the latest philippic. As a Ministry of Supply official put it to McLaughlin: 'The motor industry was of central importance. But it was a wild horse. Every time we got on the saddle it threw us off.'[80] The contrast with postwar Japan, even under occupation, could not be starker where the ever-powerful Japanese Civil Service made sure their country's great manufacturing combines were ready to move as soon as the opportunity occurred (which it did when the Korean War broke out in 1950 a hundred-plus miles from Japanese truck factories, nine thousand miles from the closest American production line).[81]

The contrast with postwar Germany is even more painful. British officials in the Occupation Control Office were cabling home as early as 1946 about the 130 man hours taken to produce a Volkswagen saloon, adding 'This figure has never been approached by any English manufacturers.'[82] What is more, we could have had the world-beating Beetle, the Kdf-Wagen, as it was known at the time, for the taking.

The VW Wolfsburg factory was in the British Zone. On 22 August 1946, Lt Colonel C.P. Boas, a British officer in the occupation authority, wrote to the Board of Trade that the car would make a 'splendid investment for this country . . . In light of my personal experience in the making and testing of this car, I consider that the acquisition of the complete plant for this country would not only satisfy the low price demand of the domestic motor user but be an extremely attractive proposition for overseas markets.'[83]

The Colonel wrote in vain. As Andrew McLaughlin noted: ' . . . the BOT was wary of the proposal because it considered that it would only reinforce the UK manufacturers' concentration on small cars which it had adjudged to be a handicap in export markets such as North America.

'Yet, even the BOT's reluctance was surpassed by the intransigence of those producers who bothered to inspect the German plant. On their return they suggested that the plant be stripped of its machine tools (which were in short supply in the UK) in a pre-emptive move against future competition. This was symbolic of the insular attitudes of the British producers which subsequently impeded the export drive.

'In reply to the control office the BOT wrote: "The car undoubtedly had many attractive features and I have no doubt that the British manufacturers have taken note of these in connection with their future designs, but it has to be borne in mind that the car was developed on a potential design and it is not considered to have a long term civilian application by our producers."[84] The Beetle has since become one of the top five best selling cars of all time.'[85]

The Beetle, which swept the American market in the 1950s as *the* second car for the affluent household was, as Jonathan Woods noted, exactly the kind of 'cheap, tough, good-looking car' which Cripps urged the British manufacturers to make in 1945.[86] In 1956, West Germany overtook the UK as the world's leading vehicle exporter. The world market was ours for the taking in the early postwar years. Despite the strictures of ministers and officials in Whitehall, the industry preferred protected, easy and ultimately ruinous business-as-usual.

Early postwar prospects seemed equally glittering for the huge industry housed in so many of these shadow factories – aircraft. Only on the electronics side had the technological leaps of the Second World War matched those made in aircraft and aero-engines. The symbol of British defiance to this day is the beautiful silhouette of the Spitfire and the sweet sound of its Merlin engine. I can remember the moment at the Duxford Air Show in June 1982 (shortly after the Falklands war had been won) when the combined Merlins of the Battle of Britain Flight (a Lancaster bomber flanked by a Spitfire and a Hurricane) started up. The crowd moved forward to the fence, mesmerised, ignoring completely the advanced technology of the Tornados and F-111s passing overhead.

War had also seen the second great technological breakthrough of twentieth-century aviation – the development of jet flight with Sir Frank Whittle's remarkable engine, operational in the RAF's Meteor by the time the conflict ended. (The Germans, too, had jets in the air but, defeated and disarmed, they were sure to be prevented from building on their breakthroughs.) Care was taken to acquire German knowhow to supplement our own once the British occupying forces were in place.

Considerable care was taken, too, to apply the lessons of the previous postwar period after 1918 when the British aircraft industry was left to its own devices. This time the state was to remain a partner in such a promising sunrise industry and not merely in the production of future marques for the RAF. The civilian side was going to be developed on a carefully planned basis to capitalise on the military-led breakthroughs – jets, the related turbo-props, stressed-metal skins, pressurised cabins and undercarriages which pulled up inside the aircraft after take-off – among a myriad of improvements which poured out of design offices turned into adventure playgrounds for engineers by Whitehall officials bearing cost-plus contracts.

The War Cabinet commissioned an inquiry led by the aviation pioneer and former Minister of Aircraft Production Lord Brabazon to plan the creation of a civilian industry after the war which would surpass many times over the converted bombers and flying boats which plied the few routes operated by Imperial Airways in Europe and the Empire between the wars.[87] It was, like many of the social aspects of postwar planning, 'a tremendous act of optimism and vision' as a member of the Brabazon Committee called it.[88]

The Brabazon exercise was a rare British example of the kind of targeting the Japanese were later to practise with such impressive results. For part of its purpose was to furnish a home-made plane to topple the domination of the Atlantic the Americans then exerted (as they were to again from the late 1950s) through the Lockheed Constellation. Even the national carrier, the British Overseas Airways Corporation (as Imperial Airways had been renamed on becoming the country's first nationalised industry in 1939) was obliged to rely on Constellations for its transatlantic routes.

The committee foresaw an industry capable of competing with the world on all levels with five types of aircraft. At the top of the range would be Brabazon 1, a monster of a propeller-driven craft. More like an ocean-liner-in-the-sky than a plane, it was to be capable of carrying fifty people to the United States with dining-rooms and sleeping quarters for all. It reached prototype stage and flew but was cancelled before it could be put on the market.

Brabazon 2, a medium-haul specification for European routes, emerged in finished form as the Ambassador and the hugely successful turbo-prop Viscount. Brabazon 3 turned into the larger-haul turbo-prop the Britannia which flourished briefly on BOAC's transatlantic run in the late 1950s. Brabazon 4 became the world's first jet liner, the Comet; Brabazon 5 the short-haul Dove which, among other things, moved the Queen and the Royal Family through the sky above the UK.

Put together with the country's postwar military requirements (big enough given imperial and occupation duties even before the cold war shut down the possibility of a genuine peacetime economy), a high proportion of the nation's scientific and financial resources were clearly going to be pre-empted by the twenty-two aircraft companies, the nine engine manufacturers and the extensive apparatus of Government R and D establishments with whom they worked. In 1945 this was regarded as an entirely natural state of affairs. The toughest test of all – aerial combat and bombardment – had shown we could compete at the highest level in every sense. To have been less ambitious in the early postwar years would have been regarded as defeatist rather than realistic.

With the coming of peace much more could be divulged about the 'boffins war', the amazing (to 1945 eyes) techniques, or 'force-multipliers' as they later became known in defence jargon, which had guided aircraft to their targets night or day in all weathers. Though it took another thirty years before Whitehall felt able to expound (or let others expound) on the achievements of British and allied code-breakers in reading the mind of the enemy during several crucial periods of the conflict.[89] It was radar, the detection of moving objects like ships or planes at a great distance by the use of radio waves, which most caught the mind of the scientifically-minded of the first postwar generation. A.P. Rowe, Director of the Telecommunications Research Establishment evacuated to a public school in Worcestershire, caught the mood when he predicted that while the Napoleonic Wars may have been won on the playing fields of Eton, this one would be won on the playing fields of Malvern.[90]

The crucial intellectual breakthrough on radar had been made by the British scientist Robert Watson-Watt in 1935. As we have seen, by the time the first air-raid siren sounded on 3 September 1939, the UK was protected by a chain of radar stations from Orkney to the Isle of Wight, one of which had been alerted by that careless RAF pilot returning from France. Great improvements in design and a multiplicity of applications were made in the six years that followed. In manpower and technology terms the British electronics industry doubled in size between 1939 and 1945. It was a sunrise activity in the classic sense of having come from virtually nowhere to predominance in a very short space of time. With the sudden and lavish application of scientific talent and research funding, the absence of a conflict-laden past of the kind that by 1939 afflicted most of the sunrise industries of the Victorian era transformed the war years into a uniquely favourable period for technology-led growth.

The boffin side of Britain at war contained what few suspected even among those the Official Secrets Acts permitted to know – the foundations of the world's third industrial revolution (the first built on coal; the second on electricity; the third on electronics).[91] In December 1942, a research team at the now legendary Bletchley Park establishment concluded that completely new techniques were needed to attack the Germans' *Geheimschreiber* (secret writer) transmissions. These were very different from the familiar morse-code standard to signal traffic and the famous German 'Enigma' machine. In essence they were a complete system capable of simultaneous encipherment and transmission of secret messages with a simultaneous reception and decipherment facility at the other end.[92] From the middle of 1941, the so-called 'Fish' traffic began to be intercepted regularly by British listening stations as a dense and baffling exchange of high-speed transmissions.

Equally fast machinery was needed to cope with this. Bletchley's first attempt, the 'Heath' Robinson machine, was, in the words of its official chronicler, Sir Harry Hinsley, 'something of a lash-up'.[93] The great breakthrough – from which a torrent of computer science and information technology was later to flow – came with the Robinson's successor, the Colossus machine, which burst into life at Bletchley in February 1944.[94] Built with the help of a gifted team of engineers from the Post Office's Research Station at Dollis Hill in north London, Colossus generated data electronically rather than mechanically and is generally agreed to have been the world's first programmable electronic digital computer. Unlike the more familiar computers of the postwar electronic age it had no memory and there was not a chip in sight (transistors and semiconductors were invented several years later). Colossus Mark 1 ran on 1,500 thermionic valves, Colossus Mark II with 2,400 (operating just in time to make a big contribution to D-Day in June 1944[95]) in huge rooms run by teams of Wrens. It was men like Alan Turing from Bletchley and other scientists from the research station at Malvern who pioneered the early postwar breakthroughs in computer technology which enabled the British company, Ferranti, to market the world's first commercial production model in 1951.[96]

Computing, its promise and its potential applications, were as arcane a subject as existed in the technological dawn of 1945. Not so radio or television. The radio age was well established when war came and hostilities were to entrench it as *the* medium of communication in the home and on the battlefield. Television was still in its tiny pioneering mode when invasion of Poland switched it off. From American experience, where it had flickered and prospered throughout the war, it was plain that peace could bring a manufacturing boom for television receivers comparable to that which in the 1930s had doubled employment in the wireless industry inside five years and brought the number of licensed sets to 9 million (almost one radio for every four members of the population) by the time that Chamberlain's voice came over the air that Sunday in September 1939. The industry was already anticipating a future era of mass production when the screens came to life again on 7 June 1946, the day before the Great Victory Parade down Whitehall ('when viewers, according to a delighted Press, could see the cuff-links on Churchill's sleeves and the bristles of Attlee's moustache'[97]) with the announcer Jasmine Bligh asking 'Remember me?' before screening the Mickey Mouse cartoon interrupted on 1 September 1939.

What electronics were to the Second World War, chemicals had been to the First World War – a kind of miracle industry. When the British Expeditionary Force set off for France in August 1914, the dye which put the khaki in their uniforms had been made in Germany.[98] More alarming still, the same plant which produced dyestuffs was also needed to manufacture the explosive to fill and propel shells. It took total war, a near fatal shell shortage and David Lloyd George at the Ministry of Munitions to 'jerk' the chemical industry 'out of 1845'.[99] That experience was the making of the modern chemical industry in Britain, a fact implicitly acknowledged by ICI when it provided Lloyd George with a London office until the end of his days. By the time ICI was created by a grand merger which brought about 40 per cent of the nation's chemical capability into a single company, Britain was on the way to catching up with the United States and Germany. In the 1930s the firm was strong enough to do a deal with Du Pont and, later, I. G. Farben. British chemicals would keep out of the United States and Europe. In return it would have the Empire and much of Asia and South America as its trading playground.

In 1939 the trauma of 1914 was not repeated. Britain was self-sufficient in chemicals. The Government, as with its shadow factories for aircraft, had collaborated with the industry in putting up new explosive factories and raw materials were stockpiled. In chemicals, at least, Britain had a well-primed war machine.

The Great War had created the industry. The Second World War transformed it. Money and brains were applied in abundance. New industries were spun-off by the war effort some of which, like modern drugs and plastics, were crucial in making everyday life easier, pleasanter and healthier after the war. The most awesome spin-off, atomic energy, brought a prospect as dramatic as it was paradoxical – unlimited power and utter annihilation.

The key raw material of the chemical industry, and advanced economies generally, was also about to change thanks to war-driven scientific breakthroughs. There was a growing realisation in the labs and on the factory floors that chemicals could be based on oil as well as coal. Refining techniques advanced and the huge petrochemical industry was born, affecting not just manufacturing but literally the kitchen sink when Shell developed synthetic detergents in 1942.

It took several years of peace before the most dramatic changes reached the kitchen front. On the land the breakthroughs were more swiftly applied in the drive for maximum food production. The chemical revolution fed into its agricultural equivalent in the form of DDT, weedkillers and ever-better fertilisers. In few sectors was a revolution more needed. Without it the British agricultural scene could have remained the 'derelict fields, rank with coarse, matted grass, thistle, weeds and brambles' of which an official Government report spoke in 1942.[100]

The collapses of farm prices in the 1920s and 1930s was dramatic. Wheat fell to its lowest price since the Civil War in the seventeenth century. Farmers went bankrupt in droves; the labour force began drifting to the cities as it had on the grand scale in the nineteenth century. Rural life was synonymous with depression until, little by little, prospects began to improve with the introduction of protection in 1932 and the first glimmering of the postwar pattern of subsidies and product organisations which began with the Milk Marketing Board in 1933. Modern equipment, such as the milking machine, was beginning to be installed. And the internal combustion engine, the bringer 'of the most fundamental changes' ever made in farm history,[101] began its transforming work.

The number of tractors increased from less than 5,000 in 1925 to 55,000 by the time war broke out. That miraculous American invention, the combine harvester, made its first appearance in Britain in the early 1930s. By 1942 there were 940 combines in England and Wales. By VE Day that figure had doubled nationally. The number of tractors multiplied fourfold in British fields between 1939 and 1945, many of them shipped from America where the Ulsterman, Harry Ferguson, had gone into partnership with Ford's to make and market his small but revolutionary design.

Pip Stanley, who farmed in Dorset for forty years, recalls that

Fergusons came over in considerable numbers because of Lend-Lease – those little grey tractors with the hydraulic lift that enables you to keep an even depth and the pressure on the ploughshare allows you to use a light tractor. If you take prewar, the number of tractors in Dorset was almost negligible. The War Agricultural Committees brought them in. The whole of agriculture post-1940 was financially motivated. If they wanted something, they put up the price and it arrived.[102]

Even the hill farmers, who had seen little change when matters improved generally after the mid-1930s, flourished during the war. In fact, in terms of real income farmers saw the greatest gains of any group – and the lot of the rural proletariat was ameliorated too by minimum wages set by a Government-sponsored board. Intervention paid off handsomely in production terms as well. By the end of the war Britain was producing 80 per cent of its own food (seventy years of free trade had pushed that figure down to 30 per cent by 1914) and the country's agriculture had entered into a direct and close relationship with the state that was only to be ruptured in 1973 when the United Kingdom joined the European Community and rural production was subject to the wider Common Agricultural Policy.

In 1940–1 a walk down a high street and a glance at the shop-fronts – the penultimate destination of all that home-grown produce – would have illustrated perfectly the paradoxical effects of the war economy. In a heavily blitzed area, the unsought bonus to our indigenous glass industry would have been jaggedly obvious. Pilkingtons of St Helens, its leading manufacturer, claimed 'that London was twice reglazed, and at one period three million square feet of glass per week was sent to the London area'. Thanks to the bombings and the virtual cessation of imports, Pilkingtons' home sales were 50 per cent higher in volume in 1941 than in 1938 despite the halting of car-making.[103]

But the shops themselves, especially the more modern chain stores, gave every sign of a commercial transformation interrupted. Shortages, rationing and near total state control by 1941 had stopped then reversed one of the most dramatic interwar economic revolutions – retailing. Its nature and impact were hinted at in a brilliantly evocative passage J.B. Priestley penned in the closing pages of his *English Journey* which he made in the autumn of 1933.

Priestley found three Englands: the 'Old England' of the cathedrals, the Cotswolds and the colleges of the ancient universities; secondly,

the nineteenth century England, the industrial England of coal, iron, steel, cotton, wool, railways; of thousands of rows of little houses all alike, sham Gothic churches, square-faced Chapels, Town Halls, Mechanics' Institutes, mills, foundries, warehouses . . .

The third England, I concluded, was the new post [First World] War England, belonging far more to the age itself than to this particular island. America, I supposed, was its real birthplace. This is the England of arterial and by-pass roads, of filling stations and factories that look like exhibition buildings, of giant cinemas and dance-halls and cafés, bungalows with tiny garages, cocktail bars, Woolworths, motor-coaches, wireless, hiking, factory girls looking like actresses, greyhound racing and dirt tracks, swimming pools, and everything given away for cigarettes and coupons.[104]

It was chain-stores like Dorothy Perkins spreading across the country as Priestley made his journey, with 5 shillings (25p) their top price for a dress, which, with cosmetics bought at Boots or Timothy White's, enabled factory girls to look like Rita Hayworth. Marks & Spencer transformed what they wore beneath. The House of Lyons put a cheap and cheerful teashop in town for their days off. Woolworths offered them virtually everything everywhere at prices made competitive by bulk-buying and economies of scale, unless it was part of the 30 per cent whose prices were the same everywhere because of resale price maintenance agreements insisted on by the manufacturer. Liptons, Home and Colonial and, in the south, Sainsbury's added to the range of foods they could buy provided unemployment did not turn them from factory girls to love on the dole.

Marks & Spencer, laying the foundations of an integrated system from raw material via carefully controlled manufacturer to well laid out high-street store (it had 234 nationwide by the time war broke out), were about to build the beginnings of an affluent society upon them when the siege economy started to redefine what was an essential and what a luxury. Expansion plans were shelved, Hitler damaged about half the M & S stores (its largest in Birmingham being destroyed completely), and the British Government set about requisitioning a large proportion of what remained upright. As the company's historian noted:

By 1944 over a million square feet of floor space in stores was being used by the Government, and in all, during the war nearly one and a half million square feet was requisitioned for the storage of foodstuffs. The company's selling area fell to half the prewar figure; after 1944, selling space again increased but it was 1953 before the 1939–40 square footage was restored.[105]

As if to rub austerity in, much of M & S's Baker Street headquarters was given over to Combined Operations and the Special Operations Executive.

What did improve in wartime, however, were wages and conditions. Bevin's wages councils fixed minima for shop workers who, like the agricultural labourers, were a scattered workforce difficult for unions to penetrate and organise. To save fuel, the 'open all hours' syndrome was ended. Compulsory closing applied at 6 p.m. What resale price maintenance had not fixed, Ministry of Food price control took care of. The country's most competitive capitalist sector became part of the mixed economy for the duration and, in the case of some scarce items, for nine years after that until rationing finally ended.

Whatever the mix of the mixed economy, goods have to be moved from port or mine to factory or foundry to retailer or customer. In what condition did war find Britain's road and rail and in what state did it leave them? In any discussion of British transport, the starting assumption is one of chaos and overstrain – of clogged roads, crowded trains, the whole overlain by delay and squalor and stress on the part of the traveller. The grim scene is usually depicted against a backdrop of other advanced countries where matters are arranged differently – clean and efficient urban systems linked by motorways that work and trains that glide in and out of mainline stations on time. But, for all the genuine chaos of interwar transport policy, the UK transport picture in September 1939 was not too bad.

Despite the staggering growth of cars and lorries since the First World War (a phenomenon entirely unforeseen inside the Ministry of Transport by the framers of the 1921 Railways Act which regrouped 120 companies into four),[106] rail still dominated the picture as war approached. Naturally, therefore, 'railways were given the dominant role when the inland transport preparations for war were drawn up.'[107]

The combined stock of capital equipment owned and operated by the Big Four – the London and North-Eastern, the London Midland and Scottish, the Great Western and the Southern – was vast: nearly 20,000 locomotives (virtually all steam), 1,300,000 wagons, 20,000 miles of track. There were problems. Ever tougher competition from road haulage and coach travel meant semi-regulated railway companies never reached the revenue targets set for them by successive Ministers of Transport. As a result capital improvements were skimped and 'the survival of a large number of private owner wagons and of goods wagons smaller than their European or American counterparts prevented, to some extent, the development of faster and better freight services.'[108] Above all, the rail system had been laid down with the needs of peacetime not wartime traffic flows in mind. But if war came it could, however, rely on home-produced fuel (coal) when its chief competitors (lorry, car and coach) were all dependent on imported propellants (petrol and diesel oil).

But, all in all, Britain's railway network was in fairly good shape in 1939 when the moment came to start carrying the traffic of war. C.I. Savage, the official historian of wartime inland transport, concluded that:

Generally, the British railway system immediately before the war of 1939 was, despite its handicaps as a competitor of road transport, an efficient machine. It compared favourably with systems abroad, particularly those of Europe and the high standard of speed and safety of British passenger trains was universally recognised. The amalgamation of the railways into four large groups and the comprehensive pooling arrangements made between the groups in the nineteen-thirties had practically eliminated competition on formally competing routes . . .

While the peacetime regulation of railways did not extend to the management of the companies, the General Managers of the four groups met regularly to discuss matters of common interest and these provided a ready-made instrument of control when war came. The existence of four unified systems in contrast to more than a hundred separate companies in 1913 provided a railway system much more adaptable to Government control in war-time.[109]

In starkest contrast to 1913–14, Britain in 1939 was the owner of a whole new transport capability – the tarmacadammed road – 4,456 'trunk road miles', a further 23,089 miles of what the Ministry of Transport called Class I roads plus 17,634 miles of Class II. All in all the British landscape was criss-crossed by over 180,000 miles of road – more road in proportion to our area (though not our population) than any other country in the world.[110]

There had been no attempt to cope with successive surges in traffic (over 3 million vehicles on the road by 1938 of which 500,000 were engaged in the haulage of goods and another 50,000 in the carriage of people) by going down the Autobahn route like Hitler's Germany. It was to be another twenty years before the word 'motorway' entered fully into the English language. But the Thirties were the era of the 'arterial road' and the 'by-pass' with their chic, art-deco 'roadhouses' as the latest mutation of that enduring artefact on the landscape, the English pub.

This, however, was not the age of trouble-free motoring. If that ever existed, it brought joy to the tiny number of Edwardians owning cars. The traffic-jam was a constant feature of the British city in 1939 and of certain notorious bottlenecks on the trunk roads, like Lancaster on the A6 or Rochester/Chatham on the A2. But the roads were generally well made and properly maintained. Again, they were constructed with moving goods from London to Newcastle or holidaymakers from Manchester to Blackpool in mind; not the movement of huge armies to the south-coast ports.

Anybody who had to endure a wartime train journey on a crowded, slow train or (and such people were far fewer) drive a vehicle across south-eastern England in 1944–5 will have first-hand testimony to offer about the condition of rail and road after five and six years of hammer. And, once peace came, matters did not improve for a very long time. Take the 'Note on first-class travel in England' penned by that indefatigable observer of the national scene, J.L. Hodson, in the autumn of 1946:

> I travelled [from London to Lancashire] on Sunday, which is a foolish thing to do in England; on Sundays trains too often take all the time there is. Nor had it any food aboard, nor was there opportunity to get any. On this train, which must surely have held a thousand seats, only twenty-seven were first class, so having paid first-class I journeyed third. Not much hardship this, except one feels defrauded. We were seventy-five minutes late, so that I had no food or drink for eight hours. Again nothing much, but we are at peace – in theory, anyhow.[111]

There is a statistical explanation for Hodson's discomfort. The planned shift from road to rail, and the use of rail as *the* wartime carrier, had been so successful that 'the railways had been overloaded . . . almost to the point of breakdown'.[112]

In the years between the German invasion of Poland and the Japanese surrender, the amount of merchandise carried by rail increased by 77 per cent, minerals by 35 per cent and coal by 9 per cent. Passenger traffic had almost doubled. This extra load had to be carried with less than a proportionate increase in manpower and resources.[113] By the end of 1942 locomotives were scarce. In 1944–5 the railway system teetered on the verge of breakdown. If anything the picture worsened in 1946–7 as the dawn of public ownership approached on 1 January 1948. In the last days of the Big Four the ravages of wartime meant the stock of coaches and wagons remained well below the last days of peace.[114]

Inland transport in 1945 was, in terms of the country's long-term economic prospects, perhaps the most kaleidoscopic industry of all. It had its sunset/temporary reprieve element in its near total overshadowing of its great rival road haulage on the freight side. It had its sunrises too in the potential applications of diesel-power and, above all, electricity, both of them proven technologies. The same could be said of bigger and faster freight wagons. Everything would depend on the level of investment, the degree of rationalisation and the effective management of change the future would bring. The road and the private car were, like the chain store, interwar boomers whose development had been thoroughly if artificially arrested. Their gradual revival would be a big factor in terms of both public (roads) and private (cars) investment as the war economy returned to a peacetime footing.

There are three dangers that accompany a Cook's Tour of British industry in the summer of 1945. One is to use hindsight to peer deep into the past in a fashion that only highlights the signs of future decline. This, to put it crudely, is the besetting sin of the Correlli Barnett school. The other is to fall too much under the spell of the glorious dawn in which it was bliss to be alive – a temptation to which fewer and fewer commentators succumbed as economic disappointment piled upon industrial setback from the mid-1960s. The third danger is to start parading the alibis for economic underachievement from the moment the War Cabinet appeared on the Ministry of Health balcony on 8 May 1945 – the overextension of a war-weakened economy by absurdly ambitious military and political commitments, the responsibilities of being a world policeman and an occupying power in the defeated Axis countries, the lack of a 'fresh-start' mentality as a victorious power, over-optimism about the costs of slaying Beveridge's 'Five Giants on the Road to Recovery'.

With that trio of dangers in mind, the summary of my own audit would be this: that in 1945 Britain's sunrise industries outshone its sunsets and its twilights; add in the City of London, the country's financial capabilities that accumulated such a rich heap of 'invisible' exports, and it is plain that we possessed an industrial and monetary base that should have sustained a nation of 46 million people with relative ease, not merely for the period in which several of our customary competitors were laid low by defeat or the wounds of occupation. To have pretended otherwise on VJ Day would have sounded defeatist and, more importantly, it would have *been* defeatist.

Having reached this conclusion I was gratified to discover, on a trip to the Public Record Office shortly after, that no less a figure than Keynes shared it at the time. In his celebrated assessment of postwar economic prospects, drafted in the Treasury in the last days of the war in Europe and circulated to the Cabinet in the first days of peace, he talked about the 'perennial' anxiety 'of knocking some energy and enterprise into our third-generation export industries which our first generation is well qualified to conduct if the capital and the organisation can be arranged'.[115]

Earlier in the paper, the same line of thought had launched Keynes upon the kind of flight of fantasy in which he revelled and made his economic assessments read like no other:

> The hourly wage to-day in this country is (broadly) 2s [10p] per hour; in the United States it is 5s [25p] per hour (reckoned at an exchange rate of $4). Even the celebrated inefficiency of British manufacturers can scarcely (one hopes) be capable of offsetting over wide ranges of industry the whole of this initial cost-difference in their favour, though admittedly, they have managed it in some important cases . . . The available statistics suggest that, provided we have never made the product before, we have the rest of the world licked on cost.
>
> For a Mosquito, a Lancaster, Radar, we should have the business at our feet in conditions of free and fair competition. It is when it comes to making a shirt or a steel billet that we have to admit ourselves beaten both by the dear labour of America and by the cheap labour of Asia or Europe. Shipbuilding seems to be the only traditional industry where we fully hold our own. If by some sad geographical slip the American Air Force (it is too late now to hope for much from the enemy) were to destroy every factory on the North-East Coast and in Lancashire (at an hour when the Directors were sitting there and no one else), we should have nothing to fear. How else we are to regain the exuberant inexperience which is necessary, it seems, for success, I cannot surmise.[116]

In fact, our industrial and financial platform represented a base not just for arresting decline or holding our own but for growth as a manufacturer and trader. It was a basis for large and sustained wealth creation. The key question was and remains how much of a load could that base carry? The actions of the new Labour Cabinet (words rarely convey intentions with the precision historians secretly crave) suggested that, in addition to sustaining the traditional activities of a world power, three new tasks would fall upon it straight away:

1 Reconstruction. Repairing war damage, rebuilding our export trade and recapturing markets lost since 1938.

2 Sustained growth that would eventually surpass prewar performance thanks to the efficiencies of a planned, mixed economy and the effectiveness of the new techniques of demand management that would avert the booms and slumps of the Twenties and Thirties.
3 The 'never again' factor, popularly known as the welfare state, which, with full employment arising from number 2, would avoid a reversion to the hardships and the conflicts of the depression.

For the new Labour ministers this third task on the road to recovery was what really put that song in their hearts. It was what had won them the election. It was what most of them had joined the Labour Party for. They really did think that Jerusalem could be builded here. War socialism had shown them the mechanics; the 'People's William' had shown them the figures; the Coalition Government had bequeathed them a fistful of White Papers; the electorate had given them the mandate to begin. The money would be found – somehow.

CHAPTER 4

Building Jerusalem

The question is asked – can we afford it? Supposing the answer is 'No,' what does that mean? It really means that the sum total of the goods produced and the services rendered by the people of this country is not sufficient to provide for all our people at all times, in sickness, in health, in youth and in age, the very modest standard of life that is represented by the sums of money set out in the Second Schedule to this [National Insurance] Bill. I cannot believe that our national productivity is so slow, that our willingness to work is so feeble or that we can submit to the world that the masses of our people must be condemned to penury.
Clement Attlee, 1946[1]

How did you get the costings so wrong? Didn't anyone listen to the Treasury? Prescription charges had to be applied within three years of the National Health Service coming into existence. Wouldn't it have been better to go for viability rather than have everything free when, in fact, nothing is for free?
Sir Kenneth Stowe, former Permanent Secretary, Department of Health and Social Security, on questions he would like to have put to Sir William Beveridge and Attlee's Ministers, 1989[2]

For its customers it [the NHS] was a godsend, perhaps the most beneficial reform ever enacted in England, given that it relieved so many not merely of pain but also of the awful plight of having to watch the suffering and death of a spouse or a child for lack of enough money to do anything about it. A country in which such a service exists is utterly different from a country without it.
Peter Calvocoressi, 1978[3]

The 1944 Education Act taught me to read and think. The National Health Service has given me nice teeth and the BBC gave me Shakespeare and Beethoven.
Gillian Reynolds, 1989[4]

She [Ellen Wilkinson] wanted Britain to become a 'Third Programme' nation.
Lord Redcliffe-Maud recalling the Minister of Education, 1945–7, in 1981[5]

Some words acquire pejorative overtones quite at variance with the original phenomenon they were coined to describe. The welfare world is especially blighted. 'Carer', for example, summons up for some a bleeding-heart image, for others a professional member of a highly unionised social work department in a local authority. 'Welfare' itself became synonymous for some prominent public spirits in the Thatcher years with a crippling burden on government finances and productive industry which served only to debilitate still further its recipients by making them ever more dependent on the state and ever less capable of taking care of themselves. By the late 1980s 'dependency culture' had become almost as familiar a phrase as 'welfare state'.

But the key word is, mercifully, still to be contaminated by partisan attack. It is 'philanthropy', the impulse behind most welfare provision wherever its location on the public-private spectrum. 'Philanthropy', according to the historian of 'the voluntary impulse', Frank Prochaska,

> is defined as love of one's fellow man, an action or inclination which promotes the well-being of others. It is usually studied from the point of view of institutions, but as it implies a personal relationship it is useful to think of philanthropy broadly as kindness. This opens up the subject to include casual benevolence within the family or around the neighbourhood, activities which often expand and lead to the creation of formal societies.
>
> It also helps us to avoid the misconceptions inherent in assuming that charity is invariably a relationship between rich and poor, particularly the view, still current among social historians, that through philanthropic agencies the wealthy simply foster a subservient class of Mr Pooters. Helping others informally is a deeply-rooted tradition in Britain, as elsewhere. A necessity in working-class communities, it is widespread among all social classes. It often springs from little more than an impulse, triggered by the needs and aspirations of people who see themselves as part of a community, whether it be the family, the neighbourhood or the nation at large.[6]

It's an impulse as old as mankind and has found expression in an immeasurable variety of institutions – monasteries, alms houses, lying-in hospitals, church schools, parish relief, even, God help the inmates, the workhouse – long before the familiar scaffolding of the postwar welfare state was constructed along lines suggested by the most celebrated of our twentieth-century social architects, Sir William Beveridge.

Even some of the terms and phrases that have a post-Beveridge ring are of considerable antiquity. For example, the man who invented the concept of

'national insurance' was not Beveridge or even Lloyd George (its first popular-
iser) but an Anglican clergyman, the Reverend William Blackley. The words
formed the title of his article in *The Nineteenth Century Review* in November
1878. 'I have long hesitated', he confessed, 'before fixing on such a title as I
have chosen for the present writing, from a knowledge that its very sound may
induce most readers to pass it over as a matter so extravagant, impracticable,
and Utopian, as to be unworthy of serious consideration.'[7]

Two other nineteenth-century Britons vie for the title of inventor of the
social worker; the Scottish philanthropist and Church of Scotland Minister,
Thomas Chalmers, who hoped that an organised system of parish visiting
would foster self-reliance on the part of the poor;[8] and Ellen Ranyard whose
'Bible Women' of the Ranyard Mission toured the backstreets of London from
the late 1850s and found selling Bibles to the poor 'to be much easier when
combined with tips on cooking, cleaning and other household matters'.[9]

The term 'welfare state', which climbed to the commanding heights of political language in the 1940s never to be dislodged, was not, as we have seen,
invented by Beveridge, the man to whose name it is most often attached. Nor
was its creator Archbishop William Temple who has often received the credit
for it (though Temple did a great deal to popularise it, contrasting it in his book
Citizen and Churchman with the 'power-state' so evident in the continental
tyrannies of central and southern Europe).[10]

It was the invention of Alfred Zimmern, Professor of International Relations
at interwar Oxford, who had used it in this sense in 1934[11] as did the economist,
Sir George Schuster, three years later when he said in a lecture: 'The best way
for what I term "welfare" states to undermine the influence of dictators in
"power" states is to show that they themselves produce welfare for their
people.'[12] Though both Zimmern and Schuster may have been picking up and
translating an even older usage in Germany in the 1920s where the word
Wohlfahrstaat was a term of abuse for the alleged failings of the Weimar
Republic.

One result of this linguistic pioneering is the impression, which still
flourishes, that Britain invented state welfare and pushed it further and faster
than any other nation in the twentieth century. That is simply untrue. It was
the Bismarckian system, as operational in the Kaiser's Germany, that Lloyd
George used as his model when constructing his national insurance legislation
in 1910–11[13] (he had visited Germany in 1908 to see it for himself[14]). In 1945
Labour intellectuals such as Dick Crossman had their eyes on the sophisticated
systems of social security created in Sweden and New Zealand in the 1930s.[15]

In fact, most of the advanced nations of western Europe had been laying
the foundations of some kind of welfare state in the interwar years. War gave
the process a shove partly, as in the British case, through a reorganisation of the
Home Front for war (Emergency Hospital Service, school-milk for children),
and partly, in the case of occupied countries like France, as a way of restoring
the legitimacy of tainted government (de Gaulle's Government-in-exile in

London was engaged in planning 'for a more socially just and economically fair French society' after the war).[16] Once a degree of self-government was restored to West Germany in the early 1950s, Konrad Adenauer picked up the pieces of the pre-Hitler Bismarckian system and developed it into 'a corporatist structure for most social benefits which the Federal Republic has gone to great lengths to co-ordinate with other German policies'.[17]

No western European nation started entirely afresh with its welfare arrangements after the Second World War. But, as the comparative historian of twentieth-century welfare states, the American scholar, Professor Douglas Ashford, has put it,

> What is crucial to understanding the changing context of policy-making after the 1945 social policy reforms is that social policy had become an integral part of the institutional life of each democracy. Henceforward, countries would be arguing *about* national social security, not *whether* it should exist. Of negligible concern in most abstract views of the welfare state, it was nonetheless institutionalized in very different ways. The aggregate effects of constructing welfare states were similar across most democracies: more income for the aged; better relief for unemployment; improved social services etc.
>
> What differentiated the democracies was that the basic decision to build a welfare state was made under such different political circumstances, and, as accomplished, had such diverse institutional form. The essential political feature of the democratic welfare states was that they could respond in different ways, and could build very different frameworks to move toward social protection and social equality.[18]

There was a special element to the British construction site in 1945. It was floodlit in a way no continental equivalent experienced. It was treated as *the* talisman of a better postwar Britain generally. To the world's and the country's surprise, it was the chief propellant behind Labour's accession to power. The 1945–51 Government – and the civil society over which it presided – was better organised than any European counterpart and it did not hesitate to proclaim the specialness of its achievements, nor did it shrink from portraying itself as a model other advanced democracies might emulate to their benefit. A measure of Labour's success was the entirely plausible conclusion reached by a Harvard political scientist, Professor Harry Eckstein, in 1959 that, a decade after its birth, the National Health Service had become accepted as an altogether natural feature of the British landscape, 'almost a part of the Constitution'.[19]

Beveridge in 1942 had mapped out the entire construction site for putting up a modern 'social service state'. Its scope was so considerable, however, it is best examined initially section by section. Labour's plan in 1945, according to the new Minister of National Insurance, the former Welsh miner James Griffiths, was 'to implement the Beveridge Plan in full within three years, and bring it into operation on the third anniversary of the great electoral victory – 5th July 1948'.[20]

'This was', Griffiths recalled, 'a formidable task. It would necessitate five Acts of Parliament, scores of regulations and the creation of a nationwide organisation.'[21] It was on Griffiths' side – social security – that matters were most advanced when the Government changed and the former collier found 'himself installed at Carlton House Terrace, once the citadel of aristocratic power'.[22] For in its last days Churchill's Caretaker Administration had put through the first of those five Parliamentary measures mentioned by Griffiths, the Family Allowance Act 1945.

Social Security

Insurance necessarily temporary expedient. At no distant date hope State will acknowledge a full responsibility in the matter of making provision for sickness, breakdown and unemployment. It really does so now, through Poor Law; but conditions under which this system had hitherto worked have been so harsh and humiliating that working-class pride revolts against accepting so degrading a doubtful boon. Gradually the obligation of the State to find labour or sustenance will be realised and honourably interpreted.
David Lloyd George, note to his Treasury private secretary, 1911[23]

We must establish on broad and solid foundations a National Health Service . . . [and] . . . national compulsory insurance for all classes for all purposes from the cradle to the grave.
Winston Churchill, Prime Ministerial broadcast, 1943[24]

In his report Beveridge warned us that 'freedom from want cannot be forced on a democracy, it must be won by them'. In the nineteen forties we fought and won a battle for the cause of social security. We rejoice that the present generation knows not the poverty and distress of the thirties.
James Griffiths, 1969[25]

In 1948 it was an idealistic set-up. There was a lot of novelty in it. The central feeling was one of 'we are creating Jerusalem'. It was epitomised by Jim Griffiths who saw himself as being Father Christmas to the postwar generation.
Basil Kibbey, former Ministry of National Insurance official, 1989[26]

By the time the tide of war had turned in early 1943, the notion of social security was an idea whose moment had come. The concept of national insurance, which struck its inventor as sounding 'so extravagant, impracticable and Utopian' in 1878, had become practical politics, a postwar necessity accepted by all the major political parties. Though, as we have seen, their degree of commitment varied according to their enthusiasm for social justice at any price and their fear as to the viability of an all-embracing, open-ended scheme. In a paper to the War Cabinet dated 15 February 1943 (between the publication of the Beveridge Report and the Parliamentary debate on its recommendations) Churchill revived a phrase that had been a favourite of his as a reforming President of the Board of Trade in Asquith's Government. 'This approach to social security, bringing the magic of averages nearer to the rescue of the millions, constitutes an essential part of any postwar scheme of national better-ment,' he told his colleagues.[27]

Churchill, as Paul Addison once put it, was in later life rather stronger on the magic than the numbers.[28] Social security policy has always involved a range of emotions and skills, from simple, warm-hearted compassion to desic-cated, actuarial calculations and parsimonious financial appraisal. Income support, with health, comprises the core of any marque of welfare state. In England the state had been involved in both since the turn of the sixteenth and seventeenth centuries.

The Tudors made a rudimentary 'attempt to see the problem as a whole'.[29] Sixteenth-century life was continually harsh and often brutal for most people. The poor, as always, experienced the same – only worse. But by the standards of the time, the Tudor schema deserves the name of a system. In 1601 there was a legislative attempt to codify the varying types of provision. It was, inci-dentally, the year in which the rates were invented as a local property tax, a system that was to survive, with modifications, until replaced, temporarily, nearly 400 years later by the community charge or 'poll tax'. The Elizabethan Poor Law could not match the rates for longevity. It did, however, endure for nearly three centuries until the industrial and agricultural revolutions of 1750–1830 shattered its fragile provisions for the deprived and the destitute.

What replaced it, the nineteenth-century Poor Law system, with its hated, ubiquitous symbol – the workhouse – was in some respects a less humane arrangement than that which it replaced. One of the final manifestations of the Elizabethan way, the Speenhamland system (named after the Berkshire parish where it was pioneered) operated for a few decades on the principle that parish relief should roughly correspond to the income of the lowest-paid workers and increase according to family size, the beneficiaries receiving relief in their own homes.

With that nineteenth-century passion for standardisation and tidy adminis-trative practice, the Poor Law Royal Commissioners, under the intellectual leadership of the thirty-two-year-old Edwin Chadwick who went on to run the new system, developed a new principle of relief enshrined in the 1834 Poor Law Act. The philosophies behind it were the need to avoid subsidising idle-ness, to save money (Speenhamland was said to offend on both counts) and to re-establish social control over the unemployed and potentially riotous poor at the time of agricultural depression. The key phrase in the Royal Commission report which underpinned the 1834 legislation was the belief that 'Every penny bestowed that tends to render the condition of the pauper more eligible than that of the independent labourer is a bounty on indolence and vice.'[30]

All future support would, therefore, be contingent on the poor entering the workhouse where conditions would be kept deliberately tough (the avoidance of starvation, not poverty, being the aim) to give the inmates an incentive to find work rather than rely on parish relief. The state would supervise the system through a Poor Law Department run by Government-appointed Commissioners and a Secretary (Chadwick). In the localities Boards of Poor Law Guardians elected by the ratepayers would run the workhouses. As the social historian and policy analyst Rudolf Klein puts it: 'The principles of the New Poor Law can thus be seen as an attempt to combine the requirements of all industrialising societies (whether capitalist or not) for labour discipline with the acceptance of collective responsibility for maintaining standards of subsistence for the whole population.'[31]

The workhouse remained a place of misery throughout the UK until the 1930s. The New Poor Law, however, was a thing of controversy from the very start – a target for social reformer and political activist alike. The Reverend Blackley's 'national insurance scheme' was aimed at its destruction (Blackley even anticipated employers putting insurance stamps on workers' cards and claimants visiting the Post Office for their benefits).[32] While it was the life work of Sidney and Beatrice Webb to place the relief of poverty on a scientific and humane basis (it was the Webbs' minority report to the main findings of the 1909 Royal Commission on the Poor Law which first spelled out the concept of a national health service).[33]

The Liberal Government, swept to power in the 1906 landslide, didn't wait for the Royal Commissioners to report before beginning the construction of a new-style system of relief. The philosophy of the 'New Liberalism', as it was called, bore little relationship to the grim suppositions of Chadwick and his colleagues. Rodney Lowe has captured the mixture of political self-interest, philanthropy and national considerations which fired Asquith, Lloyd George and Churchill over five remarkable years of legislative and practical achievement:

Philosophically, the development of socialism (the Labour Representation Committee, precursor of the Labour Party, was founded in 1900) and 'new liberalism' encouraged a more positive attitude towards state intervention. Freedom was no longer defined as freedom from state intervention but freedom from poverty. Politically Lloyd George and Churchill astutely realised that if the Liberal Party were to survive, it had to win the support of the working class which would soon be enfranchised. Humanitarian concern was also raised by the social surveys of Booth and Rowntree which showed 30% of the population to be in poverty whilst, conversely, the self-interest of the rich was aroused by Britain's declining international competitiveness and the Boer War. A healthy working class, it was realised, was needed to defend the Empire and increase productivity.[34]

In order of creation, the welfare measures of the Campbell-Bannerman and Asquith administrations began with free school meals for the children of large families in 1906, attempts to remedy low pay by trade boards in 1908, the introduction of old-age pensions and the opening of Labour Exchanges in 1909 (plus a scheme for employment-creating public works run by a Road Fund and Development Board), plus unemployment and health insurance under the National Insurance Act 1911.

The philosophical change from the Chadwick era was immediately apparent in the 1908 legislation which saw the first payment of old age pensions the following year. Pensions of between one shilling (5p) and five shillings (25p) a week were payable as of right to persons over 70 'subject to a means test but without the stigma of Poor Relief'.[35] Within a year over half a million elderly were benefiting.

When the Royal Commission finally reported, Lloyd George (by this time Chancellor of the Exchequer) rejected its suggestion that the voluntary insurance work of the trade unions and friendly societies should be extended. In putting together his insurance legislation his eyes, as we have seen, were on the Bismarckian system already well established in Germany. Lloyd George was driven by a personal loathing of poverty which he saw as arising not just from a lack of money at times of high unemployment but from ill health as well. His 1911 scheme reflected this: its first part rested on a compulsory system of insurance against loss of health, the second against unemployment.

The 1911 Act represented a conceptual as well as a legislative benchmark. Neither scheme was comprehensive (that had to wait until after Beveridge), 'but both differed from any earlier scheme in being both contributory and compulsory in expecting contributions from the State and from employees as well as from the workers, and in being state-organized'. Pauline Gregg, historian of the welfare state, is, therefore, right to see the 1911 statute as 'the direct forerunner of the health and unemployment legislation that lies at the heart of today's [she was writing in 1966–7] Welfare State'.[36]

Looked at in detail, the 1911 arrangements were, as Lloyd George admitted when he introduced the Bill in the House of Commons, only 'partly a remedy'.[37] The health side of the Act covered all manual workers between the ages of sixteen and seventy and non-manuals earning less than £160 a year. Lloyd George popularised the scheme with his famous slogan of 'Ninepence for fourpence!'[38] – insured workers would pay 4 pence (about 1½p) a week, the employer three pence and the state two pence. The benefits received in return were a place on the 'panel' of a doctor agreeing to take part in the scheme, liability for sickness and disablement benefit. The scheme only extended to the employee not to his or her family though there was provision for maternity benefit for dependent wives. Hospital treatment was part of the scheme but it was means tested.

The unemployment side of the legislation was limited only to those industries deemed particularly vulnerable to cyclical unemployment caused by the uncertainties of the trade cycle. It embraced about 2.75 million workers in iron and steel, shipbuilding, engineering and the building trades (about a sixth of the working population). The state provided about a third of the funding and benefit was restricted to fifteen weeks in any one year.

The bulk of the system was to be run by existing private insurance companies on behalf of the State. But the medical benefits were to be administered by new Insurance Committees in each county and county borough. The 'New Liberalism' did, however, have the incidental effect of changing the Civil Service from a small, policy-making élite to something approaching the great administrative instrument of today. The Labour Exchanges represented Whitehall's first regional network (there were 430 of them up and down the country with a thousand more small branch offices in rural areas) while the running of the 1911 insurance schemes required 1,800 officials divided into four Commissions, one each for England, Scotland, Wales and Ireland. As a result the Civil Service grew from 116,413 in 1901 to 282,420 by the time war broke out in 1914, an increase of 143 per cent.[39]

The Edwardian Liberals, Lloyd George in particular, the Booths and Rowntrees whose reports fired them, the Morants and the Braithwaites who converted their passion into practical schemes, deserve an equal place to the politicians, investigators and administrators of the 1940s as creators of the twentieth-century welfare state. (Beveridge spanned both as designer of the 1908 Labour Exchanges and arch-reporter of 1942.) Men and women of a certain age never forgot that. As late as the mid-1980s I heard an old man in Walthamstow refer to the pension as 'the Lloyd George'.

The interwar period is all too often and all too easily dismissed as a time of lost decades when one reforming impulse after another was stifled by smug or feeble governments as small-minded at home as they were weak-minded abroad when it came to facing the dictators. This, like most sweeping generalisations, is a parody. There was a steady increase in social service spending as a proportion of Gross Domestic Product (GDP) (from 8.5 per cent in 1924 to 10.8 per cent in 1938). From 1919 Whitehall had its own purpose-built welfare department, the Ministry of Health, which embraced local government and housing as well as the activity its name embodied.

Progress was gradual rather than revolutionary. In 1919 health insurance was extended to workers earning £250 a year bringing to 14 million the total of people within its orbit. In 1929 responsibility for the Poor Law hospitals, which had usually grown up as appendages of the workhouses, was transferred to local authorities (local government peaked in terms of functions in the interwar period with its new responsibilities for health and housing).[40]

The benefits of Lloyd George's 'ambulance wagon' were also extended on the unemployment front by the Unemployment Insurance Act of 1920 which built the original scheme up to include almost 12 million workers. There were two critical weaknesses in the enhanced 'New Liberal' welfare state that was in place by the early 1920s: it continued to exclude almost entirely the dependants of working men and women; it was too fragile a safety net to withstand the stress of large-scale and protracted unemployment which blighted Britain once the postwar economic boom subsided in 1921–2, reaching 1.5 million in 1922, 2 million in 1930 and 3 million in 1932.

For the long-term unemployed that grimly familiar form of relief – the Poor Law workhouse – was the much-feared last resort. The second Labour Government appointed a Royal Commission on Unemployment Insurance to examine the problem and its remedies. As a result of its recommendations the Poor Law finally went in 1935 to be replaced by a Public Assistance Authority which provided relief in the home but 'an applicant was expected to exhaust his savings before getting [it]; the earnings and savings of "liable relations" were weighed in the balance when considering public assistance; and a "household means test" brought the income of a whole household into the scale to assess the claims of its members.'[41]

If the impact of the Second World War on welfare philosophy had to be reduced to a single sentence, it would be this: pre-1940 what little existed was for the poor; post-1940 the principle of selection gave way to universality, to the notion of flat-rate contributions and an equality of benefit for all as a bonding of a common citizenship. Despite the changes of 1935, not until Beveridge was accepted as the basis for a new deal was the stigma of the Poor Law banished. Before 1939, as Rodney Lowe put it:

> The feeling remained strong that poverty was the fault of the individual and should be punished. During the war both its [state welfare's] extent and its nature permanently changed. It acquired the positive purpose of promoting welfare through the management of the economy and the provision of social security. Coinciding with the common experience of war, everyone was to be treated equally and, partly in consequence, services started to be provided above a minimum level. In this way services which had evolved individually over time collectively took on a new meaning, necessitating the coining of the new term 'welfare state'.[42]

The essence of the Beveridge Report was the abolition of poverty by attacking its multiplicity of causes – illness, unemployment, old age – from a variety of angles with a comprehensive array of instruments. To change metaphors, it turned a patchwork of provision into a quilt. The document marked the maturing of Beveridge's views from his early days as a surveyor of social conditions and as a technocrat of the 'New Liberalism'. As his biographer José Harris put it, the 1942 report contained

> a number of new ideas that distinguish Beveridge's views in the 1940s from those which he had held in earlier years – though in certain respects the difference was one of emphasis rather than basic principle. For the first time he envisaged that unemployment could be abolished within the context of

the existing political system. For the first time he suggested that insurance should be applied uniformly to the whole community and not merely to manual workers or those below a certain income limit. For the first time he proposed that state benefits should provide not merely a platform for private saving but a subsistence income – a subsistence income, moreover, that was geared not merely to physical survival but to current perceptions of 'human needs'. In the Report of 1942 he laid much greater emphasis than he had previously done on insurance as an instrument of redistribution – as a means not merely of 'spreading wages over good times and bad' – but of effecting a positive re-allocation of resources from single people to families and from the rich to the poor.[43]

As we have seen, the degree to which Beveridge would be implemented was the very stuff of the 1945 general election, almost certainly the chief factor which piled up the votes for the more wholehearted Labour Party. But there was one key building-block of the Beveridge temple which did not wait for the change of administration. It didn't need to, for the consensus in favour of family allowances was all but absolute – a factor which owed as much, if not more, to another, now far less known, social analyst-cum-politician, Eleanor Rathbone.

She sprang directly from the great Victorian tradition of philanthropy. The daughter of a Liverpool shipowner, as an undergraduate at Oxford in the 1890s she came under the influence of T.H. Green from whom her philosophy of social improvement was imbibed (her feminism can only have been enhanced by Oxford's refusal in those days to award degrees to women). Her encountering of deep-seated poverty as a charity worker in Liverpool during the early years of the twentieth century led her to develop firm convictions about income support specifically targeted towards the family, a view she propagated from the backbenches of the House of Commons after 1929, when she was elected MP for the Combined English Universities.

She founded a pair of pressure groups, the Family Endowment Society in 1917 and the Children's Minimum Council in 1934. Through them she took on both a sceptical trade union and political establishment. Rathbone lived long enough – just – to see her idea prevail as the first pillar of the postwar welfare state to be erected when Leslie Hore-Belisha, political chief of the newly created Ministry of National Insurance,[44] steered the Family Allowances Bill into law on 11 June 1945 on behalf of Churchill's Caretaker Government. Under its provisions every family in the land was given an allowance, payable at the Post Office, of five shillings (25p) a week for the second and every subsequent child under school-leaving age (at that time fourteen). It represented both a philosophical and a practical transformation – the benefit was payable without a means test. Universality had arrived. In that sense the Family Allowance was both a symbol and a pioneer of a new way of giving and receiving.[45]

In personal political terms, the social security torch was swiftly passed from

Hore-Belisha to Jim Griffiths. At a somewhat poignant takeover in Carlton House Terrace, Hore-Belisha bade Griffiths goodbye with tears in his eyes and with 'this is the end of my career' the words on his lips.[46]

Griffiths' priority was to bring into operation the Family Allowances Act, which he generously thought ought to have become known as the 'Eleanor Rathbone Act' just as the 1944 Education Statute became known as the 'Butler Act'. 'My first job', he wrote later, 'was to find the money, and I made the first of many visits to the Treasury. The Chancellor, Hugh Dalton, gave me the money "with a song in his heart", as he told our conference to the delight of our supporters and the fury of his critics.'[47] No Chancellor of the Exchequer, before or since, has been such a soft touch for social-spending ministers.

Griffiths fixed the first Family Allowance day for August Bank Holiday Tuesday, 1946. On day one 2.5 million families took it up. By 5 July 1948 (vesting day for the NHS and, as we have seen, target date for the full implementation of Beveridge), the figures had increased to over 3 million. 'The cost to the nation', Griffiths calculated, 'was £59 million, surely one of the best investments the State ever made.'[48]

Next off the Carlton House Terrace production line was the Industrial Injuries Bill. This effectively nationalised the system, which had grown up bit by bit since Joseph Chamberlain's Workmen's Compensation Act of 1897, as responsibility for its running and funding was removed from the employers and private insurance companies to the Ministry of National Insurance. Its reach now embraced the whole workforce and its level of benefit was set at 45 shillings a week (£2.25), much higher than the 26 shillings (£1.35) fixed for unemployment or sickness benefit, a differential that reflected intensive lobbying from the trade union movement.[49]

But the 'cornerstone of Labour's welfare schemes', as Kenneth O. Morgan called it,[50] was the National Insurance Act of 1946, the very incarnation of the principle of universality and embodiment of the idea of a 'national minimum standard' so cherished by the Webbs (only Sidney lived to see it; Beatrice had died in 1943). Its very first clause set the tone: 'Every person who, on and after the appointed day, being over school-leaving age and under pensionable age, is in Great Britain and fulfils such conditions as may be prescribed as to residence in Great Britain, shall become insured under this Act and thereafter continue to be insured throughout his life under this Act.' Or 'in plain English,' as Griffiths put it, 'it was to be all in: women from sixteen to sixty and men to sixty-five.'[51]

Griffiths' bill was not quite as all-embracing as he made it sound. It was not a measure of social nationalisation like the Industrial Injuries or National Health Service Acts. Private insurance was left alone and flourished mightily as a great financial engine of the British economy throughout the postwar period.

The 1946 National Insurance Act was, however, a considerable advance by any standards. It provided twice as many benefits as the old Lloyd George scheme and its successors and embodied the Beveridge principle that subsistence would be the standard for its array of payments for sickness, unemployment and retirement, plus widows' and maternity benefits and death grants, with allowances made where appropriate for the needs of dependants.

To ensure that the needy never fell behind again, Griffiths even considered that later phenomenon of the 1970s – index-linking. 'I shared to the full', he recalled later,

> Beveridge's view that benefits should be paid as of right on the basis of contributions and without any means test. My aim was to provide security with dignity. I considered the possibility of providing benefits on a sliding scale linked to the cost of living. This had practical difficulties in that it would require changes in contributions each time benefits were changed. I was reminded that when after 1918 war pensions had been tied to a cost of living scale it had worked well while the cost of living was rising and was abandoned the first time it fell. In the end, I provided in the Act that the minister should review the scale of benefits every five years with a view to adjusting them to changes in the cost of living and in the standard of life.[52]

In one area, however, Griffiths allowed his generous impulses full rein. Beveridge, worried by the increasing proportion of elderly people in the population as a whole (in 1901 6.2 per cent were of pensionable age; by 1942 it had risen to 20.8 per cent), recommended that pensions should be gradually raised to the new rate over twenty years. Griffiths decided to do it in one go as 'The men and women who [in 1946] had already retired had experienced a tough life. In their youth they had been caught by the 1914 war, in middle age they had experienced the indignities of the depression, and in 1940 had stood firm as a rock in the nation's hour of trial.'[53] Within three months of the Act receiving royal assent, a single pensioner was receiving 25 shillings a week (£1.25) and a married couple 42 shillings (£2.10).

The social security building site of the welfare state was cleaned up and left as planned once its final monument, the National Assistance Act of 1948 (to catch those who, for one reason or another, fell through the system; 'the sump' of the welfare state engine as Sir Kenneth Stowe would later call it[54]) had been piloted through Parliament by Jim Griffiths' fellow Welshman, Aneurin Bevan, the Minister of Health.

For all its centrality to the architecture of the postwar welfare state and the immense difference it made to the lives of all but the wealthiest of the country's citizens, the social security legislation of 1945–8 is not the part which glows mightily in the near light of popular memory. That honour lies with Nye Bevan's other creation – the National Health Service.

Health

> In the case of nutrition and health, just as in the case of education, the
> gentlemen in Whitehall really do know better what is good for the people
> than the people know themselves.
> **Douglas Jay, 1937**[55]

> Most people under the age of forty have grown up with the National Health
> Service. Born as NHS babies, they have learnt to rely on it in all the medical
> emergencies of life. While critical of this or that aspect of the service, they
> are profoundly glad of its existence and appalled by the prospect of its
> destruction. But however genuine, their appreciation is limited in one
> respect. Much as they value the NHS, they do not remember what the
> health services were like before it started.
> **Paul Addison, 1985**[56]

> It [the NHS] was the first health system in any Western society to offer free
> medical care to the entire population. It was, furthermore, the first com-
> prehensive system to be based not on the insurance principle, with entitle-
> ment following contributions, but on the national provision of services avail-
> able to everyone . . . At the time of its creation it was a unique example of the
> collectivist provision of health care in a market society.
> **Rudolf Klein, 1983**[57]

> The extraordinary nature of the commission with which Bevan was charged
> must be emphasised: it was nothing less than to persuade the most conserva-
> tive and respected profession in the country to accept and operate the
> Labour Government's most intrinsically Socialist proposition.
> **Michael Foot, 1973**[58]

> A free Health Service is a triumphant example of the superiority of collective
> action and public initiative applied to a segment of society where commercial
> principles are seen at their worst.
> **Aneurin Bevan, 1952**[59]

The National Health Service is the nearest Britain has ever come to institution-
alising altruism. It is, as Professor Rudolf Klein put it, 'the only service
organised around an ethical imperative'.[60] Aneurin Bevan knew its core philosophy transcended mere notions of socialist planning and progressive administration. 'Society', he wrote when piecing together his new scheme, 'becomes
more wholesome, more serene, and spiritually healthier, if it knows that its
citizens have at the back of their consciousness the knowledge that not only
themselves, but all their fellows, have access, when ill, to the best that medical
skill can provide.'[61]

Bevan's friend, disciple and biographer, Michael Foot, explained that

'*Serenity* was one of his favourite words. It meant something richer and more enduring than merely *security*. He had always searched for it himself and he presumed others wanted it too. His enthusiasm for removing ill-health from the frenzied arena of money-making was closely associated with his belief that people have a craving for a design in society, a settled, serene sense of order, not imposed, but co-operatively established.'[62]

Whether or not the creation of the NHS brought Nye Bevan personal serenity is unknowable. It did, however, bring him political immortality. No other politician's name is so firmly or uniquely attached to a great British institution. Few institutions, too, have taken root so firmly in the sub-soil of society. I'm sure the great achievement of 1948, which is synonymous with Bevan, has inspired in successive generations of ministers, especially Labour ones, the ardent desire to leave like him a legislative and institutional achievement that will carry their name down the ages. If not carefully controlled it can become an impulse as damaging as it is delusory.

Even in Bevan's case, crucial though he was to the eventual shape of the NHS, it is something of a distortion. The idea, as we have seen, was first mooted by Mrs Webb in her minority opinion on the Poor Law Royal Commission published when Bevan was a mere twelve years old and still at school in Tredegar. And it was run through many a powerful and seasoned mind before the new Minister of Health applied his intellect to it in the summer of 1945.

In fact, the concept of a national health service is the classic example of Laski's Law of Royal Commissions. Writing in 1938, ten years before the creation of the NHS and nearly twenty years after Mrs Webb had conceived it, as it were, the legendary (and to politicians of the right, notorious) Professor of Political Science at the Webbs' temple, the London School of Economics, claimed that 'On the average, in our system, it takes nineteen years for the recommendations of a unanimous report of a Royal Commission to assume statutory form;[63] and if the Commission is divided in its opinion, it takes, again on the average, about thirty years for some of its recommendations to become statutes.'[64]

The sequence runs like this:

1909: Beatrice Webb urges combining public health and poor law health services into a 'Public Medical Service' or 'State Medical Service'.[65]

1934: A comprehensive state health service becomes official Labour Party policy.[66]

1936: Ministry of Health examines possibility of providing specialist medical services for population as a whole.[67]

1939: The Ministry's Chief Medical Officer, Sir Arthur MacNulty, produces internal discussion paper including as an option 'the suggestion that the hospitals of England and Wales should be administered as a National Hospital Service by the Ministry'.[68]

An Emergency Hospital Scheme, staffed by an Emergency Medical Service, state funded and supervised by the Ministry, created for the duration of the war.[69]

1941: Ernest Brown, Minister of Health, announces in Parliament Coalition's objective 'as soon as may be after the war to ensure that by means of a comprehensive hospital service appropriate treatment shall be readily available to every person in need of it,' though this would be provided on 'the principle that patients should make reasonable payment, either through contributory schemes or otherwise.'[70]

1942: Beveridge includes 'a free national health service' as a crucial weapon in his attack on the 'Five Giants'.

1943: Coalition issues a commitment to ensure after the war 'through a publicly organised and regulated service, that every man, woman and child who wants to can obtain – easily and readily – the whole range of medical advice and attention, through the general practitioner, the consultant, the hospital and every related branch of professional care and up-to-date method.'[71]

1944: Coalition publishes White Paper, *A National Health Service*, based on the twin principles that such a service should be comprehensive ('every man and woman and child can rely on getting all the advice and treatment and care which they need . . . what they get shall be the best medical and other facilities available') and that it should be free ('their getting these shall not depend on whether they can pay for them, or on any other factor irrelevant to the real need – the real need being to bring the country's full resources to bear upon reducing ill-health and promoting good health in all its citizens').[72]

The principle of a national health service freely available to every citizen had arrived at last at the end of its journey from the fringe of a Royal Commission report to be set firm in the constitutional masonry of a White Paper. As so often with social policy reform, what mattered was not so much the declaratory phrases of the pieces of paper which embody them but the institutional and financial arrangements through which principle would be put into practice. Here the White Paper presented to Parliament by the Conservative Henry Willink (who had replaced Ernest Brown) was markedly less impressive. For its shape had been pummelled by all the major pressure groups in a manner which seriously distorted the whole.

At the strategic level, the Minister of Health was to be responsible for the service as a whole but the running of a large chunk of it would be delegated by Whitehall to local government, who would establish new joint authorities combining the counties and the county boroughs, which between them maintained 1,771 hospitals in England and Wales. Those other great providers of beds, the 1,334 voluntary hospitals, would retain their independence, but would be co-ordinated after a fashion by being obliged to enter into a contractual arrangement with the joint authorities for the provision of certain services.

The medical profession lived in horror both of local-authority control and being turned into public servants themselves. The Willink proposals squared them by giving the doctors something of what the BMA wanted, a parallel hierarchy of representation alongside the borough and county councillors and by flatly ruling out any notions of a state-salaried service for general practitioners. The capitation fee would remain the financial basis of the sacrosanct link between doctor and patient with its notions of independence for the physician and free-choice for his or her client. To tackle the serious problem of the distribution of the 20,000 practices in England and Wales, which tended to cluster in the better-off locations leaving the areas of greatest need thinly covered, the Willink White Paper proposed a Central Medical Board which would have the power to refuse a GP permission to set up in a location already adequately serviced.

The White Paper, a rarity in being the product of a single pen (that of John Hawton, a gifted Ministry of Health official), costed the new service at £148 million a year, some £22 million less than the figure calculated by Beveridge just over a year before.[73] Its publication in February 1944 did not still the argument.

As Rudolf Klein put it, 'Like all compromise proposals designed to reconcile multiple and conflicting objectives, the White Paper left most of the actors involved feeling dissatisfied. For all of them, the final compromise left them to tot up a complex balance sheet of gains and losses: the White Paper indeed was a triumph mainly for those, in particular the civil servants, whose prime objective lay precisely in achieving some kind of compromise formula which, even if it did not satisfy any of the actors fully, at least minimised the chances of continued conflict.'[74]

Willink was pushed into making further concessions in the few weeks of Churchill's Caretaker Government. The idea of the Central Medical Board was abandoned. There were to be no powers to shift doctors into unfashionable areas where need was greatest. The teaching hospitals, the most prestigious part of the voluntary sector, persuaded the Minister to create 'expert regional bodies' to advise on the planning of services.[75] Those who argue that the NHS as it was eventually constructed was very largely the creation of Coalition thinking tend to forget the weakling of a scheme the succession of Willink proposals had left in place when the Government changed in July 1945.

The shock of the new wholly transformed the old. Its first surprise was the man Attlee chose for Health – Aneurin Bevan. To many it was a matter of amazement that the mercurial, hyper-fluent ex-miner from the South Wales valleys should have been given office of any kind. Part of him was natural, perpetual rebel – often expelled or on the verge of expulsion for dissenting from the Party line (he was a popular frontist with Cripps in the Thirties) or for savaging the wartime Coalition (he was one of only two Cabinet ministers appointed in 1945 who had not served in it in one capacity or another). A different side of him, however, was superbly constructive – that combination of vision and administrative flair which led Ken Morgan to describe him (quite rightly) as 'an artist in the uses of power'[76] and his time at the Ministry of Health as 'his finest hour'.[77]

Indeed, so dramatic was Bevan's arrival at the Ministry that it's become the stuff of Whitehall legend, largely because he transformed it singlehanded from a Cinderella department into the shining instrument which fashioned the British welfare state. His first administrative act was to banish the well upholstered leather chair used by previous ministers: 'This won't do. It drains all the blood from the head and explains a lot about my predecessors.'[78] Far from taking a firebrand to the department and its people, he doused them in his considerable charm. 'He sold himself to the Ministry within a fortnight,' said its Chief Medical Officer, Sir Wilson Jameson.[79]

For years afterwards, John Hawton, who became Permanent Secretary at Health in the 1950s, would speak of him with adoration and admit to being 'bowled off his feet' by Bevan.[80] Bevan's widow, Jennie Lee, recalled that 'Never once during the 1945–50 Government, when Nye had to fight all comers in order to establish the Health Service, did he come home in the evening and complain about his permanent officials. On the contrary he was full of gratitude to them and was worried only by the strains he was imposing on them.'[81]

Bevan, like Bevin (with whom generations of A level candidates have confused him), is a prime piece of counter-evidence to those who argue that a long ministerial apprenticeship is necessary before a place at the Cabinet table should be offered. By 1940 Bevin had had a formidable training as the man who put the mighty Transport and General Workers' Union together and then ran it for nearly two decades. Bevan's experience was confined to local council work in Tredegar and Monmouthshire and he delighted in telling the story of a life spent in a futile chase of power. As Michael Foot recounts it, the hunt began when Nye was a young boy:

'Very important man. That's Councillor Jackson,' his father had said to him. 'What's the Council?' he asked. 'Very important place indeed and they are very powerful men,' his father had replied. 'When I got older I said to myself; The place to get to is the Council. That's where the power is. So I worked very hard and, in association with my fellows, when I was about twenty years of age, I got on the Council. I discovered when I got there that power *had* been there, but it had just gone. So I made some enquiries, being an earnest student of social affairs, and I learned that the power had slipped down to the County Council. That was where it was and where it had gone to. So I worked very hard again and I got there and it had gone from there too.'[82]

Nobody could tell stories like Bevan. He turned his stutter, his speech impediment (he couldn't pronounce his 'r's') and strong Welsh accent into gilded assets to add to his theatrical gifts of irony, posture and timing. Like his compatriot Lloyd George, his speeches were far better to hear than to read.

But for all his lack of administrative experience, he knew instinctively what it took to be a good minister – the ability to ask the right questions and the capacity, once convinced of the right course, to act decisively. These traits he demonstrated to the full in his first few months in Whitehall. As soon as he entered the department he prepared a questionnaire for officials on the key points of funding and control of voluntary provision. 'When he learned that 70 to 90 per cent of funds would come from public sources, he was not content to leave management alone.'[83]

His solution to the hospitals question was simple. He brought the lot into public ownership. In so doing he confronted head-on two of the three pressure groups which had so buffeted his predecessors – local government and the voluntary lobby. In other words, Bevan nationalised the hospitals of England and Wales. (Scotland and Northern Ireland followed suit, but Bevan was not responsible for health policy in either, that duty falling to the Secretary of State for Scotland and the Health Minister at Stormont.)

Bevan reached this fundamental conclusion, the most powerful decision he took in determining the final shape of the National Health Service, within his first month as a minister. As Sir John Hawton told Michael Foot, 'At our very first full discussion, Bevan put his finger on the hospital arrangements devised by Willink as the greatest weakness. And, of course, he was right. They would never have worked. I came away that night with instructions to work out a new plan on the new basis he proposed.'[84]

So profound were the consequences of this transforming idea that there has been a great hunt for its author. I tend to think it was Bevan himself but claims have been made for Hawton and even for Lord Moran, President of the Royal College of Physicians and Churchill's private doctor, with whom Bevan dined more than once at Prunier's in the early days of his ministry.[85] Moran had a mission – to rid the hospitals of 'consultoids', GPs who practised diagnosis and surgery part-time in the cottage hospitals, often to the detriment of the patient and the reputation of the real consultants among whose leading shop-stewards was the vain and ambitious Moran.[86]

Frank Honigsbaum, historian of the birth of the NHS, who has filleted the files of the Public Record Office, concludes that 'if Hawton did plant the idea in Bevan's head, he did so privately or else the written record has been lost. Charles Hill [Secretary of the British Medical Association at the time, later a Cabinet Minister], for one, is certain the proposal did not come from the civil service – while [Sir George] Godber [Medical Officer in the Ministry at the time] inclines to the view that Bevan, in a flash of insight, conceived the thought himself.'[87]

It would be wrong to think a nationalised hospital service was an idea whose time had come in August 1945 or that it took the entire Ministry of Health by storm. Hawton's Whitehall superior, Sir Arthur Rucker, the Ministry's experienced deputy secretary on the health side, was a vigorous opponent of the public ownership solution. From early September 1945 he peppered Bevan with minutes putting the alternative case.[88]

The voluntary hospitals should be left alone, Rucker argued. The state could make use of their skills and resources by buying them at a cheap rate. The public interest could be ensured by appointing representatives to their boards. To go further would be to destroy the voluntary sector. As for the local authority hospitals, a state takeover 'would undeniably cause the biggest reduction yet made in the power of local authorities ... It would be particularly unfortunate if there had to be a major clash between local authorities and the Ministry of Health whom they have always regarded as their principal protector.'[89]

Rucker's words are an intriguing pre-echo of the reflections on the first forty years of the NHS prepared by Sir Kenneth Stowe shortly after he ceased to be Permanent Secretary at the Department of Health and Social Security. Sir Kenneth concluded that in attempting to run such a highly centralised health service, the state's reach had exceeded its grasp: 'The burden of ultimate responsibility for health services and their institutions', he said in his 1989 Rock Carling Lecture, 'will, of course, remain with the central Department of State in some degree under any conceivable programme of "modernisation", especially while the most costly services of all are financed mainly and directly by the Exchequer. But the centre cannot manage what it does not truly own, and/or cannot grasp because of its size, and complexity.'[90] Sir Arthur would also have relished Sir Kenneth's assertion forty-four years after he put his objections to Bevan that the Thatcher Administration's White Paper, *Working for Patients*,[91] was long overdue in its 'willingness to break the monolithic structure and to make a modest start at least on dumping some of the structural garbage'[92] while 'even more important is the acceptance and promotion of diversity in institutions in the shape of Trust-owned and managed hospitals with the freedom to buy and sell services to meet the needs of the community they serve'.[93]

In 1945, in the Bevan Ministry of Health, such thoughts cut sharply against the grain and were rebuffed. The Minister instructed officials to prepare a nationalisation plan for him to take to Cabinet in the early autumn with a view to having a bill ready for Parliament by the spring of 1946.

There was much to be said for Bevan's solution in the circumstances of 1945. The chaotic overlapping provision of the local government and voluntary sectors, the limited, rate-supported funding of one and the precarious condition of the other demanded a major overhaul not minor tinkering. The Local Government Act 1929, which as we have seen abolished the Poor Law, had as one of its intentions the creation of a full municipal hospital service. But it was what is known in the Parliamentary trade as permissive legislation, as opposed to compulsory. 'A few authorities like the London County Council [the inner London boroughs were covered by this; the outer London boroughs remained outside until the creation of the Greater London Council in 1965] did much; many others did little.'[94]

The Cancer Act of 1939 was a recognition that expensive treatment, such as radium therapy, required an organisation and financial structure (the Treasury made special provision for it) which overrode the patchwork of local and voluntary cover.[95] But it was the Emergency Medical Scheme, conceived the year before as part of Whitehall's war planning, which really began the shift which made Bevan's approach fitting and logical. It did so for two reasons: first, it brought 'a regional perspective to hospital operation';[96] secondly, it led to a marked dependence on state funding by the voluntary hospitals themselves and the salaried medical staff which worked in them. By November 1944, matters had reached such a point that the magnificently named Sir Farquhar Buzzard, the Regius Professor of Medicine at Oxford University, was stating no more than the truth when he told the Press that the voluntary hospital was dead.[97]

This was the bull point in Bevan's Cabinet paper, 'The Future of Hospital Services', which was ready by 5 October 1945.[98] Already between 80 and 90 per cent of voluntary hospital funding was from public money. Accountability must follow. Experience had shown that a local authority takeover would not work. Their own hospitals were not efficient enough and financing from the rates would be too meagre. The only answer was 'the complete takeover – into one national service – of both voluntary and municipal hospitals'. Funding would involve 'the centralising of the whole finance of the country's hospital system, taking it right out of local rating and local government'. There would, however, be a degree of administrative devolution 'with the delegation of day to day administration to new regional and local bodies appointed by the Minister (after consultation with the appropriate local organisations) and responsible to him'.[99]

Bevan's paper aroused Herbert Morrison, Lord President of the Council, and the dominant figure in interwar London local government,[100] to a passionate defence of local interests in a counter-paper he prepared for the Cabinet on 12 October:

> It is possible to argue that almost every local government function, taken by itself, could be administered more efficiently in the technical sense under a national system, but if we wish local government to thrive – as a school of political and democratic education as well as a method of administration – we must consider the general effect on local government of each particular proposal. It would be disastrous if we allowed local government to languish by whittling away its most constructive and interesting functions.[101]

When the matter reached Cabinet on 18 October, Morrison said there was no authority for Bevan's scheme in the Party's election manifesto (Labour's approach pre-Bevan had been to favour the municipalisation of hospitals).

Morrison played skilfully on Treasury fears by pointing out the big shift from ratepayer to taxpayer that would be entailed. Though a clear majority of the Cabinet favoured Bevan's approach, Dalton's concern about funding led Attlee to remit the issue to the Cabinet's Social Services Committee to give the Treasury time to prepare costings.[102] The plan was finally approved by the Cabinet as a whole on 20 December (Attlee had backed Bevan strongly from the start[103]) with Dalton costing the entire service, not just the hospitals, at £122 million, up £14 million from the figure in the 1944 White Paper. (By the time the bill was ready in the following spring the estimate had risen to £134 million – £4 million more than Beveridge's original estimate in 1942.[104])

Cabinet wrangles, naturally, were secret and remained so for years. Cabinets tended not to leak in the 1940s, though Bevan would 'damn and blast' Morrison when he got home.[105] The row over the prototype NHS which is especially well remembered did not take place in Parliament (the Bill was carried on the second reading in the Commons on 2 May 1946 with a huge majority, 359–172). The key elements of the measure – nationalised hospitals, regional boards, a new deal putting doctors into under-provided areas, a salaried service and Swedish-style health centres to house group practices – commanded a high degree of Parliamentary support. The real trouble came from the GPs' trade union, the British Medical Association.

The BMA, as we have seen, were successful in persuading Willink to water down his initial proposals, especially as the new body intended to direct the profession to under-doctored areas, when the Government changed and like any recently triumphant pressure group, they had their tails up. Their annual conference was in session when the results of the election were declared on 26 July. More like political partisans than respectable professionals, they cheered the news of Beveridge's defeat at Berwick.[106] How great must have been their horror, therefore, when the arch-bogeyman of the comfortable middle classes, the Nye-devil himself, was appointed *their* Minister a day or two later.

In the late summer of 1945, the BMA were ready to put the new man straight. There they sat, sixteen of them, plus three representatives each from the Royal Colleges, eager to negotiate with the new Minister.[107] When finally they met on 10 January 1946, his initial impact was comparable to his effect on the civil servants the previous August. Bevan swept them off their feet. One of the BMA's most militant council members, Dr Roland Cockshut, was as affected as anybody:

> We assembled at that first meeting expecting that our beautiful profession was to be hung, drawn and quartered. Instead, we were reprieved. It was the most dramatic moment I can ever remember. On one point after another – control by local authorities, the free choice of patient and doctors' clinical freedom – the Minister had accepted what we were demanding before we had the opportunity of asking for it. We were jubilant and stunned.[108]

The euphoria was soon dispelled. The BMA's leaders suspected, rightly, that they would not be able to carry their membership on Bevan's insistence that the sale of practices should be abolished and that a basic salary be part of the remuneration of GPs (the remainder coming from capitation fees). The BMA's secretary, Dr Hill, prepared a critical report to coincide with the Bill's publication in March. A few days after its presentation to Parliament, Hill told a rally of a thousand doctors in Wimbledon Town Hall, 'We are on trial now. This is the most essential phase in the history of the profession . . . let us, at last, learn to stick together.'[109]

There is an irresistible parallel here with the BMA's opposition forty-three years later to the Thatcher Government's proposals to reshape radically the NHS. As in 1946, the doctors stood firmly on the status quo – this time unequivocally pro the Health Service. How Bevan (who died in 1960) would have relished the irony of their poster campaign against his linear successor as health minister, Kenneth Clarke ('What do you call a man who ignores medical advice? Mr Clarke'[110]). Kenneth Clarke, however, never had to put up with anything quite so vile as the attack on Bevan by Dr Alfred Cox, a former Secretary of the BMA, in the Association's journal in April 1946:

> I have examined the Bill and it looks to me uncommonly like the first step, and a big one, towards National Socialism as practised in Germany. The medical service there was early put under the dictatorship of a 'medical Fuhrer'. This Bill will establish the Minister of Health in that capacity.[111]

During the summer and autumn of 1946 the National Health Service Bill ground its way through the Parliamentary mill finally receiving its royal assent on 6 November. Bevan had made no concession to the BMA. In December, buttressed by a referendum of its membership which showed 54 per cent in favour of no co-operation with the Government, the BMA's leadership told Bevan it would refuse to negotiate with him on conditions of service.

A month later, however, the never very united front of the medical profession cracked when the Presidents of the three Royal Colleges – Moran for the Physicians, Sir Alfred Webb-Johnson for the Surgeons and Sir William Gilliat for the Obstetricians and Gynaecologists – wrote to Bevan suggesting compromise. Bevan replied in kind, expressing willingness to discuss questions of remuneration and the contentious issue of expulsion from the Health Service for doctors refusing to abandon the sale of practices in exchange for compensation.[112] BMA activists promptly turned on the Royal College leadership, accusing it of defeatism.[113]

Bevan and the GPs, however, remained at loggerheads throughout 1947 as the Ministry pieced its vast scheme together. The year end approached with stormy meetings between Bevan and the BMA negotiators. Dr Guy Davis, the veteran BMA Chairman, described the Minister as 'rude, blustering and threatening'.[114] Bevan told the GPs that if their campaign resulted in less than the expected 95 per cent of the population signing up for the Health Service by vesting day the following July, he would make serious reductions in their capitation fees.[115]

The BMA summoned yet another representative meeting in January 1948. It called for yet another plebiscite. As Michael Foot put it, 'If a majority refused [to serve under the Act] and if that majority included 13,000 general practitioners [out of a total of 20,500], the BMA leaders would advise the whole profession not to serve.'[116] Bevan responded by persuading the Government's business managers to stage a special debate in the House of Commons. When it took place on 9 February, Bevan made great play with the fact that every doctor had to sign his voting slip. 'This House may well feel that this procedure is a long way removed from the secret ballot and the workings of democracy as we know it in this country and it is bound to cast doubt on the validity of the result.'[117]

The Government won its Commons motion (looking forward to vesting day and expressing satisfaction that 'the conditions under which all the professions concerned are invited to participate are generous and fully in accord with their traditional freedom and dignity') by 337 to 178. The BMA leadership won theirs. On an 84 per cent turn out, 40,814 voted against the NHS (including 17,037 GPs) and only 4,734 for.[118]

Once more the consultants rode to Bevan's rescue. Later he would say he had 'stuffed their mouths with gold'[119] by enabling them to maintain pay beds in NHS hospitals for their private practice *and* by giving them salaries for the first time (previously hospital appointments for consultants had been honorary; their living came entirely from private fees). The key figure was Lord Moran, 'corkscrew Charlie', as the BMA activists liked to call him on account of his perceived role as a twister.[120]

Frank Honigsbaum has unravelled the inside story of Moran's crucial fix:

He not only urged Bevan to introduce an amending Act that would bar a salaried service but suggested that the basic salary proposal be restricted to new entrants during their first three years of service. He also thought the issuance of regulations should be subject to a special procedure because of the profession's fear of ministerial power. Bevan was swift to respond and announced [on 7 April in the Commons] his intent to include the requested ban on a salaried service in legislation that had been contemplated for 1949.

This exchange had all the hallmarks of a carefully planned manoeuvre; indeed it has been suggested [by Michael Foot] that Moran's intervention was 'partly contrived in the Ministry', though there is nothing in the Public Record Office to document it. For Bevan, the move offered an immense advantage since it swept aside all issues except the salaried payment, leaving him free to hold fast to the reform that mattered most – abolition of the sale of practices.[121]

Davis wobbled. Hill was more decisive. The BMA would be put once more through the frenzy of a ballot, a meeting of its Council decided on 15 April. Three days later, Davis had rekindled his fighting spirit. In a die-hard speech at Shrewsbury he urged the profession to reject Bevan's olive branch. BMA head office in Tavistock Square began to crumble. So did the profession beyond Bloomsbury. When the result was declared on 8 May, a majority was still opposed to the NHS (25,842 to 14,620) but the opponents included a mere 9,588 GPs, more than 3,000 short of the figure the BMA itself had set to ensure continued resistance to the will of Parliament.[122]

The BMA's Council was forced to capitulate. Moran's torpedo had crippled the dreadnought of their resistance. The Council recommended its members to join the Health Service provided Bevan kept his promise to amend the Act in a way which ruled out a salaried service. This he did, throwing them another sop – extra payment for maternity work, a smattering, if not a stuffing, of gold.

Another factor in pushing the BMA rank-and-file towards acceptance was the knowledge that their 'panel' income, present since Lloyd George's 1911 Act, would cease abruptly on vesting day. The cost of continued resistance would, for many, be simply too high. By the end of May 26 per cent of GPs in England had enrolled in the NHS, 36 per cent in Scotland and 37 per cent in Wales. By vesting day only 10 per cent remained outside. And, equally important, by the appointed day, 75 per cent of the public had put their names on GP lists and the proportion reached 97 per cent a few months later. 'There', wrote Frank Honigsbaum in 1989, 'give or take a few percentage points, it has remained ever since.'[123]

The fifth of July 1948 was one of *the* great days in British history. It wasn't like VE Day. There were no bonfires or street parties, and Bevan diminished his own glory by attacking the Tories as 'lower than vermin' in a speech the evening before during a Labour rally at Belle Vue in Manchester, a phrase which earned him a rebuke from Attlee[124] and the undying hatred of large sections of the Conservative Party. Yet it was a day that transformed like no other before or since the lives and life chances of the British people.

With hindsight, the construction of this marvellous creation had its faults which will be true of every great event until the Second Coming. Costs were underestimated consistently and, as we shall see, financing the NHS was an instant and persistent headache. By going for national, as opposed to local, public ownership, Bevan created an organisational leviathan, one of the biggest employers the world has ever seen. Yet relatively little attention was paid to the management problems that would inevitably be created during those hectic weeks in the late summer and early autumn of 1945 when dream was converted into blueprint. The most apt and memorable comment on this shortcoming came from Sir Roy Griffiths in his report on health service management forty years later. Sir Roy, a businessman from the hugely successful retailer, Sainsbury's, said that 'If Florence Nightingale were carrying her lamp through the corridors of the NHS today, she would almost certainly be searching for the people in charge.'[125]

Yet 5 July 1948 was the second of Britain's finest hours in the brave and high-minded 1940s. Like the Battle of Britain it was a statement of intent, a symbol of hope in a formidable, self-confident nation. That should not be forgotten later in this and its successor volumes when the trials and tribulations and the often fractious politics of health care are given their due place in the postwar history of the United Kingdom. The NHS was and remains one of the finest institutions ever built by anybody anywhere.

Education

Educational reconstruction ranks first because, in relation to society, a national system of education has two vital functions to perform: a tradition-preserving function and a growth-facilitating function. In a time of social flux both these functions become overwhelmingly important. They decide the future.
H.C. Dent, 1942[126]

In December 1943 I was invited, together with Chuter Ede [Junior Minister] and Maurice Holmes [Permanent Secretary], to meet the Northern Roman Catholic Bishops. Near Durham we came to the imposing parterres of Ushaw College. We were greeted by the Bishop of Hexham, in full robes, and taken almost at once into the evening meal, which in the tradition of the Younger Pitt, was served at about 6 o'clock. There was a large *gigot* and tolerable quantities of a red wine. Immediately this feast was over we were taken to see the Chapel, and a magnificent ivory figure was taken down from the High Altar for our benefit. We were all filled with a certain awe, which was no doubt intentionally administered. Chuter Ede told me he thought he was going to faint.
Lord Butler, 1971[127]

No time is ever regarded as ripe for reform, but by standing firm in Cabinet, Ellen [Wilkinson] saved the Education Act.
Lord Alexander of Potterhill, undated[128]

At a pinch you might be able to do without Parliament. You could do without the Minister: you could certainly do without Civil Servants and almost as certainly without local education authorities. Without any or all of them the world might not seem much worse. But if there were no teachers the world would be back in barbarism within two generations.
George Tomlinson, Minister of Education, 1947[129]

Just as Bevan's name will be forever associated with the Health Service, so will R.A. Butler's name be synonymous with postwar education, in some ways, more so. The 1944 Statute is universally known as the 'Butler Act'. The National Health Service Act 1946 has not travelled down the decades as the 'Bevan Act' though in many ways it should have done.

Interestingly enough, the two of them entered Parliament together in 1929. Rab always found Nye a fascinating character and, as an old man, wrote an essay on 'Aneurin Bevan and the Art of Oratory'.[130] Butler reckoned it 'a very shrewd move'[131] on Attlee's part to appoint Bevan Minister of Health.

One of the very first conversations Butler and Bevan enjoyed was on the subject of education. Rab recalled Nye saying:

'We come from different classes; my class is on the up and yours is on the down.' I said I did not agree at all; I come from a normal professional class, my father being in the Indian Civil Service. It was true that I had been able to go to privately financed schools but I did not think the general level of types of people I represented were on the downgrade. Bevan retorted, 'I had no education; all I learnt was in the mines and in the lodges, the local branches of the Labour Party and in speaking and taking the lead.'[132]

Most newly appointed education ministers declare it to be the job they always wanted. Rab was no exception. After hearing Churchill's offer in 1941, 'I then said I had always looked forward to going to the Board of Education if I were given the chance. He appeared ever so slightly surprised at this, showing that he felt in wartime a central job, such as the one I was leaving [No. 2 in the Foreign Office], is the most important. But he looked genuinely pleased that I had shown so much satisfaction and seemed to think the appointment entirely suitable. He concluded the interview by saying, "Come and see me to discuss things – not details but the broad lines."'[133]

In Butler's case the joy the new job brought was entirely genuine. His father, Sir Monty Butler, was a civil servant, it's true, but he came from a long line of scholar-administrators and himself finished up as Master of Pembroke College, Cambridge, on his return from India. Rab had exactly that rich mixture of high-mindedness, love of scholarship and desire for social progress which had made so many of the Victorian reformers what they were.[134]

Nye Bevan, of course, had a point. A gilded scion of an established family who travelled the bookish path from Marlborough to Cambridge could be expected to know little of what passed as education in the elementary schools (all-in establishments from five to fourteen) that shaped over 90 per cent of the population. That is not to say that he did not care about it deeply. His last intervention in public life in 1980 (he died in 1982) was to defend his beloved 1944 Act in the House of Lords against some of the provisions of Mark Carlisle's Education (No. 2) Bill. He teamed up with the Duke of Norfolk to defeat a clause which would have imposed school bus fares on children in rural areas.

A few years later I wrote: 'It was as if Old England had risen for a last hurrah. I can see him now on the *Nine O'Clock News*, that dry voice finding its way somehow out of that wonderfully fleshy face and saying, "Politics is largely a matter of heart." He seemed like a benign and decent beached whale washed up on the harder shores of modern Conservatism.'[135]

The slice of Old England that Rab inherited in 1941 was a thorough mess, messier if anything than the patchwork of which Beveridge and Bevan tried to make sense on the social insurance and health fronts in that decade of reform. Until the 1830s education was treated as a wholly private concern, as a charity rather than a national resource. In the opening decades of the nineteenth century every particle of it was voluntary from the ancient, medieval corporations of Oxford and Cambridge (the only two universities in England when the century began), through the public (i.e. private) schools, which reached their lowest ebb in terms of scholarship and behaviour in the eighteenth century, and the few endowed grammar schools, to the elementary level represented by the Sunday Schools and the institutions run by the National Society and the British and Foreign School Society.

Provision was hopelessly inadequate, becoming more so as the industrial revolution proceeded apace stimulating the great flight of agricultural workers and their families to the cities. Westminster and Whitehall, however, were nonchalant to the point of negligence: 'The first act of Government intervention was in 1833 when a half-empty House of Commons approved a grant of £20,000 to be divided between the National and the British and Foreign School Societies as an aid to the building of schools. For several years the continuance of the grant was uncertain. Thus in 1839, when Parliament approved the establishment of the Select Committee of the Privy Council for Education, the annual grant was passed by the slender majority of two.'[136]

This was just enough, however, to create the first piece of state apparatus for the central consideration of education – an off-shoot of the Privy Council (the creation of a Board had to wait until 1899 and a Ministry till 1944). It also brought into play the first of a remarkable line of reforming minds which gave education something approaching the crucial place it should occupy in any society. He was the Secretary of the Privy Council's Education Committee, Sir James Kay-Shuttleworth.

Under Kay-Shuttleworth a system of state assistance, as opposed to state supervision which was an early twentieth-century innovation,[137] came into being. Its underlying principle was that the Government should aid education, which was to remain in a variety of hands, all of them private and usually religious, until the 1870s. Aid would take the form of books, equipment and salaries for teachers and pupil teachers (sixteen-year-olds taken on as a kind of school-based apprentice) all paid for by public money voted by Parliament. This was, however, a mere scratching of the surface of a need, a need made up of many layers. On an individual level, most of the schools were crude and cruel, dominated by rote learning, 'chalk and talk', with institutionalised violence the goad. On an industrial level, overall provision was ruinously inadequate for a manufacturing and trading nation which, as the nineteenth century progressed, found a previously empty field suddenly crowded with competitors. On a national level, no need was properly met – not even for the military or administrative classes an imperial power required.

In the 1850s this came to be realised by the discerning in British public life who resorted to their traditional instruments, the royal commission and the committee of inquiry. There was, however, a strong tradition in British thought and politics which militated against such ideas and the nascent schemes to which they logically led. That tireless enumerator of Establishment failings, Correlli Barnett, has both encapsulated the intellectual and temperamental problems which trammelled the mid-Victorians and set them in their wider context:

> In following Britain into the Industrial Revolution, European nations operated on different political and economic principles. Whereas the British had solved the problem of the inefficiency of the State by abolishing the State as far as possible, European countries like Prussia instead modernised the State and made it efficient. Whereas the British dissolved the nation into individuals and left their destiny to the free market, European countries stuck to the old notion that the State should embody the collective will of the people and guide the national development . . .
>
> The most important – indeed in the long run decisive – contribution of the European States to their countries' industrial progress lay in elaborate and coherent systems of national education – elementary, secondary, technical and university. From the beginning European (and American) industry was served by thoroughly well-trained, well-informed, high quality personnel – from boardroom to factory floor. Its operations were based on sophisticated intellectual study, and above all on close liaison with scientific research.
>
> British industry and its 'practical' men were no more fit to meet this formidable attack than the British militia would have been to meet the Prussian army. From the very moment when British technology ceased to have the world's markets entirely to itself and had to face competition, its defeat was under way.[138]

Even Parliament was aroused. And thirty years after it reluctantly allowed a mite of public money to be spent on education and a rudimentary administrative apparatus to be constructed for its disbursement, its Select Committee on Scientific Instruction described the bleak consequences of parsimony and neglect:

> . . . the foremen are almost without exception, persons who have been selected from the class of workmen by reason of their superior natural aptitude, steadiness and industry. Their education, and that of the workmen, during the school age, has been received in the elementary schools; and owing both

to the defective character of the instruction in some of these schools, and to the early stage at which children go to work [twelve years of age at that time], it is rarely sufficient to enable them to take advantage of scientific instruction at a later period.[139]

At the summit of the system, there was cause for comparable alarm. As Matthew Arnold, the poet and scholar who doubled up as an inspector of schools, put it in the aftermath of the Franco-Prussian War of 1870 (the victory which led to a united Germany and a permanently formidable competitor for the United Kingdom), 'We have been lately witnessing in the elasticity with which every branch of Prussian organisation bore the tremendous strain upon it by the war, the fruits of the effectiveness of the German University system. Our breakdown at the Crimea [1854–6] is distinctly traceable to the ineffectiveness of our superior [i.e. higher] education.'[140]

In the generally lamentable picture of British higher education in the first half of the nineteenth century, Scotland must be differentiated from England. Its own ancient universities, Glasgow, Aberdeen and St Andrews, had a far better reputation than their counterparts south of the border and deservedly so. Paul Langford, historian of eighteenth-century Britain, has recorded that:

The universities in England gave an impression of complacency and sloth, particularly by comparison with their Scottish counterparts. North of the border, academic life was characterised by religious strife and even bigotry. But it also displayed signs of immense vigour on which the Scottish Enlightenment prospered. The Scottish contribution to the European achievement of the age in fields as diverse as moral philosophy, political economy and medical science was substantial. The English universities fell far short by this yardstick. Their function was partly to train their clergy, partly to offer a broad education to the genteel and the wealthy.[141]

Oxford and Cambridge deliberately deprived themselves of even much of the best grey matter in the 'genteel and wealthy' classes by continuing to practise bigotry of their own in the religious tests which kept non-Anglicans out until these barriers were demolished in the 1850s. Such discrimination was among the reasons for the foundation of London University in 1825, while concern about the condition of England after the Great Reform Act led the Anglicans themselves to establish the University of Durham in 1833.

As with schooling, there was a surge of mid-Victorian concern about the state of university education and a Royal Commission on the Universities of Oxford and Cambridge was appointed in 1850. As a result Gladstone, very reluctantly, put a bill through Parliament in 1854 which changed the face of the university he represented in Parliament (Oxford) whereby 'university and college government became representative; appointments were thrown open to competition; power was given to alter trusts, and to require the provision of documents and accounts. Religious tests were abolished in respect of candidates for matriculation or for a Bachelor's degree; but they were retained in all other cases.'[142]

But it is upon the public schools – in whose classrooms the officer and administrative corps were instructed and on whose playing fields, future wars (allegedly) were won or lost – that the harshest, accusing gaze has been cast by anatomists of Britain's subsequent military and economic decline. Indeed, their mid-nineteenth-century role has been depicted as doubly malign by continuing to misshape an old aristocracy based on blood and land while absorbing and equally deforming a new aristocracy sired by the sweat and money of the men who made Britain's and the world's first industrial revolution.

Few books had greater impact during the recession-hit, conflict-laden (by British standards) early 1980s than Martin Wiener's *English Culture and the Decline of the Industrial Spirit*.[143] Here the villain of the piece is Dr Thomas Arnold of Rugby, philosopher king of the ideal of the English Christian gentleman. Another would-be reformer of British education, Kenneth Baker, once said during his spell as Education Secretary in the late 1980s that 'our education system is not the product of a single directing mind – a Napoleon or a Bismarck – let alone the expression of a single guiding principle. It has grown by a process of addition and adaptation. It reflects a good many historical compromises. In short, it is a bit of a muddle, one of those institutionalised muddles that the English have made peculiarly their own.'[144]

Arnold was one of two men in mid-nineteenth-century England who had what might qualify as a Napoleonic or Bismarckian vision of what education should be (the other was the great Benjamin Jowett of Balliol who persuaded Gladstone not only to reform Oxford but to do the same for that great employer of Oxford men in the future – the Civil Service).[145] Arnold was Headmaster of Rugby from 1827 until he died in 1841. But his extraordinarily demonic personality went marching on for a century or more.

'Arnold', writes Correlli Barnett, 'more than any other individual gave late Victorian English education both its concern with moral conduct and its distinctive mark of romanticism,' while 'Arnold's Rugby was the most important and influential of the schools that served as prototypes for the numerous new public schools that opened between 1840 and 1900 to cater for the swelling middle classes.'[146]

Self-confidence marked both Arnold and his creations who came off the public school production lines during Britain's Imperial heyday – public self-confidence that is, for who can calculate what private emotions seethed in the young men that emerged from those singular forcing-houses with their peculiar mixture of learning, high-mindedness, petty cruelties and routine violence.

'It's very true', wrote Arnold, 'that by our distinctness we have gained very much – more than foreigners can understand. A thorough English gentleman – Christian, manly and enlightened – is . . . a finer sentiment of human nature than any other country, I believe, could furnish.'[147] The pomposity and arrogance of that reminds me (and answers) the question Noel Coward posed implicitly a century later in *Mad Dogs and Englishmen* when he sang:

> It seems such a shame when the British claim the earth,
> That they give rise to such hilarity and mirth.[148]

The second half of the nineteenth century saw a Britain driven by Arnold-and Jowett-like preoccupations *and*, more decisively, by pressing economic concerns and fears of military and industrial rivals, to take a succession of hard looks at all levels of education. The result was marked both by statute, institutional innovation and an ever greater flow of public money. Germany provided the model for many on matters educational as it did for the more advanced thinkers on social security. Here the Bismarckian equivalent of national insurance was the much-admired technical high school.

It was Matthew Arnold once more who acted as a kind of Marco Polo bringing educational travellers' tales back to England from the Continent. In his paper prepared for the 1868 Royal Commission's schools inquiry, he described the Prussian system as 'at once the most complete and the most perfectly adjusted to its people of all that now exist'.[149] His capture of the Commissioners could not have been more complete as their final report showed:

> We are bound to add that our evidence appears to show that our industrial classes have not even that basis of sound general education at which alone technical education can rest . . . In fact our deficiency is not merely a deficiency in technical education, but . . . in general intelligence, and unless we remedy this want we shall gradually but surely find that our undeniable superiority in wealth and perhaps in energy will not save us from decline.[150]

It's hard analysis and grimly accurate prognosis such as that which would come to mind time and again a century later when sterling crisis succeeded balance of payment imbalance in a seemingly endless cycle broken only temporarily in the early 1980s by the all too finite godsend of North Sea oil.

Though the Gladstone Administration legislated for schooling two years after those words were published, you would not have known the two pieces of paper – the report and the statute – were linked. It was partly because the 1868 inquiry was commissioned to look at endowed (i.e. grammar or secondary schools maintained by voluntary bodies) as opposed to the public schools or the elementary schools. And W.E. Forster's 1870 measure concerned itself chiefly with the latter.

His Elementary Education Act aimed only to fill the gaps in voluntary provision.[151] If a locality remained badly served, school boards, established locally to maintain a framework of elementary schools helped by funding from the rates and government grants, would step in. Here lay the foundations of the religious problem which blighted every educational reformer up to and including Butler. For, as Harry Judge put it, 'A dual system had been absentmindedly created in elementary education. In many places the parson and the school board glowered at one another, and fought for pupils and resources.'[152]

For all the upheaval of reform (and the legacy of religious conflict it bequeathed), the 1870 initiative was about administration and structure *not* the content of education with which Matthew Arnold and the Royal Commissioners were, rightly, preoccupied. 'Sixteen barren years' after they reported as Correlli Barnett tartly puts it,[153] another set of Royal Commissioners made the Grand Tour of Europe finding 'the one point in which Germany is overwhelmingly superior to England is in schools, and in the education of all classes of the people. The dense ignorance so common among workmen in England is unknown.'[154]

Their report was phrased with such force that it tweaked the nerve of insecurity already apparent in a nation whose territorial expansion was about to explode once more in a 'scramble for Africa'.

> It is our duty to state that, although the display of continental manufacturers at the Paris International Exhibition in 1878 had led us to expect great progress, we were not prepared for so remarkable a development of their natural resources, nor for such perfection in their industrial establishments as we actually found . . . Your commissioners cannot repeat too often that they have been impressed with the general intelligence and technical knowledge of the masters and managers of industrial establishments on the Continent.[155]

And what impact did the accumulated wisdom of the Victorian 'good and great' have? The Science and Art Department of the Privy Council (a separate entity from its Education Department which concerned itself with the elementary schools) carried on trying to do good piecemeal with grants paid on the basis of previous results to science classes in the grammar schools, the higher grade elementary schools and a smattering of evening classes.

The most promising step forward was the Technical Instruction Act, 1889, which empowered the newly created local councils to levy a rate of one penny in the pound for technical education. A year later, a change in Customs and Excise legislation raised a new tax on spirits. The Treasury, in a rare burst of generosity and foresightedness, handed over this 'whisky money' to the secondary schools, a windfall, amounting to more than £400,000 by 1894, which 'rescued' many a grammar school in financial difficulty.[156]

It was, however, a financial drop in the ocean of crying need – a need which, if unmet, would unleash a chain reaction with, eventually, deleterious consequences for many crucial activities in the factory, the laboratory and on the battlefield. When Cripps called for higher productivity and better management, or Bevin for a million more tons of coal, in the late 1940s, they were addressing the hard practical consequences of the educational failures in the late nineteenth century as well as what John Kenyon called 'the squalor and starvation, the abysmal relationship between master and man, which lay beneath the pompous and vulgar glitter of Edwardian England'.[157]

In the closing years of the nineteenth century it was plain that the administrative delivery of education in England and Wales (the Scottish system has always been separate, different and much admired by many to the south) was about to undergo another convulsion. For a start it was quite obvious that in central government terms, the work could no longer be carried out as a subsidiary activity of the Privy Council. In 1895 the Bryce Commission was appointed by Lord Rosebery's Liberal Government to bring order out of chaos. The Commissioners recommended a minister should be appointed with a Board of Education to help him at the centre. At the periphery the 2,500 school boards should be replaced by a smaller number of local education authorities fully integrated with the local government system.[158]

The first recommendation found statutory form with the Board of Education Act, 1899; the second with the Education Act, 1902. When Bryce reported in 1895, there were 5.25 million children in elementary schools, 4 million of them under ten years of age.[159] The odds against them going on to a secondary education were 270 to 1.[160] As the Army doctors seeking recruits for the Boer War and the first teams in operation under the school medical service (created by the 1902 Act) were to find, a phenomenally high proportion were dirty, ill or suffering from malnutrition.[161]

At the other end of the system, England had seven universities to serve a population of 31 million; Germany twenty-two for a population of 50 million; and the United States, 484 men's and 162 women's colleges plus 48 schools of technology for a population of 100 million.[162] In Britain women had scarcely secured a foothold on the university ladder. As G.A.N. Lowndes put it, 'When the Act of 1902 was passed the country possessed the nucleus of what are now the universities [he was writing in 1937 when Britain possessed twenty-one universities with 48,000 undergraduates between them][163], in those days amounting, with a few brilliant exceptions such as Owen's College, Manchester, to little more than congeries of technical and literary classes; a small number of polytechnics mainly in London: a rather larger number of organised science schools and evening science and art classes.'[164]

The name attached to the 1902 Act is that of Arthur Balfour, Lord President of the Council (and soon to be Prime Minister) to whom the President of the Board of Education, Sir John Gorst, was subordinate. But the mind behind it was that of Sir Robert Morant, a reforming civil servant of the Kay-Shuttleworth type. Morant's driving demon was not the shortcomings of technical and scientific education but the messy overlap of bodies running the system at the local level. He knew the solution he wanted and he more than any other man was responsible for hijacking the old arrangement of state assistance and replacing it by state supervision. So great a figure was he that Butler's number two, Chuter Ede, found himself grappling with Morant's ghost when piloting the 1943 Bill through the House of Commons.

In 1944 Chuter Ede, stung by criticisms of the backwardness of technical education in Britain, said, 'We had the misfortune that, when the Act of 1902 was passed, its administration was left to one of the greatest autocrats who ever dwelt in the Civil Service – the late Sir Robert Morant, of whom it is said, "He was not unprincipled but he was unscrupulous."'[165]

Morant was also dedicated to a point where he was prepared to forgo Boxing Day at home in the dying days of 1898 in order to meet clandestinely with an education official of the London County Council to set him and his authority up to challenge the legal basis of the patchwork of provision bequeathed by the Forster Act of 1870.[166] As a result of a test case brought by the LCC, the local auditor ruled that any money spent by the school boards on anything other than the *elementary* education prescribed by the 1870 Act (i.e. any of the increasingly important haphazard funding of rudimentary secondary education) was illegal. The old system was holed. A new one, embracing the secondary schools, had to be put in its place just as Morant wanted. To persuade ministers to move, however, Morant (still a relatively junior official, his patron, Balfour, did not dislodge the permanent secretary, Sir George Kekewich, in his favour until 1902) had to play the religious card. As Harry Judge explains it:

For the Church of England especially, the problem in the 1890s was essentially financial. The voluntary societies looked anxiously at what seemed to them the extravagance of the school boards in enlarging their premises, improving the pay of their teachers, extending the curriculum beyond the limits of the elementary codes – all this with the encouragement of the officials in Whitehall. The resources for church schools were straitened, and the schools themselves at breaking point.

Any attempt to increase central government grants – or, even worse, to introduce the novelty of local government grants – could be relied upon to inflame opposition. But, at a time when half the children at school were in voluntary schools, the problem could not be ignored.[167]

The Balfour Bill proposed the abolition of the school boards and their replacement by local education authorities under the wings of the County and County Borough Councils. Control of elementary education passed to them and they were empowered to aid education 'other than elementary', which meant secondary and technical education and the provision of teacher training colleges. To fund all this, Councils were allowed to levy an education vote of twopence in the pound on top of the 'whisky money'.

It was the spectre of 'Rome on the Rates' as well as 'Canterbury on the Rates' which drove the Non-Conformists wild. Why should they as ratepayers be required to pay for the teaching in schools of doctrines from which they dissented? In a materialist age in probably the most secular country in the world, it is very difficult to comprehend such passion or the force of its political expression. Non-Conformity, however, was at its height, the Liberal Party its instrument and the word-power of Lloyd George, the greatest orator of the day, its cutting-edge.[168]

Balfour got his Bill through but it was a major contributor to the Liberal landslide in 1906. Churchill not only lived through all this but became a minister because of it. In the mid-1940s he never ceased to remind Butler of its potentially explosive power as Rab did the rounds assuaging a minister here, praying with a bishop there. When Cardinal Hinsley, the Archbishop of Westminster, wrote to *The Times* in 1942 asserting the independence of Roman Catholic education and declaring 'no political party will seek to or be able to set at naught the respect of the British people for minorities',[169] Churchill cut it out and sent it from No. 10 to Butler at the Board of Education in Kingsway on a piece of cardboard with the message: 'There you are, fixed, old cock.'[170]

There was but one burst of educational reform between Balfour/Morant and Butler – that pioneered by the great European historian H.A.L. Fisher, sent to the Board of Education by Lloyd George in 1916. Fisher's idea was to build extensions at either end of the school system – nursery provision at one end and 'continuation schools' for the young adolescent at the other to which fourteen–sixteen-year-olds would go for 320 hours a year during their early days at work. The Fisher Act raised the school-leaving age to fourteen and, not before time, swept away the nineteenth-century legislation permitting twelve–fourteen-year-olds to work part-time in factories. These last two reforms stuck but the 1918 legislation was 'permissive' when it came to nurseries and continuation schools. Local authorities could provide them if they wished but they did not have to. Some did but only for a few years.

Postwar slump and the Lloyd George Coalition's notorious response – the cuts made by the 'Geddes Axe' (so-called after Sir Eric Geddes who chaired the economy committee) – was to slash the education budget by a third which put an end to most experiments pre-five and post-fourteen. Though other Fisher reforms on the examination side – the school certificate for fourteen-year-olds and higher school certificate for sixth-formers in secondary and grammar schools – did survive.[171]

During an otherwise barren interwar period, the intellectual preparation for the Butler Act was well under way. Most statutes reflect the policy Research and Development (R and D) of the previous generation. The ever-fertile R.H. Tawney, whose influence on the 1918 Act Fisher acknowledged,[172] operated as a kind of tweedy one-man pressure group, producing ideas through a haze of herbal tobacco smoke pushing them gently in one forum after another until they caught on. The Labour Party's *Secondary Education for All* published in 1922 was largely Tawney's work[173] and he was the moving spirit behind the Hadow Report in *The Education of the Adolescent*, published by the Board of

Education's own Consultative Committee in 1926 (Tawney was a member). Hadow anatomised the bone structure of the Butler Act which passed into law eighteen years later – secondary schools (a mix of 'modern' and grammar institutions) and primary schools for five–twelve-year-olds should replace the elementary system.[174]

Hadow, however, sustained the post-Morant tilt against technical education. 'Modern Schools' would have a practical bias in the scheme of things but they would be a far cry from the technical high school concept. 'The idea that technical studies should be included was anathema.'[175] This was to be of critical importance to Britain after 1945 because the Hadow Report set the tone and the parameters of the system put in place in the two decades which followed the Butler Act. For what the 1944 settlement achieved was a rationalisation and an expansion of *existing* patterns of educational provision. An improvement, certainly, but not a fresh start. And in terms of the cross–party consensus which saw it safely through Parliament, 'the lack of strictly educational innovation in the 1940s was the silent clue to much of the action'.[176]

The Hadow Report was the foundation of that consensus, but other inquiries built on it and refined it before Churchill gave Butler his chance to leave a great mark on British social policy. To their credit, Board of Education officials demonstrated an admirable faith in the future of their country during the 'standing alone' year of 1940–1. Working in the Branksome Dene and Durley Dean Hotels in their wartime headquarters in Bournemouth (the President and a small group of advisers stayed in Holborn) they prepared a plan for postwar education and summarised it in a confidential handbook known as the 'Green Book'. Paul Addison, a dispenser of justice to the forgotten in British political life, described the President of the Board at the time, Herwald Ramsbotham (a Conservative), as 'even then one of the most obscure of all political figures . . .

> But it was he who took the decisive step of circularising the Green Book to interested parties in the educational world. The traditional processes of consultation, one of the unwritten elements in the constitution, were under way, and memoranda began to pour into Bournemouth. Though not yet published, the contents of the Green Book were extensively leaked to the press, and propaganda for educational reform encouraged.[177]

Butler, who liked to quote Professor Lester Smith on the Green Book's being distributed 'in such a blaze of secrecy that it achieved an unusual degree of publicity',[178] decided to publish a summary of its contents as one of the first acts of his stewardship at the Board.

Within two months, Butler had decided the time was ripe for reform and minuted Churchill accordingly. The Old Man had vague notions that something must be done. In December 1940 he told the boys at his old school, Harrow, that 'after the war the advantages of the Public Schools must be extended on a far broader basis,' and in August of the following year he remarked to Lord Halifax that it was the secondary schoolboys (I suspect he meant grammar-school boys, given the paucity of secondary schools pre-1944) who had saved this country. 'They have', he said 'the right to rule it.'[179]

A month after imparting this magnanimous vision to his fellow aristocrat, Churchill was writing to Butler stating emphatically that:

> It would be the greatest mistake to raise the 1902 controversy during the War, and I certainly cannot contemplate a new Education Bill. I think it would also be a great mistake to stir up the public schools question at the present time. No one can possibly tell what the financial and economic state of the country will be when the war is over. Your main task at present is to get the schools working as well as possible under all the difficulties of air attack, evacuation, etc. If you can add to this industrial and technical training, enabling men not required for the Army to take their places promptly in munitions industry or radio work, this would be most useful. We cannot have any party politics in wartime . . . Meanwhile you have a good scope as an administrator.[180]

Rab, characteristically, ignored the Prime Minister and his 'compliant' Permanent Secretary, Holmes, and 'decided to disregard what he said and go straight ahead. I knew that if I spared him the religious controversies and party political troubles of 1902 and sidetracked the public schools issue, I could win him over.'[181] No wonder Butler spent so much time viewing relics or on his knees with Archbishops. The Education Act was clearly worth a Mass.

Butler appointed Sir Cyril Norwood to chair a Committee on Secondary School Examinations, to put the flesh of a curriculum on the bone structure laid down by Hadow, and set off on his travels to tell the vast network of educational organisations, institutions and trade unions about his aim of 'secondary education for all' over eleven years of age and his belief that:

> Educationally after the war Britain had to be one nation not two. So there must be an education system providing a 'training suited to talents of every individual'. This would have to be combined with more expert training for industry, with a revivified system of apprenticeship, and with a practical form of continued education, later to be called County Colleges. I did not, however, go any further on the religious side than to call for a final settlement of the 'Dual System' of provided and non-provided schools. Since this issue was a particularly thorny one, I was to spend more time in trying to reach the settlement than on anything else.[182]

Rab solved his thorniest problem by patient diplomacy, the pursuit of allies (the conversion of Archbishop Temple was an early and critical victory) and the capacity to build a compromise, brick by denominational brick.

That compromise took the form of an offer to the voluntary sector (church schools, that is, not the public schools which hardly figured at all in the 1944 settlement). They could either become 'aided' or 'controlled' schools. If the schools' managers couldn't stump up half the costs necessary for bringing the schools up to standard (the Board of Education had kept a 'Black List' of substandard buildings since 1925 when 521 church schools found themselves so fingered), effective control would pass to the local education authority, though certain religious/worship safeguards were guaranteed. Where the governors, parents and sponsoring churches could come up with more than half, they would remain independent but 'aided' by local-government finance. This effectively settled the religious question which had blighted Balfour and terrified Churchill. Not until Kenneth Baker's 1988 Education Reform Act, with its allowance for 'opting out' of local authority funding in favour of a direct financial link with the Department of Education, did the issue arise once more with the possibility that religious groups (especially in communities with a high proportion of Muslim residents) might seek to use it to create schools more to their choosing than those offered by local councils.

As so often happens with reforming bouts, the area of least controversy turns out to be the battleground for the next generation. So it was with the Butler Act. The terrain of future dispute was mapped out by the Norwood Committee and another chaired by Sir Will Spens which reported shortly before war broke out. Spens took Hadow a step forward and recommended a tripartite system of post-eleven education. In addition to grammar and modern schools, there would be technical schools as well. The Spens Committee considered the idea of 'multilateral' schools, as the comprehensive idea was then described, and rejected it on the grounds of size. All-in schools could have as many as 800 pupils and, as Harold Dent put it, 'all the Englishman's innate distaste for large schools welled up'.[183]

At this time, the 'multilateral' school was a rather different notion from that which underlay the comprehensive blueprint of the 1960s. Grammar, modern and technical schools would share a single site to facilitate transfer between them. Spens saw the utility of such an arrangement in rural areas with scattered populations and suggested experiments could be made along these lines.[184]

Such thinking blended easily with the 'official mind', to use Robinson and Gallagher's phrase,[185] in the Board of Education. Tripartitism became the core notion of the reform thinking behind the 'Green Book'. The Norwood Committee refined it, believing, as Paul Addison put it, that 'such a system . . . would correspond to a natural division of aptitudes among children'.[186] Aptitude would be judged by intelligence, or IQ tests, then at the zenith of their prestige as indicators of future potential.

The tripartite notion, the basis of the structural consensus which underlay the 1944 Act, was much criticised later, not least by Ministry of Education officials who, once their collective 'official mind' had changed once more, saw it as far too simplistic and rigid. As one of them, Sir Toby Weaver, put it with considerable disparagement:

There was a general belief, I believe totally false, that children were divided into three kinds. It was sort of Platonic. There were golden children, and silver children, and iron children.

The golden children were capable of going to a grammar school, they had minds, they could have abstract thinking. The technical children, the silver children so to speak, were technically orientated, and all the rest, they couldn't handle ideas, they had to have concrete notions.[187]

The tripartite system, the basis of the non-religious part of the educational settlement and its controversial instrument, the 'eleven plus' examination, became the battleground of the 1950s and 1960s. The comprehensive idea did not catch fire until the 1950s. But there had been sufficient pressure in favour of it in Butler's time to persuade Rab to take an agnostic line on it in his statute, thereby, in a sense leaving the door open for it as the measure left the type of post-eleven schools they operated to the discretion of the local authorities, subject to the approval of the Minister (one of the changes in the 1944 Act was the replacement of the board by a ministry and the president by a minister).

Most of the running in favour of the multilateral school was made by the National Association of Labour Teachers. In 1942 they persuaded the Labour Party Conference to pass a resolution in favour of such institutions. In February 1943 they waited on Butler to press their case, to no great effect.

The country's largest education authority, however, the London County Council, was enthusiastic. In July 1944 it included comprehensive schools in its postwar development plan, a move long regretted by Harold Dent who wrote as long ago as 1954 that 'the idea of the comprehensive school has never quite recovered from the blow dealt it when England's largest municipality decided to adopt it. Even some people not entirely averse from the idea of trying out the comprehensive, or the multilateral school, criticised the London County Council for embarking upon a total policy of comprehensive schools instead of beginning by setting up one or two as experiments.'[188]

London may have been the vanguard in planning terms. But in bricks-and-mortar terms, the Lakeland town of Windermere takes the palm as the builder of the first comprehensive school, which opened in 1945. While Anglesey was the first authority to go completely comprehensive. By the time Labour left office in 1951 there were less than twenty genuine comprehensive schools in England and Wales.[189]

In some labour movement circles, Butler's successor, Ellen Wilkinson, has never been forgiven for missing a great opportunity as Minister of Education at *the* 'revolutionary' moment in postwar history not just to push the comprehensive idea but to get rid of the public schools as well (they were exhorted to take more local authority pupils but otherwise left alone). The lack of charity towards Miss Wilkinson's memory is compounded by the memory of her fiery 'Red Ellen' of the Jarrow March days and the theory (which may have something in it) that by becoming (almost certainly) Herbert Morrison's mistress in the late 1930s, she succumbed to a less intense vision of the socialist mission. Others, like her sympathetic biographer, Betty Vernon, point out, with a high degree of justice, that Ellen Wilkinson was hard put to implement the essentials of the Butler Act given the shortage of materials for the new accommodation necessitated by the raising of the school-leaving age and her increasing ill-health for the last year before her sad (possibly suicidal) death in February 1947.

'Ellen', wrote Betty Vernon, 'had little opportunity to stand back and *think* in the face of insistent departmental demands for swift decisions and swifter action. Not for her was there to be that "generation in office" which she had envisaged as essential for implementing the 1944 Act.'[190] Her relentless Labour critics in the Commons, like W.G. Cove, might have been assuaged if they had read Wilkinson's one outburst in the Ministry which revealed her true, still fiery self and a mind instinctively opposed to what Toby Weaver called the notion of gold, silver and iron children.

The cause of her eruption was a draft submitted by an official in March 1946 for a pamphlet, *New Secondary Education*, which the Ministry was planning to publish (it was finally published after her death with a foreword she had prepared in her last, sad days in office).[191] The civil servant concerned was Sir Martin Roseveare, the Ministry's Senior Chief Inspector of Schools, a Wykehamist mathematician who had a profound impact in another sphere of 1940s life, being the same Roseveare who designed that great symbol of the age, the ration book.

After reading Roseveare's submission, she recalled,

I wondered why I felt deep down angry . . . Then I realised that Mr Squeers had given me a quizzical look across the years . . . this pamphlet is fundamentally phony because it subconsciously disguises the real question that has to be answered, namely, 'What shall we do to get miners and agricultural workers if a hundred per cent of the children able to profit from it are offered real secondary education. Answer [in Roseveare's submission] . . . give the real stuff to a selected 25 per cent, steer the 75% away from the humanities, pure science, even history.'[192]

She was appalled at the prospect of boys and girls doing practical things in their Secondary Modern Schools which they would, perforce, spend the rest of their life doing. 'Can't Shakespeare mean more than a scrubbing brush – can't enough of a foreign language be taught to open windows on the world a bit wider – I learnt French verbs [Wilkinson was a grammar school girl from Manchester] saying them as I scrubbed floors at home.' The prospect of no history being taught, quite rightly, enraged her. Could it be that it was 'too dangerous if an intelligent child asked awkward questions? (Don't worry how we got India, let's go and do some nice work at the forge!)'.

She didn't want children of different IQs going to physically separate schools. The stigma of lower IQs should not attach itself to any particular institution. As for the higher IQs, they 'will become intolerable little wretches if stamped from eleven as being superior!'

For all the formidable radicalism packed in her tiny, ailing frame, Wilkinson was a builder where Butler, Hadow, Spens and Norwood had been architects. Her monument is the standard concrete hut (in which I ate my school dinners at Our Lady of Lourdes Primary School in North Finchley in the 1950s and at Marling School, Stroud, in the 1960s), part of the HORSA (Hutting Operation for the Raising of the School-leaving Age) enterprise which had as great an impact on the 1940s landscape as the pillbox early in the decade.

That and the crash twelve-month course, the Emergency Training Scheme for teachers, are the monuments of the Wilkinson era. Though the marvellous enrichment of the teaching profession by 35,000 teachers, recruited from returning servicemen, men and women from industry and commerce (given their basics in an extraordinary variety of requisitioned buildings) was, like so much of the post-1945 workload, an idea of Coalition vintage; the author of this particular scheme being a civil servant on the Board, Sir Gilbert Flemming.[193]

As well as HORSA and his brother SFORSA (School Furniture Operation for the Raising of the School-leaving Age), the late 1940s saw a marvellously creative burst of primary-school buildings – 928 new ones between 1945 and 1950 – the product of a need and a remarkably effective partnership between Ministry of Education administrators such as Sir Antony Part and professionals like Stirrat Johnson-Marshall based on pioneering work by Hertfordshire County Council.[194]

Often ignored among the flurry of changes stimulated by the Butler Act was the first postwar surge in university education aided by the British equivalent of the GI Bill which placed several thousand returning servicemen and women on the path to a degree without the normal pre-entry qualifications. Quite apart from its place as an act of gratitude to those who had placed their lives at the disposal of the state in 1939–45, the war had heightened an awareness at all levels of the need for trained, graduate manpower.

In 1944 the Percy Report recommended a doubling of the output of engineering graduates. In the same year the Goodenough Committee urged an increase in medical education. In 1946 the Barlow Committee said the nation needed a doubling of the supply of scientists and technologists.[195] Ellen Wilkinson wanted an expansion of numbers at existing universities and a new one at York (nearly twenty years after her death there was one).[196]

Even the Treasury was moved by the spirit of the times and demographic pressure. In what John Carswell called a 'quiet measure of nationalisation',[197] it told the University Grants Committee, this previously 'highly respectable backwater'[198] created by Treasury Minute in 1919, 'to assist, in consultation with the universities and other bodies concerned, the preparation and execution of such plans for the development of the universities as may from time to time be required in order to ensure that they are fully adequate to national needs'.[199] As a result, the number of university students increased from 50,246 in 1938–9 to 76,764 in 1947–8,[200] a growth of over 50 per cent which produced a generation of undergraduates (many older than their years because of combat experience) still spoken of with nostalgia by the dons when I reached my own ancient university in 1966.

Education, as everybody knew then and knows now, is crucial to the wider social and economic well-being of the country. There is a direct link between the quality of educational investment in one generation and the industrial output, balance of payments and strength of the currency in the next and the next-but-one. However, when the economic consequences of previous governmental neglect in education are felt, it is often the current budget that becomes a victim of previous shortcomings – a key arc in the vicious circle of relative decline. So it nearly proved in the last weeks of Ellen Wilkinson's life on earth.

The Hadow Report of 1926 had recommended a raising of the school-leaving age to fifteen. In 1936 the National Government of Stanley Baldwin passed an Education Act to give effect to this. It was due to happen on 1 September 1939. Events in Poland took care of that. The Butler Act looked forward to a restoration of previous plans. The 1944 Act set a date of 1 April 1945 for this. The war was still under way as the date approached and ROSLA (Raising the School-leaving Age) was postponed for two years until 1 April 1947. This was the position Ellen Wilkinson inherited, fulfilling that pledge she regarded as her first priority.[201]

She moved quickly after the election to win Cabinet backing for its achievement. The Cabinet agreed on 23 August 1945 that the school-leaving age would be raised to fifteen on 1 April 1947 and to sixteen at an unspecified date thereafter.[202] She also persuaded her colleagues to add £100 million to the education budget for 1946. During the second half of 1946 doubts about ROSLA set in, not on Wilkinson's part (though she knew that the building programme would not be completed in time).[203] The first doubter was the Secretary of State for Scotland, Joseph Westwood, who said there would be part-time schooling north of the border by the summer of 1947 if the date was not changed.[204]

A much greater threat came from the Treasury which was preparing the first of its economic surveys as part of the Government's new planning regime. On the basis of the physical shortages predicted therein, especially in the construction industry, Dalton urged in December 1946 that ROSLA be postponed until September 1947. Wilkinson countered with a memo to Morrison who as Lord President had at this stage an overlord's role for the domestic economy, arguing that the crunch would not come until the autumn of 1948 by which time there would be sufficient numbers of teachers and huts to cope with the bulge.[205]

The matter reached Cabinet on 16 January 1947 and Wilkinson put up what turned out virtually to be a farewell performance. She reminded her colleagues that whenever governments hit trouble, education was always the first casualty.

I pledged the honour of the Government that 1 April 1947 would be the date. Just because I made the country believe that the Government meant to keep its word, the phased programme is now ready enough to do its job: we shall never get the same intensity of effort to a date again, and those to suffer most by deferment will be precisely those working class children whose education has already been so seriously interrupted by the war.[206]

She told the Cabinet quite plainly that if they failed to back her 'As a trade union official I am fully prepared to use my union, public platforms and the press to argue the case,'[207] a cause the disciplinarian Attlee would have been most unlikely to allow her had she remained a minister.

It didn't come to that. The Cabinet, including the P.M., backed her. Herbert Morrison, in an action that must have caused great hurt given their former intimacy, backed his fellow economic ministers, Dalton and Cripps. Little Ellen left the Cabinet Room immediately to issue a prepared press notice confirming ROSLA on 1 April. Her Permanent Secretary, Sir John Maud, was in no doubt that had she lost in Cabinet, she would have resigned,[208] in which case neither Attlee nor anyone could have prevented her from taking her case to the country.

There was a dramatic backdrop to her last triumph – a severe winter crisis, the coldest winter in memory *and* a huge fuel crisis which ministerial incompetence had compounded as we shall see in chapter eight. Ellen Wilkinson's last public act was to defy the elements as she had defied the Treasury when she opened the Old Vic Theatre School in south London on 25 January 1947.

A photograph of the occasion shows her looking drawn and tired; yet obstinate as ever, rather than escape from sitting in the icy building, blitzed into heatlessness and open to the sky, she elected to stay and caught pneumonia.[209]

A few days later she was taken from her flat in Dolphin Square to St Mary's Hospital, Paddington, where she died on 6 February at the age of fifty-five. Morrison, himself in hospital a couple of miles away in Hammersmith recovering from the removal of a blood clot, sent no message or flowers.[210] The BBC, however, was persuaded to delay the broadcast of Ellen's death until the news could be broken to Morrison by a doctor friend. When he heard, 'Morrison did not say anything, but he suddenly looked years older'.[211]

Though she was not there to see it (Attlee appointed George Tomlinson to succeed her), ROSLA, flanked by HORSA and SFORSA, arrived on cue seven weeks later – the work of many minds, several committees and two Acts of Parliament, but Ellen Wilkinson's memorial none the less.

Housing

We are telling them now that they are heroes for the way in which they are standing up to the strain of the mighty bombardment – and it's true. I think they will keep on being heroes, but when the war is over they will demand the rewards of heroism: they will expect to get them very soon and no power on earth will be able to rebuild the homes at the speed that will be necessary . . . I think there's going to be grave trouble, and the danger is that if the machine of government which can spend money so recklessly in engaging in war, fails to be equally reckless in rebuilding, there will be both the tendency and the excuse for revolution.
Lord Woolton, 1940[212]

We joined a stream of people who were heading up through Phillimore Gardens in the direction of the Duchess of Bedford flats. And it was a scene somewhat reminiscent of the vicinity of a football crowd on a Saturday afternoon. It seemed that thousands of people carrying all kinds of houseware, some pushing it on prams, others with it strung over their shoulders, were all heading in one direction. We joined this group and we headed to what we weren't quite sure, but a policeman directed us and we passed a van where soldiers were serving tea and cakes and we came to this magnificent red brick and marble looking building and there members of the Communist Party were directing people in through the doors.
Stan Henderson, recalling September 1946[213]

After we looked round Mary was worried and meself – would it be our luck to get one? When we came on the Friday, there was the Council people outside with a table, there was nine families lining up. 'Course Mary's got my hand and says, 'Oh, there's only eight prefabs.' 'Course, well, someone was going to be unlucky and as number two went, then number three, number four, so the tension was getting worse, but when it came to number eight he called my name to the table, I said . . . 'Yes, I'll have it' . . . And of course we took it and we moved in a week after but I did feel sorry for the person who was left out and she even cried. But it's the happiest day that ever happened.
Joe Linsell, recalling 1947[214]

We should try to introduce in our modern villages and towns what was always the lovely feature of English and Welsh villages, where the doctor, the grocer, the butcher and the farm labourer all lived in the same street. I believe that is essential for the full life of a citizen . . . to see the living tapestry of a mixed community.
Aneurin Bevan, 1945[215]

If he [Bevan] now builds the houses he is in direct line for the Premiership. If he does not, he is for the high jump.
Hannen Swaffer, 1945[216]

Of all the buildings that we make and use, it is difficult to think of any that matters more to us – and matters in a profoundly personal way. There is no kind of building that we know more about – and yet know less about. The fact is that we take it too much for granted.
Patrick Nuttgens, 1989[217]

Housing . . . differs from other fields of social administration because the aspect of it which attracts keenest attention – the building of new houses – is exposed to all the winds that blow in a draughty economic climate.
David Donnison, 1960[218]

The urban problem is as old as history, overcrowded and insanitary housing its essence. It is, as the great historian Fernand Braudel explained, the price paid for economic progress. 'Towns', he said, 'are like electric transformers. They increase tension, accelerate the rhythm of exchange and constantly recharge human life. Towns and cities', he went on,

> are turning points, watersheds of human history. When they first appeared, bringing with them the written word, they opened the door to what we now call *history*. Their revival in Europe in the eleventh century marked the beginning of the continent's rise to eminence. When they flourished in Italy, they brought the age of the Renaissance. So it has been since the city-states, the *poleis* of ancient Greece, the *medinas* of the Muslim conquest, to our own times. All major bursts of growth are expressed by an urban explosion.[219]

British cities in 1945 – as today – still bore the scars and configurations of the world's first industrial revolution which turned us into a nation of urban dwellers. The population of Britain almost doubled inside fifty years from 13 million in 1780 to 24 million in 1831. By 1801 30 per cent lived in towns or cities.

The extraordinary transformation of the British economy in the nineteenth century, based on coal, built on iron and powered by steam, 'produced a nation and an economy whose preoccupations were by 1870 largely industrial and urban. The growth of towns, which some had thought in 1851 could hardly be continued, intensified. By 1901, only one-fifth of the population of England and Wales lived in what may be called "rural areas"; that is, 80 per cent of the population was urbanised, a far greater proportion than in any European country, and one which remained little changed until the 1970s.'[220]

This intense degree of urbanisation made Britain the most proletarianised of the advanced nations by the end of the nineteenth century. The area four miles to the east of the Tower of London and three miles north of the Thames probably represented the largest, single working-class concentration in the world.[221] The north of England's plight, as every Marxist the world over knows, was captured by Friedrich Engels' description of Salford in 1844.[222] Charles Dickens did it best of all with his novelist's pen.

Coketown was 'a town of red brick', or a brick that would have been red if the smoke and the ashes had allowed it. It was a town of machinery and tall chimneys . . . It had a black canal in it, and a river that ran purple with ill-smelling dye . . . Nature was as strongly bricked out as killing airs and gases were bricked in.[223]

As we have seen in the case of health and social security, philanthropy simply could not keep pace with the consequences of Britain's economic take-off.

The state, belatedly and inevitably, was drawn in. The first statutes to regulate the housing market were a pair introduced in 1851 by the great philanthropist, Lord Shaftesbury, enabling local authorities to supervise lodging-houses. In the 1870s further legislation (the so-called Cross and Torrens Acts[224]) empowered local authorities to make the first slum clearances. As Mayor of Birmingham, Joseph Chamberlain used such legislation to clear the centre of his city for the building of a Victorian glory which lasted until the 1960s development mania flattened it.

In 1884, a Royal Commission on Housing raised the conscience of the nation and, incidentally, began a tradition of royal concern (the Prince of Wales was a member) which stretched via King George V ('an adequate solution to the housing question is the foundation of all social progress,' was how he put it in 1919[225]) through to the present Prince of Wales. The 1884 Royal Commission was a watershed in another sense – it shifted political and official opinion to a recognition that public intervention was needed as part of any solution to the nation's housing problems.

The Commissioners were strongly influenced by evidence presented by the London Trades Council which argued:

It is totally impossible that private enterprise, philanthropy and charity can ever keep pace with the present demands . . . Economic forces and population have outstepped their endeavours: hence evils accrue. But what the individual cannot do the state municipality must seek to accomplish . . . for it alone possesses the necessary power and wealth.[226]

Though the legislation which resulted from the Royal Commission, the Housing of the Working Classes Act 1885, accepted the notion of state intervention, public attempts to ameliorate the problem until the years after the First World War relied mainly on the establishment of minimum criteria for new dwellings put up once the municipalities had demolished the old.[227] It would be wrong to forget or belittle the private, charitable and philanthropic impulse in British housing in the nineteenth century, however inexorable may seem the progress towards the council house – that great, if often drab, shaper of the twentieth-century British landscape. It was, and remains, a fine tradition that began with the medieval alms-house.

Its industrial revolution manifestation began with the celebrated New Lanark experiment on the Upper Clyde in the late eighteenth century. David Dale, a Glasgow manufacturer and banker, took 500 children from the Edinburgh workhouse plus an adult workforce and placed them in the rolling countryside of Lanarkshire in what can claim to be the first industrial estate *and* new town in Britain. Robert Owen, who married into the family (and with whose name the project is mostly associated) took the experiment to a higher plane of virtue with school, shops, bakery and wash-house provided for the new community. Dale and Owen began a trail trod with variations by a long succession of industrialist-philanthropists: Edward Ackroyd in Halifax, Sir Titus Salt, creator of Saltaire near Bradford, Lord Lever with Port Sunlight on the Wirral Peninsula, the Cadburys with Bournville near Birmingham and the Rowntrees with New Earswick just outside York.

In addition, there was the industrial dwelling movement, associated with names like Sydney Waterlow and the Peabody Trust, which threw up the first multi-storey blocks of flats in an attempt to improve inner-city housing for the working class in the second half of the nineteenth century.[228] While Ebenezer Howard, building on the Port Sunlight and Bournville experiments, founded the Garden City Movement in the last years of the nineteenth century which found expression in brick-and-mortar in Letchworth in 1903, Welwyn in 1919 (both in Hertfordshire) and, it could be argued, in the twenty-five New Towns erected in Britain since the Second World War.[229]

There was a link – a human one – between the Garden City Movement and the British council house. His name was Raymond Unwin, the architect who turned Howard's vision into Letchworth. Unwin, like many people before and since (including Nye Bevan), was in love with the English village. Improvement he sought, but not by the nineteenth-century method of Coketown-style back-to-backs. His philosophy, laid out in his book *Nothing Gained by Overcrowding*,[230] was that there should be no more than a dozen houses per acre except where the cost of land was exceptionally high. This principle was adopted by housing authorities after the Great War thanks to Unwin's advocacy on the Committee of Inquiry established by the Lloyd George Coalition into postwar housing under the chairmanship of Sir John Tudor Walters.

It turned out to be the single most influential committee on this much-discussed subject in the twentieth century. As Patrick Nuttgens put it, 'The Tudor Walters Report, published in 1918, was intended to "profoundly influence the general standard of housing in this country". Its proposals were revolutionary, initiating a major innovation in social policy, and ultimately affecting the character of working class life. They were to remain a model throughout the inter-war years, and indirectly much longer.'[231]

In its century of pages Tudor Walters called for a more comprehensive method of improvement than that allowed by the succession of local authority bye-laws and late nineteenth-century legislation on the grounds that 'it is quite evident to those who have examined the facts of the case that special remedies are needed to deal with the acute housing difficulties that have arisen . . . It seems evident from these circumstances that, unless there is some supreme guiding direction, an adequate housing programme is not likely to be carried out, but that the shortage of houses for some years after the war will increase rather than diminish.'[232]

Tudor Walters ranged from aesthetic considerations (the need 'to develop the beauty of vista, arrangement and proportion') to the practical and detailed (a home with a parlour is 'undoubtedly the type desired by the majority of the artisan class'), almost all of which were adopted by the Board of Local Government in its *Housing Manual* published in 1919.[233] It was the President of the Board, Dr Christopher Addison (soon to become first Minister of the new Ministry of Health whose responsibilities included housing and local government), who picked up the Tudor Walters Report and ran with it. If any man can be described as the father of the council house it's the thoughtful medical man, one of the quietly influential people of twentieth-century government, whose service to the nation lasted until 1950 when he finally retired from the Attlee Administration.[234]

Since 1919, housing has been a political/administrative activity in which swift and enduring results can be achieved – and seen to be – within a few years of an important decision being taken. This explains why so many leading politicians since Addison have been keen to become Housing Minister. The department responsible – whether it be Health from 1919 to 1951, Housing and Local Government from 1951 to 1970 or Environment thereafter – has been the place where political monuments can be constructed or, on occasions, great reputations made (Neville Chamberlain's in the 1920s, Harold Macmillan's in the 1950s).

Addison, though now long forgotten, was the first to win such a permanent memorial for himself for, thanks to his Housing and Town Planning Act 1919:

> The change in housing standards that followed can be measured in figures but it is there for all to see in every English town – at the point where the 1919 stratum of building begins with a sudden eruption of trees, hedges, and little gardens from the asphalt, slate and paving stones. Since then, there have been improvements in the equipment of new houses – particularly their bathrooms and kitchens – but their structure and the space allotted to them have changed comparatively little.[235]

What exactly were the ingredients which made the Addison Act so effective? The crucial one involved making the permissive powers of the nineteenth-century legislation mandatory. Local authorities were required henceforth to assess the housing needs of the areas and to make plans to meet them. Central government would provide the bulk of the money. The Treasury's subsidy was looked on as a temporary cash flow needed to make good past neglect, a measure given added urgency by the Great War. After all the Prime Minister himself, David Lloyd George, had promised 'a fit country for heroes to live in'[236] which, as so often happens to the one-liners of the famous, became transmogrified into '*homes* fit for heroes to live in' which LG never, in fact, said any more than Margaret Thatcher coined the phrase 'Victorian values' or Jim Callaghan asked 'Crisis? What crisis?' in 1979.

State subsidy for public housing was, however, here to stay whatever the intention of its inventor. 'The Act', wrote Patrick Nuttgens, 'established *council housing* as we know it. In effect, the state had taken over responsibility for working-class housing since the local authority contribution was at first minimal (no more than a penny rate). It also set a precedent for the professional design of mass housing, when Addison commissioned a number of architects to submit plans for the guidance of authorities.'[237]

The 'cottage', that enduring symbol of Old England, was the model for the architect, S.B. Russell, who designed most of them. The council 'cottage' began to appear inside the big cities especially the capital where the London County Council set out to build 29,000 dwellings in five years including 'cottage estates' and modified neo-Georgian-style flats, five storey brick constructions with sloping tiled roofs, still a prominent feature of inner-city London and, given the height restriction, mercifully free of tower-block syndrome.

London, in fact, managed to achieve less than a third of its target. This, too, was the picture nationally. Rising costs and government retrenchment began what has become a familiar story ever since. Addison envisaged half a million dwellings of which 214,000 were sanctioned and only 170,000 built at a cost of one pound per week per house to the Treasury.[238] Addison was, in fact, paying about £900 for houses which, a few years later, could be put up for less than £400 apiece.[239] After fierce public criticism of waste and mismanagement, Lloyd George dropped him. But Addison had left his mark on British history. For 'he, more than any other man', in A.J.P. Taylor's judgment, 'established the principle that housing was a social service, and later governments had to take up his task [until the 1980s, that is], though they tried to avoid his mistakes.'[240]

The Addison Act was quickly modified by his two immediate successors at the Ministry of Health. In 1923 Neville Chamberlain targeted public money both to local authorities *and* private builders. If the 'cottage' council house is Addison's memorial, the mock-Tudor semi, the symbol of interwar suburbia, is Chamberlain's. In 1924, the Clydesider, John Wheatley (the most successful minister in the first Labour Government) restored the emphasis on public housing which he wished to see replace private renting as the standard form of working-class housing. Wheatley gave local councils long-term funding provided they met Ministry of Health production targets.

His successor in the second Labour Government, Arthur Greenwood, achieved a different kind of fame. His symbol is the swinging ball of the demolition gang. For the 1930 Act established the principle of government support for slum clearance. The pattern of state-subsidised destruction and rebuilding was set for the next forty years until in the 1970s the concept of conservation took a hold and, in the 1980s, the idea of state subsidy (mortgage tax relief apart) ran its course.

Housing, in fact, was one of the few success stories of interwar Britain. Despite successive economy drives (the 'Geddes Axe' in 1922; the cuts which followed the 1931 crisis), more homes were built for the heroic and the less heroic, come to that, than in any comparable period in British history. In the twenty years after the First World War, 4 million new houses were put up in England and Wales. Of these 370,000 were built as part of slum clearance schemes. As we have seen from the arithmetic of the Second World War, Hitler undid many of the best efforts of Addison and Chamberlain, Wheatley and Greenwood.

Summing up the housing balance sheet for the period 1919–39, David Donnison reckoned it was 'a much bigger output than the country had ever achieved before: measured as a percentage increase on the stock of houses available in 1919, the pace was even faster than that achieved between 1821 and 1841 – hitherto the record period of growth. By 1939 there were about 11.25 million houses in England and Wales – 12.5 million in Britain. During the next six years some 200,000 were blown up or burnt down (nearly as many were built over the same period), another 250,000 were so badly knocked about that they could not be lived in, and a similar number was severely damaged.'[241]

This would have been an atrocious legacy for any housing minister to inherit. The picture was made darker by the shortage of men and material and the forces of demography (the wartime marriage boom was about to produce its natural consequence, the postwar baby boom whose statistics I myself swelled; in the three postwar years marriages were up 11 per cent and births by 33 per cent compared to the last three years of peace).[242] The prewar labour force of the building industry, some 1 million strong, was down to under 340,000 and was concentrated in the south-east coping with the consequences of the 'second Blitz' caused by the V weapons.[243] The remainder were in the forces or war factories.

In the 1945 election campaign, Labour had promised the earth. The Coalition White Paper of March 1945 estimated 750,000 new houses would be needed after the war 'to afford a separate dwelling for every family desiring to have one'.[244] The plan was to build between 3 and 4 million houses in the first ten to twelve years after the war[245] and there was a vague pledge to put up 300,000 new homes in the first two.[246] During the campaign Ernest Bevin outbid these estimates by a big margin, promising 'Five million homes in quick time.'[247]

To meet this target would have required a supply and an organisational miracle. Both turned out to be beyond the reach of the new Government. For the first they can scarcely be held culpable. Steel, softwoods and a host of other essential items were scarce and/or dollar imports competing for precious currency reserves. The second was a true failure all the more surprising given Attlee's gifts as an operator of the central machine. He has been criticised, rightly, for not separating the housing portfolio from the Ministry of Health in 1945 as he did later when it was transferred to the Ministry of Town and Country Planning and, later still, to a new Ministry of Housing and Local Government.[248] Bevan had enough to do building the NHS, though his self-ironic retrospective shaft, to the effect that he spent but five minutes a week on housing when Minister of Health, should *not* be taken at face value.[249]

The magazine *Picture Post*, favourably disposed towards the welfare state though it was, graphically illustrated this un-Attlee like muddle after Labour's first year in office:

Mr Dalton, the Chancellor of the Exchequer, is responsible for providing the capital required to pay out the housing subsidies. Mr Arthur Greenwood, the Lord Privy Seal, has certain, vague, overruling functions. No one quite knows what he does do. Mr Tomlinson, the Minister of Works, directs the building industry, licensing private builders, controlling building materials, and providing temporary and prefabricated permanent homes. Mr Isaacs, the Minister of Labour, has to provide the manpower. The Minister of Town and Country Planning can decide against house building on any site. The Minister of Agriculture must be consulted about rural housing. The Ministry of Supply deals with materials, and especially with the provision of house components, of which there is a serious shortage. Mr Bevan's writ does not run north of the border, where the Secretary of State for Scotland controls housing. The tenth cook is Sir Stafford Cripps who, as President of the Board of Trade, is now calling upon all builders employing more than fifty men to reply to ninety questions. Everyone in this industry considers that the issue of these forms will add to the delays and costs of housebuilding.[250]

To compound those problems at the Whitehall end, Bevan relied on the individual local authorities – some 1,700 of them in England and Wales – as his agents on the ground. They ranged from the giant London County Council, with long experience at large-scale public housing projects to tiny rural district councils with little or none. Big and small alike were subjected to a blizzard of housing circulars from the Ministry of Health at the rate of five a week in 1946.[251] Such chaos cried out for the services of the management consultants Cripps was so keen on.[252] It didn't get them.

Attlee, prodded by his economic adviser in No. 10, Douglas Jay, was worried by Bevan's reliance on the local authorities for delivering so crucial a part of the Government's programme.[253] But Bevan would not hear of Jay's idea of a 'Housing Corporation' to run it and nor would Tomlinson, his colleague at the Ministry of Works.[254] Attlee took the chair at the Cabinet's

Housing Committee when it was set up at December 1945 and, in April 1946, insisted that Bevan establish a Housing Production Executive.[255]

Did Bevan do any better than Addison had after the First World War? Their experience and their approaches were rather similar (though in 1945–6, Addison, by this time a Labour Cabinet Minister and Dominions Secretary, shared Attlee's scepticism about the capability of some local authorities as housebuilders).[256] For Bevan was a quality as well as a quantity man and applied vision to the mundane materials of construction. He was, to his credit, a subscriber to the view 'that nothing is too good for the working class', though his detractors thought he took this to the point of both hedonism and consorting with the enemy in his delight at sharing Lord Beaverbrook's table.[257]

Like Unwin and Russell, Bevan was a sucker for the magic of the village in which all sorts and conditions of people lived alongside each other in harmony. He hated the private-sector ribbon development of interwar Britain with houses flanking the arterial roads – 'the fretful fronts stretching along the great roads out of London', as he aptly called them. He didn't care either for the 'twilight villages' created by the local authorities with the powers Addison gave them. And he loathed even more the creation of age ghettos within those twilight estates.

> I hope that the old people will not be asked to live in colonies of their own – they do not want to look out of their windows on endless processions of the funerals of their friends; they also want to look at processions of perambulators . . . The full life should see the unfolding of a multicoloured panorama before the eyes of every citizen every day.[258]

He wanted, too, more space for the state's tenants.

Bevan pushed up the Addison standards from 750 square feet of room space to 900, with lavatories upstairs as well as down – improvements which led Hugh Dalton, his successor as Housing Minister who was raised in the precincts of Windsor Castle, to dub Bevan, brought up in a terrace house in Tredegar, 'a tremendous Tory'.[259] For his part, Bevan was never reconciled to Dalton's abandoning the 900 square feet minimum in 1951.[260]

Like Addison, too, Bevan saw Exchequer funding as the engine of housing growth and boosted the Treasury subsidy for council housing which was to have a marked priority over new private homes (one private house for five public was the ratio talked of in Bevan's early days at the Ministry).[261] His equivalent of the Addison Act was the Housing (Financial and Miscellaneous Provisions) Act of 1946. The Exchequer would find three quarters of the subsidy, instead of two thirds as prewar, the remainder coming from local rates – and the subsidy period was extended from forty to sixty years.[262]

With his loathing of the 'rabbit hutch' house, Bevan took a great interest in the design of postwar council homes. He did not care for the temporary prefabs which began to appear on bomb sites and wasteland from 1944. But the notion of prefabricated permanent dwellings did appeal to him and in the spring of 1946 he gave his backing to two types – the British Steel and the Airey Houses. He supported the use of local material, such as Cotswold stone, even where this added to costs. Bevan believed in equality of provision ('We don't want a country of East Ends and West Ends with all the petty snobberies that involves,') as well as quality ('We shall be judged for a year or two by the *number* of houses we build. We shall be judged in ten years' time by the *type* of houses we build').[263]

Bevan's houses can still be seen in little clusters on the edge of villages as well as in the larger estates in the city. They are noticeably larger than their council house successors of the 1950s and 1960s.[264] But the largest single concentrations of new postwar public housing were not Bevanite creations. For the New Towns were the responsibility of Lewis Silkin, the Minister of Town and Country Planning.

The town and country planning movement, the lineal successor to the pioneering efforts of Ebenezer Howard and Raymond Unwin, had made great strides during the war. A ministry embodying the name and the principle had been created in 1943. But the running had been made by a local authority, the London County Council, which appointed the country's leading planner, Sir Patrick Abercrombie, to draw up a 'county plan' for the metropolis. Within two years, Abercrombie and the LCC's chief architect, J.H. Forshaw, had completed their report.[265] Shortly after, central Government asked Abercrombie to extend his gaze to the hinterland of the nation's largest conurbation. In 1944 he produced his *Greater London Plan*.[266]

The idea was to tackle four aspects of London blight – poor housing, too much traffic, too few open spaces and the lack of zoning which left homes, factories and roads to spread spaghetti-like. The solution? A series of four concentric rings – inner urban, suburban, green belt and outer country – to stop ribbon development, give London a lung and to disperse people and industry to a constellation of eight new towns beyond the green belt.

There was no whisper of the new towns in the Labour Party's manifesto for the 1945 election. But Silkin did for Abercrombie what Griffiths had done for Beveridge. He turned it into a charter or, to be more exact, the New Towns Act 1946, which planned for fourteen new towns, eight beyond the London green belt (Crawley in Sussex; Bracknell in Berkshire; Hemel Hempstead, Hatfield, Stevenage and an addition to the existing Welwyn Garden City in Hertfordshire; Harlow and Basildon in Essex). The other six went to regional development areas – Corby in Northamptonshire, Cwmbran in Monmouthshire (now Gwent), Peterlee and Newton Aycliffe in County Durham, East Kilbride and Glenrothes in the central belt of Scotland.

The residents of the pleasant, quiet home counties towns affected were less than ecstatic about the proposal of a predominantly working-class cockney influx. A Residents' Protection Association was set up in Stevenage, centre of the most militant resistance. Silkin was howled down at a public meeting there in May 1946 with howls of 'Gestapo' and 'Dictator'. Sand was put in the tank of his car and its tyres deflated. Later more imaginative protestors in the winter of 1946–7, after the new town corporation was set up, changed the signs on the railway station to 'Silkingrad'. The local policeman was persuaded to turn a blind eye. The national Press was alerted. It even made the papers in the United States, adding, no doubt, to Republican suspicions that the American Loan was being poured into a neo-Marxist social experiment.[267]

Some impressive names were recruited to chair the new town development corporations, such as John Reith in Hemel Hempstead and William Beveridge in Peterlee. Inevitably, the gap between the architects' board and the cutting of tapes was quite long. In the end twenty-five new towns were built which now house some 2 million people. But, in the late 1940s, they did little to ease Bevan's immediate headaches. When Labour lost office in 1951 most of the first batch were still building sites.[268]

The new towns, like the bulk of Bevan's housing starts, were examples of public enterprise. But it would be wrong to imagine the work was done solely by local authority direct labour organisations. The private sector was heavily involved, did well out of it and was nicely poised for the day when, as they fervently hoped, a Conservative housing minister would set them free from the strings in which those endless Ministry of Health circulars entrapped them.

Bevan, meanwhile, had to get things moving long before the 'Aireys' and the like spread across England and Wales or the fields around Stevenage sprouted bricks. He faced frustration at every turn, badgering Isaacs and Bevin to speed up the demobilisation of skilled building labour from the forces, a process which caused Bevan to explode in Cabinet and Attlee to produce one of his drier put-downs.

BEVAN: 'Where are all the people I need for my programme?'
ATTLEE: 'Looking for houses, Nye!'[269]

Bevan tried to ease the position by putting up temporary accommodation and making habitable war-damaged dwellings. In 1944 the Coalition Government had introduced a new word into the English language – the 'prefab'. Lord Portal, the Minister of Works, had promised half a million of them in March that year. The trouble was the steel frames of the Portal prefab would have deprived the rest of the industry of its metallic sinew. An aluminium substitute was designed and aircraft factories went over to prefab production as the demand for their usual output eased.

The target was scaled down to 100,000 prefabs at £600 apiece. By the end of 1945 production was booming but the cost was up to £1,000 per unit. By 1948 nearly 125,000 had been erected. They proved immensely popular with their occupants and, far from being temporary, lasted in numbers into the 1970s, a few even reaching the 1990s. They certainly didn't deserve Bevan's dismissal of them as 'rabbit hutches'.

Until 1946, when Government policy switched to the construction of new, permanent public housing, prefabs and repairs were given priority. Nearly 600,000 damaged dwellings were brought back into occupation in 1945. Over 70,000 properties were requisitioned by local authorities continuing a policy begun in the war. (I lived in a succession of these, some rather grand, courtesy of Finchley Borough Council through most of the 1950s.) Bevan appealed to people to share their homes.

There was, given the demand, a King Canute air about the housing programme in 1945–6 and Bevan's personal position looked very shaky in the summer of 1946 when the country was suddenly affected by a squatter movement which saw the peaceful occupation of empty property, led by the Communist Party in London and by the politically uncommitted but destitute in the country, where many an army camp exchanged the shouts of the sergeant for the cries of a baby. By early October it was estimated that nearly 50,000 people were occupying over a thousand military properties.[270]

In most cases, sympathetic local authorities turned a blind eye, glad to have some kind of safety valve which eased the everyday pressure on their housing departments. Bevan put his faith on his council house programme as a bringer of long-term easement. Bit by bit the number of new homes rose – 55,400 completions in 1946; 139,690 in 1947 with rapid growth expected in 1948. But the chill wind of economic retrenchment was about to freeze ambition and investment as Bevan relived Addison's experience after the Great War when the sterling crisis of 1947 seriously curtailed the housing programme.

Slaying the Giants

I can remember this particular day. Everything was in a radius of a few minutes' walk, and she [mother] went to the opticians. Obviously she'd got the prescription from the doctor. She went and she got tested for new glasses. Then she went further down the road . . . for the chiropodist. She had her feet done. Then she went back to the doctor's because she'd been having trouble with her ears and the doctor said . . . he would fix her up with a hearing aid. And I remember – me mother was a very funny woman – I remember her saying to the doctor on the way out, 'Well, the undertaker's is on the way home. Everything's going on, I might as well call in there on the way home!'
Alice Law recalling 5 July 1948 in 1984[271]

The fifth of July 1948 *was* welfare state day. The Health Service came into being and the new social security legislation came into force. For the likes of Mrs Law in Manchester, life was never the same again – it was simply better. None of the frustrations, disappointments or cash crises in the intervening years can detract from that.

A few weeks before vesting day, the Ministry of National Insurance decided to mount a simple consumer test to see if the new machine was ready. Bernard Taylor, Jim Griffiths' Parliamentary Private Secretary, and, like his boss, an ex-miner, went to the local office in his constituency, Mansfield, in the Nottinghamshire coalfield. As one of the Ministry's officials recalled:

'I used to be a miner', he told the girl on the counter, 'but I had to give it up through a strained back. Will there be anything for me in the new benefit scheme?' The counter clerk, imbued with the new spirit of helpfulness, replied 'We're all new here and we're not too sure about the industrial injuries scheme. But if you come back and see us on the fifth of July, I'm sure we'll be able to fix you up with something.'[272]

Benefits, health care, a roof over your head and education for your children – these are the basics of social provision. In an advanced society they are as much 'the essentials of life' as the 'food, water, fuel or light' mentioned in the Emergency Powers Act of 1920.[273]

There were other advances in the late 1940s that did not come into the essential category which, none the less, greatly improved the fairness or the quality of life for all. An example of this on the equity side was legal aid. The idea had a long antecedence. For centuries the courts had recognised a phenomenon known as 'the dock brief'. For the fee of a guinea a poor defendant could pick out any barrister wearing a wig in the court to defend him. When a poor prisoner called for such a brief from the dock, barristers would dash for the door.[274] The truly poor, of course, had to do without even the services of the fifth-rate lawyers prepared to take up a dock brief.

The principle of institutionalised legal aid was first recognised by the Poor Prisoners' Defence Act 1903 which, for all its theoretical advance, was hopelessly inadequate in real court life. It was up to the judge to decide whether an accused person qualified and for the judge so to decide, the accused had to disclose his case in advance. The Act didn't apply at all to magistrates' courts where most cases were heard.[275]

Widespread dissatisfaction, within the legal profession as well as on the part of the public, with the workings of the 1903 Act led to the commissioning of an inquiry from the Finlay Committee in 1925. As a result of its recommendations some improvements were made by a new Act in 1930 – legal aid was extended to magistrates' courts, the accused no longer had to divulge their defence in advance and assistance became mandatory in murder trials.[276]

Legal aid was still discretionary. It would only be granted if the judge or the magistrate was minded to award it and most weren't. In 1935, for example, 750,000 accused persons were found guilty of whom 19,500 were committed to prison. Only 335 of them were granted legal aid.[277] As in so many aspects of national life, it took the coming of war to force those in authority to rethink the habits and prejudices of a lifetime. Legal pressure groups, like the Haldane

Society of socialist lawyers, took the initial lead. In 1942 they urged that a centrally run, state-funded system of legal aid be established.[278] In 1944 the Coalition set up its own inquiry under Lord Rushcliffe.

Rushcliffe reported the following year, castigated the existing patchwork of provision as 'totally inadequate', and recommended an Exchequer-funded system which would reach a wider group than 'those normally classed as poor'.[279] The legal profession was part of the new consensus and not merely because a state-funded scheme would line legal pockets (everyone imagines that lawyers think through their wallets). The Law Society itself had recommended pre-Rushcliffe the creation of legal advice centres which would work alongside Citizens Advice Bureaux, another great invention of the war years.[280]

The new Government accepted the Rushcliffe recommendations and incorporated those dealing with criminal cases in the 1949 Legal Aid and Legal Advice Act. The courts would still decide who was granted legal aid and who was not, but there was to be a bias in favour of saying 'yes'. It was also laid down that aid would be granted in sufficient time for a proper case to be prepared.[281]

Many magistrates – who acquired their local worthiness in an era with a different approach and found it difficult to make the conceptual shift from charity to social service – continued to show reluctance to grant public money for such purposes. And that great hard man among postwar jurists, the Lord Chief Justice, Lord Goddard, revealed his displeasure in public three years after the new scheme came into operation saying he found 'there is very little gratitude among persons who get aid ... I am beginning to believe that it would be far better to leave many of the people to defend themselves'.[282]

As so often with social reform, funding problems vitiated the best intentions. The state of the economy after the sterling crisis of 1949 caused a delay in the full implementation of what Sir Hartley Shawcross, the Attorney General, called 'the charter of the little man to the British Courts of Justice'.[283] The Government announced in October that year that the scheme would only apply initially to the High Court and the Court of Appeal. Not until 1955 was it extended to county courts.[284] The claims of the 'little man', however, had been accepted – in principle at least.

In terms of the quality of life for the nation as a whole, broadcasting had become a crucial ingredient, as potentially unifying as it was universal. Radio had come of age in the war producing probably the single greatest cultural change in the country since the development of railways a century before had opened up the nation to the national newspaper, allowing, in Walter Bagehot's words, 'London ideas [to] shoot out every morning ... [carrying] ... a uniform creed to each cranny of the Kingdom', turning the county towns of England into 'detached scraps of great places'.[285]

The BBC, the single provider, had, like almost every other national institution, laid its postwar plans well before VE Day. In September 1943, a committee had been appointed under the former Cabinet Secretary, Lord Hankey, to consider the coming age of television. It reported just before the end of the war in Europe with the message, as the BBC's official historian Asa Briggs put it, that 'Television has come to stay.'[286] And, as we have seen, TV did return to screens blank for nearly six years on 7 June 1946.

But the man who mattered – that austere, Victorian, William Haley, one of the straightest men ever to work in the British media[287] – was a radio man to his last, high-minded grey cell. Haley began his media life as a shorthand/tele-phonist – a 'copytaker' he would be called nowadays – in the Brussels office at *The Times*, and finished it as Editor of that then great newspaper (old sweats during my period on the paper in the 1970s and 1980s would refer to him as 'the last Editor of *The Times*'). He took over as Director-General of the BBC after an unsatisfactory interregnum between the departure of John Reith in 1938 and his own appointment in 1944.

Haley, according to his anonymous profiler in the *New Statesman* in 1954,

> brought back administrative order, increased its already high technical effi-ciency, and took hold of its finances with a firm hand. He also restored to it a sense of mission and a belief in its cultural and educational purpose that it had begun to lose after Reith. He was, indeed, ideally suited to serve the conception of broadcasting which the British people have chosen for their own. Here was to be found satisfaction for all his own most cherished beliefs in the efficacy of self-education, in the dissemination of culture, in the per-vasive influence of honest reporting – in short, of liberalism.[288]

Haley, with the best of the Victorians, was a great reader – a convinced believer in the individual's capacity for self-improvement.[289] He was, in Asa Briggs' judgment, 'more interested in securing the full potential of sound broadcasting than in switching to television, which he believed would encour-age passivity and lead to a surfeit of entertainment'.[290]

To that end he planned a splitting of the single prewar channel into three – a Home Service, a Light Programme and a Third Programme. The idea – a wonderfully 1940s, 'Brains Trustish' one – was that, in Haley's words, the new system would 'lead the listener on to more serious things'[291] as he or she progressed from the music and variety of the Light, through the views and talks of the Home to the music and the plays of the Third.

To be sure, Haleyan high-mindedness would have stayed grounded on inter-nal BBC memos if the Attlee Government had not been prepared to fund it. They were and, by the standards of the time, generously. In 1946 the BBC's licence fee was doubled to £1. As the Lord President and minister for media matters, Herbert Morrison, put it, 'if the institution is to pay its way, it just cannot be done on ten shillings a year'.[292] For BBC people in the 1990s, a sentence like that can produce a hot flush of nostalgic emotion.

'Injustice' was not one of the five giants William Beveridge set out to slay. Legal aid was left to others to justify. 'Ignorance', however, was a Beveridge giant and, it could be argued, the BBC was an important sword to set alongside the Ministry of Education's spear in slaying it. Looking back, how well forged were those mid-to-late-Forties weapons in terms of effective giant-killing?

Bursts of reforming activity occur in British history when a tall and growing pile of resentment, criticism and anger about past inadequacies goes critical – the catalyst being the special set of political circumstances which make change possible. As we have seen, the experience of war speeded up the historical process dramatically. The new Labour Government was the beneficiary and took it a stage further. As Paul Addison put it, 'when Labour swept to victory in 1945 the new consensus fell, like a branch of ripe plums, into the lap of Attlee'.[293]

Such moments, apart from driving historians into a rich mixture of metaphors (spears, swords, critical piles and lush fruit trees), have an important characteristic which it is easy to overlook. They are as much backward looking (remedying past evils) as they are forward looking (building a better tomorrow). This is a point well brought out by Basil Kibbey, one of the technicians of the welfare state in the postwar Ministry of Pensions and National Insurance. 'For centuries', he told an international conference in 1967,

> the dominating factor in social provision had been the relief of poverty and the early schemes of social insurance were introduced to meet particular needs of people who were vulnerable to particular risks. It was Beveridge who really started looking at social provision in terms of the community as a whole.
>
> He set out to show why the existing schemes had failed to get rid of poverty and his recommendations were designed to win what he called the war on want. The weapons were modernised but the struggle itself was as old as the hills and he did not set out new aims so much as to show how the old aims could be achieved. In this sense – and with a liberal helping of hindsight – it may be said that Beveridge's analysis was backward looking and that his recommendations were more appropriate to conditions between the wars than to postwar Britain.[294]

There are three kinds of hindsight which have been liberally applied to Beveridgism. The first, to which Basil Kibbey was referring, has to do with its core principle of universality. 'The principle of flat-rate contributions and flat-rate benefits which Beveridge had put forward as a sensible and desirable social principle', Mr Kibbey explained, 'was revealed as a constricting influence on the development of a scheme in line with postwar economic and social needs. The increasing prosperity of the working population and the inflation that went with it made the position of those on fixed income – including national insurance beneficiaries – worse off in both absolute and relative terms. Something had to be done to improve provision for old age but, as the Government had recognised at the start, the level of benefits in this sort of scheme had to be geared to what the lower-paid workers could afford to pay out of their weekly earnings.'[295]

In essence the problem was this: could those at the lower end of the scale manage the contributions required of them to help fund Beveridge? Would the better-paid workers put up with such meagre (by their normal standards of life) benefits when sick or temporarily unemployed? In the 1950s the answers became increasingly problematical to both questions, hence the suggestion that the Beveridge Report was more suited to remedying the social and economic shortcomings of 1935 rather than 1955.

The second and third doses of hindsight take us deep into the political debate about the welfare state as a whole. The aspect most familiar to those with fresh memories of the 1980s is the funding – overload – dependency argument. This school of thought suggests that not only were the cost projections very optimistic, but the whole paraphernalia of welfare in all its forms (social security, health, subsidised housing and, some would argue, a rigid system of funding and managing state schooling), placed an insupportable burden on a weak, war-exhausted British economy – hence our missing out on the postwar economic miracle which brought sparkle to so many of our competitors.

The 'overload school' embraces a wide variety of people from business (Sir John Hoskyns, creator of a computer software company, adviser to Mrs Thatcher and a former Director-General of the Institute of Directors),[296] scholarship (the critic Correlli Barnett)[297] and the Civil Service (Sir Kenneth Stowe, former Permanent Secretary at the Department of Health and Social Security).[298] They have their counterparts who maintain that far from transforming the face of Britain and the power relationships which underlay it, the Attlee Government merely applied cosmetics to what a future Conservative Prime Minister called in another context 'the unpleasant and unacceptable face of capitalism',[299] thereby preserving it to fight another day.

The founding father of this school is the scholar, Ralph Miliband, whose book, *Parliamentary Socialism*, exerted a considerable sway on the minds of the young, 'New Left' of the 1960s and 1970s who could see nothing but feebleness and compromise in the postwar Labour Government. Miliband saves his toughest criticisms for Attlee's failure to present 'no serious challenge to the power of the men who continued to control the country's economic resources'.[300] But, while paying tribute to the NHS and the new system of social security ('In housing, in education, in welfare, it could well boast to have done more than any other Government had done before – and to have done it in the midst of acute economic difficulties,'[301]) he, none the less, found 'the Government's impact upon postwar Britain was profoundly ambiguous.'[302]

The fuel of the debate at this end of the spectrum is not the hard cash or the personal dependency of welfare recipients on the state which motivates the 'overload' school. It has much more to do with political linguistics – what does that term, the 'welfare state', which Beveridge (and Ernest Bevin, incidentally[303]) so disliked, actually imply: greater social justice or a profound transformation in the distribution of power and resources in society?

We are familiar with the second definition as it's implicit in every thought that came to Richard Titmuss and every line he wrote about social policy in the Second World War. Its other great philosopher was another pillar of the postwar London School of Economics, T.H. Marshall, who expressed it in a book published in the twilight of the Attlee years, *Citizenship and Social Class*,[304] his idea being that general rights of citizenship in Britain were extended first through legal means (the common law), then by the political process (extensions in the right to vote), and finally in the 1940s using social legislation. Thus the state is the agent – phase by phase – of a deliberate spreading of political and economic power through the population as a whole. Modern critics of 'Labourism', to use Ralph Miliband's dismissive phrase, would argue that the mid-1940s 'White Paper Chase'[305] and the statutes which flowed from it did not amount to anything like so deliberate and profound a change in the power and money lines of Britain.[306]

The more conventional definition, the one which forms the basis for the bulk of the welfare state debate since 1945, is that which simply sees it as 'a given range of social services provided by Government', and in particular the five '"core" services – social security, the National Health Service, housing, education and the personal social services'.[307] And, by this test, the achievements of 1944–8 – from the Butler Act to NHS/social security vesting day – do represent a profound change in British history, by the standards of what had gone before and what was to come later. Undoubtedly, on balance, it was highly beneficial to virtually everyone in Britain.

The post-Beveridge settlement was not perfection, an ideal from which we could only decline. Each of the schools of critics has its points. To take the left critique first, for all Beveridge's talk of a revolutionary era being a time for revolutions, not patching, the 1944–8 social settlement was organic and incremental – a natural and necessary tidying-up and extension of a building site on which others had long since started and one which had seen creative bursts of construction before, most notably in the 'New Liberalism' of the early years of the twentieth century.

The one potentially revolutionary document among that flurry of mid-Forties studies and White Papers – the Uthwatt Report on Land-use – led to nowhere and nothing. Uthwatt, published in 1942,[308] recommended a form of land nationalisation which, if it had been implemented, would have affected the balance of ownership in the country very substantially. It suggested the state take control of development land at a price which reflected its *existing* not its potential value. Profits made when it was sold to developers would accrue to the public purse and could be ploughed back into the public housing drive.

Understandably enough, the Coalition's 1944 White Paper on the *Control of Land Use* confined itself to pious generalities about the need to find 'a practical system whereby individual rights of land tenure may be reconciled with the best use of the land in the national interest'.[309] To have done otherwise would have aroused uncontainable tensions within the Government. Once in power in its own right, Labour did not embrace Uthwatt. Lewis Silkin's approach was to rely on his new town and country planning powers. His 1947 Act created a Central Land Board but the Treasury starved it of its most necessary resource, money. Its allocation was a mere £100,000 which does not suggest any seriousness of intent.[310]

Viewed through a very different prism, the welfare reforms of the 1940s were a gigantic leap in the dark in financial terms. As early as 1946 hard evidence began to appear to feed scepticism. The Government's own Actuary, for example, drew attention to the financial consequences of Jim Griffiths' determination to do right by *all* pensioners instantly rather than to phase the scheme in over twenty years. As Basil Kibbey recalled, 'Few public commentators bothered to study the financial structure of the scheme and many years later when the deficit which stemmed from the decision to admit existing pensioners and late entrants to full benefits began to emerge, and the long-term financial problem began to receive some publicity, no one outside official circles seemed to realise that the Government Actuary had spelt it all out in detail in his report on the 1946 Bill.'[311]

Quite apart from the 'political economy' aspects of the debate, a detached observer could not fail to see the widespread kicking into touch of several issues in the 'too difficult for the moment' category. On the education side, what to do about the public schools in the private sector came into this category. On the health side, Bevan not only stuffed the doctors' mouths with gold to get them into the NHS, he ceded clinical freedom to them too.[312] As a senior health service manager would put it forty years later, traditionally, the NHS had not been a *managed* service; it was an organisational framework within which doctors and nurses provided services for patients.[313]

And management was about to become a big, persistent problem for government. It's impossible to read H.V. Rhodes' account of putting the Ministry of Pensions and National Insurance together at top speed in 1946–8 – scouring Whitehall for staff, high streets for premises, designing and printing a mountain of forms – without realising that here were new leviathans in the making.[314] And the permanent secretaries, convened by their Chief, Sir Edward Bridges, twice in May 1946 to discuss whether a new-style Civil Service, and a more managerially minded and a better trained officialdom to staff it, was needed to cope with this changing, extending nature of the state, decided, inexplicably, that it was not. It was to be Whitehall business as usual and no minister, the technocratic Stafford Cripps apart, took the issue seriously.[315]

Caveats and hindsight-driven nit-picking, however, should not detract from the central fact of the mid-1940s: during that period the state took responsibility for the well-being of its citizens to an extent that would have amazed any serious observer a decade before. For the first time poverty was tackled as an interlocking problem to whose solution both *social* and *economic* policy were crucial. Lloyd George and many of the 'New Liberals' had seen what they called 'national efficiency' in these terms. But unlike the Edwardian politicians, those of the 1940s who mattered in the two major parties (the much vaunted consensus never embraced the outer rims of the Conservative and Labour parties), felt capable of extending the politics of the possible to such an integrated approach. The war experience was central to this. The command economy and an intensely mobilised society demonstrated as no gradual, peacetime developments ever could that the instruments of bigger Government were to hand.

As a result, fragments of prewar social provision were replaced by universal, national systems on the welfare side. On the economic side, the key commitment of the 'White Paper Chase' was the 1944 pledge that future governments would maintain a 'high and stable level of employment'.[316] For this aspiration – extraordinarily ambitious in historical terms even for an economic superpower (and we were no longer that) – to be achieved, a vigorous, robust and consistently productive economy was essential. Without it not only would unemployment return, ruining all of Beveridge's calculations, but the houses, the schools, the benefits could not be paid for.

This was not a truth that became apparent only to a generation of scholars and commentators reflecting in tranquillity. It was appreciated at the time. As vesting day – 5 July 1948 – approached for the welfare state, the Government's own propaganda, put out in a shower of leaflets from the Central Office of Information, stressed time and again, in Rodney Lowe's words, 'that state welfare and economic efficiency were interdependent: social services would make a vital contribution to economic growth which, in its turn, would finance them'.[317]

As I indicated in chapter three, it is my belief that, taken as a whole, Britain's postwar industrial base was very promising. It should have been adequate to retain its vitality, regenerate itself from its own resources *and* provide sufficient dividend to fund the new social responsibilities assumed by the state. Whether it did so was, as always, partly dependent on the performance of the world economy as a whole and the subdivisions of it on which Britain was then especially reliant (North America and the Commonwealth in particular); partly on the burdens which Britain felt it needed to continue carrying despite its slippage, temporary or permanent, from economic superpowerdom (Empire, world currency/sterling area, imperial preference, occupying power in defeated Axis territories); and partly on the efficiency with which it marshalled its own economic resources. And it is to that aspect – banishing the fifth of Beveridge's 'giants', 'Idleness' – I now turn before widening the perspective to imperial policy and the increasing strain imposed by a worsening cold war.

CHAPTER 5

Towards the Commanding Heights

There are going to be public corporations, business concerns, they will buy
the necessary brains and technical skill and give them their heads.
Herbert Morrison, 1946[1]

We weren't really beginning our Socialist programme until we had gone past
all the utility junk – such as transport and electricity – which were publicly
owned in every capitalist country in the world. Practical Socialism . . . only
really began with Coal and Iron and Steel, and there was a strong political
argument for breaking the power of a most dangerous body of capitalists.
Hugh Dalton, 1946[2]

As always when the British economy has been given a real economic task, a
task to produce and create, such as in the war years and now in the period of
postwar reconstruction, it performed magnificently.
Professor Sidney Pollard, 1982[3]

We both felt that Keynes had left behind a set of doctrines quite unfitted for
the times in which we live as for the last 20 years of his life he was preoccupied by questions of deflation instead of inflation – in a way he had been
too successful.
Robert Hall, Head of Cabinet Office Economic Section, 1948[4]

The full employment commitment which had been fundamental to post-war
Keynesian social democracy was undermined, not by economic imperatives,
but by moral and political preferences, and by the institutions which
embodied and transmitted past moral and political preferences . . . One
reason why the political class did not create a developmental state is that
Britain has lacked a state tradition of the sort which has shaped the politics
of most other European nations. Part of the reason . . . is that the doctrines,
and still more the ethos, of early nineteenth century market liberalism were
more deeply embedded in her culture than in other European cultures.
Professor David Marquand, 1988[5]

In the glossary of politics, certain phrases become fixed in a particular era and, sometimes, remain forever associated with an individual. 'The commanding heights' is such an expression, depicting those core industries which Labour had to take over on behalf of the people if economic planning was to become a reality, or so they thought. One of the most enduring images of the late 1940s comes from the countless photographs taken of the signs which sprang up outside every pit on 1 January 1947: 'THIS COLLIERY IS NOW MANAGED BY THE NATIONAL COAL BOARD ON BEHALF OF THE PEOPLE.'[6]

In a word, 'the commanding heights' equals 'nationalisation'. Its author is commonly presumed to be the great apostle of public ownership, Nye Bevan. Bevan dismissed Keynesianism in the Commons debate on the 1944 Employment White Paper as a 'thermostatic operation to occur every five or six years by which [the workers] are taken forcibly away from their normal occupation and put to do some job of public works in order to pump spending power into the system which has caused unemployment'.[7] A year before Bevan had argued for full-blooded nationalisation – the taking into state ownership of all basic industries, to be run by a 'Supreme Economic Council' of 'able men' under the general control of the House of Commons.[8]

In fact, 'the commanding heights' was Lenin's phrase not Bevan's,[9] though he was happy enough for it to be associated with his name. In his last speech to the Labour Party Conference in 1959 he quoted Barbara Castle and Hugh Gaitskell quoting him: 'Yesterday Barbara quoted from a speech I made some years ago, and she said that I believed that Socialism in the context of modern society meant the conquest of the commanding heights of the economy. Hugh Gaitskell quoted the same thing.'[10]

It's a misleading phrase in that it has become synonymous with *100 per cent* public ownership and a planned economy. Because there were a hundred and one other ways of tackling those commanding heights and applying a high degree of central management to an economy like Britain's, certainly in those early postwar days when the idea of a European Economic Community was not yet even a gleam in Jean Monnet's eye.

For seven decades – from the adoption of its new constitution in 1918 with its famous Clause IV commitment to the publication of its policy review in 1989 – the Labour Party was wholly committed to public ownership. In 1918, the formula drafted by Sidney Webb was unambiguous, as we have seen, in its determination 'to secure for the workers by hand or by brain the full fruits of their industry and the most equitable distribution thereof that may be possible, upon the basis of the common ownership of the means of production, distribution and exchange'. By 1989, this had become somewhat softened in *Meet the Challenge, Make the Change*, to 'In our view, the economic role of modern government is to help make the market system work properly where it can, will and should – and to replace or strengthen it where it can't, won't or shouldn't.'[11]

Ambiguity, both of intention and method, was already present in abundance when Labour finally took Whitehall's commanding heights – if no others – in the summer of 1945. It was instantly apparent to the senior economic advisers with whom Attlee and his colleagues had worked in Coalition days when the more avowedly socialistic sides of their natures had had to be moderated, if not suppressed altogether.

James Meade, a future Nobel Prizewinner who would succeed Lionel Robbins as head of the Cabinet Office's Economic Section in 1946, returned to Whitehall from a three-week holiday at the end of August 1945 and penned a perceptive and prescient entry in his diary.

In internal policy there is already a conflict between the different main meanings that might be given to the idea of Socialist economic planning. Broadly speaking, there are on the one hand those (led by Cripps at the Board of Trade) who believe in the quantitative planning of the economy commodity by commodity.

Such a Gosplan [the name of the Soviet Planning Commission] could not in my opinion, be carried out without socialising [synonymous with 'nationalising' in the 1940s] of all or most industries (which is expressly not the policy of the Labour Party) and, possibly, without losing freedom of choice of consumers and workers as to what they will consume and what they will work at.

On the other hand is what I think of as the Liberal-Socialist solution under which certain industries which must in any case be large-scale monopolies (e.g. electricity, railways, etc.) are completely socialised and run on 'market' principles of pricing and costing, while the rest of industry is made to compete by anti-restrictive practice legislation. Steps are taken to maintain total aggregate demand – partly (i.e. in the case of the socialised sector of the economy) by quantitative planning and programming and partly by planning certain categories of demand by such means as tax and subsidy policy, the rate of interest, the rate of exchange etc. to see that private investment, consumers' expenditure or exports are of the desired magnitude. I am pretty sure that Morrison, who most fortunately as Lord President is the Economic Section's Minister, is going to be the leader of this second school of thought.[12]

In effect, Meade was arguing (if only to himself at this stage) that the Keynesian technical breakthroughs which, it was thought, made demand management possible, had made old-fashioned socialist notions of physically controlling the economy both passé and redundant.

It should not be assumed, however, that the 'official mind' of Whitehall had jettisoned its interwar orthodoxies and thrown in its lot with the new economics. Nor should it be imagined that methods of measuring and forecasting national income developed by Richard Stone and Meade himself in the War

Cabinet Office were still anything other than experimental in 1945. Before turning to the debate within the new Labour Government which Meade perceptively foresaw, it's worth spending a moment on the economic thinking and the econometric technology which was to play such a big part in the full employment/welfare state 'consensus' which, according to 1980s orthodoxy, held intellectual sway in both Cabinet Room and Whitehall from 1944 to the late 1970s.

The publication in May 1944 of the Coalition's White Paper on *Employment Policy* has, quite rightly, been treated as 'a revolution in economic policy'[13] ever since by all parties to the enduring debate about the most desirable system of political economy for the United Kingdom. The best short account of this 'revolution' I have read is the 'Gist of Draft White Paper' sent to Churchill himself, who hadn't read it, a few days before publication. (There was a terrible rush because Beveridge was about to publish his own unofficial treatise on the subject[14] and, in the words of Lord Woolton, the Minister for Reconstruction, 'The Reconstruction Committee are unanimous that we ought not to allow him to get the credit for being the first to put before the country a policy for full employment, and we have been striving to get ahead of him.'[15])

To comply with Churchill's loathing of official paper, Woolton's officials had managed to capture the White Paper's essence within the famous single sheet of paper the Old Man demanded. It's a masterpiece of compression:

1 Government accept responsibility for maintenance of high and stable level of employment after the war.

2 *First condition* to be satisfied: maintenance of total national expenditure, both by investors and consumers, at high level.

3 Means of satisfying this first condition:
   a) Varying the rate of interest.
   b) Timing of public investment to offset swings in private investment.
   c) Raising when trade is brisk (and reducing when trade slackens) rate of weekly social insurance contributions, without impairing actuarial basis of new insurance scheme.
   d) Deferred income tax credits (payable in times of depression) might also be used.
   e) Balancing Budget over period of years, but not necessarily each year.

4 *Second condition*: stability of prices and wages and avoidance of inflation, by means of
   a) Moderate wage policy (responsibility of employers and organised labour).
   b) Industrial policy of expanding output, not increasing prices (chiefly responsibility of private enterprise).
   c) Cost of living subsidies, on certain conditions.

5   *Third condition*: mobility of labour, to be achieved by
    a) Individual initiative and adaptability.
    b) Training and re-settlement schemes.
    c) Divorce of unemployment benefit from training allowances.
    d) Availability of low rented houses.

6   *Fourth condition*: balanced distribution of industry, to maintain employ-
    ment in 'development areas' (pre-war 'special areas' policy to be super-
    seded), by means of
    a) Influencing location of new factories and factory extension.
    b) Policy regarding munitions' factories and Government contracts.
    c) Government erection of factory premises for smaller firms.
    d) Financial assistance by Government.

7   *Transitional Period*: measures
    a) to forestall danger of unemployment resulting from switchover from
       war to peace production;
    b) to ensure priority for essential needs (e.g. exports);
    c) to prevent inflation.

8   *Machinery* for applying policy:
    a) Better statistics and other information from private enterprise.
    b) Small central staff to interpret facts and figures.
    c) Annual Capital Budget of total national investment.
    d) Complementary Man-Power Budget.[16]

With hindsight, this reads like a classic of the Tommy Cooper school of
political economy – all the deep-seated travails of the British economy were
going to be remedied 'just like that'. The 'second condition' on inflation avoidance is especially touching, the more so given Keynes' admission to his Cambridge disciple, Richard Kahn, a year later that 'One is also, simply because one
knows no solution, inclined to turn a blind eye to the wages problem in a full
employment economy.'[17]

Behind the sheet of A4 which went to No. 10 lay a battle royal in Whitehall
which saw a clash of, if truth be known, unreconcilable economic philosophies
under the respective banners of the Cabinet Office's Economic Section and the
Treasury. This is beautifully brought out in 'Notes on the Draft White Paper
on Employment Policy' by John Jewkes, the former Director of the Economic
Section who in 1944 was working for Woolton as, in effect, his chief economist.

With careful understatement, Jewkes minuted Woolton in March 1944,
pointing out that 'There are a number of places in the latest draft of the White
Paper where there has been some difference of opinion between ourselves and
the Treasury as regards policy or emphasis, and where, in consequence the
[Cabinet Office's] Economic Section, in drafting the document and trying to
meet different points of view, have been forced to adopt tortuous language or
obscure presentation.'[18] For example, the Treasury was still not prepared to

admit defeat on that great 1930s battleground – the desirability of state-funded
public works as a stimulus to demand in times of depression – over which its
officials and Keynes (then a non-Treasury man, firing shafts from Cambridge
and Bloomsbury) had fought most notably during the hearings of the Macmillan Committee between 1929 and 1931.[19]

Jewkes was especially critical of a paragraph

> drafted by the Treasury, who are anxious that we should not attach too
> much importance to an expansion of the public works schemes in offsetting a
> decline in exports, and that we should stress the need for efficiency and low
> costs in the export trades. But my own feeling is that in this particular draft
> the difficulties have been laid on so thickly that the impression is created that
> an expansion of public works will have no influence whatsoever upon the
> decline in the export trade. This, I am sure, is untrue, and I think redrafting
> on a more optimistic line is essential.[20]

Backed by such evidence from the files, the economic historian, Rodney
Lowe, is surely right to say that though the 1944 Employment White Paper has
been taken by many commentators 'as an endorsement of Keynesian economics
and thus as the symbolic start of postwar consensus . . . [it] was contradictory
and flawed as a guide to postwar policy'.[21]

Building on the work of other scholars like George Peden[22] and Anthony
Booth,[23] Dr Lowe noted that as the White Paper's 'Foreword' showed,

> it did represent all-party consensus on two vital issues: the government's
> responsibility for the maintenance of a 'high and stable level of employment'
> and its achievement through the management of demand within the
> economy. However, through the rest of the text, the precise objective and
> nature of employment policy were kept deliberately obscure. Just as in its
> consideration of the Beveridge Report, the Coalition had dropped the ideal
> term 'social security' for the more pragmatic 'national insurance' so it modi-
> fied its commitment to 'full employment' to one of maintaining 'a high and
> stable level of employment'. Appendix II suggested that this meant a level of
> unemployment below 8½%, the definition endorsed in the Beveridge
> Report, rather than the 3% or 5% which were the figures respectively being
> advanced in 1944 by Beveridge and Keynes; but the precise commitment
> remained vague. So too did the means of its achievement.[24]

The final result was not even the homogenised White Paper Jewkes implied
the Cabinet Office were in the course of preparing in the spring of 1944.
Treasury thought infused the first three chapters with their concentration on
micro-economics and their emphasis on world trade and co-operation between
both sides of industry as important factors in achieving the aims of full employment in Britain (and who's to say they were wrong here?). The thinking of the

Cabinet Office's Economic Section prevailed in the last three chapters which stressed the importance of macro-economics – of maintaining aggregate demand – and displayed a much greater optimism about the potential impact of Government intervention in the economy.

'Hence,' writes Dr Lowe, 'in relation to regional policy, a policy of "bringing work to the workers" was advocated in paragraph 29, whilst the need for labour mobility was stressed in paragraph 56. Even more seriously, to combat cyclical unemployment, the deliberate planning of a budget deficit was rejected in paragraph 74 whereas, three paragraphs later, a "rigid policy of balancing the Budget each year" was dismissed as being "neither required by statute nor (as) part of our tradition".'[25]

Had the development of economic techniques in the 1930s and 1940s really provided the politicians with the instruments they would undoubtedly need if the full employment aspiration was to be fulfilled? One thing can be said with certainty: war had been a great stimulator in this particular area of intellectual R and D. Before the war, measuring the output of a whole national economy had been the scholarly preoccupation of a few pioneers such as Simon Kuznets in the United States and Colin Clark in the United Kingdom.[26] The building and running of a war economy turned it into an arm of Government in Britain especially. Sir Kingsley Wood's 1941 Budget is generally treated as the first of the Keynesian marque (as opposed to the Gladstonian variety, to borrow Ernie Bevin's terminology),[27] not least because of the simultaneous publication of *An Analysis of the Sources of War Finance and An Estimate of the National Income and Expenditure in 1938 and 1940* which led its authors, Stone and Meade, to crack a bottle of champagne that night on the grounds that 'we had accomplished something'.[28]

They had. Without the picture they painted in numbers for Kingsley Wood and other key 'Home Front' ministers, the 'inflationary gap', as Wood called it, would have led to a catastrophic rise in prices. If the armoury of Government restraints (the familiar mixture of rationing, food subsidies and commodity controls) had not been applied, the increase in incomes which came with an economy running at full pelt would have produced ever greater inflation as the consumer goods available for purchase became ever scarcer. Thanks to Stone and Meade and the 'number crunchers' in the newly formed Central Statistical Office, ministers and officials had the database they needed to target their stabilisation policy, as they called it, effectively. As a result, Keynes was able to include 'the Stabilisation Policy for domestic prices and the management of the Wage level' in the 'catalogue of success' he drew up as part of his generally grim appraisal of future economic prospects as the war came to a close.[29]

Great achievement though it was, balancing an economy is a simpler matter in wartime than in peace. As Stone himself put it in the immediate postwar period, 'The principal difference is that in wartime the brunt of economic change must for practical reasons be borne by physical controls such as rationing, restriction, allocation and direction, whereas in peacetime much more could be done to achieve social ends by fiscal and financial policies.'[30] Stone could have been speaking for an entire generation – for the technicians of the Keynesian consensus – when he said in the late 1940s:

> Anyone who believes in the maintenance of a social economy and the avoid-ance of the totalitarian direction of all aspects of economic life must be concerned at the present time with the creation of an *institutional framework* [emphasis added] which will permit a social economy, with the essential features of free markets, free choice of occupations and free choice in the spending of disposable income, to function more in accordance with con-temporary social ideals. In the achievement of this goal and in redrafting the rules of the economic game in such a way that both *laissez-faire* and overall physical control are rejected as a basis for economic organization, national income and expenditure studies and their extension to the technique of national budgeting have, I believe, a great deal to offer.[31]

Richard Stone's postwar reflections have an enduring significance. For central to the thinking of post-'consensus' political thinkers like David Mar-quand who, unlike the people associated with Mrs Thatcher's intellectual court, wished in the late 1980s and early 1990s to recreate what Harold Mac-millan would have called a 'Middle Way', is the notion that the makers of the prototype Keynesian state in Britain failed to establish the institutions it needed to develop, thereby building-in a design fault which would contribute powerfully to its eventual demise.

As Professor Marquand put it in his *The Unprincipled Society* in 1988,

> By the early 1970s, the British economy was among the most vulnerable in the developed world. But that vulnerability was not a fact of nature. It was a product of past choices, reflecting the moral and political preferences of those who made them. Unlike its counterparts on the mainland of Europe and in Japan, Britain's political class had never managed – even in its inter-ventionist periods – to create an entrepreneurial or developmental state. It had also failed to construct an enduring cross-class coalition, with the strength and will to answer one of the central questions which lie at the heart of economic adjustments: the question of how its costs and benefits are to be distributed.[32]

This is a big, sweeping claim. But there is plenty of evidence to corroborate it in sources which Marquand had not seen before he made it. Quite apart from the technical difficulty of creating the database for the new Keynesian state in 1944–5, there remained intense scepticism about the utility of the enterprise, in any of its manifestations, at the highest levels in Whitehall.

The contrast was stark between the Meades and the Stones and Treasury regulars such as Sir Bernard Gilbert and Sir Wilfrid Eady. Though Sir

Edward Bridges, the Head of the Civil Service, did crank up the Whitehall machine for Keynesian action in the last days of the war. He instructed all departments to collaborate with the Cabinet Office and the Treasury in preparing 'estimates of a future "target" level of national expenditure over the next five years', prompting a grateful Meade to reflect that 'The great steamroller of the Whitehall machine will thus actually have been put in motion to undertake national expenditure forecasting for the purposes of Employment Policy. Thus is five years' labour finally rewarded.'[33]

Bridges and his predecessor as Permanent Secretary at the Treasury, Sir Richard Hopkins, were crucial figures in the building of even a rudimentary Keynesian apparatus as Meade recognised in another diary entry in the spring of 1945:

I have this week had a very revealing conversation with [Dennis] Proctor (who has been put generally in charge of the co-ordination of Employment Policy in the Treasury) . . . Proctor was concerned because, in his words, Sir Bernard Gilbert just does not believe in Employment Policy and [Edward] Hale, who deals with local authorities under Gilbert, does so even less. Thus the outlook is not promising until some reshuffling of duties takes place in the Treasury. But I told Proctor that time was on our side, because Bridges believes in it, Parliament will certainly demand it, and there are a number of other elements . . . who are on the side of the angels.[34]

But more, much more was needed if Whitehall, Westminster and, most important of all, Britain's system of political economy as a whole were to adapt, and, where necessary, build afresh to accommodate the new Keynesian methods and to increase their chance of achieving that permanent transformation for which they were designed. This is a crucial issue, central to the whole postwar settlement and its ultimate viability.

Meade's remarkable diary (remarkable in its minute chronicling of the intellectual processes and observations of a public servant plainly exhausted by six years of war service in the Whitehall front line) gives several clues to these lacunae above and beyond the scepticism of the Treasury's old guard. For example, there is abundant evidence that Whitehall, generally, lacked officials with the technical competence to engage in the necessary economic systems-building. Which is why the departure of the innovative Richard Stone for university life in 1945 and the death of Keynes in 1946 were, in their different ways, such severe blows. As early as January 1945, Meade records 'a long conversation with Keynes' in which 'He was very amusing calling me "the only rat that was not deserting the ship" and inveighing against the Treasury officials who (with the exception of Hoppy [Sir Richard Hopkins]) he said were utterly incapable and incompetent to deal with technical economic matters. How have they the face to write long documents on economic matters!'[35]

This was a theme reprised in the late 1940s by other economically literate insiders such as Richard 'Otto' Clarke and Robert Hall. Clarke, one of the gifted 'irregulars' recruited by wartime Whitehall from journalism (he invented the FT index for stocks and shares) wrote in his diary on hearing news of his hero's fatal heart attack on the Sussex Downs at Easter 1946:

> Appalling news of the death of Keynes. Felt bereft as at death of Roosevelt [the President] and Alekhine [the chess champion]. He is the man whose career I would soonest match; I could never hope to match his all round genius, but I might hope to match his type of skill in the field of forensic economy . . . his death leaves the Treasury in a terrible hole . . . it will be interesting to see whether the Treasury relapses into habitual slovenliness and complacency or whether some new man is found for providing stimulus.[36]

Robert Hall, who succeeded Meade as Head of the Economic Section, has some eloquent passages in his diary not just about the unsuitability of many of Keynes' notions for the postwar economy but also about the lack of technique and application behind the Attlee Government's attempts at economic planning (of which more later). In the late winter of 1950, for example, Hall wrote 'It gets more and more of a bitter joke, that Ministers should believe so strongly in planning and be so anxious to do nothing about it that we have been gradually driven in despair to disinflation, to devaluation, and now are trying to get rid of controls to restore some semblance of competition.'[37]

But this is to jump the gun on a grand scale. The Whitehall picture in 1945 was summed up thirty years later by Sir Alec Cairncross who was well placed to remember it having himself been a senior economic adviser in the Board of Trade at the time. 'The co-ordination of economic policy', he wrote,

> inevitably rested heavily on the calibre of officials advising ministers, especially when, as in 1945–7, no minister (except Dalton) had any training in economics. Economic planning is by no means always undertaken by economists: but without *some* economists it is exposed to unnecessary hazards. At the end of the war, however, nearly all the economists in government service had left Whitehall and showed no inclination to return.
>
> Apart from the small group in the Economic Section of the Cabinet Office, few of whom were of much seniority, only one or two remained. Lord Keynes, the dominant figure in the Treasury, survived only until April 1946. Of those who had exercised a major influence on wartime planning, James Meade, Director of the Economic Section, and Austin Robinson, Economic Adviser to the Board of Trade, were the only two still available in 1945 . . . One or two others, such as Robert Hall and Russell Bretherton, who had served in the Raw Materials Department of the Ministry of Supply, had remained in post when their department was absorbed by the Board of Trade. Eric Roll continued to serve in the Ministry of Food. But the

Treasury in particular, and the Board of Trade in its main policy departments, relied almost exclusively on career civil servants with little or no training in economics. In the Treasury only 'Otto' (RWB) Clarke had any real flair for general economic policy.[38]

By any standards this represented a flimsy basis on which to build an ambitious, interventionist economic capability with no precedent in peacetime Whitehall. Not even the two chief economic ministries – the Treasury and the Board of Trade – could find the people they needed, partly because any awareness of that need passed by so many of the generalist, all-rounder senior civil servants in what since the late nineteenth century had been virtually a self-regulating profession.

Even if Whitehall had found the staff needed to put theoretical and practical cladding on the outline of the 1944 full employment White Paper, another huge gap would have remained which the perceptive James Meade touched on at the time. In a conversation with John Maud, another wartime temporary who stayed, becoming Permanent Secretary to the new Ministry of Education at the young age, by Whitehall standards, of thirty-nine (no one under forty has been appointed to the top Civil Service grade ever since[39]), Meade surveyed the wider changes needed in society as a whole if the new economics were to bring their intended benefits:

I argued that the technical scientific problem was largely solved. The ethical problem consisted in:
(i) suitable people taking the trouble to understand the technical problem;
(ii) persuading people that they must have the will to see that something was done about it this time, and not just let unemployment continue as they did last time: one must not just get used to an evil; and (iii) in those cases where there was a conflict between private interest and the social interest persuading people to restrain the former in preference to the latter.[40]

It was quite apparent to Meade that an ambitious attempt at public education would be necessary if the policy was to stick. Converting Parliament and Whitehall was not enough:

I argued that Employment Policy probably raised this third essentially moral problem less acutely than most other economic issues, since, in general, greater employment by leading to a larger national income could make everyone simultaneously better-off, whereas problems involving the distribution of the national income or the control of monopoly raised immediately the question of the conflict of class interests.
Nevertheless there were instances of this type of conflict in Employment Policy. For example, workers in work must exercise self-control in industrial discipline, in wage policy, in restricting entrance to new workers, etc., if the

high demand for their labour which would be associated with Full Employment was not to lead to the evils of reduced productivity, inflation, exclusion of the underpaid or unemployed from the best-paid employment.[41]

Rarely have I encountered such foresight on the part of a public servant. James Meade was, in fact, describing precisely what happened progressively in the 1950s, 1960s and 1970s. He was pretty accurate, too, when he turned his mind to the employers on the last day of 1944:

> Similar restraints would be needed on the part of producers who might, through certain restrictive practices, gain at the expense of others the high demand associated with Full Employment. It was to explain the reasons for this kind of self-restraint and 'unselfishness', if the employment policy was to succeed, that required a special moral appeal.[42]

It's not the job of civil servants to make such appeals. That is the task of politicians. Was there any political figure of public stature on the horizon in 1944–5 who could think in such terms or speak such language? Yes, there was. His name was Sir Stafford Cripps.

Cripps is a political figure whom it is near-impossible to describe for a generation that did not know him. Indeed he was a puzzle, a man of paradox, to those who did. His passage from a Conservative home (his father was a leading lawyer and a Tory MP) to a socialist activist is one trodden by many others in his generation, Attlee included. In both cases the Christian ethic lubricated the shift though Cripps was an actual, in fact, an ardent believer and Attlee was not.

For a politician, Cripps had a peculiarly rich background. It was immensely privileged – a prosperous home and Winchester College, and a marriage which brought him, through his wife Isobel, some of the fortune earned by Eno's fruit salts. He was a trained chemist, manager of a Ministry of Munitions explosive factory in the Great War (after a spell at the front with the Red Cross Ambulance Service), a hugely successful barrister after it, taking silk at the young age of thirty-seven in 1927, and something of a publishing entrepreneur in the 1930s, starting the newspaper *Tribune* to help further the cause of a 'popular front' with the Communists which preoccupied him in the last years of that decade.

Ill health dogged him all his life in the form of intestinal problems. In middle age he 'became converted to a system of "conscious bodily control" which, whatever it did for his health in the long run, gave him a peculiarly erect and detached but dedicated carriage,' wrote Roy Jenkins, a biographical essayist for whom Cripps held a peculiar fascination.[43] 'The spectacles', Jenkins continued,

> became smaller and rimless. The Cripps of his Chancellorship had (in 1937–8) assumed bodily shape. It was the Cripps who later prompted

Churchill to make his growling witticism, 'there, but for the grace of God, goes God'. It was the Cripps to whom, when he indicated dissent from the Government front bench a Tory member could say, 'the right honourable member must not shake his halo at me'.[44]

At the height of his fame at the Treasury, the political and public world perceived Cripps as a mixture of Iron Chancellor and mystic – part Bismarck, part Gandhi – exhorting the nation to greater productive effort and self-sacrifice, existing all the while off a diet of nut cutlet and carrot juice. In fact, as Edwin Plowden, close friend and economic adviser, would put it later, Cripps was 'a tremendously kind and generous man, not without a pleasant sense of humour. Moreover, until he became seriously ill (in 1949), he enjoyed a glass of wine and was a heavy smoker.'[45]

Cripps was a mixture of all the things the public and his colleagues saw in him. He was capable, too, of being utterly daft in political terms as his journey to the wild left frontier showed in the late 1930s. Attlee, whom he tried to depose in favour of Bevin in 1947 (Bevin said 'I'm sticking to little Clem' and that was that[46]) was always surprisingly forbearing towards Cripps even after the attempted putsch.[47] But there was more than a little truth in the terse assessment of 'Stafford, political goose' which Attlee gave Harold Wilson in 1949.[48]

Yet there was another side to this extraordinary man which is virtually forgotten – what one might call Cripps the management consultant. As we have seen, Cripps was keen on promoting the craft of management consultancy and, in his own way, he applied it to the processes of Parliamentary government even in his late 1930s phase when he was full of idiotic talk about short-circuiting Westminster procedures through an enabling bill to get socialist legislation through without the risk of obstruction. It was in this revolutionary mood that he raised the possibility of a capitalists' revolt which might need to be put down by force.[49]

This was partly a matter of temperament. Never had a more tidy-minded man occupied a high office of state. He once told Edwin Plowden, '"If you gave me the papers of any case I have fought in the last twenty years for one hour, I could go into court and fight it again." Then he paused for a moment and corrected himself, "No, I would not need the papers." He said this was no tribute to him, he just had a mind like that. He could put away the facts about a case in a drawer, pointing to his head, and draw it out when needed and it was all there.'[50]

In 1939 Cripps published his management consultant's report on Parliament calling it *Democracy Up-To-Date*, passing logically through 'The Problem' to 'The Solution' by way of 'Efficiency, a Pre-requisite to Survival' with a reorganisation of Commons procedure, a more effective use of Parliamentary committees and the replacement of the House of Lords by a 'committee of experts' among the recommendations.[51]

During the war as a Minister in the Coalition he plagued Churchill with schemes for improving the machinery of government causing the old man to remark about valuable ministerial time being wasted by 'academic and philosophical explanations which ought, in these times, to be the province of persons of leisure'.[52] By the time Cripps inherited his kingdom as an economic minister in the mid-to-late-Forties (first as President of the Board of Trade, then Minister of Economic Affairs before becoming Chancellor of the Exchequer in 1947), his thinking had become truly ambitious, nothing less, as he told the House of Commons, than a new notion of 'democratic planning' which 'aims at preserving maximum freedom of choice for the individual while yet bringing order into the industrial production of the country, so that it may render the maximum service to the nation as a whole'.[53] This, in the mixed metaphors of non-economic language, is the squaring of circles or having your cake and eating it.

But it would be wrong to be too hard on Cripps. At least he recognised there was a problem and that it was a fundamental one. Few others did. Most members of the political class were quite happy to carry on as before, putting constitutional or structural questions into the too dull, too difficult or irrelevant categories. This is not a matter for surprise. It merely reflects the fact, in Alan Beattie's words, 'that the British legal and political vocabulary is impoverished by its lack of notion of "the State"' and 'the curious British habit of accepting important institutional changes only when they awake to the fact that, unheralded, they have already occurred'.[54]

It was Beattie's colleague at the London School of Economics, John Griffith, who encapsulated this pragmatic approach in a single sentence when he said 'the Constitution is what happens',[55] a line which, I'm sure, owed a great deal to the view attributed to Herbert Morrison that 'socialism is what the Labour Government does'.[56] Even with Morrison's supreme pragmatism in mind, there is a danger of imposing a pattern where there was none upon the Attlee Government's initial approach to economic management and industrial reconstruction. As Alec Cairncross put it, reinforcing the impression left by Meade's and Bridges' efforts to cobble together some sort of macro-economic apparatus in the last months of war and the first days of peace:

> The very concept of managing the economy was new and little understood. While debate raged on abstract theories of planning, the practice of regulating economic activity through demand management was in course of development and improvement . . . Yet if one looks forward from 1945 rather than backwards from the 1980s [Cairncross was writing in 1984–5] the Labour Government was ill-prepared for the hectic years ahead. It was committed to programmes of nationalisation without having given much thought to the way in which the nationalised industries should operate . . .
>
> It had little idea what to do about inflation. It could not even count on the wholehearted support of key groups of manual workers such as the miners. Above all, it had not taken on board the limitations imposed on all aspects of

policy by the sheer lack of importing power. It was not conscious of succeeding to the management of an almost bankrupt economy, critically dependent on what it could buy and borrow from other countries. It took a long time to learn, if it ever did, that the 'commanding heights' of the British economy lay, not in the steel industry, but in the balance of payments and energy supply.[57]

In other words, Attlee and his colleagues had not taken on board the stark realities painted for those who served in the War Cabinet at least, by Maynard Keynes in April–May 1945,[58] or by his warning of a 'Financial Dunkirk' in the first days of the new Labour Government.[59]

During the first eighteen months of its life – until the fuel and currency crises of that desperate year, 1947, forced a rethink on several fronts and brought Cairncross's 'commanding heights', energy and the balance of payments, to the fore – the Attlee Administration pursued an economic policy which can be separated into four parts:

1 The extension of public ownership.

2 The conversion of war industries to a peacetime footing and the rapid demobilisation of that part of workforce bound up in the Armed Forces.

3 Regional policy, the idea as one of its originators, Douglas Jay, liked to put it, 'of taking the work to where the workers are'.[60]

4 The management of demand which, by extension, embraced a policy of planning (with the exhortation of the public and their education into economic realities as a key ingredient in the achievement of both).

I shall take each in turn, before looking at Government mechanics – the Cabinet Committees and departmental machinery – involved in pushing the policies forward and assessing the overseas financial position, the desperately precarious backdrop against which these economic and managerial experiments were conducted.

Nationalisation

We are seeking a combination of public ownership, public accountability and business management for public ends.
Herbert Morrison, 1933[61]

Herbert held their hands. For example Barnes [Minister of Transport] asked Morrison what to do and how to do it. He was really a rabbit stumbling along who picked up something from the Civil Service and something from Herbert. And that went for a lot of the nationalising ministers.
Christopher Mayhew, Parliamentary Private Secretary to Herbert Morrison, 1945–6, 1968[62]

He [Morrison] had that rare gift of being interested in the efficiency of the administrative machine. This made him a delight to work for as a civil servant.
Sir Alexander Johnstone, 1968[63]

These measures of ours are not theoretical trimmings. They are the essential part of a planned economy that we are introducing into this country . . . vital to the efficient working of the industrial and political machinery of this country, the embodiment of our Socialist principle of placing the welfare of the nation before that of any section.
Clement Attlee, Labour Party Conference, Bournemouth, 10 June 1946[64]

Prior to the election of the Attlee Government, public ownership had been a staple of socialist thinking for generations, a topic beloved of Fabian summer schools. It was also the subject of four important dummy runs in peacetime, as opposed to the temporary takeovers of wartime. These were Churchill's purchase of the Anglo-Iranian Oil Company (better known these days as BP) when First Lord of the Admiralty in 1912 to ensure supplies for the Royal Navy's newly converted boilers; the transformation of the British Broadcasting Company into the British Broadcasting Corporation by the Baldwin Government in 1927;[65] Morrison's creation of the London Passenger Transport Board as Minister of Transport in the second MacDonald Government in 1931;[66] and the Chamberlain Administration's refashioning of British Airways (itself a merger of three big companies) into the British Overseas Airways Corporation, BOAC, in 1939.[67]

Yet precious little thought had been given to implementing the nationalisation proposals in the public ownership shopping-list contained in *Let Us Face the Future* in 1945, as Manny Shinwell never tired of telling people:

I was asked by Attlee to go to the Ministry of Fuel and Power, with a seat in the Cabinet, and to nationalise the mines. He also asked me to nationalise the electricity supply and gas. I went back to my department, consulted with my permanent under secretary and other officials, and they said to me, 'Well, you'll have to prepare the headings, Minister.' Naturally, I looked around for some information, for blueprints, but there were none in the department. I went to the Labour Party. There was very little there. There was a pamphlet written by Arthur Greenwood . . . There were several resolutions passed at the Labour Party Conference, no blueprints. So I had to tackle it as if it was something quite new. It was very difficult indeed to do it.[68]

Morrison alone had something approaching a vision of the new public corporation and experience of an actual blueprint with his track record at bringing the Underground trains and buses of London under a single authority. He was a natural choice as co-ordinator of the Government's public ownership pro-gramme. In fact, in appointing him Lord President of the Council, Attlee made him Labour's economic overlord, a position he was to hold until the autumn of 1947 when he was eclipsed by the Stafford Cripps ascendancy.

In his political lifetime, Morrison had a gift for making enemies, Ernest Bevin in particular, and for attracting detractors, his official biographers, Don-oughue and Jones apart, since his death. In fact, he was one of the most substantial figures in domestic policy in the twentieth century. He deserved better of Attlee who, when asked by Donoughue and Jones about his achieve-ments, snapped out 'Waterloo Bridge, the LCC and the Festival of Britain', adding 'Morrison was essentially a London man.'[69] Herbert was much more than just 'a London man', though the London County Council when it was counted as one of the most progressive systems of urban government in the world under Morrison's leadership in the 1930s, had provided him with a remarkable stage on which to display his natural talents as an organiser.[70]

Morrison was in no way ashamed of his metropolitan associations. Quite the reverse. When Jim Griffiths first encountered Morrison in the course of Party work long before the war he found him 'very quick, humorous and totally absorbed in local government'. Morrison would call Griffiths a 'Welsh nation-alist'; Griffiths would counter by calling him a 'London nationalist'.[71] It must be remembered, however, that interwar local government meant a great swathe of activity – not just schooling and housing, but public health and a large chunk of the hospital service too – and London dwarfed all other local authorities.

Morrison was a big figure in Labour Party terms as well. As we have seen he was Minister of Transport 1929–31. He was, too, an innovator, one of the first to appreciate that Labour needed to appeal to a new and rising middle class if it was ever to win an absolute majority, and his protégés, like John Wilmot and George Strauss (both to become ministers in the 1945–50 governments) reflected this.[72] He was also among the first of Labour's national figures to appreciate the dividend that could accrue from cultivating the Press and, as Lord President, introduced the idea of briefing privately the Westminster lobby correspondents every Thursday.[73]

Attlee, by contrast, used to give the impression of never having read the newspapers.[74] (In fact he read *The Times* for the births, marriages, deaths and cricket scores and took the *Daily Herald* out of loyalty to the trade union movement and 'to see what the chaps are doing, ye' know,' while his very rare appearances before the lobby would be over in ten minutes, the hacks exhausted by his battery of put-downs, 'Nothing in that', 'You're off beam again', 'That idea seems bonkers to me – the Cabinet's never looked at it.'[75]) Whereas Morrison 'was very sensitive about the press. He read them all – everything about himself – and had a cuttings book.'[76]

It was the war in general and the Blitz in particular that turned Morrison into a national figure. Churchill decided Morrison was far more suitable to handle it than Anderson.[77] So the cockney sparrow replaced the calculating machine at the Home Office to general satisfaction. 'His performance here', Jim Griffiths said admiringly many years later, 'turned him into "Our Herb".'[78]

Morrison became a bit of a favourite with Conservative ministers in the Coalition (second only to Bevin) as a kind of 'cheeky chappie'. Oliver Lyttelton used to say Morrison was the man who got him through many a boring Cabinet committee meeting especially when the long-winded and platitudinous Woolton was in the Chair. When, finally, Woolton said he had come to the conclusion that the only way to deal with the housing problem was to build more houses, Morrison leaned across to Chandos (as Lyttelton became when he went to the Lords), strands of his quiff brushing across Chandos' forehead, and said 'Call me after prayers.'[79]

It was Chandos, long before the electorate had given Labour the power to extend state ownership, to whom Morrison confided his doubts about the pressures pushing Labour to take over what in a later generation would have been called 'lameduck' industries. 'Chandos', wrote Bernard Donoughue after interviewing him for the Morrison biography, 'recalled that once Morrison had asked him [Chandos was Minister of Production in the Coalition] what he would do with the coal mines? Chandos replied: "Nationalise them." Morrison immediately responded: "I know why, for the same reason that I don't want to." In other words, because it would discredit nationalisation.'[80]

Morrison's remark is highly significant. Because one of the many myths that have grown up about what's become called the 'Morrisonian model' public corporations created in that great, postwar burst of institution building is that Morrison himself was a fervent advocate of nationalisation. He wasn't. In fact there is plenty of evidence that he was going off the idea as early as the summer of 1947 as we shall see. 'Morrison', as Kenneth Morgan has rightly said, 'alone . . . had the sustained intellectual energy to provide a workable model of public ownership.'[81] Professor Morgan should in fairness have said 'models' plural. Because another myth is that Morrison was only interested in one solution of the London Passenger Transport Board variety, and applied the centralist approach uniformly.

He did not. He had a more open mind than that as was apparent to the civil servants with whom he worked. For example, Bridges believed Morrison 'deserved great credit for the solutions to the problems of nationalising industry'.[82] And Alexander Johnstone, the top civil servant on the nationalisation side of the Lord President's Office, said Morrison 'was very keen on variety and experiment. He liked to have coal, steel and gas run in different ways. He liked the fact that the London Port Authority and the airports were run by the state and not by corporations so he could compare them. He didn't want uniformity. His attitude was "Let's try something different" . . . Electricity was centralised and then gas was decentralised because Morrison thought that we now had enough centralisation.'[83]

Clearly, therefore, it would be as misleading for historians to succumb to the convenient shorthand of the 'Morrisonian model' as for them to treat the activities nationalised as in any way comparable to each other in size, scope or purpose. Equally, it would be misleading to regard the 'very conservative figure'[84] of Lord Catto, Governor of the Bank of England, the former General Secretary of the TUC, Lord Citrine at the British Electricity Authority and Lord Hyndley of the colliery company Powell Duffryn before becoming first Chairman of the National Coal Board, as three-of-a-kind because they were all creatures of a public ownership statute.

What can be said, however, is that the activities of Morrison and his colleagues on the Cabinet's Legislation and Socialization of Industry Committees in the late 1940s *did* change the configuration of British industry dramatically and alter the mix of the mixed economy fundamentally. What Labour's programme did not do (and it was never intended to) was transfer power and control to the workforce. Cripps, in what Kenneth Morgan has called 'a moment of appalling frankness'[85] in a speech in October 1946, said: 'There is not yet a very large number of workers in Britain capable of taking over large enterprises . . . until there has been more workers on the managerial side of industry, I think it would be almost impossible to have worker-controlled industry in Britain, even if it were on the whole desirable.'[86]

This statement of the truth – for nothing in the British education system or the traditional relationships between capital and labour had prepared the nation's workforce for such a task – has led to the Labour Government in general and Cripps in particular being vilified by the hard left ever since. For example, its leading historian and theoretician, Ralph Miliband, wrote in 1960 that:

As for the effective control of the nationalized industries, the Conservatives found the Government much more than half way in their own camp. Though ultimate control was vested in the Minister and provision made for a measure of parliamentary accountability more formal than real, the Government's conception of public ownership ensured the predominance on the boards of the nationalized corporations of men who had been, or who still were, closely associated with private finance and industry, and who could hardly be expected to regard the nationalized industries as designed to achieve any purpose other than the more efficient servicing of the 'private sector'.[87]

There is more than a grain of truth in this. As we have seen, Citrine apart, it was private sector figures to whom the Government turned for its chairmen or governors. And Morrison himself had made it plain to the 1945 conference that pragmatism would be all: 'You must spend substantial time in arguing the case for the socialisation of these industries on the merits of their specific cases. This is how the British mind works. It does not work in a vacuum or in abstract theories.'[88]

Attlee himself echoed Morrison. 'It had always been our practice', he wrote in his memoirs, 'in accord with the natural genius of the British people, to work empirically. We were not afraid of compromises and partial solutions . . . We realised that the application of socialist principles in a country such as Britain with a peculiar economic structure based on international trade required great flexibility.'[89] Attlee, too, highlighted the big divide in Labour's postwar public ownership programme – that between iron and steel and the rest. 'Of all our nationalisation proposals, only iron and steel aroused much feeling, perhaps because hopes of profit were greater here than elsewhere.'[90]

Equally, there was a marked ambivalence about the need for and the nature of the 'socialisation', to use the word in vogue at the time, of iron and steel within the Government itself. It was treated as a special case by the Cabinet and is, therefore, best examined separately from the first big batch of measures which passed through Morrison's Socialization and Legislation Committees. As Morgan noted, they 'included the Bank of England, civil aviation, Cable and Wireless, and coal-mining. By the autumn of 1946, all were on the statute book, as part of the seventy-five measures that the Government swept through in that astonishing first year of socialist rule; electricity was to follow. None occasioned any major dissent. The Government, armed with a huge majority, piloted these complex measures through both Houses with much ease.'[91]

The nationalisation of the Bank of England was very much Hugh Dalton's statute. It was not a Morrisonian enterprise. In its way, it illustrated the deeply paradoxical nature of that puzzling man, loathed by the Tories as a class traitor. Dalton was an Old Etonian, son of a Canon of Windsor who was also a tutor to the future George V.[92] His Treasury civil servants disliked his high-handed manner (for Otto Clarke he was 'worth about £500 millions a year to the nation's enemies'; Ernest Rowe-Dutton said of him 'He shits for England in the Olympic Games').[93] Dalton oscillated between great exuberance and genuine depression (he had a rotten private life and his sexual appetites were decidedly ambivalent). His most consistent features were the conspiratorial gossip in which he constantly indulged and the booming voice in which he conducted it.

Douglas Jay captured Dalton perfectly when recalling their days together in the wartime Board of Trade. 'Dalton's views and sympathies', he wrote, 'were beautifully simple and clear.'

> He was in favour of miners, the young, white men, socialists, New Zealand, Australia and dwellers in Durham and Northumberland. (His seat was in the mining community of Bishop Auckland.) He was against the Germans, reactionaries, the elderly and the rich. But he tended to shout at all junior or senior officials, visiting industrialists, or myself and John Wilmot his very assiduous PPS. Attlee once described Dalton's voice as a 'confidential whisper which echoes around the lobbies'.[94]

Quite the worst thing I ever heard about Dalton was that as Minister of Economic Warfare and, therefore, the politician responsible for the behind-the-lines sabotage and subversion secret service, the Special Operations Executive, he had used SOE equipment to bug a fellow Labour politician and Coalition Minister, Arthur Greenwood. According to the figure from the intelligence world from whom I heard it, MI5 discovered this and informed Churchill who promptly removed Dalton from the Ministry of Economic Warfare and 'kicked him upstairs' to the Board of Trade. If true, this story has a wider significance. Because, according to this same intelligence figure, it was what lay behind Churchill's notorious 'Gestapo' speech in 1945, the argument being that he (Churchill) couldn't conceive of Attlee or Bevin creating such a monstrosity but in Dalton's case he could.

What is certain is that Dalton had had his eye on the Bank of England for years. In his memoirs he wrote: 'Once in some Left Book Club circles I had listened to the tedious theory that the capitalists would resist, if necessary by force, a socialist government which would try to nationalize the Bank of England or anything else. Impatiently I had replied: "Make me Chancellor of the Exchequer and give me a good Labour majority in Parliament and I will undertake the nationalisation of the Bank of England over a dinner party." And now no dinner party had been necessary: only tea for two [with Catto]'.[95] As Dalton's friend and sympathiser, the self-styled 'City radical', Nicholas Davenport, later wrote: 'Of course Lord Catto would not resist, or any of his capitalist friends, because they knew that Dalton planned no real change in the management of the Bank and had no real wish to upset the financial Establishment or undermine the subtle power it exercised through its interlocking bank directorships.'[96]

Davenport was one of a handful of money men sympathetic to Labour thinkers like Douglas Jay and Evan Durbin in the 1930s and was a member of the 'XYZ' dining club where from the early days of 1932 fruitful exchanges took place on 'administrative financial problems'.[97] According to Francis Williams, an XYZ man in his capacity as City Editor of the *Daily Herald*, and Attlee's Downing Street press secretary 1945–7, the club had 'some claim to have exercised in a quiet sort of way more influence on future Government policy than any other group of the time'.[98]

This could hardly be said of the nationalisation of the Bank. As Davenport put it in his memoirs:

We had found Labour politicians before 1945 constantly talking of how they would seize 'the commanding heights of the economy' . . . We had tried to explain to them that 'the commanding heights of the economy' were all to be found within the square mile of the City clustered round and about the Bank of England. We of the XYZ Club fondly imagined that when they had got control of the Bank they would appoint a technocrat Governor outside politics who was experienced in the monetary management of a mixed economy, that they would restrict the Court of the Bank to technical experts and that they would remove the part-time merchant bank directors.[99]

Davenport and his City friends did not expect Labour to nationalise more financial institutions. But they did expect the Bank of England to take powers to direct other banks and, perhaps, put Government directors on their boards, as a way of bringing the nation's money system 'under proper public control'.

> But what Dalton did was really a great non-event. First, he asked . . . Lord Catto of Morgan Grenfell to stay on because he was such a nice friendly chap who had risen up from the ranks. Then he reduced the Court from twenty-four to sixteen and took power to appoint only four of them each year. He retained the prominent directors who had been associated with the worst disasters of Montagu Norman [the arch-deflationist who governed the Bank in the interwar years].[100]

Insofar as the Government was to take directing powers over the nationalised Bank, the Chancellor could do it where and when necessary 'in the public interest' in the vague wording of the Act.

No wonder the Conservatives did not oppose it. One of their number, the independent-minded Robert Boothby, actually voted with the Government when the measure slipped easily through Parliament in the autumn of 1945. In a peculiar way, nationalisation of the Bank was a symbolic, almost cathartic, act for both the labour movement and the City, a truce if you like – a nominal shift of power to the state; in practice, business-as-usual.

Far more symbolic, however, was coal – the most passion-laden of all the nationalisations. More than forty years later, veterans of the 1945 Labour intake would glow at the memory of it, none more so than Barbara Castle who, when she recalled it for me in 1989, was back there in the Commons Chamber with the 'young majors from the army', the 'intellectuals' and the 'working class people from traditional Labour areas . . . who filled the Voting Lobby when the nationalisation of the mines went through and the Welsh lads linked arms and started singing 'Cwm Rhondda''.[101]

Behind the passion and the rhetoric, officials in the Ministry of Fuel and Power, like their colleagues in the Ministry of Health, had, in the early months of the Labour Government had to engage in an unprecedented exercise in institution building with the vexed question of compensation for the owners, a simultaneous and constant preoccupation. There was nothing marginal about coal. At that time it met over 90 per cent of the nation's fuel requirements. It had a labour force of 700,000 plus, pits of all sorts and conditions in areas stretching from Fife in the north to Kent in the south, Selby in the east to Llanelli in the west and an eccentric range of ancillary assets including coke ovens, brickworks, farms and row upon row of tied housing – those distinctive redbrick, soot-blackened terraces of the classic pit village.[102] The whole lot, as we have seen, was hugely run down thanks to the war and decades of under investment before that. As one of the Ministry's officials put it later, 'the responsibility laid upon this new, vast and untried organisation was stupendous.'[103]

Nationalising the Bank of England, or the largely technical matter of Cable and Wireless (involving the creation of an integrated communications network between Britain and the Commonwealth), or come to that, the tidying-up of civil aviation by completing the process begun by the Chamberlain Government (a trio of corporations were established, a reshaped BOAC plus a British European Airways and South American Airways) – all these were push-overs compared to coal. As Sir Norman Chester, the official historian of postwar nationalisation, put it, 'The Coal Industry Nationalisation Bill had to be thought out virtually from scratch and put into good legal language in less than four months. And this by a Minister [Shinwell] and his senior advisers tackling major problems caused by the shortage of coal and electricity.'[104]

A price was paid for rushing the coal bill. 'However quickly everyone worked', Reuben Kelf-Cohen recalled, 'in that very short period nothing but a very crude scheme was possible.'[105] Much of it was taken up with the transfer of assets and compensation (£164.6 million was the figure eventually agreed upon). The management gap we saw in the construction of the Health Service yawned here too. The Act established a National Coal Board of nine. Beneath them were eight new regions. Below them forty-eight area groups of collieries. 'The emphasis, for all Shinwell's claims on behalf of administrative decentralisation, was on a highly unified financial and organisational structure.'[106]

The statute gave the Coal Board no guidance on how to run its industrial kingdom. An acute shortage of high quality management, brutally apparent to the industry's wartime sponsors in the Board of Trade, was made worse by an exodus at the time of nationalisation. The Fleck Committee, rightly, put its finger on this debilitating factor when it reported in 1955. 'When the industry was nationalised', the inquiry said,

> it lost many of its administrators. In particular, most of the managing directors of the larger undertakings did not choose to come into the service of the Board. Thus the industry lost virtually a complete level of management at the moment when, because of the great size of the new undertaking, managerial and administrative talent was needed more than ever before. The gap has not yet been filled.[107]

Within weeks of vesting day the new structures were tested to near destruction by the severest bout of winter weather in living memory, as we shall see in the chapter 'Ice, Dollars and New Looks'.

The public utilities, 'gas and water socialism' as they are sometimes collectively called, with their musty, late-Victorian overtones, have never set the political pulses racing. They are, however, crucial to an advanced society as the merest glance at the Emergency Powers Act 1920 confirms. There they congregate, fuel, light and 'the means of locomotion' which, with food and water (this last brought fully into public ownership only in the 1970s and privatised once more in the late 1980s), were listed as 'the essentials of life' which the state has a duty to maintain.[108]

The last rush of the first cascade of postwar public ownerships very much involved States of Emergency industries – gas, electricity and transport. The only surprising element in the nationalisation of electricity was that it hadn't happened before.

As long ago as 1882 Parliament, even before Labour was represented in it, had envisaged public ownership as the ultimate goal for the industry. Successive governments, Baldwin's especially with the Electricity (Supply) Act 1926 which created a Central Electricity Board, had moved to bring order to the chaos of separate municipal power stations. By the time the McGowan Committee recommended a national grid, two thirds of the industry was owned by public authorities to their considerable financial profit.[109] That most remarkable Scottish Secretary of State, Tom Johnston, had piloted his pioneering nationalisation bill for the public ownership of hydroelectricity in the Highlands through the Commons in 1943. It was the nearest Britain has ever come to having a Tennessee Valley Authority, a utility with a heart. It commands fierce local loyalty to this day.

Johnston, one of the most intriguing of the 'forgotten men' of British politics, virtually singlehandedly turned his country into what, with much justice, has been called 'the biggest pressure group in Britain'.[110] A Scotland-first man, he had a brisk way with dissenters. In the Commons in 1943 he threatened to give the names and addresses of the few objectors to his Hydro Act to 'the 51st [Highland] Division when it returned after the war'.[111] After the war he chose to leave politics and forsake his certain place in the Attlee Cabinet to run his beloved North of Scotland Hydro Electric Board.

Shinwell, by contrast, was the kind of partisan Scottish politician who brought the class warrior out in his opponents. Though he could not charm the system and make it yield like Johnston, nationalising electricity caused him little trouble. It was more a matter of finishing a task long in gestation. A British Electricity Authority was set up under Citrine's Chairmanship to preside over fourteen area boards which would operate on a federal basis.

Its sister utility, gas, showed that, as the nationalisations proceeded, their federalist content would increase. From 1949, when the industry came into full public ownership (a year after electricity) its twelve area boards were genuinely autonomous with a Gas Council, consisting of the area chairmen plus an independent chairman and deputy, as its umbrella body instead of a central directing staff. Ironically, the Gas Bill had a rougher passage than its precursors, given the private owners had put up no resistance and the Heyworth Committee, established by the Coalition, reported in December 1945 with the recommendation that the whole of gas supply be brought into public ownership. It is probable, however, that the protracted late-night sittings in the Commons on the Gas Bill in 1948 had more to do with the revival of the Conservative Opposition than with ideological impulses.

Nationalisation could only bring a measure of efficiency to two thirds of the industry (the remainder of which was already municipalised) which were split up into 700 companies that reflected its Victorian origins ranging from one or two giants like the Gas, Light and Coke Company to tiny outfits sometimes on a village scale. Even the arch opponent of public ownership, Kelf-Cohen, had to acknowledge that 'Many of the small companies were grossly inefficient. They operated on too minute a scale to afford competent staff and up-to-date plant, their service was often inadequate and the gas they supplied left much to be desired in its quality.'[112]

Given the romance with which the British have invested their railways in picture, book, film and song (Flanders' and Swann's 'The Slow Train' can still move me almost to tears at the memory of the rural railway station in the age of steam), the nationalisation of transport was bound to be a more exciting and excitable business than power and light. It became highly publicised, too, because of the original intention of the 'Socialisation' Cabinet Committee to embrace the small carrier, the so-called 'C Licence' operator, within the new British Road Services. As there were thousands of them (their lorries amounted to 350,000) in every town and many villages in the land, this was more of a problem than disposing of a few coal or gas companies. Alf Barnes, the rather leaden Co-op figure at the Ministry of Transport, was overwhelmed and the Government backed down.[113]

In many ways, transport was the most ambitious of the Attlee Government's public ownership projects as its ruling idea was the integration of rail, road haulage and inland waterways under a British Transport Commission, 'a giant of a kind previously unknown in any country', involving 'a vast and novel experiment'.[114] Its Railway Executive was relatively straightforward, completing the rationalisation process begun by the amalgamations of the 1920s and the effective state takeover under wartime conditions in the 1940s.

But when this was put together with the running of 3,800 road hauliers, all road and rail transport in London, the great harbours in Southampton and Hull which were owned by the railway companies plus several similarly owned hotel chains and Thomas Cook the travel agents for good measure – all this plus the duty, as Barnes put it in the Commons, 'of integrating all forms of transport covered by the Bill and . . . to see that all parts of the country are adequately served,' and you have another blueprint for unmanageability, especially in view of the rundown condition of virtually every truck and locomotive, bus and barge thanks to the war. As Lord Stamp, the outgoing boss of the London Midland and Scottish Railway put it wryly, 'the efficient management of any concern really rested upon what could be supervised by the brain of one competent person,'[115] the brain, in this case, being that of Sir Cyril Hurcomb, the Ministry of Transport's Permanent Secretary who had developed the BTC concept and became its first Chairman presiding over a board noted for its age, caution and 'drabness' of its members.[116] The same, ominously, could be said of virtually all the titans of the public slice of the mixed economy Attlee's ministers spent so much time creating in the first three years after the war which may partly explain why by 1948 so many of them had lost their zest for this element in the socialist transformation (of which more later).

Regional Policy

Labour was a mainly geographical resource and could not be rapidly moved about the country like a machine tool or a ton of steel . . . Very early at the Ministry of Supply I had been struck by the absurdity of the competing production departments . . . all crowding their labour demands into a few notoriously congested areas like Birmingham, Coventry and Luton and leaving hundreds of thousands of workers unemployed elsewhere.
Douglas Jay in 1980, recalling the war years[117]

In my years in industry I have seen the capacity of what are described as 'ordinary' people to do very complex tasks and take breath-taking responsibility . . . All through its history my own company has found that men from the farms, the mines, the shipyards have adapted perfectly readily to the needs of a high-technology business.
Sir John Harvey-Jones, Chairman, ICI, 1986[118]

There was the conversion of the old wartime ordnance factories for peace-time industrial purposes . . . In addition, the government sponsored, through the Board of Trade, a vast programme of building advanced factories, plant built with Treasury finance ahead of demand from industrialists . . . By the start of 1951, as a result, the Board of Trade's controller for Wales . . . could report that jobs for 64,000 workers had been created since 1945 and that unemployment was largely confined to a few small pockets in eastern Glamorgan and Western Monmouthshire, between Merthyr and Blaenavon.
Kenneth O. Morgan, 1981[119]

The need was to restore the competitive position of the heavy industries, or else to find substitutes which could compete. War actually increased dependence on them. Dispersal from the South and diversification at home were too limited to redress Scotland's lack of capacity in the new industries which were to ensure prosperity in other parts of industry . . . Johnston never applied his energy to correcting these shortcomings . . . In consequence there was much misdirection of effort . . . Under the imposition of central control the spring of native enterprise all but dried up.
Michael Fry, 1987[120]

Looking back . . . from the 1980s to the 1940s, it seems to me pretty obvious that industry would not have accepted, or co-operated with, this policy had

17 Sir Stafford Cripps and Dame Isobel; 'political goose' and surprising source

18 John Maynard Keynes: if only the US Air Force 'by some sad geographical slip ... were to destroy every factory on the north-east coast and in Lancashire (at an hour when the Directors were sitting there and no one else), we should have nothing to fear'

19   Sir William Beveridge, giant-killer

20   Family Allowance day, Vicarage Lane Post Office, Stratford, East London,
      6 August 1946

21–22   The Welfare State: *Above* From the cradle; *Below* almost to the grave, Nye Bevan in Preston on Health Service day, July 1948

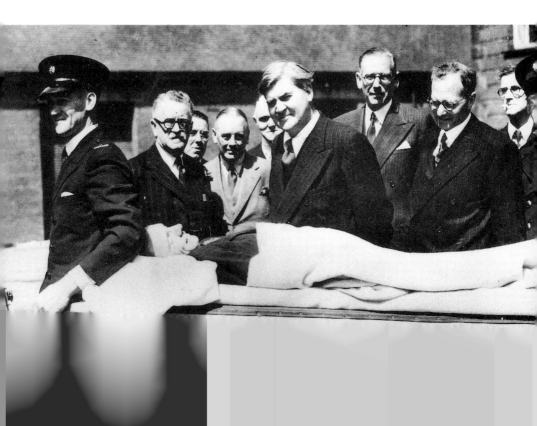

23–24 Homes for *some* heroes: *Left*
Evicted squatters occupy a
council building, Islington,
1949. *Below* Prefabs go up in
York, 1947.

25   Ellen Wilkinson – Britain as a
      'Third Programme' nation

26   Emergency training in a Nissen
      hut; 35,000 from the Forces into
      teaching in twelve months

27   Black gold: Emanuel Shinwell with miner, Lord Hyndley and Nye Bevan, 1947

28   Standard's Coventry plant, 1948; Fergusons and Vanguards for export

29 'Mortician of Empire': Lord Mountbatten with Nehru (left), Jinnah (right) and Ismay, New Delhi, June 1947

30 Jerusalem, December 1947; British policemen between Arab and Jew after bomb-blast

" WHO'S NEXT TO BE LIBERATED FROM FREEDOM, COMRADE ?"

31 Stalin and Molotov at the cold
    war switchboard

32 Bevin and Molotov. 'What are
    you after? ... You are putting
    your neck out too far.'

it not first grown accustomed to Government controls in war, often administered by its own people, the businessmen who made such a large contribution to the war effort, working within the government departments. It is surely unlikely also that either the IDC [industrial development certificate] or the building licence preference would have been considered politically acceptable outside the atmosphere of the war and the euphoria of the immediate postwar years.
Dame Alix Meynell, 1988[121]

From the late 1920s, successive British governments became concerned about what geographers call the 'spatial' consequences of Britain's vicissitudes as a world economic power – the concentration of problems associated with manufacturing decline and persistently high unemployment in those areas associated with the mining and manufacturing triumphs of the Victorian years. Starting with Baldwin's Industrial Transference Scheme of 1928 and progressing through the Special Areas Act 1934 taken through the Commons by Chamberlain as Chancellor of the Exchequer, a mild degree of intervention, mainly social rather than economic in impulse (i.e. temporary relief rather than long-term reconstruction), became a standard element in central government activity.

Almost from the outset, there were those who appreciated that the application of social Elastoplast was no remedy for such deep and festering economic wounds. Dalton was prominent among the politicians in arguing this case. To the embarrassment of the National Government, the industrialist it made special commissioner for the English depressed regions, Malcolm Stewart, Chairman of the London Brick Company, pushed hard for a policy of economic regeneration in the distressed areas to the palpable alarm of the Treasury.[122]

Partly in response to such proddings, partly for fear of what German bombing might do to an overcrowded south-east, the Chamberlain Government in 1937 commissioned Sir Montague Barlow to inquire into the distribution of industry and population. The Barlow Report of 1940 began the rise of the regional planner in Britain, an ascent not checked until the 1970s and only reversed in the 1980s. It 'recommended that for the first time the government should take responsibility for the pattern of land use throughout the country, restricting factory development in the South-East, dispersing congested populations to new towns and garden cities, inspecting plans put forward by local authorities, and encouraging the location of industry in areas threatened by unemployment.'[123]

But for the war, a menu of this magnitude would have proved too rich for the country's political or administrative classes to digest. At the very moment Barlow reported, the supply, production and manpower ministries found themselves engaged in putting together the most ambitious – and successful – regional policy ever. Its stimulant, of course, was Hitler not Barlow. As Alix Meynell, a senior Board of Trade official, later put it, out of the 'extraordinary scramble' for factory space at the turn of 1940–1 grew 'an extempore location of industry policy covering the country as a whole'.[124]

Douglas Jay has described how 'the near-total mobilization of manpower' enabled Whitehall to direct not just men but materials as never before or since to the depressed areas by dividing the country into scarlet, red, amber and green areas – scarlet being overcrowded localities where no new production was permitted, and green, the depressed areas, to which new production and mobile labour were sent. 'For instance,' he remembered, 'by 1944 Dundee became almost a Ministry of Supply preserve. The lesson was also indelibly impressed on my mind that what was true of wartime was equally true of peacetime. You could not have full national production, any more than full employment, unless the production was located where the workers lived.'[125]

The lesson was not lost either on Dalton who, as President of the Board of Trade 1942–5, found himself in possession of the bureaucratic instrument to pursue his most cherished notions of regional policy. 'I was', he recalled, 'sure from the start that legislation would be needed to establish permanent postwar control of location.'[126] And despite the non-interventionist traditions of his department and the Conservative majority inside the Coalition, he drove this thoroughly democratic socialist policy through the War Cabinet and its committees until he got his Distribution of Industry Act 1945 which extended the prewar special areas policy to a far wider swathe of 'development areas' embracing 13.5 per cent of the population where the prewar 'special areas' had accounted for 8.5 per cent, with far tougher directional powers for Whitehall.

Instead of merely providing 'government-sponsored trading estates which gave firms the great advantage of not having to sink capital in bricks and mortar'[127] which had been the basis of prewar policy in places like Speke on the fringe of Liverpool, the Board of Trade would forbid any manufacturer wishing to extend his factory by more than 5,000 square feet without an industrial certificate. Alix Meynell, 'in that fertile thinking area, my bath', dreamed up another powerful inducement in that era of shortages:

Why not add to the IDC control the inducement of a building licence! The building industry was over-stretched as a result of the enormous destruction during the war, and in consequence . . . the right to use building labour and building materials was strictly rationed. If we could offer building licences with our IDCs we should get quick industrial expansion in our Development Areas.[128]

This was, in its way, a British version of Roosevelt's New Deal in the United States. During the war, the UK equivalent of FDR's dams, rural electricity schemes and works programmes was the siting by the Ministry of Supply of its huge Royal Ordnance factories in areas of high unemployment such as the filling factory at Bridgend in South Wales, the cordite factory at Wrexham in the North, the TNT factories at Sellafield in West Cumberland and Irvine in the central valley of Scotland.[129] IDCs and building licences were the same policy by another means.

Cripps, who replaced Dalton at the Board of Trade (with the brief interlude of Churchill's 'Caretaker' Administration) inherited a tried and tested system which was absolutely critical to the achievement of full employment. The first two years after the war were its heyday – war socialism extended. And the results were impressive. The 'development areas' contained some 10 per cent of the country's population. Between 1945 and 1947 they received 50 per cent of new building investment. As a result of such targeting, and what had gone before in the war, unemployment in these localities fell from an average figure of 22 per cent in 1937 to single figures.[130]

Dalton regarded this as his greatest achievement. When D.W. Parsons flipped through his notes for his 1946 Budget Speech he found this passage forcefully underlined in red ink.

The battle for the Development Areas is not yet won, but we mean to win it. We mean to wipe out the evil heritage of mass unemployment in these areas, due to long years of political neglect and private enterprise . . . I have told my colleagues that I will find, and find with a song in my heart, whatever money is necessary.[131]

If anything, the Government may have overdone the policy in those first postwar years. So many advance factories were put up by 1947 that no more were constructed until 1959.[132]

When the Government published a White Paper in the autumn of 1948 spelling out its achievements in the formerly depressed areas,[133] Dalton wrote, 'All this was victory indeed . . . My dreams of twenty years ago, when I first came to Bishop Auckland . . . were coming true at last. Now at last mass unemployment was on the way out. Now I could rest content in deep joy.'[134] That makes painful reading for anyone who visited the once-more depressed regions of Britain in the 1980s. Ironically, Dalton penned those words at a time when the Labour Government was in retreat not just from public ownership (which he strongly believed in) but from physical controls in favour of a more hands-off, demand management approach, or what became known as 'Keynesianism' to postwar generations, for whom it was first the established norm, then an object of intense dispute as ideology re-entered the British political bloodstream in the 1970s. From a forty-year perspective, that impressive war inheritance of IDCs, building licences and 'song in heart' Treasury funding looks much diminished – temporary palliatives that produced fleeting success in areas the world economy would increasingly pass by.

Planning Versus Managing

When Hugh Dalton arrived for the weekend at Hinton on 5 August 1945 on his way up to the Treasury, my misgivings deepened . . . I had to explain to him the functions of the Government broker . . . I had also to explain the difference between jobbers and brokers on the Stock Exchange about which he knew nothing . . . Here was one of the big men in the Labour Party taking up high office who seemed to be utterly ignorant of the workings of the monetary system.
Nicholas Davenport, 1974[135]

On the Monday morning my wife and I motored Hugh Dalton . . . up to the Treasury for his first day in office. It was an uncomfortable journey because the silencer had broken down and the noise was deafening but Hugh did not appear to notice . . . He boomed away about his job and when we got to Great George Street he said to me: 'I have got your XYZ papers in my bag and I am going to put them on my desk, press the button for my new slaves and ask them why we should not put them into practice.' I knew that the slaves would soon become his masters.
Nicholas Davenport, 1974[136]

Long meeting of the Economic Survey Committee to consider the second edition of National Plan for 1946. Great division of opinion between people who want *real* planning and people who want thermostattery. Great unwillingness to accept the view that for the short-term we need a forecast, which will throw up what will actually happen unless the Government intervenes further.
Otto Clarke, diary entry, 1 February 1946[137]

The Budget must be regarded as the main instrument for implementing the Plan. In a Liberal-Socialist economy it is fiscal policy, *par excellence*, which must be used in order to ensure that the level of personal expenditure, investment etc. is right. Success or failure depends . . . on whether or not we manage to get this the accepted Treasury doctrine.
James Meade, diary entry, 31 March 1946[138]

Despite Britain's immense problems, Labour were determined to maintain Britain as a world power. They added to these problems when they committed themselves to honouring the objectives of both the 1944 White Paper on *Employment Policy* and the Beveridge Report on the Social Services. All this was to be realised by a rather nebulous economic policy which they referred to as 'democratic planning'. It can best be described as a mixture of physical controls, nationalisation and exhortation, laced with a dash of Keynesianism and a liberal dose of wishful thinking.
Lord Plowden, former Chief Planning Officer, 1989[139]

Alix Meynell and her colleagues in the Board of Trade engaged on regional policy had life easy compared to 'thermostatters' like James Meade in the Cabinet Office or 'Gosplanners' like Otto Clarke in the Treasury, who invented the two terms and complained he was obliged to put in a sixty-hour week thanks to his interventionist convictions.[140] Though in fighting for the minds of ministers, both had the additional handicap of treading where no public servants had trodden before. As Sir Alec Cairncross put it: 'The very concept of managing the economy was new and little understood. While debate raged on abstract theories of planning, the practice of regulating economic activity through demand management was in the course of development and improvement.'[141]

Much of this took place beyond the attention span of ministers. Dalton had at least written a book on public finance,[142] Cripps had managed an ordnance factory and Morrison had run the world's largest local authority and, according to his economic adviser, Max Nicholson, 'had deep-down . . . a hankering to be a sort of civil service permanent secretary'.[143] None the less, several officials felt a sustained lack of guidance on many economic matters, large or small.

This could be as much a frustration to a 'thermostatter' like Cairncross (who concluded that 'the economic problems encountered by the Government were not, as a rule, those which it had expected. Equally, the solutions to the problems were rarely of the Government's devising,'[144]) as to a 'Gosplanner' such as Clarke who put this illuminating piece of cathartic writing into his diary in the opening days of 1946:

> Cotton bulk purchasing meeting . . . This is the height of rule by officials. Ministers have demanded a report on bulk purchase. Here we are at the nub of socialism; the decision whether imports are bulk purchased or whether the futures markets are restored is crucial; it really makes a difference in a fundamental sense, unlike nationalisation of the Bank of England or transport. But ministers have no policy and ask officials to produce one for them.[145]

Thanks to yet another irony of institution building, the Government only got round to creating a formal apparatus for economic planning when it recruited Sir Edwin Plowden (as he then was) to Whitehall to preside over a Central Economic Planning Staff and to chair an Economic Planning Board made up of Whitehall, industry and trade union representatives, a few months before the financial crisis of 1947 changed the leading ministerial personalities in the economic departments and, to a significant extent, the policy as well.

It still baffles me that such a natural organisation man – or staff officer as I suspect he would have put it – as Clem Attlee could allow such a chaotic structure of decision-taking to continue until severe trouble obliged him to rethink. It may well have been yet another legacy of wartime Whitehall simply running on, which split economic policy-making between the Board of Trade (industry/regions), the Treasury (finance), the Ministry of Labour (manpower budgeting of still the crucial resource) and the Ministry of Supply (raw materials). Also there was one set of economic thinkers in the Cabinet Office under Meade and another in the Lord President's Office under Nicholson with the hapless Morrison, Chairman of the Lord President's Committee, charged with co-ordinating the whole lot into coherence. The entire problem, it could be argued, was compounded in 1945–6 by a reluctance to concentrate on the key economic factors like overseas financial policy, once the American Loan was in the bag, and growing fuel shortages.

Yet, the British economy did well in 1946 – despite the confusion in what should have been the command posts of the siege economy. Exports boomed – up to 111 per cent of the 1938 total while imports remained at wartime levels (some 70 per cent of prewar totals) thanks to tight rationing and the general shortage of consumer goods even for those who had the money to purchase them. Despite the rapid pace of demobilisation there was work for all. It was not back to the Thirties even in the most forsaken locations of the economy. Dalton, hubristic as ever, told the Commons in November 1946 the export drive had 'succeeded beyond expectation and beyond estimate'[146] (although it was true enough, the balance of payments deficit was £344 million, half of the Treasury's estimate when negotiating the US Loan).[147] Giving even greater hostages to fortune in a speech the month before, the crooner-at-the-Exchequer had said: 'I have been able, as Chancellor, to meet all the demands on the public purse literally with a song in my heart. If we keep going together as we have since V-J Day, the shortages and frustrations which still afflict us will disappear like the snows of winter, and give place to the full promise of springtime.'[148]

There were those close to power, such as Douglas Jay (now a Downing Street economic adviser) who thought that if snow came, we could freeze thanks to the absurd over-optimism of Shinwell at the Ministry of Fuel and Power. In June 1946, Jay warned Attlee that falling coal stocks could be reduced 'to the impossible level of 3,000,000 or 4,000,000 tons by next spring. This clearly means uncontrollable dislocation before then. This easily predictable and avoidable disaster is likely to occur at exactly the moment when the National Coal Board takes over the first great nationalised industry in this country.'[149] He was only a month out in this forecast.

Equally, Jay put the welcome export boom (the product of a country and a world rebuilding and restocking after the war providing full order books to one of the few stable, up-and-running economies in Europe) into perspective when he minuted Attlee in April 1946 in what was, at the time, regarded as an optimistic fashion, that 'by [July 1947] as present prospects our exports should be paying for all our foreign commitments'.[150] Here in a nutshell, was the bind of a great power in trouble: without its colonial possessions and the trading and financial networks which went with them, it was a mere European power of the kind it had not been since the sixteenth century. Yet the economic and industrial horsepower which had driven the bounds of Britain and Europe to the corners of the globe was much diminished. To make matters worse, the exigencies of war had obliged the UK Government to run up huge debts in its dependent possessions (over £1 billion in India alone, £356 million in Egypt and the Sudan, £122 million in Australia) – the so-called 'sterling balances' totalling £2.39 billion according to Keynes' estimate when the European war ended.[151] Could the imperial position be restored without jeopardising domestic recovery and Britain's long-term performance as a trader and manufacturer?

Few, very few, were aware of this imperial bind when the British Empire emerged victorious in 1945. It simply could not be back to business-as-usual but, the anti-Colonial Left excepted, everyone who thought or cared about such matters believed it would be, India (always a special case) apart. It is to this extraordinary, much debated, multi-faceted phenomenon – the tangible expression of British superpowerdom – that we must now turn.

CHAPTER 6

Jewels from the Crown

As long as we rule India we are the greatest power in the world. If we lose it we shall drop straightaway to a third-rate power.
Lord Curzon, 1901[1]

He took it without a murmur. You can't imagine old Queen Victoria sacrificing the Imperial Crown without a struggle, not a bit of it. But George VI didn't mind at all.
Lord Attlee, 1965[2]

'Do you mean that, after beating the Germans and the Japs, you are going to be chased out of India by Hindu lawyers?'
North-west Frontier tribesman to officer of the Frontier Scouts, 1947[3]

Britain's decision to quit India was not intended to mark the end of empire. Quitting India has to be seen in the light of the simultaneous decision to push British penetration deeper into tropical Africa and the Middle East . . . so the same Labour Government which had liquidated most of British Asia went on to animate part of British Africa. Africa would be a surrogate for India, more docile, more malleable, more pious . . . No one really knew what geological jackpots Africa contained, because general neglect had skimped the necessary surveys. Here might be God's Plenty which would rescue the Pilgrim British economy from the Slough of Despond.
Professor John Gallagher, 1974[4]

I do remember him [Arthur Creech Jones, Colonial Secretary] on one occasion coming back from the Cabinet . . . and he shook his head and said 'The Foreign Secretary (who was Ernest Bevin) thinks you develop Africa by putting Africans in lorries and letting them drive into the bush.'
Sir Leslie Monson, former Colonial Office official, 1988[5]

While the British party was alone and discussing rearmament prior to attending some meeting [in Washington in December 1950], Attlee turned

to Slim [Chief of the Imperial General Staff] and asked how long it would take him to create from the African colonies an army comparable in size and quality with the Indian Army, an army which we could use to support our foreign policy just as the Indian Army had done. Slim, who had spent his life in the Indian Army, said he could do something in eight or ten years, but to do anything really worthwhile would take at least twenty or probably more.
Lord Plowden, 1989[6]

Putting a date to the end of the British Empire is the ultimate 'trivial pursuit' of the historical profession. For some the Boer War, when a small group of expatriate Dutch farmers organised in guerrilla bands, drove the cream of the British Army to distraction in South Africa for three years at the turn of the nineteenth and twentieth centuries, is the moment when our 'imperial over-stretch' became plain for all to see.[7]

For me the turning-point is a richly ludicrous episode in the history of Empire which took place on the roof of the world three years after an accommodation had been reached in South Africa. For no real reason at all, Sir Francis Younghusband, mystic, explorer and 'prominent player of the Great Game'[8] of Empire, set off from India to pacify Tibet and to keep it out of Russian hands in the teeth of disapproval from London. As the expedition approached Lhasa, the Dalai Lama fled. That incomparable miniaturist of the imperial scene, James Morris, takes up the story:

> For several weeks nothing much happened. The Dalai Lama was well on his way to Outer Mongolia, and the National Assembly of senior lamas was frightened to reach decisions without him. The British set up their main camp outside the gates of the city, and soon erected the familiar parapher-nalia of Empire. The flag flew, the bugles sounded. Servants polished officers' boots in the sunshine, grooms combed ponies' manes, troops drilled on the dusty parade-ground, the gunners greased their beloved guns, whitewash and regimental crests blossomed on the scree. They organized gymkhanas, race meetings and football matches . . .[9]

At last the lamas caved in and agreed to receive Younghusband. In full fig, with escort party dressed to match, he rode across Lhasa to the foot of the vast Potala Palace with its steep stone ramps which the horses could not manage. The pro-consul dismounted as did his companions. Within seconds the British Empire overstretched itself in an unforgettable spectacle symbolic of internal collapse:

> For the cobbles of the causeway were so slippery that in their nailed boots they could hardly get up it. They were like men bewitched in a fairy tale. Slithering all over the place, their plumes erratically waving, their Sam Brownes and decorations pushed awry, the representatives of advanced

civilization clambered farcically up the hill of bigotry, to disappear at last, panting with the altitude and hastily straightening their accoutrements, into the dim and dirty corridors of the palace . . .[10]

Tea was drunk. Dried fruit nibbled. The Tibetans sternly lectured. The lamas managed to keep straight faces, but not for long.

As the departing officers scrabbled and slid away down the ramp, almost convulsed themselves with the ridiculousness of it, they heard guffaws and high-pitched laughter somewhere above them, and looking up to the great face of the palace-monastery, saw the monks of the Potala, high on their serried terraces, merrily observing their predicament.[11]

Never has there been a better illustration of Lord Salisbury's view that too much time poring over maps drives men mad, or the old Premier's distrust of the top military and their Younghusband-like tendency to see threats where there were none. 'If these gentlemen had their way', he said, 'they would soon be asking me to defend the moon against a possible attack from Mars.'[12]

As with all territory-based empires – the Roman before it or the Soviet after – the British Empire carried on long after the fuse was lit under it by changing economic or military circumstances both within it and outside. The British Empire was always a bit of a myth in the sense that it was never anything other than overstretched – held together by a string of naval bases and coaling stations with small concentrations of British civil servants and military, in tenuous and spasmodic touch with Whitehall, administering and policing vast native populations. The myth of unchallengeability, resting very largely on the Royal Navy, was preserved for a remarkably long time. Not until 1942, when both symbol and territory fell to the Japanese in the Far East, was the myth punctured as W.R. Louis, an imperial analyst of the tough American school, put it when he said, 'The sinking of the *Prince of Wales* and *Repulse* together with the fall of Singapore brought an end to the illusion of both the power and prestige of the British Empire in the Far East.'[13]

Two things held Britain's extraordinary imperial enterprise together – will-power and firepower. The firepower was of two kinds; the heavy guns of the Royal Navy and the small arms of British troops in India and the colonies. The loss of the two great capital ships in 1942 changed the world's and Britain's perception of the former. The waning of the latter was less obvious, more gradual. But there was no question that it happened and that it was crucial to the end of Empire.

I shall never forget the conversation between old Empire hands on a winter's morning in London in December 1988 when the seminar discussion got round to the inescapable realities of power. There they sat, men in their seventies and eighties, wearing the tweeds and the Savile Row of a past generation in the Menzies Room of London University's Institute of Commonwealth History, the last of an extraordinary breed.

'You can rule by force or by consent,' said Sir John Johnston, 'and consent can be pretty attenuated. But once consent is withdrawn, you can't rule by force in the middle of the twentieth century, you've got to hand over.' 'There was', added Sir Leslie Monson, 'the great remark of Paul Marc Henri of the French Colonial Service: "You either shoot or you get out."'[14]

The turning-point, in Sir John's and Sir Leslie's terms was rather earlier than the mid-twentieth century, on 13 April 1919 to be precise at a time when, thanks to victory in the Great War, the territorial expression of British power was at its zenith. The place was Amritsar, the Sikhs' holy city in the Punjab. Trevor Royle, historian of 'the last days of the Raj', sets the scene:

> After the First World War there was unrest in many parts of India, particularly in the Punjab which had supplied most of the men for India's war effort. Amritsar . . . had been the centre of much of the agitation and after an English lady missionary doctor had been assaulted by a mob the Governor-General, Sir Michael O'Dwyer, decided to use force. His agent was Brigadier-General Reginald Dyer, a dyspeptic dug-out of the old school who arrived in the city with military reinforcements.[15]

Dyer began a process which was to win him the kind of unwanted immortality he shares with Captain Boycott or Vidkun Quisling. His first response was to ban political meetings,

> a decision that was bound to bring him into confrontation with the local Sikh community. On Sunday 13 April 1919, in defiance of those orders, a large meeting took place on the Jallianwala Bagh and Dyer decided that he had no alternative but to respond with force. Without giving any warning to the crowd his men moved into position and opened fire. The official death toll in the Jallianwala Bagh was put at 379 but was probably higher as the Gurkha riflemen fired 1,650 rounds of ball ammunition in an enclosed space. The following day Dyer introduced a series of demeaning punishments – Indians passing the scene of the assault on the doctor were forced to crawl on all fours . . .[16]

There was, quite rightly, an outcry in India and Britain. The Government ordered an inquiry, Dyer was dismissed (though the readers of the Conservative *Morning Post* were persuaded to part with £25,000 as a retirement gift for him). Matters were never the same again within the independence-seeking Congress Party, the Viceroy's Lodge in Delhi or the India Office in London. It was plain to all that, unlike the aftermath of the Indian Mutiny in 1857, the country could not be held by firepower alone. The road to accommodation through dialogue – and to eventual independence for the sub-continent – was trodden from that moment on. Ironically, Dyer's Gurkhas had fired the starting gun for British withdrawal and, if Curzon was to be believed, the home country's descent to third-class status.

Again, as with the Correlli Barnett school of irresistible economic decline, the perils of retrospective determinism are apparent at this point. Nobody in authority sat down in 1919 and said quietly to themselves, 'Let's face it, Kipling's "Great Game" is up. Now is the time to start the process of graceful withdrawal.' It's not just the Barnetts who have been prone to hindsightedness. A different sort of Englishman – often with a touch of the 'New Jerusalems' which so enrages the auditor of war – became in the 1960s and 1970s rather prone to depicting the withdrawal from Empire as a particularly graceful and skilful British triumph. I can recall a conversation as late as 1989 with one of the Queen's closest advisers in the postwar period in which he said, 'The Commonwealth is the most civilised method yet devised for the dismembering of an Empire.'[17]

There is much in this view. But the Commonwealth idea was invented originally as a way of sustaining British imperial power – letting the white 'dominions' of Canada, South Africa, Australia and New Zealand move to a position of self-government while remaining part of the military and economic networks of Empire.[18] Once invented, however, it became an immensely useful instrument when the lowering of the Union Jack became a routine ritual in all corners of the former empire. As Patrick Gordon Walker put it, 'There could have been no Commonwealth had there not been a British Empire. Equally there could have been no Commonwealth but for the negation, withdrawal and transformation of British imperialism. The evolution of the Empire into the Commonwealth came about because British imperial rule increasingly assumed such a nature that it could fulfil itself only by annulling itself. Otherwise the normal historical process of imperial disintegration would have taken place: instead of being a Commonwealth, the Empire would have extinguished itself in a trail of Americas, followed by a trail of Burmas.'[19] (Burma after 1947 retreated into the isolation of a siege economy outside the Commonwealth.)

India was always a special case because of its size and its role as provider of *the* army of Empire. It should be remembered as the sword as much as the jewel in the crown. Unsurprisingly, therefore, its path to independence was special too. From the 1920s, the only question – despite the efforts of Churchill and a smattering of other Parliamentary die-hards – was when independence would come and in what form? The most likely possibility was as a brown version of the white dominions, a process recognised and begun by the 1935 Government of India Act. Whether without the Second World War it could eventually have been achieved without partition and massacre is an unanswerable question. War, in this instance, both speeded up and complicated the historical process.

As premier, Churchill managed to face both ways. It was quite plain from the time of the Cripps Mission in the spring of 1942 that India would be independent fairly swiftly after the war (an offer Gandhi famously dismissed as a post-dated cheque offered by a failing bank). Yet the Prime Minister the following November could tell the Lord Mayor of London's Luncheon at the

Mansion House that 'We mean to hold our own. I have not become the King's First Minister in order to preside over the liquidation of the British Empire.'[20]

The Cripps initiative was a response, not just to the need to keep India relatively quiet for the duration of the war, but to pressures within the Coalition, not least from the Deputy Prime Minister, Attlee, who was something of an India-hand having served on the Simon Commission to the sub-continent in the late 1920s.[21] Generously enough, Attlee was to say later that 'It was greatly to the credit of Winston that he accepted that, when he didn't like the idea of any change in India really. The idea was to set up a great constitution-making body immediately after the war with a firm promise of Dominion status . . . Cripps did as good a job as any man could possibly have done and there seemed a real chance that Nehru would co-operate. But Gandhi turned difficult.'[22]

Yet nobody in the War Cabinet had the slightest notion that the juggernaut of postwar nationalism would flatten the British Empire *everywhere* within most of their lifetimes, Churchill's and Attlee's included. Eight days after his Mansion House speech Churchill told his colleagues that given American criticism of Britain's colonial policy (a phenomenon which affected much of that country from President Roosevelt down) 'it might be a good plan that a full statement should be drawn up for publication on the development of the British Colonial Empire, vindicating our past and present policy, and indicating the probable trends of future policy'.[23]

To return to those key sustainers of Empire, firepower and the phenomenon Max Beloff described as mattering most in imperial history – 'the will to Empire, or the lack of it'[24] – both were waning south of the Himalayas. But in Africa, the Far East and the Caribbean they were most certainly not. Once Hitler, Hirohito and Mussolini had been taken care of, the idea was that imperial life should be business as usual or, to be precise, even more business as usual. For at the moment of its greatest peril, the British Government had taken on board the idea of positively developing its tropical empire with the passage of the Colonial Welfare and Development Act.

It should not be thought that this was the result of any rational cost-benefit analysis of Empire. That had to wait until almost the last hours of colonial rule during Harold Macmillan's premiership seventeen years later.[25] It arose from squalor and neglect in the British West Indies and the collapse of sugar prices in the interwar period which led to a series of riots in the 1930s in what one commission of inquiry called 'the slums of the empire'.[26] The initial sum available, £5 million a year, was tiny, but it was to be built on substantially as the Forties progressed and ministers, Labour ones especially, came to regard the colonies as the source of 'geological jackpots' in Jack Gallagher's words, or, as in Bevin's case, developed the hallucinatory view that 'if only we pushed on and developed Africa, we could have the United States dependent on us, and eating out of our hand in four or five years . . . [as] . . . the United States is very barren of essential minerals, and in Africa we have them all'.[27] It was this kind of thinking which led to the ill-starred attempt to grow peanuts in the Tanganyika bush – the notorious 'Ground Nuts Scheme'.

In 1941 the Government had been advised by Lord Hailey that African politics were quiescent with little sign of discontent apart from pockets in the Gold Coast (Ghana after independence in 1957) and southern Nigeria.[28] The War Cabinet's collective view is neatly summed up by the minutes of one of its committees from May 1943: 'Many parts of the Colonial Empire are still so little removed from their primitive state that it must be a matter of many generations before they are ready for anything like full self-government. There are other parts inhabited by people of two or more different races, and it is impossible to say how long it will take to weld together these so-called plural communities into an entity capable of exercising self-government.'[29]

Naturally, there were some – a tiny few – who actually saw the writing on the wall in the mid-1940s. There were many more, especially in the Labour Party (the Fabian Society set up its Colonial Research Bureau in 1940 with Arthur Creech Jones as its Chairman and Rita Hinden as its Secretary), who *wanted* the writing to appear on the wall, which is a very different thing from detecting its faint outline.

Keynes, for example, posed some hard questions about the economic value of Empire in his celebrated paper on overseas financial policy prepared for the Cabinet in the last days of the European war. 'Our financial embarrassments', he wrote,

have been, and still are, and look like being even after the war, mainly the result of the cash expenditure of the Service (i.e. military) Departments in Africa, the Middle East, India and the Southern Dominions . . . there remains a vast cash expenditure overseas – local expenditure incurred on the spot . . . which is poured out, not only with no effective Treasury control, but without the Treasury knowing either beforehand or afterwards, what it has been spent upon . . .

I am chiefly alarmed by the apparent prospect (if nothing is done about it) of the appalling rate at which this expenditure will be running on the day at which the final Cease-Fire in Asia brings with it the end of American lend-lease and Canadian Mutual Aid . . . When we had thrown the Germans out of Africa, and the Middle East was no longer in danger, our expenditure in those parts remained much as before. The Major-Generals in Cairo look like becoming chronic . . . the *prima facie* evidence of the global statistics is that unless it is advisable and practicable to bring this expenditure under drastic control at an early date (and perhaps it is not), our ability to pursue an independent financial policy in the early post-war years will be fatally impaired.[30]

Keynes, flying at full intellectual horsepower, concluded that:

At the very best, even assuming a fabulous improvement in the above weak spots (including financial arrangements within the sterling area), we should do well to assume that complete financial independence of the United States would require:–

(a) the continuance of war rationing and war controls *more* stringent than at present for (say) three to five years after the war;

(b) the national planning and direction of foreign trade both imports and exports, somewhat on the Russian model; and

(c) an indefinite postponement of Colonial Development and Far Eastern rehabilitation and a virtual abandonment of all overseas activities, whether military or diplomatic or by way of developing our trade, wealth and influence, which involved any considerable expenditure.[31]

How much of an impact this, India apart, had on the imperial mind-sets of those to whom it was directed is a moot point.

The Colonial Office was not used to such sophisticated, iconoclastic economic analysis. Though in 1943, it recruited an economist from the Ministry of Food, the LSE-trained Aaron Emanuel, to help with postwar economic planning for the Empire, a move that Mr Emanuel believes probably increased the number of economists in Dover House, which then accommodated the CO, by 50 per cent (the other was the man who recruited him, Sydney Caine).[32] 'It was an innovation,' he told me nearly fifty years later. 'Certainly there was a dichotomy at the time between those who had to deal with economic matters and those who knew anything about economics.'[33]

When he joined the Colonial Office, a mere two decades before the Empire and, shortly thereafter, the CO itself disappeared, Aaron Emanuel was not given the impression that it was his job to plan the sprucing up one last time of an institution about to be put on the international market or, to be more accurate, subject to a buy-out by its workforce. Quite the reverse. 'We were planning', he recalled,

> things like the reoccupation of Malaya and Hong Kong and we were also planning the economic development of the West Indies and how to use the welfare money which we couldn't use effectively during the war . . . I think one might have expected, if there had been any clear-cut policy towards independence of any of the colonies, that it might have seeped down that we shouldn't take too long-term a view. Whereas everything that I was instructed to do and did of my own volition was concerned with putting the colonial territories on a much better economic footing without any expectation that that wouldn't last for a very long time, so long that we didn't occupy our minds . . . with the forthcoming demise of the colonial empire.[34]

In the mid-1940s there were one or two Empire-hands whose minds were so occupied, but they were extreme rarities. Among them was John Bennett, a

Cambridge historian who joined the Colonial Office in 1936, served in the Middle East during the war and returned to the CO as an assistant secretary after it.

Mr Bennett emphasises, rightly, the need to treat with care successive phases through which Colonial Office thinking passed in the late 1940s and always to separate in-house thought from that of the politicians or the public at large. At the 1988 seminar of Colonial Office veterans and scholars of the end of the Empire he said, 'You historians have to distinguish between the immediate postwar – up to 1948 – and the subsequent phase.

> It's very easy, especially in retrospect, to run the two together. Now, I saw it, both as a citizen and an official in the period up to 1948 or, indeed, a little longer. The general assumption was that we were still a great power and were going to be one again.
>
> I didn't believe that myself. But the general assumption in the Office . . . was that our intentions were splendid . . . that we had control of the time-table, that history would march according to what we thought, that we had the time and the power and the resources to do all this splendid development. That, as I remember saying in a paper I wrote in 1947, is unlikely to be true and, therefore, we must get out quick everywhere . . . But I don't think that was the general realisation in the country at large, and whatever political party happened to be in power, was in sympathy with that view until the 1950s and really not until after Suez.[35]

The evidence supports John Bennett's contention – and Jack Gallagher's. The appetite for Empire, albeit a modified one with less stress on firepower and more on welfare-cum-economic development, continued to excite the 'official mind', especially when it turned to Africa.

Take two key indicators of bureaucratic intent – people and buildings. The Colonial Office after the war was thinking big about both. The key individual in terms of recruitment for nearly forty years (1910 to 1948) was one of the Colonial Secretary's private secretaries, Major Sir Ralph Furse. He brought the same approach (and the same attire) to the job through the reigns of four King-Emperors and no fewer than twenty-two Colonial Secretaries. 'His only absence', Colin Cross wrote of Furse,

> was during his military service in the 1914 war when there was practically no recruitment anyway. At the end of his career in 1948 he still on occasion wore the same suit of brown West of England tweed in which he had arrived at the Colonial Office in 1910. He had been to Eton and to Balliol College, Oxford, where he had obtained a third-class degree in 'Greats'. In choosing staff he admitted to a weakness in sympathising with others who had got thirds.[36]

His methods of selection, at least until a Colonial Service proper was created in 1930 with a Personnel Division in the CO to run it, were singular in the extreme, eclipsed only by Sir Mansfield Cumming, navy man and first head of the Secret Intelligence Service, MI6, who would test the mettle of the would-be recruit by pulling up his trouser leg, striking a match on his wooden stump (the real thing had been lost in a motoring accident) and lighting his pipe with it. If the young man from Oxford or Cambridge so much as hesitated in the account of his prowess on the river or the cricket pitch while this performance was in progress, he was out.[37]

Furse, unlike 'C' (as Cumming and every MI6 chief after him was known) did not fly solo when interviewing. As he was a bit deaf he placed great emphasis on the appearance a candidate gave.

> In the 1920s Furse and his assistants worked together in a big room next to that of the Secretary of State. Their desks were far enough apart for them all to be able to conduct interviews at the same time; out of the corners of their eyes they looked at each other's candidates. Furse found this a sound arrangement. 'Interviewing boards normally sit on one side of a table, with their victim on the other,' he wrote. 'For instance, a man's face may not reveal that he is intensely nervous. But a twitching foot, or hands tightly clenched under the table, will tell you this, and you can make the necessary allowances and deductions.'[38]

Colin Cross was exaggerating when he said of Furse, 'He had been possibly the most influential British civil servant of his generation.'[39] He simply cannot be compared to Maurice Hankey, the first Cabinet Secretary, Edward Bridges, the second, or Warren Fisher who headed the Treasury from 1919 to 1939.[40]

But Cross captured his true importance when he wrote: 'By the time of his departure it could be reckoned that almost every senior administrator in almost every British colony had originally been recruited by him. His standards had been those of the British public school. What neither he nor anyone else had foreseen was that his postwar generation would find their most crucial function not in routine administration but in handing over power to new masters.'[41]

In fact, Furse and his fellow observers of twitching feet could have been forgiven for thinking after the war that their young men were about to take the Colonial Empire to new heights. For a start, an ever greater stream of them passed through the selection boards and on to the Empire Flying Boats which continued to carry them from Southampton Water to, in W.S. Gilbert's words, 'wherever country's banner may be planted'.[42]

In the interwar period, Colonial Service recruits had varied from 551 in 1919 to 70 in 1932. In the first five years after the war the numbers sent out to the colonies were 1,715, 806, 957, 1,341 and 1,510. And they went not just as district commissioners in the field, but as members of increasingly sophisticated administrative machines. 'The appointment of more and more technical specialists accounted for part of the increase but the major factor was a trebling in general administrators. Areas once controlled by a single district commissioner were now split up into fractions, each under its own commissioner. In the colonial capitals the old "secretariats" were split up into separate government departments on the pattern of a European state.'[43]

A peculiar fate awaited the young men sent forth in the 1940s. I can recall one of them, Mike Power, who came back from Kenya in 1963 to join the Admiralty, telling me in the early 1980s that I really ought to read James Morris's trilogy on Empire, especially the last volume, *Farewell the Trumpets*, as it was truly brilliant (he's right; it is). For example, said Mr Power, Morris's description of the unease experienced by the colonial servant each time he returned on home leave to find an ever stranger England, was *exactly* how it was.

Here it is, neat and unadorned.

Let us then, since it is almost our last chance, take a walk through Westminster, one morning in the later 1950s, in search of homo imperialis. It is a relatively prosperous moment of British post-war history, the nation standing for the moment between economic crises, and the civil servants hastening from the St James' tube station look, for the most part, well-dressed, well-fed, ordinary kind of people – not so very different from Belgians, say, or Norwegians. Up on the morning train from Beckenham or Guildford, they are settled into the mould of western urban man, and want nothing much more than a quiet life, a television set and an annual holiday, with pension rights assured. Among them, it is true, are more colourful figures to remind us, even now, that London is a world capital – black men in white robes and curious hats, an Arab or two, Malay or Chinese, a few huddled Indians: but then in a world now encircled by the jets one may just as easily meet a sheikh in Zurich, a Jamaican waiter in Manhattan or a Nigerian doctor completing his training in Dusseldorf. It is a cosmopolitan crowd, but in the middle of the middle of the twentieth century any great city is cosmopolitan, and London looks scarcely more imperial than Stockholm.

But there, look, swinging briskly around the corner from the Abbey, courteously stepping into the gutter to overtake the pavement secretaries, oblivious it seems to the curses of taxi-drivers – there is a figure you will not find in Copenhagen! He is not a young man now, in his fifties perhaps, and he is slightly stooped, as though a succession of fevers has warped his spine. But he is slim, stringy, rather rangy, and his face is so heavily tanned, not simply a sunburn but a deep, ingrained tincture of brown, that physically he scarcely looks like an Englishman at all. Yet British he unquestionably is, the most British man in sight, his expression, his movement, his every gesture reflecting a Britishness that has almost vanished from England. Even his clothes are yesterday's. He wears a brown floppy trilby hat, looking as though it has been repeatedly soaked in rainstorms and dried in the sun, and slightly scuffed suede shoes. His overcoat looks like a reconstituted British warm. Tucked under his arm to read in the bus (for one suspects he seldom uses the underground, disliking the fog down there), he carries a book from Harrod's library – General Slim's new volume of memoirs, perhaps, or Alan Moorehead's *The White Nile* – he doesn't go in for fiction much. On his finger he wears a signet ring, and as he swings his arm one can just see, beneath the sleeve of his tweed sports coat, the glint of oval cuff-links. He wears braces, one wouldn't wonder.

Is there something wistful to his worn if still agile figure? There is. He looks out of touch, out of time. He meets nobody he knows, for he has few friends in London now; even at the Office it's all new faces, and he's never bothered with any of those damned clubs. He averts his eye from the passing crowd, for to be honest he doesn't much like the style of Londoners these days. He is not much looking forward to his interview with Sir What's It, who doesn't know a bloody thing about Totseland anyway. He doesn't like the climate. He doesn't like the traffic. He detests what they've done to the South Bank. The young men need a haircut. That play at the Royal Court was a load of old rubbish.

He is a foreigner in his own capital. He is a true exotic among the cosmopolitans. He is the last of the British Empire-builders, home on leave and hating it.[44]

Mike Power, though younger than Morris's paradigm, was just like that. He couldn't wait to get back to his district in East Africa.

The British Empire expanded at home as well as in the field. In 1939 the CO's staff complement in London was 465. By 1950 it had almost trebled to 1,289.[45] New premises had to be found for them in Church House, just behind Westminster Abbey, a fine brick building leased from the Church Commissioners as a temporary measure until an imposing new Colonial Office was built on the bomb site bounded by Storey's Gate, Victoria Street and Parliament Square, the place occupied today by the Queen Elizabeth II Conference Centre where heads of Government meet when it's Britain's turn to chair an economic summit or a European Community meeting of a certain grandeur.

On one level, the plan was reasonable enough. The Colonial Welfare and Development Act with its later accretions had changed the nature of the bureaucratic beast. Sir Duncan Watson, Creech Jones' Private Secretary, reckons that 'After the war the Colonial Welfare and Development Act was an absolute turning-point . . . It made possible the working out of originally 10 year [then reduced to five] comprehensive development plans for each area which were exhaustively looked through and argued out with each [colonial] government and then went to the Treasury.'[46]

Its future Permanent Secretary, Sir Hilton Poynton (who, in fact, wound the CO up in 1966), described the postwar Colonial Office, with some justification, as a 'miniature Civil Service in itself . . . which had responsibilities for every gamut of public administration'.[47] As a result, it had its own singular style, a special *esprit de corps* that, in the mid-1940s at least, had nothing of the undertaker about it. As Sir Jack Johnston put it long after the trumpets had sounded their last farewell, 'Coming in in 1947 I certainly had no sense of the Colonial Office being in any way under oppression or pressure from any department . . . We fought them all . . . We had a sense of being something very different because, when everybody else was chasing tea-leaves, in the Colonial Office you dealt with every aspect of government, no matter what it was, all over the world. It was the most marvellous job. We felt ourselves as a band of brothers.'[48]

This was not a feeling shared by the rest of Whitehall nor, more importantly, in No. 10 Downing Street at various stages during the long march away from Empire. A file only declassified in 1990 shows No. 10's interest in the running story of the new Colonial Office, the building-that-never-was.[49] Churchill for one took a great deal of persuading that the new development and welfare responsibilities of the CO necessitated a trebling of its staff.[50] It was to be an imposing affair providing 'about 138,000 square feet of accommodation, a Citadel to protect Colonial Office communications and essential staff in war, a library, hall, garage and storage space'.[51]

But for the economic recession in 1949 (which put pressure on sterling and precipitated the devaluation of the pound) the foundations of the new office would have been well and truly laid by the time Churchill returned to Downing Street in October 1951.[52] In 1948, a glance at the Storey's Gate bomb site stimulated two thoughts in Sir Jack Johnston's mind – 'For Pete's sake to get them to put some squash courts in the basement . . . And only about that time, I think, did it start dawning that perhaps this wasn't the time to build a new Colonial Office.'[53]

Sir Jack can be forgiven for not foreseeing the rush to decolonise between 1957 and 1965. For Palestine apart, the Colonial Office was not in the disposal business in the late 1940s. The India Office, however, had by this stage come to exist for no other purpose.

Folk memory of the great imperial withdrawal coalesces around four phases – America in the 1770s, Ireland in the 1920s, India in the 1940s, Africa and the Far East in the 1960s. In fact it was not the 'Great Dependency', as India was known, which set the pace in the mid-1940s (though naturally it overshadowed everything). It was Burma which, on the recommendation of the Simon Commission, had been spun off from the Indian Empire in 1935. Its fate in the immediate postwar years had a special importance for Attlee, always very much in the lead in the affairs of the sub-continent.

As his official biographer puts it:

Attlee's policy in Burma was important not only for its effect on Burma but because it became a model for policies elsewhere, including India. Burma was the first former colony to be liberated from the Japanese, and the first to be given its independence. In the process Attlee learned lessons – including those from his mistakes – which he applied in other countries. In particular, he came to prefer Mountbatten's judgment about Asian nationalism, and his ability to manage it, to that of the . . . experts. The path along which Mountbatten advanced to become Viceroy of India in 1947 began in Rangoon two years previously.[54]

Mountbatten, the dominant politico-military figure in Britain's south-east Asian territories as the war drew to a close, took the breath away from the colonial administrators with whom he dealt. With reason, for not only did he actively favour indigenous nationalism, he had no intention of handing liberated land back 'to a handful of landowners and . . . industrialists'.[55] He was also in the habit of informing visiting Labour ministers that he was a socialist just like them.[56]

In the Burmese context, Mountbatten found himself at loggerheads with the Governor, Sir Reginald Dorman-Smith, a former minister in the Chamberlain Government, over whom to back once the Japanese were driven out. Mountbatten's choice was Aung San, the former student leader whose anti-colonialism had led him first to fight alongside the Japanese before his anti-fascism persuaded him to lead the local resistance to the Japanese and to switch sides to the Allies. Dorman-Smith (and Churchill) thought him little better than a collaborator and favoured political elements who had been loyal to the British throughout.

For the first ten months of the new Government Labour ministers vacillated before Attlee backed Mountbatten's judgment and replaced Dorman-Smith with a very surprised Brigadier Hubert Rance, Mountbatten's civil affairs officer. Aung San became minister of defence in the new Executive Council Rance set up in Rangoon to prepare the way for independence, but not before British hesitation had convinced him that the new Burma would exist outside the Commonwealth, something Attlee, a great Commonwealth man, always regretted, believing that had the Government 'been in touch with Aung San from the start' Burma would have stayed in.[57]

It was Attlee's announcement in the Commons in December 1946 that Aung San was coming to London for discussions that drew from Churchill a word that would ring down the decades of decolonisation from the lips of the die-hards. 'It was said', Churchill began,

> in the days of the great administrator, Lord Chatham, that you had to get up very early in the morning not to miss some great acquisition of territory which was then characteristic of our fortunes. The not less memorable administration of Mr Attlee is distinguished for the opposite set of experiences. The British Empire seems to be running off almost as fast as the American Loan. The steady and remorseless process of divesting ourselves of what has been gained by so many generations of toil, administration and

sacrifice, continues. In the case of Burma, it is hardly a year since by the superb exertions of the 14th Army and the enormous sacrifices of British and Indian blood, the Japanese were forced to surrender . . . and the country liberated. Yet there is this extraordinary haste . . . in order that we should take the necessary measures to get out of Burma finally and for ever . . . This haste is appalling. 'Scuttle' is the only word that can be applied.[58]

By the end of January 1947, an agreement was signed. The Burmese leaders, accompanied by the young junior minister at the Dominions Office, Arthur Bottomley (sent by Attlee to help sort out one of the remaining knotty problems – the incorporation of the frontier area peoples into the new nation), took off from Poole for the obligatory uncomfortable flying-boat trip home. Bottomley's ginger beer froze over France.[59]

In one of those revealing behind-the-scenes touches which were to illuminate the withdrawal from Empire, U Tin Tut, Aung San's adviser, sought the aid of a friend he had made through sporting contacts while at school in Dulwich. Through Arthur Bottomley he approached Sir Eric Machtig (who had been at St Paul's) for advice on how to write a constitution. Machtig just happened to be Permanent Secretary at the Dominions Office and was reluctant in case the still suspicious Burmese leadership heard about it and scented imperialist intrigue. Instead he gave Bottomley a copy of *Constitutions of All Countries* to pass on to U Tin Tut.[60]

In one of the less appealing touches that sometimes accompanied the turbulence of the independence process, Aung San and his Cabinet were assassinated in July 1947, three months before the transfer of power officially took place and six months before Burma formally withdrew from the Commonwealth at the end of a long-forgotten but, in its way, highly significant and (the Commonwealth aspect apart) prototypical imperial disposal.

It's difficult now to appreciate the magnitude of the Indian problem, which overshadowed all other imperial questions in 1945–8, as it confronted Attlee and his ministers. There was simply no precedent for the handover of a subcontinent. The American Colonies were tiny by comparison. What is more, they liberated themselves by force and were a fairly united society within their own borders. None of that was true of India.

After the failure of the Cripps mission in 1942, India was put on ice for three years by British politicians preoccupied by the war. Attlee chaired the Cabinet Committee on India but, like the rest of the War Cabinet, deferred to Churchill's strong antipathy towards independence.[61] Wavell, the Viceroy, sent to India in 1943 as a kind of job-creation-scheme when Churchill removed him from the command of British Forces in the Middle East, tried in vain to entice fresh instructions from his political chiefs in London.

Wavell, a quiet, scholarly, poetry-loving soldier remembered for his gem of an anthology, *Other Men's Flowers*,[62] was hopeless in dealing with politicians face-to-face. He was at his best on paper and tried to shift Churchill with a letter in October 1944 which contained an early (and non-Communist) version of the 'domino' theory: ' . . . the future of India', he wrote,

> is the problem on which the British Commonwealth and the British reputation will stand or fall in the post-war period . . . Our prestige and prospects in Burma, Malaya, China and the Far East generally are entirely subject to what happens in India. If we can secure India as a friendly partner in the British Commonwealth our predominant influence on these countries will, I think, be assured; with a lost and hostile India, we are likely to be reduced in the East to the position of commercial bag-men.[63]

Not until May 1945 was Wavell authorised to make a move towards Indian independence. He immediately released Nehru and the Congress Party leaders from jail where they had been incarcerated because of their opposition to the war. Instantly Wavell was overwhelmed by the tangle of religious animosities, territorial disputes and personal rivalries which punctuated the passage to independence. His idea for an executive council, consisting of equal proportions of Hindus and Muslims, meeting under his chairmanship to pave the path to self-government, foundered on the cold calculation of Mohammed Ali Jinnah and the Muslim League. The League's proclaimed policy was the creation of a separate PAKISTAN (the only nation to be built on an acronym: P for Punjab, A for Afghanistan, better known as the North-West Frontier, K for Kashmir, S for Sind and TAN for Baluchistan).

It was this problem to which two of the tidiest minds of twentieth-century British politics – Attlee and Cripps – applied themselves when the new Government's India and Burma Committee met for the first time on 17 August 1945. Lord Listowel, one of its members, recalls the India-effect on Attlee: ' . . . quite unlike his usual habit of listening and doodling while others talked, [he] became the dominant personality when India was on the agenda . . . [He] made it plain to us from the very start that our job was to replace British by Indian rule within the five-year lifetime of the Labour Government.'[64]

Stripped to its essentials, the aim of achieving Indian independence provided Attlee and his colleagues with four problems: carrying Parliamentary and public opinion with them at home in a nation not yet accustomed to disposing of its territorial assets nor yet aware of its diminished status as a world power; finding a solution that would hold over an area of 1,581,410 square miles occupied by a mixture of 255 million Hindus, 92 million Muslims, 6 million Indian Christians and 5.5 million Sikhs; finding it before what remained of British power was overwhelmed by (possibly violent) events; and finding it in such a way that the rest of the Empire could be insulated from its consequences.

Attlee had long believed in self-determination for India and the Labour Party enjoyed a close relationship with Congress politicians (Jinnah's people thought, with some reason, that Labour ministers were in the Congress's pocket). But underlying the sentiment was a calculation based on the realities of power. As the Military Secretary to the Cabinet, Lord Ismay, later put it, 'How could a Commissioner of a district the size of Wales maintain law and order, preside over the Law Courts, collect taxes and carry out the multifarious duties that fell to his lot, with the aid of a handful of assistants and a few score of Indian policemen, unless he enjoyed the goodwill of the masses? To have attempted to stay in India for a moment longer than the majority of the population desired would have broken us financially and militarily.'[65]

This, in varying degrees, was the calculation which lay behind the subsequent thirty-four-year withdrawal from Empire which began with Burma in 1946 and ended with Zimbabwe in 1980 (Hong Kong, Gibraltar and the Falklands were rather different special cases). And if any doubts remained inside the Attlee Government they were, Bevin apart, soon dispelled. First by the inability of the authorities in 1946 to carry through the trials of the leaders of the Indian National Army, who had collaborated with the Japanese (Wavell warned London it would be unwise to test further the willingness of the Indian Army 'in the suppression of their own people' after popular demonstrations in their favour[66]), and secondly by the wave of inter-communal massacres which began after Jinnah called his people to a 'day of action' on 16 August 1946 and which the Army were powerless to prevent. (Wavell visited Calcutta, scene of the worst massacres, and prepared a plan which he forwarded to Whitehall for a phased military withdrawal with or without a political solution.[67])

To his credit, Attlee strove hard to find a political solution. Despairing of Wavell's political capabilities, he despatched a 'Cabinet Mission' to India in February 1946 which arrived in March and stayed for seven weeks. It consisted of Cripps, A.V. Alexander, First Lord of the Admiralty ('affable, direct and a great man for singing at the piano'[68]) and the elderly, pro-Congress Lord Pethick-Lawrence, Secretary of State for India who, inevitably if cruelly, became known as 'pathetic Lawrence' among the sub-continent's political class.

Cripps took up where he had left off in 1942. The 'Mission' talked to 472 political figures. It endured Jinnah's lack of punctuality and Gandhi's quietude (on one occasion he passed them a note which read: 'Please go on. It is my day of silence.'[69]) They almost pulled it off. An ingenious solution, 'a kind of three-tier cake of a constitution' as Brian Lapping put it, was 'cooked up' in which 'the eleven provinces (the bottom tier) were to be allowed to form themselves into groups (the middle tier), thus enabling the Muslim provinces to club together into a kind of Pakistan-without-sovereignty. The all-India federal government (the top tier) would have responsibility for foreign policy, defence and communications.'[70]

Jinnah and Liaquat Ali Khan were at last persuaded. But Nehru and the Congress politicians raised a last minute quibble about the composition of the interim government. It really was a last chance lost. In India Jinnah resorted to the kind of direct action which triggered fifteen months of massacre and counter-massacre between Hindu, Muslim and Sikh in which up to a million died in unspeakable circumstances. In London Attlee decided on his own equivalent version of *force majeure*.

First, Wavell had to go. Attlee recoiled from his 'extraordinary' 'Breakdown Plan': 'They were going to move all the British out of India, up the line of the Ganges, and put them on ships in Bombay. Winston would have been right to call it "operation scuttle". Out of the question. Indians would have assumed the Raj was on the run.'[71] In early December Wavell travelled to London accompanied by Nehru (Jinnah refused to come). By the end of the month, following a meeting with the P.M. in No. 10 which Wavell described as 'disastrous' (Attlee would not contemplate the 'Breakdown' proposals), the King was informed that a new Viceroy would be needed as, in George VI's report of Attlee's view, 'he [Wavell] does not realise it is a political problem and not a military one'.[72]

The new man was to be the King's cousin, Mountbatten of Burma. As Attlee told his biographer:

We weren't getting anywhere. The only thing that was clear was that if we let the Congress have their way, the Muslims would start a war to get their Pakistan. Apart from that, nothing was in sight. Both parties were asking for everything and blaming us for not getting anything when they should have been blaming themselves. I decided there was only one thing to do – give them a deadline, and tell them 'on that date we go out. So you'd better get together right away'. It was the only thing that would bring them together. Next thing was to find the right man to carry out the new policy. Dickie Mountbatten stood out a mile. Burma showed it. To me, the so-called experts had been wrong about Aung San, and Dickie had been right.[73]

Two people with large egos – Ernest Bevin and Mountbatten himself – might have thwarted this classic and hugely significant example of Attleean decisiveness (when asked in old age what he would be remembered for, he would reply 'Don't know. If anything, India possibly.'[74]). Bevin, as Lord Listowel, Pethick-Lawrence's successor as India Secretary, put it, 'was at heart an old fashioned imperialist, keener to expand than contract the Empire'.[75]

As we have seen, Bevin could not bear the prospect of a 'scuttle' from India 'without dignity or plan'. On 1 January 1947 he wrote a private letter to Attlee on the only occasion when the two of them disagreed fundamentally on a major matter of policy. Whether he knew it or not, Bevin, in opposing Attlee's idea of fixing a deadline for the transfer of power, was echoing Curzon on India's indispensability to Britain's great power status:

. . . you cannot read the telegrams from Egypt and the Middle East nowadays without realising that not only is India going, but Malaya, Ceylon, and the Middle East is going with it, with a tremendous repercussion on the African territories . . . Why cannot we use the United States to put pressure on Nehru and Jinnah? . . . I would impress you with this fact. I can offer nothing to any foreign country, neither credit nor coal nor goods – I am expected to make bricks without straw. And on top of this, in the British Empire, we knuckle under at the first blow and we are expected to preserve the position. It cannot be done . . .[76]

Attlee made no attempt to appease his personal friend and political protector replying tartly the following day: 'You suggest that we are knuckling under at the first blow but this entirely ignores the history of the past 25 years . . . We are seeking to fulfil the pledges of this country with dignity and to avoid an ignominious scuttle. But a scuttle it will be if things are allowed to drift . . . If you disagree with what is proposed, you must offer a practical alternative. I fail to find one in your letter.'[77]

Mountbatten's ego drove him in the opposite direction. He insisted Attlee gave him unprecedented 'plenipotentiary powers' to take decisions on the spot in India or he would not go. Attlee, taking, in Lord Listowel's words, 'the greatest risk in his political life', agreed.[78] It was not the gigantic concession Mountbatten in later life would like to depict it. Attlee chose Mountbatten because they thought alike on the essentials of policy. The moment they ceased to, Mountbatten would have been on the plane home. Attlee had no doubts where crown servants sat in the constitutional firmament, however gilded their connections.

The Mountbattens in India is the stuff of which movies are made. From the moment they arrived in Delhi at the end of March 1947, he turned on his heady cataract of physical presence, personal charm and political radicalism. Edwina captivated all and sundry and, most important of all, Nehru in a web of intense personal intimacy which she would later describe to her husband as 'the strange relationship – most of it spiritual – that exists between us'.[79]

Events moved very fast. Within days Mountbatten cabled home reporting 'The only conclusion that I have been able to come to is that unless I act quickly I may well find the real beginnings of a civil war on my hands . . . I am convinced that a fairly quick decision would be the only way to convert the Indian minds from their present emotionalism to stark realism and to counter the disastrous spread of strife.'[80]

'Fairly quick' soon became dramatically fast. The timetable for independence swiftly shortened from mid-1948 to mid-August 1947 and its basis – inevitably by now – was partition into the two new nations, India and Pakistan, built on religious as well as nationalist lines. It was probably too much to expect that the twin motivaters of much of the world, God and country, could be kept separate south of the Himalayas.

Mountbatten, that genius at 'closing things down', 'pre-eminent *de*-imperialist' and first of a long line of 'morticians of empire' who saw their jobs as 'to pull down the flag and to hand over power with dignity and decency', as David Cannadine describes him,[81] caused immense adjustments on-the-spot and at home by his dash for independence. Even before he reached the Viceroy's House, the manner and purpose of his despatch had a profound effect on the geopolitics of the world. On 20 February 1947, when Attlee rose in the Commons to announce Mountbatten's departure and June 1948 as the deadline for independence, power shifted, not just between Whitehall and Delhi.

To some, its impact was total and devastating and remained so. Forty-two years later, Enoch Powell could describe the moment to me as if it had been yesterday. As a member of the Conservative Research Department he sat in the Parliamentary Gallery that day for Attlee's announcement. He left in a state of bewilderment: 'I walked the streets all that night. The world as I had known it was coming apart. Occasionally,' he told me in that apocalyptic voice of his, 'I sat down in a doorway, my head in my hands.'[82]

Once the deadline of 15 August was fixed, the race was on in Whitehall to draft the Indian Independence Bill. Attlee, delicately, had to seek Churchill's co-operation in getting it through Parliament in time. It was given with great reluctance. Thereafter, as Philip Noel-Baker, the Commonwealth Secretary, recalled, 'Anthony Eden's job was to keep Churchill away from the House while the Bill went through because if he came into the Chamber he might be unable to stop himself speaking against. One day he came in and I thought trouble was in store. But he just glared at me and went away.'[83]

The problems in London were as nothing to those in India. Everything had to be split and labelled into India and Pakistan pieces, even the office furniture of the legendary ICS, the Indian Civil Service. To the horror of Lord Auchinleck, the Commander-in-Chief of that military jewel in the Crown, the Indian Army, that, too, must be broken up. It had been kept carefully non-sectarian, the impartial instrument of authority when religious hatreds spilled into violence in village and city. Auchinleck had worked out a plan for 'nationalising' it as independence approached through the gradual withdrawal of British officers. Now at the very moment when it was most needed with intercommunal rioting becoming endemic in Bengal and the Punjab, its officers and men, too, had to decide on which side of the line their future loyalties lay.

The man with the most impossible job of all was the drawer of that line, Sir Cyril Radcliffe, lawyer, public administrator, high-minded Victorian and pillar of the Good and Great. He arrived in India in early July and had just over a month to make his recommendations (which all parties had agreed to accept) in the knowledge, as Mountbatten's biographer Philip Ziegler put it, 'that his [would be] a butcher's, not a surgeon's operation'.[84] 'It was a curious task,' wrote Brian Lapping:

Where thousands of British officers had tramped the hills and valleys of India, producing maps of the entire subcontinent, Sir Cyril sat in a house on the Viceregal estate, with little time to go out and tour Delhi and less to inspect the heavily populated areas whose borders he was defining. He had commissioners, mostly Indian high court judges, sitting simultaneously in

Calcutta and Lahore. As he could not sit with both groups he sat with neither. Instead he studied the written evidence submitted to them and the transcripts of the hearings.

The commissioners, selected from the rival communities, predictably disagreed. Therefore Radcliffe made the final awards himself, sitting alone in Delhi, poring over old maps and census data and the claims of residents. He had to decide whether the most populous city in the Empire, Calcutta, should go to India or Pakistan. The majority of the population were Hindu, but East Bengal's only source of foreign exchange was jute and all the mills that processed it were in Calcutta. Without the mills, the Muslims of East Bengal argued, they would be throttled, their territory left a 'rural slum'. Calcutta went to India.[85]

Radcliffe took thousands of decisions like that in the knowledge that pogrom lurked either side of almost every line he drew. His was one of the most robust minds I ever encountered. Yet, when I talked to him about India on a freezing January morning in his Warwickshire country house in 1976 not long before his death, Lord Radcliffe was clearly still haunted by events in Bengal and the Punjab nearly forty years before.[86]

Those events overshadow the jumble of images of India's 'tryst with destiny' as Nehru put it in Delhi in his famous speech on the night of 14 August, saying that 'At the stroke of the midnight hour, while the world sleeps, India will awake to life and freedom.' When I was a young man on *The Times* my boss, Louis Heren, would tell me stories of the last hours of the Indian Empire, the brilliant sight of British troops 'marching through the Khyber Pass with bands playing and colours flying while the tribesmen watched from their hill crags',[87] the ghastly sight of the trainloads of slaughtered Hindus and Muslims desperately trying to get from one side of Radcliffe's line to the other. Another veteran British journalist, the BBC's Wynford Vaughan Thomas, like others of his profession, did what he could to prevent the massacres.

> I had a small portable recorder and a jeep. Again and again I used to see these massacres taking place on the Grand Trunk Road. People tried to cut people down, I'd lift up the microphone and say 'The BBC is watching you,' and they'd stop.[88]

But, in the end, the journalists, like the soldiers of the Punjab Boundary Force or even Gandhi, who visited the worst hit areas in the cause of peace, were quite incapable of preventing the bloodshed which went with the great migrations of the summer and autumn 1947. Wynford Vaughan Thomas again:

> The trains ran a serious risk. Anglo-Indian drivers would shunt into a siding and go off to water the engine. That would give the Sikh bands a chance to come in and they would go right through the train and kill everybody. And

the train would then shunt on to Lahore where on a siding they'd have to take the dead out. They were a terrible sight. I don't want to think over it. You could see them coming with fly swarms around them. And when the bodies were taken out and laid down, there would be about two thousand at a time.'[89]

Compared to such scenes other unfinished business, like the future of the 565 Princely States, nearly all of whom were eventually coaxed into joining one or other of the two new nations by Mountbatten, were trivial. So was the skill of Attlee and Cripps (whose original idea it was) in getting round the problem of republics inside a monarchical Commonwealth (India, Pakistan, Burma though not Ceylon, which was content with the dominion status it achieved in February 1948 'without shedding one drop of blood', as D.S. Senanayake, its first premier, pointed out[90]). Cripps' fix was to suggest that George VI be given a new and extra title, 'Head of the Commonwealth', which would enable the republics to recognise him and the post-imperial show to stay on the constitutional road. This, after a bit of difficulty from the New Zealand premier, Fraser, was agreed to at the Commonwealth Prime Ministers' Conference in London in 1950.[91]

Was the Attlee/Mountbatten solution the right one? If the pace had been slowed down rather than speeded-up could that body count have been avoided? Louis Heren, who saw the killings and described them graphically and unforgettably in his memoirs, has always agreed with the Assistant Police Commissioner in Lahore, a Muslim, who told him in the middle of those terrible scenes, that 'a few British battalions could have saved the Punjab'.[92]

Heren witnessed the Gurkhas successfully protecting some 200,000 refugees, mostly Sikhs, as they 'moved in a single column from the Lyallpur district of the West Punjab to India . . . By any standards, it was an impressive operation, and it proved the point of the assistant police commissioner in Lahore . . . I still find it impossible to agree with the complacent assertion,' Heren continued, writing in the late 1970s, 'that Britain withdrew with honour and dignity from India because in 1947 I was overwhelmed by the horror of it.'[93]

It is impossible to make a definitive judgment. If that crucial will to Empire had, perhaps, endured until its last minutes in India and the Government in London had been prepared to contemplate delay and to find the troops and money for a thoroughly supervised partition, the bloodshed would have been diminished. What is certain is that however long Radcliffe had had to draw his lines, great – and vulnerable – shifts of population would have been inevitable.

India, the most momentous of all the imperial disposals, showed more than any other that burying an empire could be a far more vexing, time-consuming and bloodstained business than acquiring one in the first place, however decisive 'morticians' like Attlee and Mountbatten proved to be. That other late-

Forties disposal, Palestine, demonstrated another lesson – just how ruinous indecision and imprecision could be when the Union Jack came down.

Palestine, the territory we now know as Israel, has the misfortune, as has Germany 2,000 miles to the north-west, of being a patch of terrain of intense geopolitical sensitivity. Such places often called 'crossroads' tend to be fought over by powers, ideologies or faiths. Palestine has been like this for 3,500 years, ever since it was a critical arc in the 'fertile crescent' which linked the two ancient civilisations of Egypt and Mesopotamia (now known as Iraq). In the millennia that have elapsed since, Palestine, for its pains, became a sacred place for no less than three of the world's great religions, Islam, Judaism and Christianity. 'It has', as Brian Lapping aptly put it, 'proved the most fertile spot on earth for religions . . . No territory on earth has aroused such passion.'[94]

Responsibility for ruling it, one of the great poisoned chalices in world politics, fell to the strongest power in the Middle East which is how Britain became involved when the collapse of the Ottoman Empire at the end of the First World War transferred the lines of responsibility from Constantinople to London. The British, in an imperial sleight-of-hand many in Whitehall came to rue, added their own dash of strychnine to the chalice shortly before the cup passed to them. Wishing for so strategically important a territory to be in reliable, pro-British hands, the Foreign Secretary, Arthur Balfour, pledged in 1917 the Government's support for the dearest wish of the Zionists. In a letter to Lord Rothschild of 2 November 1917, Balfour declared: 'His Majesty's Government view with favour the establishment in Palestine of a national home for the Jewish people, and will use their best endeavours to facilitate the achievement of this object.'[95] Bevin, in a moment of intense exasperation with the Palestine problem nearly thirty years later, wrote of his predecessor's promise: 'It was a unilateral declaration . . . [which] . . . did not take into account the Arabs and was really a Power Politics declaration.'[96] He was absolutely right.

In the years between Balfour and Bevin, governing Palestine on behalf of the League of Nations (it was a so-called mandated territory, not a British colony) brought nothing but grief to policy-makers in the Colonial and Foreign Offices as they tried to reconcile the irreconcilable – Jewish aspirations for a national home (heightened by Nazi persecution in Europe after 1933) and the resentment of Palestinian Arabs displaced by Jewish immigration. 'Managing' Palestine was made progressively more difficult, too, by the growing importance of Middle East oil to the British economy and the need to appease the oil-rich Arab states to the east of Jerusalem. Civil disorder in Palestine after the Mufti incited his followers to anti-Jewish riots in 1929 stretched the authorities to the limit. (The first riots had started in 1921 as the pace of Jewish immigration quickened; between 1922 and 1926, 75,000 Jews settled in Palestine doubling the previous Jewish population.[97])

Labour's victory in 1945 was the perfect result for Chaim Weizmann and the would-be makers of a Jewish state. He knew the Labour leaders personally and the bulk of the party supported Jewish hopes, including Ernest Bevin. Yet Bevin's memory in Israel is a sour one, as, at best, the man who bent his mighty will to frustrating its birth and, at worst, as a crude anti-semite. It's certainly true that within days of filling the Foreign Secretary's seat, Bevin had changed his mind. He waddled across Downing Street to No. 10 to set to work on Attlee. 'Clem,' he said, 'about Palestine. According to my lads in the office we've got it wrong. We've got to think again.'[98]

As for the alleged anti-semitism, Bevin always said, 'The Jews are a religion, not a race or a nation.'[99] He suggested at a Labour Party conference that the Americans were pushing for a Jewish state in Palestine because 'they did not want too many Jews in New York'. And he could indulge in extraordinarily crude humour on diplomatic occasions as during a power cut in the fuel crisis of February 1947, which plunged the FO into darkness, and led Bevin to remark there was no need for candles as they had the Israel*ites* present.[100]

This makes for pretty unappetising reading. How much of it can be laid at the door of anti-semitism, it's difficult to say. Even with the memories of the Holocaust so fresh, there remained an unhealthy awareness in Britain of who was a Jew and who was not. Attlee was no exception. When discussing the appointment of new ministers with Dalton in February 1951, the Prime Minister said, 'There were two who were always being recommended as knowing about industry – Mikardo and [Austen] Albu – but they both belonged to the Chosen People, and he didn't think he wanted any more of *them*.'[101]

In Bevin's case these unsavoury outbursts could have been occasioned by sheer frustration (to be fair to his memory, Jews were included in 'my people' whom he was not going to allow Hitler to persecute in his great anti-Nazi outburst at the Grosvenor House in 1939[102]). In 1945, with the supreme vanity of the century's most successful trade unionist, he said he would stake his 'political future' on negotiating a settlement in Palestine.[103] By the early months of 1947, Bevin was confessing that 'I am at the end of my tether' in trying to impose a solution on Jews and Arabs.[104]

But to understand Bevin's Palestine policy you have to grasp first his, and (by extension of that domineering personality) the Cabinet's, grand strategy for the Middle East as a whole. It was bound up with the guts of imperial policy post-India, part of that cherished notion of an oil and mineral rich Empire from Cape Town to Iraq which would sustain Britain in its great powerdom long after the Indian Army marched to a different drumbeat.

For one brief moment an adjustment to what Paul Kennedy would later call 'imperial overstretch' was contemplated including a withdrawal from the Middle East. The Prime Minister himself made the running and, in Alan Bullock's words, 'showed himself a radical and persistent critic of the services' plans'.[105] He simply did not believe the country could afford the finance or the people the Chiefs of Staff were demanding for their postwar establishments. Supported by Dalton and Morrison, he took them on at a series of Defence Committee meetings in the early months of 1946.

Dalton, taken aback by the boldness of Attlee's 'large view . . . which aims at considerable disengagement from areas where there is a risk of clashing with the Russians', summarised the P.M.'s strategic vision as

> giving up any attempt to keep open the passage through the Mediterranean in war-time, and to pull out from all the Middle East, including Egypt, and, of course, from Greece. We should then constitute a line of defence across Africa from Lagos to Kenya and concentrate a large part of our forces in the latter. We should face the prospect of going round the Cape in war-time and, the future attitude of India being somewhat uncertain, we should concentrate a great part of the Commonwealth defence, including many industries, in Australia. We should thus put a wide glacis of desert and Arabs between ourselves and the Russians. This is a very bold and interesting idea and I am inclined to favour it.[106]

The Chiefs of Staff were not, nor was the 'official mind' of Whitehall as a whole. Nor, crucially, was Bevin. *His* dash of radicalism was a wish 'to clear right out of Cairo as soon as practicable' (he was to make mighty and almost successful efforts to negotiate British troops out of the vast base in the Suez Canal Zone). His reasons for insisting that Britain should remain a Mediterranean and a Middle Eastern power were political and economic. As so often, the dry Cabinet Committee minutes make him sound like Lord Curzon by another means:

> The Mediterranean is the area through which we bring influence to bear in Southern Europe, the soft underbelly of France, Italy, Jugoslavia, Greece and Turkey. Without our physical presence in the Mediterranean, we should cut little ice with these states which would fall, like Eastern Europe, under the totalitarian yoke.[107]

Gradually the Bevin view prevailed. The Middle East remained, in Roger Louis' nice phrase, 'a region honeycombed with British military installations',[108] a price worth paying if you believed, as Bevin did, that it was now the chief prop of Britain's position in the world.

To be fair to Bevin, he was not the crude *nineteenth*-century imperialist he is often portrayed as, the 'working class John Bull' as Churchill once called him.[109] His was a very late Forties imperialism – one based on partnership rather than domination, which would raise the living standards of the peasant and curb the tyranny of the pasha while, naturally, serving the strategic needs of Britain for oil and bases to keep the Russians contained to the north.

Initially Palestine fitted neatly into this bounteous vision. 'Not only was the equable Palestine climate conducive to the permanent garrisoning of troops but also the air base at Lydda and the naval installations at Haifa had a strategic value that might help to offset, if necessary, an eventual withdrawal from Egypt.'[110]

By the spring of 1946, when Bevin was beginning to convert the withdrawal symptoms of Attlee and Dalton into a 'staying on' frame of mind, this charming picture of a Palestinian future began rapidly to turn into a nightmare. Truman had never accepted Bevin's turnaround, prompted by 'my lads in the office', which led to a ceiling of 1,500 a month on Jewish immigration along the lines of the 1939 White Paper, a curb Labour had previously opposed. The American Administration did not accept the Bevin line that the solution to Palestine lay in Europe, in creating the conditions whereby the Jews would stay there as resettled displaced persons, rather than sail in leaky flotillas from Marseilles to Haifa, provoking an Arab uprising with repercussions throughout the Middle East upsetting that grand, strategic vision.

Within a month of Labour's taking office, Truman was urging Attlee to admit 100,000 Jewish refugees into Palestine immediately. An Anglo-American Commission, established jointly by the two countries in November 1945, reported on 1 May 1946 and backed Truman on the 100,000 entry certificates. Though it ruled out the early establishment of a Jewish state adding, piously, that 'Jew shall not dominate Arab and Arab shall not dominate Jew in Palestine'. This must have struck Bevin, as the Balfour Declaration did, of trying 'to ride two horses at once'.[111]

The grim cycle of terrorism and counter-atrocity in Palestine between the two communities, with British troops inevitably drawn in, continued. The British HQ in the King David Hotel in Jerusalem was blown up on 22 July 1946 by the Irgun gang, an operation planned by Menachem Begin, a future Prime Minister of Israel, to the horror of traditional Zionists like Weizmann. Bevin told Weizmann, 'I do not want any Jews killed either, but I love the British soldiers. They belong to my class. They are working people.'[112] A year later, when the Irgun captured two British sergeants, Clifford Martin and Mervyn Paice, and hanged them in retaliation for three of their own members executed for terrorist offences, British soldiers and policemen went on the rampage in Palestine, and anti-semitic riots broke out in London, Liverpool, Manchester and Glasgow.

Bevin, too, found himself pilloried in the United States for turning back the immigrant ship, *Exodus*, off Palestine and forcibly returning its 4,500-strong human cargo to refugee camps in the British Zone in Germany. Pictures of passengers being carried off at Hamburg and put on trains inevitably revived revolting recent memories, and stimulated journalists' reports 'suggesting that the British Government had either gone mad or turned viciously anti-semitic'.[113]

Security forces even of 100,000 (80,000 troops plus 20,000 police) could no longer keep the lid on in Palestine. Persistent American pressure undid any British effort to negotiate a solution at international level. The vision of British Tommies, free of the stinking summer heat along the Suez Canal, basking in a new and permanent base in Palestine, had vanished in the dust of the King David Hotel when the Irgun's milk churns packed with explosive went up. Now the best that Attlee, Bevin and Creech Jones could hope for was a dignified withdrawal. Even this was denied them.

Bit by bit the initiative slipped from Whitehall to the United Nations where the crucial vote in favour of partitioning Palestine was taken at the end of November 1947 (the United States and the Soviet Union, voting together for once, helping to muster the necessary two thirds majority needed for a change of status in a mandated territory). Britain, still administering Palestine in the name of the UN, made it plain it would not implement the partition resolution until its troops, policemen and officials could be withdrawn in good order.

'Thus', wrote Brian Lapping, 'Britain ducked out. Although thirty more British policemen were killed before the final departure, the British were no longer the principal target: Arabs and Jews now faced each other, with no effective force to separate them. Britain refused even to keep the peace. The High Commissioner, Sir Alan Cunningham, repeatedly begged to be allowed to bring in extra police, particularly to Jerusalem, to stop bloodshed. But the Cabinet forbade it.'[114]

The attitude and actions of Cunningham and his colleagues in those dreadful last days in Palestine in a strange way corroborated the views of Sir Isaiah Berlin, who knew well the minds of both the Zionists and the colonial authorities, about the Mandate. He compared Palestine to a minor English public school: 'There was the headmaster, the High Commissioner, trying to be firm and impartial: but the assistant masters favoured the sporting stupid boarders [the Arabs] against the clever swot dayboys [the Jews] who had the deplorable habit of writing home to their parents on the slightest provocation to complain about the quality of the teaching, the food and so on.'[115]

Rather in that tradition, I'd long savoured the story of Sir Henry Gurney, Chief Secretary of the British Administration, at a press conference in the King David Hotel on the last day of the Mandate. 'And to whom', according to the legend, 'do you intend to give the keys of your office?', Sir Henry was asked. 'To Nobody. I shall put them under the mat,' he replied.[116] Sadly, reality was rather different – less witty, more bitter. Gurney's diary entry for 14 May gives the true story:

> The Police locked up the stores (worth over £1 million) and brought the keys to the UN, who refused to receive them. I had to point out that the UN would be responsible for the administration of Palestine in a few hours' time (in accordance with the November resolution) and that we should leave the keys on their doorstep whether they accepted them or not, which they did.[117]

It's a pity. If Gurney *had* spoken as legend had him speaking on that grim, chaotic day, it would be the wittiest exit line of any in the long sequence of imperial departures that followed, a procession influenced in no small part by the Palestine experience which was watched closely by nationalists throughout George VI's domains. It was an infinitely more potent message than Indian independence which, after all, had been foreshadowed and discussed endlessly between the two world wars. When the second ended Bevin was still thinking of Palestine as a safe haven for British regiments and squadrons.

As so often, James Morris conveys raw, harsh geopolitical reality in graceful, atmospheric prose:

> It was in Palestine that the British imperialists, for the first time, frankly abandoned the imperial responsibilities, and there the last retreat began . . . and in a way the possession of the Holy City, and the establishment there of the first Christian government for a thousand years, had marked the summation of the Empire itself. Jerusalem had set a seal upon the adventure, and the governance of the Holy Land had been the crowning privilege of Victorian imperialism. Yet there the Empire had first admitted impotence. The withdrawal from India could be rationalised, even romanticised: the withdrawal from Palestine was without glory.[118]

Morris is right, too, to claim that 'Palestine was a declaration. The British would no longer fight to a finish.'[119]

Yet like most of the 'great turning points of history', this one is much more clear-cut in retrospect than it appeared at the time. As Cunningham, his soldiers, policemen and administrators prepared to leave Haifa in an evacuation fleet of Royal Navy frigates, the journalist, Fellow of All Souls and imperialist romantic, H.V. Hodson, was already writing of 'a Fourth British Empire' emerging from the débris of the third (the first, according to Hodson, ended with the American revolution; the second with the emergence of the dominions; the third with the close of the Second World War and Indian independence). Hodson admitted that:

> At present it lacks the individuality which is given to political institutions by a name, a formula or a statement of principles. This very lack of formula is typical of the Fourth Empire. The key words of the British Commonwealth of Nations were equality and co-operation, and the stress was on status. Today the stress is on function.[120]

In other words, shared interests, economic and political, would keep the remaining imperial show on the road.

Hodson's view was not that different from Bevin's notion of partnership in the Middle East. Even Creech Jones, more susceptible than either to the claims of nationalism, thought the Empire had another fifty years to run.[121] There was hard necessity behind the wishful thinking. The Empire as farm, larder and mine, was crucial to postwar calculations of economic recovery, more so even than defence, as was shown in those discussions about withdrawal behind a glacis of sand and Arabs.

Since the final end of Empire in the 1960s, the economic historians have discovered a rich seam of retrospection as they mercilessly subject this kaleidoscopic phenomenon to the spartan rigours of cost-benefit analysis. Scholars have rediscovered the celebrated Edwardian critique of Empire by J.A. Hobson, the Liberal journalist, whose *Imperialism* saw the enterprise as an expensive and ineffective substitute for social reform and economic modernisation at home.[122]

On top of the Hobson line, they place a new argument: that Britain's primacy in the world economy of the early and mid-nineteenth century was so great, that its industrial and trading requirements could have been secured by financial muscle. In other words, the whole costly, time-consuming apparatus of *territorial* Empire – the frontiers, the district commissioners, the garrisons, the colonial civil services – were an energy-sapping irrelevance.

As Patrick O'Brien, author of an influential article on 'The Costs and Benefits of British Imperialism', put it:

> Modern economic historians have reopened this venerable discussion by resorting to their favourite heuristic device, a counterfactual question. Predictably they now ask what might have happened to British exports (visible and invisible), to its imports and to flows of capital and labour (the entire nexus of economic connections between Britain and her empire) as well as to the defence budget and taxation *if* the dominions and colonies had become *independent* polities from the middle of the nineteenth century onwards.
>
> After all, commercial relations with France, Spain and the United States, even with Brazil, were not predicated upon similar degrees of political intrusion by the British government. Might not British businessmen, with or without the raj, have been engaged in similar levels of commerce with India? With or without the Colonial Office might not trade with Jamaica have been much the same as it was over the period 1850–1914?[123]

Such deliciously subversive thoughts would not have troubled Bevin or Creech Jones for a moment for the simple reason that in 1947–8, no one was thinking them let alone committing them to paper. If they had Bevin would have told them to 'stick to history' just as he advised Patrick Blackett to 'stick to science' when he questioned the wisdom of manufacturing a British atomic bomb.[124] Bevin was determined to husband every ounce of British power wherever it lay, at home or on the imperial landscape. Nothing would be given up unless Hindu lawyers or Jewish scholars (and guerrillas) forced him to – and then only with extreme reluctance.

He was, as we have seen, a late empire man. Yet, like those British Army regulars who regarded Hitler and Mussolini and Europe as a diversion from 'real soldiering' in the Empire,[125] Bevin's concentration was increasingly drawn away from the jackpots of the colonies to the wrecked and desolate landscape of Europe, darkened by the shadow of the Red Army. Cold war, not colonial war, became and remained the overriding preoccupation of foreign and defence policy as the Forties crept towards the Fifties.

CHAPTER 7

Chill from the East

Molotov, Stalin, they are evil men.
Ernest Bevin to Christopher Mayhew, *c*. 1946[1]

The fundamental aim of the Soviet leaders is to hasten the elimination of capitalism from all parts of the world and to replace it with their own form of Communism. They envisage this process as being effected in the course of a revolutionary struggle lasting possibly for many years and assisted, should favourable conditions arise, by military action . . . The Soviet leaders are, however, also convinced that the capitalist world, aware of the growing strength of Communism, is likely eventually to resort to force in an attempt to avert its own collapse. This belief inspired the more immediate aim of Soviet policy which is to ensure, by all possible means, the security of the Soviet Union.
Joint Intelligence Committee assessment, 1948[2]

All that the Red Army needed in order to reach the North Sea was boots.
Denis Healey, recalling pre-NATO Europe, in 1969[3]

We sit under the shadow of the Nine O'Clock News, nursing our sense of doom.
Dr Jacob Bronowski, 1948[4]

Vast enterprises acquire a life of their own. They spawn cultures, grow mind-sets, acquire clients, create dependents and are terribly difficult to halt or even reform once the original circumstances of their birth are forgotten. As Lord Hailsham once said, 'Nations begin by forming their institutions, but in the end, are continuously formed by them or under their influence.'[5]

The cold war was like that. In its forty-year life, from the Berlin Air Lift of June 1948 to Mikhail Gorbachev's speech at the United Nations announcing unilateral cuts in Soviet conventional forces in central Europe in December 1988, it stimulated huge and seemingly permanent military and industrial establishments on both sides and fixed itself as the ever-present, and overriding priority of ministers, diplomats, chiefs of staff and intelligence analysts. In the British context it ensured that something between 5 and 12 per cent of gross domestic product went on defence year-in, year-out.

A valuable rule of thumb for the historian when confronted by such phenomena is to repair to the archive to find the key document, the founding charter as it were, of the endeavour. It usually takes the form of a piece of work analysing the new picture which is so persuasive and all-embracing that large, long-term adjustments are made to it, often with no expense spared.

The nearest I have come to it in the context of the cold war, as perceived and coped with from Britain, is a seventy-page Joint Intelligence Committee assessment of the Soviet threat drawn up in the summer of 1948, a few months after the Communist coup in Czechoslovakia, while the Dakotas of the Royal and United States air forces built their air bridge over the Soviet ground blockade into Templehof with the food and fuel needed to keep their Berlin zones alive and in the western orbit.

By this time, three years down an ever-grimmer road of east-west confrontation from the Potsdam Conference, the British intelligence services reckoned they had got 'Russian interests, intentions and capabilities' pretty well taped. The JIC assessment is worth lingering over. Because upon it, and the revised versions which periodically went to carefully selected ministers on a 'need-to-know' basis, was built the British branch of the cold war business. If the Soviet threat had been perceived differently, a great deal of treasure (and not a little blood in Korea and Malaya) would have been saved.

JIC (48) 9, as we can call it for short, set itself to answer the questions 'What is Russia trying to do? How far is she capable of doing it?'[6] Rightly, the intelligence services reckoned the Soviet Union had no time for reformist democratic socialists like Attlee and his Foreign Secretary, Bevin, whose roughest language was reserved for the hated 'Mowlotov'.[7] He was regarded as something far more offensive than Lord Palmerston in a cloth cap by his Soviet counterpart at their interminable and increasingly acrimonious Foreign Ministers' Conferences between Potsdam and the autumn of 1947 when the attempt at reaching a postwar settlement was effectively abandoned (not until 1990 was a peace treaty concluded between Germany and the wartime Allies).

In JIC-speak, this read:

> It should be emphasised that in Russia's eyes the United Kingdom is still a capitalist and imperialist country, despite its Labour Government. In general the Soviet leaders are especially hostile to 'reformist socialism' of the British pattern, which they regard not only as an opponent to Communism but also as a dangerous competitor for working-class support in many countries.[8]

One day, in some kind of historical nirvana or conference-to-end-all-conferences, it may be possible to match the perceptions of east and west in

1947–8, assessment for assessment, to see how valid were the suspicions of some old Whitehall intelligence hands, such as Michael Herman, that the intelligence services of each side were mirror-imaging each other in serving up the worst-case scenarios to their customers in the foreign and defence ministries.[9]

As we have seen, the British intelligence community *circa* 1947–8 was convinced that the long-term aim of the Soviet Union was worldwide domination based on the Communist system. The short-term preoccupation was with the security of its existing redoubt from external attack. So much for 'intentions', or the 'software' of intelligence as it became known in the computer age.[10] What about the all-important 'capabilities' or 'hardware'?

The JIC summarised these under five headings[11] for the purposes of busy ministers who couldn't be ·expected to absorb over 400 paragraphs and 70 pages:

> It is unlikely that before 1957 the Soviet Union will be capable of supporting her armed forces entirely from the natural resources and industrial potential now under her control in any major war, except one in which extensive operations are not prolonged. Nevertheless, if Russia wished to go to war, economic considerations would not in themselves be enough to prevent her from doing so if she felt confident of attaining her objectives rapidly.[12]

This is an early version of the ultimate nightmare of western defence planners right through to the Gorbachev era – that the Red Army could make a push to the North Sea from a standing start without warning, Denis Healey's 'boots' image. Under the second heading, however, the JIC dismissed any idea that the Soviet Union would, like Japan in the 1930s, feel impelled 'to use methods which might lead to a major war in order to acquire external economic resources'.[13] But now the JIC confronted what seemed *the* ultimate nightmare of mid-1948, those legendary 175 divisions of the Red Army. (Actually they put the figure at 170 divisions but 'the very scanty evidence at our disposal indicates that in the event of mobilisation, this total . . . could be increased by about 60 per cent, and the personnel strength doubled in 30 days'.[14]

> The Soviet land forces, with their close support aircraft, are sufficiently strong, at the present time, to achieve rapid and far-reaching successes against any likely combination of opposing land forces. In view of the present reduced effectiveness of the navies of the British Commonwealth, United States and the Western European Powers, the Soviet Union may appreciate that within the next few years her relative naval strength will be as great as it is ever likely to be, and that her naval situation is therefore in itself no additional deterrent against engaging in a major war.[15]

The west, or, more accurately, the United States had one strength to neutralise such overwhelming Soviet ground force – atomic weapons and the means to deliver them.

The strategic air situation . . . remains adverse to the Soviet Union in that she has at present no satisfactory answer either to atomic weapons or to strategic bomber attacks. She can thus not yet count upon a reasonable degree of immunity for her centres of population and industry from serious air attack. Her future readiness to embark upon a major war is likely therefore to be conditioned by considerations of her own air power in relation to that of her probable opponents.[16]

The atomic bomb was so crucial an element in strategic calculations in the late 1940s (as we shall see in a moment Attlee and Bevin had given production of a British weapon a high priority from early 1947) that it's worth pulling out the full, not the summarised, JIC assessment of future Soviet nuclear capability according to the best (almost certainly negligible) information available in the summer of 1948.

The manufacture of atomic weapons demands not only a high standard of scientific knowledge and the application on a very large scale of difficult industrial techniques, but also the use of large quantities of uranium. The most reliable present estimate that can be made of Russian progress indicates that the limiting factor is their supplies of uranium. At the present time it is considered to be most misleading to attempt to forecast how much uranium will be available to any Russian project beyond January 1952 since this depends on two unpredictable factors:

a) the discovery within Russian-controlled territory of new high-grade deposits, which is believed to be unlikely, and
b) the success the Russians will have in developing a practicable process for large-scale extraction of the small percentages of uranium present in oil-shales, large deposits of which are available to them.

Existing estimates of the date when the Russians began their programme and of their ability to overcome the technological difficulties involved suggest that they may possibly produce their first atomic bomb by January 1951, and that their stockpile of bombs in January 1953 may be of the order of 6 to 22 . . . These figures, however, are the maximum possible based on the assumption that the Russian effort will progress as rapidly as the American and British projects have done. Allowances for the probably slower progress of the Russian effort will almost certainly retard the first bomb by some three years.

On these assumptions it is improbable that the Soviet Union will have sufficient atom bombs by the end of 1956 to defeat the United Kingdom by this means alone. Even though the Russians may take a different view about the number of bombs required for this purpose, the defeat of the United Kingdom would still leave them with the greater problem of defeating the United States, which such an attack on the United Kingdom would involve.[17]

After a brief consideration of biological weapons, the JIC wrapped the intelligence parcel up within an overall conclusion that 'failing the early development of biological or other new weapons, to a point which she believed would ensure her rapid victory, the Soviet Union's economic situation is likely to be decisive in making her wish to avoid a protracted major war at any rate until 1957.'[18]

What are we to make of these insights? We know they were wildly wrong about the bomb. The Soviet Union's first atomic explosion took place much sooner – in August 1949, a mere thirteen months after this prediction that it would be January 1951 at the earliest. By the summer of 1953 Russia had developed the vastly more powerful hydrogen bomb. Very few thermonuclear explosions are required to wreck the United Kingdom (one dirty burst off St David's Head and the south-westerly air stream will do the rest according to one old defence hand).[19]

Just how firmly based was *any* of the material in this vast assessment with its unmistakably cold warrior conclusions? To be fair to its compilers, they warn their readers throughout that hard knowledge is scarce. On aircraft, for example, 'there is little information upon which to base a reliable estimate of present output'.[20] In those pre-satellite days, as we have seen, evidence was 'very scanty' even on the number of divisions available to the Red Army's commanders.

As I live on the eastern side of London, I should dearly love to know the source for one truly bizarre paragraph in JIC (48) 9 which declared, 'Communists have their distinctive approach to all problems of politics, economics, ethics and culture. Thus, in achieving their political ends, they make use of a remarkable variety of instruments, ranging from national governments in Eastern Europe to "jitterbug" clubs in the East End of London.'[21]

This must be a contribution from MI5 whose Director-General, Sir Percy Sillitoe, former Chief Constable of Glasgow (who wrote a ghastly memoir called *Cloak Without Dagger*[22]), sat on the JIC and was a signatory to the 1948 assessment. God knows why they attributed American bebop dancing in the East End to Communist subversion!

Michael Herman, a former member of the Defence Intelligence Staff, has cast an insider's eye over those projections and estimates of Soviet capability in the period, as he rightly puts it, when 'the cold war attitudes were set'.[23] These were the years, too, in which intelligence came into its own as the shaper of foreign and defence policy. There was no sign after 1945 of the rapid rundown of the country's espionage and code-breaking capacities as had happened after 1919.[24] Even the Second World War behind-the-lines capabilities, immortalised by the many and glorious tales to come out of the Special Operations Executive,[25] carried on after SOE's demise as part of MI6's Special Operations Branch and its Political Action Group.[26]

'The Cold War', as Michael Herman put it, 'was in a special sense an intelligence conflict . . . Never before in peacetime have the relationships of competing power blocks been so influenced by intelligence assessments. Never before have the collection of intelligence and its denial to the adversary been such central features of an international rivalry. The Cold War transformed intelligence into a major element of the peacetime international security system.'[27]

So what does Herman make of JIC (48) 9? With hindsight, he and other experts have scaled down those nightmarish '175 divisions'. Such calculations, he argues, have always been bedevilled by counting rules – the degree to which civil defence, railroad and construction workers have been included in the military totals as well as the tendency to ignore the difference in strength levels between a Soviet and a western division:

> But the central error was the assumption up to the early 1960s that ground forces Divisions were active units, rather than a mixture of active and reserve forces. The 1948 JIC paper quoted 170 Divisions (plus 25 artillery Divisions) which in the event of mobilisation could be increased by 60% with a 30% increase in personnel. As is well known, the general estimate of active Divisions was subsequently scaled down to something like the current figures [Mr Herman was writing in 1989] of 90–100 Category A or B divisions and rather more cadre formations. Paul Nitze has suggested that actual Soviet strength in the late 1940s was of the order of one-third full strength, one-third partial strength, and one-third cadre. Most western estimates for the total size of Soviet forces at that time were of the order of four million; the JIC paper quoted 3.685 million. Khrushchev in 1960 put the size of the Soviet forces after the final stage of early demobilisation in early 1949 as 2.874 million, and it has been argued that the West probably did not perceive the extent of Soviet demobilisation.[28]

We must be careful here. Even if the Government Communications Headquarters' listeners at Bletchley and Eastcote, the MI6 watchers behind the Iron Curtain, and the army sergeants in the British zones of Germany and Austria picking up scraps about Soviet and satellite military formations from refugees from the east, *had* between them produced estimates around the 100 Division mark, it would still have been enough to alarm the JIC's political and Whitehall customers. For that figure represented an overwhelming conventional, as opposed to atomic superiority, and would do for the whole cold war period.

The key issue here, however, is not the figures, but the assumptions that were drawn from the counting and their implications for policy. JIC (48) 9, in Herman's words, 'formalised the idea that there was a military opportunity for Russians to overrun Europe quickly if no countervailing forces were created. This led in time to the dogma that Soviet force levels had been set for that purpose – rather than for other reasons – and therefore showed a Soviet political intent to keep this option open, however remotely. Secondly, by focusing on worst-case estimates of what Soviet military power *could* be in the period from 1956 onwards, it laid the seeds for the long-running assumption that maximum Soviet military investment *had* to happen.'[29]

The tendency to fear the worst was heightened in the late 1940s by two factors – the lack of confidence that comes from having so little to go on (the absence of reliable evidence from the east was acute); and the livid, very recent memory of what can happen to whole nations once armies march and aircraft fly on the orders of tyrants.

The shortage of high-grade intelligence in the pre-satellite era has been known for some time from declassified Chiefs of Staff papers and from insider memoirs like *Time to Explain* written by Bevin's junior minister, Christopher Mayhew. Mayhew was well plugged into the intelligence side as the minister responsible for the Information Research Department, a new Foreign Office division for countering Soviet propaganda by both overt and covert means which Mayhew himself had persuaded Bevin to set up.[30]

'At that time', Mayhew recalled, 'our knowledge of the Soviet Union, and especially of the blacker elements of Soviet oppression, was extremely limited. We had few secret sources of intelligence; defectors were few and far between; the movements of western visitors were strictly controlled, and the Soviet media gave little or nothing away.'[31]

JIC material declassified almost certainly by accident at the India Office Library (JIC (48) 9 comes into this category, incidentally[32]) shows in the words of its discoverers, Richard Aldrich and Michael Coleman, that 'Britain enjoyed no postwar equivalent to the extraordinary achievements of Ultra during the Second World War . . . The evidence for British success against high-priority signals intelligence targets . . . suggests that the results were, at best, disappointing.'[33] According to Aldrich and Coleman, 'JIC papers for the late 1940s appear to display very detailed knowledge of Soviet dispositions in only two areas: the capabilities of the Soviet Air Force and Soviet troop movements in South East Europe.'[34]

Their windfall in the India Office Library spells out in detail what Whitehall's intelligence chiefs really wanted to know about Stalin's Russia. In fact, it contains the complete menu of Britain's postwar intelligence requirements. As no other document like it has reached the public domain covering any other patch of the postwar period, it's worth examining in detail.

Entitled 'SIGINT intelligence requirements – 1948' it was circulated by the JIC to all providers of signals intelligence in the armed forces as well as GCHQ on 11 May 1948.[35] Four targets were listed in 'Priority I':

1 Development in the Soviet Union of atomic, biological and chemical methods of warfare (together with associated raw materials).
2 Development in the Soviet Union of scientific principles and inventions leading to new weapons, equipment or methods of warfare.
3 Strategic and tactical doctrines, state of training, armament and aircraft of:–
    (a) Soviet long-range bomber force.
    (b) Soviet metropolitan fighter defence force . . .
4 Development in the Soviet Union of guided weapons.

Priority II embraced political matters, such as who would succeed Stalin, the construction programme of submarines and aircraft, the condition of strategic industries in the Soviet Union, the organisation and operations of the Soviet secret services, Soviet intentions in Germany and Austria and what assistance Moscow was giving Communist guerrillas in the Greek civil war.

Not until you reach Priority IV do you find a non-Soviet target in 'Arab nationalism and relations of Arab states with UK and USA'. The Chinese do not get a look-in until the penultimate item, and the last one, almost as an afterthought, sweeps up 'Zionist movement including its intelligence services ... clandestine right-wing French and Italian movements ... Right-wing movements in the satellite countries.'

Let's return now to the kind of political, military and official minds into which were fed such fragments of intelligence as there were in the fraught late Forties. 'This was a generation', wrote Alan Bullock, 'for whom war and occupation were not remote hypotheses but recent and terrible experiences. The fear of another war, the fear of a Russian occupation, haunted Europe in those years and were constantly revived – by the Communist coup in Czechoslovakia, by the Berlin blockade, and by the outbreak of war in Korea in 1950 which produced near panic in France and Germany. It is unhistorical to dismiss these fears as groundless because the war and occupation did not occur.'[36]

The brutal events in Prague in February 1948 and the prolonged war scare over Berlin throughout the summer helped finally to shove British public and political opinion to the point Bevin had reached long before during the many hours spent across the table from Molotov. So much so that by 1949, the foundation year of NATO, 'it came', in the judgment of Bevin's biographer, 'as near consensus as any British foreign secretary has been able to count on in time of peace'.[37] It would be wrong, however, to think either that there was anything inevitable about this crystallisation of view or that it was engineered by clever men in Whitehall, the Chiefs of Staff Committee or the intelligence services who had regarded the Soviet Union all along as *the* enemy, even when Hitler was still issuing orders from Berlin.

Not just they, but Bevin, if he were in a position to read late twentieth-century reappraisals built on a careful reading of the archive, would surely say that's all very well, we may have been a bit off-beam in those JIC assessments, but it was *events*, undeniable and nasty developments in places like Prague and Berlin, that really persuaded us that Russia really was a threat, that Stalin and Molotov had ambitions that must be contained. The intelligence material merely corroborated that. To have acted otherwise, not to have eased the United States back into Europe and to have kept them there by locking them into NATO, would have been to take an appalling risk.

And, of course, in their terms they were right. How can we know that the Red Army wouldn't have put on its boots and marched to the Channel at some point in the early postwar period if it had appeared to their politicians and military planners to be a cost-free exercise? In late twentieth-century jargon,

NATO's 'performance indicator' was fixed by 'Pug' Ismay, the first Secretary-General of NATO. According to legend, he told a group of Conservative back-benchers in 1949 that 'NATO exists for three reasons – to keep the Russians out, the Americans in and the Germans down'.[38] It did all three for exactly forty years. Again, in modern management terms, you couldn't have left 'a control group', say Norway or Denmark, outside NATO's protection to see if the T-34s would roll. International politics isn't like that.

But this is to race ahead. None of this was foreseeable early in 1942 when Ismay himself, Churchill's Chief of Staff, circulated inside the defence world a request from the Foreign Office that the military planners turn their mind to postwar strategy and the likely threats to Britain's security.[39] The ebb and flow of inputs into the three-year process of postwar planning, from the Foreign Office, the Chief's Joint Planning Staff and from ministers produced a kaleido-scope of possibilities, some assuming the proposed international organisation, the United Nations really would sustain the co-operation of the Allies, includ-ing the Soviet Union, deep into the peace. (The War Cabinet had, in fact, accepted this 'as the present basis of our foreign policy' in November 1942.[40]) Others, like Gladwyn Jebb of the FO's Economic and Reconstruction Depart-ment, argued that should wartime collaboration break down under the strains of peace, 'we should inevitably be driven into forming some kind of anti-Soviet front, and in doing so we should eventually have to accept the collaboration of Germany'[41] (all of which had come to pass within ten years of the war's ending when West Germany was admitted into NATO).

Christopher Warner of the FO's Northern Department (which covered the Soviet Union) counselled patience in the autumn of 1942 on the grounds that Whitehall lacked 'any real evidence as to what is Russian policy as regards the future' and, when it came to *their* postwar intentions, 'The Russians are in fact likely to have two alternative policies and not to make up their minds finally until they can assess the results of co-operation with us during the war.'[42]

The Chiefs of Staff, naturally enough, did not place much faith in the ability of the new world organisation to protect the security of Britain and the Empire. As late as February 1944, with the creation of the United Nations a matter of weeks away, the Chiefs told Jebb 'it was a most unrealistic conception and bore no relation to reality . . . How could the World Council or whatever it was "dispose" of the national forces concerned?'[43]

The Armed Services tended to take a dimmer view of the Soviet Union than the diplomats. William Cavendish-Bentinck, an FO man who chaired the wartime JIC, drew on his long experience of the Chiefs of Staff to explain their doubts to his fellow diplomats in a beautifully even-handed memo.

I have seen it said in minutes that the Service Departments are violently anti-Russian. I do not think that this is quite correct. They are peeved with the Russians because the latter have been on the whole unco-operative. Moreover there is an unbridgeable gulf between the mentality of our own soldiers and sailors and that of the Russians. However the Service Departments are not confident that we shall be indefinitely on good terms with the Russians and that our interests will not clash both in Europe and the Middle East.

Though this did not mean, however, Cavendish-Bentinck concluded, that the military wanted a war with Russia.[44]

Other FO men were less understanding. One reprised the famous Lord Salisbury quote from the 1890s: 'If you believe the soldiers, nothing is safe. Some of them want to occupy the moon, in fear of an invasion from Mars.' In an uncannily accurate forecast of the worst-case scenario syndrome which later drove down the temperature in east-west relations, this particular diplomat (name unknown) minuted 'The Russians are unlikely to fulfil the Chiefs of Staff fears unless they became suspicious of us, and they will not justify our suspicions of them. We are threatened by a vicious, suspicious circle. Let us not describe the first arc.' Years later one of the FO sceptics said benignly of the military, 'They always have to have somebody to plan against.'[45]

Just who did describe that first arc – east or west, Stalin or Truman (aided and abetted by the British) – has fuelled one of the 'great debates' of the postwar period with 'traditionalist' historians locking horns with 'revisionists'. With more and more archives being broken open, 'post-revisionists' took over the running in the 1970s telling each set of historical combatants that reality was nothing like as simple or clear-cut as they had supposed.[46] The swirl of secret argument between the diplomats and soldiers, Whitehall's 'post hostility planners' of 1942–5, was in many ways a pre-echo of the great cold war controversy which has racked the historical profession since D.F. Fleming and William Appleman Williams began to challenge western orthodoxy in the late 1950s and early 1960s.[47]

If we had to fix on one document among the hundreds which can be said to reflect the 'official mind' about the postwar Soviet Union, it's Christopher Warner's paper prepared in January–February 1944. It assumed that the 'fixed point' of Russian foreign policy would remain what it had been since Stalin disposed of Trotsky – 'the search for security against any Power or combination of Powers which might threaten her while she was organising and developing her own domain'. The Soviet Union would avoid major conflict unless she 'suspects' us of having designs hostile to her security.

After the war Russia would treat Germany brutally and 'she would be constantly manoeuvring to increase the strength of her own position in Europe by establishing her influence in European countries through Left-Wing Governments and by interfering in their internal affairs both through intrigue and through power politics. Outside Europe, too, she would no doubt follow a similar aim.'[48] Warner was spot-on here. He was less so when he predicted that for the first five years after the war, Russia would concentrate on recovering from the war and would co-operate with the USA and the UK in the new postwar security system.[49] The history of the UN turned out very differently.

How much did ministers imbibe the balance of the Warner appraisal? As the Red Army advanced across eastern Europe establishing its own kind of governments in its wake (a few short-lived exceptions apart) ministers, like the Chiefs of Staff, tended towards a darker view, especially after the Red Army halted to the east of the Vistula and waited for the Nazis to put down the Poles during the Warsaw uprising, an event which left a lasting scar on all minds, political, official and military.[50] As early as May 1944 when the Warner report reached the Foreign Secretary's desk, Eden wrote next to the paragraph predicting Soviet interference in the internal affairs of European countries, 'Is she not doing this now?'[51]

Attlee and Bevin were privy to the internal Whitehall debate. They sat on the War Cabinet's committees on postwar reconstruction.[52] 'And it was this experience of two years' preparatory discussion of the postwar international settlement,' wrote Alan Bullock, 'discussions conducted in office not in opposition, as members of a coalition not a party administration, with all the resources of governments, including a mass of secret information, and their minds focused on the national interest in a world dominated by power politics, not on hopes of a European revolution or the principles of a socialist foreign policy, which shaped the Labour leaders' and particularly Bevin's and Attlee's views when they came to formulate the policy of a Labour Government after the election.'[53]

There's a danger here of becoming too determinist, or teleological as historians like to say – of reading too much certainty into the story too soon. Just because the cold war became a fixture, it would be wrong to suppose this outcome was, barring the odd lapse into wishful thinking, inevitable. In fact an alternative course was seriously considered, especially by the new Prime Minister, Attlee himself, as we shall see to the surprise and intense irritation of the Whitehall professionals.

The Foreign Office welcomed Bevin's arrival in the last days of July 1945 for two reasons. Bevin, as a senior ambassador confided to his diary, 'impresses one as a man who knows what he wants and knows how to get it'.[54] Another FO diarist, Oliver Harvey, for a long time Eden's private secretary, gives the clue to the second reason. 'Bevin', he wrote, 'is bent on a foreign policy we can only approve, much of what Anthony's policy would have been if he had ever been allowed to have one.'[55] For Eden and the FO simply could not control the imposing yet mercurial figure across Downing Street in Number 10.

One minute Churchill was the victim of deep pessimism about western Christendom's ability to resist the godless barbarians of the east. The next, especially when they met, he was succumbing to the charms of 'Uncle Joe' Stalin with whom he'd attempted his famous spheres of influence deal in October 1944.[56] As Raymond Smith says, the FO, where orderly consistency is all, had to put up, even in Churchill's last weeks as premier, with 'the enormous leap from Churchill's position at the end of May 1945 in seeking a report from the Joint Planning Staff on the possibility of taking on Russia, to his willingness to welcome Russia's appearance on the oceans during the Potsdam Conference'.[57]

Whitehall, however, should not have been surprised by Attlee's tendency to take on military and diplomatic orthodoxy. As chairman of a clutch of War Cabinet committees on postwar problems, his radicalism had already shocked them. As a convinced United Nations man, Attlee had suggested on 20 March 1945 that manning the Suez Canal would be too costly for Britain alone after the war and an irrelevance as well. For, under the terms of the new world organisation, the other great powers would share in such tasks.[58] This drew from Eden the prophetic retort (given the cause of his ruin at Suez eleven years later) that the Middle East 'is an area the defence of which is a matter of life or death to the British Empire since, as the present war and the war of 1914–18 have proved, it is there that the Empire can be cut in half . . . We cannot afford to resign our special position in the area – and allow our position to be dependent on arrangements of an international character.'[59]

Attlee, as we have seen, continued to hanker after a British withdrawal from the Middle East well into 1946. His internationalist tendencies brought forth a deep scepticism of Whitehall's darkening appreciations of the Soviet threat which, with little difficulty, persuaded Bevin on whom the diplomats and the Chiefs of Staff came to rely in speaking reality to the little man in No. 10 and to the Cabinet as a whole. The former American Secretary of State, Edward Stettinius, now the US representative at the UN, caught the difference precisely. 'Attlee', he wrote, 'had his heart in the United Nations Organisation . . . Bevin thought the emphasis would be more on power politics of the world in the immediate future than anything else.'[60]

Bevin and the Chiefs constantly stressed the dangers of Soviet expansion south into the Eastern Mediterranean and the Middle East. Attlee would retort, as he did at a meeting of the Cabinet's Defence Committee on 21 January 1946, that 'there was no one to fight'.[61] To the First Sea Lord, Admiral of the Fleet Lord Cunningham, such thinking was 'past belief'.[62] Attlee persisted in arguing that the priority given to keeping Britain's air and sea communications through the Mediterranean, the Suez Canal and the Red Sea were based on old imperialist impulses which the United Nations had made redundant. In early March 1946, he told the Defence Committee, 'We must not for sentimental reasons based on the past, give hostages to fortune.'[63] For Lord Alanbrooke, Chief of the Imperial General Staff, this was simply 'defeatist'.[64]

Alanbrooke was among the military figures in the last years of the war whose attitudes had caused a frisson in the Foreign Office. In 1944 he had written in his diary that 'Germany is no longer the dominating power in Europe – Russia is . . . She . . . cannot fail to become the main threat in fifteen years from now. Therefore, foster Germany, gradually build her up and bring her into a Federation of Western Europe. Unfortunately all this must be done under the cloak of a holy alliance of Russia, England and America.'[65]

By the time Attlee and Bevin were on their way to Potsdam to replace Churchill and Eden across the negotiating table from Stalin and Molotov, the mainstream view of the Foreign Office had caught up with that of the soldiers. On 11 July, Sir Orme Sargent, number two to Sir Alexander Cadogan at the FO (whom he would shortly replace) prepared an influential reappraisal of the post-Hitler scene (Sargent, to his credit, had been against appeasing the Nazis throughout the 1930s[66]).

Experts on Britain and the early cold war, like Anne Deighton, are right to describe the Sargent memorandum as 'central to an understanding of the real agenda of the immediate postwar world'.[67] Sargent was the obverse of Attlee, most definitely not a UN man. According to one more internationally minded official, Sargent represented 'the FO of say 1910 . . . He laughs at the United Nations as he did the League [of Nations] and the Southern and Northern Departments which, with Reconstruction, are the kernel of the FO, take their lead from him.'[68]

'Stock taking after VE Day', writes Anne Deighton,

is full of references to the nature of the threat that Hitler posed before the Second World War. In the same way that the Nazis demanded Lebensraum in the 1930s, Sargent thought that Stalin intended 'to obtain his security . . . by creating what might be termed an ideological Lebensraum in those countries which he considered strategically important'.[69] Hitler had explained in *Mein Kampf* both his objectives and his methods, but 'in the case of the Soviet Union Stalin is not likely to be so obliging. We shall have to try and find out for ourselves what is his plan of campaign.' British foreign policy makers had an obligation to stand firm in any diplomatic trial of strength that the Soviet Union might care to try. Sargent, unlike some of his other colleagues, still hoped to retain a Western influence in Eastern Europe by keeping 'our foot firmly in Finland, Poland, Czechoslovakia, Austria, Yugoslavia and Bulgaria even though we may have to abandon perhaps for the moment Rumania and Hungary'. He further feared the capacity of the Soviet Union to 'exploit for their own ends the economic crises which in the coming months may well develop into a catastrophe capable of engulfing political institutions in many European countries . . . It is not overstating the position to say that if Germany is won this may well decide the fate of liberalism throughout the world'.[70]

There was evidence to justify this stance. The Russians were utter hell to negotiate with. From the Teheran Conference of 1943 through Yalta in February 1945 to Potsdam in the ruins of Hitler's empire, Stalin and Molotov had appeared to win on the big issues – and still they asked for more as if, like textbook Marxists, they really expected history's plums to fall into their laps.

Christopher Mayhew wrote of Bevin's poor health at the last of the abortive Foreign Ministers' Conferences (into whose lap the heads of Government had deposited Potsdam's failures) in Moscow in December 1947, 'But even if he were fit, it would be hard to beat Molotov at this conference. The man's a genius in his own perverted form of diplomacy. Ernest keeps saying, "Will anyone tell me what to do next?" at the delegation meetings.'[71]

Those in the Labour Party at the time and in the historical seminar room since who think Bevin was too ready to ask the likes of Orme Sargent what to do next, underestimate the effect on that powerful but raw intellect of sitting opposite Molotov and Vyshinsky day-in, day-out, and the impact of events on the ground in eastern Europe and the Soviet Zone in Germany as all but the most reliable (i.e. pro-Soviet) local politicians were gradually excluded from the political process.

As Alan Bullock has pointed out, a deal with the Russians would have suited Bevin. It would have suited the Labour Party, the British Treasury and the Americans who, at political and official level at this stage, were way behind Whitehall in their sense of urgency about containing Soviet power in central Europe.[72] But Bevin could not get Molotov to do what Stalin had done with Churchill.

'When Bevin tried to get Stalin or Molotov to say what it was they wanted, to put down a line on the map between Soviet and British spheres of influence which could provide a basis for negotiation, they evaded him, preferring to keep their options open. Why not?' Alan Bullock asks. 'They were well aware that Britain was overstretched and would have to abandon some of her commitments. It was in Britain's interest as a power in decline to try and define the situation, and in theirs to leave it undefined, not to forego opportunities which might arise, particularly if (as the Russians firmly believed) the Americans faced a severe slump which might lead them to show less interest in Europe and the Middle East.'[73]

As late as December 1947 in Moscow, Bevin told Mayhew 'he just had no idea of Molotov's mind and intentions – whether or not he intended agreement after this initial fighting. Our delegation is in no better shape. I feel ashamed at not being able to suggest a thing – but have the excuse that Germany is only a small part of my job, while the others are specialists.'[74]

Lord Mayhew's diary, however, is in many ways at variance with the mountain of declassified files accumulated by those same 'specialists'. Certainly by the spring of 1946, when Attlee was still infuriating the Chiefs of Staff with his internationalism, the leading FO professionals were putting detailed ideas to Bevin about how to combat Stalin in Germany and in the world as a whole. In the first weeks of 1946, the JIC, the Foreign Office and the British Embassy in Moscow undertook substantial reassessments of the Soviet threat.[75] They were unreservedly sombre. They were pulled together by Christopher Warner in a paper entitled 'The Soviet Campaign against this Country and our Response to it' which won Bevin's approval and was sent to Attlee in a shortened version (the full Cabinet were rarely consulted on the most sensitive east-west issues at this stage).[76]

Bevin also approved a new brainchild of Warner's, the Russia Committee,[77] a high-level FO group, established, in Warner's words, to 'pool recent information regarding Russian doings affecting their various areas in order to get a collated picture and consider what action political, economic or in the publicity sphere should be taken as a result'.[78] In fact, it was rather more than that. The idea was to do to the Soviet Union what the 'permanent government' in Whitehall now almost universally believed the Russians were trying to do to us. In Orme Sargent's view (as paraphrased by Warner) 'It would be valuable to have a Joint Planning Committee of this kind for matters concerning the Russians since the Russians themselves clearly planned their campaign and therefore it made sense to try to assess their plans and make Joint Office counter plans.'[79]

The FO's hope in August 1945 that their new Foreign Secretary would 'stand up to the Russians all right'[80] was not disappointed. Though in the spring of 1946 Bevin curbed the wilder notions of officials like Ivone Kirkpatrick who wanted an anti-Soviet campaign comparable to the wartime operations against Hitler's Europe when 'the V sign was emblazoned all over the world . . . [and] we parachuted men, money and arms into occupied territory'.[81] And as late as April 1946, when Bevin left for the second Council of Foreign Ministers' meeting in Paris, they still worried that their man might succumb to a softer Soviet line.

Warner committed his doubts to paper in a telegram to Frank Roberts who had travelled from Moscow to Paris to join Bevin's team. 'We have foreseen', Warner wrote, 'that the Russians would pretty soon realise how clumsy they have been in the last few months, and would attempt to pull a velvet glove over their iron hand; and that public opinion and many important people both here and in America might well be misled into thinking quite erroneously that the iron hand had been discarded or even that it had been a figment of the imagination of wicked Foreign Office and Foreign Service officials.'[82]

Those 'wicked' officials needn't have worried. Molotov never softened, nor did that other granite negotiator of the postwar period, Andrei Vyshinsky, the prosecutor at the Moscow show trials before the war. There is a wonderful photo in Alan Bullock's biography of Bevin, fag in the mouth, his great peasant face beaming with mirth, joshing Vyshinsky (as they would have put it in those days) at a meeting of the UN Security Council in London in February 1946. His interpreter is smiling, but Vyshinsky shows not a flicker of mirth. Even George VI had a brave go at lightening the gloom. When Andrei Gromyko, the stony face of Soviet diplomacy for over forty years, dined off the 'massive gold cutlery' at Buckingham Palace while in London for the UN General Assembly early in 1946, he found himself 'alongside the King, evidently not by accident. Suddenly I heard him say: "Let's go into the middle of the room for a little chat."

'On his own initiative, the British Sovereign started urging me earnestly that it was essential that the wartime contact between the USSR and Britain not be lost. Naturally, I supported this view.' But, what mattered more to Gromyko was that though Churchill and Eden had gone, under Attlee and Bevin 'the class face of power remained the same'.[83]

Over eighteen months later, Bevin's junior ministers, Christopher Mayhew and Hector McNeil, tried again as Mayhew recalls:

In October 1947 Hector McNeil and I left for New York to represent Britain at the UN General Assembly. Hector was the delegation leader. He was almost as young and inexperienced as myself, a Scotsman, a former Beaverbrook journalist, courageous, a great mixer. Our fellow passengers included many other delegates bound for the UN Assembly, including a large party led by Vyshinsky . . . Hector set out to establish a personal relationship with this repellent man. It was a forlorn hope. He sent a bottle of Scotch and a friendly note to Vyshinsky's cabin, but there was no acknowledgement. He then sent some flowers to the cabin of Vyshinsky's daughter, but with no better result.[84]

Vyshinsky probably thought the flowers were bugged.

Bevin's mind almost certainly was finally made up about Stalin, Stalin's negotiators and the Soviet Union's intentions in the spring of 1946. Just occasionally, one can become a retrospective fly-on-the-wall at a seminal meeting when, out of the give-and-take, a long-lasting line finally hardens. One such took place in the Foreign Office on 3 April 1946.

It was called to hear a report from John Hynd, the Minister for the British Zone in Germany. Hynd said a decision was needed on future policy. The Russians were putting pressure on the democratic parties in the western zone who were 'rapidly losing their grip on Western Germany and the Communists are going ahead'. The Government in London was 'faced with the question whether we are to go ahead with setting up central administrations or whether we shall give up all interest in Eastern Germany and settle down to develop Western Germany'.[85]

Everyone present knew that this was a turning-point. If the victors of 1945 split Germany into two it would freeze their policy divisions in an especially enduring territorial fashion in what was then the cockpit of world politics (it was to remain *the* heartland of the cold war; not until the Berlin Wall came down in 1989 did the world truly appreciate it was over). As the minutes record:

Mr Hynd . . . said that the question must be faced whether we should now proceed to establish a German Government in our own zone with full powers of Government including economic powers.

Mr Arthur Street remarked that this amounted to a partition of Germany and *Sir Orme Sargent* said that such a step would be irrevocable.

Mr Bevin said this meant a policy of a Western Bloc and that meant war. *Sir Orme Sargent* said that the alternative to this was Communism on the Rhine.[86]

'It is clear', writes Anne Deighton, the leading historian of Britain and the postwar division of Germany, 'that the intervention of Sargent, a senior official with an unblemished track record as an opponent of appeasement, was critical. His theme was that Britain's economic weakness and the vulnerability of her position in Germany actually increased the obligation on her to act decisively and with speed towards her own zone, for "we might, by failing to take a decision now, merely drift along until we found ourselves obliged, under American pressure added to our own manpower and financial difficulties, to hand over suddenly to a German Government which would be under Communist influence".'[87]

Bevin was persuaded by his Permanent Secretary. He confronted the difficult task of 'carrying' the Americans 'with us'. But first he had to carry the British Cabinet and he prepared a long paper for them which they discussed in his absence (he was in Paris facing Molotov) on 7 May 1946, the first time they had tackled the central cold war issue since the Government had been formed ten months earlier. He broached the possibility of a 'western strategy to stall both Communism and Russian influence'. Eighty million pounds a year (the cost of subsidising the still shattered British Zone) would be a price worth paying to keep Communism east of the Elbe. 'We are not prepared to leave the field to Russia,' Bevin concluded.[88]

Several ministers did not buy the Bevin line. In this they reflected a substantial slice of public and newspaper opinion which, as the reaction to Churchill's famous 'Iron Curtain' speech two months earlier had shown, was far from ready to substitute for the image of the brave, defiant Russian ally at Stalingrad in 1942 the threat of a predatory Soviet Union armed to the teeth and ready to swoop in western Europe.[89] (Of those polled by Gallup in the days after Churchill's speech in Fulton, Missouri, 89 per cent had heard of it or read about it, they were made up of 39 per cent who disapproved of its facing-up-to-Russia theme, 34 per cent who approved and 16 per cent who were of no opinion.)[90]

In the Cabinet Room the dissenters were the Chancellor, Dalton, who wanted neither heavy *British* public expenditure in Germany nor a drift 'into an anti-Soviet policy' and the left-wingers Bevan and Shinwell who accused Bevin of exaggerating the Soviet threat. They argued that Soviet power weakened the further west it stretched and that the Germans should be allowed to evolve their own political structure. Even a right-winger like Morrison thought that Bevin was pushing his arguments too far and that harmonious relations were possible with Russia.[91]

Interestingly, only Attlee defended his absent Foreign Secretary (arguing with him in private was one thing; but Bevin, Attlee's political mainstay, had to be backed in the presence of the colleagues at least in their full Cabinet manifestation). Almost a year to the day after the Germans had surrendered, neither the Cabinet, Parliament, public opinion nor the Truman Administration in Washington was ready to contemplate confrontation with Russia which might lead to war. Sargent, Warner, Roberts and, to a very large extent, Bevin himself, were the prototypical cold warriors.

Attlee, however, chose to pursue his dissenting line in the Cabinet's Defence Committee and on the terrain of the Middle East. He continued to do so tenaciously for the rest of 1946 influenced by private briefings from the original and independent strategic thinker, Sir Basil Liddell Hart.[92] The Chiefs of Staff tried to shift their stubborn Prime Minister by tackling the Middle East in the context of the cold war and not in the imperial terms of which Attlee was so disdainful.

As there was 'little or no obstacle in Europe to a Russian advance to the western seaboard',[93] the only way to deter Stalin from so moving was to be able to hit his 'important industrial and oil producing areas' in southern Russia and the Caucasus.[94] Attlee observed in July 1946 that 'it was becoming difficult to justify our staying in the Middle East for any reason other than to be prepared for a war against Russia',[95] a concept the Prime Minister believed to be both wrongheaded and dangerous. 'At the present stage of international negotiations', he told the Defence Committee, 'it would be most dangerous to create suspicion in the minds of the Russians that we were threatening their security in the Middle East.'[96]

As late as December 1946, Attlee, at his most candid in a personal letter to Bevin, was, unlike the JIC, the FO or the Chiefs, still keeping an open mind about the true impulse behind Soviet foreign policy. 'I do not think', he wrote, 'that the countries bordering on Soviet Russia's zone viz. Greece, Turkey, Iraq and Persia can be made strong enough to form an effective barrier. We do not command the resources to make them so. If it were possible to reach an agreement with Russia that we should both disinterest ourselves as far as possible in them so that they become a neutral zone, it would be much to our advantage. Of course it is difficult to tell how far Russian policy is dictated by expansion and how far by fear of attack by the US and ourselves. Fantastic as this is, it may very well be the real grounds of Russian policy. What we consider merely defence may seem to them preparations for an attack.'[97]

Remember, too, the word 'atomic' was by now associated with the idea of such attacks. As early as April 1946, the Joint Technical Warfare Committee had prepared for the Chiefs a detailed plan for atomic attacks on sixty-seven Soviet cities containing 88 per cent of its population with the RAF flying twenty-six raids, twelve from England, thirteen from Cyprus and one from Pakistan.[98] Julian Lewis's study of postwar military planning has the target map as its grim frontispiece.

The irony of such planning papers – and those protracted 1946 discussions about the strategic value of the Middle East – is that the Government had still to decide formally to make a British atomic bomb, though it looked inevitable; what a senior Ministry of Defence official was later to call an 'of course' decision.[99] Why?

To answer that one has to go back far beyond the Chiefs' planning to drop bombs on Moscow and Kiev, beyond even the Manhattan Project which gave the US Air Force the weapons to drop on Hiroshima and Nagasaki, deep into the interwar period when several of the world's leading scientists had pondered the potential of atomic energy, a fair proportion of them in British laboratories.

In 1932 Cockcroft and Walton split the atom at the Cavendish in Cambridge in what has been called the '*annus mirabilis* of nuclear physics'.[100] Cockcroft derided anyone who saw in this the potential for releasing vast quantities of energy as 'talking moonshine', a view which, when he read it in a newspaper, set the refugee Hungarian scientist, Leo Szilard, pacing the streets of Bloomsbury. 'As he waited for the light to change . . . on Southampton Row', writes Professor Lewis Wolpert, 'the idea came to him that was to change history – a neutron chain reaction, in which atoms would split and liberate energy on an industrial scale and could, he realised with a shock, also be used to construct atomic bombs.'[101]

This was a notion the king of science fiction, H.G. Wells, had advanced in his novel *The World Set Free*[102] in the year the Kaiser launched his armies on Belgium. But not until Hitler was about to do the same in 1940 was the crucial theoretical breakthrough made which showed such a nightmare to be in the realms of the practical. Unknown to the British Government, a pair of refugee scientists working in a Birmingham University laboratory – Otto Frisch and Rudolf Peierls – discovered, in the words of Margaret Gowing, official historian of the British bomb, that 'instead of the tons of uranium which scientists had previously envisaged when they considered the possibility of a bomb, 1 Kg of metallic U235 would . . . suffice'.[103]

Years later I interviewed Sir Rudolf in a basement studio in BBC Broadcasting House. Scholarly looking, in a battered corduroy jacket, ill-fitting trousers and scuffed Hush Puppies, he looked every inch the absent-minded professor of popular imagination as he told me, in his quiet Austrian accent, of the sequence of events in Birmingham in 1940. The conversation, the only one I have ever conducted with someone of whom it could be said that they truly changed the world, went like this:

Nobody had really thought hard about how much separated uranium would be required to make an explosion – what was a critical size? And then one day it occurred to us to ask what would happen if you had a large quantity of separated isotope? And, to our surprise, if you worked this out on the back of an envelope, the amount came out quite small.

Then we asked ourselves, now if you could make such an explosion, what would happen? And again on [the] back of another envelope it came out that while you couldn't predict the exact power, the effects would be enormous. We also then pointed out the consequences of this weapon, including the fall-out, including the fact that it would probably be very difficult to use it without killing a lot of civilians. And, we added, for that reason, it might never be a suitable weapon for use by this country.[104]

I asked Sir Rudolf how they felt the day they completed their 'back-of-an-envelope' research. 'We were elated in some sense, but also frightened,' he replied.

Incredible though it now seems, they merely showed the results of their research to Professor Mark Oliphant who passed it on to Whitehall in March 1940 where 'interest about the uranium bomb which had been waning now waxed rapidly'.[105] In the deepest secrecy Whitehall set to work with a policy committee and a technical committee on which Frisch and Peierls sat. By July 1941, the results were presented in the so-called 'Maud Report' to Churchill and the handful of ministers and civil servants admitted to the secret.

In research terms, it placed Britain ahead of the United States where investigations were also under way (prompted in large measure by Leo Szilard and Albert Einstein who had approached President Roosevelt through an intermediary shortly after the outbreak of the war in Europe about 'extremely powerful bombs' which might be made if 'nuclear chain reactions' could be engineered[106]). The Maud Report was passed to the Americans. It was almost certainly the most important British gift to the USA. Even though they were not yet in the war, it was imperative that if an atomic bomb was going to be made, Hitler shouldn't be the first to do so.

As Margaret Gowing put it: 'If it had not been for the brilliant scientific work done in Britain in the early part of the war, by refugee scientists, the Second World War would almost certainly have ended before an atomic bomb was dropped. It had been the cogency and clarity of the British Maud Report in 1941 which had persuaded the Americans of the practical possibility of an atomic bomb and the urgency of making one.'[107]

It was this knowledge that caused such intense resentment in Whitehall when the United States unilaterally suspended atomic collaboration with Britain after the war. The special atomic relationship, however, was bumpy from the start. The Americans were impressed by the Maud Report, but the British were reluctant to go into partnership with them. Why?

Lord Sherfield who, as Roger Makins, was the most important atomic diplomat of the 1940s (the Americans called him 'Mr Atom')[108] reckons 'it was partly psychological. We thought we had all the information, we could probably get on pretty well on our own and we could be willing to exchange information with the Americans but not really go into a joint project. The result of that was that the Americans were not very much impressed with the British attitude, so they decided to go ahead on their own. And, of course, when Americans decide that they really are going to have to do something, they really get on with it . . . so, by the time collaboration was really established in 1944, the Americans had gone miles ahead.'[109]

That collaboration, which involved a small team of British scientists travelling to North America, resulted from an agreement struck between Churchill and Roosevelt at Quebec in 1943. The two leaders also bound their governments not to use the bomb without the consent of the other and Britain undertook not to proceed with a civil nuclear power programme without American agreement.[110] In the following year, a note of another conversation between the two men at Roosevelt's upstate New York country home, Hyde Park, pledged the continuation of Anglo-American atomic collaboration in peacetime.[111] But, given wartime secrecy, no hint of either the Quebec Agreement or the Hyde Park aide-memoire reached the United States Congress or the British Parliament – a factor of great significance in the early months of the peace.

When Truman and his War Secretary, Henry Stimson, moved towards the decision to use the atomic weapon on Japan, a secret channel was opened up to London to secure Churchill's agreement via Field Marshal 'Jumbo' Wilson, the British representative on the key atomic body, the Combined Policy Committee, in Washington, who was Makins' boss in Washington, and Sir John Anderson, the minister in London to whom Churchill delegated much of the work on 'Tube Alloys', as the project was code-named.

As Britain was involved in the awesome decision which led to the destruction of Hiroshima and Nagasaki, the only time nuclear weapons have been used in war, it's worth taking a look at how it was done. Neither the War Cabinet (most of whom had no idea of the bomb project) nor the Chiefs of Staff (who had) were consulted. 'The Prime Minister', writes Margaret Gowing,

> was anxious that the British should not have to insist on any legalistic interpretation of the appropriate clause of the Quebec Agreement. Some of the Americans have grave doubts about the wisdom of this clause, partly on constitutional grounds and partly on political grounds. There might be considerable criticism that the United States Government had spent two billion dollars on the most expensive weapon yet devised and yet had accepted an obligation not to use it without the consent of another power.
>
> Nevertheless, Mr Stimson and Field Marshal Wilson agreed amicably at the end of June 1945 to record the decision to use the weapon against Japan in a minute of the Combined Policy Committee. Anderson asked the Prime Minister for his authority to instruct the British Representative on the Combined Policy Committee to give their concurrence, Mr Churchill simply initialled the minute and on July 4th the Combined Policy Committee in Washington duly noted the British agreement.[112]

Wilson said the Prime Minister might want to talk to the President about it at Potsdam, and that was that. For Churchill, this too was an 'of course' decision. It was, however casual, a genuine consultation though, surely, Truman would have launched the atomic strike anyway if Churchill had said 'no'. The Quebec Agreement was not a treaty – nor did more than a handful of people know of its existence. Just how lightly the Americans regarded it quickly became apparent. For no sooner had the bombs been dropped on Hiroshima and Nagasaki and the British scientists returned home, than, to all intents and purposes, collaboration ceased. The Anglo-American partnership had always had an on-and-off air about it. But now, with Germany and Japan defeated, the Americans regarded the bomb as their exclusive property.

From Attlee to Makins, the British bent every effort to restore collaboration in the autumn of 1945. By the time of the Prime Minister's visit to Washington in November, it was plain Truman was under the influence of General Groves, the bustling army engineer in charge of the Manhattan Project who wanted to ease the British out. Attlee spent much time with Truman discussing international control of the bomb through a proposed UN Commission on Atomic Energy. He persuaded himself that a general statement from the Americans pledging 'full and effective co-operation in the field of atomic energy'[113] meant what it said.

It was already becoming plain to Makins, the official responsible day-to-day for defending Britain's atomic interests, that this was not so. 'The trouble with the Hyde Park Agreement', he told me over forty years later when he was at liberty to divulge pretty well the whole story,

> was that the American copy of the agreement was lost. I had the rather invidious task of taking a copy down to the State Department because they couldn't find it . . . What had happened, in fact, was that the President's Secretary, or whoever was with him at Hyde Park, had passed it down the line. And whoever got it in the Administration looked at it. The code name was 'Tube Alloys'. And this official thought, 'Well, Tube Alloys, that must be something to do with naval engineering.' So they sent it over to the Navy Department.[114]

To make matters even worse, as these difficult negotiations proceeded, Senator Brian McMahon, Chairman of the Senate Committee on Atomic Energy, in complete ignorance of the Quebec and Hyde Park undertakings, was busy pushing legislation through Congress prohibiting co-operation with any country on nuclear matters. Makins, however, did have copies to brandish in front of his American counterparts.

> Of course we made the most of it. But, in fact, they were very weak documents and they had no legislative backing. They were not capable of being ratified, or even produced to the Parliaments. So it wasn't really a very strong hand. However, we did in fact make a draft and submitted it to the Combined Policy Committee in, I think it was April [1946], and the Americans just threw it out, out of hand.

By that time the McMahon Act had either been passed or was in the process, and they said 'We can't sign this. It's impossible. We can't have an agreement.' Now Mr Attlee sent a long message to the President rehearsing the whole background of our collaboration in the war, and so on, and saying that this really was an intolerable situation – a very strong document. He never got an answer.[115]

Some years later Senator McMahon told both Attlee's Defence Minister, A.V. Alexander, and Winston Churchill that had he known about the Quebec Agreement he would never have put his Bill through Congress.[116] Lord Sherfield is not convinced. 'If they'd seen the Quebec Agreement . . . I think they would have been taken aback by it . . . They would have thought it was a document which probably ought never to have been written. I don't think it would have made the slightest difference.'[117]

The barren result of these negotiations made a great difference, however, to a Britain exhausted by six years of war. The difference was not so acute on the theoretical side. Several British scientists had been involved in the minutiae of the uranium and plutonium bombs dropped on Japan. William Penney, for example, the British expert on blast effect, carried home the details of the Nagasaki bomb in his head from where not even the McMahon Act could expunge them. It was on the vast industrial infrastructure needed to produce fissile material for the warhead that the Americans had so much to offer their former partner. A British bomb would have been a far easier proposition if collaboration had continued, particularly on the industrial side.

Once the McMahon Act was law, Britain, as Attlee put it simply, 'had to go ahead on our own'.[118] His Cabinet Committee on Atomic Energy had already put in place much of the essential groundwork (as had the Civil Service Commissioner, the scientist-cum-novelist, C.P. Snow, who encouraged Penney to stay in government service, and not to return to university life, for just this purpose).[119] In December 1945 a special Cabinet Committee GEN 75, at the prodding of the Chiefs of Staff, had authorised the building of an atomic pile to make plutonium at Windscale[120] (known as Sellafield nowadays; it was this pile which caught fire in 1957 briefly threatening the Lake District with intense fall-out). The same meeting of ministers decided 'The Chiefs of Staff would submit a report on our requirements for atomic bombs and the possibility of making consequential reductions in other forms of armament production.'[121]

Perhaps Attlee was not as confident of American collaboration as he had pretended in Washington the previous month. It was Bevin, however, who was the real patron of the British bomb. Unlike Attlee, he never put much hope in internationalising control of atomic energy either through the UN Commission or the American Baruch Plan. He told GEN 75, 'Let's forget about the Baroosh [his usual trouble with foreign-sounding names] and get on with the fissile.'[122]

In October 1946, however, there was a political hiccup in the Cabinet Committee when ministers were asked for money to build a gaseous diffusion plant in addition to the Windscale pile to improve the supply of fissile material for the bomb. Sir Michael Perrin was present as assistant to Lord Portal, controller of the bomb project in the Ministry of Supply. 'When the meeting started', he recalled,

> the Foreign Secretary, Bevin, had not turned up. Two of the other ministers, Dalton, the Chancellor of the Exchequer, and Sir Stafford Cripps [President of the Board of Trade], were very much against this, because they said, we haven't got the money to do it, we haven't got the materials. We want building materials for the present crisis in the country . . . I was there with Portal and I was sitting between the two of them [the Minister of Supply, John Wilmot, and Portal].
>
> He [Wilmot] said to me, 'Look, I think we'd better withdraw this paper.' And Portal said, 'Go on talking.' And he did go on talking. And at that stage Mr Bevin came in and apologised for being late . . . The Prime Minister summed up very much on the lines of what Dalton and Cripps had been saying . . .
>
> Bevin said, 'No, Prime Minister, that won't do at all. We've *got* to have this.' And one of the reasons he gave was a very striking one. Quite bluntly, he said: 'I don't mind for myself, but I don't want any other Foreign Secretary of this country to be talked at, or to, by the Secretary of State in the United States as I have just had in my discussions with Mr Byrnes. We've got to have this thing over here, whatever it costs.' And, I think I'm right in remembering, he ended up with saying, 'We've got to have a bloody Union Jack flying on top of it.' And that swung the meeting right round.[123]

The occasion was pure Bevin. He'd had a heavy lunch and had fallen asleep (the 25 October meeting of GEN 75 began at 2.15 in No. 10). He waddled in, caught its sense, recoiled and, as Roy Jenkins said of him in another Cabinet context, 'simply stopped the engine in its tracks, lifted it up, and put it back facing in the other direction. He got what he wanted. He was concerned neither to give himself the pleasure of delivering a great Cabinet oration, nor to save the faces of those whose time he had wasted by being late. The bad manners were incidental. The exercise of power on the side of good sense (as he saw it) was central.'[124]

No matter that the Cabinet's two most important economic ministers said £30–£40 million over four to five years for a gaseous diffusion plant was a bad investment[125] (the cost of the whole bomb programme was £100 million[126]). Bevin knew the reality of power. He had to take the brunt of Byrnes' disregard for Britain and dislike of its Empire at international gatherings.[127] For the 'working class John Bull' it was a matter of simple patriotism to put a Union Jack on the atomic bomb. Great powers had to have great weapons.

There is another significant truth lurking in the accounts of GEN 75 in autumn 1946 (which was a far more significant meeting than the occasion the following January when a formal decision was taken to make a bomb because in October 1946 the economic and great-power fundamentals were addressed). There is no mention of the Russians, the Soviet threat, the Iron Curtain or any of the perceptions that infused the telegrams of Roberts or the memos of Warner and Sargent. It's *America* that Bevin bangs on about – as he was to again on the day the bomb was given the specific go-ahead. Even if the wartime alliance had not been crumbling because of events on the ground in eastern Europe and Bevin's growing conviction that in Molotov he was dealing with the worst kind of Communist in a local Labour Party ('If you treated him badly, he made the most of the grievance, and, if you treated him well, he only put up his price and abused you the next day,'[128]) some time in the first two years after the war, a group of British ministers would have opted for a bomb with a Union Jack on top of it. General Groves and Senator McMahon, not Stalin and Molotov, were the reasons for that. The bomb became a central element in Britain's cold war strategy (it already was at the level of the military planners). But it was a quite different set of impulses which gave it the first ministerial seal of approval.

Attlee has often been criticised for failing to take the bomb decision to full Cabinet.[129] Even Churchill was amazed on returning to No. 10 in 1951 to see how Attlee had concealed its £100 million cost from Parliament.[130] Why did he keep it away from the Cabinet? Not, I think, because with a dash of dissent from Dalton and Cripps on economic grounds, and from Bevan and Shinwell on cold war grounds, he would have failed in the end to get his way. But because, as he told John Mackintosh in old age, he 'thought that some of them were not fit to be trusted with secrets of this kind'.[131] He was persuaded by the total secrecy argument Portal (wartime Chief of the Air Staff turned Ministry of Supply atomic controller) and the Ministry of Supply put to him.[132] When a sparse announcement was finally made in Parliament in May 1948,[133] the Government only came clean on the bomb in order to motivate the workforce by telling them the national importance of their task (previously the true significance of their individual input had been left unsaid, but many must have guessed).

Even after Bevin had seen off Dalton and Cripps, the scientists still hadn't been alerted to the drift of ministerial thinking on the bomb. Penney was only summoned by Portal to be told he was to design the warhead in May 1947.[134] But the military pressed ahead apace. In November 1946 the Air Ministry drew up the specification for a new long-range bomber with the capacity to carry a single 'special bomb' of 10,000 pounds 'to a target 2,000 nautical miles from a base which may be anywhere in the world'.[135] This was the beginnings of the V-bomber force, carrier of the first generation of British nuclear weapons.[136]

It's an awesome moment for any country when its Government decides to become a nuclear power. Great responsibilities fall upon its political leaders and defence chiefs. The cost and technical complications involved have a profound impact upon its industrial capacity and research establishments. Its relationships with other nations change. Yet it was a civil servant, Lord Portal, who nudged ministers into that decision. As he told them when they gathered in the Cabinet Room on the afternoon of 8 January 1947,

> so far as he was aware, no decision had yet been taken to proceed with the development of atomic weapons. He had discussed the matter with the Chiefs of Staff who were naturally anxious that we should not be without this weapon if others possess it. About three years' work would be needed to solve the problems of nuclear physics and engineering involved in the bomb mechanism.[137]

A glance at the faces around the table as Portal spoke would have shown some significant absences from the normal Cabinet Committee on atomic matters, GEN 75.

Dalton and Cripps, the economisers and husbanders of civilian resources, were gone. The Defence Minister, A.V. Alexander, had arrived. In fact, Attlee deliberately moved the key bomb decision out of GEN 75 (to which, with Dalton and Cripps back, atomic business later returned) and put it in a special new ministerial group, GEN 163 which met only once and for the specific purpose of giving Portal and the Chiefs the green light. It consisted of Attlee and five colleagues – Bevin, Morrison, Alexander, Wilmot from Supply and the Dominions Secretary, the venerable Lord Addison, for whose wisdom Attlee had a great regard.[138]

Again, not a whisper of the Soviet threat. Once again the superpower talked about was the United States. 'We could not afford', rumbled Bevin, 'to acquiesce in an American monopoly of this new development. Other countries also might well develop atomic weapons. Unless therefore an effective international system could be developed under which the production and use of the weapon would be prohibited, we must develop it ourselves.'[139]

Attlee never agonised over atomic matters. In his way he was as decisive as Truman, a comparison made by Lord Sherfield who saw them both in action.[140] Sherfield, back in London from 1947 as the FO's 'Mr Atom', chaired the official committee which shadowed GEN 75 in 1948–9.

> I reported direct to the Prime Minister. The papers came back in two or three hours inscribed 'CRA' in red ink. Only once or twice did he put 'See me', and this was to make a political point for my guidance.
>
> I never had a more efficient chief. His mastery of the Cabinet was proverbial. I saw him in action in the Cabinet Committee on Atomic Energy, of which all the big guns were members. The Prime Minister sat hunched in his chair while all the salvoes were firing, drawing geometrical designs with a multi-coloured chalk pencil. After he thought the discussion had gone on long enough, he would look up and say 'Yep', and announce the decision in a few crisp sentences. It was a vintage performance.'[141]

Attlee's atomic decisiveness never left him. Years later he recalled the thinking behind the GEN 163 decision for his official biographer, Kenneth Harris. As for Bevin at the time, it was all about America and Britain as a great power: 'If we had decided not to have it, we would have put ourselves entirely in the hands of the Americans. That would have been a risk a British government should not take. It's all very well to look back, and to say otherwise, but at that time nobody could be sure that the Americans would not revert to isolationism – many Americans wanted that, many Americans feared it. There was no NATO then. For a power of our size and with our responsibilities to turn its back on the Bomb did not make sense.'[142]

It is important to remember this crispness and decisiveness on atomic weapons was possible partly because the bomb decision at this stage was isolated from cold war policy-making where, as we have seen, Attlee was most definitely not in step with his Foreign Secretary and his Chiefs of Staff throughout 1946. Just as Portal was getting GEN 163 to concentrate its mind on matters atomic in January 1947, the Chiefs and Bevin were moving in on Attlee across the wider terrain of foreign and defence policy.

Matters were brought to a head[143] by Attlee himself on 5 January 1947 when he sent Bevin a long memorandum reprising his doubts about the costs of a substantial Mediterranean/Middle Eastern commitment and the wisdom of planning to bomb the Soviet Union from airfields in the region. 'I regard the strategy . . . as a strategy of despair. I have the gravest doubts as to its efficacy. The deterrent does not seem to me to be sufficiently strong. I apprehend that the pursuit of this policy so far from preventing may precipitate hostilities.'[144]

In what Alan Bullock described as 'the most radical criticism Bevin had to face from inside the Government during his five and a half years as Foreign Secretary',[145] Attlee went on to suggest an alternative strategy which led to his being compared to Chamberlain by his closest Cabinet ally. 'Unless', Attlee told his Foreign Secretary, 'we are persuaded that the USSR is irrevocably committed to a policy of world domination and that there is no possibility of her alteration, I think that before being committed to this strategy we should seek to come to an agreement with the USSR after consideration with Stalin of all our points of conflict.[146]

In his reply to Attlee, four days after receiving his memo and one day after they had decided, in perfect harmony, to make a British atom bomb, Bevin reached straight for the most potent weapon available in a foreign affairs discussion in late-Forties Britain. 'It would be Munich all over again', he said of Attlee's plan to parley with Stalin, 'only on a world scale, with Greece, Turkey and Persia as the first victims in place of Czechoslovakia. If I am right about Russian ideology, Russia would certainly fill the gap we leave empty, whatever her promises . . . If we speak to Stalin as you propose, he is as likely to respect their independence as Hitler was to respect Czechoslovakia's and we shall get as much of Stalin's goodwill as we got of Hitler's after Munich.'[147]

That afternoon Attlee cancelled a planned meeting with the Chiefs and consulted Bevin and the Defence Minister, Alexander, privately. According to a Foreign Office account of the meeting he was 'still not satisfied' with the case for Britain carrying on in the Middle East.[148] Yet, by the time the Chiefs of Staff gathered in No. 10 on 13 January for their postponed meeting on Middle East strategy, he had caved in.

Why? Because all three Chiefs – Montgomery for the Army, Tedder for the Air Force and Cunningham for the Navy – threatened to resign if he didn't. This was ironic in Monty's case for he had just returned from a visit to Moscow, which included a conversation with Stalin, which led him to believe (as he told a War Office debriefing) that Russia would be unable to fight another major war for twenty years.[149] To the Chief of the Imperial General Staff, however, the Prime Minister's ideas about Middle East strategy smelt of defeatism. 'We must hold it [the Middle East] in peace and fight for it in war,' was Monty's view.[150]

Monty's military diarist recorded the crucial occasion at which the military ganged up on the Prime Minister. 'At the first Chiefs of Staff meeting which he attended after his return [from Moscow], he asked the other two Chiefs of Staff if they were prepared, with him, to resign rather than give way over the Middle East. He told them that he would do so with or without them, but this was unnecessary as they both agreed wholeheartedly with him. General Hollis [Secretary of the Chiefs of Staff Committee] was accordingly instructed to convey, by private methods, this information to the Prime Minister.'[151]

Attlee probably received the message on Sunday 12 January. The following day the Chiefs turned up for their meeting ready to go. They stayed. 'We heard no more about it,' wrote Montgomery in his memoirs.[152] The most important of Britain's cold war dissenters had succumbed to the new Whitehall/military orthodoxy at the beginning of a year in which many of the familiar rhythms of postwar Britain were first played to a still exhausted people living off a frayed and stretched economy. It's to the pivotal events of 1947 that we now return.

CHAPTER 8

Ice, Dollars and New Looks

I have asked Mr Attlee 3 times now if he is not worried over the domestic situation in this country. But he won't tell me he is when I feel he is. I know I am worried.
King George VI, diary entry, 30 January 1947[1]

Britain very suddenly advertised to the world she could no longer play her role . . . The wind that blew down the scaffolding rose at the end of January 1947 . . . an area of high pressure somewhere above Archangel began moving in an arc over Scandinavia and down towards England, sucking Siberian cold with it . . . If ever a nation was paralysed it was Britain in her winter crisis. Millions were unemployed. War-time blackout was reintroduced over 80 per cent of the country. Domestic use of electricity for heating was restricted on pain of heavy fines. A newspaper stated the alarming truth that at that moment a country so small and weak as Portugal could have invaded and conquered England prostrated by cold . . . If ever a people deserved a happier fate . . . it was the common people of Britain.
Howard K. Smith recalling 1947 in 1950[2]

In the 1947–8–9 harvests to run no risks of insufficient labour . . . might mean radical interference with educational arrangements, we should go forward with a 'famine' food programme and, if necessary, direction of labour to agriculture.
Secret Treasury contingency plan in case American Loan ran out and Marshall Aid did not arrive, July 1947[3]

The summer of 1947 comes back to mind for the settled perfection of the weather for weeks on end, the visit of Alan Melville's South Africans, and the triumphal progress of Denis Compton, whose eighteen hundreds and 3,816 runs broke all records.
E.W. Swanton, 1974[4]

We were very cross about it [the 'New Look'], because there was Christian Dior, lowering the hemlines almost to the ankle with enormously full skirts and little slim tops . . . and nothing that we had in the cupboard was any longer in fashion and an awful lot of us said, 'Oh we can't afford it, and we can't buy it', but of course we did.

Mrs June MacDonald, Secretary of the National Housewives' League, recalling 1947 in 1985[5]

In the first few years after the war, everybody, from the highest to the lowest in the land, shared the same fixation. 'Food, clothes and fuel are the main topics of conversation with us all,' the King wrote to his brother the Duke of Gloucester.[6] He could have added strikes, especially when industrial action threatened the rations as it did in the early days of 1947 when the Smithfield lorry drivers took unofficial action and Attlee sent the Army in to keep the meat moving.[7] George VI raised the possibility of going on strike himself at one of the Prime Minister's weekly audiences. 'The liberty of the subject', he stammered, 'was at stake if a strike interfered with home life. Essential services such as gas, electricity and water should never be used for those purposes in an unofficial strike. He and I could easily go on strike. He would send me no papers and if he did I would not sign them. But we don't.'[8]

Types of food, commonplace before the war and positively humdrum now, could be an object of magical veneration in the late 1940s. Take a banana. 'The first time I ever heard of a banana', recalled Terry Alford, a schoolboy at the time,

> was when my sister came home from the theatre. She was a junior dancer on the stage in Covent Garden theatre . . . and she'd spoken to one of the porters in Covent Garden market and he said there was a consignment of bananas into the market the next day and she said that he'd promised to give her one.
>
> So, anyway, she went off to the theatre that night and I sat at home waiting and waiting and getting excited about this prospect of seeing a real banana, because up to that time I'd only seen them on a film. And eventually she came in and as the door opened she had this piece of cloth . . . then she took off this cloth and revealed this banana and we both stared at it and we put it on the table and to us it was like a piece of sculpture, it wasn't a piece of fruit, we was touching it and moving it around. But my mother, because she'd seen bananas before the war, she came in and she says, 'You're not eating all that on your own,' and she chopped it in half and destroyed the whole image of it.[9]

As a ten-year-old I can remember going on holiday to the Isle of Skye in 1957 and the excitement of the Hebrideans at the first consignment of bananas to reach them since 1939 (I still can't understand why it took so long for them to reappear up there).

Everybody, again from the highest to the lowest, tried to find a way round the rigour of the ration. Ernie Bevin had his own luxurious retreat, much beloved by his wife Flo, at the sumptuous home of the Italian-born film producer 'Del' Giudice, near Marlow. 'Rationing', said the historian Geoffrey Warner (whose father was Giudice's personal projectionist), 'might as well not have existed at Del's place.'[10] Bevin's private secretary, Sir Nicholas Henderson, has described an afternoon in Giudice's personal cinema in a converted barn on his estate.

After a heavy and liquid lunch, during which Del presented Ernie with a box of a hundred cigars 'and a trousseau of ties, socks and coloured braces' which he had picked up on a recent trip to America, they staggered off to the barn. 'From the outside', writes Henderson,

> it did not make much pretence at age, but no Tudor effort was spared within: beams as numerous as zebra stripes, plenty of oak and iron-work, electric logs in the grate, and all round the walls antlers and tiger skins. There was also a bar. The lights of the barn went out and cigars were handed round as the Dolly Sisters came on the screen.
>
> After the film footmen served tea in the bar. Del and the Foreign Secretary talked about their insides and, at the former's request, I agreed to arrange for Bevin to see a certain Madame X in London the following day. 'It's only a lavage', Del confided to me, 'but it'll cleanse the whole business. Royalty and lots of nice people go there . . . ' It could not be denied that Bevin liked food and drink, and he said to me once that he would never have got where he did, had the good things of life been available to him when he was a young man. But more than anything, I think he mixed with people like Del to please Mrs Bevin.[11]

Cripps was also a friend of Giudice's.[12] In fact, the austere Sir Stafford was not quite the prim, carrot-chewing puritan of popular imagination. As we have seen, 'Until he became seriously ill, he enjoyed a glass of wine and was a heavy smoker.'[13] Attlee was probably the greatest puritan in the Cabinet. His ministers and their wives lived in fear of invitations to Chequers because of the freezing bedrooms and the thimblefuls of sherry the Attlees served.[14]

Richard Hoggart, newly demobbed and starting out in life as an adult education lecturer in the north-east with a young family to nurture, has captured the reality of early postwar consumption of those who could not count a Del Giudice among their friends.

> In 1946, to be a newcomer in a place like Redcar could bear hard on you. You didn't know a butcher or a grocer so had no place in the queue for titbits off-rations.
>
> An essay could be written on the power accrued by butchers especially, during the war and for as long as rationing lasted . . . Even if they were not corrupt, and I imagine most were not though some were 'keen', sentimental

folklore set in so that a butcher would say – or his wife more likely, since she usually served – that Mrs So-and-So had been loyal to their shop throughout the war and naturally they would see her all right now.

We were succoured by coincidence. Our regimental MO [medical officer] . . . was practising in Redcar, with an established family. One of their many kindnesses, in that notoriously bitter winter, was an introduction to their butcher, which meant that when the Old Loyalists had been served we might be offered, very much *sotto voce*, half a rabbit.[15]

'I doubt', adds Hoggart, 'if we have had a rabbit since rationing stopped; it says too much.'[16]

An especially sharp blow to public morale came in the summer of 1946 when bread was rationed. It hadn't happened in the war. It lasted two years and almost everybody, including the official historian of the Ministry of Food, now thinks it was unnecessary.[17] Bevin, Cripps, Morrison and the new Minister of Food, the former Marxist intellectual John Strachey, all thought it a needless mistake from day one.[18]

It was, however, introduced for remarkably altruistic reasons – to help alleviate famine in Asia and defeated Germany, the bulk of whose population concentrations were in the British Zone. Throughout 1946 the extraction rate of flour from the wheat increased until it reached 85 per cent, darkening an already grey loaf. Bevin hated the so-called 'British Loaf'. He said it made him belch.[19] As an extension of this anti-famine programme, Strachey announced on 27 June that as from 21 July 1946 adults would be restricted to 9 ounces of bread a week, though factory workers would get more.

There was uproar, from millers, from housewives (the celebrated British Housewives' League was already becoming a thorn in ministerial flesh); and from the Conservative Opposition who went to town on the inevitable anomalies of the scheme. On 29 June J.L. Hodson noted in his diary:

Bread rationing is historic. We avoided it in two major wars, we come to it after a year of peace that bears some resemblance to war in its hardships and uneasy international relationships. Master bakers growl bitterly, housewives, already sorely pressed, must assume yet another burden. But I do not think it will be so troublesome and harsh as at first blush it sounds. There will be households – mine is one – where the ration will be greater than we now eat, and we shall be able, so they say, to exchange the surplus for other 'points' to give us extra tinned milk, sardines, dried fruits, biscuits, and so on. The conscience of some people will be easier . . .[20]

And so it proved. Strachey and Morrison between them had negotiated sufficient supplies for Britain in Canada and America. The ration was adequate. So, in the event, consumption was only reduced a little.[21]

There was, however, a genuine feeding problem in the first two years after the war. In March 1947 a report went to the full Cabinet from Dr Magnus

Pyke, later a gesticulating television personality of the 'mad professor' type, then a scientific officer in the Ministry of Food, which claimed that nutritional standards had fallen so badly as to have halted the physical improvements made by children during the war.[22]

When cold weather and the fuel crisis fused in a cruelly malign fashion towards the end of January 1947, it produced a loss of faith in the Government of competence and fair shares. 'Shiver with Shinwell and starve with Strachey' became the inevitable (and, up to a point, plausible) headline in the Conservative Press.[23] For Dalton 1947 was Labour's *'annus horrendus'*.[24] For Attlee and his ministers, wrote Dalton, the fuel crisis was 'certainly the first really heavy blow to confidence in the Government and in our postwar plans. This soon began to show itself in many different and unwelcome ways. Never glad, confident morning again.'[25]

The God of politics can be mercilessly cruel. That holy grail of the British labour movement, nationalisation of the mines, became a reality on 1 January 1947. 'Two months later power supplies across the country had almost broken down. Over 2,000,000 people were thrown out of work; people worked in offices by candlelight; fires and traffic lights went out; lifts stopped; the national newspapers were cut to four pages; and periodicals did not appear for three weeks. Exports were disrupted and firms like Austin were forced to close. No one was allowed to cook on an electric stove from 9 a.m. to 12 p.m. and from 2 p.m. to 4 p.m.'[26] Why? It wasn't just the most severe winter weather in living memory which struck on 23 January 1947. There was more to it than that. Much of it had to do with the political mismanagement of the country's black gold – coal – supplier of 93 per cent of the nation's energy.[27]

As we saw in our survey of the British industrial base when war ended, the condition of the mining industry was parlous even through the years of state direction in both the management and the manpower senses. The industry and the country just squeaked by during the first postwar winter (for planning purposes the 'coal winter' ran from 1 November to 30 April) with a mere 6.8 million tons left in reserve for a nation at that time consuming just under 200 million tons a year.[28]

Whitehall split into two camps on the coal problem – the Minister of Fuel and Power, Emanuel Shinwell, versus the rest. Shinwell appeared to take at face value the assurances of miners' leaders (he sat for Seaham, a coalfield seat in the north-east) that once the pits were nationalised on New Year's Day 1947, a new spirit underground would raise all the coal the country and the Government needed. In one of the most spectacular examples of individual political complacency in the postwar period, Shinwell told a lunch of coke-oven managers as late as 24 October 1946 that 'Everybody knows there is going to be a serious crisis in the coal industry except the Minister of Fuel and Power. I want to tell you there is not going to be a crisis in the coal industry, if by crisis you mean that industrial organisation is going to be seriously dislocated and that hundreds of factories are going to be closed down.'[29]

This is precisely what happened four months later. There were those in Whitehall who had predicted as much, notably James Meade in the Cabinet Office and Douglas Jay in No. 10. Jay, Attlee's personal economic assistant until he left to fight and win the Battersea North by-election in July 1946,[30] warned the P.M. in one of his last memos the previous month that current coal production would only build up stocks to 11 million tons by October, 20 per cent below the comparable figure a year before which had only just seen Britain through. After that, Jay warned, the winter run-down would reduce reserves to 3–4 million tons, or about a week's supply. 'As things are going at present', he concluded, 'industry, transport and domestic consumption is bound to be dislocated on a wide and uncontrollable scale by December or a little later.'[31]

By the end of July Attlee was treating coal as 'now the most urgent economic problem'.[32] Dalton and Morrison agreed with him but, so strong is the position of a stubborn departmental minister in Whitehall, Shinwell did not shift his ground and exhibit a sense of urgency about the position until November despite regular prodding from the Cabinet's Coal Committee.[33] Even without that pall of freezing air from Archangel which reached London and the Home Counties at the end of January, there would have been a winter crisis in the mines, the power stations and the factories in the early months of 1947.

One of the pitfalls of writing history is the difficulty of channelling all the pressures bearing down on hard-pressed ministers into a single barometer. All too often specialist accounts wonder at the slow speed and superficiality with which the author's preoccupation was handled at Cabinet or Cabinet committee level. How could they have failed to appreciate the significance of X's or Y's line? In 1983 Andrew Arends and I tried to counteract this tendency by summarising the flow of Cabinet business in the first fortnight of that crucial year of 1947.[34]

Our survey, though far from comprehensive, was revealing of heavy duty preoccupations from India to the bomb, from the meat lorry drivers' strike to the housing shortage. It's worth rereading not least as an illustration of the political overload that has burdened most British ministers most of the time since 1945:

WEDNESDAY, 1ST JANUARY, 1947.
    Defence Committee, DO 1(47). Chairman: Attlee.
    Agenda:
    1   Palestine – Use of armed forces.
    2   Defence co-operation between Canada and the USA.

THURSDAY, 2ND JANUARY.
    Cabinet Meeting, CM 1(47).
    Agenda:
    1   Peace Treaties – Italy, Trieste, Balkan States, Finland, Forces of
        Occupation.

2 Germany.
3 Austria – Preparations for Peace Treaty.
4 UN – Meeting of the General Assembly.
5 Food Supplies from the USA.
6 Future Meetings.

Legislation Committee, HPC 1(47). Chairman: Greenwood.
Agenda:
1 Town and Country Planning Bill – draft approved.

FRIDAY, 3RD JANUARY.
India and Burma Committee, 1B 1(47). Chairman: Attlee.
Agenda:
1 Future Policy in India.
2 Problem of how to withdraw.

MONDAY, 6TH JANUARY.
Cabinet Meeting. CM 2(47).
Agenda:
1 Peace Treaties.
2 Germany. Preparations for Foreign Ministers' Meeting in Moscow. Socialisation of Ruhr Industry.
3 Austria Peace Treaty.
4 Spain and France.
5 France – Economic co-operation needed.
6 UN – Use of veto in Security Council.
7 Albania – Corfu Channel.
8 Egypt.
9 Publication of Cabinet Minutes – no information to be released.

Coal Committee, CC 1(47). Chairman: Dalton.
1 Coal and Electricity allocation to power stations and industry: both to be rationed.

India and Burma Committee, 1B 2(47). Chairman: Attlee.
Agenda:
1 Mountbatten worried about Europeans being trapped as breakdown of 'law and order' likely.

TUESDAY, 7TH JANUARY.
Cabinet Meeting, CM 3(47).
Agenda:
1 Coal and Electricity. Critical Shortages. Power Stations to be favoured.

Committee on Service Land Usage, GEN 160. Chairman: Greenwood.
Agenda:
1 White Paper on training programme of the services.

Colonial Affairs Committee, C 1(47). Chairman: Greenwood.
Agenda:
1 Legislative Council in Singapore.
2 Malta's Constitution.

Committee on Economic Planning, MEP 1(47). Chairman: Morrison.
Agenda:
1 Economic Survey for 1947.
2 Wages and Prices Policy.

Legislation Committee, HPC 2(47). Chairman: Greenwood.
Agenda:
1 Electricity Bill.

WEDNESDAY, 8TH JANUARY.
Cabinet Meeting, CM 4(47).
Agenda:
1 India.
2 Persian Gulf – Relations with Arab States.
3 Food – Wheat Supplies from Turkey.

Committee on Atomic Energy, GEN 163. Chairman: Attlee.
Agenda:
1 Decision to build a British Atomic Weapon.

India and Burma Committee, 1B 3(47). Chairman: Attlee.
Agenda:
1 Sir Gilbert Laithwaite's Report on his visit to Burma.

Machinery of Government Committee, MG 1(47). Chairman: Morrison.
Agenda:
1 Advisory Council on Scientific Policy to be set up.

THURSDAY, 9TH JANUARY.
Committee on Economic Planning, MEP 2(47). Chairman: Morrison.
Agenda:
1 Lord President's Report on the 1947 Economic Survey.

India and Burma Committee, 1B 4(47). Chairman: Attlee.
Agenda:
1 Burma.

FRIDAY, 10TH JANUARY.
India and Burma Committee, 1B 5(47). Chairman: Attlee.
Agenda:
1 Burma.
2 Compensation for Officers in India.

Transport Strike Committee, GEN 165. Chairman: Alexander.
Agenda:
1 Maintenance of Food Supplies during present unofficial strike.

Lord President's Committee, LPC 1(47). Chairman: Morrison.
Agenda:
1   Penicillin Legislation.
2   Local Authority Investment Programmes.
3   Building Industry Wages to be held down.
4   Reduction in working week for road transport industry should be prevented.

Coal Committee, CC 2(47). Chairman: Dalton.
Agenda:
1   Supply of Coal to power stations versus industry.
2   Road Haulage Vehicles to be made available for coal transport.
3   No sports special trains to be allowed for duration of crisis.
4   Mid-Week football matches banned.

MONDAY, 13TH JANUARY.
Cabinet Meeting, CM 5(47).
Agenda:
1   Road Haulage Strike.
2   Leakage of Information – Details of GEN 165 meeting on 10th January had been leaked. Lord Chancellor to conduct a leak inquiry.
3   Production of ground nuts in East Africa.
4   Japanese reparations.
5   Malta constitution.

Housing Committee, HG 1(47). Chairman: Attlee.
Agenda:
1   Raw Materials Shortages.
2   'Finish the Houses' Campaign.

TUESDAY, 14TH JANUARY.
Defence Committee, DO 2(47). Chairman: Attlee.
Agenda:
1   Defence Estimates for 1947–48.

Fuel Supplies Committee, GEN 161. Chairman: Morrison.
Agenda:
1   Supply of solid fuel to industry.
2   Road transport of coal to power stations.

Legislation Committee, HPC 3(47). Chairman: Greenwood.
Agenda:
1   Legislative programme for 1946–47 to be increased – more medium sized bills to be introduced.

As that flow chart of Cabinet business shows, its Coal Committee was planning drastic interference with the nation's life and leisure *before* the steady, silent, white downpour put much of the south-east under 6 inches of snow over the night of Thursday 23 and Friday 24 January. Within two days virtually the whole of the British Isles was blotted out by a blanket of white. Pathé News hired a plane which flew up and down the Midland Railway main line from London to Leicester and back – town and country alike, frozen, inert. The newsreel archive shows Luton looking like Siberia, trains cut off somewhere in Northamptonshire.[35]

The east wind blew for a month without stopping. The Kew Observatory recorded no sunshine at all from 2 to 22 February. The temperature didn't rise above freezing between 11 and 23 February. The Thames froze. Coal boats, bound for London, were icebound in the north-east ports. The RAF dropped food for people and animals. Coal was frozen at the pits. There were no trains to shift it. Thousands were laid off work and went home to houses dark and chilled. Unemployment shot up from 400,000 to 1.75 million. Big Ben, the sound of the nation throughout the war as it 'bonged' listeners into the *Nine O'Clock News* on the Home Service, was silenced, its mechanics frozen solid.[36]

It was a winter which could move sophisticated men to emotion nearly forty years later, men like Lord Bancroft, the former Head of the Home Civil Service who could tell an audience at the London School of Economics in 1983 that 1947 'was the cruellest winter . . . The Earl's Court bed sitting-room soon had no heat, no light, no water . . . 20 January was the day I joined HM Treasury reasonably fresh from the Armoured Division and a brief return to Oxford. It was twenty months after Hitler's suicide. Harry S. Truman had still to face his first US Presidential election. Frederick S. Trueman was still only fifteen years old . . . '[37]

Contemporary diaries tell the story even more vividly. The journalist J.L. Hodson:

February 9, 1947

Several further inches of snow during the night, and toboggans out this morning. Meanwhile the incorrigible English are slowly having it drummed into their heads that we really do have a winter. Drifts fifteen feet deep in Northumberland, railways in parts impassable, and queues of professional women in St John's Wood with buckets at a water-tap in the road, like a night after a blitz.

Meanwhile also the incorrigible Mr Shinwell was jaunty at his press conference yesterday, telling us unless we conform to his orders and don't use electricity we shall face complete disaster. He is a modern phenomenon – muddling, insouciant, and a yoke round our suffering necks.[38]

Comparisons with the privations of war, that touchstone against which subsequent developments were measured throughout the period spanned by this volume, were especially frequent and heartfelt in the first weeks of 1947. Hodson again:

We are sitting over this fire of stone and slate and coal and rubbish that passes for a coal-fire these days and looking out on the driving snow . . . We suppose we made a mistake in thinking the war was over in England. Or is it that one war is over and we're now in the middle of another one? A civil war? We wonder sometimes if the Government are on the telephone, so to speak, or whether they're permanently cut off – young ex-service men and women saying: 'Austerity this, austerity that, we've had it. We're off.'[39]

Mass Observation picked up such sentiments first hand from an ex-serviceman using the British equivalent of the 'GI Bill' to study at college:

What the crisis means to me is: 1.30–3.30: lie without lights; my bedroom is rather dark so this means I cannot read. I cannot listen to the radio. I cannot sit up in bed and do anything since the power is off and I cannot use my electric fire. The place is almost unliveable in from the point of view of heating, from early morning to six at night. I hate cold. I wish I were back in Egypt. I wish I were anywhere but in this goddamned country where there is nothing but queues and restrictions and forms and shortages and no food and cold. Flu' and the fuel crisis is the last straw . . . [40]

For some, of course, fame – and cash – provided the escape route for which so many naturally longed. Noël Coward fled for a Cunarder and New York. On the January day Hodson and his family shivered before their sputtering grate, 'The Master' experienced 'a nightmare morning owing to there being no hot water, everything frozen and the car not arriving in time. Finally it did get to the house and off I went in a frenzy to Waterloo, only to find that owing to the cold the train was two hours late starting. Gladys [Calthrop] and Bert were with me. We perished, and finally arrived at Southampton at 2.30. Waited in a queue for ages. Finally got on board and had a fantastic lunch, with white bread and every luxury.'[41]

It *was* a deeply depressing time and not just for sybaritic, blithe spirits like Coward. Louis Heren, a tough, patriotic cockney on *The Times* who, back from the Forces, covered the haulage strike for his paper and experienced the kind of union intimidation which went with a show-of-hands at a mass meeting (though never a T and G man, he had to put his hands up, too, for reasons of personal safety).[42] Louis found life in 1947 Britain so 'austere and, I felt, mean-spirited' that he got as far as the emigration desk at Australia House with his wife, Pat.[43] Happily (for me, that is; Louis was one of the best bosses I ever had) *The Times* kept him where he belonged by making him their man in India, hence those chilling accounts of the Punjab massacres cited earlier.

I was born into that winter crisis alongside the North Circular Road in Edmonton; the North Middlesex Hospital, to be precise. To my great joy I discovered a generation and more later that my birthday, 28 March 1947, found that ailing and tubercular pessimist, George Orwell, at his Lion-and-

Unicornest in *Tribune*:

> For the last five minutes I have been gazing out of the window into the square,[44] keeping a sharp look-out for signs of spring. There is a thinnish patch in the clouds with a faint hint of blue behind it, and on a sycamore tree there are some things that look as if they might be buds. Otherwise it is still winter. But don't worry! Two days ago after a careful search in Hyde Park, I came on a hawthorn bush that was definitely in bud, and some birds, though not actually singing, were making noises like an orchestra tuning up.
>
> Spring is coming after all, and recent rumours that this was the beginning of another Ice Age were unfounded. In only three weeks' time we shall be listening to the cuckoo, which usually gives tongue about the fourteenth of April. Another three weeks after that, and we shall be basking under blue skies, eating ices off barrows and neglecting to lay up fuel for next winter.[45]

Orwell may have been unsurpassed on the texture of English life, but, on the basics of climatological physics, he was an innocent. He forgot the medium which would inevitably link the winter freeze with the summer ice-cream – water.

The spring floods of 1947, like the snow, were record-breaking. In the second week of March the great thaw began. Between the eleventh and the twentieth, the flow of the Thames at Teddington Lock (below which it's tidal) increased from 3,600 million gallons a day to 13,500.[46] The worst of it struck Britain's own Low Country in East Anglia. The banks of the Ouse and the Wissey crumbled in the areas to the north and south of Ely as agricultural workers and servicemen fought and failed to stem the flow.[47]

An aerial photo taken from 16,000 feet by an RAF plane on 25 March shows isolated farms in the Hoddenham area sticking out of a vast sea, like Bangladeshi hamlets after a hurricane.[48] Rescue and repair teams worked round the clock. Huge pumps were sent from Holland to get the liquid up and off the rich agricultural land which normally produced high yields of sugar beet and vegetables. As with the snow, the differences between town and country diminished. The River Lea to London's north-east burst its banks, contaminating the huge reservoirs that flank it. By one of those cruel ironies which accompany natural disasters, a million Londoners were without drinking water.[49] In Yorkshire, Selby was cut off as the Ouse and the Aire roared to the North Sea with Pennine meltwater. The Army fed 20,000 people from emergency field kitchens set up in the middle of Yorkshire's tiny, new island kingdom, as Army 'ducks', built for chasing the Wehrmacht across European rivers, carried its citizens away from over 2,000 flooded homes.[50]

It was against this grim, mind-concentrating backcloth of ice, water, dole queues and silent factories that the Government moved towards a series of tough decisions on India, Palestine and Britain's position in the Mediterranean. Bevin, Montgomery and the Chiefs may have forced Attlee into a more

Lord Curzon-like position on the Middle East – but something had to give. It turned out to be Greece, or, to be exact, the British commitment to its maintenance outside the Soviet orbit. David Watt, using the material available in Dalton's diary, has reconstructed the scene when the Foreign Secretary finally conceded:

> On a day in mid-February Bevin had arrived at a Cabinet Committee meeting in Great George Street, his vast frame heaving from the exertions of walking with a weak heart up two flights of stairs. The electricity was cut off and the lifts were not working. He found Dalton determined to bring to a head the long-standing question of Britain's expenditure in Greece. Bevin had been told by his officials that a withdrawal would mean disaster in the Balkans, and had fought a rearguard action since the previous autumn. Now, suddenly, he gave way to Dalton's demand that the Americans should be told that Britain was definitely determined to leave. Dalton was puzzled, and wondered whether Bevin quite realised what he was agreeing to; but at any rate the Chancellor got his way.[51]

Dalton shouldn't have been surprised. Bevin knew exactly what he was doing. The Foreign Office had been working for months on getting American dollars and GIs into Greece to replace pounds sterling and British 'Tommies' (who numbered 16,000 with Royalists and Communists fighting around them for supremacy). As Bevin was telling Dalton and the Cabinet Committee on 18 February 'We get no help from the Greeks',[52] an American mission was already in Athens and the State Department in Washington was slotting the final paragraphs into a 'crisis' contingency plan should the British presence in Greece 'collapse'.[53]

In Washington, a new Secretary of State, that thoughtful war hero and strategic planner General George Marshall, was playing his way in as Truman's choice to replace the spiky Byrnes, ever suspicious of rescuing Britain with money, troops or nuclear know-how. Marshall was up at Princeton receiving an honorary degree when, three days after Bevin's battle with the Cabinet Office steps, the eccentric British Ambassador, Lord Inverchapel (he insisted on bringing his Russian valet with him from Moscow to the fury of the FBI), rang to request an urgent meeting. Marshall being away a pair of notes were sent about Greece and Turkey. Their gist? That Britain's commitment to their support would cease on 31 March. As a member of the State Department staff later wrote, somewhat melodramatically, 'There was nothing that afternoon in the cables, or in circulating memoranda, or even in anybody's mind to suggest that the most revolutionary advance in United States foreign policy since [the Monroe Doctrine of] 1823 would occur within the next fifteen weeks.'[54]

Joseph Jones's breathlessness is justified, however. For those 'fifteen weeks' saw the promulgation of the Truman Doctrine ('it must be the policy of the United States to support free peoples who are resisting attempted subjugation by armed minorities or outside pressures'[55]) and the development of the Marshall Plan for the economic recovery of western Europe as a whole. It marked the *peacetime* assumption of superpower responsibilities by the United States and their *de facto* relinquishment by Britain. All this was triggered, though not, of course, caused, by the pair of notes delivered on that dull Friday afternoon in February by H.M. Sichel, First Secretary, British Embassy, to Loy Henderson, Director of Near Eastern Affairs, and John Hickerson, Deputy Director, Office of European Affairs, US State Department.[56]

Marshall complained to Bevin about the suddenness of this *démarche*.[57] But the Truman Administration did everything the British Foreign Office wanted them to. For Gladwyn Jebb it wasn't a moment to mourn the passing of superpowerdom. It was 'a red letter day' for Britain.[58] For the rest of the world, too, it was a day the earth moved, including the patch beneath Moscow. For Andrei Gromyko, Marshall simply 'gave his name to the plan to carry out the Truman Doctrine in West Germany and other countries of western Europe, its aim being to consolidate capitalism and prevent progressive social change from taking place'.[59]

Needless to say, to those feverishly knitting policy together in Whitehall and Washington in the winter and spring of 1947, the careful construction of such a reactionary masterplan was not how it struck them at all. If their state of mind had been convertible to cartoon form it would have emerged very like David Low's picture of Stalin and Molotov. Stalin, a photo of Marshall on his desk, sits in front of a vast switchboard with the switches beneath Czechoslovakia, Rumania, Hungary, Poland, Yugoslavia, Finland, Bulgaria and Albania already depressed, his finger hovering over the switch marked 'France', asking Molotov (whose finger spins a globe) 'Who's next to be liberated from freedom, Comrade?'[60]

In fact, as the ringing phrases of the Truman Doctrine were going through their drafting process, Bevin was setting off for Moscow on a long train journey (his health precluded him from flying) to try once more to patch up a deal with his fellow foreign ministers. After pausing at Dunkirk to sign an Anglo–French Treaty for mutual defence (the first of a series which would lead to the great prize of NATO) he took another four days to reach the hospitality of the British Embassy across the Moscow River from the Kremlin under the spartan regime of Sir Maurice and Lady Peterson.

It was a far cry from Del Giudice's barn. Bevin liked to tell the story of Brindle, the Petersons' elderly Scotch terrier, and how he, Bevin, suffered in the pursuit of His Majesty's Foreign Policy. 'Towards the end of our little meal', Ernie would recall, 'they gave me, with the cheese, what I took to be a dog biscuit, so I said, by way of a joke like, and quite unsuspecting: "Lady Peterson, these look to me like dog biscuits." "As a matter of fact they are, Secretary of State," she said, "but we like them." Well, after a bit of a pause, I said, "Lady Peterson, I 'ope I'm not depriving Brindle of his dinner?" And do you know what she replied? "That's quite all right, Secretary of State, Brindle won't eat 'em." '[61]

At the time, the Moscow Conference of March 1947 was seen as the last chance for the victors of 1945 to salvage the peace. But, just as Germany had united them between 1941 and 1945, it finally pushed them apart less than two years after the German surrender. The consequence? A forty-year cold war in Europe which finished where it began, in Germany. A particularly prescient American politician, Senator George Sadowski of Michigan, said at the time, 'Instead of the Big Four being strong enough to decide the fate of Germany, it is the Germans who in the long run will decide the fate of the Allies.'[62]

In fact, all Britain's diplomatic planning had been based on the eventual breakdown of Allied co-operation for almost a year. It was as if Attlee's dissent had emanated from a peace group rather than from No. 10. In July 1946, Bevin had seized on Byrnes' idea that the British and American zones should merge which they duly did on 1 January 1947. It was not that Bevin's heart went out to the famished and unemployed Germans scratching a living amid the ruins of the Ruhr. 'I tries 'ard, Brian, but I 'ates 'em,' he told General Robertson, the British Military Governor in Germany.[63]

It had to do with two factors: the need to save money in the populous British Zone (22 million Germans run by 16,000 UK administrators) then costing the British taxpayer £80 million a year (plus bread rationing at home to prevent real starvation on the Rhine) and the desire to balance what remained of the north-west's industrial capacity with agricultural output from the US Zone to the south; plus the overarching requirement of keeping Germany out of Communist hands for, ideology apart, whichever of the world's post-1945 superpowers held sway in Germany, the geopolitical advantage would swing overwhelmingly to them. Equally there remained a fear, especially among the nations overrun by the Nazis, of what a re-united Germany could do.

You did not need to be on the circulation list of JIC assessments to appreciate this as Bevin munched his way through Brindle's biscuits before setting off to do battle with Molotov. The American journalist, Howard Smith, a perceptive foreign correspondent of New Dealish tendencies, expressed perfectly the twin-track German problem at the time. 'Next to the two giants who now hold world initiative', he wrote,

> Germany is the most important country in the world. The German vacuum by itself would have caused serious dissension between the powers. When it merged with the Western European vacuum, good relations for a long time became well nigh impossible.
>
> Germany dominates the central plain of Europe. If she were allied with a great power of East or West, that alliance could geographically dominate most of Europe . . . If Germany's industrial potential were allied with that of any other great power, the unit could dominate all European economy.[64]

The problem to late 1940s eyes was the appalling immaturity of the Germans. 'Germany today', Smith went on, 'is like a strong handsome young man, superb at sports and with a quick mind – but guided by the values of a brash, self-centered, barbaric five year old.'[65] In London Noël Coward might sing 'Please Don't be Beastly to the Germans' and in Hamburg, the resident British Minister Lord Pakenham (better known as the Earl of Longford he became) might plead for Christian charity towards the defeated, but few then would have quarrelled with Smith's description of Germany as an industrial giant and a political primitive.

There *was* much in it. For me, a great deal of the perpetual debate about who was to blame for the cold war which has plagued history departments in American and British universities almost since the Moscow Conference of 1947 has been of supreme irrelevance. I have always agreed with that American revisionist *sans pareil*, William Appleman Williams. In that sacred text of cold war dissenters, *The Tragedy of American Diplomacy*, written as long ago as 1959, he argued that 'If anyone can be said in that sense to have caused the cold war, then the responsibility rests primarily if not exclusively upon Adolf Hitler and Nazi Germany.

'What might or might not have happened if those protagonists had not torn central and eastern Europe to pieces in a vain effort to unify them is not . . . a very useful kind of hypothetical question. It is not a matter of what Hitler might have done. Hitler and Nazi Germany did make that attempt. And it was in the course of defeating their ignoble ambition that the United States and the Soviet Union came into direct and sustained confrontation from the Baltic to the Black Sea.'[66]

Such fundamentals must be borne in mind, as an antidote to high-minded and retrospective censoriousness which can afflict present-day scholars when they come across Machiavellian-sounding memos between members of the British team in Moscow like this one from Patrick Dean to Pierson Dixon. The truth, said Dean,

> is that . . . the gulf between us (and I hope and think the Americans) and the Russians is unbridgeable at present. We must be careful therefore not to get into detailed discussions which the public everywhere may expect to lead to a compromise. The sooner the width of the gulf is realised . . . the better. We want to be in the position of pointing out, faintly but unmistakably now, and with ever increasing clarity why we can't agree at this Conference and that Russian intransigence on these matters is the cause . . . unless the Russians came the *whole* way to meet us, and that they won't do at this Conference.[67]

By the time Dean put pen to paper, there was no danger of that. Five days earlier Truman had delivered his message to Congress which 'burst' like 'a bombshell' on the Moscow Conference.[68] You didn't need to work for the KGB's cryptographic department to decode who was the enemy to whom the President was referring.

'Although the Truman Doctrine was barely mentioned' at the Moscow

Conference, writes Anne Deighton, 'there can be no doubt that it sent a tremor of alarm through the Kremlin, as the propaganda outpourings show'.[69] She may be right in arguing that 'Soviet fear of the United States was now greater than their fear of an immediate resurgence of German power,'[70] but Stalin and Molotov were not going to be pressured into an acceptance of the British and American positions on German reparations (crucial to Soviet recovery after the poor harvest of 1946), not to mention the ruinous effect of four years of war on the Russian economy, and the merging of the Anglo-American zones and the revival of German industry.

In a letter from Moscow to Attlee shortly before the Conference broke up in mid-April, Bevin told the P.M.: 'It looks as if we are getting perilously near a position in which a line-up is taking place . . . There is courtesy, there are no high words being used, no tempers, but all of it is cool, calculated and between the two big boys looks to me to be pretty determined.'[71]

By this stage, as we have seen, Bevin was in no doubt about Molotov's intentions. The quiet, contained Marshall was another matter. The British delegation in Moscow could not read him as yet. Edmund Hall-Patch, the leading Treasury economic diplomatist of the age, told a colleague on his return to London that 'Mr Marshall arrived new to the subject and feeling his way. His advisers were hopelessly divided and he had to make up his own mind without sufficient background. He was very conscious of the danger of Congress cutting his appropriation, a danger which imposes on the United States a kind of artificial poverty,'[72] a brilliant phrase which, in the postwar period as a whole, could apply even more to Washington's attitude to social spending.

The thoughtful soldier, in fact, was educating himself fast. 'When Secretary of State Marshall returned from the recent meeting of the Council of Foreign Ministers in Moscow', his number two, Dean Acheson, told a gathering of small farmers and businessmen in Mississippi on 8 May 1947, 'he did not talk to us about ideologies and armies. He talked about food and fuel and their relation to industrial production to the organisation of Europe, and the relation of the organisation of Europe to the peace of the world.'[73] What Acheson didn't tell the farmers of the Mississippi Delta was that, even now, the State Department was working on the most ambitious aid programme since Lend-Lease, only, this time, it would involve an economic life-line to the whole of western Europe not just Britain.

Bevin and his team may have come back from Moscow with the outcome they wanted, but, as Bevin would say in his black moments, he had no money or goods to offer those he was trying to influence. To adapt the celebrated wag at the American loan negotiations, we may have had a high proportion of the brains used in developing the new western strategy, but there was no doubt where *all* the moneybags were stored. Just before Bevin left for Russia, figures circulated in Whitehall showed a burgeoning dollar deficit and the proceeds of the American Loan running out fast, a position (made much worse by the big freeze and its associated widespread industrial stoppage) so dire that Orme

Sargent privately predicted a 'Greek' situation in Britain when the loan ran out.[74]

The outflow of gold and dollars quadrupled between 1946 and 1947 from $900 million to $4,100 million. Unlike the coal crisis, where prompter action in Whitehall (not least the facing down of the Miners' Union and the employment of refugee Polish miners in the pits who, unlike many demobbed British pitmen, were actually keen to go underground) would have made a substantial difference, it's difficult to see what Attlee and his ministers could have done to reduce that mountainous dollar deficit of $8 billion in 1946.[75] Given the US dominance of the world economy in those first postwar years, there was nowhere else to buy the goods needed for the reconstruction of British industry.

Even if the Cabinet had ordered a dramatic withdrawal of British forces from around the globe, shed imperial commitments with abandon and settled for a kind of Scandinavian status (not an option in 1945), or if they had turned their back on the Health Service and the apparatus of the welfare state (which would have amounted to a political death-wish), it's virtually certain that some kind of economic blizzard would have followed the climatic one in 1947. Why? Simply because sterling would have been unable to survive the convertibility into dollars imposed upon it by the tough terms exacted by the US Treasury for its money in December 1945.

As 'C' Day – 15 July 1947 – approached, however, the Bank of England exuded an almost Shinwell-like complacency about the prospect, arguing that most sterling holders had discounted the change-over in advance, though, to his credit, Dalton at least contemplated an approach to the Americans about the convertibility commitment in February. Not until June, when Will Clayton, the leading US economic diplomat, visited London, was the possibility broached. Clayton explained it was too late as Congress was about to go into its summer recess.[76]

To place the problems of the Attlee Government in their wider context is not, however, to absolve ministers from justified accusations of drift and indecision. Nor is this hindsight. Otto Clarke at the Treasury was in the thick of policy-making *and* highly sympathetic as an individual to the Government's aspirations. In a diary entry for 20 April 1947, all the frustrations of the previous quarter (when he'd had no time to put pen to paper) poured out: 'For fifty years and more the best of the working class have fought and suffered and struggled so that Labour should rule; by the miracle of a war they had gained power . . . ; now the chosen leadership of the workers was sitting there, not only baffled by the problems but apparently disinterested, not seeming to appreciate that there was a crisis at all.'[77]

The specific focus for Clarke's frustration was the effort to produce Labour's first plan, the *Economic Survey for 1947* which was largely drafted by him and appeared in the middle of the fuel crisis selling an amazing 300,000 copies in a short space of time.[78] Churchill, to Clarke's delight, was so taken with its phraseology about the need to compete with the rest of the world in design, quality and price that he asked Cripps in the House 'who was the civil servant who wrote this for his Socialist masters. Out of the 2,000,000 we have at present, he should be the last one to be sacked.'[79] 'As a matter of fact,' Clarke wrote in his diary, 'it wasn't a bad paper, but bricks without straw.'[80]

It was his dealings with ministers 'in the middle of this drafting process [when] the power crisis broke [and] industry was brought to a standstill, a thing which the Nazis had never succeeded in doing' which doused Clarke in disillusion amounting almost to despair:

> It was bricks without straw, for there was no known plan and no known means of implementing a plan even if there had been a plan . . . Very hard work with Bridges [Head of the Treasury] for a long time and two absolutely frightful meetings with ministers. These made me very nearly abandon hope for the success of the Labour Government. With Morrison ill, Ministers have virtually abdicated.
>
> The Chancellor was not trying. Mr Shinwell was in a state of hopeless fog. The PM pottering away. Not an ounce of will to govern or ability to control the situation. Lengthy discussion about whether they would use prison labour. Mr Shinwell very optimistic about coal. Not a single one of them with the shadowiest concept of what they meant by planning. I went away from 10 Downing Street terrified [this was early February].[81]

By the end of April, Clarke, at the very heart of policy-making with the best data available flowing routinely across his desk, felt the country was peering into an economic abyss: 'The balance of payments has been rapidly deteriorating. The rise in prices (40% since December 1945) together with the loss of exports due to the fuel crisis has made the prospective balance of payments [deficit] look like £700 millions in 1947 instead of £250 millions. On this reckoning, the [American] Loan will be through by mid 1948 – an impossible situation . . . so much has been happening and really fundamental things too. We are getting to the Finland Station.'[82]

It was against this grim background that Bevin broke free of the pattern of ministerial supineness in the face of overlapping adversities by seizing the opportunity offered by General Marshall's thoughts on the road from Moscow and the subsequent efforts of his backroom planners. 'When Bevin grabbed at what became the Marshall Plan' is, in the judgment of Alec Cairncross, the moment which was the exception to the late 1940s norm whereby 'the economic problems encountered by the government were not, as a rule, those which it had expected. Equally, the solutions to the problems were rarely of the government's devising . . . they were slow to grasp the true options of policy and had great difficulty in reaching sensible conclusions.'[83] Bevin also demonstrated what a fine Chancellor he would have made if Attlee had stuck to his original plan in July 1945 and sent him to the Treasury instead of the Foreign Office. Central to the Bevin legend is his response on hearing of General

Marshall's Harvard Speech of 5 June 1947 on the tiny wireless by his bed the following morning. Marshall told his alumni audience in Harvard Yard:

> The truth of the matter is that Europe's requirements for the next three or four years of foreign food and other essential products – principally from America – are so much greater than her present ability to pay that she must have substantial additional help or face economic, social and political deterioration of a very grave character . . . [84]

'It would be neither fitting nor efficacious', Marshall continued, 'for this government to undertake to draw up unilaterally a program designed to place Europe on its feet economically. This is the business of the Europeans. The initiative, I think, must come from Europe.'[85]

With sublime indifference and parsimony, 'the British Embassy in Washington did not think it worth the cable charges to send an advance copy of the speech to London'.[86] The American Press was equally indifferent. But Acheson had tipped off three British correspondents as to the importance of Marshall's speech and it was one of them, Leonard Miall of the BBC, whose voice Bevin heard that June morning.[87]

Bevin later told a group of American journalists that Marshall's speech 'was like a life-line to sinking men'.[88] 'It is arguable', in his biographer's view, 'that Bevin's action in the next few days was his most decisive contribution as Foreign Secretary to the history of his times. Without any advice from the British Embassy in Washington, and to the surprise of his officials, he came into the Foreign Office next morning and seized upon what was no more than a single sentence in Marshall's speech – 'the initiative, I think, must come from Europe'. Relying solely on his own intuitive judgment, he threw all his energy into conjuring up a European response of sufficient weight and urgency to give substance to Marshall's implied offer of American support.'[89]

To be fair, the British Embassy had been given advance warning of the Harvard speech plus an idea of the common European response which the State Department hoped for and had sent a telegram to this effect on 2 June.[90] Information is one thing, action quite another. Only a minister of Bevin's gifts and power could have made things happen quite so fast – that is the point, not whether the Foreign Secretary heard it first on his wireless or courtesy of the Foreign Office teleprinters.

In its way, the miniature historical dispute about just who, when and what alerted Bevin to the possibility of this new transatlantic life-line,[91] is symptomatic of the way in which Marshall Aid has become a scholarly battleground as this remarkable piece of geopolitical engineering has faded into folk memory. What remains at issue is the *degree* of the Marshall Plan's importance in reviving western Europe, reducing its vulnerability to Russian aggression from without or totalitarianism from within, and the extent to which it set in train the forces which led to the creation of first, the European Coal and Steel Community, and, later, the European Economic Community.

The most faction ridden section of the historical dispute has, inevitably, turned out to be the prime motivation of the Plan. Was it, to borrow Churchill's description of Lend-Lease, one of 'the most unsordid' acts 'in the history of any nation',[92] or was it a cynical and successful American instrument for prising Europe open for US business to penetrate while effectively driving the Soviet Union out of the reconstruction business and into its own grim and impoverished redoubt behind the Iron Curtain – the final stage on the two-year trail from Potsdam which doomed Europe to four decades of cold war?

What all the protagonists agree upon is this: that there was a crisis in Europe in 1947 and that the policy choices and outcomes (not always the same thing) *were* crucial for the next forty years, not just for Europe but for every part of the world where the reach of the superpowers could be felt. Yet it's a year that is hard to pin down. No wars were declared or peaces concluded. No empires fell. No major heads rolled. The political personnel remained much the same pretty well everywhere you looked. It was, as Otto Clarke noted in his diary in April 1947, 'one of the big periods in history – the period of a revolution without any revolutionaries'.[93] There is a second historical certainty about 1947, however. The succession of British crises – fuel, food, currency, balance of payments (even the brief threat to Attlee's premiership in the autumn) – cannot be treated in isolation from the wider, European one to which Marshall and his officials turned their minds.

Motive first, what was in these minds belonging to the Washington geo-politicians in the spring of 1947? A mix of ingredients went into the making of the Marshall Plan – Marshall's own experience and judgment, Clayton's account of a prostrate Europe. The wordpower behind the speech was Chip Bohlen's but the mind which blended the mix was that of the most sophisti-cated of postwar State Department intellects, George Kennan, the philosopher of 'containment'. 'He did succeed', wrote his biographer David Mayers, 'in helping to shape the Marshall Plan in three distinctive ways: The West Euro-peans assumed the major responsibility for devising a programme of economic relief; the Soviets bore the embarrassment of refusing an offer of apparent American generosity and had to accept much of the onus for the partitioning of Europe; West Germany's economic and political rehabilitation was achieved within a framework of general European recovery.'[94]

Mayers might have added a fourth – the economic integration of Europe, for only through this substantial and permanent development could the American planners foresee a time when Europe could banish its dollar famine and cease to be a drain on the US economy while becoming an ever more effective buffer against Soviet expansion. Marshall mentioned this in his Harvard speech, tact-fully saying it was Churchill's idea in his Zurich speech on a United Europe in Zurich the previous September.[95] (There are huge chunks of irony in this as insistent American pressure on Britain to integrate with its European neigh-bours set the Atlanticist and Commonwealth nerves of every occupant in No. 10 from Attlee to Eden, Churchill's included, on edge.)

From Kennan's private papers as well as from the official State Department archive, we now know for sure what many suspected at the time – that Marshall Aid was offered to the Soviet Union with the intention that it would be turned down. That Stalin and Molotov would refuse was regarded as a near certainty because acceptance of the US terms would mean the beginning of the end of their closed economy and its branches in the satellite countries.[96] In a memo 'Measures Short of War' drawn up in September 1946 and preserved in his personal archive, Kennan foreshadowed what in fact happened forty-three years later when, though he doubted Russia itself was vulnerable to economic warfare, America's and, eventually, the west's dazzling economies could lure the satellites from the Soviet grip, a view which became the conventional wisdom the following year in the influential Policy Planning Staff Kennan ran in the Department of State.[97]

Kennan persuaded Marshall of his logic and the tactic of offloading the blame for a divided Europe on to Stalin. On his return from Europe, Clayton thought the only way to break the malign cycle of balance of payments and associated political crises in Europe would be to recognise that '*The United States must run this show*'.[98] Kennan's and the Planning Staff's approach was to make an offer to the whole of Europe to come up with a plan. The offer would be 'in such a form that the Russian satellite countries would either exclude themselves by unwillingness to accept the proposed conditions or agree to abandon the exclusive orientation of their economies . . . '[99]

It's easy to see why Marshall acceded to this line. It would be a victory for American policy either way. Bevin was equally concerned that the Soviet Union should not partake of Marshall Aid. On 13 June he said during an after-lunch speech in London, with that gift, for which many Foreign Secretaries have become famous, of saying one thing in public and the reverse in private: 'We are glad to know that any possible source of misunderstanding has been eliminated by including Russia in the American proposal and therefore removing any idea that there is anything ideological in this proposal.'[100]

In reality, Bevin, like his French counterpart Bidault, was desperately keen for the Russians to be kept out. He couldn't see how the plan could work if they were in, as he told Clayton at a series of meetings in London at the end of June, following Molotov's acceptance on 22 June of an invitation to a conference in Paris to discuss European recovery. Clayton assured Bevin that 'there would have to be a radical change in the Russian position regarding European recovery and other related matters before the American people would approve the extension of financial assistance to Russia'.[101]

In many ways, that meeting in No. 10 on 24 June 1947 was a classic vignette of the dilemmas of early postwar British foreign policy (Attlee, Cripps and Dalton were there as was Lew Douglas, the Arizona copper magnate turned US Ambassador to London).

Bevin got his assurance about the real US intentions towards the USSR but was deeply disturbed by the Marshall Plan's implications for Britain's relationship with America. If the UK was to be treated as just another country in western Europe, it could be to the USA what Yugoslavia was to the USSR. 'Britain with an Empire is on a different basis,' he insisted.[102] Dalton said Britain was different because it had its own occupation zone to run in Germany. Cripps said a high proportion of our trade was with non-European countries while Attlee reminded the American envoys that Britain had global responsibilities as had been shown during the Indian famine the year before when Australian wheat, badly needed in the UK, had been diverted to the sub-continent.

Not for the last time, a British Foreign Secretary played his trump card. It had Stalin's head on it. 'If the UK was considered just another European country', Bevin told them, 'this would fit in with Russian strategy, namely, that the US would encounter a slump and would withdraw from Europe; the UK would be helpless and out of dollars, and as merely another European country, the Russians in command of the Continent, could deal with Britain in due course.'

Britain, Bevin went on, could not stay aloof from a European recovery plan as this would remove the 'little bit of dignity we have left'. Equally, the idea of Britain joining a European customs union (i.e. a Common Market) was out of the question as a 'full blue print for Europe would take too long for the present emergency'.

The Americans were unmoved. In one sense the candour does show there was a special relationship between the US and the UK. As Alan Bullock observed, 'so outspoken an exchange could hardly have taken place between the representatives of any two other countries and it illustrates what Attlee meant by his cryptic remark when I asked him once, without notice, what was Bevin's greatest contribution as Foreign Secretary. His reply, without a moment's pause, was 'standing up to the Americans.'[103]

Yet, as Lord Bullock put it, 'The conflict between poverty and pride was obvious. The British were financially dependent on the Americans for their own economic survival, yet wanted to be treated as an equal partner in dispensing aid to the Europeans. Ministers complained vigorously of the terms imposed by the Americans at the time of the loan to Britain, particularly the clause directed against trade discrimination; yet even now Dalton and the Treasury team, although hinting at the difficulties ahead, were still not prepared to come out openly and admit that the UK would not be able to face the strain of making sterling convertible.'[104]

Such relative weakness was, in the summer of 1947, easier for the Whitehall insider to see than the backbencher in Parliament or the voter in the country at large. To all external appearances, Britain was still unquestionably a Top Table power.

Wasn't it a British official after all – Sir Oliver Franks, star wartime civil servant brought back from Oxford for the purpose – who chaired the Marshall Plan discussions when they began in Paris in early July? Thirty years later he told me that he had no illusions that the really big players were the Americans and the Russians that sticky summer. Britain still had a voice, 'but it was a junior voice', a perception not shared by the bulk of his fellow countrymen until the Suez Affair nine years later brought it home suddenly and starkly.[105]

As the British planners had predicted and hoped, Molotov quickly left Paris, dragging the reluctant satellites in his wake convinced, as a *Pravda* comment put it at the time, that 'From retail purchase of several European countries Washington has conceived design of wholesale purchase of whole European continent.'[106] As expected, Molotov had fiercely resisted suggestions that details of the Soviet economy be given to the Committee of European Economic Co-operation, as the sixteen-nation gathering was officially known, on the grounds that it would be an intrusion on national sovereignty. His alternative proposal – that a calculation of the composite needs of all sixteen be made – was unacceptable to the men with the dollars. As Bevin reported to the Cabinet on 8 July, 'from a practical point of view, it is far better to have them definitely out than half-heartedly in . . . Any other tactics might have enabled the Soviets to play the Trojan horse and wreck Europe's prospects of availing themselves of American assistance . . . at least the gloves are off, and we know where we stand with them.'[107]

The gloves *were* off between east and west and remained so in pretty well every quarter of the globe where (from then on, ideology seeped into a variety of conflicts, regional and local, great and small) until the Korean War armistice in July 1953 showed that de-escalation was at least, possible. I regard those six years which began on 2 July 1947 when Molotov and the east Europeans walked out of the Paris talks as the 'high cold war', years of extraordinary peril when hot war was possible at any moment, even after 1949 when the beginnings of a crude atomic balance of power began to be put in place after the Soviet test explosion in Kazakhstan. The course of the Paris negotiations had an enduring significance way beyond Europe.

That the outcome, in strictly European terms, was crucial to the extraordinary, unprecedented, cornucopic postwar economic growth from the Rhine to the Pyrenees, from Narvik to Naples is not in doubt. Yet economic historians like Alan Milward have, by tracing back and forth across the flows of trade and payments in the reconstruction years after 1945, set the nature of the European recovery in a different perspective. According to Professor Milward, the upward track of postwar growth (Germany apart) began pretty well instantly in 1945. What Marshall Aid did was to allow the liberated western European nations and Britain to avoid choking off their nascent booms in the pivotal year of 1947 when dollar famine and balance of payments problems caused nightmares in their finance ministries. The European Recovery Programme, like Lend-Lease for Britain, in effect enabled these countries to 'throw good housekeeping to the winds' and to reconstruct regardless. They were driven not merely by the pressing need to turn rubble into factories and homes and roads, but by powerful political compulsions in pretty well all their politics to ensure that never again would slump and economic depression be allowed to distil the social poison that made fascism possible. In other words, Marshall Aid was the classic example of pump priming which enabled a reconstruction boom to transform itself into a succession of economic booms, consumer goods and export-led, which, Britain somewhat apart, fed one into another in an unsurpassed miracle of production until the late 1960s when the pace began to slacken.

This, plus the security infrastructure put in place after the signing of the North Atlantic Treaty (the NATO Charter) in 1949, represents in American eyes to this day, the supreme achievement of US diplomacy at the start of what in 1945–7 was expected to be an 'American Century'. The foreign policy and military setbacks after the turn of the decade (especially the Vietnamese ensnarement in the 1960s) led to a casting back of nostalgic eyes to the Marshall era.

Take J.K. Galbraith, the seer of Harvard and economic guru for many a mid-century social democrat in Europe. Writing in 1971, with the Vietnam War still raging, he suggested that:

> had Italy and France remained economically distraught, politically disorientated and militarily a vacuum in the years from 1946 on, their large and cohesive communist parties might have taken over, and without any particular encouragement from the Soviets. One of the errors of the period was in exaggerating the power of a superpower, American or Soviet, to control such events. For better or worse (my own orthodox instinct is to think for better) this did not happen, and its failure to happen coincided with a vast and many pronged initiative by the Democratic administration in Washington; the Truman doctrine on behalf of Greece and Turkey in 1947, the Marshall Plan in 1948 and numerous military steps leading to . . . the creation of NATO in 1949.
>
> Of these actions, the Marshall Plan made the most profound and lasting impression. Here was free enterprise, supplemented by a sizeable infusion of capital, combined with sound American leadership. Something great could be expected. Expectations were justified; western Europe came back with marvellous speed. Whether it would have gone to the communists without the Marshall Plan will never be known. The fact is that with the Marshall Plan it did not. Improved economic wellbeing was accompanied by greater political stability. Support for violent solutions waned . . . additionally, the European military forces, strengthened by American aid, and the NATO forces deployed across western Europe, helped guarantee internal tranquillity as well as the frontiers.[108]

There was, Galbraith argued, something in this for everybody. The mistake after 1950, when the Korean War convinced the United States the cold war conflict was global, was to assume the concoction of economic and military aid would work everywhere, even in economies and societies which had nothing of the European capabilities which proved so easy to revive in the late 1940s after the depredations of the first half of that decade, hence the frequent and misguided calls urging a 'Marshall Plan for . . . well, everywhere'.

Galbraith is right about the unknowability of Europe 1948–50 without Marshall Aid. It was the constant reporting from US diplomats in Paris and Rome that France and Italy would go red without star-spangled aid that helped create a true sense of urgency in Washington and enabled the Truman Administration to sell both the Truman Doctrine and the Marshall Plan to the wider American public on that basis.

In fact, without the Soviet threat, perceived as such in dark shades of red by American public opinion until deep into the Gorbachev era, America would, at best, have been indifferent to the needs of postwar Europe and, at worst, hostile not just to the never again, welfare statist impulses of Attlee and his ministers in London, or Jean Monnet and his interventionist planners in Paris, but to the aspirations of centrists and Christian democrats in most of the western European capitals.

As Alan Milward put it:

> If the great stir of public opinion in the United States against nationalization or against the restrictions on 'free enterprise' or against planning were not translated into political action by Congress this was not just because of a sensible and accurate understanding of these policies within the American government, although such an understanding was very often there, it was because the immediate problem was not seen merely as a crisis of the world payments system but as the need to prop up in America's strategic interests all forms of western European capitalism and democratic governments, even socialists and planners, against communists and the Soviet Union.
>
> These strategic necessities meant that what the government of the United States actually paid for with Marshall Aid was not to increase the rate of recovery in European economies and to prevent Europeans in dislocated and deteriorating economies from starving, but to sustain ambitious, new, expansionary economic and social policies in western European countries which were mostly already in full boom conditions. Those countries, driven in many cases by overwhelming historical forces to run a risk which was economically wholly unjustified, found their gambler's throw made successful by the changed circumstances of great power politics.[109]

In fact, in terms of *realpolitik* as opposed to the wider interests of humanity in avoiding a forty-year cold war, Bevin was right in the line he put to the Cabinet in July 1947. Thanks to the external Soviet threat, which everyone in positions of authority in the west largely agreed upon at that time, Europe was acting in its best interests in putting aside the hope of an all-embracing peace settlement after the Second World War, concentrating on its own needs and dragging as much American money, goods and equipment as it could get beneath what Alan Milward calls its 'painfully constructed roof of inter-dependence . . . [For] let all those who wish to reconstruct the roof on funda-mentally new principles think first that never except beneath that roof has western Europe known so long a peace nor a life so prosperous and so humane'.[110]

It would be wrong, however, to assume that all this was set in train as part of a desirable and irresistible aim towards a united Europe as Marshall and the State Department wanted. In many ways, the states whose negotiators remained in Paris after Molotov had left were engaged more in the business of postwar national reassertion (especially those overrun by the Axis powers seven years before) than in moves towards greater international co-operation. They undertook only as much economic integration as was necessary to sustain their home-grown reconstruction programmes. Attlee and his minis-ters were not alone in resisting the wider European vistas being sold them by Clayton and Marshall in 1947 and, in fact, by mid-1948, when Congress at last had voted for the first Marshall Aid appropriations, the Americans had begun to soft-pedal their united Europe theme.[111]

Though we cannot know if Maurice Thorez or Palmiro Togliatti would have been leading communist governments in France or Italy by the end of the decade had not Marshall said what he did at Harvard in 1947, we can glean a fair idea of what would have happened in Britain in that event. Harry Pollitt and the Communist Party of Great Britain would not have replaced Attlee and Labour in the Cabinet Room that's for sure. But everyday life would have been fiercely spartan and the Government hard pressed to put together the necessary siege economy. How do we know this? Because the Treasury, the Cabinet Office, the Central Economic Planning Staff (which had just come into existence under Sir Edwin Plowden to put some apparatus behind the Government's rhetoric), the Bank of England, the Board of Trade and the Ministry of Food pieced together a Top Secret contingency plan in 1947 if Marshall Aid failed to materialise. Its author? The ubiquitous Otto Clarke.

Like no other document, T 229/136, 'Marshall Proposals. Alternative action in event of breakdown', declassified at the PRO in 1978, gives the feel and flavour of the economically fraught summer of 1947. It's also quite the most alarming economic policy file I've encountered in the entire postwar period.

Clarke called the first meeting of what one official called Otto's 'If Marshall fails (hush-hush)' group for 16 July. On 15 July – the day sterling became freely convertible into dollars under the terms of the Loan Agreement – he circulated the first draft of his plan. The central problem, he said, would be financing imports from North and South America in 1948–9 if substantial aid was not forthcoming from Washington (a real possibility given the difficulties expected in Congress when it got down to the details of the Marshall Plan).

The trade deficit with the United States, Canada, Argentina and Central America would be so large, at least $2,000 million in 1948, that it would not be bridged by what Clarke called 'wangling'.

What could be done about it? The United Kingdom could put itself first by 're-empting' (*sic*) supplies, taking American wheat from India, Rhodesian copper from France and Persian oil from sterling bloc countries. A 'new sterling area' might be created embracing the United Kingdom and its colonies, Australia and New Zealand, the Republic of Ireland and Denmark. In effect, Clarke was outlining a new trading block which would pool its resources, i.e. its goods and its precious dollars with 'violent direction of exports to USA, Canada, Argentina and certain Central American countries . . .'

The new trading group, Clarke wrote,

> would behave entirely selfishly in pre-empting non dollar supplies. But countries could enter it if they were willing to pool import policy and resources. For practical purposes, however, one would start with a very narrow and informal grouping. The non-dollar countries outside the group would have to be dealt with individually, presumably with some form of payments agreement or clearing. In general, we should not have a large adverse balance with such countries. Within the non-dollar world, we should try to avoid direction of exports as far as possible. Special steps would have to be taken to ensure that the countries in the 'new sterling area' got the supplies they would not get from the USA.[112]

The implications of this were quite plain to those who gathered in the Treasury on 16 July – the end of the open, postwar world trading system established at Bretton Woods as well as a 'complete breach of the US Loan Agreement commitments', though it was 'less certain whether withdrawal from IMF [International Monetary Fund] would be imperative . . . Congressional action would be necessary to release us from our commitments. The practical difficulty is to secure such release before our reserves are gone.'[113]

But it was in the final section of this paper, on what would have happened to the domestic economy, that Otto Clarke peered into an abyss of austerity which would have shocked even a British public accustomed to wartime privations. To get by, Clarke said, a famine food programme would have to be introduced, schoolchildren taken from their classrooms to help bring in the harvest plus military-style conscription to bring adult labour back on to the land. It's so desperate a vision that it's worth quoting in its entirety. Nothing that I have seen in the Public Record Office archive brings home so clearly the weakness of postwar Britain at this most precarious and pivotal moment of recovery. 'The practical problem for the United Kingdom', wrote Clarke in a staccato drafting fashion which suggested, even for him, an unaccustomed speed and urgency, would be to ride the storm with lower imports. We cannot make great adjustments quickly in our economic structure without considerable distress. We should run risks of a downward spiral of activity, with cumulative frustration. It would be of prime importance to give people something to look forward to and to show that a plan existed for getting us through. For this reason it would be necessary to present a plan for recovery by our own efforts by 1950.

The crucial questions would be:

1   Agriculture. In the 1947–48–49 harvests to run no risks of insufficient labour; this might mean radical interference with educational arrangements. We should go forward with a 'famine' food programme and, if necessary, direction of labour to agriculture.

2   Building. The building and investment programmes generally should be drastically cut down, to save timber and steel and manpower. We should not have resources for satisfying our elementary consumption needs plus exports plus investment. There will in any case be substantial investment programmes connected with the recovery plan (e.g. copper refinery, housing for miners and agricultural workers etc).

3   Textiles. Woollen textiles would be of prime importance.

4   Coal. As always, fundamental.

Some element of direction of labour would almost certainly be necessary. But for agriculture it could be treated as a specific national service (like military conscription) and there would probably be advantage in restricting direction to this.[114]

Later drafts of the plan amended the last paragraph to read: 'It is difficult to see how this could be done without direction of labour and indeed a complete and total mobilization as far reaching as that of 1940.'

I was so struck by the starkness of Clarke's diagnosis of the problems Britain would confront with the American loan exhausted and no Marshall dollars to replace them when I first read T 229/136, that I had photocopies made which I sent to the survivors of his 'hush-hush' group. The actual file preserved at Kew is the one which belonged to the Central Economic Planning Staff whose man on the Clarke committee was Professor Sir Austin Robinson. Indeed it contains a note in Sir Austin's hand addressed to his boss, Sir Edwin Plowden, explaining the significance of these mid-July discussions as sterling poured across the exchanges when its holders, free at last, fled for dollars. 'You will realise', Sir Austin told Sir Edwin, 'that the situation we were considering would be so desperate that all obligations, legal and moral, would have to be in the melting pot. The decisions to be made are so formidable and irrevocable that what we most fear is procrastination which might exhaust the few remaining resources that might help us to survive.'[115]

Recalling the atmosphere in Whitehall thirty-two years earlier, Lord Plowden told me in July 1979 he remembered 'that someone was asked to do a study of what the British ration would be when there were no more dollars. The answer was 1,700 calories a day, over a 1,000 calories less than the minimum ration during the war.'[116]

When Sir Austin received his set of photocopies in the post, he rang me from Cambridge and said, 'The mess we were trying to deal with then was infinitely greater than that applying now [i.e. the summer of 1979, shortly after Mrs Thatcher had assumed the premiership]. The possibilities of a major crash were so much greater. But we had not then lost the power to take decisions.'[117]

Sir Austin's thinking was echoed by Sir Frank Figgures. In 1947 he was a young Treasury principal working for Clarke.

I do not think that those who were taking part in these discussions felt very frightened. Whether or not it was the moment of our greatest economic peril is perhaps better judged now than then. I doubt whether many of those round that table . . . felt that it was unmanageably dangerous.

Although in the Treasury we perhaps more fully appreciated than most the state in which we had emerged from the war . . . we were not at that time suffering from a major lack of confidence in ourselves. Most of those in senior positions in Government had been engaged in the mobilization of our economy in the war effort . . . its performance in the war years had been quite remarkable by our own standards . . . there were at hand instruments which had worked, and which, no doubt, in such circumstances, could go on working.[118]

One of the 'hush-hush' group, Sir Harry Lintott, the Board of Trade's representative, reckoned there was an element of deliberate exaggeration in the exercise: 'Officials felt that Ministers were being too timid about imposing further import-saving restrictions in order to help spin out the use of the US credit and our other $ resources; I fancy Clarke's paper of 17 July was largely intended to make Ministers' flesh creep.'[119]

I doubt that. It wasn't Otto Clarke's style. His amended paper went to Dalton on 22 July.[120] There is no evidence that any other ministers saw it though Dalton undoubtedly drew on it when he tried to impress upon the Cabinet on 29 July 'the urgency of it all and the need to take big, bold measures'.[121] The Civil Service didn't need to make the Chancellor's flesh creep. As 1947 progressed, he had become obsessed by what his biographer, Ben Pimlott, called 'the date ringed in red on the Chancellor's calendar' – 15 July, convertibility day.[122] 'Very often during these months', Dalton recalled, 'I lay awake at night doing mental arithmetic. We had so many dollars; last month we spent so many; if we spend the same next month, we shall only have so much left. But we mustn't let our dollar reserves fall below so much, or we shall be sunk.'[123]

Dalton, a sick man near breaking-point, lived in terror of a repeat of the 1931 crisis which had destroyed the second Labour Government and split the party consigning it to the political wilderness for the remainder of the decade (a very green memory for every Labour minister in 1947).[124] Observing the dollar reserves haemorrhaging, he told a friend, was 'like watching a child bleed to death and being unable to stop it'.[125] He 'saw spectres of mass unemployment, mass starvation, mass imprecations'.[126]

The wretched man was covered in boils.[127] High on Benzedrine,[128] he stormed round his office asking 'Why can't life get better?' and why 'his dollars' should be wasted on 'Strachey's food, Shinwell's fuel and Bevin's Huns?'[129] His Treasury private secretary, Burke Trend, said 'his body and his mind had turned inward on themselves'.[130] His mind returned repeatedly to the possibility of resignation as he pressed in vain for deep defence cuts, only to be defeated by 'mulish resistance from Bevin and Alexander who have been half backed up by the PM himself. The simple point is not so much the money, as the number of people kept in uniform and out of production.'[131]

Dalton was so enraged with his colleagues' lack of decision and unwillingness to face the stark implications of the dollar outflow that he couldn't sleep. He almost cracked on the night of 30 July:

Big Five meeting at 10 p.m. with Bridges and [Sir Wilfrid] Eady [senior Treasury man on overseas finance]. A most shocking performance. I put before them my draft of the paper for tomorrow's Cabinet proposing a variety of actions. Bevin, who had obviously had a very good dinner – he said next day that he had been entertaining the Afghanistan Minister – was at his worst. Morrison, after an hour of this, left the room in indignation, declaring almost audibly that he had 'had enough of this drunken monologue'. The PM, Cripps and I – and of course, both the eminent officials – showed infinite patience and good manners. Very late in the proceedings we got to the more important parts but discussion was, I thought, most inconclusive. Attlee showed no power of gripping or guiding the talk. We adjourn at half an hour past midnight, Bevin enquiring as he lurched toward the door . . . 'Where do we sleep tonight – in 'ere?'[132]

The Big Five were all exhausted, the victims of 'overload', the occupational disease of most senior British ministers for much of the time in the postwar period. In truth, in one of the least impressive patches of the Attlee Government's life, the Cabinet had no real idea of what to do as the gales of the world economy roared in through the door opened by the restoration of convertibility.

It couldn't last. On 13 August Dalton retreated to his country home, West Leaze, in the Wiltshire Downs, as Eady prepared to set off for Washington to warn the Americans that the US Loan would be exhausted by October and that the Government would no longer be able to abide by the terms of the 1946

Agreement.[133] As so often in postwar sterling crises, for which 1947 set a grim pattern, events moved more swiftly than anticipated.

On 15 August, in a journey Trend never forgot, he and Bridges drove down to Wiltshire to confront Dalton with the inescapable need to suspend convertibility as soon as possible. 'It was quite inevitable,' he told me a generation later. 'But I also remember feeling in my bones that it was almost inconceivable that the Americans would, in fact, not come up with something.'[134]

Dalton accepted the inevitable. Morrison, the supposed economic overlord of the Government, was left in charge in London when the Cabinet dispersed for their holidays in the middle of a heat wave. 'The situation was out of hand,' his biographers wrote.

On his first weekend in control, 15–16 August, Morrison conducted frantic telephone calls with Attlee in Wales, with the Chancellor in his Wiltshire retreat, and with officials in Washington. An emergency Cabinet was summoned for the Sunday afternoon [17 August]. Aircraft and cars were despatched to remote parts of the Kingdom to collect ministers from Inverness and the Channel Islands, to bring back Attlee from remote Wales, Bevin from pretty Swanage, Dalton from West Leaze.[135]

They arrived by a variety of back doors to avoid creating an impression of crisis for the waiting press and public, met at five and sat for nearly three hours.

The Cabinet was confronted by a set of figures prepared by the Treasury the day before which told the story.[136]

Week ending:-	Net drawings:- $ millions
July 5	94.6
12	112.1
19	155.0
26	91.9
August 2	114.5
9	124.5
5 days ending August 15	175.9

Eady had set off for Washington on the Saturday. He would need different instructions from those previously agreed. In effect he would have to inform the Americans Britain was proposing to break the Loan Agreement. It was important that he win their concurrence or the US Treasury might block the $850 million of credits still left. There was concern, too, that the shock would 'impair the coherence' of the Marshall Plan discussions in Paris.[137]

During the Cabinet discussion, Bevin said the Americans must be told this was 'a temporary precautionary measure under *force majeure*'. Nye Bevan wanted

33 Hard Crust Café

34 Transport strike, January 1947. Soldiers deliver horses to Brixton.

35 1947 Part I: the Big Freeze near Westerham, Kent, in January

36 1947 Part II: the Big Thaw; the Birmingham train leaving Nottingham Station in March

37   Butlins, Clacton, 1946. 'Egg and bacon for breakfast and fresh peaches for lunch ..
an absolute dream.'

38 Denis Compton and Bill Edrich. 'There was no rationing in an innings by Compton.'

39 The age of the big screen: 30 million regular cinemagoers

40   Relaxation amid exhortation: cricket on a bomb site

41   Bevin on a train: 'A turn up in a million.'

42   *Below left* Dalton, the loudest whisper in Westminster

43   *Below right* Morrison: 'Socialism is what the Labour Government does'

44   Saving the West: Bevin, Marshall and Schuman, Paris, October 1948

45   Cripps and Bevin arm in arm aboard the *Mauretania*, off to negotiate devaluation and to argue about a loaf

46   Devaluation closes the Stock Exchange. Brokers do business in Throgmorton Street, 19 September 1949.

Eady to set 'our own problems . . . against the background of the steady contraction of world trade caused by the shortage of dollars. It should be brought home to the United States Government that unless the British Government took steps now to protect the residual sterling position, world trade would break down completely within a short period with results which would cause serious harm to the United States economy.'[138]

As Eady's Constellation completed its journey across the Atlantic, the Cabinet decided that he should inform the US Government of the plan to suspend (while making 'it clear that he was not asking for . . . prior agreement'), and that 'His Majesty's Government had come to the conclusion that they had no option but to make temporary arrangements . . . to limit for the time being the convertibility of sterling into dollars by a system of rationing.' After a post-Cabinet dinner, Dalton, Bridges and Makins sat down to draft fresh instructions for their negotiator who arrived to find Washington sweltering in 110 degrees of heat.[139]

After a bumpy few days of negotiation, Eady persuaded the Americans to accept the inevitable. Dalton exchanged notes on 20 August with his American opposite number, John Snyder, who took 'sympathetic note' of the dollar drain from Britain's reserves. Dalton reaffirmed that the 'full and free convertibility of sterling' was still 'a long-run objective'.[140] Suspension was announced. Convertibility remained an aspiration for another eleven years until, three prime ministers and six chancellors later, it was finally restored.

A great deal changed that day. The Attlee Government came of age. Never again would *external* economic reality be far from their minds (Dalton 'wilfully shut his eyes to the relation between internal and external finance', said Burke Trend[141]). It also marked the end, for the foreseeable future, of the open financial system which the makers of Bretton Woods saw as the Siamese twin of an open world economy. Indeed, for economic historians like Alan Milward, the dollar famine and balance of payments difficulties which underlay the 1947 crisis across western Europe (not merely in the UK), can be 'seen as the inevitable outcome of the failure of the post-war peace settlements and the Bretton Woods Agreements to tackle adequately the problems of reconstruction'[142] '. . . the policies which the European governments pursued in 1947 showed those agreements to have solved nothing and to have practically no value or use as the basis for post-war reconstruction. If the Bretton Woods system had ever operated it ended in that year.'[143]

Dalton, outwardly ebullient as ever, was inwardly shattered. As so often when under severe stress, he forsook his shell-like marriage and his wife, Ruth, who, according to Nicholas Davenport, 'seemed incapable of looking after Hugh at their cottage . . . she could hardly boil an egg',[144] for the Davenports' sumptuous hospitality. 'When we had arrived at Hinton on 25th August 1947 after the drive from the cheering crowds of Downing Street,' Davenport later wrote, 'I had noticed that Hugh was emotionally exhausted. After a few drinks he was holding my wife's hand and tears were running down his face.'[145]

Yet, by concentrating on the *sturm und drang* of life in the Treasury and the Cabinet Room, it's possible to give a wholly misleading impression of life as it was lived by ordinary people in that glorious postwar summer of 1947. If indeed there is a folk memory of it, it's of Compton and Edrich at the crease at Lords not Dalton or Attlee at the despatch box in the House of Commons. Years after, Ian Bancroft (a young Treasury insider during that crisis summer) warned me against portraying the late Forties as drab, austere and joyless:

> True there wasn't much in the shops and there was even less money around to spend in them. But to be young, alive and unwounded was a joyous experience and there was, too, a great deal of hope. There was a great relief at the war being won and coming through alive. The weather seemed pretty good, too. Every Saturday, in that golden summer of 1947, we would go to Lords with our packets of sandwiches to watch Compton and Edrich.[146]

Denis Compton and Bill Edrich acquired at the time an image they have never lost since as 'not perhaps Mars and Jupiter in conjunction', as Sir Neville Cardus put it, but almost. 'Compton's mastery is easy and young and was not obtained by scorning delights and living laboriously,' wrote this greatest of cricket's wordsmiths. 'He was touched by the grace of genius in his cradle. Edrich, even at his most punitive – and he has many times bludgeoned bowling to a shambled condition – must needs watch closely and keep his head down and obey commonsense.'[147]

Compton, *the* 'Brylcreem Boy' in the postwar hair tonic adverts, was once depicted by Cardus as a kind of talisman of hope amid the drabness of much of life in 1947 Britain. 'Never', he recalled,

> have I been so deeply touched on a cricket ground as I was in this heavenly summer, when I went to Lords to see a pale-faced crowd, existing on rations, the rocket bomb still in the ears of most folk – to see this worn, dowdy crowd watching Compton. The strain of long years of anxiety and affliction passed from all hearts and shoulders at the sight of Compton in full flow, sending the ball here, there and everywhere, each stroke a flick of delight, a propulsion of happy, sane, healthy life. There was no rationing in an innings by Compton.[148]

'Denis', wrote the crusty cricket commentator of the *Daily Telegraph*, E.W. Swanton, 'made his runs gaily, and with a smile. His happy demeanour and his good looks completed a picture of the beau ideal of a sportsman. I doubt if any game at any period has thrown up anyone to match his popular appeal in the England of 1947–1949.'[149] (I only saw Compton once at Lords in the late Fifties when he was past his best; but I know what his eulogists mean.) No matter that bowling was weak that 1947 summer with prewar arms past their best required to do much of it,[150] Compton could do no wrong as if touched by the God of the swards. Swanton again:

> In the match between Middlesex, as champions, and the Rest of England at the Oval, Denis Compton (246) and Bill Edrich (180) between them made 426 out of their side's total of 543. This enabled them to win a handsome victory which in this match only one other county, Yorkshire, have ever achieved. In his innings Denis made what even for him was a phenomenal stroke. As he strolled out to play a ball from Goddard on the full pitch the studs of his right boot got somehow caught in the laces of his left and he toppled headlong forward. As he did so he remembered the ball and, in the act of falling, flicked it sweetly away for four. Have you ever tried walking on water, they asked him.[151]

Compton was that postwar phenomenon, a first class professional footballer as well as cricketer, like my own schoolboy hero, the left hander Willie Watson who played for Yorkshire and England and at wing half for Sunderland and England.

Naturally, the Brylcreem Boy himself gazes back at 1947 through a golden haze:

> Everybody in fact was absolutely starved of sport, so what was wonderful from our point of view, then you might say in our heyday, was that we played all our cricket and our football in front of capacity crowds and that to me was absolutely marvellous . . . The football crowds were absolutely marvellous, I mean at Highbury, the Arsenal, pretty well every Saturday we used to get 60,000 people and we used to get the young boys, children of even eight, nine, ten, eleven, twelve all going with their parents and, in fact, at times not going with their parents, going on to the terraces which were absolutely packed and you know you used to see them being pulled down over the heads of the crowd down to the front so they could get a jolly good seat. Nobody was ever hurt, the atmosphere I thought was absolutely electric . . .[152]

Compton's may be a gilded view but it is not a distorted one. In the early postwar years, crowds were huge and almost entirely violence free. If you glance at a photograph of a terrace in any football annual dealing with the first postwar decade you are struck by the absence of banners and the homogeneity of appearances. Young men dressed like their fathers and grandfathers – jackets, mackintoshes and caps. Young boys wore school uniform. Not until the first glimmerings of affluence put money into young pockets in the mid-Fifties did the external expressions of a youth culture come to distinguish the generations in a sporting crowd.

When it comes to a drab uniformity, did you notice how even Neville

Cardus's paean in praise of Denis Compton brought in rationing? The shadow of food – or, rather, its absence – dimmed even the brightness of that summer and the pen portraits which have captured it for future generations. Jim Swanton's contribution was squarely in this tradition. Writing of the South African touring side which adorned the pitches in that Compton summer, he said: 'They were extremely popular and contributed their full share to the delights of a vintage season. They brought over a good deal of tinned food as a gesture of sympathy for the ration situation, but, despite the tins, the captain's [Alan Melville's] efforts over the summer – and he was slim in the first place – cost him a couple of stone. Such hardships, all but forgotten now [he was writing in the early 1970s], were real enough at the time and they struck no one more forcibly than our visitors from overseas.'[153]

They strike me forcibly every time I read a contemporary account, especially a diary. Dennis 'Dicky' Bird was a teenager in the Forties. His schoolboy diary is filled with revealing one-liners about the changes in everyday life as war slipped into peace. Dicky lived in Shoreham near Worthing on the Sussex coast. On 17 January 1945 he recorded 'Street lamps lit in Mill Lane for first time since 1939.' For Dicky's street, the blackout was over. (The German airfields had been pushed well to the east by the Allied armies by this stage.) Not until 1 August 1946, however, did he note 'Got rid of gas-masks.'

With the peace, it's dramatic events at the dinner table which excite Dicky Bird the diarist. Take the first postwar Christmas Day: 'Wiz lunch, (chickens etc.).' 'It was a rare delicacy,' recalled Dicky. 'During and after the war, beef and lamb were the cheap foods; poultry was scarce and costly.'[154] On 8 April 1946, he shared that precious banana moment when he ate his first in five and a half years; 'one of the things I missed most'. (The previous November he'd been given oranges as a birthday present by his sister Joan though these had turned up three or four times a year during the war.) Like everyone else, the sixteen-year-old Dicky found bread rationing 'one of the biggest psychological shocks in 1946' and the Bird family 'all remembered Lord Woolton and wished he were back!'[155]

E.W. Swanton is only partly right when he said the privations of the postwar table had been all but forgotten a quarter of a century later. The folk memory may have dimmed for people of my age, but it hadn't (and never did) for people of my parents' generation or for the one between them and me. Their conversation remained peppered by what Richard Hoggart called 'the built-in rules of thumb of the permanent siege economy'.[156] 'There is still', Hoggart wrote in the late 1980s, 'behind every dealing with money and things, the fear and the hatred of waste. That old phrase . . . "you'll pay for this" . . . is joined by "it's a sin and a shame to be so wasteful"; "fancy good food being thrown away"; "he doesn't seem to know the value of money"; "I had to work hard for every penny I've got and am not going to squander it"; "a penny saved is a penny earned"; "take care of the pence, and the pounds will take care of themselves"; "put something aside for a rainy day"; "waste not, want not"; "I mean to get me money's worth"; and dozens of others expressing the fear of excess.'[157] How those phrases resonate for me, the domestic standbys of my childhood. I still notice how the war and postwar generation are reluctant to throw *anything* away (a characteristic I share with them).

It's easy to forget how long rationing lasted – in the case of meat until nine years after the war ended. There was no easement of any consequence until 1949. In 1947, as we have seen, it was at its tightest. Heaven knows what the reaction would have been if Otto Clarke's contingency plan had leaked to the Press with its talk of a 'famine food programme'. As Paul Addison put it, 'leisure . . . had to compensate for many other things'.[158]

In fact, as Addison himself has shown in his social history of postwar Britain, it's very easy to impose an overly grey patina of gloom on the late 1940s. 'There are stock images for every period,' he writes.

> For postwar Britain they are black and white images of hardship and high endeavour. They conjure up a land in which it was usually winter and people were digging themselves out of snowdrifts. The middle classes had disappeared and the male population, driven on by the exhortations of the government, were all digging coal or building ships. The women, meanwhile, were queuing for offal at the butcher's. In such spare time as they had left the people were grappling with social problems and were either squatting or looking forward to a set of NHS dentures. But the cinema brought relief – with the latest Central Office of Information documentary on the progress of the social services.[159]

In that near perfect 'Movietone' newsreel composite, Addison has captured the partly (but only partly) mythological memory of the high thinking/plain living late 1940s. With gentle irony he adds 'Only one item is missing from the received impression: the fact that there was plenty of fun to be had in the Attlee years. It was often summer and the summers were long and hot. And whatever the season peace brought with it a sustained outbreak of pleasure.'[160]

Can both impressions exist in paradoxical juxtaposition? Certainly. It's partly to do with age groups. For the children of the war – the Dicky Bird generation – it was, as Susan Cooper noted in the 1960s, a *different* experience from that of their elders, especially for those touched by middle class interwar prosperity.

> For those who remembered the years between the wars, the gradual climb back to prosperity was a long, dispiriting haul, echoing with prewar memories of better days. For the wartime children, it was different. Those years were not a return, but a revelation. They were lit by surprises; between 1945 and 1951 we saw not only the first pineapples and bananas of our lives, but the first washing-machine, the first fountain, the first television set. The world opening before us was not a pale imitation of one we had lost, but a lucky dip of extraordinary things we had never seen before.[161]

That's a view corroborated by Susan Cooper's cousin, Ken Morgan, who grew up to be a leading historian of the period: 'This was precisely my reaction, too, as a young schoolboy brought up in a home of no particular affluence, initially in a village in mid-Wales, subsequently in a London suburb. Indeed, I would add professional football matches, test matches, and Christmas pantomimes and circuses to the new delights of the postwar years.'[162]

Inevitably in the afterglow of the 'People's War' there were attempts by those in authority to regulate leisure in socially beneficial directions especially where it spilled over into culture. It may well be that the chamber music and the poetry brought to factory canteens by the Council for the Encouragement of Music and the Arts (a voluntary body founded in 1940 but with an increasing Treasury subsidy which had reached £175,000 a year by 1945) had an impact exaggerated by the passage of time; perhaps it's the cultural equivalent of the myth that the Army Bureau of Current Affairs delivered the election to Mr Attlee.

Years later, we learned of the true impact of the royal counterpart to this high-minded enterprise when the Queen Mother told a London dinner party of the effect of T.S. Eliot on the highest placed middlebrows in the land at a wartime poetry evening arranged by the Sitwells. The Queen (as she then was) explained to her dinner companion, the poet and author A.N. Wilson, that she was worried that her daughters, Elizabeth and Margaret, 'marooned in Windsor Castle for most of the war', were not 'having a very good education'.

QUEEN ELIZABETH . . . Kind Sachie [Sacheverell] and Osbert said they would arrange a poetry evening for us. Such an embarrassment. Osbert was wonderful, as you would expect, and Edith, of course, but then we had this rather lugubrious man in a suit, and he read a poem . . . I think it was called 'The Desert'. And first the girls got the giggles, and then I did and then even the King.

A.N. WILSON: 'The Desert' Ma'am? Are you sure it wasn't called *The Waste Land*?

QUEEN ELIZABETH: That's it. I'm afraid we all giggled. Such a gloomy man, looked as though he worked in a bank, and we didn't understand a word.[163]

I suspect the Royal Family were typical in this as they were in their adherence to their wartime ration books.

When Keynes persuaded the Coalition Government in 1945 to transform CEMA into a permanent, state-funded body, the Arts Council of Great Britain, he, as its first chairman, saw it as another arm of the welfare state. 'We look forward', he said in a broadcast in July 1945, 'to a time when the theatre and the concert hall and the art gallery will be a living element in everybody's upbringing, and regular attendance at the theatre and at concerts a part of organised education.'[164] It was a kind of full enjoyment policy to go with full employment. When inflation and a change of political philosophy hurled the Arts Council into a decade of convulsion after 1979, its mid-Eighties Chairman, Lord Rees-Mogg, said the Council had, in fact, been conceived as part of the welfare state 'which adopted the principle that the arts like education, health and social security, are universal goods which ought to be generally available regardless of the ability to pay'.[165]

The fledgling Arts Council recruited some brilliant spirits such as the future broadcaster of genius, Huw Wheldon, who evangelised Wales on its behalf.[166] It managed to boost the budget to over half a million pounds by 1949 and helped sponsor exhibitions of Spanish paintings which could attract a quarter of a million viewers even in the dreadful winter of 1946–7 and assisted at the birth of long-lasting festivals at Aldeburgh and Cheltenham in 1945 and at Edinburgh in 1947. 'Yet', as Paul Addison wrote, 'the temporary wartime bridge between the arts and the masses was in fact crumbling. The unorthodox wartime arrangements for taking the arts into the factory canteen or town hall were superseded. When factory concerts ended in 1946 in April the Arts Council appointed "industrial music organisers" to set up clubs which workers could attend outside the workplace. The clubs flopped and the music organisers had to be redeployed. After the war, the Arts Council concentrated naturally enough on the support of permanent organisations such as Covent Garden, the Old Vic, the big orchestras and the leading provincial theatres. It was still the aim of the Council to make the arts available to a wider audience, especially in the regions. But inevitably the arts based themselves after 1945 on a regular constituency of enthusiasts.'[167]

There was, however, already in existence a vast, state-funded organisation whose mission had been to bring education and enlightenment as well as entertainment, to the mass of the British people for the previous twenty years: the BBC. As the end of the war approached, that austere autodidact, William Haley, its Director General, began to plan postwar provision through a trio of programmes which were as much a part of my childhood as 'welfare' orange juice and those third-of-a-pint bottles of milk in metal crates which followed me round from kindergarten to primary and to grammar school. The division of radio output into a Home Service, a Light Programme and a Third Programme had been discussed as early as 1943. Haley pushed it through to the point where the Light was ready to replace the Forces Programme on 29 July 1945 even before the war in the Far East had ended (the Home Service was a continuation of the wartime domestic channel).

Haley, as we have seen, had a kind of Crippsian moral halo around him which, for a journalist, was quite remarkable. When the papers were declassified, I admired his robust way with the Attlee Government when the Home Office complained of the BBC's coverage of industrial disputes. (He told its Permanent Secretary, Sir Frank Newsam, that if the Ministry of Labour drafted its press releases in comprehensible English there would be a greater chance of the BBC making use of them.[168]) I only met him once as he was backing out of a broom cupboard in *The Times* office in Grays Inn Road. In for a lunch, he had mistaken it for the Gents. Even in these circumstances his dignity remained intact. So great was that dignity that those who dealt with him – even those who saw him in the most intimate circumstances – found it difficult to believe he could be wrong about anything. His wife would recall the impact on the Haley family of the bomb blast that shattered one of their windows during the war. Haley had regarded it as sufficiently protected. 'It was the only time in our lives when Daddy wasn't right.'[169]

Haley was sure he was right about the superiority of radio as a medium of communication. He never cared much for television. He had no compunction in shutting it down again, a few months after its postwar restoration, to save power during the fuel crisis. He left the BBC because he had no stomach for competition with ITV. Haley was a wireless man and the late Forties were Britain's radio days.

Haley, no doubt, would have wanted them remembered for the pioneering, unique Third Programme, the kind of cultural gem that could only have been produced in early postwar Britain under conditions of broadcasting monopoly. In their way, Haley and George Barnes, the first Controller of the Third, were licence-funded Medicis. It went on the air on 29 September 1946. 'C for Culture', declared *The Times*. 'The timeless wonder', sneered Beaverbrook's *Daily Express*[170] which couldn't abide culture, pursuing slavishly its proprietor's vendetta against the country's cultural arm abroad, the Foreign Office funded British Council, always referring to its staff as 'the Culture Boys' or 'the long-haired lads and lassies of the British Council' bringing 'madrigals' to Outer Mongolia.[171]

It's easy to see why the Beaver's hacks salivated at the discovery of another sitting target. 'The programmes for the first evening', recalled the BBC's official historian Asa Briggs, 'had included the first performance of Benjamin Britten's *Festival Overture*, Bach's *Goldberg Variations*, talks by Field Marshal Smuts, Max Beerbohm and Haley himself, and a feature *How to Listen . . .* devised by Joyce Grenfell and one of the most ingenious specialists in "programmemanship" as in "gamesmanship", Stephen Potter.'[172]

Beerbohm had persuaded Evelyn Waugh to buy a wireless for the occasion. He sent his wife out for one, tuned in for the first night and declared, 'I have listened attentively to all programmes and nothing will confirm me more in my resolution to emigrate.'[173] Waugh, it should be said, couldn't abide Mr Attlee's England, generally. On 8 June 1946 he wrote 'Victory Day. At home, having refused an invitation from the *Empire News* to report a masquerade which Mr Attlee is organizing in London. He is driving round in a carriage with Churchill, behind the Royal Family, at the head of a procession of Brazilians, Mexicans, Egyptians, Naafi waitresses and assorted negroes claiming that they won the war. It has rained most of the day. I hope it rained hard in London and soaked Attlee.'[174]

The Third Programme, though it never netted the big audiences baited by cultural shrimps on the Light and Home, did gain and retain a small dedicated following. Over forty years later, Richard Hoggart, recalling for me what he called the 'bump of social purpose' so evident in the postwar years and so absent as we talked in the Hotel Russell in 1990, spoke of the Third Programme and the huge contemporary circulations of the quality weeklies (the BBC's own *Listener* peaked at 151,350 in 1949)[175]: 'I would be loth to let go of the idea that that great surge was to do with the feeling that there was a moral dimension to society and its problems. It was an act of faith to listen to the Third Programme and to read the *Listener*.'[176] Remember what Ellen Wilkinson said just before she died about wanting to make Britain 'a Third Programme nation'?

In that same conversation, Richard Hoggart developed a thesis of his about the British absent-mindedly inventing some superb masterpieces (a kind of cultural equivalent of Seeley's view that the Empire was acquired 'in a fit of absence of mind').[177] He built it around the 1944 Education Act which 'symbolically seemed such an opening. The question is, did Butler realise it? That's one of the things about the British cultural hierarchy. They do things without quite knowing what it is they're doing or what the consequences will be ... Despite all our terribly bad habits and our refusal to admit to class problems, we do have some extraordinarily good ideas – the BBC, the Open University, the Emergency Training Scheme for teachers after the war.'[178]

Haley knew what he was doing. Minority audience or no, great claims can be made for its trickle-down effect, not least the cascade of popular appreciation for classical music which has irrigated Britain since the war, enabling a fleet of first class orchestras to remain afloat and keeping the quality end of the record industry buoyant. In its way, the Third Programme did for the whole country (geographically speaking) what Sir Thomas Beecham, thanks to his genius, his rudeness and his personal (Beecham's Pills) fortune had managed to do for selected audiences in a few locations during the interwar years.[179]

But it's not for the Sartre or the Wagner to be found on the Third that Britain's radio days are remembered by the listeners of the period. If you were young at the time it would be *Dick Barton, Special Agent* on the Light; if middle-aged, it would be *Have A Go* with Wilfred Pickles (who caused a stir when, after reading the news in the war, he finished with a homely 'good neet' in his Yorkshire accent[180]). If there's one tune that, even now, can drag me back instantly to earliest childhood memories it's Violet Carson striking the piano keys with the audience, Wilfred, his wife Mabel, his producer Barney Colehan and, so it seemed, anyone who happened to be passing, suddenly launching into

Have a go, Joe, Come and have a go.
You can't lose owt, it costs you nowt
    To make yourself some dough.
So hurry up and join us,
    Don't be shy and don't be slow,
    Come on, Joe! Have a go![181]

The idea, dreamed up in his front room in Didsbury by John Salt of the BBC's northern region, was to reproduce the success Pickles had had with his Civil Defence quiz shows in the war. The programme was a huge success, touring the church halls, collieries and women's institutes. Wilfred would ask fresh questions to the younger ladies – 'Are yer coortin'?' – ask a few simple questions and declare 'Give 'er the money, Mabel,' if the answer was right.

One of the classic photos of the 1940s is Wilfred persuading a reluctant 'knocker-up' (who tapped the windows of the mill workers with a long pole at some ghastly hour of a northern morning) in Wigan to come to the front and 'Have a Go'. It was 'great radio' as Colehan said. It was, said Pickles himself, 'a memorial to ordinary people', and it lasted well into the 1960s.[182]

It wasn't just the public sector, still running on the fuel of wartime unity, which made great efforts to bridge the culture equivalents of Britain's entrenched class divides. That great symbol of private communal entertainment – the Butlin's holiday camp – did the same with all the flair that Billy 'Mr Happiness' Butlin could bring.

Butlin was a cheery-faced man who had done well out of the war. A bantam weight, energetic entrepreneur with a fairground background, he was to write himself into British popular folklore almost from the moment in the mid-1930s when he gazed out over a stretch of turnip fields between the road and the North Sea in Lincolnshire and decided 'that this was it', the site of the country's first holiday camp, home of the first battalion of redcoats.[183] Skegness opened in 1936. By the time war came, Clacton had joined Skegness in the Butlin empire and Billy was a household name thanks to his ardent courtship of sportsmen and entertainers (he paid Len Hutton, fresh from scoring 364 off the Australians at the Oval in 1938, £100 to come to Skegness and have Gracie Fields bowl at his bat sculpted from Skegness Rock).[184]

Early in the war, Leslie Hore-Belisha rang Butlin from the War Office. Was it true he could build huts for £75 a head when his army architects were talking in terms of £125 per squaddie? Yes, said Butlin, that was the going rate at Filey, his half-built camp just south of Scarborough. 'Finish it,' said the Minister of War. 'The Government will pay part of the costs. We will use it for the services now, and, at the end of the war, you may have the opportunity of buying it back.'[185] Butlin gambled. He'd do it provided he could buy back the camps at three-fifths of their original cost even if the Luftwaffe had bombed them to rubble. It paid off. The taxpayer finished Filey for BB and put up Ayr and Pwllheli for him. The Luftwaffe left them alone. By the end of the war, Filey was well on the way to reconversion from RAF to holidaymaker use at a time when building materials were like gold. Within two years of the war ending all four camps were fully operational, the only trace of their former inhabitants being the HMS *Royal Arthur* insignia embroidered on the blankets of Skegness.[186]

Butlin wanted more. He wanted his camps to move up-market. A new kind of PR was required. He hired the San Carlo Opera Company to put on *La*

Bohème at Filey. He invited 400 top people from politics, public life and the arts. How to get them there in 1946 when a journey from London to Scarborough was only for the brave? He asked the London and North Eastern Railway to take the Yorkshire Pullman out of mothballs. For £1,100 they agreed. The celebrities all turned up at Kings Cross (who could resist Puccini in Filey?). They swept up the main line in style until the train, its not so tiny pistons far from frozen, caught fire at Doncaster. Butlin had a personal message of apology waiting for all 400 in their VIP chalets.[187]

He despatched the San Carlo Company to all the camps. He brought the Old Vic to Filey to do Shakespeare. Ballet dancers appeared among the comics, Vic Oliver came up with the London Symphony Orchestra. Throughout the late Forties, the good and the great (Dr Cyril Garbett, Archbishop of York and Lady Violet Bonham Carter) the svelte (Anthony Eden photographed looking like Jermyn Street man outside the famous celebrity chalet, A7, at Filey), the noisy (Hugh Dalton) and the proletarian (Will Lawther of the Miners and Nye Bevan of the Ministry of Health) all passed through to add – well who knows what Butlin or his normal customers (half a million of them in the summer of 1947) thought they were adding?

It's easy to sound patronising about Billy Butlin and to send him and his little wooden huts, his artificial flowers and his glamorous granny contests up. It would be wrong to. He was a showman and a celebrity hunter but he was a genius as a pleasure-giver to ordinary people who more than deserved a week or two in his pleasure domes beside the North and the Irish Seas. The customers loved it:

> We had what I thought then was marvellous food . . . eggs and bacon for breakfast and fresh peaches for lunch, it was an absolute dream.[188]

Campers gave in their ration books at the beginning of the week, and Butlin's chefs clipped the coupons; they, more likely he, clearly knew how to make bulk buying stretch to those parts where the woman-in-the-queue could not hope to reach.

> Butlin's was the best thing that happened to ordinary people. To get them a holiday outside their areas. To go up to Kings Cross. To get on a train [I can remember seeing the Butlin specials to Skegness roaring through Oakleigh Park in North London on Saturday evenings in the late Fifties]. It was a wonderful feeling. And Butlin's cashed in at the right time, they really did.[189]

It wasn't just ordinary people who crossed the thresholds of the camps. An element of wartime solidarity continued here too as Ted Young, a trainee manager at Skegness remembers: 'The greatest cross-section of the community came through the centres . . . let us take the knobbly knees competition, it was nothing weird to see a barrister, doctors, and many professional men queuing up with the road sweeper or the refuse person, all getting together and having a very good time.'[190]

More important than the classless solidarity of the bomb shelter transported to the coast, I suspect, was the sheer, blissful convenience for parents of all backgrounds of having your children off your hands in the care of Butlin's redcoats for hour after hour in what was, deliberately, a non-stop frenzy of entertainment and diversion. What Butlin was cashing in on was an economic niche created by the Holidays with Pay Act of 1938. By 1946, over 12 million employees (about 80 per cent of the workforce) were within its orbit. The economies of scale practised so brilliantly by Butlin brought his camps within reach of millions (it was to be another 15 years before the package holiday shifted the summertime queues from Kings Cross to Luton and the knobbly knees from Skegness to Benidorm).

Paul Addison sees in the postwar leisure boom an outlet for pent-up purchasing power which, as long as rationing lasted, the shops could not release: 'An initial boost was given by the millions of returning service personnel, each with a gratuity to spend. In conditions of full employment, the collective spending power of the working classes was greater, and the relatively higher proportion of married women at work compared with 1939, gave many families spare cash to spend. But what could it be spent on? With many commodities on the ration and others in short supply, leisure was the most powerful magnet, and the leisure industry a licence to print money.'[191]

The late Forties were, in fact, the ne'er-to-be-repeated boom years for British spectator sports. People queued from early morning to get into test matches. Over 40 million filed through the soccer turnstiles in the 1948–9 season. Some 300,000 a week went to watch motorcycle speedway. Over half a million regularly visited the dog tracks. Towns boasted packed dance halls and several cinemas (1946 was the boom year for the pictures with a staggering 1,635 million visits by a population of only 46 million). At weekends thousands took to their wheels as cycling clubs swept down roads bereft of cars thanks to tight petrol rationing.[192]

It was as if six years of lost pleasure had to be crammed into as many postwar golden summers (1946, remember, was a washout) before Stalin took over where Hitler stopped (no wonder people were jumpy about developments in eastern Europe). As if to reinforce that impression, it was largely prewar pastimes which scooped the pool in the first years of peace. On the fringe there was jitterbugging in the dance halls (an American wartime import much frowned on by bouncers as the girls' high heels carved up the wooden floors) and a dash of the illicit in the handful of cellars where fashionable young men like Humphrey Lyttelton (Old Etonian nephew of top Tory, Oliver Lyttelton) and the not-so-fashionable like Chris Barber and Ken Colyer played New Orleans music to a faintly bohemian intelligentsia. 'Mothers', Lyttelton recalled, 'used to ring me up and say they were extremely worried, their daughters had expressed the intention of coming to my club . . . I used to say, "Well, the only thing you're likely to get hung up on in 100 Oxford Street is Tizer." '193

Such 'new looks' as there were would be found in the mannequin world of fashion. Indeed it was the arrival in February 1947 of Parisian 'swirling skirts' with 'Renoirish curves and flounces . . . wasp waist and bustle' which brought the phrase into common and lasting currency in Britain and gave Harry Hopkins the title for his evocation of early postwar life. 'The volume of the outcry', he wrote,

> at what was basically merely a return to traditional feminine lines was indeed a remarkable tribute to the grip which the puritan discipline of Austerity and Fair Shares had gained in our island life. The chorus of disapproval grew as it became known that the new fashion required thirty to forty metres of material, not to mention new corsets, still firmly classified by the Board of Trade as 'luxury garments' . . . There were indignant questions in the House. The Government was rumoured to be considering legislating against the new skirt length. In the meantime Sir Stafford Cripps made an appeal for moderation, receiving emphatic support from Miss Mabel Ridealgh, MP for North Ilford. The New Look, declared Miss Ridealgh, was 'too reminiscent of the "caged bird attitude". I hope our fashion dictators will realise the new *outlook* of women and give the death blow to any attempt at curtailing women's freedom.'194

Such extraordinarily violent language (most fashion 'dictators' looked scarcely capable of crushing a grape let alone delivering a 'death blow' to anything) had not the slightest effect. Popular culture has never taken much notice of Parliament.

The Parisian shock of 1947 became the London norm of 1948. The process, however, included Cripps' successor at the Board of Trade delivering a singularly arch speech, appearing before the newsreels as 'the youngest Cabinet Minister since Pitt'. Harold Wilson declared, with his wife, Mary, in the background, that 'I have my own private views on that matter . . . [but] at this present time, with the shortage of materials and of manpower, most people would agree that it doesn't make sense to have skirts longer.' His peroration was conveyed in an extraordinarily clipped voice (replaced by his original mild Yorkshire accent by the time he became Prime Minister in 1964) which suggested a desperate attempt at Oxford- and Whitehall-induced upward mobility.195

For those who prefer their pleasures – visual, aural and read – especially refined, early postwar Britain has been depicted as a bit of a desert with an occasional BBC-watered oasis. If it were true, it would not be surprising. Creativity, after all, requires intense, sustained endeavour. Total war had affected and exhausted all except, perhaps, Noël Coward (encountered by Harold Nicolson in his bath at the Grand Hotel in Leicester in 1943, where a new play was being tried out at a local theatre, where 'A valet was opening endless scent bottles and folding clothes. There was a large apparatus in the corner, in front of which Noël, clad only in a triangulo, seated himself with an expression of intense desire and submitted himself to five minutes of infra-red, talking gaily all the while. So patriotic he was, so light-hearted, and so comfortable and well-served'[196]). Rather as great cricketers like Wally Hammond of Gloucestershire and England had had probably their best years pre-empted by Hitler, artists and writers, like ordinary mortals – like, to be utterly prosaic, the British economy – needed a period at less than full throttle.

There were one or two novelists such as Evelyn Waugh or Angela Thirkell who made a thing of decrying the Britain of Attlee and Cripps, of pandering profitably to a bygone age where consumption was conspicuous and unrationed for the few. It was, however, if anything, the era of the middle-brow. 'Labour's middle-brow Prime Minister' was an Agatha Christie fan 'and Agatha Christie largely set the tone: her stories were cunning crossword puzzles filled out to book length, without sex and without gratuitous violence.'[197]

Perhaps we have succumbed too readily to the first drafts of early postwar cultural history which were written even before the decade came to a close by some of the most powerful pens then in motion. The best remembered epitaph belongs to the lugubrious ex-bank clerk in a suit who made the Royal Family giggle in uncomprehending embarrassment. Eliot declared in his *Notes Towards the Definition of Culture* published in 1948 that 'We can assert with some confidence that our own period is one of decline; that the standards of culture are lower than they were fifty years ago; and that the evidences of this decline are visible in every department of human activity.'[198]

J.B. Priestley, in many ways *the* voice of the 1940s, was back in his role of pessimistic curmudgeon by the summer of 1949. 'We are revolutionaries who have not swept away anything,' he told the readers of the *New Statesman* (which, whingeing away to the left of mainstream Labour, had virtually doubled its circulation in eight years, reaching 80,000 at the turn of the Forties and Fifties with a strong following in the Civil Service and the education world).[199]

We are Tories loudly denouncing taxes and regulations chiefly invented by Tory ministers. We are socialists busy creating Peers and cheering pretty Princesses. We are a dreary self-righteous people with a passion for gin, tobacco, gambling and ballet. We are a nation of Sabbath-keepers who do not go to church. We toil to keep ourselves alive, with three tea-breaks, a five-day week and Wednesday afternoon off for the match. We spend so much time arguing about food we have no time to cook it properly. We spend fourpence on our culture, and several million pounds a year advertising it. We get free spectacles and false teeth and, for lack of hospital beds, may die in a ditch. We have probably the best children and the dullest adults in Europe. We are a Socialist-Monarchy that is really the last monument of Liberalism.[200]

As for Cyril Connolly, editor of *Horizon*, the literary magazine which blazed across the decade that almost exactly encompassed its life, for him, '"Nothing dreadful is ever done with, no bad thing gets any better; you can't be too serious." This is the message of the Forties from which, alas, there seems no escape, for it is closing time in the gardens of the West and from now on an artist will be judged only by the resonance of his solitude or the quality of his despair.'[201]

How oddly all this reads forty years later. My first reaction is to say, retrospectively as it were, 'you ain't seen nothing yet'. If Priestley found the Forties a disappointing decade, what disappointments life must have brought him in the remainder of his long life (he died in 1984).[202]

In fact, almost everywhere you touch the written remains of late Forties cultural life a whinge comes up to greet you. You can forgive the complaints about the activities of the Board of Trade's Controller of Paper when already tight rations were tautened in the fuel crisis of 1947 pushing the smaller publishers and a constellation of tiny literary magazines to the wall. Inevitably such physical conditions led existing publishers to allot their paper quotas to safe bets (Churchill's publishers, Cassell, hoarded their stock against the huge sales they anticipated for the old man's war memoirs[203]) and prevented new houses from starting up (new magazines were technically prohibited because of the paper shortage but the guileful, like George Weidenfeld, got round this by publishing what were called miscellanies[204]).

The publisher Geoffrey Faber distilled the gloom from the Bloomsbury atmosphere (where his and a host of prestigious houses could be found between the Charing Cross and Euston Roads), in a *Spectator* article in 1948:

> During a routine conference for the purpose of going over my own firm's forthcoming publications, I found myself wondering aloud where 'literature' had got to. Almost every book seemed to deal with some more or less specialised subject. That evening I attended a meeting of a society whose members include editors, critics, librarians, authors and literary agents as well as booksellers and publishers. We were addressed by the editor of a famous periodical; and the burden of his utterances was precisely the doubt I had expressed in the afternoon. There were one or two dissentients in the discussion that followed; but the general opinion was overwhelmingly with the speaker.[205]

Why? Faber partly answered the question: 'Signs of exhaustion are only to be expected. As a nation . . . we have suddenly exchanged riches for poverty, and power for insecurity. This change in our status and prospects has come as a reward for our "finest hour". Until we have realistically and courageously adjusted ourselves to it, we are not likely to produce very much worthwhile literature.'[206]

There was more to it than that. After the ideological and literary excitements of the Thirties with its Marxist tinge, its sense of menace and the stimulus that danger brought in the dénouement when conflict burst over Europe, some kind of hangover, of anti-climax was inevitable. It was made worse by a corrosive, gradual disillusion on the part of those who had believed, traceable in the odysseys of Victor Gollancz, whose Left Book Club had been its very incarnation, and of his prize author, John Strachey, who had exchanged revolution for ration book (a process begun by Gollancz's *The Betrayal of the Left*, to which Strachey contributed, in 1941, continued by his *Our Threatened Values* in 1946 and completed, most famously of all, by the galaxy of contributors – André Gide, Richard Wright, Ignazio Silone, Stephen Spender, Arthur Koestler and Louis Fischer – to *The God That Failed* in 1950).[207]

There was benefit in the British intellectuals being weaned from their 1930s 'Trahison des Clercs'. George Orwell had great difficulty finding a publisher in 1945 for his anti-Stalinist satire, *Animal Farm* (it was turned down by Gollancz, Cape and Faber, finally being published by Secker and Warburg).[208] There was no such problem with his *Nineteen Eighty-Four*, a grim extrapolation from 1948 into a totalitarian future dominated by perpetual war between superpowers with Britain reduced to 'Oceania's' 'Airstrip One', which, almost as soon as it was published in 1949, became *the* cult novel of the age and gave the ailing Orwell his permanent place in popular, as opposed to literary culture.

Painful intellectual readjustment, if not repentance, there was bound to be. So why the accusations of whingeing instead of expressions of sympathy and pleasure at scales falling from eyes? Because even from men I admired, like Priestley or Tom Harrisson (the Mass Observer), there came forth a drizzle of complaint which makes me suspect that nothing would have satisfied them. Just listen to Priestley in his 1947 pamphlet, *The Arts Under Socialism*:

> The artist wonders rather dubiously about the Socialist atmosphere of co-operation, committees, and common sense . . . He is doubtful about a society that no longer has either magnificent palaces or picturesque hovels but only nice bungalows and tidy communal flats; and he is ready, secretly perhaps, to regret the dramatic values that will disappear from a society abolishing all terrific social inequalities.[209]

As for Harrisson, within four months of the Third Programme's appearance and just before its temporary disappearance during the fuel crisis, he was writing to the *Listener* talking it down as 'cliquey, a bit of a mutual admiration society . . . A relatively small number of persons, nearly all between the ages of thirty and fifty, and many of them personal friends, exercise a major influence on the cultural side of a large proportion of our newspapers, weekly journals, arts bodies and the plethora of new monthlies and quarterlies. The Third Programme has further helped those who have "arrived" to widen their prestige and to ensure their getting a larger slice of the income cake.'[210]

Much the same was said of the ballet (Covent Garden ceased to be a Mecca dance hall and reverted to its original use in February 1946) and the theatre, that they were dominated by the familiar and the safe, *La Bohème* and *Tosca*, Wilde and Shakespeare, with the theatre world controlled not by some remote licenser in the Board of Trade but by Prince Littler and 'The Group', with Littler's colleague, 'Binkie' Beaumont exercising an unhealthy degree of patronage.[211]

Of course there were cliques, whether they be 'The Group' or the regulars in the diaspora of pubs around Broadcasting House where who you were and who you knew counted for more than it should as it has always done in any patronage society. To expect otherwise merely because a kind of socialism had come to Britain was as delusory as shop steward, Fred Kite (Peter Sellers) in *I'm All Right Jack*, the Boulting Brothers' Fifties classic send-up of trade union power, telling 'the Major' (Terry-Thomas) of the workers' paradise in the Soviet Union – 'all that waving corn and ballet in the evening'.

Culture, however, was treated in an atomised fashion by those who took up their pens in lamentation at the postwar scene. It was a much wider phenomenon, even at its higher levels. The universities, for example, exist as a cultural bank in which the riches of the past are stored for the scholars of the present to draw on and add to. These as we have seen were swelled to overflowing by returning servicemen and the first beneficiaries of the 1944 Education Act (the number of state scholarships was increased in 1947).

This being Britain, the rapid 50 per cent increase in numbers produced its own version of the later 'more means worse' controversy (the phrase belongs to Kingsley Amis; at this time he was in his more egalitarian, *Lucky Jim* phase). Its most elegant expositor was Michael Oakeshott, the gentlemanly, Conservative political philosopher who was soon to move from Cambridge to the London School of Economics and the chair vacated on his death by Harold Laski. Rebutting the plea for university reform contained in the earnest collection of essays (bewailing the waning of a Christian morality in the seats of learning) edited by Sir Walter Moberly, Chairman of the University Grants Committee, and published in 1949 under the title *The Crisis in the Universities*,[212] Oakeshott rejected any utilitarian concepts, treating it instead as a uniquely enriching interlude in an otherwise humdrum and frantic existence.

'The great and characteristic gift of the university', he wrote in probably the most romantic evocation of such an institution ever penned by an Englishman,

was the gift of an interval. Here was an opportunity to put aside the hot allegiances of youth without the necessity of acquiring new loyalties to take their place. Here was an interval in which a man might refuse to commit himself. Here was a break in the tyrannical course of irreparable events; a period in which to look round upon the world without the sense of an enemy at one's back or the insistent pressure to make up one's mind; a moment in which one was relieved of the necessity of 'coming to terms with oneself' or of entering the fiercely trivial partisan struggles of the world outside; a

moment in which to taste the mystery without the necessity of at once
seeking a solution . . .

And all this, not in an intellectual vacuum, but surrounded by all the
inherited learning and literature and experience of our civilization; not as a
sole occupation, but combined with the discipline of studying some recog-
nized branch of learning; and neither as a first step in education, for those
wholly ignorant of how to behave or think, nor as a final education to fit a
man for the day of judgment, but as a middle.[213]

Given such a view it's not surprising that Oakeshott did not relish the arrival of
the postwar university bulge, though, heaven knows, British colleges remained
ultra élite institutions compared to almost everywhere else in the advanced
world.

In a conclusion, where my own convictions do not follow his, Oakeshott
added, 'Anyone who has worked in a contemporary overcrowded university
knows it to be an illusion that there was any large untapped reserve of men and
women who could make use of this kind of university but who never had the
opportunity of doing so.'[214] A view belied, I think, by the testimony of any
adult educator, whether it be that pillar of the Workers' Educational Association and Oakeshott's colleague at LSE, R.H. Tawney, or Richard Hoggart,
E.P. Thompson and Raymond Williams in those outhouses of the British
university system, the extra-mural departments.

Wartime university departments were run on a care-and-maintenance basis,
their best and brightest plundered for the war effort in Whitehall, if not the
North African desert. In many disciplines there was by British standards, a
postwar Renaissance. British philosophy may have succumbed to the paralysis
of linguistics and lost its most coruscating luminary, Isaiah Berlin, on the
grounds, 'that I should prefer a field in which one could hope to know more at
the end of one's life than when one had begun; and so I left philosophy for the
field of the history of ideas . . . '[215] But it gained incomparably from the arrival
at LSE in 1945 of Karl Popper, *the* philosopher of the open society (he stayed
there for a quarter of a century, the bulk of it as Professor of Logic and
Scientific Method), the most persuasive (to my mind) defender of free inquiry
against totalitarianism both in its intellectual and its political forms. Popper, an
Austrian, who had escaped Nazism, reached England via a spell in New
Zealand which saw the completion of his masterpiece, *The Open Society and Its
Enemies.*[216] He began the book 'on the day he received the news he had so long
dreaded, of Hitler's invasion of Austria' and finished in 1943 when 'the
outcome of the second world war was still uncertain'.[217] So great was Popper's
spell (it was still very real when I encountered it at the LSE in his eighty-
seventh year) that it entranced both the libertarian right and the democratic
left. His intellectual vigour was quite exceptional but it was his sense of morality, which mattered most to him, that placed him a class apart – 'Man has
created new worlds – of language, of music, of poetry, of science; and the most

important of these is the world of the moral demands, for equality, for freedom, and for helping the weak.'[218]

When peace came, the study of English was already enlivened by controversies stimulated by another great moralist (with a puritanical side absent in Popper), F.R. Leavis. When the greatest adornment of postwar Cambridge philosophy, Ludwig Wittgenstein, came up to him one day and declared, without preliminaries, 'Give up literary criticism!'; 'I abstained from retorting "Give up philosophy, Wittgenstein!"' Leavis said later, 'largely because that would have meant telling him that he had been listening to the talk of a dominant coterie, and ought to be ashamed of supposing that Keynes, his friends and their *protégés* were the cultural *élite* they took themselves to be.'[219] Already by 1943, in his *Education and the University*,[220] Leavis had begun an assault on thoughtless, heartless technocracy which squeezed the meaning out of life, on the more modern kind of university administrator and on his fellow labourers in that vineyard known as the Cambridge English Tripos which was to envenom him for the rest of his life.[221]

History, too, was lining up for some battles royal (controversy is not the be-all and end-all of scholarship, but it's a true sign of life). J.H. Plumb was back from code-breaking at Bletchley Park itching to rescue history from the narrow, obsessive methodology of Lewis Namier and his 'veneration for monarchy, aristocracy and tradition'.[222] Hugh Trevor-Roper, having poked around the ruins of Berlin and reassured MI6 Hitler really was dead[223] was limbering up for his great assault on Tawney's theories of the gentry and the rise of the Protestant ethic in England,[224] and the incomparable A.J.P. Taylor was at work on updating his *The Habsburg Monarchy*,[225] the prelude to a ten-year assault on the orthodoxies of the British way of writing diplomatic history. This was the golden age of history not just in the British universities but among a wider reading public: the *Penguin History of England* (to which Plumb himself,[226] as well as S.T. Bindoff[227] and David Thompson,[228] were brilliant contributors) carried on a tradition begun by Macaulay with his *History of England*[229] and developed by G.M. Trevelyan and his *Social History of England* which sold over 300,000 copies when Longmans finally found sufficient paper in 1944.[230]

War had turned Whitehall into an adventure playground for economists and statisticians,[231] but postwar university expansion proved such a magnet that even the Whitehall of Morrison and Cripps, with all its emphasis on economic planning, couldn't attract the pool of technocrats it needed. On almost his first day as head of the Economic Section, Robert Hall had to tell the Cabinet Secretary, Sir Norman Brook, that 'many economists felt that the present Government was hopeless. In any case all universities had raised their salaries and the Economic Section was not as attractive as it used to be.'[232]

Economics as a subject had come of age. It was difficult in the late Forties to remember just how great had been Alfred Marshall's struggle to get it accepted as a discipline even in Cambridge where it was to find the most fertile soil in Britain and, in Keynes' prewar heyday, the world.[233]

Keynes and his posthumous 'ism' didn't entirely sweep the board in every economics department in the land in the postwar period. The LSE remained a citadel of the old *laissez faire*/free market orthodoxies. Friedrich von Hayek was a recruit second only to his fellow Austrian, Karl Popper, in eminence. (His *The Road to Serfdom* went through several reprints and a popular edition when it appeared in 1944; what would now be called a 'guru' book, it was seized on by all who detested the drift to collectivism they saw, rightly or wrongly, all about them.) 'The important thing now', he wrote, 'is that we shall come to agree on certain principles and free ourselves from some of the errors that have governed us in the recent past ... The guiding principle, that a policy of freedom for the individual is the only truly progressive policy, remains as true today as it was in the nineteenth century.'[234]

The LSE also boasted Lionel Robbins, another formidable free marketeer, whose friendship with Keynes was restored during Whitehall war service. After helping secure the American Loan, this enormous, leonine figure returned to Houghton Street to give the most celebrated introductory lectures in economics in the postwar period and to build LSE up into a postgraduate, as well as undergraduate institution, of world class.[235]

In the more fledgling social sciences, too, postwar LSE was the kind of place which scions, such as A.H. Halsey and Ralf Dahrendorf, would, years after, recapture for me with affection and reverence. To home grown demographers like David Glass and Alexander Carr-Saunders, were added the international perspectives of Edward Shils and Karl Mannheim.[236] T.H. Marshall, whose concepts of citizenship continued to influence the likes of Halsey, Dahrendorf and Frank Field[237] for another forty years, was succeeded in 1950 by Richard Titmuss, the intensely sensitive chronicler of the wartime Home Front, the first and almost certainly the last person to hold an LSE Chair without the adornment of a first degree. Titmuss and the 'Titmice' he nurtured had a profound impact on social policy until the Thatcher years.

That other great group of intellectuals for whom the war machine was one giant theme park – the scientists – returned to their universities with ideas in their head of a richness and promise that six years of peace is most unlikely to have nurtured. In some cases, like the 'boffins' from Malvern who helped build the world's first civilian computer at Manchester University in the first three years of peace, they came out with bits of illicit equipment too.[238] It's impossible, given the mercurial nature of brainpower and the untrackable paths of serendipity, to make any precise linkage between what Churchill called the 'strange sinister resources' of wartime British science (a war-winner, he said)[239] and the taking of so many Nobel Prizes by British scientists in the forty years that followed, a haul second only to the Americans.[240] It had, no doubt, as much to do with that egalitarian republic of the intellect attitude in British labs which so distinguished them from, say, the Japanese.[241]

It was widely thought in 1945 that, thanks to the wonders of the boffins' war, the hour of the scientist had come. It was not to be, not even in Whitehall. Scientists and professionals generally remained, in the power plays, very inferior beings to their largely arts-trained administrative colleagues. They remained at a disadvantage despite the sustained importance of big science and R and D which the cold war and huge civilian procurements, such as the development of *civil* nuclear power, made a regular feature of Cabinet agendas and a constant nightmare for the Treasury.

Solly Zuckerman, one of the most brilliant scientists recruited as a temporary civil servant in wartime Whitehall, was made a member of the Barlow Committee on Future Scientific Policy commissioned by Herbert Morrison shortly after the Government took office (as Lord President, Morrison was the nearest thing there was to a Minister of Science).[242] Sir Alan Barlow, unusually for a Treasury man, 'had cultivated scientific interests, particularly through friends and acquaintances in the Athenaeum'.[243]

Zuckerman prepared for Morrison, at the Lord President's request, what was, in effect, a manifesto for postwar British science. He could turn a mean phrase; he was one of a pair of anonymous authors (the other was the crystallographer, J.D. Bernal) who had produced inside a fortnight a Penguin Special, *Science in War*, in 1940.[244] Bernal was involved in the drafting of Zuckerman's 'Memorandum on the need for a central Governmental Science Secretariat', as were Patrick Blackett and C.H. Waddington, the animal geneticist.[245] Its style was rather like that of the Beveridge Report though, unlike Beveridge, it wasn't published, didn't lead to a public or political debate and had almost no impact. Its opening declaration could have been written (and justified) at any time since:

> Scientific affairs in Great Britain are badly integrated and planned. Yet the economic condition of the country today is such that it demands the fullest possible use and extension of our scientific resources in the restoration of industry and agriculture, in the development of the social services and in the determination of defence politics – which in turn calls for a large measure of forward-thinking and bold and energetic planning.[246]

Zuckerman recommended a full-time science secretariat answerable to the Lord President with an input to the Cabinet comparable to the Joint Intelligence Committee and the Central Statistical Office. Not only would it drive Government science, it would co-ordinate a national effort, 'plan for the supply of the much larger number of university-trained scientists necessary for the full development of our national resources' and 'ensure that an appreciation of science is adequately provided for in our schemes for general education'.[247]

Very little of this came to pass. The Government acted on the Barlow Committee's recommendation that an Advisory Council on Scientific Policy be established.[248] On one or two 'big science' projects, the drive and effectiveness of wartime were sustained, most notably the nuclear weapons programme which combined the leadership talents of a remarkable trio of 'atomic knights'; William Penney, Christopher Hinton and John Cockcroft.[249] But the search for an integrated science policy, like its counterparts for regional or transport policy, became one of *the* great postwar holy grails, much dreamed of, never found.

For all the great wartime boom in books, especially paperback buying (did shortage create the appetite? The popularity of the *Brains Trust* on radio suggests there was more to it than that – or was it the boredom of many a Force's existence), George Orwell was surely right in the implication of what he wrote in his *The English People* in 1947. 'The English', he declared, 'are not sufficiently interested in intellectual matters to be intolerant about them.'[250] In terms of *mass* communication, the great cataracts of information supply came from the films, the newspapers and the film equivalents of newspapers, the newsreels.

The first two of these were the stuff of political activity in the postwar period. In the film world it was largely as an offshoot of the dollar problem that the industry came to the attention of ministers. Thanks to the ABC cinema chain's close links with Warner Brothers and J. Arthur Rank's comparable ties with Twentieth Century Fox, American distributors were siphoning $70 million a year from dollar-starved Britain. During the Convertibility Crisis, the Board of Trade put a 75 per cent import duty on foreign films with the double aim of saving currency and encouraging indigenous talent. By the spring of 1948, the resulting American boycott of Britain had induced a change of policy. The American companies agreed to restrict their British earning to £4.25 million a year. Later that year, Harold Wilson set up the National Film Production Council with £5 million to invest and imposed a requirement that 45 per cent of the films shown in Britain should be British-made.

Though this was the era of the Ealing Comedies, of *Brief Encounter* and *The Third Man*, the British Film Industry could not rise to the stimulus of Government protection and fell well short of the 150 feature films a year that would have been needed to meet Wilson's quota.[251] Unwisely, perhaps, though patriotically, even high-mindedly, the Attlee Government took powers in the Film Act 1948 to compel cinema chains to screen meritorious, home-produced productions. Del Giudice's *Chance of a Lifetime*, starring Bernard Miles, whose story line was workers' control in a factory after the boss had invited his labour force to run the business, was shown by the Rank chain after Government intervention.[252] (Rank thought it was propaganda and, according to some, was keen to put Giudice out of business which quickly happened.)

Apart from such occasional eruptions, there was little political friction over the cinema. Though, if psephology were a perfect science, it would be nice to know how much Ealing Studio's brilliant *Passport to Pimlico* fanned resentment of rationing in 1949 and contributed to the dramatic shrinkage in Labour's majority the following year. I have a hunch that the Conservatives owed a great deal to T.E.B. 'Tibby' Clarke's gem of a script based on the (fictional) discovery that an area of London (just down Victoria Street from the hated Whitehall) belonged to Burgundy, thus enabling the residents (led by Stanley Holloway) to free themselves of rationing which 'perfectly caught the contemporary mood' and caused Clarke to be nominated for an Oscar. Perhaps Churchill realised this. Tibby Clarke was made an OBE in 1952![253]

The newspapers, however, *were* seen as instruments of political warfare; much more so probably than in any subsequent period. Despite Attlee's effective put-down of Churchill's 'Gestapo' gibe, the radio was not seen as a poll-turning issue (and not until 1955 did Britain enter the age of the television election). Papers, rightly or wrongly (wrongly, in my assessment) were. The most celebrated Press one-liner of the era was Beaverbrook's confession to the Royal Commission on the Press in March 1948 that 'I ran the paper [the *Daily Express*] purely for propaganda, and with no other purpose . . . '[254]

It was under pressure from former Beaverbrook journalists, such as the new MP for Devonport, Michael Foot (who, in fact, adored his Max), that Attlee was persuaded to set up the Royal Commission in 1947 under the Chairmanship of the Oxford Don, Sir David Ross, Provost of Oriel.[255] It has been a stand-by of Labour politicians ever since the formation of the Labour Representation Committee that the Tories enjoy a perpetual advantage in the existence of a capital Press, just as they believe that all changes in constituency boundaries go the Conservative way (the Conservatives have their equivalents in seeing the teaching profession, in both its school and college branches, as unpaid agents of Labour headquarters and, as for the BBC . . .).

Rather eccentrically, the compilers of the 1945 general election study, McCallum and Readman, totted up a rough equilibrium in newspaper circulations supporting Attlee and Churchill in 1945 – roughly 6 million for Labour and some 6,800,000 for the Conservatives.[256] This calculation has been challenged on the grounds that McCallum and Readman excluded both the evening papers and the weekly journals from their calculations and that they failed to differentiate between degrees of support, putting the Liberal *News Chronicle* in, for example, with the *Daily Herald* and the *Mirror* as Labour supporting.

I doubt if newspaper coverage of the 1945 election affected the outcome to any significant degree. In my view, the great shift of opinion owed more to the nation's experience of total war (in terms of both the necessity and effectiveness of state power in achieving results, and fair ones at that, in conditions of stress and shortage). As neither of the major parties' leaderships foresaw such a conclusive result, which newspapers said what took on a considerable importance at the time. In fact, newspaper criticism of the war effort or strategic policy had a capacity to enrage Churchill long before the election was in prospect. Churchill saw the influence of the leftist leader writer, the scholar E.H. Carr, in *The Times* attacks on his policy of supporting the Royalists against the Communist-dominated resistance in Greece in 1944–5. In retaliation he attacked the paper in the Commons in January 1945.[257] Nor could he bear its pro-welfare line on social policy, what he absurdly described as 'your Christian Communism' when he lunched with the paper's Editor, Robin Barrington-Ward, in February 1944.[258]

Attlee apart, the Labour leadership was similarly inclined. We have already encountered Morrison's obsession with the Press. Bevin hated Beaverbrook even more than he loathed Morrison (Bevin, too, had a direct interest in the newspaper world as the TUC controlled the *Daily Herald*). When he became Foreign Secretary he was as tough on *The Times*' line on Russia and Greece as Churchill had been. Barrington-Ward took a note of his private meeting with Bevin on 11 March 1946:

> . . . he turned to an extraordinary attack on T.T. [*The Times*]. He said it had no policy. It was 'spineless'. It was 'a jelly fish'. It was neither for him nor against him . . . But it was always 'balancing' – (he made the gesture of twisting his hand with outstretched fingers). (All this of course was about Russia) . . .
>
> *The Times* did great harm. It was taken abroad for a national newspaper. He was going to tell the H. of C. that it was not, and that it was pro-Russian and not pro-British. I had a lot of pink intelligentsia down there and he didn't believe I was in control . . . He had a plan . . . Give him three years and he would build a new Commonwealth without regard to Russia or America. 'I would build it up just as I built up the Union' (i.e., the T and G) . . .
>
> We also clashed over Greece. I told him that I had only supported the postponement of the elections when I found that reputable and responsible Greeks considered it essential. He said 'Have you ever known a reputable Greek!'[259]

The only difference between Churchill's tirade and this one is the accent in which it was delivered. (Note, too, the Curzon-like vision of a 'new Commonwealth' which would enable Britain to conduct its affairs without regard to the USA and the Soviet Union – extraordinary!) Pinkoes in Printing House Square is also a classic example of the paranoia of the powerful. Bevin's was a very different impulse from that of Michael Foot or the National Union of Journalists in urging a Royal Commission.

The implications of the terms of reference given to Ross and his Commissioners were faintly radical: 'With the object of furthering the free expression of opinion through the Press and the greatest practicable accuracy in the presentation of news, to inquire into the control, management and ownership of the newspaper and periodical Press and news-agencies including the financial structure and the monopolistic tendencies in control, and to make recommendations thereon.'[260]

Beaverbrook, for one, was taken in by the inquisitorial flavour of these instructions. He left a message on his famous 'Soundscriber' for E.J. Robertson, general manager of his newspaper stable, which has preserved his paranoia for posterity:

> Mr Robertson. I will be glad to hear about the Royal Commission on the Press which is one of the Government Agencies in the persecution of newspapers. Sorrow, sorrow ever more. There is nothing I can say about it except to bow my head in misery. It wouldn't be a bad thing if the Socialists cut off all newsprint entirely.[261]

Beaverbrook was not the only pro-Tory proprietor alarmed by the mere existence of the Ross Commission.

Gomer Berry, Lord Kemsley, the dim, social-climbing son of a Merthyr Tydfil estate agent (who, miraculously, sired not one but two Press Lords, the other being Gomer's elder brother, William, Lord Camrose of the *Daily Telegraph*), was an unthinking kind of Conservative with a face like Groucho Marx and a genius for circulation and advertising.[262] By the time war came, Kemsley had built up a vast provincial and national newspaper empire which included the *Sunday Times*. He made sure everyone knew one of his titles when they saw one by emblazoning 'A Kemsley Newspaper' beneath every masthead. He was thus seen to be ubiquitous and slavishly pro-Tory to boot. Herbert Morrison described him as owner of the 'gramophone press'.[263]

Kemsley, however, had recently acquired the services of one of the nicest and shrewdest men in postwar Fleet Street, Denis Hamilton. Fresh from a brave and distinguished war, Hamilton found 'I soon had to advise him on how to face the Royal Commission . . . this gave me an unexpected leverage to do something revolutionary . . . I was able to suggest a scheme which, at any other time, he would have slipped into the side drawer in the hope that it would go away. Thus, the Kemsley Editorial Training Plan was born. It was expensive, it demanded enormous effort, energy and concentration, but it laid the foundations of professional training in journalism, being taken up and copied not only by all the press in Britain, but in many foreign countries too.'[264]

It was one of the few beneficial, enduring effects of the Royal Commission. Its other recommendation was the creation of a 'General Council of the Press', a self-regulating body for the profession 'which would derive its authority from the press itself and not from statute' and 'by censuring undesirable types of journalistic conduct and by all other possible means, should build up a code of conduct in accordance with the highest professional standards'.[265]

Spurred on by the threat of a Private Members' Bill in the House of Commons, the industry finally created a watered-down version of this in 1953 when the Press Council was born.[266] Apart from this, the Ross Commission scarcely scratched the paintwork of a Press Lord's Rolls Royce. Though it did have tough things to say about the perpetual problem of journalists going native on their regular suppliers of information, especially in Whitehall, the kind of client relationship Attlee's press secretary, Francis Williams, so effectively pilloried in his *Parliament, Press and the Public* published in 1946.[267]

'The evidence put before us', Ross reported, 'does not suggest that up to now any harmful influence is being exerted on the Press through the medium of the Government Information Services; but if newspapers get out of the habit of finding their own news, and into the habit of taking all or most of it unquestioningly from a government department, they are obviously in some danger of falling into totalitarian paths. Future developments, therefore, need to be carefully watched.'[268] Mind you, this trait is not removable by any remedy within the grasp of a Royal Commission. It has everything to do with the in-house, professional shortcomings of the British political Press.[269]

This is not to say that everyone in every news room was supine in the late 1940s. In a Cabinet Office leaks inquiry file declassified by accident, it's plain for all to see that Paul Einzig (that rarity, an economically literate political journalist) of the *Financial Times* and Freddie Kuh of the *Chicago Tribune* caused the Attlee Government such trouble that MI5 was called in to tap their telephones. Einzig was leaking embarrassingly accurate information about Cabinet flounderings on iron and steel nationalisation; Kuh, through, it's suspected, the medium of Francis Williams' secretary, his girl friend, was very well informed on policy towards Palestine.[270]

By subsequent standards, Attlee's Cabinet was relatively leak-free. There was, however, one persistent trickle whose source MI5 could never trace, not surprisingly, because it was almost incredible. It was Dame Isobel Cripps. The story only came out in the posthumous study of politicians and the Press, *The Anatomy of Power*, written by the wonderfully wry and dry James Margach of the *Sunday Times*. The beneficiary of Dame Isobel's indiscretions was Hugh Massingham, who, as 'Political Diary' columnist of the *Observer*, pioneered the modern form of political commentary.[271] 'For several years', wrote Margach thirty years after the event,

Massingham recounted in his *Observer* precis what took place at the Cabinet meetings every week, a highly personalised account of what everybody said, a count-down of what looked like the Cabinet minutes. No 10's official spokesman of the day (Francis Williams . . .) confided to me that Massingham's diaries of the Cabinet secrets were so accurate that even the security and intelligence experts were called in to discover the source of the constant inspired leaking. Close checks were made on the distribution of Cabinet documents; even expertly doctored papers, with slips and inaccuracies worked in, were channelled to suspected Ministers to see if the errors might be repeated in the Massingham version.

All such counter-espionage traps failed to spring. Years later I discovered the source. Every Friday afternoon he had tea at a moveable rendezvous with Lady Cripps. She was devoted to advancing the career of Sir Stafford Cripps and wanted him to become Prime Minister. Cripps, one of the three most powerful Ministers in the first Attlee Government, confided to his wife what had been happening. In due course she reported to Massingham what Attlee, Herbert Morrison, Aneurin Bevan and Ernest Bevin had said.[272]

I only got to know Jimmy Margach in his last days. He didn't tell me the Massingham/Lady Cripps story so I couldn't ask him how he found out. I suspect Massingham, in *his* last days, told Margach. Jimmy was right in the moral he drew from this gem of a tale – 'that good Lobbying is essentially a one-man business'.[273] But no Royal Commission could teach it to a political corps determined to a man virtually (until a brief interlude in the late 1980s when the *Independent* and the *Guardian* temporarily broke free) to take its briefings non-attributably and *en masse* from the press secretaries of successive Prime Ministers.[274]

It's very hard now to capture the pre-television era in every sense, not just the political. The hunt for bias, not just by politicians but by early media analysts like Political and Economic Planning,[275] was then targeted on newspapers whereas their late twentieth-century equivalents in the Glasgow Media Group are riveted by television bulletins.[276] There was for much of the postwar period, however, a medium which bridged the two eras in a singular way – the newsreels which ran between the feature films in the packed cinemas of the late 1940s.

Movietone and Pathé reached huge audiences. With an astonishing 4,500 cinemas the length and breadth of the land, and a regular audience of 30 million out of a population of 46 million,[277] their black and white items on home and foreign affairs brought the news home in a way papers and radio could not match and only television, eventually, would surpass. To anyone with a message to put over, Movietone and Pathé mattered as the most vivid image setters of them all.

They had a style all their own which can still summon up the flavour of the Forties, even for people not born at the time, so basic a staple have old newsreels become for any documentary dealing in any way with the period. There was a constant backdrop of jolly music, upbeat in a stiff sort of way – a mixture of military band, *Workers' Playtime* and Percy Grainger. The narrators always had clipped, good chap voices – very male, very 1930s and often very sexist too.

Take Pathé's report from Oxford in September 1945, from the No. 1 Civilian Repair Unit at Cowley as 'the last part goes into the last Spitfire'. War production was giving way to civilian in one of Morris Motors' shadow factories. And 'here they come! Britain's postwar cars,' the 'good chap' declares jauntily. 'You can have any colour you like . . . so long as it's black' (pronounced 'bl*e*ck'). Film of prewar-designed Morris 10s coming off the Cowley line and here, too, comes the arch sexism. 'Already a few thousand wives are getting in their applications for backseat-driving lessons.'[278]

Royalty, too, was a great obsession, the King and Queen opening exhibitions, planting trees, sailing to South Africa on HMS *Vanguard*, the Princesses playing 'tag' with young officers beneath Atlantic skies. Naturally the Royal engagement and wedding (July and November 1947 respectively) proved a wonderful and hyperbole-laden diversion from austerity as the perfectly newsreelogenic Princess Elizabeth and Lieutenant Philip Mountbatten charmed their way from one marvellous picture opportunity to another.[279] The Windsors, too, couldn't touch English shores (even if only *en route* from America to France) without the cameras pouncing and commentators drooling over the Duchess's wardrobe.

The war still dominated the newsreel editor's psyche. There were the protracted trials of German and Japanese war criminals. In March 1947, Pathé made much of newly discovered footage of Hitler and Eva Braun at Berchtesgaden in 1942.[280] There were a good deal, understandably, of lest-we-forgot shots of prominent Nazis in the dock at Nuremberg, which would be intercut with footage of mass funerals in Coventry in 1941 or concentration camp victims piled high in 1945.

Heathrow, the new London Airport, opened by Civil Aviation Minister, Lord Winster, on New Year's Day 1946, was another favourite backdrop. Air travel was very glamorous even though much of it was in Lancastrians (converted Lancaster bombers) and the departure lounge was often a tent. Churchill was forever on the move, though usually by sea, to make a speech in America or receive a medal in France.

British Tommies under fire abroad were another stand-by, especially those engaged in the increasingly nasty conflict in Palestine. In those days, news reporters were actively pro, not just sympathetic to British troops in difficult circumstances. In August 1946, for example, shots of a Jewish arms cache uncovered in Tel Aviv were screened to this voice-over:

> Britain's hard-working ambassadors, the ordinary Tommy and policemen, uncover yet another hoard of illegal weapons . . . another dirty job well done.[281]

And Pathé's commentators were not slow to give advice to other great powers when it came to international troublespots. Another report from Palestine in March 1947 declared, in truly stentorian, almost pompously Parliamentarian tones, 'others, like the Americans, are ever ready with advice. Now is the time for them to share the responsibility.'[282]

Food shortages and rationing were sure to strike a chord with the cinema-going millions. The newsreel-makers obliged. Often stilted conversations were manufactured and memorised as between the Lord Mayor of Bristol and a young girl when the first shipload of bananas arrives at Avonmouth Docks in 1947. 'Would you like one?' says the Mayor. 'Thank you,' says the little girl. 'And jolly good they are, too,' opines His Worship.[283]

Occasionally Pathé would slip into an anti-Government tone as when its glamorous fashion correspondent visited a nylon factory in November 1946, talked its boss out of a pair for herself which she coyly puts on while berating the failure of the manufacturers to meet their pledge of nylons for every woman who wanted them by the previous June. 'The Board of Trade said nothing,' she adds censoriously.[284] The Board's President was singled out for a bit of mockery when Pathé filmed the King opening the *Britain Can Make It* exhibition at the Victoria and Albert Museum in September 1946 (complete with shots of a bizarre bicycle and ladies' shoes made with perspex from bomber gun turrets). The Royal Family were accompanied by Mr and Mrs Attlee and the President of the Board of Trade. 'For "Austerity Stafford"', the commentator quips, 'so many luxuries must bring quite a headache.'[285]

Yet, for the most part, Pathé's coverage of controversial political issues was sensitive. Charles Hill berating in March 1946 Bevan's plans for the medical profession would be balanced by Dr Haden-Guest, a Labour MP, explaining what the Health Service would mean for the ordinary person.[286] In January 1947, when the lorry drivers' unofficial strike halted meat deliveries, a 'vox pop' of housewives on the fringe of a troop-filled Smithfield had one put the case for and another against the striking men.[287] While in March, 'Austerity Stafford' was given a good run before the cameras when the *Economic Survey for 1947* was published. 'No doubt, we're in a bit of a tight spot,' he says in that poised, courtroom voice. 'We'll take a year or two before we get out. But we've done it before and we can do it again', a view backed up by an upbeat Pathé voice at the end of the feature declaring, 'For seven years [the war, in fact, lasted six years], we, the people of Britain, fought a war for Mankind. Today we fight for our own survival. This battle also we shall win.'[288] So unlike a late twentieth-century *Panorama* or *World in Action* or, come to that, *The Nine O'Clock News* or *News at Ten*. But in 1947 that was quite normal.

'Austerity Stafford' couldn't have complained about Pathé's treatment of his production crusade from the Board of Trade. In private, however, he spent a great deal of 1947 complaining not about the media, but about the way the Government was run. Yet, until the '*annus horrendus*', the Attlee Government experienced little serious internal trouble. The party in Parliament and in the country, however, soon experienced the usually very public effects of what Ian Mikardo has called 'the division between the socialists and pragmatists in the Labour Party which has persisted ever since'[289] and which, in my judgment, has been the single most potent factor in keeping Labour out of office for much of the postwar period.

The Keep Left group, of which Mikardo was a leading light, was the prototype dissent-cum-ginger group from which the Bevanites and, later still, the Tribunites grew. From a small collection of sociable leftists, complaining in a corner of the Members' Smoking Room about pretty well every aspect of the Government's progress (no purge of bosses and no workers' control in the nationalised industries, no genuine economic planning, too many men under arms with service ministers in the pockets of the Chiefs of Staff, too much economic servility to the Americans – 'if we needed their goods, they needed our market'[290]), they shot to international prominence when they put down an amendment to the King's Speech in 1946 on foreign affairs. Keep Left urged the Government to 'Review and recast its conduct of international affairs so as to . . . provide a democratic and socialist alternative to an otherwise inevitable conflict between American Capitalism and Soviet Communism'. 'We were great half way housers', recalled Dick Crossman, one of the amendment's sponsors, 'and we were to lead a third force in Europe. This was the concept.'[291]

To Bevin, away in New York negotiating with Molotov, this wasn't just pie-in-the-sky. It was, as he told the Party Conference the following spring, a 'stab in the back'. Molotov, Bevin later told Arthur Bottomley, had used the fact that fifty-seven Labour MPs had signed the Crossman-Mikardo amendment as ammunition saying, 'Yes, well, you can't speak with much authority, you haven't even got the support of your own Party.'[292] History, for once, has recorded Bevin's reaction when Hector McNeil broke the news to him in the daily telephone call from the FO to New York.

MCNEIL: There's been some trouble in the Commons today, Minister. An amendment was put down on the King's Speech criticising the conduct of foreign policy and . . .
BEVIN: Who are they?
MCNEIL: Well, Minister, there are rather a lot of them . . .
BEVIN: Who are they?
MCNEIL: Do you want . . .
BEVIN: Who are they?
MCNEIL: Richard Crossman.
BEVIN: I'll break him.
MCNEIL: Michael Foot.
BEVIN: I'll break him.[293]

And so on, through all fifty-seven varieties of dissenter (only a few of whom, contrary to some contemporary views, were pro-Communist fellow travellers, though, even if the MI5 archive was open, it would still be impossible to be sure who truly was or was not one of Stalin's Englishmen).

Bevin didn't break the 'Keep Left group', as they became known from the pamphlet they produced in a rush over Easter Weekend 1947 in time for the Party's Margate Conference.[294] They were up, running and waiting for the charismatic Nye Bevan when he resigned from the Cabinet in April 1951 to join those, in Mikardo's words, who had been depressed almost from day one by the Attlee 'Government's downward slide from the peaks of its socialist promise to the flatlands of conformity and conventional respectability'.[295] But events – cold, chilling, Stalinist ones in Budapest, Warsaw and Prague – marginalised their never more than minimal influence outside the corners of Labour Party activism. (The early and mid-Fifties were their hour, not the late Forties.)

Denis Healey, that most bruising of postwar intellects, produced an effective retort to *Keep Left* with *Cards on the Table*, a broadside from Transport House where Healey was the Party's international secretary. 'I had taken care to make sure it was approved by Hector McNeil and Chris Mayhew, Bevin's junior ministers, who were my main channel of communication with him,' Healey wrote later.[296]

Bevin endorsed Healey's pamphlet strongly at the Party's Margate Conference with its denunciation of the 'sustained and violent offensive against Britain by her Russian ally . . . in Trieste, Northern Persia and the Dardanelles, Greece, Turkey and Eastern Europe'.[297] Interestingly, Gladwyn Jebb, that 'lordly radical' as Healey called him,[298] was candid enough to send Bevin a note about *Keep Left*, identifying Crossman ('C') as one of its authors and reminding the Foreign Secretary just how far he and his department had shifted since the end of the war.

'Much of what C says', wrote Jebb, 'would have appeared sensible two years or even eighteen months ago. Indeed all our own papers were then based on the assumption that there should in no circumstances be any Anglo–US line up against the USSR or indeed against Communism, until such time at any rate as the Soviets should have made it abundantly clear that they did not intend to co-operate with the West. It will be recalled with what passionate conviction the FO represented this thesis to the Chiefs of Staff and what care was taken to prevent even the smallest whisper getting round that we favoured the Americans rather than the Russians . . . '[299]

Much more serious than the public grumblings of *Keep Left* were the private complaints about Attlee's leadership on the part of Cripps and Dalton during the months of setback and drift in 1947, complaints which, by summer, had turned into plotting. Cripps was conspirator-in-chief. He had long had reservations about the way Attlee was running his Cabinet. On his return from the Cabinet mission to India he was appalled, when catching up on the minutes (as Bridges was told by Cripps' Permanent Secretary), 'by the amount of time and energy taken up in the Ministerial Committees with the discussion of quite minor matters which individual Ministers ought to settle in their discretion'.[300] As 1947 progressed, Cripps became convinced that the only man decisive enough to cut through the muddle and delay was Bevin.

In April Cripps confided in Dalton that without a change and Morrison's removal from his economic overlordship 'we shall be sunk' as Morrison was 'incapable of handling planning'.[301] At the end of July, Bevin and Dalton shared the long car journey back to London from the Durham Miners' Gala, accompanied by a police car in case the Foreign Secretary was attacked by Jewish terrorists with Palestine on the boil. Bevin complained about Attlee as 'very weak, we can't get him to make up his mind'.[302] But he would not hear talk of replacing him himself. Bevin's line, as we have seen, was 'I'm sticking to little Clem.'[303]

And stick to 'little Clem' big Ernie did – when Dalton and Cripps called on him just before the emergency Cabinet called to suspend convertibility on 17

August. ('What's Clem ever done to me?' he asked. 'Who do you think I am, Lloyd George?'[304]) Three days later the *Daily Mail* carried the erroneous heading 'Attlee Resigning Soon. Bevin to be PM!' (The Royal Commission on the Press tried and failed to discover its source.) Undeterred, Cripps called on Attlee after dinner on 9 September and told him flatly he should make way for Bevin so that Bevin could lead a great assault on Britain's economic problems and resolve them to the great benefit of socialism worldwide. Attlee simply picked up the phone and got through to the Foreign Secretary: 'Stafford's here: he says you want to change your job.' Bevin said he did not. Attlee offered Cripps the economic overlordship. He went away purring as the new Minister for Economic Affairs. 'What a man,' Bevin said later of Attlee to the P.M.'s Parliamentary Private Secretary, Arthur Moyle. 'He plucked victory from disaster. I love the little man. He is our Campbell-Bannerman.'[305]

Some good did come out of the 1947 leadership crisis. Attlee used it not only to put Cripps into a position where his considerable gifts could be deployed on an even bigger field, he used the occasion of the resulting reshuffle to promote the young and gifted with a pair of economically literate technocrats, Harold Wilson and Hugh Gaitskell, taking over the Board of Trade and the Ministry of Fuel respectively (Shinwell, sulkily, accepting the job as War Minister outside the Cabinet).

Perhaps most important of all, Attlee rationalised and streamlined the Cabinet machinery for taking economic decisions. As he wrote to Morrison, softening the blow to his authority and easing him out of his overlordship,

> I propose to have now a single Economic Committee over which I should preside . . . Its functions would be to take decisions within Cabinet policy on the working of the Economic plan which go beyond the scope of what can be decided by a single Minister. It should not be overburdened with documentation. With regard to your own work, you have a very heavy task on the Home Front and with AG [Arthur Greenwood] retiring there is too much for one man, however efficient, especially when he is the second man in the Cabinet who, like the PM, must have time to think of matters of major policy.[306]

The creation of the Economic Policy Committee, to give it its full title, in September 1947 at last ended the undesirable state of affairs at the heart of decision-taking in phase one of the Attlee Government whereby, in Alec Cairncross' words, 'Financial policy was split off from economic policy when it lay increasingly at the heart of economic planning; and overseas economic policy was separated from domestic when it was beginning to dominate domestic economic management.'[307]

In the collective memory of official Whitehall, the early autumn of 1947 is the time the Attlee Government came of age. According to Lord Croham (who as Douglas Allen, was on loan in 1947 from the Treasury of the Central Economic

Planning Staff), 'for the first two years of the 1945–50 Government the Ministers and officials were living in different worlds . . . Stafford Cripps had a more realistic approach to the economic problem than many of his colleagues and the tendency to let things drift was halted after his appointment as Minister . . . for Economic Affairs in September 1947.'[308]

To the Keep Left Group and to later commentators like Ralph Miliband, this is the period of radical decline when 'the Government's reforming zeal was all but exhausted'.[309] For them, the talisman was iron and steel nationalisation, 'the only one which entailed a serious threat to the private sector'.[310] At the end of April, the Cabinet agreed to the headings of a nationalisation bill produced by the Minister of Supply, John Wilmot. It would be introduced in the 1947–8 session of Parliament and the Government would take the industry into public ownership while leaving the current company structure intact.[311]

This was not good enough for the Cabinet's full-blooded nationalisers like Dalton and Bevan. Yet as crisis piled upon crisis, events played into the hands of the compromisers like Wilmot and, most important of all, Mr Socialisation, Morrison, who, as we saw in chapter five, was swiftly going off public ownership on the centralised model. Bevin, who could have swung the issue Morrison's way, was compromised by his policy of nationalisation in the Ruhr (of which the US Government was constantly critical).[312]

Morrison and Wilmot, after discussions with the formidable Sir Andrew Duncan, top baron among the steelmasters, came up with an even more diluted version of public ownership whereby a new Control Board would own and run the central core of the industry, with private enterprise continuing to operate on the periphery.[313] On 24 July the Cabinet collectively floundered on the issue, agreeing only to call for another paper.[314] On 7 August, against the background of the raging dollar crisis, the Cabinet finally resolved to press ahead with nationalisation but not before the 1948–9 session of Parliament. To placate Bevan and the other Clause IV ministers, it was agreed that the Parliament Act should be amended to reduce the power of the House of Lords to delay a bill from two years to one, thereby ensuring that, despite the postponement, steel could be in public ownership before the next election.[315]

Miliband is right to see this as a crucial turning-point, not just in the politics of the Attlee Government, but in postwar history as a whole. Despite the decision of 7 August 1947, 'everyone tacitly assumed that steel would be the government's last measure of public ownership. There would be no "Second wave", as there was briefly in France in 1948 or Austria with electricity in 1947. 'For the nationalisers', wrote Kenneth O. Morgan, 'the party was already over.' He is surely right, too, to underscore just how short was the life of public ownership as a widely applicable economic solution in Britain (contrary to the impression given by Sir Keith Joseph, Mrs Thatcher and others thirty years later). 'Like Mark Twain's death, the role of nationalisation in British history is often exaggerated. It was, in fact, a relatively brief encounter.'[316] Its monuments, however, largely remained in place until the tide of privatisation swept over the public sector after 1983.

The unfortunate John Wilmot, one of the few businessmen in the Attlee Government, was made the sacrificial lamb upon the altar of steel and perished in the October 1947 reshuffle to be replaced by another steel merchant, George Strauss. The reconstruction of the administration and the building, at last, of some adequate decision-taking machinery on the economic side, did not complete the process of rebuilding. Fate had to take a hand before Cripps fully entered his economic kingdom, and with him, the Treasury at last regaining the Whitehall primacy it lost in 1940. This time the lamb (an unlikely image for the ebullient Hugh) was Dalton.

Dalton, to his credit (though 'wary of Cripps – Cripps seemed to want to plan the economy without any concern about the domestic policy for which Dalton cared,' said Lord Trend[317]) managed to work well enough with him in the few weeks they were in tandem. Dalton was, however, still in poor shape, physically and mentally. On 12 October he recorded in his diary, 'I am haunted by the thought of a people starving, unemployed and in revolt! And of the end of our Socialist experiment and of all our dreams!'[318] A week later, after staying in bed all day on the Saturday, he was buoyed up by the outcome of a meeting of the 'Big Five' at Chequers on the Sunday. At last an attack was to be made on dollar imports.[319] He got down with relish to the details of his forthcoming emergency budget scheduled for 12 November. On the way to the Chamber, he paused for a brief word with John Carvel, the Lobby Correspondent of the London evening paper, the *Star*. Dalton gave him a brief outline of the budget: 'no more on tobacco; a penny on beer; something on dogs and pools but not on horses; increase in Purchase Tax . . . Profits Tax doubled'. Carvel phoned it over to his paper which managed to get it on the streets a few minutes before the unfortunate Dalton delivered the words in the Commons.[320]

After exchanges in the Commons the following day, the P.M. accepted Dalton's offer to resign, largely, according to Dalton's biographer Ben Pimlott, 'because he wanted to be rid of him'. The Press and the professional economists were after him. He had plotted against Attlee. He was a gossip. 'The truth was', wrote Pimlott, 'by the autumn of 1947, the Government inner circle no longer needed Dalton, who had allowed himself to become fatally isolated.'[321]

'Perfect ass,' said Attlee a generation later. 'His trouble was he would talk. He always liked to have a secret to confide to somebody else to please him. He did it once too often.' 'If he hadn't resigned would you have fired him?' 'I would have had to.'[322] I think he would. After all, in the Whitehall constellation of secrecy, Budget secrets are the tops. 'They're like Holy Communion,' a permanent secretary once told me, 'they come no higher.'[323]

Few wept for Dalton. His wit, his indiscretions had penetrated too many skins. The Davenports rallied round and offered to put him up in their small flat in London, as, having resigned, he couldn't bear to spend another night in No. 11. 'We dined that night in Soho,' Nicholas Davenport recalled.

Perhaps we had too much to drink to ease the strain of the moment. But by midnight we had seen Hugh to bed and I lay awake meditating on the sadness of his downfall. In the middle of the night I heard him go to the bathroom. Then I heard a thud . . . I rushed to the lobby and found him lying prostrate on the floor . . . With difficulty I dragged the big man back to bed. I then fetched my wife. When she came he had just recovered consciousness and caught hold of her hands making her sit on his bed, and poured out all the feelings which had been suppressed during his crisis years at No. 11. The frustrations and anxieties of his office had been a slow torture and now that the tension had been broken and he felt released he cried his heart out.[324]

Though Attlee brought him back into the Cabinet as Chancellor of the Duchy and, later, Minister of Town and Country Planning, Dalton was never much of a force in Labour or national politics again, dying, raving, in a geriatric ward in St Pancras Hospital,[325] in February 1962 a week after his (by the standards of those days) sensational memoirs of 1945–51, *High Tide and After*, were published. He was indiscreet – and controversial – to the end.

Dalton was the biggest human casualty of the 1947 crisis year. Without him Attlee's inner Cabinet was duller but almost certainly more effective. Cripps, however, was a great improvement as Chancellor. As Robert Hall, not an official to be soft on ministers, wrote early in 1948, 'In the past 3 months there has been a revolution in Government policy since Stafford Cripps has been the undisputed master in the field . . . All the old barriers are coming down between the Treasury and other policy . . . The more I see of SC the more highly I think of him – he is anxious to tell the truth, he is a man who is completely fair in his outlook, and completely bold if he is convinced that a particular course is right.'[326]

How much credit is due to Cripps personally for the pronounced improvement in the British economy over the winter of 1947–8 is impossible to measure. Certainly the decrease in inflationary pressures can be attributed to the effects of Dalton's last budget. By the end of March 1948, the 'dollar drain' had turned into an inflow. Production boomed, the British economy took on a four-year spurt, real gross domestic product growing by 3 per cent a year between 1947 and 1951.[327]

The Attlee Government had entered its mature, second phase. 'The Big Five' effectively became 'The Big Three' with Dalton gone and Morrison eclipsed. These were the years of Attlee, Bevin and Cripps – a turn-up that would have astonished people had the future been disclosed to them a decade earlier with Cripps removed from the Labour Party for advocating a Popular Front, Bevin contemptuous of politicians and content to run the T and G, and Attlee the most underwhelming Leader of the Opposition in memory. They were also the years when Britain played a crucial role in building one enduring postwar international institution, NATO, and refused to have anything to do with another, the nascent European Community.

CHAPTER 9

Partners, Pounds and Productivity

Mr Bevin considers that the most effective steps would be to take very early steps, before Norway goes under, to conclude under Article 51 of the Charter of the United Nations a regional Atlantic Approaches Pact of Mutual Assistance, in which all of the countries directly threatened by a Russian move to the Atlantic could participate . . . We could at once inspire the necessary confidence to consolidate the West against Soviet infiltration and at the same time inspire the Soviet Government with enough respect for the West to remove temptation from them and ensure a long period of peace. The alternative is to repeat our experience with Hitler . . .
Aide-memoire from Ernest Bevin to George Marshall, 11 March 1948[1]

Well you know, Chris, we've got to give them something and I think we'll give them this talking shop in Strasbourg – the Council of Europe – we'll give them this talking shop.
Ernest Bevin to Christopher Mayhew, 1948[2]

At one point Secretary Snyder made some very – well, remarks which I thought were wholly undiplomatic and rude and showed his lack of concern for the UK problem (the general sense of them was why didn't the UK get a hold of itself, and why didn't its people do some work for a change and why don't you cure these productivity problems in the United Kingdom and why don't you get off your butt). That so irritated Ernie Bevin that he held forth for about five minutes in defence of the United Kingdom and a description of why Snyder was wrong. I was trying to keep minutes. There were just words, no sentences of any kind . . . but when Ernie Bevin had finished I looked up at Secretary Snyder and there were tears in his eyes. Honest to goodness, I couldn't believe what I saw.
Paul Nitze, recalling the Washington negotiations which preceded the devaluation of sterling in September 1949[3]

We work or Want.
Ubiquitous Government poster, 1948–9

We said we thought that any extra profits which accrued from better productivity should be shared between the management, who had provided extra money for machinery and facilities, the customer, he should have a share, and the workmen should have a share. They should find a little bit extra in the pay packet. But we were surprised when Sir Stafford didn't agree with us at all. He said, 'I don't agree to the men having extra money in their pay packets. I think that if a man put up a good performance on the shop-floor and you found that he was doing a good job, then he should be given a medal. Then everyone else would try and emulate him to have the medal.'

Eddie Daybell, member of the Steel Foundry Association productivity mission to the United States in 1949 on their debriefing with the Chancellor of the Exchequer[+]

The fate of nations and peoples is more tied up with institutions than they usually realise or care to admit. Great men or women, grappling with powerful forces and shaping destinies at dramatic moments in history make for much more appealing and easily understood reading than grey administrators plodding cautiously on in drab organisations distinguished one from another only by their forgettable acronyms. Yet much of history most of the time is moulded to a large degree by such mundanities. NATO and the EEC are classic examples of such phenomena. Of course the political genius of a Bevin and the resolution of a Truman, or the vision of a Jean Monnet and the capacity to fix politically of a Paul Henri Spaak, are crucial in getting such bodies up and running. But, once in motion, it is the nameless men and women who conduct regular diplomatic, military and economic exchange on the international scene who take over until a sudden crisis once more draws Press, and therefore, political attention to the sphere of activity.

The military alliance of the countries of the North Atlantic Treaty Organisation and the trading arrangements of the nations of the European Economic Community became two of the greatest 'givens' of the postwar period, the two key sets of scaffolding erected in the wreckage left when Hitler's attempt to impose *his* economic, political and military solution on the rest of Europe failed. Neither NATO nor the EEC was foreseeable in 1945. Neither was an inevitable outgrowth of the early cold war, the failure of the United Nations as a mechanism for underpinning international stability, the deepening rupture between the eastern and western members of the wartime Grand Alliance or even as a way of handling the German problem for the next generation or two.

In both, Britain could have played a leading part. It chose to do so only in one – NATO. Its view of itself, its place in the world led it instinctively to emphasise its Atlantic links almost as strongly as its Imperial bonds in 1948–50 and to place its European connections at a discount then and for many years after. The third, fourth and fifth years after the war were those in which the parameters of Britain's overseas relationships were drawn as various combinations of the western nations engaged in a spurt of institution building. It was the last moment in world history when British ministers, officials and military had the wherewithal to make a decisive contribution. For the rest of the century their successors, for good or ill, had to live with the consequences of their predecessors' instincts and their analysis, their impulses and their actions. To find out why they went this way on NATO or that way in Europe is not just instructive, it's critical to understanding the whole of postwar British history.

But for the Russians, of course, it would not have happened. Had the postwar attempt at world order guaranteed by superpower condominium not fallen apart at Potsdam and in the succession of Foreign Ministers' Conferences which followed, western European reconstruction would have been part of a pan-European recovery programme. And without the near-constant perception of Soviet-inspired danger from the east, from the collapse of the Marshall Plan negotiations until the stalemate in Korea in 1951–2, the stimulus would have been lacking for any truly ambitious attempts to put new military and economic roofs over western Europe. For ambitious they were, both on the part of the United States (which had to give up a hundred and fifty years of its history to conclude a ten-year military pact with eleven other nations when the NATO treaty was signed) and on the part of Britain (which had to acknowledge it could no longer fight a major war without American assistance, i.e. that it was no longer a superpower) and even more so of France (which made the first crucial moves towards a permanent pooling of its economic sovereignty as well).

To late 1950s eyes such developments were, in retrospect, something of a commonplace. To late 1930s eyes, they would have appeared startling, almost miraculous. In the part it played in their shaping, Britain, in Jean Monnet's phrase (borrowed by Michael Charlton), paid 'the price of victory'. Its policymakers, with very few exceptions, were convinced that whatever the new political, military and economic arrangements, all could and should combine to the special advantage of the United Kingdom as a great power. In this they were plumb wrong. Here was the greatest and, in its unravelling, the most painful of the postwar illusions. And, ironically, it was the greatest of those policymakers, the incarnation of standing alone, of persisting until victory was won, Winston Churchill, who (as so often) distilled its essence most powerfully into words.

His image was of three interlocking circles with the United Kingdom as the link between all three – the genetic code of Britain's postwar foreign policy. The grand old man unveiled it to the grandest young man of late Forties diplomacy, Oliver Franks. 'Mr Churchill', Lord Franks recalled,

> . . . gave me a lecture on the three intersecting circles – those represented by the United States, by the Commonwealth and by Europe. And he said to me, 'Young man, never let Great Britain escape from any of them.'

Now [Lord Franks explained in 1980 with a perspective of thirty years plus] if you come to the question of priorities, that is more difficult. If you are thinking in strategic and military terms there is no question that our relationship with the United States was the priority. On the other hand, in terms of tradition, emotion and affection, the Commonwealth came first; and in terms of our neighbours without whom we were literally not safe or secure, then Europe came very much into the picture.

So . . . what Winston Churchill said to me, and this would be in early 1948, represented the way a great many people in Britain thought and felt at the time. I think that he hoped it would be possible for Britain to have a foreign policy, both political and economic, of a kind which permitted Britain to live in all three circles satisfactorily.[5]

There was a profound drawback to this three-ring vision of Britain's place in the world. The rest of the world did not share it. Even superpowers find it difficult to prevail in isolation. Nineteen-forty-eight Britain was no superpower.

From the moment the bump on Molotov's forehead swelled, as it always did when he was under pressure,[6] on the day in July 1947 when he ordered his delegation to leave the Marshall Plan negotiations in Paris, west and east began to order political, economic and military life in each of their own geopolitical zones on the assumption that the other was not just irredeemably hostile in attitude but, in the worst case, might launch actual hostilities across the 1945 truce lines.

We have seen already the cocktail of recent experience and future fears which shaped the JIC professionals in London when putting together assessments of Soviet intentions and capabilities for their customers in Whitehall. At the time of writing, the break-up of the Soviet Union had not proceeded sufficiently far in Moscow for comparable KGB assessments in 1947–8 to be put in the hands of western historians. But a quick brained, open-minded former British intelligence official, Michael McGwire had, while working as an analyst at the Brookings Institution in Washington in the late 1980s, made an imaginative and persuasive stab at getting inside the cranium of the Moscow intelligence analyst forty years before, based on what Soviet material was available in the shape of speeches and their actual dispositions on the ground. He, too, sees the Marshall Plan negotiations as the moment when the cold war slipped into irreversibility.

> If there were still doubts in Stalin's mind about the thrust of Western policy after the Foreign Ministers' meeting in Moscow, these would have been finally dispelled by the proposed European Recovery Programme . . . Although the use of US economic strength was not unexpected, it seems that the Soviets assumed initially that Marshall's proposals were primarily prompted by the need to find markets for American output. It soon became clear, however, that something more threatening was involved. It appeared that Britain and France, under the guise of co-ordinating European recon-

struction, were acting as US agents in an ambitious scheme to lure as many countries as possible into a binding relationship with the West, by integrating their economies into the capitalist bloc . . .

The Anglo-French stance at the Paris meeting, following as it did on the heels of the Truman declaration, the stonewalling on reparations at the Council of Foreign Ministers, and the eviction of the Communist members of the French and Italian coalition governments, appears to have finally convinced Stalin that the West was indeed on the offensive against Communism. Not only was co-operation no longer a practical option, but even the possibility of 'peaceful co-existence' was in doubt. The hard-line pessimists therefore moved into favour in Moscow.[7]

This is the beginning of the mirror-imaging of worst-case scenarios with which rival sets of intelligence analysts put the fear of God into their consumers each side of the east-west divide. Naturally, each took the other's resultant behaviour as proof that their worst nightmares were justified with ideology – the capitalist/Communist divide – constantly inflaming both perceptions and superpower rivalry.

The result of the reassessment in Moscow after the breakdown of the wider European negotiations on the Marshall Plan (the result, remember, profoundly wished for in Washington and Whitehall), was the extension of Stalinism throughout eastern Europe, the progressive disappearance of non-Communist elements from governments in Warsaw, Budapest, Sofia and, most alarming of all to the west, in Prague in February 1948. And those western fears of Soviet-inspired subversion did not appear so fanciful when Communist-led strikes erupted in France and Italy in 1947–8 in an undeniable attempt to wreck the Marshall Plan and western European recovery. The Cominform (the Communist Information Bureau) was established in September 1947 to replace the legendary Comintern (formally stood down by Stalin during the Second World War) as the feared instrument of revolution and subversion beyond Russia's borders and those of its new empire in eastern Europe. As a result, strings of cold war clichés did not seem far wide of the mark in 1947–8.

Was the west right to see this as yet another milestone in the triumphant march of Communism which began at the Yalta Conference, when Stalin allegedly bamboozled the dying Roosevelt, despite Churchill's best efforts, into giving away half of Europe (it wasn't as simple as that, of course; the Yalta Declaration was unequivocal about free elections in eastern Europe after the war), a process only halted by the brilliant logistics and firm resolve of the western powers during the 1948–9 Berlin Air Lift? No, it was not.

The post-Paris developments in 1947 represented, as Mike McGwire puts it, 'a massive failure of Soviet foreign policy, both in terms of shaping the international environment and in forecasting the behaviour of other states. The United States had not withdrawn into isolationism . . . the "arsenals of capitalism" had not slumped back into the predicted recessions, nor had the need for markets proved to be a constraint on its foreign policy. And, despite conflicting interests, America and Britain were working together as an effective and aggressive team. As for shaping the international environment, the situation was now the opposite to what the Soviets had hoped for, wartime co-operation having been replaced by bellicose confrontation.'[8]

Stalin was well placed when it came to understanding the ups and downs of Anglo-American co-operation for he had a spy at the heart of it. Donald Maclean, in Sheila Kerr's words, had 'a secret hotline to Moscow' though, as she points out, it's impossible to know what he passed down it.[9] It could have been a great deal. As a young, high-flying diplomat in the Washington Embassy 1944–8, he was on *the* inside track of what nuclear collaboration survived after 1945 as a member of the US–UK–Canada Combined Development Committee on atomic energy. He also took the minutes at the meetings which nudged the western powers towards the NATO alliance. He would have been in a position to report on personalities, plans and intentions, invaluable as events unfolded swiftly and dangerously at the time of the Berlin blockade. He would know, too, of developments in deception techniques which proceeded apace in 1948 as the FO's Information Research Department got into its stride.[10]

Stalin suspected intelligence officers, diplomats and ideologically motivated spies (along, one feels, with the whole human race including his family). He once told Marshal Zhukov, 'You can't believe everything you read in intelligence reports.'[11] If I were Stalin, I would have believed Maclean's reports for two reasons: he was superbly well placed in the area of the dictator's greatest current preoccupation; and he was one of nature's tidy-minded bureaucrats with a fusspot's passion for accuracy (a great tribute to the country and the diplomatic service that made him) as the slightest acquaintance with his FO files, carefully preserved at the PRO, shows. The only exception was when the drink had got to him the night before and the meticulous handwriting deteriorates.[12] It's quite plain from JIC assessments like the mammoth seventy-page paper circulated in July 1948 that western intelligence had nobody comparable in the Soviet bureaucracy.

If we ever do gain access to Soviet intelligence archives, one important test of Maclean's value to Stalin will be the degree to which he was able to tell Moscow just how real were some of the *differences* between Washington and Whitehall. On one level – the military – the US and the UK were, to borrow Mike McGwire's phrase, an increasingly 'effective and aggressive' team. On another – the economic – the differences were and remained pronounced. Marshall and Acheson may have ceased to denigrate the Commonwealth as an evil empire as Byrnes liked to do (its possible contribution to containing the Soviet Union was more appreciated), but they substituted for earlier US efforts to break imperial preference a sustained campaign to push Britain into an ever more integrated European economy. This kind of dollar diplomacy was anathema even to that incarnation of the special relationship in the FO, Roger

Makins (though in old age, as Lord Sherfield, he once said to me and a pair of equally incredulous BBC producers that he'd no idea what this 'special relationship' was about which people had talked for so long).[13]

Makins, who was so influential with Bevin in the late Forties that he has been called a 'quasi-minister',[14] remained unrepentantly passionate when defending his and Bevin's convictions about Britain's true interests in 1947–9. When talking to Michael Charlton thirty years later about both US and European pressures to go further with economic integration after the war, he said, 'We were fighting a rearguard action – but we were determined to fight it!'[15]

Why? The pull of that still glittering circle among the intersecting trio – the one marked 'Empire'. 'At the time we're talking about', Lord Sherfield recalled, the nations of the Commonwealth and the sterling area 'were assets, no question about it. They were not only assets, they were obligations and what we were being asked to do was . . . to have a forced liquidation of our assets and a false repudiation of our obligations. Clearly our position had changed substantially,' Lord Sherfield continued,

> particularly on the economic front. For example, we'd been cut off [during the war] almost completely from our side of American trade which was an enormous loss. On the other hand the Commonwealth, the colonial empire, even the sterling area outlook – that was more or less intact. The independence of India and Pakistan had made a tremendous difference in the strategic sense which was not immediately apparent, but apart from that the Commonwealth structure was more or less intact.
>
> I'm sure the record shows that a great many people in the United States and influential people, wanted to see us, and regarded us, as a purely European power. They were not sympathetic to our colonial obligations; they wanted to get us out of our colonies, and pushed us far too hard, I think, in that respect. They never understood the sterling area and regarded that as our impediment to the free world economy which they wanted to achieve.[16]

The record does indeed show that the pressure was on from Washington to lever Britain into an economically united Europe from the moment in late September 1947 when the sixteen nations of the Committee for European Economic Co-operation presented its estimate of its combined four-year dollar deficit ($19.33 billion) to the Americans. Oliver Franks, who led the delegation from the Paris talks which crossed the Atlantic to negotiate with the Americans in October, gracefully and tactfully summed up the difference of approach by telling his hosts: 'American thought is clearly much preoccupied with the extent to which the reduction or elimination of quantitative restrictions and tariffs might bring benefits to Europe through the creation of a larger domestic market and concentration of productive effort. They appreciate the magnitude and importance of the problem of European trade with the rest of the world, but perhaps not so clearly the limited extent to which Europe's essential requirements from the rest of the world can be affected by a development of intra-European trade.'[17]

Sir Oliver's subtleties had little effect on the wielders of the dollar weapon, even upon as Anglophile and sophisticated a dollar diplomat as Averell Harriman. When he arrived in Paris in May 1948 to head the US agency for disbursing Marshall Aid, the Economic Co-operation Administration, he told Edmund Hall-Patch that, as Hall-Patch summarised it for his Foreign Office colleagues, the British Government 'over-rated the importance to us of the Commonwealth and the Sterling Area and that we would probably do much better for ourselves by making up our minds to integrate at once with Europe'.[18]

The first battleground was the nature of the CEEC itself. The Americans wanted it to be truly supranational and driven forward by a powerful secretariat run by that arch integrationist, the Belgian Paul Henri Spaak. The British resisted fiercely (knowing where that would lead) and suggested a much looser arrangement of national delegations. Whitehall, on this occasion, won. The Americans settled in January 1949 for a Consultative Group of Ministers which would meet occasionally between gatherings of the CEEC's Executive Committee.[19]

Bevin cabled Franks (by now Ambassador to Washington) in March 1949 asking him to have a quiet word with Dean Acheson (Marshall's successor as Secretary of State) about Harriman's high-handed ways as Washington's economic overlord in Europe, adding, with a mixture of candour and deception that, 'The United States must understand our difficulties and you might remind [Acheson and co.] that we have an isolationist mentality to watch here. It is very difficult to make the British European-minded,' (which was profoundly true), 'we want to do it but we must be helped and understood,'[20] (which was not).

There was, however, no danger that the Americans would halt the flow of Marshall Aid unless the British Government agreed to send the receiver in to the Empire. The chief impulse in the US was the desire to create a dollar curtain to confront Stalin's iron one. And, at the very time Harriman was jockeying for position with the FO's economic diplomats in Paris as the European Recovery Programme was converted from words into food, goods and money, another set of negotiations – intensely secret ones – was beginning to preoccupy the practitioners of statecraft in Whitehall and Washington, negotiations in which the UK was making the running rather than applying the brake.

With hindsight, it's possible to put a precise time and place on the moment of NATO's conception – six o'clock in Bevin's room in the Foreign Office on the evening of 17 December 1947 – when Marshall called on Bevin to discuss the way forward from the London Foreign Ministers' Conference. It had been an especially pointless conference even by the standards of those gatherings, memorable only for its complete deadlock over Germany and Bevin's tirade against Molotov after he'd invited him back to his flat for a heart-to-heart chat. 'What is it you want?' the Foreign Secretary asked.

What are you after? Do you want to get Austria behind your iron curtain? You can't do that. Do you want Turkey and the Straits? You can't have them. Do you want Korea? You can't have that. You are putting your neck out too far, and one day you will have it chopped off . . . If war comes between you and America in the West, then we shall be on America's side. Make no mistake about that. That would be the end of Russia and of your Revolution.[21]

Marshall had been summoned for his drink as the first stage of the greatest strategy Bevin had ever put together – to ensure that if war came in *Europe*, America would be bound to come to its aid, thereby ensuring that, too, would be the end of the Soviet Union and its Revolution.

It took nearly one and a quarter years from his first pass at Marshall over the whisky to reach the culmination – the signing of the North Atlantic Treaty – and very possibly it would not have happened at all if Molotov's people, as if on cue, hadn't snuffed out democracy in Prague or cut the road and rail link to Berlin, thereby reminding US policy-makers, legislators and its thinking public that now really was the time to change the diplomatic and military habits of a lifetime.

All this lay ahead. The first touch had to be an especially delicate one on the part of the big man, whom Marshall respected but did not like,[22] thinking him clumsy, as indeed he had been, missing his cue two days earlier for the carefully rehearsed move which would have enabled Marshall to put the blame on the Russians for adjourning the Foreign Ministers' Conference.[23] That night in his office, however, Marshall if anything found him too delphic, with all his talk of a 'spiritual federation of the west'.[24] A formal treaty? Nothing could have been further from Bevin's mind.

His own idea was that we must devise some western democratic system comprising the Americans, ourselves, France, Italy, etc., and of course the Dominions. This would not be a formal alliance, but an understanding backed by power, money and resolute action . . . He preferred . . . the British conception of unwritten and informal understandings. If such a powerful consolidation of the west could be achieved, it would then be clear to the Soviet Union that having gone so far they could not advance any further.[25]

It didn't quite end up like that. But the DNA Bevin mixed that evening was made flesh when Truman welcomed the NATO signatories to the [State] Departmental Auditorium on 4 April 1949 as the US Marine Band played Gershwin, including 'I got plenty of Nothin'',[26] an apt commentary in its way as not until the great war scare of Korea did the United States put fresh ground troops into Europe. In 1949, the line-up of forces in central Europe, according to estimates then current, was Stalin thirty-five divisions; the west eleven.[27] (Worst-case military planning contemplated a conventional withdrawal from the Rhine to the Pyrenees; the expected war winner, until the Russians tested their atomic weapon in August 1949, was thought to be the US Air Force B29 carrying the A-bomb from East Anglian bases to Moscow.)

The three great war-scare years of the postwar period are 1948 (Berlin), 1950 (Korea) and 1962 (Cuba). Both British and American intelligence in 1948 didn't think war was a serious possibility in Europe until the mid-Fifties when Russia would have both recovered from the Second World War and built itself a war-making machine capable of striking west with a capacity to wage sustained conflict. But it didn't seem quite as reassuring as that to the secret groups of NATO-builders working first in the Pentagon (US, UK and Canada) and later in the State Department with the European nations added (who were themselves in the course of agreeing the Brussels Treaty, a mutual defence pact for western Europe, crucial to the process of persuading the Americans that they were dealing with more than a set of supine, defeatist scroungers). Sir Nicholas Henderson, in the FO's private history of the NATO negotiation, describes vividly how the Czech coup in February and Soviet pressure on Norway in March 1948 concentrated minds in Washington.[28]

It concentrated them, too, in western outposts much closer to the Red Army. On 5 March, General Lucius Clay, the US military governor in Germany and, in many ways, the maker of modern West Germany (after he left the Army to run the Continental Can Corporation he liked to say he was the only man on Wall Street to have created a government),[29] despatched a telegram to the Director of Army Intelligence in Washington which set alarm bells ringing throughout the capital's national security apparatus (which was precisely the purpose of his writing it, said Clay in his memoirs).[30] 'For many months', Clay told General Chamberlin,

> based on logical analysis, I have felt and held that war was unlikely for at least ten years. Within the last few weeks, I have felt a subtle change in Soviet attitude which I cannot define but which now gives me a feeling that it may come with dramatic suddenness. I cannot support this change in my own thinking with any data or outward evidence in relationships other than to describe it as a new feeling of tenseness in every Soviet individual with whom we have official relations. I am unable to submit any official report in the absence of supporting data but my feeling is real.[31]

This report, said Avi Shlaim, anatomist of the Berlin Crisis, 'caused a veritable war scare in Washington'.[32]

Marshall judged the position to be 'very, very serious'.[33] On 8 March the Senate voted funds for the European Recovery Programme. On 17 March the

UK, France, Belgium, Netherlands and Luxembourg signed the Brussels Treaty, creating a Western European Union, a military alliance for mutual defence (it later gave Attlee a heaven-sent opportunity to replace Montgomery as Chief of the Imperial General Staff by Slim after the Field Marshal had proposed himself as Chairman of the Western Union's military command).[34] At the end of March the CIA assured Truman the Red Army would not march – for two months![35] On 22 March the Americans, the Canadians and the British began talks in 'the bowels of the Pentagon', the delegations arriving in the underground car park to avoid attracting attention. With them was Donald Maclean.[36] The business of probing Bevin's idea of an 'Atlantic Approaches Pact of Mutual Assistance' was under way with the ink on the Brussels Treaty still as fresh as paint.

On 25 February, with the news of the Prague coup coming over the wires in the FO, Bevin had told the US Ambassador, Lew Douglas, 'We are now in a crucial period of six to eight weeks which will decide the future of Europe,'[37] a line he had been pressing upon the Cabinet[38] and the House of Commons.[39] On the prompting of Mayhew, he virtually read into Hansard the ringing words Gladwyn Jebb had put in his pair of Cabinet Papers (Jebb was horrified as his phone was jammed with the diplomatic community asking what this phrase or that word actually meant[40]). One item Bevin did not impart to Parliament was the *real* thinking behind his metaphysical talk of Britain's role of mustering the spiritual resources of the west to save European civilisation. 'Provided we can organise a Western European System', Bevin told his Cabinet colleagues,

> ... backed by the power and resources of the Commonwealth and the Americas, it should be possible to develop our own power and influence to equal that of the United States of America and the USSR ... By giving a spiritual lead now we should be able to carry out our task in a way which will show clearly that we are not subservient to the United States or the Soviet Union.[41]

Here we have the true leitmotif on Bevin's policy once more. His 'spiritual union of the west' would fulfil two cardinal purposes – keeping the Red Army east of the Elbe *and* providing a breathing space until the economic buoyancy of Britain and the Empire could be restored and, with it, equality of great power status with the US and USSR. For one so practical, so earthy with so natural a feel for economics that even Keynes was impressed when he saw him in action on the Macmillan Committee in 1930,[42] this vision was as crazy as it was noble as it was – deluded.

What Bevin did not foresee, however, for all his feeling that the spring of 1948 would prove *the* turning-point in the jostling for power and territory in the protracted series of after shocks following the Second World War, was the Berlin Blockade, the moment when many sensible people (not just the logrolling General Clay) thought the Third World War was about to erupt three years after the Second had subsided.

Though the Russians had been engaging in minor harassment against western vehicles, trains and passengers passing through the corridors to the US, UK and French Zones in Berlin,[43] and Marshal Sokolovsky, the Soviet military commander in the Eastern Zone, had threatened dire consequences if the three western zones created a new and single currency (which they did on 21 June 1948 at a rate of one Deutschmark for ten old Reichsmarks), the western authorities did not expect the Soviets to retaliate for their surprise by giving the west a menacing surprise of their own in return. At 11 o'clock on the evening of 23 June the tickertapes of the news agencies tapped out this message:

> The transport division of the Soviet Military Administration is compelled to halt all passenger and freight traffic to and from Berlin tomorrow at 0600 hours because of technical difficulties.[44]

Clay rushed to US headquarters in Heidelberg and started to put together a military convoy to force its way down the autobahn to Berlin. The British Commander, General Sir Brian Robertson, told him: 'If you do that, it will be war – it's as simple as that.' Mercifully, Clay's superiors in Washington thought the same as Robertson. There would be no shoot out on the autobahn.[45]

Bevin was holidaying on the Isle of Wight when the blockade began, so little was this particular crisis anticipated, and he was rushed across the Solent by torpedo boat *en route* for London where he quickly issued a statement saying the policy was to resist and to stay in Berlin on the grounds, as he told Douglas, 'that the abandonment of Berlin would have serious, if not disastrous consequences in Western Germany and throughout Western Europe'.[46]

It's all too easy for historians to get sucked into the world of the Ernie Bevins, the Lew Douglases, the General Clays and the General Marshalls. Attention to the official written records, with that special 'Top Secret' cachet, can have such a whirlpool effect. It's one of the several manifestations of that occupational disease of historians, archivitis. June 1948 is a good moment to pause and ask just how menacing did the world seem to the thoughtful not privy to the cables, the intelligence reports and the Cabinet papers of those on the most inner of the inside circles?

Two generations later a young civil servant, who had had what used to be called 'a good war', and was working in the Admiralty in 1948 organising 'Operation Zebra', the despatch of sailors to the London docks to break the unofficial dispute,[47] could still recapture the peril of that Berlin summer. He remembered 'August in particular as a period of pressure, tension and urgent preparation against the risk of war or some form of military aggression of the Russians in Berlin'. Sir Pat was due to be married in mid-September and, at one point, thought developments might cause the wedding to be postponed.[48]

Sir Pat's memory is corroborated by the contemporary account of the ever perceptive J.L. Hodson, who had been a war correspondent in the Second World War and, like everybody else, couldn't bear the prospect of a third. His diary entry for 11 March 1948, recording the 'suicide' of Czech Foreign Minister, the gregarious, pro-western Jan Masaryk (it's now established that, as many suspected at the time, he did not fall from his bathroom window but was pushed to his death by the secret police[49]), says it was 'like an accusing finger pointing at the Kremlin . . . a sky as black as thunder. Imagine a young couple asking themselves whether they shall bring children into this tormented world. Imagine those of us who have lived through three wars, hearing the distant rattle and clangour of the juggernaut's wheels.'[50]

Berlin, naturally, deepened Hodson's pessimism. On 27 June he noted: '"There's a smell of Munich in the air," says *The Observer* today. Last week my friends the "Cherrypickers" were patrolling Berlin in their armoured cars and the Worcesters had mounted machine guns and dug themselves in. The Russians are striving to push us out of Berlin. If we go, we shall (says the *Observer*) be out of Germany altogether inside two or three years. I would agree that if that happened, with Germany Communist and within the Russian orbit, our days would be numbered.'[51] On 10 July Hodson was recalling he had

> told a Russian friend recently, in amicable talk, that if, in order to preserve our English way of life, I had to revive the Ruhr and make allies of the Germans against the Russians, I would do it. All the same, do we have to woo the Germans in public? General Brian Robertson has told them they have proved they are a civilized people (I wonder when precisely they did that) . . . Mr Churchill was busy saying, when speaking of the future of Germany, that it would not help the world if we continued to nurse feelings of hatred. The time has come, he said, when we should turn our faces against the terrible past.
>
> All this coincides with the arrival in this country from USA of sixty Superforts, which are the sort of machines which carried atom bombs to Hiroshima. This is a demonstration to the Russians to behave more reasonably or else . . . R. rang up the other day and spoke about the black-out she will need for her flat. She was almost in tears, dreading war. A friend said today that his wife, who was like a lion in the last war and drove an ambulance through it, is very frightened now.[52]

She was not alone. This was the time when, in Jacob Bronowski's words, the British sat 'under the shadow of the Nine O'Clock News, nursing our sense of doom'.[53]

Churchill, in fact, in the months before the Soviets closed the roads and rails to Berlin, was thinking in terms of much more apocalyptic solutions than merely stopping being beastly to the Germans. Years later it emerged that he had been urging an atomic solution on the Americans. Lew Douglas cabled back to Washington on 17 April the gist of several conversations with the old man:

> When and if the Soviets develop the atomic bomb, war will become a certainty, even though by then Western Europe may have become again the seat of authority and a stable political part of the world. He believes that now is the time, promptly, to tell the Soviet that if they do not retire from Berlin and abandon Eastern Germany, withdrawing to the Polish frontier, we will raze their cities. It is further his view that we cannot appease, conciliate or provoke the Soviet; that the only vocabulary they understand is force; and that if, therefore, we took this position, they would yield.[54]

This kind of talk was commonplace in 1948, the last year, as it turned out, of the American monopoly of atomic weapons. Even Bertrand Russell had succumbed to it briefly just after the war.[55]

At the time Douglas transmitted Churchill's views to Washington, the US Air Force had only a dozen useable atom bombs (though a production drive was to push that up to fifty by the end of 1948[56]), far fewer than those outsiders imagined and nowhere near enough to devastate the Soviet Union's cities and production centres. Oliver Franks told Robert Hall in March 1948 that 'he was very optimistic about the outcome of any war, largely on the grounds that ABs [atomic bombs], whatever else they might do, could immolate railway junctions'.[57] Stalin, however, was probably reckoning on a greater number even though Maclean was near perfectly placed for atomic intelligence purposes in early 1948. He could pass to his controller the tonnage of uranium the Americans were buying in, 2,547 tons for 1947–8, which Kurchatov's people would have translated into roughly fifty bombs by 1948.[58]

Maclean would have known, too, that production was being stepped up and that, in the words of an intelligence report from Washington to London in April 1948, there was 'a sharpening sense of military preparedness' inside US nuclear circles.[59] So when the B29s arrived in East Anglia in July, just about everybody, from Stalin to the English newspaper reader, would have got the message Hodson recorded – that the A-bombers had arrived and were within striking distance of Moscow. From 18 July 1948 there was to be a permanent American nuclear presence on British soil. It was a huge step for both nations as General Leon Johnson, who led the bombers over, was fully aware. 'Never before in history', he said later, 'has one first-class Power gone into another first-class Power's country without an agreement. We were just told to come over and "we shall be pleased to have you".'[60]

It was an extraordinary arrangement, as casual as it was momentous, long reviled by those of the Left in Britain who have been cold war dissenters. Tony Benn, for example, has consistently resented the 'commanding position in the deployment of its own nuclear weapons in Britain',[61] the UK of Attlee and Bevin ceded to the USA of Truman and Marshall. ('No Cabinet in which I have served has ever been told the true position and I can only suppose that the key US/UK arrangements are in effect only known to the President and the Prime Minister.')[62]

For just as long, it has been defended as a prime and beneficial piece of pragmatism by defence insiders like Sir Frank Cooper who told a group of American alumni at Oxford in 1990 that in 1948 he 'was then Private Secretary to one of the Air Ministers and it seemed sensible on both sides of the Atlantic to make provision for the USAF to be able to use facilities in Britain. Following talks with that splendid US Ambassador to the Court of St. James – Lew Douglas – it was decided there should simply be a brief exchange of letters saying that the USAF could have the use of 4 airfields in Britain "as long as it was in the interests of both countries". Though there have been adjustments in detail that is still the basis on which US Forces are here . . . I have always thought, at least in a bi-lateral sense, that simple arrangements are best and the longest lasting.'

What Sir Frank had in mind, as he made plain later when interviewed for the BBC Radio 4 *Analysis* programme, *Moneybags and Brains*, were the arrangements for USAF planes to use RAF bases in an emergency, not the much more complicated and vexed question of the use of any nuclear weapons they might carry which caused difficulties between Attlee and Truman in 1950–1 and which, eventually, was resolved by an entirely separate agreement.[63]

The original idea of supplying the whole population of West Berlin by air, not just its military garrisons, originated with an RAF officer, Air Commodore Waite. General Robertson, keen to buttress his arguments against Clay's impulse to despatch an armed convoy east down the autobahn, backed it as did Bevin. The Foreign Secretary pressed the possibility strongly on the Americans and, in the same conversation with Ambassador Douglas, raised the possibility of the B29s coming to Europe.[64] The initiative, which took General Johnson's breath away, was *Bevin's* idea. It was not a case of 'Britain as a Colony', to use the title of Tony Benn's chapter in his *Arguments For Democracy* where his objections to US bases on British soil are spelled out.

The Americans seized upon it with, as is quite plain from Defence Secretary Forrestal's diary, a degree of amazement. Douglas was instructed 'to ask Bevin whether he had fully explored and considered the effect of the arrival of these two [bomber] groups in Britain upon British public opinion'.[65] The only consultation Bevin felt obliged to undertake was with the handful of ministers on the Cabinet's 'Berlin Committee' set up to manage the crisis. (It consisted of Attlee, Bevin, Morrison, A.V. Alexander and the Chiefs of Staff.[66]) Not until 13 September did Bevin give a full report to the Cabinet's Defence Committee on the B29 story by which time, of course, it had been all over the newspapers.[67] Before the Defence Committee met, Sir Norman Brook briefed Attlee in a manner which conveys the mixture of cold war urgency and constitutional casualness which infused the entire episode. 'You saw', the Cabinet Secretary reminded the Prime Minister, an exchange of correspondence between the Secretary of State for Air, the Foreign Secretary and the Minister of Defence, discussing the possibility that the three American Heavy Bomber Squadrons now in the United Kingdom might continue to be based here more or less indefinitely, and asked that this matter should be brought before the Defence Committee before Parliament meets.

In this paper the Foreign Secretary outlines the present position in regard to these heavy bombers and makes it clear that no definite proposal has yet been made by the United States Government to station any of them in this country on a permanent basis. Two of the three groups are here as a political gesture and a third has been transferred from Germany because the Americans felt that it was too close to a potentially hostile frontier; but the question of their staying any longer than is warranted by the Berlin crisis has not yet been mooted.

The Foreign Secretary suggests that all three groups might be allowed to remain here for the time being on this basis, leaving the possibility of their more permanent location here at a later date.[68]

The story, contrary to the impression conveyed by Sir Frank Cooper, did not continue happily ever after from this point.

The question of joint control over those bombers ran on for another three and a half years. Contrary to the impression deliberately conveyed in July 1948, the B29s were not at first nuclear capable. Not until the summer of 1949 did some of them carry the necessary conversions to fly with the atomic bomb on board. But, by the summer of 1950, they all did.[69] By this time the question of their use was a live issue between Washington and Whitehall. In January 1948, as part of the *modus vivendi* on atomic energy signed by the British Government in the hope of restoring a modicum of technical exchange (it was very modest, though, as we shall see, the arrangement for pooling intelligence on what Russia was up to proved of great value to British scientists in the mid-1950s), the UK had given up all rights to be consulted by the US before the President authorised the use of nuclear weapons.

Lord Sherfield, who led for Britain in the negotiation, always maintained that it was the best deal possible in the circumstances and that it had the added advantage of removing *American* influence from any civil nuclear programme the UK might mount, a control ceded to Roosevelt by Churchill at Quebec. 'My own view', he told me forty years later, 'is that a great power cannot allow another country to prevent it doing whatever it needs, or thinks it needs, for national security; and that, therefore, that provision was really in practice not in fact enforceable; and that the other provision, about the President controlling our civil programme, was totally unacceptable on our side; and that, therefore, by cancelling those two provisions out, nothing was lost, something indeed was gained. I think we gained more really.'[70]

Good bargain or not, American atomic bombs based on British airfields, however, were a different matter. Bevin became concerned to safeguard the British position in 1949 when the US asked for more bases in Oxfordshire.[71] The outbreak of the Korean War in June 1950 increased British worries. As almost his last act as Foreign Secretary, Bevin's successor, Morrison, told Dean Acheson in September 1951 that it was intolerable for Britain to risk annihilation because of a US atomic strike from the UK over which British ministers had no control.[72] Not until Churchill, back once more at the British end of the special relationship, met Truman in Washington in January 1952, did the President acknowledge there was no question of British bases being used for an atomic raid without the prior consent of the UK Government, an assurance made public in the communiqué after their meeting.[73]

The phrases agreed on 9 January 1952 have governed whatever US nuclear delivery systems have since rested on English runways and launchpads or Scottish sea lochs (B29s, B47s, B52s, Thor missiles, Polaris submarines, F111s, Poseidon submarines). They consist of a mere thirty-four words (though there are, I know, a sheaf of classified papers putting operational flesh on the bare linguistic bones)[74]: 'The use of these bases in an emergency would be a matter for joint decision by His Majesty's Government and the United States' Government in the light of circumstances prevailing at the time.'[75] Whatever emphasis each side may have cared to place on it at any point in the cold war years, the only certainty built into it was – however you read it – that it did not amount to a UK veto over the US of the kind explicit in the 1943 Quebec Agreement.

Mercifully, the brilliant technical fix of building an air bridge to Berlin worked so successfully in 1948–9 that the issue did not arise. The Prussian sky was dark with transport aircraft, military and civilian for almost a year. The problem was solved with an ease which even the fertile mind of Air Commodore Waite could not have anticipated at the end of June 1948. By the time Stalin called the blockade off, the supplying of 2 million people by a flight every ninety minutes with a turn-round time of six minutes on West Berlin's airfields had almost come to seem business-as-usual.

When the Berlin crisis broke it was a remarkable concentrator of minds in the committee rooms of the west, not least in Washington where the NATO-builders were at work. As the British Embassy's in-house historian noted, the seven-power negotiations (US, UK, Canada, France, Belgium, Netherlands and Luxembourg) got under way on 6 July 'against the setting of the Soviet blockade of Berlin and the Western Air Lift: eloquent testimony to the reality of the Soviet threat and to the determination of the West to withstand it, whatever the cost and hardship'.[76]

Even though their deliberations took place in the constant shadow of the Air Lift, they were by no means smooth or inevitable in their conclusions even at this stage. There were influential voices with the ear of the mighty in Washington who continued to press the case *against* a formal alliance bonded by a treaty, most notably the two State Department Soviet specialists, Chip Bohlen and George Kennan. The latter was concerned that if the cold war became institutionalised it would prevent the seeds of the Soviet bloc's eventual decay from sprouting and flowering and saw NATO as a pure cold war institution. He was eventually reconciled to it, though he left Washington when the Truman Administration's cold war stance hardened still further and claimed for ever more that his 'containment' idea had been hijacked and distorted by the hawks.[77]

Kennan and Bohlen were taken on in debate by the State Department's European experts, Jack Hickerson and Ted Achilles (with Franks and Lester Pearson throwing British and Canadian weight discreetly behind them). But even the Washington Europhiles found the French fractious and difficult (early shades of the French reservations which led de Gaulle to remove French forces from the NATO command structure in the 1960s). The question arose, too, of who to include and exclude – Italy, a recently defeated Axis power? Greece, which had no Atlantic shore? Portugal, a tyranny, but the Azores, like Iceland and Greenland would be a necessary stepping stone for American forces 'crossing the pond' if war came in Central Europe? Ireland – yes, but only if they kept the NATO question separate from the unification question (they didn't, so they stayed out).

There was also the political paralysis which always afflicts Washington in the run-up to a presidential election. The Republican Chairman of the Senate Foreign Relations Committee, Arthur Vandenberg, had almost become an honorary member of the NATO negotiations so important did the Washington bureaucracy regard the need for bipartisanship; and Thomas Dewey was expected to win for the Republicans in November 1948. As election day approached, Robert Lovett, the chief State Department figure in the Chair, frustrated the Europeans by stalling more and more. Once Truman had, to everybody's immense surprise, won re-election, the logjam unfroze fast. The President declared in his inaugural in January 1949, 'I hope soon to send to the Senate a Treaty respecting the North Atlantic Security plan. In addition, we will provide military advice and equipment to free nations which will co-operate with us in the maintenance of peace and security.'[78]

Four months later the Treaty was signed. The United States signalled to the world its unequivocal assumption of a superpower role, at least for the ten initial years of NATO's life as specified in article 12. Article 5 was the key, and the one whose wording had most stretched the negotiators:

The Parties agree that an armed attack against one or more of them in Europe or North America shall be considered an attack against them all and consequently they agree that, if such an armed attack occurs, each of them, in exercise of the right of individual or collective self-defence recognised by Article 51 of the Charter of the United Nations, will assist the Party or Parties so attacked by taking forthwith, individually and in concert with the other Parties, such action as it deems necessary, including the use of armed force, to restore and maintain the security of the North Atlantic Area.[79]

It was ratified by the USA, Canada, Belgium, Denmark (then responsible for Greenland), France, Iceland, Italy, Luxembourg, the Netherlands, Portugal and Norway. Franks and Bevin signed for Britain.

For Bevin it was an extraordinary triumph. America was locked into Europe, fulfilling his primary aim in a manner that would have seemed impossible in 1945–6 during his endless prickly sessions with Byrnes and improbable even in the first six months of Marshall's tenure.

As Nicholas Henderson noted in a foreword to his contemporary official history written long afterwards in the early 1980s,

> The facts recorded in my account will, I believe, help to dissolve any remnants that remain of the revisionist view according to which the Americans were responsible for the Cold War and hence were the instigators of the North Atlantic Treaty. The document shows in fact how reluctant the Americans were in the first six months of 1948, when the West Europeans and Canada were urging upon them the need for some new security arrangements in the face of Soviet threats, to countenance the idea of a commitment to defend Western Europe; and how much effort the British and Canadians had to exert to try to convert the Americans to this need in the face of the widespread and persistent opposition that existed there, not least in the high ranks of the State Department.[80]

Henderson is right, too, to identify Bevin as the great 'canalizer of mood' which led to NATO and the filling of the gap left in Central Europe by the collapse of Hitler's empire.

As Bevin signed the Treaty he said, 'I am doing so on behalf of a free and ancient parliamentary nation and I am satisfied that the step we are taking has the almost unanimous approval of the British people.'[81] 'This', writes his official biographer, 'was not only the climax of his career as Foreign Minister but – with a German settlement at last secured [the Federal Republic came into being on 23 May 1949] and the prospect of the Berlin Blockade being lifted – the greatest ten days of his life.'[82] In fact 'one week after the NATO Treaty was unveiled, the State Department received from Moscow the first direct word from Stalin that he was ready to discuss calling off the Berlin Blockade.'[83] On the evening of 11 May 'the lights came on all over Berlin.

> At a few seconds after midnight a corporal of the Royal Corps of Military Police opened the iron gate at Helmstedt and a procession of cars and lorries moved through ... At 1.23 a.m. a British military train set off from Helmstedt station bound for Berlin, pulled by a west German locomotive, driven by a west German driver. It was laden with occupation officials, soldiers back from leave and a crush of journalists. It chugged east to a rousing chorus of 'It's a Long Way to Tipperary'. The blockade of Berlin was up.[84]

Bevin had put a military-security roof over western Europe. The need for it was, to him, a self-evident truth. The Americans wanted an economic and industrial one as well. To their way of geopolitical thinking, they made a natural pair. Bevin and, it must be said, virtually the entire British political and administrative class not only failed to see the connection, they regarded the idea as both undesirable in terms of British interests and naive in its assumptions about Europe's capabilities.

Public pronouncements are one thing, private another. Postwar British statesmen developed a nice line in constructing glittering images of a future Europe while refusing to lay down anything amounting to foundations for the new European home. Admittedly in the first five years after the war it was Winston Churchill, permitted by loss of office to become a freelance statesman extraordinaire, who laid on most of the rhetorical plaster with his lavish oratorical style.

In 1947 he used a great rally at the Albert Hall to launch the movement for a United Europe. His aim, he told Stafford Cripps, was 'to lift this whole business above our Party politics and try to make a real brotherhood of Europe, overriding all national, class and Party frontiers'.[85] He was writing to Cripps in a vain attempt to persuade him to come to the Hague for the European Conference, to launch the European Movement and to press for the establishment of a European Parliamentary Assembly in Strasbourg. It was classic Churchillian stuff, guff about 'all the little children who are now growing up in this tormented world', intermingled with passages which went to the heart of the debate which rent British politics for the next forty years.

> We shall only save ourselves ... by rejoicing together in that glorious treasure of literature, of romance, of ethics, of thought and toleration belonging to all, which is the true inheritance of Europe ...
>
> It is said with truth that this involves some sacrifice or merger of national sovereignty. But it is also possible and not less agreeable to regard it as a gradual assumption by all the nations concerned of that larger sovereignty which can also protect their diverse and distinctive customs and characteristics and their national traditions all of which under totalitarian systems ... would certainly be blotted out forever.[86]

This kind of talk made the man who counted in 1948 queasy and brought forth some classic Bevinese. Of the proposed Council of Europe he said, 'If you open that Pandora's box, you never know what Trojan horses will jump out.'[87] It was in response to what Christopher Mayhew called Churchill's 'great song and dance' at the Hague that Bevin agreed to give the Europeans a 'talking shop',[88] a far cry from Churchill's vision of it as an 'instrument of European government',[89] all of which, of course, fell away completely when the old man got his proper job back on the change of government in 1951.

But the best way of illustrating the true direction of British foreign and economic policy, when it was on what could be called its private automatic pilot, is to examine the real world of secret meetings and diplomatic exchanges and compare the hard nosed, we–mean–business attitude of the British in the Washington negotiations which led to NATO with the series of private meetings between British and French officials in the weeks just before and after the North Atlantic Treaty was signed. The key figures were the economic planning chiefs for the two countries, Edwin Plowden and Jean Monnet.

The French made the first move after both countries had done what the Americans required and submitted their long-term programmes to the OEEC in Paris in order to qualify for Marshall Aid. The French, as one of the British team in Paris, Eric Roll, admitted, 'were the only ones who had a fully-fledged planning machinery and a domestic plan for economic renewal and invest-ment'.[90] Monnet, too, as Directeur of the Commisariat du Plan in Paris was a quasi-political official with the kind of clout Plowden neither wished for nor could have had in the Central Economic Planning Staff in London, a point Monnet seems never to have grasped. The two men's styles were very differ-ent: Monnet, an evangelical, one-idea-a-minute man with a long-term vision of a United Europe as the only guarantor of peace and prosperity to which every-thing, including national sovereignty, was subordinate; Plowden quiet, under-stated, a progressive in his way but no visionary and certainly no hustler of the mighty like Monnet (it was Monnet who almost pushed the French and British Governments into a national union as the Wehrmacht rolled towards the English Channel in June 1940 and suddenly, there was no independent French nation to fuse with).

The Foreign Office were horrified by Monnet's suggestion of joint talks in February 1949 and even more by the huge delegation he proposed to bring to London with him. Plowden, who had no doubt about Monnet's place in world history ('he had [when he died in 1979] done more to unite Europe on a permanent basis than all the emperors, kings, generals and dictators since the Fall of the Roman Empire,[91]) persuaded the FO that a small, low key gathering could do no harm. He also, characteristically, tried to disabuse the Frenchman that he was dealing with a British plenipotentiary: 'Monnet was convinced that I would carry sufficient weight with senior Cabinet ministers for our recommendations to be taken seriously. I had to tell him, however, that while it might be possible for him to do such an exercise independently of the main French Civil Service machine, it was quite impossible for the CEPS to do so.'[92]

The French kept up the pressure regardless of Plowden's soft-pedalling. In March they met again in Paris this time with Cripps present after the Chan-cellor and his French counterpart, Maurice Petsche, had agreed to allow their planning staffs to talk about the Marshall Plan's long-term programmes. Lord Plowden paints a beautiful miniature of the French thinking about the future of the world and the British preoccupied with pounds, shillings and pence (as they then were):

During this second series of meetings Monnet elaborated on his hopes for the talks. Subsequently, I reported his views thus: 'M. Monnet explained that in his view Western Europe was a vacuum, on either side of which were the two great dynamic forces of communism and American capitalism. He felt that this vacuum could be filled either by one of these two outside forces, or by the development of a Western European Way of Life.'[93] At the time we were becoming increasingly preoccupied with the problem of devaluation and the difficulty of persuading Ministers of the need for it. Consequently, I fear we did not pay enough attention to Monnet's analysis.[94]

Plowden did agree, however, to carrying on the conversation the following month in Monnet's farmhouse at Bazôches on the outskirts of Paris. But, as for that Monnet vision of a European way between the great dynamos of east and west, Plowden responded in a totally *English* fashion: 'Well, this of course was a very typical Jean Monnet view. I'm afraid I was used to his rather higher flights of this kind and I didn't pay a great deal of attention to that analysis.'[95]

Matters were no different when Plowden, accompanied by his CEPS deputy, Alan Hitchman, and Robert Hall from the Cabinet Office, turned up at Bazôches on 21 April 1949 to talk with Monnet, Etienne Hirsch and Pierre Uri in what the Press, had they known it, would have called the 'relaxed surround-ings' of 'the long, low stone-floored drawing-room with its family bibelots, its paintings by Madame Monnet and its tall French windows overlooking the fields towards Rambouillet'.[96]

From Robert Hall's diary account, the three days at Bazôches did not even amount to a footnote in European history:

> Monnet felt that we must do something to catch the imagination of ECA [Marshall Plan] and our own people, by way of economic co-operation. He had various suggestions, notably that we might deliberately plan for a big coal-meat swap, they changing their agricultural plan from grain to meat . . . I did not feel that we got very far somehow – the talk was too much in general terms and I doubt if it will get as far as discussions in detail.[97]

Plowden's account in his memoirs was equally prosaic and low-key, noting that 'when on our return . . . we put these proposals to Bevin via Cripps, they were immediately rejected as Bevin felt that even these would go too far in the direction of a surrender of British sovereignty.'[98]

For the French, however, those three spring days near Rambouillet repre-sented a turning-point in theirs – and Europe's – postwar history. Monnet recalled in his memoirs the impossibility of leading the three British civil servants on to broader themes, adding that 'it could not have been more clearly or authori-tatively stated that the British Government had no desire to commit itself, however loosely, to an economic relationship which might have led to a closer union with France – or, indeed, any other country. Time was slipping by, and my attempt to create a nucleus around which a European Community might be formed had met no response from the one great power in Europe which was then in a position to take on such a responsibility [the United Kingdom].'[99]

Plowden always insisted that Monnet had simply not spelled out this vision to his British visitors – 'he was never this explicit about his hopes for the talks and we in the British delegation did not realise how far, in fact, he wanted to go. But, in any case, this does not mean that had we known, a different outcome would have resulted; indeed I think such knowledge would have made us even more cautious.'[100] Why? 'We still were thinking in terms of Britain, and of standing between the United States and Western Europe and Russia and so on; as being an independent great power ... I don't think ... that we really believed in the vision he had of forming a nucleus around which a new Europe could be built. After all, for I don't know how many hundreds of years Britain had kept out of Europe. And suddenly to ask it to change, to give up its external, its worldwide role in order to join with a Europe which was *down and out* at the time, required a vision which I'm quite sure I hadn't got, and I doubt whether very many people in the United Kingdom had. Some may now *think* they had, but I don't think they *did*!'[101]

Before considering the consequences of the Bazôches misunderstanding (which can be stated quite simply – France turned to Germany as its partner in shaping what became the European Economic Community and one of three great economic forces in the world, with Britain finally admitted as a junior partner in 1973, still searching for its elusive postwar economic miracle), the question needs to be asked: did anyone knowledgeable and possessing a degree of authority in public life think another outcome was possible in 1949? Because the reaction of Plowden, Hall and Hitchman, Cripps and Bevin at that time indicated precisely what the answer would be a year later when Robert Schuman, the French Foreign Minister, asked the British Government formally if it would care to join France and Germany in creating a new, Monnet-patented supranational body, the European Coal and Steel Community.

The records show that at least one man broke the official intellectual mode, no less a figure than Edmund Hall-Patch, the FO's top economic diplomat, who replaced Franks as Chairman of the Marshall Plan negotiations in Paris in 1948, a figure with a rich past. Indeed, Alan Milward's A.J.P. Taylor-style footnote on him is virtually a biography in miniature:

Sir Edmund Hall-Patch, 1896–1975. A most interesting person. Born in Russia and brought up in Paris, a spasmodically successful musician and a failed novelist. Served with the Reparations Commission after the First World War. Became financial adviser to the government of Siam from which post he was driven by Montagu Norman, the Governor of the Bank of England. Played the saxophone in New York before rejoining the Treasury in 1935, on whose behalf he served most of the time in China and Japan. Seconded to the Foreign Office in 1944. Deputy Under-Secretary of State and leader of the British delegation to the OEEC in 1948. Executive Director of the IMF 1952. A Catholic bachelor in whose imaginative advice Bevin placed much reliance: 'Send for 'All-Patch,' he would say, ''e'll make yer flesh creep.'[102]

Would that *Who's Who* entries read like that.

In a memo to Bevin in August 1947 written during the Convertibility Crisis, Hall-Patch, with what strikes hindsight-tinted eyes as extraordinary, perhaps in 1947 Whitehall unique, prescience, declared:

> There is a well-established prejudice in Whitehall against a European Customs Union. It goes back a long way and is rooted in the old days of Free Trade. It is a relic of a world which has disappeared, probably never to return. The Board of Trade is overstating the case against it. One of their most potent arguments is that we have to *choose* between a European Customs Union and the Commonwealth. However that may be, the Board of Trade have successfully blocked for two years our efforts to look at these proposals objectively. As a result of Marshall's proposals [i.e. OEEC] European imaginations have been fired. It may be possible to integrate in some measure comparable with the vast industrial integration and potential of the United States, which the Russians are trying to emulate. If some such integration does *not* take place, Europe will gradually decline in the face of pressure from the United States on the one hand and the USSR on the other.[103]

Have we found the British Monnet? Yes and no. The vision is similar but Hall-Patch, unlike the Frenchman, could not shift minds or inspire hearts, at least not in the passion-free zones of the Whitehall ministries.

As Lord Franks, with whom he had 'discussed these issues . . . exhaustively,'[104] said thirty years later, 'Now Hall-Patch had these opinions and, if you look at them over a larger period of time, fifteen or twenty years, of course he was seeing ahead with very considerable accuracy. But if you're asking yourself, as I am trying to do now, what we thought and what the possibilities seemed to be in, say, the five years after the war, then I don't think the views which he puts forward so lucidly there carried as much weight as he would have liked them to.'[105]

Franks said this had nothing to do with Hall-Patch being an unconventional person by Foreign Office or Treasury standards. He was listened to. But his thinking cut against the grain of Whitehall thought because, Lord Franks explained to Michael Charlton, 'We did not see how we could both preserve the sterling area and be full members of a European Customs Union.'[106] Lord Franks is absolutely right. Every ounce of British history and Whitehall conventional wisdom weighed against Hall-Patch.

It would be wrong, in one sense, to put the postwar policy-makers in the dock for a retrospective mass trial on the charge that they wilfully ignored the beauty and poetry of the European vision. To Monnet it was a vision, but the hard-headed politicians and civil servants in most of continental Europe, like the British, would only go along with it so far as it suited their national interests and their postwar recovery programmes. As Alan Milward bluntly put it, 'The European Community came into existence to settle domestic political and economic problems.'[107]

It suited Britain to join the European Payments Union in 1948 to benefit from a common European attempt to cope with the dollar shortage. Much further it was not seen in our interests to go whereas for Belgium and the Netherlands it made sense to think of tacking their small markets on the large French and soon-to-be-large German one. For some European nations, the Schuman Plan represented a supranational development which dovetailed naturally with their own national push towards economic recovery. Not for Britain juggling with its three overlapping circles.

For the Americans this was a cause of profound irritation and regret. Acheson wrote in 1969 that Britain's failure to join in the Schuman Plan negotiations in 1950 was our 'great mistake of the postwar period . . . It was not the last clear chance for Britain to enter Europe, but it was the first wrong choice.'[108] Monnet couched his explanation in a brilliant aphorism – 'Britain had not been conquered or invaded. She felt no need to exorcise history.'[109] This was the lesson he began to learn in his own drawing-room as the vision, however opaquely he put it, simply passed over the heads of Plowden, Hall and Hitchman through the French windows and into the atmosphere. Etienne Hirsch later told Plowden that 'they hoped up until December 1949 that something might come between England and France. And then, by then, he [Monnet] became completely convinced that we were not going to do anything. It was then that he turned towards trying to form the Schuman Plan, the Coal and Steel Community',[110] and to Konrad Adenauer, Chancellor of the newly created Federal Republic of Germany.

We've felt already the pull that the Empire still exerted on British policy-makers. But what about that other interlocking circle which they consistently rated above the European ring? What was it about the 'special relationship' that held them in such thrall by mid-1949 and which led them to treat Europe and America as either/ors for the bulk of the postwar period (quite erroneously as US administrations attempted to push successive British governments into a more fully integrated Europe from the Marshall Plan negotiations onwards)?

It's perfectly possible to make a case *against* the 'special relationship' (the phrase was used and popularised by Churchill in his 'Iron Curtain' speech at Fulton, Missouri, in 1946),[111] even in its early years, especially when Britain's economic interests are weighed in the balance along with its military needs. Robert Cecil was a First Secretary in the Washington Embassy in the early years after the war and replaced his friend Donald Maclean as head of the FO's America desk when the latter defected to the Soviet Union in 1951. He never succumbed to the great partnership notion on which so many British diplomatic careers were built.

Cecil remembers the FO's postwar notion as another version of the celebrated 'they have all the moneybags, but we have all the brains' idea (as described by the anonymous poet when the American loan was under negotiation) – 'the special relationship, in our view, would be a means of making sure that if this little British gunboat was following in the wake of the American battleship, nevertheless, on the bridge of the battleship, the Americans would be receiving messages from the British who had this long experience of international affairs and knew so much more about things than the Americans did, or so we liked to think.'[112]

The test of such assumptions, whatever the metaphor in which they are couched, is to ask if, at any point, Whitehall actually changed Washington's mind on an issue of substance, persuading the Americans to do something that, but for us, they would have done differently or not at all.

'I don't think there was such an occasion,' said Robert Cecil when invited to do an audit for BBC Radio 4's *Analysis*. 'There certainly wasn't an occasion when the Americans cancelled Lend-Lease without any notification to us; not when, in spite of Keynes' pleading, they decided that the loan to Britain would be accompanied by [the pound] going convertible; not when the wartime agreements about atomic power were ignored and the McMahon Act was passed . . . On none of these occasions, in my recollection, were we successful in dissuading the Americans from what they intended to do anyway.'[113]

There's a danger here of looking at this singular relationship in a monochromatic fashion. For it was, in reality, a cold war partnership, a military and intelligence phenomenon not an economic one. But for the cold war it would not have revived after 1945 for all Churchill's rhetoric at Fulton about the shared sacrifices of war and the common experience of the English speaking peoples. Beyond the boundaries of the cold war relationship, the Americans were reluctant to go when it came to slapping the label 'special' on this or that bilateral activity.

Dean Acheson was happy to 'talk regularly, and in complete personal confidence, about any international problems we saw arising' with Sir Oliver Franks in Washington[114] but he lost his temper when Foreign Office and State Department officials tried to capture its essence on paper in May 1950: 'My immediate and intense displeasure with this document', he said later,

caused its origin to become obscure. It was not the origin that bothered me, but the fact that the wretched paper existed. In the hands of troublemakers it could stir up no end of hullabaloo, both domestic and international, within the [Atlantic] alliance.

Of course a unique relation existed between Britain and America – our common language and history insured that. But unique did not mean affectionate. We had fought England as an enemy as often as we had fought by her side as an ally. The very ease of communication caused as many quarrels as understandings . . . for all copies of the paper that could be found were collected and burned, and my colleagues, after a thorough dressing-down for their naiveté, were urged to channel their sentimental impulses into a forthcoming speech of mine before the Society of Pilgrims, which, by tradition, was granted dispensation for expressions of this sort.[115]

In fact, very little of the 'special relationship' has been put on paper in the formal sense (though reams upon reams exist in speeches delivered on the White House lawn as presidents and prime ministers have heaped the saccharin both upon each other and each other's countries). There are exceptions – the secret intelligence treaty of 1947, the 1952 communiqué on the use of US nuclear weapons based in Britain and the 1958 agreement on atomic collaboration which repaired the damage done to the very special nuclear relationship by the McMahon Act.

This is the way that Acheson wanted it. It suited the British guardians of the partnership as well. 'I don't awfully like the term "special relationship",' the former Cabinet Secretary, Lord Hunt of Tanworth, told me. 'I'm not sure I can invent a better one, but "special relationship" seems to imply a number of things. First of all, it seems to imply symmetry. Second, it also implies something like an agreement or a treaty – that you do this or you don't do that and you have to consult on this or you have to consult on that. With a very few exceptions, of which intelligence and nuclear matters are the two obvious examples, that simply doesn't exist.

'But, between the United States and the United Kingdom, you have got a reservoir of language, of law, of all sorts of academic links, of experience, and, I think, a habit of consultation, a habit of tending to see things the same way. And that is a reservoir which is certainly important to our side and, I think it's equally important to them to be able to draw on.'[116]

Lord Hunt's reflection captures perfectly both the informal nature of the 'special relationship' and the degree to which it became a constant, an accepted backdrop to British policy-making (aberrations like Suez apart), from the days of Attlee and Truman to Thatcher and Reagan. And in those early postwar days, there was something in Robert Cecil's metaphor of the clever little British gunboat and the great, cumbersome American battleship. I shall always remember how angry Acheson's assistant Luke Battle became when I reported to him Sir Nicholas Henderson's view that 'I think NATO was a British invention. In fact, I know it was a British invention.'[117]

'Well,' said Mr Battle, one of those craggy US diplomats with the build of a football player, 'I thought we did it, but we might get into some competition here. I thought this was one of the few really creative things that we did after the war without being told by you to do it.'

'What', I asked him, 'do you think Dean Acheson would say if he heard one of those silky Brits from that era claiming that they invented NATO?'

'It wouldn't be usable on this network [i.e. the BBC],' said Mr Battle.[118]

Such spats should not obscure the significance of the enduring defence relationship with western Europe, not just Britain, into which Bevin enticed the Americans in 1948–9. Of course it wouldn't have happened if Truman, Marshall and Acheson had not wished to be persuaded and had not wished to persuade Congress in turn. But raising the possibilities and the mapping of the terrain on which NATO was to be built, represent the greatest single achievement of British diplomacy since 1945 and one from which the UK and the whole of western Europe benefited enormously, until the cold war ended at last with a solution to the German problem in 1990. In General Ismay's terms, the Americans stayed in, the Russians stayed out and the Germans posed no military threat to the democracies throughout that undeclared forty years' war.

The blindness to Europe apart, there were beneficial spin-offs of practical use to British policy-makers in areas beyond the simple boundaries of the cold war. With Byrnes gone from the State Department, crude American attempts to destabilise the Empire ceased. From the Korean War onwards, the Americans began to appreciate the global role of the British of which the Commonwealth was a symbol, as in Henry Kissinger's words, 'It is not appropriate for the United States and too dangerous to be the country that makes all the global decisions . . . it is important for us to have a European partner that can broaden our horizon, particularly one with wide experiences.'[119] For the American intelligence services, too, it was immensely valuable to have British imperial possessions on which to plant National Security Agency aerials for signals interception purposes and strips of colonial territory from which the CIA could mount clandestine operations against potentially hostile nations.[120]

In general terms, Paul Addison is surely right to say that 'from the point of view of people who were in charge of [UK] government, the special relationship was simply necessary in order to keep the show on the road.'[121] As we have seen, without the dollar life-line the Attlee Government would simply not have been able to provide the basics of survival for the British people *and* build a new welfare state. That life-line was, under various guises – Lend-Lease, American Loan, Marshall Aid – the means of injecting more than a billion dollars a year into the British economy throughout the 1940s. As Robert Hall noted in his diary in mid-1951: 'We have had . . . an average of over a billion dollars a year one way and another since 1946 and of course under Lend/Lease we had a great deal more. In fact our whole economic life has been propped up in this way.'[122]

Of course there were strings attached to this dollar diplomacy. Crudely put, the Americans were always keen for us, in financial and trade terms, to get out of Empire and into Europe. But, thanks again to the overriding priority given to fighting the cold war, when push-came-to-shove, the Americans, on the larger economic issues, could usually be persuaded to make allowances for what the British saw as their special national/imperial interests.

This became apparent to the most successful and influential special relation of them all, Sir Oliver Franks, when the pound sterling was devalued in

September 1949. Lord Franks accepts that early postwar dollar diplomacy had its ruthless side – that the attempts to break up the sterling area were real when the American Loan was under negotiation. By the summer of 1949 when the pound came under intense pressure on the foreign exchanges, the picture was much less clear. Lord Franks recalls the visit the US Treasury Secretary, John Snyder, paid to Downing Street in July 1949 for money talks with British ministers:

> The British at that stage refused to devalue and asked for short-term assistance in various ways which was not forthcoming, at which point the British said they would have to withdraw into the sterling area, look after their reserves, separate the pound from the dollar – there would be two world trading areas.
>
> When this got back to Washington there was absolute consternation because it threatened to put a total halt to the progress of . . . bringing France and Germany together, the liberalisation of [import] quotas and the European Payments Union that Hoffman, the ECA [Marshall Plan] Administrator, was so keen on – threatened to put a stop to the whole lot.
>
> Now there were people in Washington who wanted to put pressure on the British. Acheson said 'No'. He said, 'We need Britain. She has her commitments, she's a worldwide power. I'm not prepared to try to make her do things which are against her nature. What we have to do is to find ways of accommodating her and yet getting her into the European Payments Union.'[123]

Why this sudden and remarkable forbearance in Washington in the summer of 1949 which had been conspicuously absent in the autumn of 1945 when Keynes and Clayton locked words and ideologies across the table in the Federal Reserve Building? The answer can be found in the words 'cold war' which had changed everything in the intervening four years.

In 1949 the Americans still had 'all the moneybags' but Washington's most influential 'brains' were by now in tune with Whitehall's. Acheson despatched his European Affairs deputy, George Perkins, to Europe to persuade the big US 'proconsuls', Harriman in Paris and McCloy in Bonn, who, as Lord Franks put it, 'were inclined to favour bringing Germany and France together and, therefore, to put pressure on Britain. George Perkins said to them, "No, the Secretary of State has decided to respect Britain's commitments overseas and to have regard to her historical position in the sterling area. We have to do this because she is a partner of the United States and the Pentagon say that we cannot possibly do without her."'[124]

Interestingly enough, in the protracted and fractious debates inside the Cabinet's Economic Policy Committee over whether to devalue or not in June and July 1948, only Bevin (who didn't initially wish to alter the exchange rate) appreciated the importance of playing the cold war/special relationship card.

At an all day emergency session in No. 10 on 1 July (which Franks attended) Bevin said, 'The Government should make it known that they were determined to stabilise the level of employment and the standard of living in this country, and should point out that, while the United States might not be unduly alarmed at the prospect of seven or eight million unemployed, the development of serious unemployment in Western Europe would have disastrous effects on the policy which culminated in the negotiation of the Atlantic Pact. The problems confronting us could not be settled on a purely financial level, and must be discussed on the political plane. The question was whether there would be three separate economic systems viz. Eastern Europe (re the Soviet bloc), the sterling area and the dollar area which might be extremely dangerous.'[125]

This was exactly the ploy Bevin used in Washington two months later when, in a fashion veteran American diplomats like Paul Nitze could 'recall as though it were yesterday', over forty years later,[126] he swung even the sceptical US Treasury into line by switching the discussion away from narrow money channels to the glories of Britain and her place in the wider world.

'Snyder', Nitze recalled, 'was very tough. He was from Missouri and he made some very cutting remarks about England in particular – England had caused no end of trouble and was costing no end of money; and he thought it was totally unjustified and there was no excuse at all for England to have asked our help [in] getting out of a problem they'd gotten themselves into. Ernie Bevin was offended by the way in which Snyder put this and he began to castigate Snyder . . . and defend England's record as having had courage and having stood up against the world . . . It was just an outpouring of emotion. And it was so strong and he was so powerful in what he said. I was looking at Snyder and, suddenly, Snyder began to cry. There were tears in his eyes. That was the end of Snyder's revolt. From that point on he decided we would do what we could to help Britain in that crisis.'[127]

The devaluation crisis of 1949 did not only produce tension between Britain and the ally on whom it relied for so many of the essentials of life – financial, industrial, edible or military. It split the Cabinet and Whitehall too. And it was harder to reduce a British Treasury man to tears than an American. He'd lived here and experienced the blitz and rationing at first hand rather than through the nightly evocations of Ed Murrow on the radio.

In retrospect the 1949 devaluation looks inevitable. At $4.03, sterling's postwar rate was clearly out of line with the mighty dollar *and* the underlying weakness of the British economy. It's surprising it took four years to come after the shooting stopped. In fact the Treasury had been thinking about the possibility since the end of 1941 but the balance of thought tilted against the idea. 'The Treasury view', wrote Alec Cairncross, ' . . . was that devaluation would be of little help in dealing with the problem of the sterling balances and would provoke unhelpful reactions among American bankers. The [Cabinet Office's] Economic Section initially took a somewhat similar line, seeing no great value in devaluation when overseas income was denominated in sterling and imports were limited by controls rather than by price.'[128]

The first official to run the idea of devaluation as a beneficial step was Otto Clarke. He argued in June 1945 that an early and modest devaluation would help postwar trade and enable Britain to balance her accounts by 1949–50. Keynes disagreed, maintaining that the *dollar* was overvalued and, therefore, British exporters would enjoy an advantage in the postwar years.[129]

The Convertibility Crisis of 1947 and its aftermath clearly had an impact. As part, no doubt, of the general banishment of wishful thinking, the Treasury began to prepare a contingency plan for devaluation – or the 'Sterling War Book' as Ernest Rowe-Dutton, its author, called it in a highly secret memo to Sir Wilfrid Eady in January 1948.[130] By mid-February a first draft was ready – who should be told and in what order plus the simultaneous technical and financial adjustments that would be needed.

Commenting on a further draft in early June, Otto Clarke declared himself 'very largely convinced of the desirability of this [a deliberate, unforced devaluation of the pound], as the only means of mobilising ordinary commercial incentives for the task of righting our dollar balance of payments'.[131] On 17 June, for reasons that are difficult to divine, the Treasury's secret planners decided 'the exercise was unrealistic and we should leave it on one side' until further discussion of the pros and cons of devaluation had taken place.[132] At no point, if the files are any guide, was anybody but the Bank of England alerted to this secret planning. Ministers certainly were not.

Not until early 1949, when the beginnings of an economic depression in the USA caused renewed fears about the prospect for British exports in North American markets, did devaluation begin to move once more up the most secret agendas in Whitehall. Robert Hall was an early and influential convert to devaluation. Plowden and Makins soon followed. Cripps, however, would have none of it. By May the Chancellor was making public speeches trying to damp down devaluation talk while complaining privately that the Americans were fostering it.[133]

At Franks' suggestion, Hall and Wilson-Smith travelled to Washington in early June to test administration and financial thinking. Bill Martin, Snyder's number two, told them 'practically all officials of the US Government were firmly convinced that devaluation of sterling was inevitable'.[134] It was the relaying of such views to the Cabinet's Economic Policy Committee which confronted ministers for the first time with the notion that devaluation was a real and serious possibility. In short, they panicked.

As usual, the EPC minutes for 15 June 1948 convey no feel for the occasion in that cool, bland Cabinet Office style. Dalton's diary tells the real story:

Very serious dollar situation. Gap widening and reserves running down . . . Cripps says that the danger is that, within twelve months, all our reserves will be gone. This time there is nothing behind them, and there might well be 'a complete collapse of sterling' . . . We meet again in the afternoon, without officials. Cripps gets authority to stop all purchase of gold and dollars . . . As we go out, Addison says, '1931 over again'. I say 'It reminds me awfully of 1947? Shall we never get free?'[135]

As before in 1947, and as would happen on many later occasions, sinking reserves concentrated minds. On 1 July EPC was due to meet all day on the dollar crisis. The influential Hall attempted to concentrate Attlee's quick but uneconomic mind with a personal memo. 'The country', he told the P.M., 'is now facing a major crisis . . . Our difficulties in the end can be reduced to two. We have been trying to do too much at home, and we have been trying to support an overvalued currency . . . I am one of the officials . . . who consider that we should devalue sterling in the very near future. It is agreed that our costs are too high for the North American market and that we must get them down somehow. I do not believe that there are any measures other than devaluation which will do this in time to be of any use.'[136]

Hall stressed to Attlee that he was among the *pro*-devaluation officials because EPC ministers were being circulated with a summary of the division of opinion inside the Treasury. Bridges, like the fine, traditional civil servant he was, had allowed his top officials to give their views individually to Cripps (they are all beautifully preserved in the 'Caliban File', 'Caliban' being the secret code for devaluation, which Sir Edward had produced and bound in leather after the event; he called it 'Caliban' because, for him, devaluation stood for all that was unsavoury and underhand).[137]

The argument raged from the traditionalist Sir Wilfrid Eady ('No country devalues its currency except out of weakness. No Government which has been forced to this step can expect, however plausible its arguments, that its political credit will be unaffected among plain, and nervous people, in its own country, and over a large part of the world. The £ will be "worthless".'[138]) to the Keynesian Hall ('It would indeed be a fantastic reversal of all we have striven for in economics since 1931 if we now go in for a substantial deflation. No Government ought to do so.'[139]).

Both men knew their Chancellor and played on Cripps' sentiments mercilessly and note how political their views were for allegedly neutral civil servants. Eady, in fact, said 'a major change in the value of a currency must always be about 60% "politics" (or policy) and 40% "economics"'.[140] Eady knew Cripps could not abide the thought of cheating the holders of sterling given his fierce personal standards of morality. Equally, Hall understood the horror that severe deflation as the alternative to depreciating the pound would mean for a man who was deeply committed to full employment and for whom the scars of 1931 were still livid.[141]

When Cripps, spinning all the inputs through that beautiful, albeit by now exhausted mind, came to place his thoughts on paper for the Cabinet committee, he reduced the possible courses of action open to the Government to three:

(1) The policy we are now pursuing of attempting to increase productivity so as to reduce costs, accompanied by the maintenance of a very high standard of Social Services, subsidies on food, and other beneficial transfer payments.

(2) A policy of severe deflation internally such as was pursued in 1921 [presumably a reference to the 'Geddes Axe' when the Lloyd George Coalition inflicted huge cuts across a swathe of public services,[142] or it could be a typing error, '1931' being the date intended] which would reduce internal and external prices with the consequences especially in terms of unemployment that were then experienced.

(3) A devaluation of sterling which would make our exports cheaper in terms of all currencies which did not similarly and simultaneously devalue. All my advisers however agree in the view that devaluation alone is not the answer.[143]

When the Economic Policy Committee met on 1 July, neither Cripps nor his colleagues, Morrison excepted, were ready to plump for the devaluation option. Cripps, according to the minutes, 'did not consider that sterling should be devalued at the present time, since it was impossible to determine to what level it should be devalued and whether that level could be maintained. He might, however, be prepared to contemplate such a step as part of some larger scheme which would guarantee the reserves of the sterling area.'[144] Even Morrison was lukewarm: 'He would not welcome devaluation as a solution, but it was in fact taking place, and it might therefore be better to devalue sterling as a matter of deliberate policy than to be forced to do so by outside pressure.'[145]

As usual it was 'outside pressure' that prevailed. But it took another two months before the Cabinet finally accepted the inevitable on devaluation. In early July they were still furiously engaged on what would these days be called 'displacement activity'. As Hall noted, with a touch of desperation, in his diary on 8 July:

After a long and violent series of arguments, Plowden and I managed to convince the other Treasury officials and those of the Bank what was needed. However Ministers would not take our prescription. They agreed reluctantly to announce import cuts, though not really to make them. And to have talks with the US. But nothing on expenditure, money or exchange rate – no fundamentals in fact. It is a tragedy that SC [Stafford Cripps] should be so ill at this time, it is almost impossible to get anywhere with him and he told P [Plowden] that he felt suspicious of all his advisers and had to read all their stuff to see that they did not slip anything over on him that was flatly against his party beliefs.[146]

Cripps' health, as Lord Plowden recalled, was, by this time, 'failing fast. He was suffering from a serious gastric ailment which made it difficult for him to sleep or eat. Moreover, the strain of the last few months, added to his insatiable appetite for work, meant that he was close to the end of his tether. He had made arrangements to enter a sanatorium in Switzerland on 19th July.'[147]

Two days before Cripps left, Douglas Jay, Cripps' junior and one of three ministers Attlee asked to take over economic policy in Cripps' absence (the other two were Gaitskell, the Minister of Fuel, and Wilson, President of the Board of Trade), finally became convinced of the need to devalue while 'meditating on the whole horrid situation on my usual Sunday walk round Hampstead Heath . . . Next morning I called on Gaitskell alone in his Ministry of Fuel and Power office in Smith Square and told him what I thought. He replied he had reached the same conclusion on the day before for exactly the same reasons [the need to halt the dollar drain and to make exports more competitive], and we decided there and then to talk with Wilson *à trois* on the Thursday. Before this there was just time for me to see Cripps before he left for Switzerland and tell him I favoured devaluation. "What, unilaterally?' he said, and left it at that.'[148]

Wilson vacillated to the fury of Jay, Gaitskell and Hall (the Gaitskellites were to regard Wilson as devious for evermore).[149] At last Attlee asserted his authority. 'At this morning's Cabinet', wrote Hall on 29 July, 'which Oliver [Franks] attended, the PM said he would do whatever was needed during the holidays as it would look bad to summon Ministers. So he got carte blanche – this is the best thing he has done yet that I have seen.'[150]

Attlee instructed Jay and Gaitskell to draft a letter to Cripps which Wilson would deliver to the sanatorium in Zurich on the way to his own holiday in the South of France. They took it to Chequers on 5 August on a perfect day (the devaluation summer was a scorcher) and Attlee signed it. 'I have been considering further', the P.M. told the Chancellor,

> . . . the question of devaluation. All of us are now agreed, including the responsible officials, that this is a necessary step (though not of course the only step) if we are to stop the present dollar drain before our reserves fall to a level so dangerous as to impair the Government's ability to handle the situation.
>
> Although the weekly dollar drain since you left London has not exceeded expectations, we have all been strengthened in this conviction by three main considerations:
>
> 1. The ever-accumulating evidence that universal expectation of devaluation is holding back purchases of British exports day by day and discouraging the holding of sterling all over the world. 2. The now evident fact that the United States and Canada are not likely to take short-term action which will materially affect the dollar drain in the next few weeks. 3. The clearly emerging probability, confirmed by Sir Oliver Franks, that substantial help by the Americans is not likely to be forthcoming as a result of

the talks in Washington in September sufficiently early to prevent the
reserves falling to a dangerously low level.[151]

Cripps, reluctantly, concurred. At a specially summoned devaluation
Cabinet on 29 August, for which he had returned from Switzerland, he took
the view 'that it was impossible to show arithmetically that devaluation would
prove an advantageous step to take, and it was doubtful whether any considerable benefits would accrue by way of increased dollar receipts. An atmosphere
had, however, been created in this country, in the United States and in other
countries in which the pound could not reach stability without devaluation. If
there was a reasonable prospect that stability could be secured by this means,
and if assurances could be obtained from the United States Government that
they would not take measures that would defeat the purpose of devaluation,
then he believed devaluation would on balance be of advantage to this
country.'[152]

The Cabinet 'agreed in principle that the pound might be devalued if satisfactory understanding on consequential United States policy could be reached
[and] authorised the Foreign Secretary and the Chancellor of the Exchequer to
inform the Governments of the United States and Canada accordingly in the
Washington talks and to discuss with them the extent to which the pound
should be devalued.'[153]

Hence the Cripps-Bevin trip to Washington which produced the memorable
exchange with Snyder. Amazingly the news of devaluation did not leak in the
nearly three weeks which elapsed between the Cabinet's decision and the
announcement, though the British Embassy in Washington was shaken when
the Bank of Brazil informed *them* on 12 September that 'they heard that we
were going to devalue to $2,80 on 18 September'.[154] The Brazilians were spot on.

Notice how special the 'special relationship' was in 1949. The Americans
and the Canadians were on the inside track. The idea of informing or consulting our European partners in the OEEC wasn't even considered. As Henry
Pelling, historian of Britain and the Marshall Plan, put it: 'The operation had
been conducted with an effective degree of secrecy, but inevitably it left the
British Government open to criticism from its OEEC [the Organisation for
European Economic Co-operation] partners, particularly the French, for the
precipitate nature of the decision. The French Prime Minister, Henri Queille,
complained to the American Ambassador in Paris of what he called a "complete
lack of loyalty" by the British to the continental countries. Acheson received a
personal note from an American official in Europe [David Bruce] saying that
"the way in which the devaluation of sterling was handled constituted a severe
setback to the cause of European co-operation".'[155]

The Cabinet had, in effect, given Bevin and Cripps *carte blanche* to negotiate
the new sterling-dollar rate with the Americans and they set off on the *Mauretania* (Bevin's heart trouble precluded him from flying) for the USA. Cripps
may also have been in failing health but the first thing he did on boarding was

to pace the decks calculating how many circumnavigations of the liner would be required for him to complete his daily three-mile run. His private secretary, William Armstrong, was not obliged to don his own plimsolls but Cripps insisted he accompany him in the *Mauretania*'s pool even when the Atlantic swell reduced it to a succession of tidal waves![156]

Cripps and Bevin reached Washington on 7 September. Next day they began talks. What they wanted from the Americans was more Marshall Aid, a loan from the Export-Import Bank, a tap on British drawing rights at the IMF and a reduction in US tariffs to stimulate UK exports.[157] Once Bevin's outburst had cleared the air, officials were asked to leave the room. 'When the door was shut', Acheson recalled, 'we were told of the forthcoming devaluation and pledged to secrecy, except that we Americans insisted, and the others agreed, that the President must also be told.'[158]

With the Canadians acting as a kind of midwife, the Washington talks by and large yielded what the British wanted – lower US tariffs, simpler customs procedures, more US investment abroad and more American dollars for the purchase of Canadian wheat under the terms of Marshall Aid.[159] It only remained for the British delegation to fix the rate. (They had a wonderfully horticultural code invented by William Armstrong for communicating their decisions to London; the 'London Rose Show', Armstrong called it – 'cabbage' equalled gold and 'orange' meant $2.80.[160])

There then took place on the evening of 12 September a richly ludicrous yet highly serious meeting in Bevin's room in the vast Lutyens mansion which houses the British Ambassador on Massachusetts Avenue in the fashionable north-west area of Washington. Lord Plowden recalled it for me when the devaluation files were declassified:

> Ernie was in his dressing gown. He hadn't been well. He was taking pills for his heart . . . The time came when we had to settle the rate. We had two alternatives, $3.00 and $2.80. We had assembled in Ernie's sitting room at the Embassy – myself, Robert Hall and Oliver Franks.
> Ernie's roots were in a time when bread was the staff of life. Ernie said what would $2.80 do to the price of a loaf? I said it would raise it from 4½d to 5½d (old pence). Ernie said, 'That's all right.' If he had said $3.00 it would have been $3.00.[161]

Bevin was obsessed with food, bread especially, partly because of his genuine sense of working class needs and also because, as we have seen, he didn't like the austerity 'British Loaf'. It made him belch.[162] As William Armstrong (present at the same meeting with Cripps) put it, 'He believed almost that the Government would stand or fall by whether the British working man got his jam butties and what he had to pay for them.'

This led to an absurd confrontation – a pre-echo of the health debate which later grew with affluence in Britain – between that prototypical eco-freak,

Stafford Cripps, and tribune of the people, Ernie Bevin. 'He suddenly said',
Armstrong remembered,

> he felt the British working man would accept an increase in the price of
> bread if he could have a whiter loaf. We had this national flour and . . . it
> was a sort of dirty brown colour and he reckoned that if we raised the
> extraction rate and produced a whiter loaf, people would accept that they
> had to pay more for that.
>
> He got into a terrible argument with Stafford about all this because Staf-
> ford was prepared to agree that the price of bread was an important matter
> but he thought Ernie's gimmick for getting over it was absolutely dreadful
> because he didn't believe in white bread, he believed in brown bread, being
> a bit of a food fad. And the idea of selling the British public an inferior
> product that would do them harm, and, at the same time, charging them
> more for it he regarded as little short of immoral.[163]

Five days later the Cabinet gathered for a Saturday evening meeting to hear
the terms of the devaluation broadcast the following day, Sunday 18 September. 'There was a Cabinet at once,' Hall recorded in his diary, 'very secret
with the Ministers coming in at the old Treasury door in Whitehall and going
to No 10 through the tunnel. The main changes were bread to be 5½d instead
of 6d and the family allowance scheme dropped.'[164]

Cripps summoned Churchill to No. 11 Downing Street and told him of the
intention to devalue shortly before the broadcast. The old man, William Armstrong recalled, broke down and wept, saying to Cripps: 'I just hope to God
that if I had been in the position you are in I would have been strong enough
to do what you have done.'[165] Later, after Churchill had accused Cripps of
misleading Britain's allies by his change of stance on devaluation, he refused
to talk to him and would not even receive an honorary degree from him as
Chancellor of Bristol University[166] (Cripps sat for Bristol South-East, the seat
which Tony Benn was to inherit from him).

When Cripps addressed the nation that late summer Sunday, he told his
listeners that devaluation had been chosen as the alternative to 'heavy
unemployment' and 'the drastic cutting down of the social services . . . It
gives us a convincing hope that with our own efforts, thus made effective, we
shall finally emerge out of our postwar difficulties.'[167] But the end of those
'difficulties' would depend only partly on exchange rate policy. In the long
term what really mattered to the postwar British economy was another factor
which was the subject of Crippsian eloquence on Devaluation Sunday –
productivity.

'We must', said Cripps, 'at all costs avoid anything that increases costs of
production. Indeed, we must continue with as much or even more vigour than
ever, the drive for greater efficiency and lower costs of production. This
change is not instead of all the policies we have already been following to earn

more dollars, but in addition to them, because they of themselves have not been enough.'[168]

Cripps, as we have seen, was a productivity man, something of a prototypical supply-sider in his convictions about the need for R and D training and management science. Productivity was given a prominent place in the first of the Labour Government's *Economic Surveys* in 1947. By 1949 it had become its centrepiece. In 1946 Cripps had launched his Production Campaign from the Board of Trade which 'ranged from general media advertising, high-level conferences [to] factory-distributed notices and newspapers'.[169] In 1947 the Government appointed Sir Henry Tizard to chair a high-powered committee on industrial productivity. As Chancellor of the Exchequer Cripps was an enthusiastic backer of the Anglo-American Council on Productivity, efficiency teams, consisting of both sides of industry, set up at the suggestion of Paul Hoffman, the former President of Studebaker and now running the ECA, the Marshall Plan body, in Paris.

Teams were despatched to America. Forty-seven reports were produced. One of the first groups to go dealt with the steel industry. Both sides of the industry were impressed by the lack of confrontation on the shopfloor and the degree of consultation with the labour force. 'There was', recalled Douglas Aston, a British employer who sailed with the steelmen in the *Queen Mary*, 'never any . . . resistance to the introduction of machinery to save manpower and to save effort. In America the application of power in its widest sense, that is to relieve the drudgery, or to speed the job, was universally accepted . . . I walked through one of the plants to be confronted by a huge placard on the notice-board, issued by a trade union, the CIO [Congress of Industrial Organisations] and this said, "The greatest crime a company can commit against the employees is failure to make a profit." '[170]

It was Mr Aston's steel foundry team which was summoned to brief Cripps on their return from America – the meeting which so outraged its trade union members when the Chancellor said people should get a medal rather than more pay if productivity went up and greater profits resulted. When each team returned its report was circulated widely through industry. Yet, as the historian of the postwar productivity drive, Jim Tomlinson, put it, 'overall it would seem the Government's attempt to use the AACP to engage the enthusiasm of employers and unions for the productivity drive failed. There is little evidence the AACP reports had much impact except upon the already converted.'[171]

What of the Development Councils, tripartite bodies set up as a purely British initiative? Apart from the Cotton Development Council, where it rested on a previous consensus built up around the old wartime Cotton Board and the knowledge that only Government assistance could save the industry, they, too, had little impact. The Joint Production Councils, another wartime offshoot, were only slightly more effective.

Why? Because employers very largely did not care for the Government's democratic socialist ideology and preferred to operate through their trade associations rather than through joint bodies foisted upon them by Whitehall or Marshall Plan administrators. On the trade union side, the benefits of a handful of full employment years had yet to soften tough attitudes – and the restrictive practices that went with them – after decades of recession and unemployment. The AACP report on the cotton industry captured this very well when it concluded: 'Because memories still remain of the dark days of unemployment, short time, the Means Test and hundreds of other vestiges of the past, trade unionism in Britain is falling short of the responsibility for the future that has been placed before it.'[172]

There is, I think, another reason which stands out vividly when you compare postwar Britain with postwar France. One had a mechanism for converting an economic plan into a productivity drive, the other did not. Monnet's Commissariat du Plan made a big difference to the long-term economic regeneration of France – to the cutting of coal and the milling of steel – whereas Plowden's Central Economic Planning Staff was, at best, marginal.

Even allowing for the genuine modesty of Lord Plowden, his reluctance to take the job of Chief Planning Officer in the first place, his determination that it should be nothing more than a small, advisory co-ordinating body, the uselessness of the liaison officer system with other Whitehall departments and the failure of the tripartite Economic Planning Board all add up to something very far short of the body the bustling Monnet was building on the other side of the Channel.[173]

The Economic Planning Board was an example of British machinery-of-government ad hocery at its worst. Nobody – not Government, industry, trade unions or Whitehall – ever really knew what it was *for*. Two extracts from Robert Hall's diaries for 1947 tell us really all we need to know:

Thursday, September 4th

Planning Board. The TUC members were away at the annual conference and we had quite a pleasant time discussing methods of *cutting* investment [italics added] – the FBI [Federation of British Industry] members want industry to do their own but it is hard to see how this would work. However even an exhortation might help.

Thursday, September 18th

Planning Board took the current review [of the economy prepared for them by Hall himself]. A useless discussion but they broadly accepted the conclusions and Plowden persuaded them to ask for draft recommendations to the Government on the additional measures needed. Afterwards I saw Plowden and said that I thought we ought not to be discussing the failings of the Government with outsiders unless we had *first* told Ministers. The Planning Board was really a new constitutional development and quite contrary to all Civil Service practice: however it seemed that Ministers had intended this.[174]

Plowden himself admitted in his memoirs that 'the Economic Planning Board never became much more than an adjunct to the policy-making process. In its early days the EPB was a support to ministers in getting difficult and unpopular policies accepted. From the beginning ministers never came to meetings and later showed little interest in it. These meetings, in turn, became less frequent and more sparsely attended.'[175]

Contrast this desultory performance with the French Modernization and Investment Plan and the Planning Council, with the French Premier taking the chair, presiding over top businessmen, trade union leaders and bureaucrats.[176] Like the CEPS, Monnet's Commisariat in the Rue de Martignac was small in number but, unlike Plowden's people, they set out to make up for the locust years of the interwar period, the destruction of the war and to put France in the vanguard of the advanced technological nations by concentrating on a clutch of industries which would provide a platform for take-off – energy, transport, steel, cement and agricultural machinery. 'Satisfying the chronic needs for housing, consumer goods and a more radical plan for improving agricultural efficiency were postponed.'[177]

Far from cutting investment, Monnet strove to protect his long-term plans from short-term crisis, utilising every scrap of dollar credit he could lay his hands on from the postwar loan he and Léon Blum negotiated with the Americans in May 1946 to France's tranche of Marshall Aid. Despite deep political instability with a rapid change of governments in the Fourth French Republic (Britain's was, by contrast, a highly stable system), successive administrations stuck to their investment targets, preferring to devalue rather than to cut.[178] If there is one single reason why the road, rail and social infrastructure of France in the 1990s compares so favourably with British conditions, it is this, the 'thirty glorious years', as Faurastic called them, of sustained investment between 1945 and 1975.[179]

Another factor of considerable importance seeped up between the lines in Robert Hall's diary. The British Civil Service was not in the business of modernising our economy. Steering it through fiscal means they knew all about, but wrenching it to new levels of performance left them both uneasy and ignorant of the techniques for so doing. This need not have been the case.

During the war the Civil Service had recruited talent heavily from outside, with an emphasis on men and women with practical skills rather than all-round administrative ability, and had run a highly effective (and thoroughly interventionist) Home Front as a result. Early in 1946, Bridges, in his capacity as Head of the Civil Service, summoned his fellow Permanent Secretaries to a meeting in the Treasury to consider whether the skills and lessons learned during the Second World War had an institutionalised place in the peace. In a memo circulated in advance, his thoughts turned to what had happened in the Great War and its aftermath:

Speaking for myself, I have been disposed to think of the change-over from war to peace, as it affects the Civil Service, largely in terms of what happened at the end of the last war. In that war, too, large numbers of business men, industrialists and others came into the Civil Service, and at the end of it, when the war problems came to an end, they packed up and went back to their businesses.

It is true that in this war we have made far better use of the industrialists and others who have come to our assistance, and we have greatly regretted the loss of their help when the time came for them to go. But have others – like myself – been working on the general expectation that Civil Service problems would in a year or so resume more or less the same general pattern which they took before the war?

That may or may not have been a reasonable working hypothesis a year or so ago (i.e. before the formation of the Labour Government). But is it not clear that the Government's legislative programme will more and more confront the Civil Service with problems which require a far closer degree of contact with industry than ever before, and that this will have important consequences on the experience and type of qualities which will be required in many sections of many Departments?[180]

Apart from Sir Oliver Franks, still the young Permanent Secretary at the Ministry of Supply, nobody in Bridges' room on 2 March 1946 spoke up in favour of a new-style Civil Service. They were determined to return to business-as-usual.[181] They were utterly wrong. The country, the scope and requirements of Government had changed for ever. They simply refused to face up to it – a classic illustration of the myopia that can befall a largely self-regulating profession.

Attlee and his ministers were equally culpable. With the possible exception of Cripps, they simply failed to make a link between the demands of their kind of state and the refashioned Whitehall needed to help run it. As a result, until Mrs Thatcher's management reforms in the 1980s, the country was stuck with a Civil Service devoted to a combination of policy advice and what Tony Benn, in his early days as a minister, called 'care and maintenance'.[182] It had its virtues (it was clean, decent, honest and honourable), but it wasn't a 'can do' organisation like its French equivalent, highly trained and motivated thanks to the *grandes écoles*, especially the new postwar one, custom-built for the purpose, the *Ecole Nationale D'Administration*.

This again was part of a wider failure to construct the apparatus needed to underpin a modern, Keynesian-Beveridgite mixed economy-welfare state, of the kind David Marquand calls in his *The Unprincipled Society* a 'developmental state',[183] part of that phenomenon of running the *existing* state and industrial machine flat out to rebuild exports to 1938 levels and to win the supreme prize – full employment.

As Martin Chick has put it, 'In allocating resources, priority was given to high and immediate export earners such as motor vehicles, textiles, engineering and chemicals, and also to such basic industries as iron and steel, especially those where supply bottlenecks were appearing. This pattern of allocation was given added emphasis during 1947 by the fuel and balance of payments crises.'[184]

Herein lies the crucial difference with France and the Monnet approach: 'Investment resources as allocated by [the UK] government overwhelmingly flowed towards production rather than infrastructure or long-term reconstruction. One of the few instances in the private sector of resources being allocated to a long-term investment project was the backing given to the expansion of domestic oil-refining capacity.'[185]

Contrast this with Monnet in 1946: 'I proposed that the [Planning] Council include in the Plan the targets which we believed could be attained if conditions were right: to get back to our 1938 production level by 1948, and to the 1929 level, 25% higher, by 1949; then, in 1950, to improve on the 1929 level by a further 25%. To this end, the Council approved the target which the Coalmines Commission had set itself: 65m. metric tons by 1950, plus guaranteed deliveries of German coal. Hydro-electricity output was to be doubled. Steel production was to reach 12m. metric tons. 50,000 tractors were to be produced annually in the next five years.'[186]

Monnet's motivating idea, for which he found a willing father in France's first postwar premier, Charles de Gaulle, was that his country faced a triple task – to repair the damage of war, to overcome the decades of decline which preceded it *and* to put France on the path to sustained, long-term, technology- and productivity-driven economic growth. In other words, an economic miracle which would start with 'a long campaign of explanation [which] would be needed before the country could be persuaded to invest in essential capital goods rather than squander its resources on immediate satisfactions'.[187]

Monnet looked at what the Attlee Government was doing before deciding to steer France on another course: 'We had studied the operation of Cripps's "working parties", which brought together industrialists, trade unionists and technical experts; but this democratic attempt to steer the economy seemed to us seriously handicapped by the absence of civil servants representing the public interest, *as well as by its lack of general objectives* [emphasis added]. Improving on this precedent, we quickly hit upon what seemed the right formula, that of our "Modernization Commissions".'[188]

In so far as Labour had a long-term re-equipment and modernisation strategy it was nationalisation of the 'commanding heights', a notion on which, as we have seen, several key ministers had cooled by as early as 1948. As to thinking about the residual private sector, especially its crucial medium-sized firm segment, beyond vague thoughts about voluntary co-operation associated with the development councils, the issue only surfaced in the twilight years of the Attlee Government when ministers debated how much permanent control to legislate for when the Supplies and Services Act expired in 1951. Harold Wilson managed to face both ways, engaging in his famous 'bonfire of controls' (so called because he announced them on 5 November 1948) while arguing for 'certain basic controls essential to the maintenance of full employment, to the proper location of industry, to the maintenance of our economy on an even keel'.

Such controls, he told the House of Commons during the devaluation debate on 28 September 1949, 'will remain a permanent instrument of our national policy . . . What we want to get rid of as quickly as possible . . . are those controls which are a hang-over from the wartime administration, which restrict the handling or sale or manufacture of goods to specified firms engaged in their manufacture at some date in the past . . . limiting competition between those firms and preventing the entry of often enterprising, progressive, efficient firms from outside.'[189]

To be fair to Attlee's economic ministers, they were the first to introduce legislation on competition policy with the Restrictive Practices Act of 1948, though this was weaker in its provisions than even the Coalition Government had envisaged in its planning for the postwar. A Monopolies and Mergers Commission was set up but, 'where Labour intervened it was a matter of persuasion, jollying along and patriotic exhortations,' according to Dr Helen Mercer.[190] Ministers were reluctant to tackle head-on those companies and trade associations deemed critical to the export drive.

It's not surprising, therefore, that the Attlee Government declined to launch any assault on the restrictive practices of that other great institutionalised player in the British economy – the trade unions. In fact, as we have seen, an early statute restored those privileges they had lost after the General Strike. Cripps' strategy was to tackle the consequences of trade union power at the output not the input end by curbing the high wage settlements which such power tended to produce. Here, in the first of a long line of postwar incomes policies, he met with considerable success.

It's a measure of the never-to-be-repeated unity of the labour movement in the late 1940s that Cripps' White Paper, the *Statement on Personal Incomes, Costs and Prices*, published in February 1948,[191] should the following month have received the overwhelming support of the TUC at a special delegate conference in the Central Hall, Westminster, on 24 March (the voting was 5,421,000 to 2,032,000[192]) because the unions were, in effect, accepting a wage freeze for the foreseeable future.

'In present conditions', the White Paper declared, 'and until more goods and services are available for the home market, there is no justification for any *general* increase of individual money incomes. Such an increase will merely raise costs of production, without making more goods available, and so can only have an inflationary effect.'

For a time, until the Korean War blew every economic calculation out of the Treasury's adding machines, it worked. The first incomes policy did mitigate the consequences of the still novel full employment policy, the jewel in Labour's crown. Within a year the rate of wage increases almost halved as the

Minister of Labour, Isaacs, reported to the Cabinet on 15 February 1949.[193] Cripps did equally well in persuading over 90 per cent of private firms to restrain dividends which helped the Government's allies in the TUC to hold the line for the policy throughout 1949.[194]

As Ken Morgan put it: 'On balance, it was a remarkable exercise in industrial consensus. Cripps won support not only from right-wing union bosses such as [Arthur] Deakin, but even from Aneurin Bevan in the Cabinet. The latter regarded a wages policy as an intrinsic part of a socialist economic strategy, and was prepared to take tough action in suppressing unofficial strike leaders who were endangering a Labour Government, which provided a beacon of hope to the civilised world.'[195]

Such a view received surprising (and secret) endorsement at the time from a group of people not normally disposed to regard socialist governments as 'beacons of hope' to any part of the world. In June 1949, the Central Intelligence Agency, as part of its periodic 'Review of the World Situation' for the President, produced an accurate and prescient account for Truman of both the importance of the UK to the US as its 'most powerful and important ally'[196] in the struggle to contain Soviet power, *and* the 'major element of uncertainty' in that relationship. The CIA questioned

> the capacity of the UK to maintain the economic strength required to support, not only the commitments it has in its own policy account, but the position it occupies in the overall pattern of US security. The relative weakness of the UK at the end of the war, instead of being merely a condition caused by the war and corrected by the recovery of 1947–48, may be the result of long-term trends that were only momentarily halted. If so, the weakness which, at the start of 1947 made Greece and Turkey a US responsibility, may develop progressively and call for progressively major adjustments on the part of the US.[197]

The CIA's analysts, accurately enough as it turned out, reckoned Britain was 'approaching the end of the first phase of its postwar history', a phase which they portrayed to the President in remarkably sympathetic terms.

> This phase can be described in retrospect as a period of reorganising the national economy in relation to the concept of a welfare state and the national potential in relation to profound changes in the international sphere. The adjustments called for were essentially political and economic.
>
> A large measure of democratic socialism has quietly revolutionised the national life of Great Britain. The Commonwealth and the Empire have undergone major political alterations of a realistic kind without any suggestion of collapse. The national economy has, with tremendous effort, been momentarily adapted to the demands of a welfare state. The speed and success of these adjustments have been an undeniable factor in the develop-

ment of the more favourable security position in which the US now stands.[198]

Truman's secret advisers believed, however, that by the summer of 1949 'the peak' of British economic success, on which its other roles and its international value to America depended, may have been reached. In terms of the UK's share of world trade 'the signs are as follows':

a Overseas markets are being increasingly satisfied by restored domestic industries and by competitors.

b Japanese industry, revived to reduce US occupation costs, implies future serious competition.

c German industry, similarly revived, but with its prewar outlets in Eastern Europe still blocked, implies an even severer competition.

d Demand in the US has perceptibly receded and there is no early evidence of its revival.[199]

They were, in the long term, absolutely right about a to c. It was d, as we have seen, that tipped sterling into devaluation three months after Truman received this assessment. But the 1949 recession did not develop into the protracted postwar slump so many still feared on both sides of the Atlantic. Far from it.

'The moment', the CIA concluded, 'at which the first postwar phase will give place to the second cannot be specified, but it is believed close at hand. Curves of production, exports, and national income are already losing their upward trend. When they flatten out, the UK will be in the second phase. Whether or not they turn downwards depends mainly upon developments over which the UK can exercise no control and very little influence.'[200] And so, in 1950–1, it was to prove as the first era of British postwar history came to an end amid the shot and shell of the Korean War, economic crisis and its associated political change at home.

CHAPTER 10

Shot and Shell

The result of the meeting? Oh, we're carrying on. That's all.
**Clement Attlee, Outside No. 10 Downing Street, 24 February 1950,
after Labour's majority had been reduced to five.**[1]

I believe that the shock to our export drive was such that we lost much of the
momentum which we'd been able to gain in 1948–49 . . . And, in a sense, we
never recovered that momentum.
**Lord Croham on the economic consequences of the Korean War,
1990**[2]

If the question is, 'did it [the Korean rearmament] harm Britain economically?' the answer is 'yes'. But the question that has to be answered is,
'how far was the perceived threat on a world scale there?' and, therefore,
'harmful or not, was what we did necessary?'
Lord Franks, 1990[3]

We thought the British interest in Iran had to be saved and we thought the
British Government, led by the Anglo-Iranian Oil Company, was behaving
with crass stupidity and that the British really had to be saved from themselves.
Paul Nitze, on the Mossadegh Crisis of 1951–3, in 1990[4]

You have always got certain quite genuine left wingers and you have always
got a number of queer birds. Sometimes you can use them, like Aneurin
Bevan, and sometimes you can't.
Clement Attlee, 1967[5]

I therefore say, with the full solemnity of the seriousness of what I am
saying, that the £4,700 million arms programme is already dead. It cannot
be achieved without irreparable damage to the economy of Great Britain and
the world.
Aneurin Bevan, Resignation speech, 22 April 1951[6]

It's no good. We cannot do it: the Durham Miners won't wear it.
**Herbert Morrison on hearing of the Schuman Plan for a European
Coal and Steel Community, 1 June 1950**[7]

In the first days of the new decade, George Orwell died, alone in University
College Hospital in Bloomsbury. On the night of 21 January his lung hae-
morrhaged and he was gone at only forty-six. His *1984* gloom about the totalitarian future that might await his England was belied by events. How we
needed him to do a *Lion and the Unicorn* for us, not just in 1950, but in 1960,
1970 and 1980 too. I have a feeling he would have regarded the Eden of Suez
with contempt, loathed the affluent society of Macmillan, despised the shallow-
ness of Wilson. But who knows?

Just how much he would have disliked 'modern Britain' preoccupied me in
May 1990, just over forty years after his death, when I stood by his grave in the
'heart' of the English countryside. To the surprise of his friends, he had asked
to be buried 'according to the rites of the Church of England'.[8] His friend and
patron, the editor/proprietor of the *Observer*, David Astor, secured a plot for
him in the graveyard of All Saints, Sutton Courtenay near his family estate in
what would then have been a very rural part of Berkshire. It was very much a
last-minute affair. Malcolm Muggeridge thought meeting his wish would be
impossible. Astor, though not himself a Christian, asked for twenty-four hours
and persuaded the young vicar of All Saints, 'an admirer of Orwell's', to oblige.[9]

Having recently completed a written fiftieth anniversary tribute to his *The
Lion and the Unicorn*,[10] I stopped by, that fine May morning on my way to
Oxford. 'The stone', I recorded in my diary, 'was just what he'd asked for in
his Will – plain, brown . . . with the inscription "Eric Arthur Blair, 1903–
1950". It was an exquisitely English setting – old stone church, graveyard
surrounded by trees in full spring leaf. If the trees had been bare, the huge
cooling towers of Didcot Power Station a mile or so to the south would have
overshadowed the scene (as it was the muck from the chimneys passed directly
overhead).

'A couple of miles to the north is Culham and the Joint European Torus
complete, I noticed, with its own "European School". In a sense it illustrated
to perfection Orwell's thesis in *The Lion and the Unicorn* that everything and
nothing changes in England.'[11] I could have thrown in two more intrusive
artefacts of the post-Orwell countryside on the Oxfordshire-Berkshire border
close by that beautiful churchyard (where Asquith is also buried) – the sound
of the motorway-style A34 to the west and, overhead, Boeing 747s climbing out
of Heathrow along the line of the Thames Valley on the way to North America.
In such a fashion can four decades of progress be measured in postwar Britain.

How much of it was foreseeable as Orwell was lowered into the ground that
day in January 1950? Surprisingly, most of it. Roads like the modern A34
already existed in Germany with its autobahns and had for fifteen years. The de
Havilland Comet had already flown 50 miles along the chalk downs in Hatfield.

Everybody in Bevin's England knew the economic importance of both coal and electric power. As for atomic energy, wasn't it going to solve a whole swathe of problems? As Tony Benn, once a believer now a dissenter, put it in 1990: 'After the war we all thought let's use this extraordinary power for peace – swords into ploughshares and all that. We were wrong. It was neither safe, nor cheap, nor peaceful.'[12]

Symbolic though Orwell's death was, it's erroneous to categorise periods according to crude calendrical considerations. In terms of natural breaks in the postwar period, in domestic terms it was the end of rationing, the spurt of housebuilding and the rise of affluence and consumerism in 1953–4 which was far more of a genuine divide than the Forties slipping into the Fifties. In defence and foreign policy terms it was the Suez crisis rather than any of the spate of defence reviews between 1949 and 1954 which marked the true turning-point in attitudes and aspirations.

Yet, politically, the rim of the decades was important. Even while ministers were grappling with the devaluation of sterling, their thoughts were on the timing of the election. On 18 August Gaitskell minuted Attlee with the suggestion he should go to the country either in November 1949 or June 1950 and that anything in between would be 'most unwise'.[13] On 7 December Attlee summoned his senior Ministers to No. 10 to reach a decision. Bevin, now a seriously ailing man, sent a message from Eastbourne saying he would leave the date to his colleagues as he was 'no politician',[14] a fiction he maintained to his dying day (he was no Parliamentarian, which is not the same thing). Cripps seems to have swung the meeting by adamantly refusing to introduce another budget before the nation voted.

Ever after, Douglas Jay maintained it was Cripps' fault that Labour went too soon in 1950, that if they had gone in May, when the weather was better and the beneficial effects of devaluation would have had time to work through the economy, they would have got back with an adequate majority and have become the natural governing party in Britain as the terms of trade became steadily better as the 1950s progressed. But, on matters of morality, like *not* bribing the electorate with a pre-election budget, Cripps would only commune with his spiritual Maker, not his political colleagues.[15] Who knows. This is counter-factual history with a vengeance. Gladstone apart, there has never been a Chancellor of the Exchequer like Cripps. Certainly none of his successors would turn to the Almighty as the arbiter of their party's electoral fortunes.

The outcome of the process begun in the Cabinet Room that December morning did, however, mark the beginning of the end of an era even though Labour was to stagger on in Government for almost another two years. On 10 January Attlee called the election for 23 February, the first winter contest since 1910 with, by modern standards, an extraordinarily long run-up to polling day.

It was a lack-lustre campaign. Vi Attlee drove her husband, with her usual behind-the-wheel mania (legend has it the Special Branch car was regularly left in the dust of the Attlee's old Humber) some 1,300 miles as, in that pre-television era, he sold the contents of Labour's manifesto, *Let Us Win Through Together*, at traditional meetings (often seven or eight a day) in town, village and city. I have a photo of him electioneering in Hoe Street, Walthamstow, a few hundred yards from where this volume is being written, Homburg on his head, shaking the hand of a Gas Board worker in a hole just across the road from the Snooker Hall (which still survives).

Labour's 'shopping list' for the next tranche of nationalisations illustrated perfectly its running out of steam on public ownership – sugar, cement and industrial assurance. It had effectively exhausted its collective impulses in the still incomplete attempt to bring the country's steel mills within the parameters of the state. All the manifesto did was to stimulate a quite brilliant political advertising campaign by Tate and Lyle which placed a 'Mr Cube' drawing on every packet warning of the perils of nationalisation. 'Mr Cube' thus brought political argument to every breakfast table in the land. He was almost certainly my first encounter with politics.

The only really constructive feature of the official Conservative campaign was Churchill's call, during a speech in Edinburgh on 14 February for 'another talk with Soviet Russia upon the highest level. The idea appeals to me of a supreme effort to bridge the gulf between the two worlds . . . It is not easy to see how things could be worsened by a parley at the summit, if such a thing were possible.'[16] It was the first time the phrase 'the summit' had been used and a new concept entered the language of diplomacy (such gatherings had, of course, been occurring since time immemorial as had 'working dinners' and even 'working funerals').

The Conservative manifesto, *This is the Road*, *was* of long-term significance, however, because it endorsed implicitly the Attleean settlement, that famed 'postwar consensus' about which there was to be so much politico-theological argument thirty years later.[17] As that supreme connoisseur of general elections, David Butler, put it: 'Although the document promised to stop and, if possible, reverse the process of nationalisation and to end socialist waste and bureaucracy, it did completely accept the newly enacted welfare state legislation and promised to maintain full employment.'[18] The Keynesian and Beveridgite essentials would be intact whatever the outcome.

During the campaign Attlee came as close as he ever did to defining what makes democratic socialism distinctive and meritorious. Characteristically, he did it by default. 'Communism', he told a meeting in Sheffield, 'denies the dignity of the individual, Conservatism ranges the individual in classes.' As usual, he pitched his appeal towards the higher morality (there never was a more ethical premier) telling a meeting in Falkirk: 'I get rather tired when I hear that you must only appeal to the incentives of profit. What got us through [the war] was unselfishness and an appeal to the higher instincts of mankind. What is getting us through in these difficult days is a far greater sense of responsibility due to the fact that men and women feel they have a far greater stake in the country than they ever had before.'[19]

Electoral arithmetic worked against both Attleean morality and his Government's record. 'Because of the redrawing of boundaries, Labour was bound to lose seats (nineteen of the sixty-two constituencies in the heavily Labour London County Council area disappeared altogether).'[20] Limehouse was among them and Attlee moved the few miles north to Walthamstow.[21] In later life Attlee said, when asked about the slump in Labour's majority, 'in view of the change of boundaries, which seemed very heavy against us, I wasn't too surprised'.[22]

There was a huge turnout (at 84 per cent a postwar record) which tends to favour Labour. The party increased its vote by over 1.25 million but lost ground in the south of England. Most Labour ministers thought they would make it back with a reasonable working majority.[23] The margin of five was a surprise. An early example of Galbraith's Law that centre left parties do themselves out of a job by making more and more people secure, comfortable and, therefore, conservative?[24] Though, interestingly enough, Kenneth Younger, MP for Grimsby and a rising star in the Government, wrote in his diary an intriguing and plausible reflection which rather works against the Galbraith line: 'We have done badly in the prosperous Home Counties and suburban seats. That was partly expected. Those are the areas that never really knew the slump, and consequently they resent the minor annoyances of the last few years and cannot compare them, as the north can, with serious hardships before the war.'[25]

More widely, the electoral shift was the natural reaction to a decade of rationing and constant exhortation towards personal sacrifice for the greater cause of the common good, plus the effect of going to the polls in February rather than in the spring and the unavoidable impact of the redistribution of seats reflecting the flight of populations out of the big cities (another Labour policy, ironically). Attlee always maintained that honour required him to accept the recommendations of the Boundary Commissioners. ('It was the responsible thing to do at the time; and if you do the right thing at the right time you may have to pay a price for it later.'[26]) *At* the time a majority of five seemed precariously slender. Forty years later, to Attlee's successor-but-five as Labour Party Leader, it seemed anything but after his office-starved 1980s experience. 'If I'd have been Clem,' he told me, 'I'd have carried on to get a crack at the 1950s.'[27]

The four-month period between the election and the outbreak of the Korean War has, looking back, a curious limbo feel about it as if the Labour Government was living, not just in reduced political circumstances, but in the rain-shadow of a great and menacing international event. This, however, is erroneous. The starting of hostilities in the Far East was entirely unexpected even though the consequences of China falling to the Communists in September 1949 were still being absorbed (the British Government recognised Mao in

January, deciding to do so in December in the knowledge that this would place them at odds with the Truman Administration; Bevin told Acheson, 'We feel that the only counter to Russian influence is that Communist China should have contacts with the West . . . ').[28]

That same CIA Assessment for President Truman in June 1949, which showed such prescience about the true economic and political condition of Britain, had this to say about Korea almost exactly one year before the North invaded the South:

> The scheduled start of US troop withdrawals produced so much official apprehension, publicly communicated, that symptoms of mass hysteria appeared. Unless the Republic [of South Korea] assumes an air of confidence – justifiable at least for the short run – hysteria can easily grow into panic. Actually, since the Republic's armed forces are at least the equal in number and superior in equipment to those of North Korea, an immediate test of strength is not likely. Popular panic, stimulated by hysterical government publicity, has recently done more to prepare the ground for the destruction of the Republic than have direct acts of the Communists.[29]

And the spring of 1950 had a considerable international importance quite apart from the latest menacing wrinkle of the cold war. It was the time when Monnet's European vision part one, the Coal and Steel Community, was sprung upon a suspicious and sceptical Cabinet in Whitehall by the French Foreign Minister, Robert Schuman.

Looking back, it's very easy to see the European Coal and Steel Community (ECSC) as *the* dramatic yet self-evident breakthrough which, in the form of its lineal development, the European Economic Community, was to change not just the political economy of western European nations but the geopolitics of the entire world. To be fair to those in 1950 Whitehall and Westminster who were neither captivated nor persuaded by Schuman's initiative, such developments were not merely unforeseeable, they were beyond fantasy. It wasn't obvious until the mid-Fifties that the bolt-from-the-Parisian-blue in May 1950 effectively terminated British leadership of postwar Europe.

Though events moved with extraordinary rapidity in May–June 1950, they take a lot of explaining, not least why a prototype 'Common Market' (the phrase has its origins in the Schuman Plan) for coal and steel had such strategic implications in mid-century Europe. As Monnet, the architect of the Schuman Plan, put it in his memoirs: 'Coal and Steel were at once the key to economic power and the raw materials for forging the weapons of war. This double role gave them immense symbolic significance, now largely forgotten . . . To pool them across frontiers would reduce their malign prestige and turn them instead into a guarantee of peace.'[30]

There were strong French reasons for Monnet to push as hard and as fast as he did for a Franco-German coal and steel pool. His cherished modernisation plan might founder without guaranteed coal supplies from the Ruhr for French steel mills and the occupying powers had failed to agree on the level of production they would allow. As Monnet noted in the diary he kept whilst developing his thoughts on an Alpine walking holiday in March 1950, 'France's continued recovery will come to a halt unless we rapidly solve the problem of German industrial production and its competitive capacity.'[31]

For him, a coal and steel community, however, would be a kind of all-purpose solvent for France's immediate economic problems (to reach an agreement with a still politically trammelled West Germany before its economic growth once more outstripped that of France), those of peace within western Europe (fusion of their war-making industries would guarantee that France and Germany never again endured a rerun of 1914–18 or 1939–45), those of peace between east and west ('other countries', wrote Monnet, 'were treating her [Germany] as the stake in their power games . . . We must not try to solve the German problem in its present context. We must change the context by transforming the basic facts').[32] As an added bonus in Monnet's eyes, a step would be taken towards the ultimate prize of a federal Europe. It was this which caused the alarm bells to clang so furiously in London when civil servants and ministers cast their eyes down the 104 pregnant lines of the plan when it was unveiled to them in May 1950: 'By the pooling of basic production and the establishment of a new High Authority whose decisions will be binding on France, Germany and the countries that join them, this proposal will lay the first concrete foundations of the European Federation which is indispensable to the maintenance of peace.'[33]

For Konrad Adenauer, the elderly Christian Democrat still in the early stages of piecing together a new West German state from the ruins left by Nazism, defeat and occupation, the Schuman Plan was a glittering prize, a godsend. As Walter Hallstein, a close adviser to the old Rhinelander in 1950, put it: 'What was Adenauer's hope when the Schuman Plan came? We were no state any more. We were occupied zones governed by foreign military powers. And here was a chance . . . of establishing a first, rather mighty force which included Germany.' Adenauer, Hallstein added, saw it as the chance to rebuild the German state.[34] When he read the text of the Schuman Plan, Adenauer instantly grasped that it offered Germany a road back to international respectability. 'This is our breakthrough, this is our beginning,' he said to an aide.[35] To Monnet he said, 'I regard the implementation of the French proposal as my most important task. If I succeed, I believe that my life will not have been wasted.'[36]

The reaction in London could not have been a greater contrast. To Monnet this was no surprise. It was the failure of his private talks with Plowden and Hall in 1949 that convinced him that looking to Germany was the only way forward.[37] He knew, too, the British 'character' inclined her negotiators 'to seek a special position that will save them from having to change'.[38] Above all, he knew that Britain, unlike France and Germany, who both shared recent, livid memories of defeat and occupation, would be resistant to dramatic moves which diminished her sovereignty. 'She felt no need to exorcise history', Monnet wrote in his *Memoirs* – a brilliant phrase which sums up so many British attitudes in the early postwar period.[39] 'It was', he would tell Michael Charlton many years later, 'the price of victory – the illusion that you could maintain what you had, without change'.[40]

As a civil servant in the *British* War Cabinet Office less than a decade earlier (one of his assistants was a young statistician from Oxford called Harold Wilson),[41] Monnet knew the ways of Whitehall and the British political and administrative culture as well as any foreigner. This is why, when he captured first Schuman, then the French Cabinet, the Germans and the Americans for his plan, he made it UK-proof. If the British come in, fine. If not, it would go ahead anyway, as Schuman and Monnet made plain in private and public when they brought the Plan to London in May.[42] The one outcome Monnet would not – could not – contemplate was the British coming into the Coal and Steel negotiations, taking them over and leaving the original idea watered down beyond recognition (which, given the near universal antipathy to federalism and the pooling of sovereignty in Whitehall and the Cabinet Room, is exactly what would have happened). It's quite plain that the French never intended to let Britain play for time which is why it was presented in a rush and a time limit imposed so swiftly (the famous ultimatum of 1 June 1950 which lingered in Whitehall folklore for generations); the whole enormous, deeply significant shift taking place in a blur, though the consequences would dog Britain for the remainder of the century.

It was, in truth, never really a runner. But the manner in which the Schuman Plan was disclosed to the British and handled thereafter made the chances of Britain joining the first European community that much slimmer. Dean Acheson was due in Paris for consultations with Schuman over the weekend of 6–7 May ahead of the NATO Council Meeting in London on 10 May, the trigger for the Monnet-Schuman initiative. That Sunday in the American Embassy in Paris, Schuman unveiled the Plan to Acheson and swore him to secrecy. Acheson at first recoiled, fearing it was a revival of the prewar European steel cartel which had been anathema to the United States. Further conversations with David Bruce, the US Ambassador to France, the highly influential John McCloy (who had taken over from a disgruntled General Clay when the American Occupation Authority in Germany had been civilianised on the creation of the Federal Republic) and Monnet himself convinced Acheson that this was precisely the inter-European initiative the Americans had been seeking since General Marshall's Harvard speech three years before. Acheson had come to despair of this, not least because of British reluctance to let the OEEC develop into anything approaching a supranational body. He called Truman accordingly.[43]

The immediate problem was twofold: the British, deliberately, had not been consulted or informed; and the Americans were prohibited from telling them.

This was compounded by Bevin's serious ill health (he was away from the Foreign Office for long periods and would often fall asleep at meetings when he was there[44]). There was also a residue of real bitterness in Whitehall, felt most acutely by Bevin and Cripps, built up by successive and repeated attempts by the American Marshall Plan administrators in Europe, Averell Harriman and Paul Hoffman in particular, to push the UK into a closer relationship with the rest of western Europe and to appoint the Belgian Paul Henri Spaak, as an 'independent chairman' of the OEEC, a kind of 'Mr Europe' with whom Washington could deal as a plenipotentiary. Or 'superman' as Bevin himself put it.[45] So serious had this invitation become that Julius Holmes, the number two in the US Embassy in London, cabled Acheson about it in January 1950 in that peculiar telegraphese standard to American diplomats and in terms so striking that Acheson showed the telegram to Truman.

In its way, the Holmes signal sets the scene perfectly for the reception with which Acheson – and Schuman – were greeted in London four months later. The British, Holmes told Acheson,

> resent a common American attitude that they are just another European power. They see Britain as the hub of a vast and complicated political, military and economic mechanism, occupying a position in the world and a relationship with us which is quite different from the other European powers. There is a constant wonder here [in London] that we should think it in American interest for them completely to integrate with Europe.[46]

Holmes went on to pre-echo, almost, the impact of Acheson's explosive visit to the Foreign Office after his private briefing in Paris on the Schuman Plan: ' . . . there has been a stream of American visitors, public and private, demanding to see top leaders of Government, asking impertinent or intrusive questions, raising the spectre of what Congress may do to the ECA [Marshall] Aid unless the Brit agree to this or that case of special pleading, and in general acting maladroitly.'[47]

Acheson may or may not have had Holmes' telegram in mind when he turned up at the Foreign Office in Whitehall on Tuesday 9 May. He was distressed at Bevin's physical condition and by the fact that 'I didn't feel able to inform our British friends of what Schuman might be doing at that moment'.[48] Over lunch with Attlee and his Foreign Secretary, Acheson witnessed Bevin receiving a message that the French Ambassador to London, René Massigli, wanted to see him as he had an important message to deliver – 'My embarrassment grew as the company speculated about this mystery.'[49]

By the time Acheson resumed his discussions with Bevin that afternoon, Schuman had launched his Plan in the French Assembly and Massigli had given the Foreign Secretary its details. So much for the US-UK 'special relationship'. So much for Britain as a world power – or even as *the* dominant nation in western Europe. To Bevin it was an outrageous insult on every level. To Acheson it was a 'stupid' mistake on his and Schuman's part:

I kept a four o'clock appointment at the Foreign Office with dragging feet. Bevin asked me to see him alone. He was in a towering rage, and at once charged that I had known of Schuman's plan and had kept it from him. This, of course, was true and I said so. But before I could explain, he rushed on to accuse me of having conspired with Schuman to create a European combination against British trade with the Continent. This was quite untrue, but I had certainly behaved suspiciously.[50]

When Schuman followed the text of his plan to London two days later on Thursday 11 May, Acheson engaged in a spasm of top-flight diplomacy to ease the hurt and, if possible, heal the breach between the British and the French Foreign Ministers.

Sir Roderick Barclay's note of the meeting at Lancaster House on 11 May survives in the files at the PRO. Bevin's anger blazes out of the customarily understated FO prose. He had been embarrassed in the Commons which assumed he knew all about the Plan. What is more, Britain, France and the USA 'were administering Germany and he had thought that the principle of consultation had been established. He wondered whether this had been intended to set a new precedent, and what deductions he should draw.'[51]

Acheson deftly suggested that all governments sometimes had to act secretly, as the British themselves had the previous September when they had told the Americans, though not the French, of their intention to devalue the pound. Schuman said the French Government had itself only been considering the Coal and Steel Plan for a week. It was merely a proposal. Nothing had been decided about Germany's economic future. Rather tactlessly, he added that 'The French Government had wanted to produce a psychological shock both on the European and the German plane. He hoped Mr. Bevin would be prepared to regard the matter in its proper proportions.'[52] (The fastidious Acheson, as part of the process of Bevin assuagement, even accepted and consumed 'Uncle Ernie's revenge', a vile tumblerful of gin, vermouth and water *sans* ice.[53])

Within hours of his Lancaster House meeting Bevin was reporting on his discussions with Schuman and Acheson to a special Cabinet Committee, GEN 322, convened by Attlee to consider the proposed 'Franco-German Steel and Coal Authority'. The minutes of that meeting in Attlee's room at the House of Commons on the evening of 11 May (such meetings became a frequent occurrence as, in the absence of a reliable majority, ministers, to borrow a phrase of Enoch Powell's, often 'had to dance attendance on the division bells') make for instructive reading, for most of the fundamental objections to a genuinely close relationship with Europe then current in mid-century Britain surfaced.

After Bevin had reported on Schuman's excuses for keeping the Government in the dark, and that Acheson 'had welcomed the proposal and had tended to belittle the procedural irregularities', ministers found it hard to decipher the motives of the French. France, it was pointed out (by whom is not recorded) had been reluctant to spend money on defence and 'certain groups in France might be hankering after a Third Force which could, in certain contingencies, enter into some kind of understanding with Russia'.

Equally the Cabinet Committee (which consisted of Attlee and Bevin, Morrison and Cripps, Wilson from the Board of Trade, Shinwell from Defence, Philip Noel-Baker from Fuel and Power and the steel minister, Strauss from Supply) was concerned that a European coal and steel pool would jeopardise the newly nationalised British enterprises:

> If the Franco-German authority was built up on a basis of private owner-ship, it was difficult to see how the British iron and steel industry under public ownership could be integrated with the continental combine . . . If eventual integration of the iron and steel industries of Great Britain, France, Germany and Benelux [Belgium, the Netherlands and Luxembourg] were effected, a position might be reached in which the iron and steel industry of this country was seriously reduced in size . . . Moreover if this country entered a scheme of this kind it could not easily retrace its steps if it disliked the effects of the scheme. A fully integrated Western European industry had, however, profound political implications; and, indeed, political feder-ation might be an essential pre-requisite of such a scheme.[54]

Added to the suspicion of French motives, the concern about possible soft-ness on confronting Communism, the dislike of capitalism and determination to protect public ownership and to keep both economic and political sover-eignty at home was another fear of the world beyond Dover, the kind of fear not to be spoken of on respectable occasions such as Cabinet committee meetings – the fear of Catholicism.

Bevin most certainly distrusted it. Gladwyn Jebb recalled a journey with the Bevins to a trade union conference in Southport: 'The train was rather full and people often went by in the corridor, including from time to time a Catholic priest in a soutane. Whenever this happened Mr and Mrs Bevin became uneasy and Mr Bevin muttered 'black crows'. I understood that he believed that Catholic priests brought bad luck and nothing that I could say had any effect.'[55] Even his deputy, the intellectual Kenneth Younger, was affected by it. He described Schuman in his diary as 'a bachelor and a very devout Catholic who is said to be very much under the influence of the priests'.[56] In the same entry, Younger, who was among the handful of people in the Government and the Civil Service genuinely sympathetic to the Schuman Plan, recorded on 14 May that:

> Privately we all have doubts and misgivings. In view of the political com-plexion of the French and German governments and their links with heavy industry, one cannot but expect that this will develop along old fashioned cartel lines. It need not do so, however, and if we can get the scheme executed

in a way which safeguards the public interest and limits the power of the vested interests in the international authority, then it *may* be a step forward. On the other hand, it may be just a step in the consolidation of the Catholic 'black international' which I have always thought to be a big driving force behind the Council of Europe.[57]

This anti-Catholicism is another of those mid-century phenomena which needs explaining to those under forty who live in late-century Britain and are familiar with the post-Vatican Council Catholic Church. Years later, the genuinely internationally minded Denis Healey explained that the France of Schuman, the Germany of Adenauer and the Italy of Alcide de Gasperi had 'political and . . . religious views very different from ours. Don't forget that they were all Catholic parties and that at that time the Catholic Church had a very ambiguous attitude to Labourism. The Dutch Social Democratic Party had completely reconstructed itself after the war and turned itself into a Labour Party with no Marxist dogma at all. Yet, in the first election after the war in Holland, the Dutch Catholic hierarchy excommunicated people who voted Labour.'[58]

None of this, of course, was uttered even in the privileged confines of GEN 322 which decided on 11 May that officials should make contact with Monnet in the hope that he could provide the kind of detail about the Plan which its nominal author, Schuman, had proved incapable of doing and on which a judgment could be reached as to 'whether the proposal represented an economic scheme which had been put forward at this juncture for political reasons, or whether the project was primarily political in character'. A committee of permanent secretaries was commissioned to collect and collate information with a view to briefing ministers on the effect of the Schuman Plan on the UK 'assuming the continuance of the present Government policies relating to the planned economy and full employment', on the economy of the Commonwealth and the sterling area and on defence aspects.[59]

This put the Civil Service in an immensely strong position – nothing less than the preparation of the Whitehall playing field on which the issue would be fought out. Younger, deputising for Bevin who was in the London Clinic for a fistula operation, and with both Attlee and Cripps taking Whitsun holidays, ironically enough, in France, found himself 'nominally in charge of the proceedings with only occasional reference to Herbert Morrison who was acting for the P.M. In fact of course the officials had the bit very much between their teeth. Every move was discussed between Sir E. Bridges, Plowden, Strang [Sir William, Permanent Secretary to the Foreign Office] and Makins, and by the time I had a hand in it it had become pretty hard to make much impact.'[60]

The official committee, known as FG (initials for Franco-German) in Cabinet Office parlance, was chaired by Bridges and included Makins, but not Strang from the Foreign Office, Plowden from the Planning Staff and Hall from the Economic Section as well as civil servants from the Board of Trade, the Ministry of Defence, the Ministry of Supply and the Ministry of Fuel and Power. It was Plowden and Makins who would conduct the discussions with Monnet once he had arrived in London to explain and cajole.

It's normally very difficult to syringe from the minutes of meetings the real, personal views of these influential figures and the files of the Schuman Plan are no exception. In this instance, however, we have Younger's diary to tell us just how many intellectual barriers the thinking of Schuman and Monnet encountered in 1950 Whitehall. 'I was very much impressed throughout', wrote Younger,

> with the importance of trying to make some scheme work, and consequently of finding some basis upon which we could participate from the start. In this I was virtually alone. Strang said frankly he thought the whole thing non-sense and a mere French attempt to evade realities. Makins, though less hostile, felt that we should not get committed, that the Franco-German talks would inevitably break down sooner or later, and that we would then have a chance of coming in as deus ex machina with a solution of our own. In addition, Makins was the main protagonist of the view that the plan is largely designed to get away from the 'Atlantic' conception and to revert to a 'European third force neutral between the USSR and the USA'. I have no doubt there is some force in this view. Quite certainly that is the notion of one big group of Frenchmen and possibly also of the Germans.[61]

Of the other big Whitehall figures advising ministers, Plowden 'predicted wrongly, that the setting up of a common authority as proposed would most likely lead to the formation of a cartel "of the more or less conventional type". If this was the case, I was convinced that it would be foolish if we declined to join as it would mean that our coal and steel industries would be subject to unfair competition.'[62]

Robert Hall, who recorded in his diary how the Schuman Plan 'caused us great alarms and excursions',[63] briefed Attlee on 11 May to the effect that: 'There are immense practical and administrative difficulties in carrying through any scheme of this kind. But if it were in fact carried through, the important factor for us would be the change in the whole European picture which would be implied by the fact that France and Germany had proved themselves willing and able to take a step of such importance. If we really think that they are likely to do this, we ought at once to examine the implications of the step for the whole of our policy, in economic as in other fields.'[64]

To be fair to Attlee and his ministers, they did take Hall's point that the Schuman Plan was about fundamentals and one fundamental in particular – the implications of the proposed High Authority for the development of feder-alism in Europe and a consequential diminution of sovereignty in Britain – swiftly emerged as *the* sticking point inside the Cabinet's Economic Policy

Committee. Equally vexing to ministers was the French insistence that nations should indicate their willingness to (a) participate in the ECSC and (b) accept its implications for sovereignty before negotiations began.[65] Monnet made this very plain when Makins, Plowden and Hitchman called upon him at his suite in the Hyde Park Hotel on 16 May.

The British record of the meeting says: 'M. Monnet made it abundantly clear that the French Government recognise that the establishment of an Authority on these lines means the surrender of national sovereignty over a wide strategic and economic field and that they are prepared to do this in the interest of furthering European unity.'[66] As usual, the minutes give but a faint impression of the clash of personalities and what Braudel would call *mentalités* over breakfast that spring morning in the Hyde Park Hotel. Makins, as Lord Sherfield forty years later, was able to relive it for me as if it were yesterday:

> It was, so to speak, sprung on us and, of course, there was American involvement there. I mean the Americans were informed and encouraged it. Then Monnet came over to London and Edwin Plowden and I went to see him in the Hyde Park Hotel and we said 'Now, Jean, what's all this about?' And he said, 'Oh, it's all here, I've got it, here's the bit of paper.' It was a sheet of paper and so we read it and we said: 'But, Jean, it says here that in order to come into this, we've got to submit ourselves to the concept of a federal Europe. Now does that mean that if we're not prepared to do that, you don't want us in?' And he said, 'Yes.' And so we said, 'Well, you know, I don't think that the British government is going to, at this stage, commit itself to a federal solution for Europe. I don't think they'll do it.'[67]

The precise Plowden, a fine-print man *par excellence*, was clearly vexed by Monnet's philosophical woolliness. 'We found it hard', he recalled, 'to separate the *dirigiste* from the liberal in his thinking. Above all it was the political principles of the whole arrangement that were sacrosanct. The technical details were all secondary.'[68] (If Hall's diary is any guide, Whitehall's understated chief planner was pretty fed up with his evangelical French counterpart: 'Plowden has had every meal with Monnet since he arrived and is getting weary of it.'[69])

None the less, he told Bridges' FG Committee next day that Britain should go in: 'On present advice it seemed clear that the advantages of the United Kingdom participating in some form in the proposed Authority outweighed the disadvantages: if the proposals were successful, the United Kingdom should be associated with them. It would only be possible to find out whether the proposals, which were extremely nebulous at the present stage, would be advantageous to the United Kingdom by taking part in the initial discussions.'[70]

Bridges' committee delivered their completed interim report to the Cabinet's Economic Policy Committee on the same day. The civil servants warned ministers that the Schuman Plan, if accepted, would 'involve some abatement of British sovereignty so far as concerned the coal and steel industries of the United Kingdom' and this was not something to which Britain could 'commit ourselves in the dark'. The Government, however, should seek to associate itself in further negotiations between the French and the Germans.[71]

It was, however, the mystical Monnet who brought matters to a head and converted the 'official mind' of Whitehall from its cautious, semi-open approach to a resentful dismissal of British participation on French terms. After his conversations with Makins and Plowden, Monnet concluded 'that haggling would lead nowhere, and that we must simply press ahead'.[72] He proceeded to Bonn where he experienced his crucial tryst with Adenauer. While Bridges and co. in London smothered the Schuman Plan with caveats Monnet and Hirsch on 31 May briefed the French Government in unequivocal language: 'To accept British participation on these terms – i.e., in a special capacity – would be to resign oneself in advance to the replacement of the French proposal by something that would be a mere travesty of it.'[73]

'We had to make an end of it,' Monnet wrote later.[74] Which is precisely what the French Government did. It was its ultimatum of 1 June – that all countries which intended to join the Coal and Steel Community should indicate their intentions of doing so by 8 o'clock the following evening – which closed the matter for the British almost without exception. Though one distinguished dissenter was Oliver Franks in Washington who thought that the idea of bringing 'France and Germany together, as Schuman described it to me "in an embrace so close that neither could draw back far enough to hit the other" . . . was worth everything for the peace of Europe,' but nobody in Whitehall asked his opinion.[75]

Bridges and his team briefed ministers once more. The 'official mind' 1950 vintage now became transparent. Britain *was* different from the rest of Europe. Its place in the world *was* special. 'The main issues are really political,' the committee of top civil servants and diplomats said in a Cabinet paper hastily prepared on the morning of 2 June for the special Cabinet meeting convened for that afternoon.

The exchanges with the French Government have brought out that their proposals, which started in a Franco-German context, have now been given a wider application. It is not merely pooling of resources, but also, in the first place, the conception of fusion or surrender of sovereignty in a European system which the French are asking us to accept in principle.

M. Schuman's original memorandum said in terms that his plan would be a step towards the federation of Europe. It has been our settled policy hitherto that in view of our world position and interests, we should not commit ourselves irrevocably to Europe either in the political or the economic sphere unless we could measure the extent and effect of the commitment. This is in effect what we are now being asked to do. It is a commitment of this kind which in essence the French Government is now seeking, and at the very moment when the decision has been taken to develop and give greater meaning to the Atlantic Community.[76]

It's quite plain from this, by Whitehall standards, passionate declaration of the 'permanent government's' view of Britain's place in the world that of Churchill's three interlocking circles, the Atlantic and Commonwealth loops were paramount and the European loop nowhere.

Much has been made of the fact that the meeting of ministers which finally rejected British membership of the prototype European Community was a 'skeleton Cabinet'. It's true that its three big figures were absent – Attlee and Cripps did not feel the need to break their Continental holidays, though at least Bevin bed-ridden in the London Clinic could be consulted face-to-face. In fact, a hospital and a restaurant have a secure place in the legend of Britain and the Schuman Plan.

When the French ultimatum arrived on the evening of 1 June, Younger contacted Plowden who said it must be shown to Morrison who was deputising for Attlee. Morrison, at the theatre that evening, was finally traced to the Ivy. 'We retired', Lord Plowden recalled, 'to a sort of passage at the back of the restaurant where spare tables and chairs were stored.'[77] It was in this bizarre setting that Morrison delivered his famous phrase about the Durham miners not wearing it, a remark which takes some explaining to generations unaware probably that any miners are left in County Durham and unaware, too, of the fighting qualities of the Durham Light Infantry in the then still recent defeat of two members of the Coal and Steel Community (Germany and Italy) and the liberation of the other four (France, Belgium, the Netherlands and Luxembourg).

The next day, Younger recorded, 'Morrison and I were able to see Ernie Bevin in hospital and got his view which was of the simple "I won't be dictated to" variety.'[78] Younger got a classic Bevin bollocking for his pro-European pains, as Bevin later told the *Daily Herald* journalist Leslie Hunter.

> Bevin, always keen to bring on the junior ministers, turned to Younger and asked, 'Well, young man, what do you think of it all?' Younger was all for Britain joining in.
>
> Bevin listened attentively and then heaved a sigh. 'Splash about, young man, you'll learn to swim in time', he commented and then turning to Morrison he began 'Now 'Erbert . . . ' and got down to the details of how to keep out of this embarrassing offer.[79]

Morrison had no difficulty in persuading the rump of the Cabinet to do as Bevin wished.

Younger opened the discussion at 2.30 that afternoon in No. 10 keeping his own views to himself, summarising events since the Economic Policy Committee had met on 25 May and the report from Bridges and his colleagues. Morrison summed up Bevin's views as related at the bedside – that the French proposal should be rejected 'since they were still without any information about the practical details of the scheme and were therefore unable to estimate its possible effects on their programmes for economic development and defence'.[80] The Cabinet backed this line. Once more suspicion of French motives surfaced: 'They might perhaps envisage this plan as a means of avoiding the additional commitments for the defence of Western Europe which had been foreshadowed in the recent meeting of the North Atlantic Council.'[81] Douglas Jay, standing in at Cabinet for Cripps, later declared 'no British Government – certainly no Churchill Government – could have acted otherwise than we did, and no Cabinet would have seriously considered sending any other reply to the French ultimatum.'[82]

For all Lord Jay's legendary and lifelong aversion to British membership of the European Community, he's right. In Opposition, the Conservatives made pro-European noises but in one of his first Cabinet papers as Premier in 1951, Churchill told his colleagues: 'We should have joined in all the discussions, and, had we done so, not only a better plan would probably have emerged, but our own interests would have been watched at every stage. Our attitude towards further economic developments on the Schuman lines resembles that which we adopt about the European Army. We help, we dedicate, we play a part, but we are not merged and do not forfeit our insular or Commonwealth-wide character. I should resist any American pressure to treat Britain on the same footing as the European states, none of whom have the advantages of the Channel and who were consequently conquered.'[83]

Would the outcome have been different if Bevin had retained the creativity of earlier years and not lain ill and exhausted in hospital? No. He shared Churchill's view of Britain's specialness, its place in the three interlocking circles and the primacy of the Atlantic, as opposed to the cross-Channel link. What's more, he genuinely recoiled at the manner of the French proposal. As he cabled Franks three days after the ultimatum was rejected, 'Where matters of such vital importance are at stake, we cannot buy a pig in a poke . . . '[84]

Nor did Attlee's absence from the 'skeleton Cabinet' make any difference. On 7 June, at Massigli's request, he lunched with the French Ambassador and (as he told Bevin when he returned to No. 10) 'explained to him pretty fully the grounds on which we had come to the conclusion that it was quite impossible for us to sign a blank cheque. At the same time I assured him that we were in broad agreement with the conception of building up European unity, and that this was obviously one of the matters on which progress might be made. He agreed that one of the difficulties was the nature of the [Coal and Steel] Authority and the degree to which power could be handed over to them.'[85]

Can Attlee, his ministers and their official advisers, be faulted for their actions in May–June 1950? Certainly, there was a great deal of delusion about Britain's continued great powerdom swirling around in departments and committee rooms and embassies. How hubristic and patronising Sir Oliver Harvey now sounds in the Paris Embassy on 3 June, the day after the Cabinet had rejected the Schuman Plan: 'There are precedents of international organizations set up with fanfares of trumpets which encounter only difficulties and disappointments when the time comes to put them into practice.'[86] Though Sir Roger Makins simply cannot remember telling Monnet in the Hyde Park Hotel, 'We are not ready; and you will not succeed,' as Etienne Hirsch recalls him saying, and Lord Sherfield, as he now is thinks it most unlikely that he would have used such language.[87]

But in strictly economic terms, the conclusion that Bridges and his team reached in June 1950 has been corroborated by the most astringent of historians of postwar western Europe. 'Our provisional view', declared the official committee in its final report to ministers, 'is that the economic arguments in favour of coming in or staying out of an international association of the kind contemplated by the Schuman Plan are not conclusive one way or the other, and on this score there need be no cause for alarm if at this stage the French decide to proceed without us.'[88] As Alan Milward put it more than a generation later:

> The events of 1950 and the signing of the Treaty of the European Coal and Steel Community on 18 April 1951 made no difference whatsoever at the time to the British economy and even the opening of the Common Market for certain of the products on 10 February 1953 made very little. No proper economic answer to the question can be given except by considering almost the whole span of time during which the framework created by the treaty has survived, and in that span of time so many other variables would come into account that the question would lose all precision and force.[89]

Looking *back* from 1950, is more revealing. With memories of 1940 so fresh, why should the British policy-making community have been prepared to throw in their lot with that same group of nations which had either precipitated aggression or succumbed to it in short order? The great overriding fear in 1950 was that if the Russians moved, it would happen again. Monnet knew this perfectly well and committed his view to paper at the time:

> Britain has no confidence that France and the other countries of Europe have the ability or even the will effectively to resist a possible Russian invasion . . .
>
> Britain believes that in this conflict continental Europe will be occupied but that she herself, with America, will be able to resist and finally conquer.
>
> She therefore does not wish to let her domestic life or the development of her resources be influenced by any views other than her own, and certainly not by continental views.[90]

Monnet knew his Britain.

For the original six nations which went on to form the European Economic Community eight years later, there was something substantial in the ECSC for each of them. The Franco-German interest we have already considered. Italy, too, needed both international respectability and a more integrated market in which to trade. The politicians of the Benelux nations knew that their postwar recoveries depended, in the end, on access to their bigger, immediate neighbours, their resources and their markets. For Britain, with half its trade then with the Commonwealth, a mere quarter with Europe – none of these overriding factors applied.

Oddly enough, a kind of backhanded vindication of the British view in the spring of 1950 came a decade later from the one man who *could* have brought the ECSC to nought at the time. When Konrad Adenauer and Harold Macmillan met in Bonn for talks in August 1960, 'Der Alte' told the British Prime Minister:

> . . . he would like to speak frankly as regards Franco-German relations. The old difficulties and enmities of many centuries were well known. In 1945 France had thought that Germany might embark on a war of revenge with the assistance of the Soviet Union. The Coal and Steel Community had been worked out precisely in order to prevent this happening. When the ECSC was set up the United Kingdom was invited to join but the British Government refused, probably rightly, since in fact the ECSC was really a political organisation to overcome Franco-German hostility.[91]

Adenauer, I think, was right both about the nature of the Schuman Plan and in his exoneration of Britain's attitude to it at the time. It's the next section of his peroration in the Palais Schaumberg with which, if he meant it and was not merely flattering Macmillan, I take issue:

> Then, after several more years, people in Europe found there were three main economic groups in the world, the United Kingdom and the Commonwealth, the United States and the Soviet Union. The European countries decided that they could not be competitive if they were not united and therefore formed the EEC and EURATOM, although not as supra-national authorities. The foundation of the EEC was not at all aimed against the United Kingdom or the United States but was an act of self-preservation.[92]

Adenauer must have known – as the British knew – at the time of the Messina Talks in 1955 out of which came the Treaty of Rome in 1957 and the EEC in 1958, that far from being an economic bloc to frighten Germany alone, let alone the Six as a whole, the UK and the Commonwealth, at least, were in serious and growing difficulties as a trading and currency unit. That was the real difference between the rejection by Britain of the ECSC in 1950 and the unwillingness to take part at Messina in 1955 which cannot be explained away however much one tries to occupy the skulls of the ministers and civil servants who mattered at the time. More on that later.

From the moment an outline of the Schuman Plan appeared in *The Times* on

9 May 1950, Europe and Britain's place in it would hum as an issue of domestic politics for the next forty plus years, sometimes rising to a deafening roar (forty years later in November 1990, it would be a crucial factor in dislodging the most domineering premier of the postwar period from Downing Street, so central had it become to both the political and economic life of the nation). But back in June 1950, the 'problem' of Europe quickly faded, thrust into the background by the outbreak of war in Korea and the need for political, official and military Britain to do what it thought it did best – stand in the breach alongside the United States as *the* most dependable ally in the wider interests of the world, not merely the European community.

Korea is sometimes called 'the forgotten war'[93] but it has had a remarkable and enduring resonance in postwar British history. For example, almost exactly forty years after its outbreak I found myself flying from Hong Kong to Seoul over the very same East China Sea over which the British 29th Brigade had been rushed in August 1950 to stand alongside the Americans in the still shrinking 'Pusan Perimeter' on the southern tip of South Korea. The Communist North Koreans all but won the war in their first great incursion across the 38th parallel, the cold war dividing line fixed when the now antagonistic Allies of the Second World War finally turned their attention to this bleak, neglected peninsula which had suffered so much as a Japanese colony for the bulk of the twentieth century.[94]

The parallels that struck me with what was then a still-unfolding crisis in the Persian Gulf (following the Iraqi invasion of Kuwait) were uncanny. In 1990 as in 1950 a small contingent of high quality British troops and advanced equipment were first in the breach alongside the Americans; in 1990 as in 1950 resources were diverted to war-making against the background of a shaky domestic economy; in 1990 as in 1950 many saw it (including me) as the price British governments occasionally have to pay for the 'special relationship'. In 1950, Sir Oliver Franks, a highly influential factor in persuading the Labour Government to go to war quickly and decisively, wrote to Attlee from Washington saying the commitment of British troops in Korea would keep Britain separate from 'the queue of European nations and demonstrate to the Americans that we were one of the two world powers outside Russia'[95]. What Franks later described as the 'traumatic devaluation' of 1949[96] plus the Americans' increasing irritation with Britain's reluctance about further integration with Europe had caused something of a recession in the 'special relationship' even in the period which is now regarded as its high tide.

In early 1990, before the invasion of Kuwait, the Press had been full of the retreat from the Reagan-Thatcher partnership.[97] According to the new conventional wisdom, under George Bush, the link between Washington and a newly united Germany was what mattered when American eyes turned towards Europe. The war in the Gulf changed all that. British diplomats in the Massachusetts Avenue Embassy were embarrassed in January 1991 when the *Washington Post* claimed that 'Britain has quickly reasserted its role as the

United States' closest and most reliable ally through its intimate diplomatic, military and intelligence collaboration with Washington during the Persian Gulf War.'[98] It was 'hype' according to one British diplomat, to say it was the Second World War all over again but 'Having said that, there is an undoubted closeness . . . There is a different set of rules for the Brits . . . it's as if it's one bureaucracy.'[99] For a time Sir Antony Acland, the British Ambassador, seemed to enjoy almost the kind of access to the Bush White House that Franks had used to such great effect in Truman's time, an extraordinary example of continuity in postwar British history.

As in 1950, eyes and ears were diverted from the committee rooms where the new Europe was being pieced together (the Coal and Steel Community in the summer of 1950; the Intergovernmental Conferences on economic and political union at the turn of 1990 and 1991). 'Take two films,' suggested *The Economist* evocatively in the opening days of the Gulf War. 'One is about the passing of cold war comradeship, fading American interest in Europe and an uneasy British conversion to European Union. The other is about an alliance restored, in an old colonial stamping-ground, for as good a cause as you get, with those continentals dodging and weaving. Guess which cinema the British will flock to.'[100]

Given the return to Anglo-American business-as-usual in the Gulf, that trip of mine to Korea in August 1990 was a sobering experience. Take two Americans on the Cathay Pacific Tristar between Hong Kong and Seoul. First, a lawyer in his late twenties keen to 'nuke' Saddam Hussein. 'Did the British have many troops in Korea?' he asked, surprised to know we'd been involved at all. Second, an American businessman in his late fifties, an ex-marine who had fought in the Korean War and visited the British NAAFI regularly up in the Haeju peninsula to buy Rose's Lime Juice to make the water palatable. He talked about the combination of 'cold and fear' which gripped him and his comrades, of how the younger generation in South Korea had no idea of this and regarded the substantial American forces still there as 'an army of occupation'.[101]

Korea has always meant a great deal to me. An uncle of mine fought there. Its most celebrated engagement, in terms of British folk memory, is the heroic stand of the Gloucestershire Regiment in the spring of 1951. (Unnecessarily heroic, as it turns out in a bitterly ironic way thanks to the difference between American English and English English: Brigadier Tom Brodie, CO of the 29th Brigade, was an understated man like most of his brother officers, to a degree that the Americans in the chain of command above him could not decode; 'When Tom told Corps that his position was "a bit sticky", they simply did not grasp that in British Army parlance, that meant "critical".'[102]) By the time the Americans did realise, 29 Brigade was surrounded by vastly superior Chinese forces. On the famous Hill 235, above the Imjin, the Gloucesters held back the Chinese north of Seoul for several days before succumbing to the inevitable, the survivors suffering mightily for two years in North Korean prisoner-of-war camps.

All this meant a great deal to me as I grew up in Gloucestershire a decade later. When I made a pilgrimage in the summer heat to the Imjin forty years later with the British Council's Representative in Seoul, Tom White and his wife Danielle, close to what was, in effect, the last frontier of the cold war, I recorded in my diary:

> North of Seoul the military traffic increases substantially both American and Korean. As you approach the River on Route One you pass through a series of defensive walls, military police direct you at junctions. Just south of the river, which is as wide as the Thames at Woolwich, we head off north-west through a series of villages and more defensive positions until, well into the mountains, we turn south into the valley where the Gloucesters made their stand in April 1951. The memorial is very scruffy . . . but very moving. A plaque is set into the side of the mountain where they grouped on the third night completely surrounded by the Chinese 63rd Army.
>
> Long forgotten now, the war up here was significant to us in ways more profound than the obvious. [Some 750 British troops lost their lives in the three-year war.] There is a good case for saying our economic miracle died in these hills. Quadrupling the defence estimates in the belief that Korea represented the opening shots of World War III, choked off the export led boom begun by the 1949 devaluation. I'm sure it was our best moment for a post World War II economic take-off.[103]

Others disagree. The economic impact of Korea has become one of the 'great debates' of British history since 1945.

Before assessing its consequences, it would be as well to examine the war's causes and the decision-making process which led the British Government to meet what, at the end of the crucial Cabinet meeting on 27 June 1950 (which decided to heed the UN call for assistance to South Korea), Norman Brook called this 'rather distant obligation'. 'Distant – yes,' Attlee told him, 'but none the less an obligation.'[104]

Of all the cold war flashpoints anticipated by the military planners in what all suspected would be a fraught decade of confrontation, Korea was not even in the minor league. Dean Acheson, famously, had by implication ruled it beyond the US's defensive perimeter line in the Pacific in a speech in 1950.[105] An elaborate conspiracy theory was built up among cold war dissenters – most powerfully by the radical Washington journalist I.F. Stone in his *The Hidden History of the Korean War*, published while the war was still in progress – which made much of the presence of John Foster Dulles in Seoul shortly before the outbreak and suggested that the Americans had provoked it for wider cold war purposes.[106] Given the meagre number and poor quality of the US occupation troops in South Korea, this always seemed highly improbable. We know from Khrushchev's memoirs that Kim Il Sung, the Communist leader in the north, came up with the idea and sold it to both Stalin in Moscow and Mao in Peking on the grounds that if he were allowed 'to prod South Korea with the point of a bayonet' it would 'explode and the power of the people would prevail'.[107]

Plainly it was seen in Moscow, Peking and Pyongyang as a swift and virtually cost-free advance in the forward march of international communism, one which the United States was unlikely to reverse by force once northern troops had reached Pusan and toppled the feeble, corrupt and reactionary southern regime of Syngman Rhee.

Certainly news of the invasion which took place in the middle of the night on 25 June 1950 took Whitehall completely by surprise. Kenneth Younger, writing in his diary on 6 July, captured the shock and the precariousness of the new crisis which took Britain to war again less than five years after hostilities had ceased in the Far East at the end of the Second World War.

> These last three weeks have been even more hectic than usual. Not only has the follow-up on the Schuman Plan . . . been giving us all a great deal of work, but right in the middle of it . . . a North Korean army invade South Korea, and set in motion a whole train of action of which the consequences are still largely guesswork . . .
>
> The Korean situation has now knocked Schuman right into the background of public consciousness. It is a fortnight since the invasion, and we are only at the very beginning of what promises to be a difficult business. Over 40 nations have weighed in behind the United Nations in approving resistance to the aggression. US troops are, however, still thin on the ground and are having a bad time and retreating. They may need considerable forces to restore the position, but they can scarcely afford to fail now and everyone seems convinced that the thing will have to be seen through.[108]

The Korean 'thing', as Younger called it, was to last for another three years. It saw out both the Attlee and Truman Administrations and was one of the handful of truly perilous moments in the cold war. Each side, east and west, miscalculated prewar the importance of Korea to the other, each misread the other's intentions once it started, believing it to be a feint, a Far Eastern diversion, before a decisive cold war-winning thrust was made across the central front in Europe. Each side had a small enough arsenal of atomic bombs to do each other severe, though not terminal, damage. Hence there was a possibility in that pre-hydrogen age of nuclear weapons being used.

By a lucky chance the Russians were boycotting the United Nations in June 1950 in protest at the Security Council's refusal to displace Nationalist China in favour of Red China (Mao's forces had taken Peking the previous summer), which was another indication that Stalin did not expect Truman to respond in the decisive way he did. Though the war could, therefore, be portrayed as a United Nations peacekeeping operation, it became increasingly hard for the Attlee Government to manage the tensions between the US and its number one ally.

From the start Whitehall feared Washington would 'unleash' Chiang
Kai-shek, thereby bringing China into the war. After General MacArthur's
brilliant recapture of the initiative after the Inchon landing in September,
Attlee and his ministers reluctantly went along with the hot pursuit of North
Korean forces north of the 38th parallel for fear that that, too, might draw in
China, which it did the following month. By the end of November substantial
forces of Chinese 'volunteers' had caused MacArthur to retreat from the Yalu
and stimulated a casual remark of Truman's at a Press conference which
seemed to suggest the United States might use the atomic weapon in Korea on
30 November.

Attlee, in an early example of shuttle-summit diplomacy, flew across the
Atlantic (Bevin was too ill to accompany him) for discussions with Truman,
propelled by a weight of distorted opinion in both Cabinet and Parliament. He
received the assurances he sought on the bomb and seemed, to Acheson's
horror, to have persuaded Truman to restore a British veto over its use generally.

Lord Franks recalled the moment in December forty years later as if he had
just returned from the White House:

> Acheson was appalled. He thought about all the things Truman had said
> about his having unfettered discretion in decision about this. He thought
> about the views of the Congress and this mystical weapon placed in
> American hands ... And he decided – his language – to 'unachieve' the
> agreement ...
>
> I had to draft a revised communiqué and there wasn't a table ... Presi-
> dent Truman pulled out a flap of his desk and I knelt to write (the President
> turned to me and said 'I think it's the first time a British Ambassador has
> ever knelt before a President of the United States!'). I wrote out something
> which was to the effect that the President hoped that the atom bomb would
> never need to be used and he undertook to keep the British Prime Minister
> continuously informed of all developments which might lead to any change
> in the situation.[109]

'I think Attlee was comfortable,' he added. Certainly the assurances Attlee gave
to Parliament on his return had a soothing effect.

By the summer of 1951 the war was stabilising just north of where the
Gloucesters made their stand around the 38th parallel where it had started a
year before. Truman sacked MacArthur. The bomb remained in the bays of
the B29s. The stalemate lasted another two years before the new President,
Eisenhower, brought the GIs back home. East and west had been to the brink
but the abyss of the Third World War had been avoided.

But the international consequences were profound and long-lasting. Korea
stimulated both the United States and the Soviet Union to rush through their
programmes to manufacture the hugely more powerful hydrogen bomb (the

US achieving the capability in 1952, the USSR a year later). It caused, too, real troops and weapons to be draped on the NATO framework in Europe, bringing both Eisenhower (briefly) and his GIs (seemingly permanently) back into Germany.[110] It was this commitment – the NATO, European one – which caused the Attlee Government to rearm so furiously, expensively and (in an economic sense) ruinously. As Sir Anthony Farrar-Hockley points out tirelessly, the arms and ammunition the 29th Brigade used in Korea was largely old Second World War stock nearing the end of its shelf-life. The big money was spent on NATO and the central front where it was feared the Red Army might strike at any moment, and in Sir Anthony's words, 'it was the seven divisions Britain pledged to NATO in Europe that proved far beyond our means.'[111]

Domestically, too, a price was paid. Senator Joe McCarthy had launched his crusade against alleged Communists in the US State Department in February 1950, but it was Korea which gave him his lift off and mesmerised Capitol Hill with his venomous vapour trail for another four years, building conspiracy theory upon fantasy and suggesting America had 'lost' China – and almost the whole cold war – because of Reds in high places.[112]

Britain, mercifully, avoided such excesses thanks to its more phlegmatic political tradition, the power of the party machines, the tacit agreement of party leaders not to make it an issue at election time and the determination of the Whitehall security authorities not to make martyrs out of Communists and fellow travellers in the public service.[113] The right-wing Conservative MP for Orpington, Sir Waldron Smithers, received short shrift from the Government bench (whether Attlee or Churchill was P.M.) when he called for the establishment of a House Committee on Un-English Activities.[114] The Cabinet toyed briefly however, with promulgating a draconian Press law banning journalism which brought aid and comfort to North Korea and which would have put the Communist *Daily Worker* out of business. They were talked out of it largely by Norman Brook who brought his Home Office experience to bear on where the line between liberty and licence might best be drawn.[115]

The defections of Guy Burgess and Donald Maclean in May 1951 caused a scandal of major proportions. Maclean as Head of the FO's American Department at the time of the Attlee-Truman Summit had been in a position to give Stalin pure gold.[116] While Burgess was much more than the drunken buffoon in a minor grade the authorities portrayed him as. His membership of the FO's Far Eastern Department before his disastrous booze-and-semen-laden posting to the British Embassy in Washington, gave him access to sensitive JIC assessments at a critical phase in the Chinese Civil War.[117] Their disappearance, coupled with American pressure following the exposure of the atom spy, Klaus Fuchs, in January 1950, led to the creation of 'positive vetting', the security screening system for top officials and military still used (with modifications) to this day.[118]

But the real debate about Korea – as substantial as it has been long-lasting – is what it did or did not do to Britain's long-term economic performance.

There is now almost universal agreement that Korea did overstrain the British economy, even among those on both sides of the Atlantic who were keenest for us to rearm. Paul Nitze, for example, told me, 'you can call it hubris or you can call it courage – I think we have much to admire the British for for what you could call hubris but which I consider to be breathtaking courage,' though he did admit 'I think it *is* possible that it was during that period that the United Kingdom overstretched its base.'[119]

Lord Franks agrees but insists, rightly, 'that you have to remember the context. As the Korean War went on', he explained in his North Oxford farmhouse four decades after telegraphing his crucial advice to Attlee and Bevin,

> there was a massive rearmament programme both in the United Kingdom and in the United States and France, and, of course, what it was about was not Korea, it was about Western Europe . . .
>
> [The Americans] felt certain that it [the invasion of South Korea] had happened either with the backing of the Russians or at least their letting it happen. And in this . . . subsequent knowledge tells us the Americans were right . . . Their trouble was that they feared Anglo–American/Soviet relations [were] entering on a new and much more dangerous phase when armed aggression couldn't be ruled out and, therefore, they had to build up defences in Europe.[120]

It was a fear widely shared in western Europe during that Korean summer which, as we have seen, 'produced near-panic in France and Germany'.[121]

It's important to recapture the sequence of events which led intelligence analysts in Washington and Whitehall and the politicians they briefed to conclude that there was a genuine danger that Stalin was using Kim Il Sung's forces as a feint to draw the west's attention from the central front across which the feared Red Army might move at any time. The Berlin Air Lift, certainly, had been a triumph but since the summer of 1949, the setbacks had been crowding in. In quick succession the Russians tested an atomic bomb, way ahead of the best estimates of western intelligence, in August 1949. Within a few weeks Communist forces had taken Peking. It's very hard indeed to conceive of these developments in such terms now, but to sane and sensible people it *did* look like an international conspiracy which was on the march.

The policy planners in Washington, led by Paul Nitze had drafted NSC-68, a global strategy for containing Communism by force if necessary which President Truman had accepted in April 1950.[122] There was no exact British equivalent to NSC-68, but declassified intelligence material shows the analysis was almost identical in Whitehall. The Joint Planning Staff were in the process of updating for the Chiefs of Staff Committee a 1948 survey of 'the spread of Communism' when the Korean War broke out. It was swiftly rewritten to take account of the new and unforeseen emergency. It corroborates Lord Franks' memory of how it looked to policy-makers at the time.

The planners still stuck to their and the JIC's estimate 'that war is not inevitable but that the circumstances in which war is most likely to occur will be when Soviet leaders may consider themselves strong enough to risk a major war of indefinite duration regardless of Western reactions; this may be for 1955 onwards but the estimate is based on very slender evidence.'[123] Clearly their sources had not improved since the great 1948 JIC assessment of the Soviet threat.[124]

The planners went on to warn the Chiefs, however, that 'the possibility that war may break out at any time before or after 1955 cannot be disregarded', and they outlined the four cold war methods of extending 'Russian Communist control' the years since 1945 had already demonstrated:

a by supporting a coup d'état by pseudo constitutional means as in Czechoslovakia;
b by political pressure as in Poland;
c by the support, either directly or indirectly, through Satellites, of communist rebellion as in China;
d by Russian inspired military aggression by a Satellite as in Korea.[125]

For Whitehall, as for Washington, the time had come to draw the line and Korea was the place to do it.

'Whether Soviet expansion is achieved by the method of the bayonet or the leaflet, the strategic effect on Commonwealth defence is the same, as by either method the area or the country falls under hostile control. The present extension of Soviet control and domination has now begun to impinge directly on Commonwealth ability to defend its vital interests and to meet its commitments to its allies. Further expansion must be resisted.'[126]

The planners presented a check list of 'important cold war areas . . . whose loss in peace would be a cold war defeat', and 'vital areas . . . whose loss would jeopardise our basic strategic requirements and prejudice the ability of the allies to fight a major war' – a kind of football league of threats. As Lord Franks recalled, Europe was at the top of League Division One as 'the unification of Germany aligned with Russia would make the defence of Europe problematical'.[127]

Though Korea was in Division Two, its loss would have a knock-on effect in Division One: 'If the forces of the United Nations were to fail to stem the drive of militant Communism in Korea it would be a major defeat for the Western Powers, and would shatter the faith of the free countries of the Far East and South East Asia in the ability of the Western Powers and the United Nations to defend them from Russian domination. Repercussions would, in fact, be felt in other parts of the world notably Western Germany.'[128]

Reflecting in his Oxonian tranquillity on the initial Korean crisis, Lord

Franks recalled the thinking that went into what one historian has called 'perhaps the most important telegram of his ambassadorship'[129]:

On 23 July, Ernest Bevin sent me a telegram asking me for my views so I had to give them. I felt a weight of responsibility because I knew what I was dealing with was other men's lives. But I decided in the end to put that from me and say what I thought. I said two things, really. The first one was that the Americans regarded us as their dependable ally. They would not understand it if we didn't stand with them on the ground in Korea and I thought that the damage would be deep and long lasting.

Secondly, I said something quite different – that there's something in the psychological make-up of the American nation which makes them like to have company when they're in trouble and, from this point of view, they wanted, under the United Nations' flag, allies to help them and they turned to Britain as the key. If we helped them, others would also. This went back and the Cabinet decided to send the Gloucesters. That's how it happened.[130]

Franks added that war in Korea had shifted the American image of Britain from one of economic weakness to the older one of an ally from whom much should be expected and demanded.[131] In other words, the Truman Administration was at last treating Britain as Attlee and his ministers had insisted they should whenever Marshall Aid administrators arrived in London to patronise – as a great power not just as another European nation.

Before turning to the long-term economic price paid for that psychological balm, let's engage, with that crucial adviser Lord Franks, in a little more reflection in tranquillity. In 1990 he was, he said, 'fairly clear' that:

The Russians were weaker than the United States thought they were. I think they were prepared to take advantage of situations where they thought there was no risk or small risk . . . probably the Russians thought that they were on a low-risk activity in Korea.

Why? Because the Americans reduced their troops in Korea. Speeches had been made suggesting it wasn't a vital part in the world for them, and, therefore, I think that Moscow got it wrong. But I also think that we got it wrong in the sense that it wasn't part of a concerted stepping-up of a Russian threat. I don't think this was there.

On the other hand, in the circumstances of the time, it was terribly difficult to leave things as they were in Western Europe – half-a-dozen divisions, most of them occupation divisions, badly armed . . . Were there trouble, what could they do? And this is why they put fighting divisions on the ground, American, British, French.

Now, if I look back, it's quite easy for me to say 'I doubt whether all that was necessary'. You couldn't possibly have thought it at the time. It seemed mere prudence.[132]

And, as Sir Anthony Farrar-Hockley has pointed out, it was that wider rearmament which Korea inspired that put such a strain on Britain's economic base, a strain which the less-than-expected 'burden-sharing' financial relief from the United States did little to offset.[133]

There was a strain of another kind too – a kind that history all too often forgets – a human one, the stress on those who found themselves in danger of going off to die on that inhospitable Korean peninsula of which so few people had heard. I can remember one of my schoolteachers, Brother Michael Ball (later the Bishop of Truro) recalling for me more than a decade after the event the anguish he felt doing his national service as a clerical officer in the Army sorting out who would and who would not be posted to Korea from his own age-group.

The call-up was especially stressful on the still young veterans of the Second World War barely five years after demob and the building-up of new lives and, very often, new families. Richard Hoggart has captured the scene at the Hull Paragon Station in the summer of 1951 when he was summoned to a camp in Wales to learn to be a soldier again. 'I can still see clearly the stances and experiences of the family at the barrier – Mary, newly pregnant, looking tense but "putting on a brave face" for the children ("only two weeks after all"), the children, at five and three, holding one of her hands each and observing not altogether comprehensively and certainly unhappily their father going off; not for a few days lecturing but to be a soldier again.'[134]

And what Hoggart found waiting for him confirms Sir Anthony Farrar-Hockley's point about old equipment despite the huge rearmament already under way: 'We were in some ways professionally refreshed in the two weeks, but I doubt if the North Koreans or, later, the Chinese would have noticed. The most astonishing aspect of the whole enterprise was the sight of our guns and gear. In all important respects they were those on which we had trained in the early Forties and dragged through the war. No magnificent and sophisticated new electronics from the arms industry in the intervening years. Standing on those bleak Welsh coastal hills, shouting old orders, time was collapsed.'[135]

In a strange way, the same could be said of the committee rooms in Whitehall. Apart from one or two, younger, dissenting voices, nobody seriously queried the need or the capacity for going over once more on to a war footing. Perhaps the most influential single voice at official level, as he himself admitted in his diary, was that of Sir Robert Hall. Even before the Korean War started, he and Sir Edwin Plowden were pushing for a greater defence effort.

In his diary entry for 26 May 1950 Hall, on a visit to Washington, noted: 'P [Plowden] asked me to talk to Oliver [Franks] about the defence problem which hasn't had much impact in the UK yet. I had taken Jo Alsop [influential American commentator and cold war hardliner] to dinner there [the British Embassy] a week ago and we had both tried to put a sense of urgency into him.

The trouble is that we are so pre-occupied with the internal situation that we have been holding down tight on defence. Now it seems that there is much less time than we thought, because of China and the atom bomb: so we must change our priorities.'[136] When war came less than a month later, Hall expressed 'very great relief' as it 'may well be a turning point in the history of this period. If it stops the USSR they will lose, and the US gain, a great deal of face. If not, we will have the war when on the whole I think we are relatively stronger now than we will be later.'[137]

Hall's admission of direct, personal, decisive influence – rare for a public servant, even in private – came in the spring of 1951 at the height of the rearmament row which propelled Bevan from the Cabinet. In his diary Hall recalled:

The Ministry of Defence agreed or perhaps put forward the £4.7 bn figure [for the revised, expanded defence estimates over a three-year period]. Supply and Trade more or less reluctantly went along. The Chancellor [Gaitskell] with a little help from the PM [Attlee] and the Foreign Secretary [Bevin] and Morrison pushed it through largely on a belief in the Nitze [burden-sharing] exercise. But in a sense it all went back to Plowden and I being convinced by Jo Alsop that we needed to re-arm about last April. Of course I know that two civil servants could not push the country into anything – it is international affairs and Korea and American pressure and so on. Yet if we hadn't said we could stand it it might have been £3.7 [billion] or a smaller figure, and if we had not pushed the 4% productivity idea or had said it was all going to be disastrous, I doubt it would have gone nearly as far. I think we were quite right, naturally enough. And Ministers have said over and over again that we must re-arm and they seem to believe it. But yet it is true that if we had taken different views the outcome would almost certainly be quite different.[138]

Sadly for Hall's reputation (and he was a fine, decent, liberal-minded public servant), virtually nobody sustains his arguments now – not Lord Franks, not Lord Sherfield ('looking back on it, I think it did put too heavy a burden on us').[139]

The survivor of that highly influential Hall-Plowden duo, however, maintained to the end that the real, vital, defensible argument in favour of that huge British rearmament was to keep the Americans committed to the defence of Europe. 'One forgets what the feeling was,' he told me forty years later. 'I agree our defence programme was too large. But suppose we hadn't adopted it and we had failed to get the Americans really to be involved. There wouldn't really have been much of a defence . . . in Europe.'[140]

There were still intelligent, albeit small (in terms of their place in the Whitehall pecking-order) voices expressing disquiet even at the height of the Korean War, even inside Lord Plowden's own Central Economic Planning

Staff. The young Douglas Allen (later Lord Croham and a Permanent Secretary to the Treasury) was engaged on making the figures add up in a way which buttressed the Hall-Plowden thesis and the Attlee Government's case. 'I remember', he recalled,

> researching the consequences of the proposed increase in defence expenditure on our balance of payments and reaching the conclusion that our balance of payments would suffer enormously from what was proposed. We published a White Paper[141] which I had some hand in drafting, which suggested we could save our trade balance by a massive increase in the export of consumption goods. I was quite certain this was impossible, and, therefore, that our balance of payments would suffer very severely. Others felt that if it did, the United States would be able to give us sufficient financial support to make our position tolerable.[142]

We got the balance of payments crisis but not the support.

The dramatic turnaround, from a payments surplus of £307 million in 1950 to a deficit of £369 million in 1951[143] was especially tragic as this was *the* golden opportunity in the entire postwar period for a sustained export-led boom which, with luck, might have put the British economy on to a higher and sustainable trajectory before Germany, in particular, recovered to the point where our export markets were once more highly vulnerable. Counterfactual history has its dangers, but there are powerful reasons for supposing our best hope for the kind of postwar economic miracle enjoyed by so many western European countries was scattered in fragments in the committee rooms of Whitehall, on the hills above the Imjin in Korea and along the Rhine in Germany as British occupation forces were rearmed in readiness for a Stalinist assault.

Lord Croham, while acknowledging that such things are 'a matter of belief rather than proof',[144] reckons there were 'by 1949–50 so many encouraging signs to suggest that the economy was turning, such as increasing domestic output, fewer bottlenecks and a marked improvement in exports . . . The inability of British export industries to entrench themselves in export markets before competition from Germany and Japan returned certainly owes a lot to the sudden change of priorities in 1950–51 . . . Of course exports did pick up again, but momentum was lost and the British engineering industries were never able to realise the possibilities that seemed open to them in 1949.'[145]

Lord Croham concluded: 'It may be too much to claim that, but for the headlong rush into defence in 1950, the UK would have enjoyed an economic miracle; but there would have been much less stop-go and a much better balanced economy.'[146] Certainly, the Treasury believed that analysis of the Korean experience, generation in, generation out, thereafter.[147] And economic historians have found it hard to fault it.

Most agree with Sidney Pollard that 'it was precisely in these years that other countries, above all Germany and Japan, could begin to build up a technical lead and start on their own process of wresting one export market after another from Britain. While we built tanks and planes, they built machinery with which to achieve their later success.'[148] Lord Plowden, however, was right in his memoirs to point out that the Korean-overload was but one of several factors which kept the postwar British economy a miracle-free zone. 'Even', he wrote, 'if there had been no Korean War, the obstacles to an economic miracle were and still are [his book was published in 1989] formidable. Perhaps the most important are a national resistance to change, poor management in much of industry, reactionary trade unions, the poor education and training of much of the workforce and too great a concentration on old and declining industries.'[149]

That said, the economic consequences of the Korean War-inspired re-armament *were* too lightly taken and *were* enduringly damaging to a British economy still fragile but definitely on-the-turn towards greater vitality and robustness. There was a political fall-out, too, which did much to poison the internal life of the Labour Party for the rest of the 1950s. For it was defence spending which pushed Nye Bevan out of the Cabinet, gave the dissenting left the leader it had lacked as well as a new name ('Keep Left' became 'The Bevanites') and caused an intra-party civil war of a ferocity Labour was not to experience again until the even more electorally ruinous early 1980s.

Bevan's resignation, along with those of Harold Wilson and John Freeman, junior Supply Minister, ranks as perhaps the most dramatic Cabinet farewell of the postwar period (prime ministerial departures are a class apart), rivalled only by Sir Geoffrey Howe's in 1990. It was, as such things always are, an unstable mixture of personality, politics and policy which those engaged in the business of political story-telling have changed with each retelling.

In Bevan's case it was a seething cocktail of accumulated frustrations – of being in office for over five years, his mercurial temperament crammed into a constricting bottle labelled 'collective responsibility'; of being passed over in favour of a younger man when Gaitskell went to the Treasury; of a special loathing of Gaitskell and the Gaitskell type who seemed to do so well, so effortlessly and so fast out of British democratic socialism compared to those who had risen via classic working class politics; a genuine belief that the pace and cost of rearmament was too great and an equally genuine horror about the financial impact of that rearmament on his beloved Health Service.

Bevan, as we have seen, had been eloquent on the gallons of medicine pouring down British throats in the first years of the NHS. But he had always put that, and the initial surge of expenditure, down to the inevitable catching-up effect as a formerly deprived population made good on decades of want.[150] The Treasury took a less optimistic view. Alarmed by spending out-turns way above the early forecast of £134 million (£225 million in 1948–9 and £272 million for 1949–50),[151] they successfully lobbied for a Cabinet committee with a brief to curb runaway health expenditure, which Attlee set up, with himself in the chair, in April 1950.[152] As the official historian of the NHS put it, 'Bevan's critics within the Cabinet were running out of patience with him, while his patience with them was also virtually exhausted,' even before the Korean War broke out and before Bevan's reluctant transfer to the Ministry of Labour in January 1951.[153]

'The clash', as Bevan's biographer Michael Foot called the showdown with Gaitskell,[154] came in the run-up to the 1951 Budget. When the Chancellor, Gaitskell, determined to curb social service spending generally and became convinced 'that the only possible place where big enough savings could be made was in the Health Services',[155] he would not brook compromise. Though he was only six months in Cripps' chair, Gaitskell would have gone rather than give in though, in the end, the sum at issue was a mere £13 million.[156]

It would be quite wrong, as Labour mythology often had it, that the great clash of 1951 was a showdown between a passion-driven working class socialist and an upper middle class desiccated calculating machine determined, even then, to wean Labour away from its more sacred collectivist shibboleths. It's true that, after Bevan blurted out under questioning at a rowdy meeting in Bermondsey that he would 'never be a member of a Government which makes charges on the National Health Service for the patient'[157] his old confidant, Archie Lush, travelled down from Tredegar to tell him how strongly his people in the South Wales valleys were backing his Bermondsey declaration,[158] which must have had a powerful effect on him.

It's equally true that the comparable experience for Gaitskell occurred when his Treasury Permanent Secretary, Sir Edward Bridges, broke all the rules of Civil Service impartiality and told him, 'I have really nothing to say and certainly no advice to offer. But I want you to know that not only all those in the Treasury who know about it tremendously admire the stand you have made, but that all the others who do not at present know but will know will feel the same way. It's the best day we have had in the Treasury for ten years.' 'I was so overcome with emotion', Gaitskell recorded in his diary '... that I could not say a word.'[159] Both Gaitskell and Bevan were deeply passionate people but the sources of their passion came from utterly different well-springs.

Bevan regarded charging for teeth and spectacles as a betrayal of the fundamental principle of a free NHS. Gaitskell saw it as both common sense and an aid to good housekeeping. The unfolding story had elements of the tragi-comic. It was fought out in Cabinet Room, party meeting, hospital bedside and even Windsor Castle where the Gaitskells were staying with the King and Queen. Dora Gaitskell told the King her husband was 'rather right wing' (a remark His Majesty found hilarious),[160] and George VI told Gaitskell, waving his foot at his Chancellor, that 'I really don't see why people should have false teeth free any more than they should have shoes free.'[161] (Just think what an Establishment conspiracy the Labour left would have made of the King and the

Head of the Civil Service had they known of their private support for Gaitskell.)

The bedside element of this Ealing comedy came when Attlee, in St Mary's Paddington with ulcer trouble, received Gaitskell on the morning of Budget Day. The Chancellor explained his position and, for a moment, became the victim of Prime Ministerial mumbling: 'Finally, he murmured what I took to be "Very well, you will have to go." In a split second I realised he had said, "I am afraid they will have to go." '[162]

For their part, *they* (Bevan and Wilson) thought they were home and dry when another invalid, the fast-fading Ernie Bevin, asked to see them. Wilson, cleverly suggesting that the acting Prime Minister, his successor as Foreign Secretary, was behind the whole dispute, produced one of the last roars of defiance to emerge from that shrunken frame: 'Morrison did you say? Morrison. Oh well, in that case, why didn't you tell me? I am not having this and I'll see that Clem don't.'[163]

The ploy failed. Even if Bevin had survived, it's far from certain that even he could have fixed it. The issue was far bigger than any Morrisonian scheming and Bevin was an admirer of Gaitskell's. As the teeth and spectacles row raged in Cabinet and Cabinet committee, Bevin told Lord Longford, 'I hope Hugh Gaitskell will remain Chancellor for five years at least. He knows what he wants and will get it.'[164] Bevin sat next to Gaitskell throughout his Budget Speech on 10 April. 'When I sat down', recorded Gaitskell, 'he said, "That was a great speech," and he held my hand for quite a long time.'[165] Four days later he died in Carlton Gardens, the Foreign Secretary's London home Attlee had let him keep on, his Red Box of papers on his lap in bed, its key locked in his great fist; he worked for 'My People' right to the end.[166]

Attlee from his sick bed in Paddington tried to use Bevin's death as a healing factor, writing to Bevan on 18 April: 'The death of Ernie has rather overshadowed these differences and I hope that everyone will forget them.'[167] To no avail. Gaitskell pressed on with his Bill to permit Health Service charges. Bevan said he could not vote with the Government. On 20 April Attlee reminded him of the requirements of collective Cabinet responsibility. The following day Bevan resigned.[168]

On the rearmament issue, the centrepiece of a rather lacklustre resignation speech in the House of Commons when he extemporised too much, his brilliance on his feet and his gift for making use of interruptions letting him down for once,[169] Bevan was proved right. Later the incoming Churchill Government scaled down the huge rearmament programme so dear to Gaitskell. As for prescription charges, they came and they stayed. The lasting effect of the Bevan resignation? Perhaps more than any other factor, it doomed Labour to the political wilderness for the remainder of the decade (even though Bevan and Gaitskell had publicly – and genuinely – healed their rift in time for the 1959 general election). As Denis Healey never ceased to remark, if Labour had deployed the time it spent fighting itself on fighting the Conservatives, the electoral history of postwar Britain could have been very different.[170]

Even in his moment of victory in the spring of 1951 Gaitskell was aware of this grim possibility. 'I said', he wrote in his diary, 'in the middle of one discussion to Hugh Dalton, "It is really a fight for the soul of the Labour Party." More people understand that this was so now. But who will win it? No one can say as yet. I am afraid that if Bevan does we shall be out of power for years and years.'[171] Neither Labour faction 'won' it. If anybody did it was Churchill, Eden and Macmillan in the next three elections.

But, as is the way with domestic political drama, the ripples may be felt for years, but, in the short term, attention is quickly diverted by the next crisis wave crashing in. In this instance it was not from Korea, but from Persia and at the centre of it was a political figure whose personality made even Nye Bevan's emotional spasms look like a demonstration of British sangfroid.

By the standards of some more recent Middle Eastern figures determined to use the oil weapon against 'satanic' or 'colonialist' nations in the west, Dr Mohammed Mossadegh was a benign, if eccentric, figure. When a reluctant Shah appointed him Prime Minister of Iran in April 1951, after the assassination of General Razmara, Mossadegh, to almost universal acclaim across the Iranian political spectrum from the Communist Tudeh Party to the fundamentalist Ayatollahs, nationalised the Anglo-Iranian Oil Company (better known these days as British Petroleum), and became a figure of contempt, parody and hatred in Britain on a scale that only Nasser would surpass in the 1950s, that decade of painful psychological adjustment in a nation that still marched to the drumbeats of Empire.

Mossadegh had the habit of conducting business from his old iron bed (both Attlee's envoy, Richard Stokes, and Truman's, Averell Harriman would be received by 'Old Mossy', as Harriman called him,[172] in this Churchillian fashion). Like Churchill he wept a good deal; like Churchill, too, he was a romantic aristocrat enjoying a tremendous rapport with the common people. Unlike Churchill, he would often faint on grand public occasions. Sometimes this was genuine. On other occasions it was not and he would wink at doctors who wished to attend to him.[173] To the British Ambassador in Tehran, Sir Francis Shepherd, he was simply 'a lunatic' whose breath gave off 'a slight reek of opium' and whose mind gave 'the impression of being impervious to argument'. Shepherd warned London, 'We shall have to watch him carefully because he is both cunning and slippery and completely unscrupulous.'[174]

Shepherd's views found a sympathetic hearing in some, though not all, of Whitehall, parts of the Cabinet Room and much of the British Press, but not, significantly, in Attlee's Downing Street, Truman's White House or Acheson's State Department. Had fast failing health not precipitated the sad departure of Bevin on his seventieth birthday on 9 March from his beloved Foreign Office,[175] to eke out his last few weeks as Lord Privy Seal with vague, unexpressed 'domestic' responsibilities, it's likely the reaction of the FO to events in Persia would have been significantly different.

For where Bevin had been sympathetic to the idea of partnership with progressive nationalists in the Middle East and firm against the use of force,[176] his successor, Herbert Morrison, in the words of his biographers, was not only a narrower, more insular man with a mind more attuned to political minutiae than grand global themes, he also 'grew increasingly attached to long-standing British institutions, such as the monarchy and Empire, and revered them in an almost Kiplingesque way. He had always been a patriot in the best sense. Now he became something of a little-England jingo. Within twenty-four hours of taking office he asked for a life of Palmerston, and ostentatiously carried Guedalla's volume round with him for weeks afterwards.'[177]

At various moments in the crisis, which absorbed a great deal of the Attlee Administration's failing energies in the last five months of its life, Morrison, like the Defence Minister, Shinwell, would itch to use military force against Iran, not just to teach the Persians a lesson and, hopefully, to pitch 'The Man in Pyjamas' from his bedstead, but to preserve Britain's position throughout the Middle East and to dissuade the Egyptians from pursuing any designs they might have to nationalise the Suez Canal.[178] But for Attlee's calmness and wider judgment it's distinctly possible that Churchill's yearning for 'the splutter of musketry'[179] might have been fulfilled round Abadan, at least, the island groaning under the weight of Anglo-Iranian's installations which, at that time, constituted the world's largest oil refinery.[180]

Like all Middle East crises – past, present and, no doubt, future – the 1951 episode was made up of several tangled layers – the share of oil revenue between exploiting company and exploited territory, nationalism-cum-anti-colonialism and imperial atavism, personality and religion and, in this case, the cold war. For the Americans the overriding issue was that Iran's vast oil reserves should not fall into the hands of the Soviet Union. Mossadegh, therefore, was preferable to chaos, revolution, a Tudeh Party Government and, by extension, Stalin. The cold war fixation – at fever pitch given the backdrop of the Korean War – blended most inconveniently from the British point of view with more traditional American anti-imperial sentiments held firmly, openly and irritatingly by the US Ambassador in Tehran, Henry Grady.[181]

It was, in fact, the Americans who had done most to precipitate the Persian Crisis of 1951 by transforming the entire financial edifice built upon the sands above the world's greatest storehouse of energy. Once Aramco had concluded its fifty/fifty profit-sharing deal with Saudi Arabia in December 1950, midwifed by the brash, brilliant George McGhee of the US Department of State,[182] the writing was on the wall for Anglo-Iranian. No upping of the *royalty* share (crucially different from *profit*-sharing), no placing of token Iranians on the AIOC Board, was going to stem that volatile tidal flow of anti-colonialism and revenue lust in Iran for long.

Sir William Fraser, Anglo-Iranian's Chairman, might not have been quite the rigid, purblind autocrat the Foreign Office diplomats he so disliked usually imagined him to be,[183] but, for the most part, the top management of the Company did deserve the renown accorded them by their colleague Sir William

Leggett (AIOC's labour adviser and an old friend of Bevin's from trade union days). They are, said Leggett in early 1951, 'helpless, niggling, without an idea between them, confused, hide-bound, small-minded, blind'.[184] Dean Acheson's acid assessment – 'Never had so few lost so much so stupidly and so fast'[185] – is a charge which sticks, its memory assuaged only by the splendid (if futile) British-Bulldog manner in which the Company's servants took their leave of Abadan in the final evacuation on 4 October 1951, a few days before the Attlee Government expired:

> The ship's band [they were on board the Royal Navy cruiser, *Mauritius, en route* for Basra and safety], 'correct' to the end, struck up the Persian national anthem and the launches began their shuttle service . . . The cruiser . . . steamed slowly away up the river with the band playing, the assembled company lining the rails and roaring in unison the less printable version of 'Colonel Bogey' . . .[186]

That it ended (temporarily), in bathos rather than bloodshed (Mossadegh was toppled in 1953 by a joint CIA/MI6 engineered *coup*[187] and BP came back into Iran, not as monopoly extractor, but part of an international consortium[188]) is to the Government's credit and especially to Attlee personally. Assisted by Gaitskell, who kept in close touch with the Americans throughout,[189] the Prime Minister managed the Abadan Crisis of 1951 in the way that Eden should have handled the Suez crisis five years later but failed to do so.

As Roger Louis put it, 'In the critical Cabinet discussions, in July while deciding not to intervene and in September when faced with eviction, it was Attlee who steadied nerves and guided his colleagues towards restraint. During this time of crisis he demonstrated genuine insight into the sources of Middle Eastern nationalism and the way in which British influence might be preserved. He not only believed in "partnership" but saw the need of a real and not a superficial end to the old system of concessions.'[190]

Attlee treated Persia in 1951 rather as he had India in 1946–7, as an area of personal Prime Ministerial responsibility. As he told Dalton in mid-September, 'I am handling Persia; I've made it quite clear that troops are to go in only to save lives.'[191] Significantly, he made it plain that if Labour won the election, 'our little pseudo-Pam' [i.e. Palmerston], as Dalton called Morrison,[192] would not be going back to the Foreign Office: 'His ignorance, PM said, was shocking. He had no background and knew no history.'[193]

Persia apart, the Attlee Government cut a sorry figure in its last months. With the Crippsian incomes policy defunct, wage claims crowded in. With the wartime anti-strike Order 1305 finally repealed (Bevan was being heckled by dockers on this very subject when he brought forth his reckless pledge on Health Service charges),[194] the possibility of a rash of industrial action was preoccupying Whitehall. As the last hours of the Government passed, the

Treasury fretted about the balance of payments and a shortage of coal.[195] It was almost as if nothing had changed from the crisis summer of 1947.

On top of this the ministerial stock was depleted with Bevin dead and Cripps retired through ill health. Attlee himself was the victim of intestinal trouble and 'Dalton's diary mercilessly dwelt on the physical debility of a group of leading ministers who were well into their sixties' while 'the Government was balanced on a knife edge. With its precarious majority, it needed every vote, the ambulances queued in Palace Yard as the halt, the sick and the lame were wheeled through the lobbies.'[196]

It was the Monarch, however (himself dying of cancer), who brought election timing to the fore. At an audience with Attlee on 24 June, George VI expressed concern about 'the Government's unstable position'. Attlee told the King he would ask for a dissolution in the autumn. On 1 September George VI wrote to the Prime Minister making it plain he did not wish to embark on his planned six-month Commonwealth tour with political affairs still so uncertain in Britain (in the end illness prevented him from travelling). On 5 September Attlee told the King he would ask for a dissolution in the first week of October.[197] Election day was fixed for 25 October.

The Conservatives started with a huge lead over Labour in the opinion polls (50.5 per cent to 43.5 per cent on 5 October according to Gallup).[198] Gaitskell thought at the beginning of the campaign the Conservatives would get back with a majority of seventy-five (by the end of the campaign he'd brought it down to around fifty).[199] Whitehall thought much the same and began to prepare frantically for the kind of complete change they had not experienced since 1929 (apart from the brief interregnum of the 'Caretaker Government' of 1945, there had been an element of continuity with some ministers surviving from the previous Government into the next).[200]

It's possible that the course of the campaign really did make a difference in 1951. A row soon developed about who was and who was not 'warmongering' over Persia, which climaxed in the last three days of the election period with the *Daily Mirror*'s 'Whose Finger on the Trigger?' campaign, suggesting that the peace was not safe in Churchill's hands,[201] an enterprise which brought the paper a libel writ from the new Prime Minister when the Conservatives won.[202] It is also possible that, for all the attractions of Conservative rhetoric about 'setting the people free', easing rationing, building 300,000 houses a year, the *Mirror*'s campaign had bite in that very tense autumn atmosphere of 1951.

Labour did far better than anyone predicted. On a high turnout of 82.6 per cent, it won more votes than any other British political party before or since (13,948,883) but 'it took the genius of the electoral system to give the Tories . . . a majority in Parliament'.[203] (Thanks to our first-past-the-post voting system and a flight from Labour in key suburban marginals, Labour finished up with 295 seats to 321 for the Conservatives and 6 for the Liberals.)

Paradoxically, Labour's very success in carrying out its intentions may have contributed to its fall. As Anthony King has pointed out, 'The fit between what the Labour Party said it would do in 1945 and what the Labour Government actually achieved between 1945 and 1951 is astonishingly close. Most of "Let Us Face the Future" reads like a prospective history of the immediate postwar period.'[204] Its historic mission seemed to be fulfilled, a fact the exhaustion of its leaders and the intellectual bankruptcy of its 1950 and 1951 manifestos seemed to confirm. As Peter Clarke has commented, with a wry perceptiveness, 'since the Labour party had now fulfilled its agreed aims, only the aims on which it could not agree remained . . . The Government had eliminated a huge area of accord within the party, as enshrined in the 1945 programme by carrying out its election promises – a hazardous procedure which most of its successors prudently avoided.'[205]

Sam Watson, Leader of the Durham miners, whom, briefly, Attlee had considered as Bevin's successor at the Foreign Office ('Sam never wanted to travel south of Durham. Would have been a drawback in a Foreign Secretary,'[206]) told the Labour Party Conference in 1950: 'Poverty has been abolished. Hunger is unknown. The sick are tended. The old folks are cherished, our children are growing up in a land of opportunity.'[207]

But had a decade of 'war socialism' and the social, economic and administrative infrastructure the Attlee Government erected to underpin and extend it really changed the face of mid-century Britain? If so, why is 1951 not seen as the best kind of historical full-stop (when a dark era of inequality, deprivation and human waste was cast for ever into a past best forgotten) instead of a mere comma in a depressing story of slow, inexorable relative decline? What could have – should have – been done in those early postwar years that was neglected, attempted too feebly or not even thought of at all? Why was that political generation – the makers of the fabled postwar consensus – so deluded in thinking that the biggest domestic problems had been cracked?

CHAPTER 11

Mid–century Britain

Nothing would happen so long as the British lacked a view from within. Looking on [Europe] from the outside, they lulled themselves with illusions of grandeur. They had not known the trauma of wartime occupation; they had not been conquered; their system seemed intact. In reality they suffered paradoxically – from not having had their pride broken and their factories destroyed.
Jean Monnet, 1976[1]

The most extraordinary thing is that the one Government which one would have expected to go in for planning – a Labour Government – didn't do it. It dismantled what there was of it from wartime . . . I suppose in the last analysis, they believed that essentially the British economy was sound whereas the French knew that unless there was a huge national effort to turn France from an also-ran back into a main racer it would stay down on the floor.
Professor Eric Hobsbawm, 1991[2]

We had won the War and we voted ourselves a nice peace.
Sir Kenneth Berrill, 1991[3]

Where . . . we went wrong in 1945 was in thinking that the Government actually had a major contribution to make in taking over business decisions – how to organise production, how to distribute, how to run transport and so on. I think that that was a false idea, that Governments are, in fact, very bad at this.
Lord Rees-Mogg, 1990[4]

What the postwar Labour Government really did at the crucial period is complete the interwar policies of redistribution rather than prepare the ground for a new period of growth. 1945–51 is a postscript to the interwar period. All that they did was wonderful but clearly wrong – right in

social terms, wrong in economic terms. There was something great about the postwar Government. It was the right government at the wrong time.
Sir Ralf Dahrendorf, 1990[5]

I see Europe going by default: Free economy Germany will be forging ahead; with all their gifts of efficiency displayed to the full. And we, in our mismanaged, mixed-economy, overpopulated little island, shall become a second-rate power, with no influence and continuing 'crises'.
Hugh Dalton, 1952[6]

In his twilight years, Attlee was asked by the *Observer* newspaper to prepare an obituary of the man whose spells in No. 10 sandwiched his own. Of Churchill he wrote he was 'rather like a layer cake. One layer was certainly seventeenth century. The eighteenth century in him is obvious. There was the nineteenth century, and a large slice, of course, of the twentieth century; and another, curious, layer which may possibly have been the twenty-first.'[7] In an even more curious way, mid-century Britain as a whole was like that, a mirror-image of its new/old Prime Minister.

The Festival of Britain, shimmering on its South Bank site where a mountain of blitz-blown rubble had lain but a few years before, reflected it too – the conscious celebration of a settled, successful society vindicated in twentieth-century war with its eye (in imitation of the Great Exhibition of 1851[8]) on the technologies and markets of the century to come. 'There,' between Waterloo Bridge and the LCC Headquarters in County Hall, 'the story of Britain was to be represented in a series of pavilions, each devoted to a significant aspect of national life – the home, school, industry, transport, the countryside etc. Local exhibitions and festivities were also organised throughout the country, making it a national jamboree with virtually every community involved.'[9]

It was Herbert Morrison's show. He picked up the idea and ran with it, selling it to the Cabinet on the grounds that 'we ought to do something jolly . . . we need something to give Britain a lift'.[10] As opening day approached he put Mossadegh, Europe, the cares of the Foreign Secretaryship on one side and enjoyed himself. Eden rebuked him for it, as did the *Daily Telegraph*,[11] but Morrison didn't care. He sat in his box at the shiny, new Festival Hall (the occasion's lasting monument) at the opening concert, surrounded by members of the Royal Family, as the massed choirs belted out 'Land of Hope and Glory'.[12]

The wags, as well as the Conservative Press, had a field day however. The Skylon, a kind of 'luminous exclamation mark'[13] which towered over the site, was likened to the parlous state of the balance of payments-hit British economy ('no visible means of support').[14] The Beaverbrook Press attacked the whole idea as socialist extravagance, 'Morrison's Folly', an absurd waste of £11 million of public money.[15] Noël Coward sent it up in the Lyric Revue of 1951 with his 'Don't Make Fun of the Fair':

Take a nip from your brandy flask,
Scream and caper and shout,
Don't give anyone time to ask
What the Hell it's about.[16]

Its brilliant display of the latest in British architecture and design (Gerald
Barry and Hugh Casson turned out to be patrons of flair) caused the Festival to
be described as 'all Heal let loose'.[17]

Too much symbolism has been loaded retrospectively on to 'Morrison's
Monument'. Christopher Booker is stretching too far in dumping responsibility for the environmental and planning failures, symbolised by the hated
tower blocks (which were a feature of Macmillan's Britain and after, not
Attlee's), on to the Festival and its creators.[18] As Arthur Marwick put it:

> Charles Plouviez has written of the Festival that: 'It might be said to mark
> the beginning of our "English disease" – the moment at which we stopped
> trying to lead the world as an industrial power, and started being the world's
> entertainers, coaxing tourists to laugh at our eccentricities, marvel at our
> traditions and wallow in our nostalgia.' This is a wild judgement which
> ignores both the genuine and justified pride in real achievements made by
> 1951, and the preliminary indications of the transformations which were to
> come to full flood in the 60s.[19]

Marwick had in mind the cultural transformations which did not burst
through for another decade, until British tastes, life styles and social attitudes
finally sloughed off the Thirties and Forties straitjackets in which they still
remained largely imprisoned when the crowds, confounding the critics,
swarmed to the South Bank between May and September 1951. What the
Festival did throw into sharp relief, however, was a long-standing divide in
British society (which has done much to condition twentieth-century politics,
too) between what Michael Frayn, in a celebrated passage, called 'the Herbivores' and 'the Carnivores'. 'With the exception of Herbert Morrison', Frayn
wrote a dozen years after the labourers of the Ministry of Works had moved in
and cleared the site (London's first skyscraper, the Shell Building, stands on
the spot),

> there was almost no-one of working-class background concerned in planning
> the Festival, and nothing about the results to suggest that the working-
> classes were anything more than the lovably human but essentially inert
> objects of benevolent administration.
> In fact, Festival Britain was the Britain of the radical middle-classes –
> the do-gooders; the readers of the *News Chronicle*, the *Guardian*, and the
> *Observer*; the signers of petitions, the backbone of the BBC. In short, the
> Herbivores, or gentle ruminants, who look out from the lush pastures which

are their natural station in life with eyes full of sorrow for less fortunate creatures, guiltily conscious of their advantages, though not usually ceasing to eat the grass. And in making the Festival they earned the contempt of the Carnivores – the readers of the *Daily Express*; the Evelyn Waughs; the cast of the Directory of Directors – the members of the upper and middle-classes who believe that if God had not wished them to prey on all smaller and weaker creatures without scruple he would not have made them as they are.[20]

Frayn saw the Festival as a kind of elegy for Mr Attlee's Britain. Just over a month after the closing ceremony (with Geraldo and his Orchestra, Gracie Fields at the microphone, Kenneth Horne and Richard Murdoch cracking the jokes),[21] the Labour Government fell and with it, in Frayn's depiction, the decade 'sanctioned by the exigencies of the war and its aftermath' in which 'the Herbivores had dominated the scene. By 1951 the regime which supported them was exhausted, and the Carnivores were ready to take over. The Festival was the last, and virtually the posthumous, work of the Herbivore Britain of the BBC News, the Crown Film Unit, the sweet ration, the Ealing comedies, Uncle Mac, Sylvia Peters . . . all the great fixed stars by which my childhood was navigated.'[22]

There is a trap, into which most historians and all political commentators fall, of placing too much significance on electoral benchmarks. Nineteen fifty-one is usually seen as a great turning-point. Yet, paradoxically, Lord Croham (rightly) was to depict it as the election in which less change occurred in the direction of economic policy-making than at any other transfer of political power since 1945.[23] The more important question, interestingly enough, was posed by the in-coming premier twenty-one years earlier when the scars he had acquired as Chancellor of the Exchequer were still livid. 'It is no longer a case', Churchill said in 1930, 'of one party fighting another, nor of one set of politicians scoring off another. It is the case of successive governments facing economic problems and being judged by their success or failure in the duel.'[24]

In that context, the Festival of Britain has an altogether deeper and more alarming significance. For like its great precursor in the glass palaces shining in Hyde Park in 1851, it was as much the creation of nervousness as of confidence. Hadn't Prince Albert intended the Great Exhibition to be a warning to British manufacturers not to rest on their laurels?[25] Wasn't a certain Alfred Krupp of Essen the man whose material caused heads to turn (especially those interested in the weaponry needed to sustain great powerdom) at this celebration of British manufacturing prowess?[26] What would the more thoughtful visitor to the Festival have made of Churchill's 1930 judgment as he or she gazed at the big steam locomotive made in Britain for export to India[27] or looked at the '25,000 photographs illustrating the wide range of British manufacturers' in the Design Review Pavilion?[28] Would they have noticed, in Paul Addison's words, that: 'In a whimsical fashion the Festival celebrated tradition as much as change. Though John Betjeman had no part in the Festival, a Betjemanesque affection for Victoriana was evident in the Emett railway, or the section of the South Bank devoted to the English seaside holiday.'[29]

In the summer of 1951, despite the general air of economic crisis within the Treasury and without (Rab Butler never forgot the briefing Bridges and Armstrong gave him in the Athenaeum when he took over as Chancellor that autumn. 'Their story', he recalled, 'was of blood draining from the system and a collapse greater than had been foretold in 1931'[30]), a vigorous case for optimism about the long-term prospects could have been mounted, especially by those who took the entirely justified view that it's the new technologies which count in the long-run.

Six years on after Keynes presented his coruscating paper to the War Cabinet on Britain's economic future, with its division of the industrial base into inefficient old staples like cotton and coal and new, hoped for staples such as aircraft and radar where 'we have the rest of the world licked on cost',[31] it really did seem as if we might have the world licked in these areas. In 1951, Ferrantis sold the world's first commercial mainframe computer. As an old man, Vivian Bowden (a minister in the first Wilson Government and Principal of the University of Manchester Institute of Science and Technology) would relive the glorious moment of salesmanship for me as if it was the highspot of his career. It was sold to Joe Lyons, the catering firm of Corner House fame, hence its name, 'Leo'. The company was so impressed that it set up a firm to make and sell the machines.[32] Britain really did look favourably placed to be a pace-setter in the 'third industrial revolution' (the first being based on steam; the second on electricity; the third on electronics).

The air, too, appeared to be Britain's. The four-engined turbo-prop Vickers Viscount, one of the Brabazon Committee's progeny, 'was so smooth, quiet and economical that it became the most successful British airliner ever made',[33] selling well even in the highly competitive American market where, in the words of its designer, Sir George Edwards, there was nothing like it on the horizon.[34] Some 400 Viscounts were sold worldwide in the ten years after 1948.[35]

The greatest hope of all, with an immense dollar-earning potential in that greenback-starved era, was the jet airliner planned for by the Brabazon group – the Comet – which showed every sign of being able to 'hold the world market even against American competition'.[36] De Havilland's lead over Boeing was thought to be about three years (a cause of considerable alarm to the Americans),[37] and both Whitehall and the main national carrier, BOAC, 'were so confident' about the design 'that no prototype was felt to be necessary. Fourteen were ordered for BOAC straight off the drawing board.'[38] When Pathé's cameras recorded the Comet's test flight at Hatfield in August 1949, the voice-over declared: 'Begun three years ago, the airliner that makes every other out of date.'[39]

In 1951 it was in sight of going into service. As a child in north London in the early 1950s, I can remember scanning the skies above Finchley in the hope of glimpsing it. The newspapers and the children's comics were full of it when, in smart blue-and-white BOAC livery, it went into service from Heathrow in 1952. Nobody foresaw the two disastrous crashes which would see it grounded in 1954, not to fly again until 1958 when the problems of metal fatigue had been put right, by which time a new light-blue-and-white phenomenon had come to dazzle young eyes in the London surburbs, the 707 in Pan Am livery, which put Boeing on a growth trajectory in civil jet aircraft which continues to this day. Future British attempts, such as the Vickers VC10, failed to break back into this highly profitable market. A mere fifty-four VC10s were built compared to 962 Boeing 707s.[40]

Not one paragraph of this depressing story, however, was foreseeable in Festival of Britain Year. Nor did the arms salesmen pushing the virtues abroad of the Gloster Meteor, the de Havilland Vampire and the soon to enter service Hawker Hunter and English Electric Canberra have anything to fear from their American rivals despite the successes of the Lockheed F86 Sabre Jet, star of the air war above Korea.[41] Here, so it seemed, was one legacy of Second World War-stimulated R and D which would help to put the balance of payments right and stabilise the pound sterling once the temporary, rearmament-induced troubles of 1951 were past.

A similar story could have been told for the motor trade. Hadn't the Motor Show at Olympia in 1948 shaken the world, not least with its superb new high-performance models from Jaguar? The legendary XKs were the fastest production models in the world, to which even the French accorded 'the "Blue Riband" of the road'.[42] (To this day it's the only car I've ever really craved.) Even those who might, with justification, have pointed out that it was mass production, the volume, not the specialist side of the industry, that counted in pounds, shillings and pence for the nation, could have been silenced by the complacent pointing out that 1951 was the third year in succession in which Britain had taken the palm as the world's leading exporter of cars and trucks.

For complacency was the real problem and it was a hydra-headed monster with limbs spread far beyond the production lines. Very few had any sense of our long-term economic vulnerability. Hugh Dalton's outburst in 1952 was a rarity and, one suspects, as much motivated by his Germanophobia as the perceptiveness of his economic insights. Thanks to the war, Britain's exporters could sell virtually anything they could make in the first six years of peace while the world re-equipped and the Germans and the Japanese picked themselves up off the floor. The longer-term, structural weaknesses of the British industrial base were deeply concealed under the satisfactions of a tremendous perform-ance under conditions of war and a rapid regaining of prewar export levels. The dramatic need not just to rebuild capacity damaged by the war, but to replace it with new equipment – the platform for a sustained production drive that would surge well beyond the needs of recovery – was what was missing from British perceptions, British factories and the economic ministries in Whitehall.

Lord Plowden, forty years on, insisted it was 'cloud cuckoo land'[43] to think that Attlee and his ministers could have built a French-style planning apparatus in the United Kingdom. It's certainly true that, given prevailing political attitudes, a free market, German, Ludwig Erhard approach to economic efficiency was a non-starter. But hadn't the Labour Government been elected on a planning ticket in 1945? Wasn't this still Attlee's boast in 1950 about what distinguished Labour from the Conservatives, that their record had shown that 'orderly planning and freedom are not incompatible'?[44] Yet, consistently, even the most production-minded, best-led and managed Labour Government ever failed to create the instruments it needed to put leverage behind its language. Why remains a mystery and not just to Eric Hobsbawm. Could it be that even Attlee and Cripps, Bevin and Dalton (Bevan I think was different), felt that queasy ambivalence when it came to harnessing the power of the state, that suspicion of it which has afflicted virtually all who have come within touching distance of the Whitehall machine, from Gladstone to Major? Such intriguing questions are not susceptible to historical or any other kind of measurement.

The handling of science and technology policy, one of the most crucial ingredients in an advanced nation's economic performance in the twentieth century, is perhaps the *locus classicus* of British ambivalence about the role of the state. The importance of science was not at issue in mid-century Britain. Hadn't it been one of the key war-winners?

As we have seen, the Attlee Government commissioned a fistful of reviews of its organisation. There was, perhaps, an over-simple faith in the efficacy of the linear model of scientific and industrial progress – the assumption, in Jon Turney's words, 'that scientists make unexpected discoveries, technologists take them up and apply them, then engineers and designers turn them into new products or processes. Thus, nuclear physics spawned the atom bomb . . . [and] . . . solid-state physics led to the transistor . . . '[45]

Very little came of the postwar reviews in terms of strategic planning for a national scientific effort or a ministry to give it political clout. To be fair to Attlee and his ministers, the scientists themselves 'were deeply divided on the issues and were unable to present a collective view about the problems or to provide a concerted response to subsequent central initiatives in the field of civic research'.[46] These initiatives included the creation in 1947 of an Advisory Council on Scientific Policy and a year later the National Research and Development Corporation 'to foster the development of inventions that would not otherwise attract financial backing from private sources'.[47] The NRDC was an early and 'a conscious attempt', in Tom Wilkie's words, 'to break what was then already perceived to be a prevailing British disease: the British are good at inventing things, but poor at turning them into products that customers would like to buy'.[48]

This, in many ways, was a corollary of the nation's propensity to groom and train what George Steiner would call 'the Grand National Winners'[49] of the

British higher education system, those alpha-plus minds, capable of lifting, perhaps, a Nobel Prize but not the overall performance of the British economy. This was illustrated rather neatly by the atomic bomb project. The device was delivered on time but the problem which caused the greatest trouble was not the design of the warhead but the creation of the industrial infrastructure needed to produce the few deadly billets of plutonium.[50]

The bomb project was one area where there was no ambivalence about the state's role in forcing the pace of scientific development, bound up as it was with the impulse to great powerdom.

Attlee, Morrison, Wilmot and Alexander survived long enough to see their labours in the bomb committee, GEN 163, come to its resounding result at Monte Bello off the north-west coast of Australia, but they were in opposition by the time the atomic explosion was detonated in October 1952. In a piece of unintended, if bizarre symbolism, HMS *Campania*, 'a mongrel ship laid down as a merchantman, and converted to an aircraft carrier while it was still on the stocks' in the Second World War,[51] was the floating exhibition ship of the Festival of Britain. A year later it carried the men and the material of Britain's top secret atomic establishment to Australia where it sat off the Monte Bello Islands as flagship of 'Operation Hurricane'.[52]

It's the great power assumptions of virtually the entire postwar political and administrative classes that strikes successor generations as so utterly misplaced. When in 1949 Sir Henry Tizard, the Chief Scientific Adviser to the Ministry of Defence, warned, in the deepest Whitehall privacy naturally, of the dangers of great power illusions, his advice was met 'with the kind of horror one would expect if one had made a disrespectful remark about the King'.[53] Yet what Tizard said seems both wise and commonsensical to those familiar with what Churchill would have called 'our island story' since the turn of the Forties and Fifties.

'We persist', wrote Tizard, 'in regarding ourselves as a Great Power, capable of everything and only temporarily handicapped by economic difficulties.' A perfect summary of the official and political mind. 'We are not a great power', Sir Henry continued remorselessly, 'and never will be again. We are a great nation, but if we continue to behave like a Great Power we shall soon cease to be a great nation. Let us take warning from the fate of the Great Powers of the past and not burst ourselves with pride (see Aesop's fable of the frog).'[54]

Yet, historically, it would have been a truly amazing turn-up for the history books if Tizard's view *had* been the early postwar orthodoxy. Attlee, Bevin, A.V. Alexander – these men were as much Victorians as Churchill was. They disagreed with the grand old man about India, but, the sub-continent apart, they were by no means ready to call in the imperial receivers. Even celebrated and much publicised failures like the Ground Nuts scheme in Tanganyika (the hope of cheap and abundant vegetable oil from the African bush died in the scrub among the wreckage of tractors and earth-movers),[55] did not dampen overall hopes of colonial development and the easement that would bring to dollar shortage and imbalance of payments.

As a Colonial Office official put it as the Indian Empire slid away: 'Africa is now the core of our colonial position; the only continental space from which we can still hope to draw reserves of economic and military strength.'[56] As we have seen, as late as December 1950, even the realistic Attlee could be heard asking his Chief of the Imperial General Staff, Field Marshal Slim, in Washington during a break in the Korean War talks with the Truman Administration, 'how long it would take him to create from the African colonies an army comparable in size and quality with the Indian Army, an army which we could use to support our foreign policy just as the Indian Army had done'. (Slim said eight to ten years; but 'anything really worthwhile' would take twenty years or probably more.[57])

Fantasy? Certainly. But would it have seemed so utterly delusory at the time as Labour ministers sought to strengthen simultaneously the UN position in Korea and the NATO position in central Europe? No. As Paul Kennedy, clinician of the psychosis of great powerdom, put it sympathetically: 'It's very difficult, psychologically and culturally, to be in the first generation, or the first or second generation, of the decision-makers who confront relative decline and feel that they have to do something about it. And it seems to me perfectly natural, knowing how human beings behave, that they tend to deny it and say "Well, look, all it needs is a patch-up job or a little bit of a change here, not a major transformation."'[58]

Where the first postwar generation of decision-makers are culpable, however, is that they didn't even reach that queasy condition described by Professor Kennedy. For them, as Tizard intimated, deep trends were treated as temporary handicaps. Yet to argue that taking a Scandinavian course, and settling for a prosperous, inward-looking northern European existence, was a runner in 1945–51 is to succumb to another set of delusions. The whole weight of British history and recent experience was against that – not to mention urgent necessities and inescapable responsibilities with which the Attlee Government was confronted.

As Alan Bullock has put it, the question of Britain's postwar role in the world would have been answered for us, as it was for the Germans, if we had gone down to defeat. But the British had not lost:

> However misguided it may appear now, they thought they had won. Unlike General de Gaulle, Attlee and Bevin found vacant seats waiting for them at Potsdam. Britain was one of the victor states occupying the territory of her former enemies; a Permanent Member of the Security Council with the power of veto; still head of a large empire with widespread possessions; well ahead of any other state except the two superpowers in military, industrial and technological resources. Her interests and responsibilities were world wide, at least as wide as those of either Russia or America. For her to

47–50   The advisers: (clockwise) Sir Orme Sargent, Sir Oliver Franks (and Lady Franks), Sir Edwin Plowden (and Lady Plowden) and Sir Roger ('Mr Atom') Makins

51 Mr Attlee electioneering in Hoe
    Street, Walthamstow, February
    1950

52 'Now, Jean, what's all this
    about?' Monnet guides Schuman,
    June 1950.

53 Korea: the Shropshires land
    courtesy of the US Navy

54 Bevin says goodbye to Attlee, off
    to talk to Truman about Korea
    and the Bomb, Heathrow,
    December 1950

55 Sir Robert Hall, advocate of rearmament. 'If we had taken different views the outcome would almost certainly be quite different.'

56 Hugh Gaitskell at the Treasury, 1951. Putting guns before spectacles.

57 From *Empire Windrush* to Clapham Common, June 1948

58 Arsenal v. Manchester United, Highbury, 1946

59–60   Taking on the world market. *Above* The Comet, Hatfield, July 1949. *Below* The Motor Show, Earls Court, September 1949.

61   Festival of Britain, South Bank, 1951. The Skylon, like Britain, had 'no visible
means of support'.

62   End of an era: Attlee leaves Downing Street for the Palace, 26 October 1951

abandon these, or even seriously reduce them, at short notice was out of the question. Apart from its effect abroad, it would have been a blow to national morale that no newly elected government could be expected to strike after a war from which Britain had emerged victorious.[59]

This summation of attitude fits not just 1945 but 1951 as well, despite the removal of India and its Army from the Empire, an almost unbroken succession of currency and trading crises and the division of global politics into hostile, competing camps and the beginnings of a cold war arms race with which Britain simply could not keep up.

The lessons were there to be read – Tizard's among them – at the turn of the decades. They were not, as Whitehall's and the Cabinet's almost contemptuous dismissal of the Schuman plan, and the European possibility generally, showed most graphically.

It wasn't just the imperial drumbeat, the captivating threnody of great powerdom that explains the lack of critical self-awareness in mid-century Britain. It was part of the warp and woof of our institutional life whose essential soundness had been proven between 1939–45 when the spiritual and practical bankruptcy of those 'modern' movements across the Channel had been exposed for the world to see. Hadn't Churchill repeatedly made this point when he stressed the triumphant survival of Parliamentary democracy in Britain even under conditions of total war?

As Peter Morris has perceptively observed: 'Whereas 1940–45 in France demonstrated the bankruptcy of France's institutional culture and the intensity of her internal divisions, in Britain it signalled the vindication, almost the apotheosis, of the institutional and national consensus. Constitutional liberalism proved capable of surmounting not only the challenge of Hitler but a substantial leftward shift in public opinion. The victory of the Labour Party in the general election of 1945 seemed to many foreign observers an almost revolutionary event. In reality it marked the strength of the institutional consensus in Britain at the same time as it created a new set of policy priorities that would become the guiding maps of the postwar order . . . '[60]

Institutional continuity is something of a prize especially in an era when crude and murderous 'isms' on the Continent had, and, in eastern Europe, still were sweeping traditional redoubts of professional and political decency into the ashcan of history. But the British problem was not the flimsiness of its institutions – quite the reverse. It was their resistance to reform and the lack of public and political will to tackle them which compounded the problem mightily. Some contemporary critics were aware of this even among the ranks of the traditionalists. That great Victorian[61] and lawyer, Lord Radcliffe, opened his Reith Lecture on 'Power and the State' in December 1951 with the declaration that: 'The British have formed the habit of praising their institutions, which are sometimes inept, and of ignoring the character of their race, which is often superb. In the end they will be in danger of losing their character and being left with their institutions; a result disastrous indeed.'[62]

Of course, it would be absurd to have expected the Attlee Government, beset by the basic, fundamental problems of scarcity and supply, the need to convert the war economy to a peacetime one and the imperatives imposed by the overriding requirement to hoist exports and restore the external balance of the British economy, to tackle such citadels of 'class' privilege as the public schools or the ancient universities or those great professional standing armies such as the law. The real mystery remains the unwillingness to modernise those institutions whose high performance was central to the Government's priorities such as the Civil Service. Disdain, if not incomprehension greeted Wing-Commander Cooper's suggestion to Attlee that he imitate Roosevelt in 1933 and take a hard look at the adequacy of the state machine. He met with Attlee for an hour at his room in the Commons. 'I was pleading with him,' Wing-Commander Cooper recalled. '"If you let the Civil Service set up the nationalised industries, they will just create Civil Service departments." He said "I'll refer the matter to my officials and go into it with them." Nothing came of it.'[63]

For all the columns of Hansard devoted to the new language of planning, the Attlee Government, even before the switch under Cripps from a controlled economy to a managed one, largely restricted its genuine efforts at planning to coping with scarcity. 'Planning', says Keith Middlemas, 'meant allocating scarce resources, budgeting for manpower and raw materials, using the annual budget as regulator to manage national income and expenditure.'[64] This was entirely deliberate. There was no intention at any level to operate a more ambitious definition of planning for economic regeneration. Even Bevin, that superb political manager of the wartime command economy, was heard to say of French postwar planning: 'We don't do things like that in our country; we don't *have* plans, we work things out practically.'[65]

Even in those areas whose importance Bevin felt in his bones – education and training – there was neither an attempt to modify the philosophy of the 1944 Act towards the needs of a great, if faltering, industrial power nor to ensure that the statute's County College clauses, which allowed for day-release of the youngest strata of the workforce, were implemented. As Eric Hobsbawm has written, 'The Labour Government of 1945 actually came closer to tackling the problems of Britain's decline than any administration before or since.'[66] But, he believes, 'the massive economic achievements of Labour were thrown away by the Cold War', Korean rearmament in particular.[67] To that I would add the failure to modernise the industrial base and the state machine, whose prior reform was a necessary condition of any wider economic transformation.

I suspect the answer to that mysterious absence at the heart of Labour's recovery strategy – and the postwar settlement as a whole – lies in the more general phenomenon of profound institutional conservatism so powerfully strengthened by the experiences of the national emergency which seemed to just about everyone, from 'Tibby' Clarke whose Ealing Comedy scripts tilted gently, lovingly at us and our funny little ways, to Churchill, to Attlee, sub-scribers all to that perfectly fitting image of Orwell's of England as a family.

It was exceptional to find anyone anywhere seriously questioning it, apart from the Communist Party of Great Britain and other ultra-groups outside the practical pale of the constitution. To be sure there were sharp minds like Geoffrey Cooper's or, occasionally, Robert Hall's, which would focus on the institutional shortcomings of the Attleean revolution, but, in their way, on this issue at least, they were as isolated as Tizard's lonely crusade against the illusions of great powerdom.

The occasional foreigner, as Anglophile as he was perceptive, saw mid-century Britain for what it was. A mature example was, as we have seen, Jean Monnet. A precocious one was a young American Rhodes scholar at Oxford, Mancur Olson whose early experience of 1950s Britain set him off in pursuit of his theory of 'institutional sclerosis', the centrepiece of his classic work, *The Rise and Decline of Nations* thirty years later. 'I was very impressed with Oxford and Britain,' Professor Olson recalled. But it was travelling to Germany in his vacations and observing how much faster their economy was advancing compared to ours that intrigued him.

'The poor performance of the British economy puzzled me', he added,

because I was so much impressed at the same time with Britain and with Oxford . . . One of the things that I observed in Britain in the Fifties was that there was a well developed sense of certain positions, certain occupations, certain industries as belonging to certain people. One got a quick sense it was considered rude and pushy for a new person . . . to home-in on something established.[68]

As a young economist Olson was struck by the contrast between 1950s Britain and the 'stereotype' of the enterprising Industrial Revolution the British economic history books pieced together in his mind: 'I began to think that any explanation which talks about "British culture", as though that comes down from on high and is not an outgrowth of the history and experience of the country, is wrong. We had to explain what are the mechanisms for excluding people; what are the mechanisms for controlling an occupation; for controlling an industry; for controlling a union – and how did they get to be there . . . My belief is they got there through the accumulation of collective action over a long period of time.'[69]

A case could easily be made for mid-century Britain as the most settled, deferential, smug, un-dynamic society in the advanced world. The fundamentals of its constitution – Crown, Parliament and the Civil Service at the centre, strong municipal tradition at the periphery – were unquestioned apart from a tiny handful of Welsh or Scottish Nationalists. (These latter had a brief revivalist flurry in the early postwar years which caught the headlines on Christmas Day 1950 when the Stone of Scone was taken from Westminster

Abbey and temporarily removed to the Kingdom of Fife from where it had originally come). Northern Ireland, for all its institutionalised inequalities practised on the nationalist community since partition, was dormant both in terms of terrorist activity and any place on the mainstream UK political agenda.

Britain was a society still 'Victorian' in its pretence at public and private morality, a society easily shocked by a gilded bird of paradise such as the critic Ken Tynan or a grubby one like the spy Guy Burgess, whose private life was only marginally less shocking to those who knew of it than his espionage activities. Mid-century Britain was still marked by that deference which, a century before, Walter Bagehot had seen as so critical to the successful bonding of Victorian England. War too had vindicated both the monarchy and the wisdom of 'the Establishment' at engineering the departure of the entirely unsuitable Edward VIII, still by far the most successful twentieth-century operation of that shadowy, but occasionally puissant, entity.

Such institutionalised staidness, which would go largely unchallenged even in cultural terms until the mid-Fifties 'Angry Young Men' outbursts in the theatre and literature,[70] and in sexual/moral terms for another five years plus after that, made Attlee the ideal personification of that quiet revolution between 1945 and 1951 which, ostensibly, had nothing to do with a transformation of personal mores or public morals (though you could argue that 'Mr Attlee's children', the beneficiaries of his 'settlement', were those who eventually turned the values of Buckhurst Hill or Stanmore on their head). The P.M., as we have seen, had been an angry young man only in his hatred of East End poverty. He never questioned the institutions that formed him – Haileybury, Oxford, the Army, the Labour Party – Old England, if you like. The only item missing from this traditionalist list is the Church of England and, even here, the sceptical premier, as he put it so succinctly to his biographer, 'Believe[d] in the ethics of Christianity. Can't believe in the mumbo-jumbo.'[71]

This delightful exchange ended as follows:

HARRIS: Would you say you are an agnostic?
ATTLEE: I don't know.
HARRIS: Is there an after-life, do you think?
ATTLEE: Possibly.[72]

How typical was such a pick-and-mix of notions and habits in mid-century Britain?

Increasingly so. There was yet to be the flight from belief which marked the 1960s, but mid-century Britain was still a Christian country only in a vague attitudinal sense, belief generally being more a residual husk than a kernel of conviction, though Roman Catholicism was the exception to the rule now and for some time to come. Much of the wartime rhetoric of defiance had used Christian values as a call to arms against the Godless tyranny sweeping all before it across the English Channel. 'It has often been said', said William Temple, the soon-to-be Archbishop of Canterbury, in 1940, 'that we are fighting for a Christian civilisation. My whole contention is that it is our duty to prove that to be a true claim.'[73]

Two years later, Temple's Penguin Special, *Christianity and Social Order*, sold over 140,000 copies;[74] its assertion that the Church had to make itself heard in matters of politics and economics caught the same tide ridden by that other high principled William (Beveridge), though the churchman was more radical than the social scientist in his anti-capitalist animus, arguing in 1941 that 'the State does not, and cannot, stop short at the maintenance of order. Indeed the very conception of "order" expands as it becomes relatively secure. At first the maintenance of order may seem little more than the prevention of riots or of physical violence. But when personal immunity from attack is secured, the question arises whether cut-throat competition is not in the same category of disorder as the cutting of throats.'[75]

The indistinguishability of the two Williams and, say, Stafford Cripps can, however, all too easily create the impression of a new fusion of Church and, if not quite state, then at the very least of Church and consensus, even after Temple's death in 1944 and his succession the following year by the more conservative Geoffrey Fisher. Indeed, some, like Kenneth Morgan, have gone further and implied that the 'social gospel' had become so much a part of the new welfarism that the decline of religion was itself furthered.

'The Protestant churches,' he wrote, 'Anglican and more especially non-conformist, all felt the pressure of falling numbers and of secular challenges. The Church of England mourned the early death of Archbishop William Temple, a known Labour supporter. The Roman Catholics still rested largely on their Irish clientele in the big cities. The pronouncements of Archbishop Fisher and other Church dignitaries no longer attracted the awed submissiveness that had greeted Davidson or Cosmo Lang in the past. Even the drab sabbath of Wales and Scotland was under some threat, with pressure for opening cinemas in Wales and golf-courses in Scotland. In this serious, if somewhat baffled, age the moral religion preached by the government and its unimpeachable public servants, supplies the substitute secular gospel for which the people craved, or so it was fondly believed.'[76]

Certainly the official pronouncements of the postwar Church of England stuck closely to the philosophy and prescriptions of the two Williams, though, invariably, a rider was added to the effect that 'there must be constant endeavour to resist encroachments by the State which endanger human personality'.[77] The same Lambeth Conference which entered that caveat in 1948 went on to affirm the belief 'that the State is under the moral law of God, and is intended by Him to be an instrument for human welfare. We therefore welcome the growing concern and care of the modern State for its citizens, and call upon Church members to accept their own political responsibility and to co-operate with the State and its officers in their work.'[78]

It's fascinating to see how, in the late 1940s, the welfare state is treated as a bonding concept central to the relationship between the state and its citizens. Here it is cited by the hierarchy of the Anglican Faith, the Established Church, as a reason for its communicants to 'co-operate' with the 'officers' of the state. A year later Attlee told the Cabinet that National Service in the Armed Forces was a reasonable thing for the state to ask in return for the welfare state.[79]

The Church's belief in the welfare state (remember it was a clergyman who first coined the phrase 'national insurance') was to remain a constant through all the vicissitudes of the second half of the twentieth century. It brought them, famously, into conflict with the state in its Thatcherite manifestation when the urban renewal debate took on a moral dimension in the mid-1980s with the publication of *Faith in the City*, the report of the commission established by Dr Robert Runcie as Archbishop of Canterbury.[80]

For all its easy fusion with the spirit of the age, the early postwar Church was decidedly uneasy about just how deeply Christian faith, as opposed to a vague Attlee-like ethic of decency and social justice, penetrated the British people. 'Seen from a distance', declared the Evangelist Committee (established by Archbishop Temple in 1943 but reporting in 1945 when he was no longer in Lambeth Palace to read it),

> Britain is the country which seems most nearly to approach the ideal of a Christian community. The ceremony of the Coronation, the regular open- ings of the sittings of Parliament with prayer, the Mayor's Chaplain, the provision for religion in the services and in all State institutions, the relig- ious articles in popular periodicals, the Religious Department of the British Broadcasting Corporation, and many similar phenomena, go to show that the ethos of the State remains Christian . . . the Established Church is 'still entwined by countless subtle threads around the life of the realm and nation'. The English are still more deeply influenced by Christianity than they themselves know . . . But behind the facade the situation presents a more ominous appearance.[81]

There is evidence to justify such suspicions that commitment was shaky, to the Established Church at least, both anecdotal and statistical.

In his memoirs, Sir Denis Hamilton recalled how the attendance at Sunday church parade dwindled to a handful the moment it ceased to be compulsory when the war ended. So moved was he by the injustice to the Chaplain who had lived dangerously with his men across Europe to Germany that he went round as Brigadier, playing on the consciences of the other ranks (with some success) until numbers improved.[82]

A two-year inquiry into the views of officer cadets in the last phase of the war found that more than half believed in Christianity.[83] Maurice Reckitt was probably close to reality in 1941 when describing England (Scotland, Wales and Northern Ireland have always been more theistic societies), both military and civilian, as a Christian country only if the definition of Christianity was kept vague. 'We can', he wrote, 'at least claim with some confidence that the vast majority of our people are in some real, if shadowy sense, theistic in conviction, and at least show no desire to replace the Christianity for which their "National Church" stands by any other faith.'[84] There were, of course, in the late 1940s as in every cluster of years since, customary paragraphs in any study bemoaning the rise of licentiousness and the fall of standards and *Towards the Conversion of England* was four-square in that tradition putting much of the blame on the inevitable mobility of a population at war, a fluidity, its authors claimed, which revealed 'a wholesale drift from organised religion'.[85]

The statistics, for the Church of England at least, darkened the gloom of Temple's evangelists. In 1935, membership of the Church of England stood at 3,598,522. Ten years later it was down to 2,989,704. By 1950 it had dropped to 2,958,840. The Catholic Church, by contrast, was on an upswing, standing at 2,933,294 in 1935, rising to 3,036,826 in 1945 and to 3,557,059 by 1950.[86] The gap between the two traditions continued to widen steadily over the next forty years. In every sense of the phrase, a secular trend was well under way for the Anglicans. But, to be fair, statistics are simply not applicable to spirituality. Church 'membership' bears little relation, in truth, to the spiritual vitality of an era. To expect it to is like Stalin asking, famously, 'How many divisions has the Pope?' Yet it is the only indicator we have to distinguish between the more or less secular societies. Similarly the pro-welfare state pronouncements of a church's top brain may not necessarily reflect 'what is cooking in the pew', to borrow a phrase of Fraser Steel's.[87] Like any consensus, the legendary postwar one was very much a top brass affair. Politically, too, it never permeated that far into the rank-and-file of the Labour or Conservative parties. If the rhetoric of party conference or ward meeting is anything to go by, prejudice, nasty and simple, has persistently ruled at that level.

Mid-century Britain was a time of harbingers in other demographic senses than the religious for it saw the beginnings of the United Kingdom as a multi-racial society. Some 8,000 West Indians had been based in Britain at various stages of the war serving in the Armed Forces, the RAF in particular, as a result of its active recruiting campaign in Jamaica.[88] The authorities could not compel the Caribbean servicemen to leave at the end of the war, but they were 'encouraged' to return home and free passages were laid on as an incentive.[89]

High unemployment and poor economic prospects, in Jamaica particularly which was still suffering from the effects of the 1944 hurricane, persuaded several of the veterans to attempt to return to Britain as soon as their savings and travel opportunities allowed. Among them was Sam King, a Leading Air-craftman with the RAF in the war and a future Mayor of Southwark. The opportunity he was seeking came a year after he was demobbed and sent home to Jamaica in 1947, when the '*Empire Windrush* dropped off soldiers in Jamaica on its way from Australia to England in May 1948 and we took our chance.

There was no regular passenger service at the time. The fare was £28–10/ and my family had to sell three cows to raise the money.'[90]

That 'little Mayflower'[91] as Sam King calls the old troopship, bursting at the seams with its 492 legitimate passengers, and eighteen stowaways, sailing up the Thames to Tilbury in the mist of an English summer morning on 22 June 1948, is seen, rightly, as a turning-point in British history. 'Few of these passengers', wrote Stuart Hall on the fortieth anniversary of their arrival, 'understood at the time either that this was to be a "one-way trip" or the historic significance of their voyage. Nevertheless, the great wave of postwar migration from the Caribbean to the UK can be symbolically said to have begun with that fateful voyage. The history of the black diaspora in Britain begins here.'[92]

According to Sam King, the main preoccupation of those on board was that the Royal Navy might turn them back:

> As we got closer to England there was great apprehension on the boat because we knew the authorities did not want us to land. I got two ex-RAF wireless operators to play dominoes outside the radio room on the ship so we could keep informed of the messages coming in. We heard on BBC News that if there was any disturbance on the immigrant ship, HMS *Sheffield* would be sent out to turn us back. It was a Labour Government and the Colonial Secretary, Creech Jones, said, 'These people have British passports and they must be allowed to land.' But then he added on, 'There's nothing to worry about because they won't last one winter in England.'[93]

Creech Jones, or more accurately, the Home Secretary, Chuter Ede, could not have kept the Jamaicans out even if the Cabinet (which was as surprised as anybody else by the voyage of the *Empire Windrush*) had been minded to. The British Nationality Act, which was just completing its passage through Parliament, declared that citizens of any United Kingdom Colony were British subjects, entitled, like any other of the King's subjects, to a British passport.

It's intriguing to speculate whether the legislation would have been so 'open door' in its philosophy if the Parliamentary draftsmen had set to work on it *after* the *Empire Windrush* had turned up at Tilbury, given the tizzy into which central Government was thrown by its arrival and the serious consideration the Cabinet gave to halting further immigration from the colonies in 1950–1. For the 1948 legislation was stimulated not by any prospect of the Empire coming home, but by the need to co-ordinate Commonwealth policy after Canada had acquired a new Citizenship Act in 1946. 'There followed a conference of experts in 1947 at which it was agreed that each independent Commonwealth country would determine its own nationality laws, but all Commonwealth countries would recognise that citizenship of any Commonwealth country was a sufficient qualification for a common status of Commonwealth citizen, or British subject.'[94]

The first reaction in Whitehall to 'the 400 Sons of Empire', as the *Daily Mirror* called them,[95] was a furious spate of buck-passing between the Colonial Office, the Home Office and the Ministry of Labour. No department wanted to take responsibility.[96] A Colonial Office spokesman, in a burst of candour, had told the *Daily Herald* on 9 June when news reached London that the *Empire Windrush* had set sail from the West Indies, that: 'This unorganised rush is a disaster. We knew nothing about it',[97] even though the authorities in Jamaica could hardly have failed to hear about the sudden spurt of people in Kingston seeking permission to leave the colony and asking Justices of the Peace and the police to sign the relevant affidavits as to good character.[98]

As the ship approached British waters, the Colonial Office contacted Baron Baker, a former RAF policeman, just demobbed from the service and active in community work. Baker was about to set in train the sequence of events which were to lead to his being dubbed 'the Man who discovered Brixton'. 'At that time', he recalled,

> I was the only link between our people and the Colonial Office. I was told about the *Windrush* by Major John Keith and so I went to see him: I asked him what preparations the Colonial Office was going to make for these people and he said 'none'. So I suggested he use the Clapham Common Deep Shelter. They had used the Air Raid Shelter to house Italian and German prisoners of war and even myself when I came to London sometimes and couldn't get a bed. I had to use it. So why not open it for the people on the *Windrush*?[99]

In the end Baker had to force the authorities' hand.

On 22 June he told Keith he was going on board the boat and unless a telegram reached him saying the Clapham Shelter was open, no one would disembark. The telegram arrived. Over 230 of the passengers moved into the shelter. The nearest Labour Exchange was in Coldharbour Lane, Brixton.[100] A new community was born. Like the Irish who settled in Kilburn before them (a short walk from Paddington and the boat train from Fishguard) and the Indians and Pakistanis who settled in Southall later in the 1950s (the personnel manager of Woolfe's rubber factory had been a policeman in the Punjab[101]), a combination of chance, personality and logistics determined where the new immigrants would settle.

The arrival of the *Empire Windrush* quickly brought home to the Ministry of Labour the possible consequences of the brand new British Nationality Act. By coincidence, the United Nations General Assembly in the summer of 1948 censured the British Government for letting too few immigrants into the UK from Europe.[102] Faced with a choice between admitting more Europeans or more West Indians, the Ministry opted for the former (so much for the Commonwealth link). An official explained. 'It is one thing to maintain the traditional policy under which British subjects are free to enter

Great Britain without restriction, but it is quite another thing to organise migration from one part of the Empire to another . . . the 500 men from the *Empire Windrush* have caused considerable political embarrassment by their mass arrival.'[103]

In the next two years, however, the rate of immigration continued at roughly the same level (1,200 in 1948, 1,000 in 1949 and 1,400 in 1950) rising to 2,200 in 1951,[104] despite Whitehall's efforts to persuade governors in the West Indian colonies to stress the housing and employment difficulties immigrants would find if they insisted on sailing to Britain.[105]

By the spring of 1950, with the immigrant population of Britain standing at 25,000 (seamen who had settled in Liverpool and Cardiff since the First World War; those ex-servicemen who had stayed on after 1945, a handful of stowaways and the post-*Windrush* arrivals), the Cabinet considered what was already being treated as a social problem. On 20 March the Cabinet noted 'the difficulties of finding suitable employment for the coloured people who had come to this country in recent years from the West Indies and the view was expressed that serious difficulties would arise if this immigration of coloured people from British colonial possessions were to continue or increase.'[106] Creech Jones was instructed to prepare a memorandum on the matter.

On 19 June the Cabinet considered immigration again. Ministers were worried lest high-quality social services in Britain 'should attract here an undue proportion of the surplus population of the West Indies and other colonial territories'. Administrative action such as tightening up the rules for stowaways was deemed ineffective. Ministers regarded it as no substitute for specific legislation if the flow of immigration demanded it. Within two years of the British Nationality Act receiving royal assent, the question was raised at that Cabinet meeting, 'Whether the time had come to restrict the existing right of any British subject to enter the United Kingdom?'[107]

As a result of ministerial disquiet, a special Cabinet Committee, GEN 325, was commissioned under Chuter Ede's chairmanship to consider the matter, advised by a parallel committee of senior civil servants. They sat between July 1950 and January 1951. Not a whisper of their work reached the public domain until their papers were released in January 1982. If it had, it could have seriously embarrassed leading Labour politicians, such as Hugh Gaitskell, in the later Fifties and early Sixties who fiercely attacked attempts to control Commonwealth immigration.

In fact the Cabinet on 12 February 1951 accepted GEN 325's advice that statutory action to amend the 1948 Act would have incalculable consequences for Britain's relations with her colonies and the Commonwealth in general, especially as the by now non-Commonwealth citizens from the Irish Republic would continue to enjoy unrestricted access to the UK. GEN 325 was, however, worried about the possibility of a future increase in immigration and the possibility of 'Communist-inspired' mass migrations from south-east Asia.[108] The Cabinet took the point and instructed the Colonial Office to keep a close watch on the pace of immigration with a view to possible legislation to curb it in the future.[109]

At one stage, Cabinet discussion of the immigration question became bound up with imperial policy abroad thanks to the case of Seretse Khama, heir to the chieftaincy of the Bamangwato tribe in the British Protectorate of Bechuanaland. Seretse, while a student in the UK, had married an English woman, Ruth Williams. His tribe accepted both her, and her husband Seretse as their Chief. The issue was sensitive in the Government's eyes because Bechuanaland was surrounded by South Africa, a Commonwealth member which had switched to a policy of official apartheid after Field Marshal Smuts went down in defeat to Dr Malan's Nationalists in the 1948 general election.

Attlee, to his credit, initially refused to go along with the policy of the Commonwealth Relations Office that Seretse should renounce his claim to the chieftaincy and go into exile. 'In effect', the P.M. minuted in January 1950, 'we are invited to go contrary to the desire of the great majority of the Bamangwato tribe, solely because of the governments of the Union of South Africa and Rhodesia. It is as if we had been obliged to agree to Edward VIII's abdication so as not to annoy the Irish Free State and the USA.'[110] Nevertheless, the Commonwealth Relations Office line prevailed and the Khamas spent the bulk of Seretse's remaining years in London.

It was the linkage of the outrageous treatment of Seretse to the housing and employment grievances of the new immigrant population in the UK by the Seretse Khama Fighting Committee which caused the Cabinet in the spring of 1950 to treat the two issues together.[111] In its way it was symbolically prophetic because for the next three decades British Cabinet ministers would become increasingly preoccupied by the time-consuming business of exporting independence to former colonial territories abroad and to handling the social, economic and legal consequences of the Empire coming home, not just in successive reviews of entry policy but in establishing a net of employment and housing protection over a group of people whose skin colour made them far more vulnerable to racial discrimination than any previous wave of immigrants, whether Jewish or Irish.

It's perhaps both easy and mildly misleading to connect overdramatically the Colonial Office's reactions to riots in the Gold Coast in February 1948 (which stimulated the Arden-Clarke proposals for constitutional reform in 1949 that, in turn, set the colony on the road to becoming independent Ghana in 1957, the first British territory in Africa to receive its freedom),[112] or its response to the arrival of the *Empire Windrush* four months later to the great changes which occurred later. But links there certainly were. Equally the divergence of British and American policy over both oil and Middle Eastern nationalism during the Persian crisis is undoubtedly a harbinger of the far greater trauma to come at Suez in 1956. And is it entirely fanciful to suggest that the grim postwar cycle of balance of payments and sterling crises was not well set in by 1951?

The chorus of pre-echoes is quite deafening if you listen hard enough to the sounds of mid-century Britain. The battles over the cost of the social services, health in particular, seem utterly familiar as do the related ones that defence spending should be cut to ease the pressure on them. Supermarkets had been sighted, though, as we have seen, rationing had to end before they became as familiar a sight as the high street provisions store or the corner shop with their utterly different sights and smells (plastic changed the olfactory sensations of a Saturday morning dramatically). Similarly high-rise flats were still a gleam in the architects' eyes, with the occasional exception such as the new blocks alongside Rosebery Avenue in the old London Borough of Finsbury which you can see as the medical students' rag procession makes its unruly way through the streets, with Dirk Bogarde in handsome attendance, in *Doctor in the House*. All but a fraction of the new building remained houses or low-rise flats in 1951.[113]

What about human harbingers of the individual kind? Where-were-they-then exercises can be intriguing and not entirely uninstructive. On 28 February 1949, a certain Margaret Hilda Roberts was adopted as prospective Parliamentary candidate by the Dartford Conservative and Unionist Association.[114] At twenty-four she was the youngest woman candidate in the 1950 general election.[115] Mrs Thatcher was on her way.

In October 1951, nine-year-old Neil Kinnock watched his grandfather weep as Labour went down to defeat. During the campaign he'd gone round the streets of Tredegar with the other kids banging on an old biscuit tin and singing:

Vote, vote, vote for 'Neirin Bevan,
He's the boy to beat the band.
If you're workers, now's the day,
To make the bosses pay,
And Labour rule throughout the land.[116]

About a hundred and fifty miles away in Surrey a wholly unexceptional eight-year-old with a passion for football and cricket, spent his days at Cheam Common Primary School and his evenings in Longfellow Road, Worcester Park, its garden filled with concrete birdtables and ornaments his dad made for a living.[117] Forty-and-a-half years on, John Major and Neil Kinnock would be the first Butler Act grammar school boys to face each other head-on in a British general election. As Mr Major said at his first Cabinet meeting as premier: 'Who would have believed it?'[118]

An over-concentration on harbingers, however, would create a profoundly misleading impression of mid-century Britain. For all the talk of the atomic and jet ages to come (a British aeroplane always seemed about to or to have just broken the world air speed record), it was in many ways a profoundly backward-looking society, as aware of the problems of modernity as it was of the promise of things to come. For example, in common with virtually every other swathe of the postwar period, the country felt itself in the grip of a crime-wave. As usual the picture was multi-faceted. The war years had seen a 69 per cent increase in indictable offences, from 283,220 in 1938 to 478,349 in 1945.[119] Yet the increase in London had, bafflingly, been only half the national average.[120] The greatest increase occurred in property crimes such as larceny (+ 62 per cent), breaking and entering (+ 120 per cent) and receiving (+ 195 per cent).[121]

Crime actually fell between 1945 and 1950, both in terms of indictable offences (− 3.6 per cent) and per head of the population (− 4.8 per cent),[122] though 1951 turned out to be the peak year in early postwar crime with 524,000 indictable offences reported.[123] 'It was because crime readily featured as a newspaper staple', wrote the criminologist, Terence Morris, 'that references were made to a "crime wave" when the matter was debated in Parliament, or when judges pronounced on what they perceived to be an astonishing increase in the incidence of a particular type of offence. The streets of British cities in 1945 were almost certainly safer places than they had been in 1845 and were scarcely more dangerous than in 1935.'[124] Yet it was these 'particular types of offence' − crimes associated with black market spivvery and juvenile delinquency in particular − which led to the sensation that standards and civil culture generally were declining in ways which spoke volumes about the national fibre. No other area, perhaps education apart, is so vulnerable to amateur sociology on the part of public and commentator alike, each diagnosis complete with favourite insight into the darker side of human nature and pet punishment to set it right. No other area is so intensely effective as a popular barometer of national well being. In no other area is there such a mistrust of 'the expert' or so great a reliance placed on 'commonsense'.

The French historian, Michelle Perrot, caught the special flavour of a nation's discussion of matters criminal when she wrote, 'there are no "facts of crime" as such, only a judgmental process that institutes crimes by designating as criminal both certain acts and their perpetrators. In other words, there is a discourse of crime that reveals the obsessions of a society.'[125] In any nation, crime is 'a central metaphor of disorder and loss of control in all spheres of life'.[126]

Yet, writing of mid-twentieth-century Britain, Martin Wiener, capturing perfectly the *international* perspective on the UK's susceptibility to criminality, serves equally well to bring out the growing *national* neurosis about crime with which it contrasted quite starkly in the late 1940s and into the early 1950s:

Even as both the nation's world power and economic dynamism obviously began to falter, the criminal law remained an area of unquestioned success. The English way of reconciling respect for individual liberty with a very high degree of public order and co-operation was the envy of the world. Rare was the foreign visitor who failed to remark upon the uncoerced yet pacific and law-abiding character of everyday life.[127]

At this period, too, 'it could confidently be said that, with the probable exception of those sections of society who because they lived by or in the shadow of crime had no reason to respect the police, the overwhelming majority of ordinary people held the police service in high regard and were consequently minded to place their sympathies with them when complaints were made about police behaviour.'[128]

When 'ordinary people', to use Terence Morris's phrase, reach their judgments on whether things are, or are not, what they used to be, it's not the Home Office statistics that spring most readily to their minds. It's the general atmosphere – an atmosphere influenced most of all by *causes célèbres* as presented by the ever-prurient Press. For example, the figures show that offences against property fell by 6.1 per cent between 1945 and 1950,[129] yet this was seen at the time (and still is) as the era when the spiv swaggered the land and the backstreets echoed to the sounds of goods 'falling off the back of lorries'.

What visitors from overseas did or did not make of British orderliness was neither here nor there. The British only compared their present with folk memories of their own past, no one else's. Though if a 'foreigner' was involved in a spicy case so much greater the aroma as with that most cosmopolitan of spivs, Max Intrator, who, in 1947, shot to brief fame as the man through whose hotel bedroom the rich trooped to satisfy their material wants on his Europe-wide black market.[130] When black market met violent death as in the case of the Warren Street second-hand car dealer, Stanley Setty, in the Finchley Road flat of fellow racketeer, Donald Hume,[131] all the fears of a society in menacing decay rolled into one gory mess (Setty's head was severed and, according to legend, placed in a baked bean carton to be later dropped from a plane over the North Sea). Scandal even briefly touched the incorruptibly austere Attlee Government when ex-railway clerk John Belcher, junior minister at the Board of Trade, was obliged to resign because of his association with Sidney Stanley, a bizarrely hilarious spiv who kept the nation entertained during the five weeks of hearings held in Church House, Westminster, by the tribunal of inquiry under Mr Justice Lynskey in November–December 1948.[132]

Sometimes public perceptions were borne out by the crime figures. The Ealing Studios' *The Blue Lamp* of 1950, in which that incarnation of British bobby decency, Jack Warner (whose character rose from the grave to star in the interminable BBC Television series, *Dixon of Dock Green*), is murdered by a nasty young criminal played by the multi-parted Dirk Bogarde, drew a direct connection between the dislocation of family life in wartime and postwar juvenile delinquency.[133] The motivations attributed to criminals notoriously tell as much about the judge as the judged. 'Solutions to the problem of social order', as Martin Wiener rather grandly puts it, 'as embodied in policies for crime and other forms of deviance are also solutions to the problem of knowing human beings and, indeed, the cosmos.'[134]

When Home Office statistician, Leslie Wilkins, took a retrospective look at mid-century Britain, he found a pronounced war-effect on the young – a dramatic rise in offences in the 8–17 age group between 1938 and 1944 (+ 70 per cent for boys; an amazing + 120 per cent for girls).[135] Add to this the potency of the popular postwar view that a general decline in parental discipline plus the malign impact of American-imported gangster films and horror comics was turning Britain into a hot house for delinquency and you have a near-perfect all-embracing theory. Though, in fact, the figures suggest that crime among the young did not really take off until the consumer booms of the late 1950s and early 1960s created an abundance of 'occasions of sin' (to revive a phrase from my own Catholic childhood) and the means (cash and mobility included) to succumb to their temptations.[136]

The Attlee years saw a degree of reform in the penal system with the Criminal Justice Act 1948, a measure shaped almost entirely by prewar thought and, indeed, drafting, which had been interrupted by hostilities. As usual it was a reform driven by the professionals of the system not by the force of public opinion which has always lagged where easement of punishment was involved. Criminals could no longer be flogged by order of judges or magistrates (though prisoners offending in jail could still be by order of the Board of Visitors). Probation was developed as a notion and a practice. The House of Commons voted narrowly to suspend the death penalty for a trial period. The House of Lords, devotees of the rope until life peers began to dilute the punitive impulses of the hereditaries and the Law Lords after 1958, threw it out. Attlee kicked the issue into touch by appointing a Royal Commission under Sir Ernest Gowers.[137] Kindness and gentleness extended only so far when Victorians like Attlee and Chuter Ede held sway in the Cabinet Room.

Almost wherever you look across the spectrum of social attitudes and the cultural patterns which reflected them, you find as much, if not more, in common with Thirties Britain than Fifties Britain and far more than with Sixties Britain. This was true even for vanguard areas like pop music where swing, big bands, crooners and balladeers held sway, their near cultural monopoly buttressed by the conservative attitudes of the dominant recording labels – Capitol, Mercury, Columbia, Decca and RCA – whose immensely fragile products continued to whirl round at 78 revolutions per minute, while long-playing discs were still a transatlantic rumour.[138]

There were, of course, exceptions to what looks retrospectively like a stunningly staid norm. Jazz, and the semi-underground 'beatnik' culture that went with it, could be found in the occasional Soho basement such as 'Club 11', on the corner of Windmill and Archer Streets, which opened in 1948 and offered a select audience the delights of Ronnie Scott and Johnny Dankworth.[139] But, as P.J. Kavanagh noted in his review of Max Hastings' *The Korean War*, the GI who said 'We went away to Glenn Miller. We came back to Elvis Presley',[140] spoke for a generation and a generational change.[141]

Broadcasting, potentially the most potent maker of cultural change, presented an equally staid face (for the tiny television audience – still less than a million sets in 1951)[142] and a traditional ear to the listener. Although some pre-echoes of the 'soaps', *Mrs Dale's Diary* (first transmitted in January 1948) and that extraordinarily long-lived phenomenon, *The Archers* (first broadcast on New Year's Day 1951), were finding their regular place within the real-life experience of their avid followership.[143] Only when the fictional Grace Archer perished in a fire in 1955 (as a spoiler operation to attract audience away from the first night of Independent Television) was it generally appreciated just how real such literally disembodied radio folk could be to those of genuine flesh and blood.[144] Again there were joyously unstaid hints of unstuffiness to come of which the most magnificent was *The Goon Show*, first broadcast in May 1951 as *Crazy People*.

'The Goons' – Peter Sellers, Spike Milligan and Harry Secombe – fashioned the humour of my generation from the Prince of Wales down, with its hilarious debunking of institutional types, a kind of decade-long 'other ranks' revenge on the Empire and its officer class with a parody, complete with funny name and funny voice, for grotesquerie and pomposity of all kinds. As the *Observer*'s anonymous profile writer put it in 1956 (appropriately enough in the week when the last British troops quit the Suez Canal in the final act of US imposed humiliation after the invasion of Egypt the month before):

> The essential thing [about *The Goon Show*] . . . is the combination of a quite special, ultra-modern humorous idiom with a nostalgia for our Victorian, imperial past. It is as though Britannia were having not a nightmare but a sort of comic dream; it is as though Dali, Kipling and Dickens had co-operated.[145]

Celebrating the fortieth anniversary of the first *Goon Show* in that same paper, Dave Gelly, exaggerating but not too outrageously, put the event on a par with the Festival of Britain, declaring: 'There is a case for claiming that the Fifties actually began in May 1951, with the opening of the Festival of Britain and the start of the *Goon Show*. The Festival laid out the future pattern for architecture, town planning and design, while the Goons set about reducing to rubble the redundant edifice of British Imperial smugness,'[146] – this last a role I would attribute to Colonel Nasser in 1956 rather than to Major Bloodnok in 1951.

The Report of the Beveridge Committee on Broadcasting – yet another carrying the name of the 'People's William' – published early in 1951, over the protest of one of its members, the Conservative MP Selwyn Lloyd to whom the victory ultimately went[147] – found against commercial television and in favour of a continued BBC monopoly of both sound and vision,[148] with Sir William, as his committee began its task, 'looking back nostalgically to programmes he had broadcast in 1932'.[149]

Essentially the philosophy Beveridge and, in its dying days, the Attlee Government accepted[150] was Haley's. The BBC's Director-General, insisting that as with Gresham's Law, competition from commercial channels would ensure that 'the good, in the long run, will inescapably be driven out by the bad', told the Committee that:

> So long as broadcasting is continued as a public service, conducted by one independent, impartial, single instrument, that organisation will be free, without any over-riding obligation, to discharge all the responsibilities to the community that broadcasting involves . . . They include the responsibility for impartiality, for the greatest possible freedom at the microphone, for the preservation of standards and the re-establishing on a broader basis of a regard for values, for the use of broadcasting as an educational medium and a means to raise the public taste, for the discharge of broadcasting's duty to and in all the arts, for the encouragement of all artistic endeavour whether of creation or performance, for the use of broadcasting to develop true citizenship and the leading of a full life.[151]

Reith could not have capped that. Not only was it vintage Haley, it cries out with the official spirit of that age – ambitious, high-minded, proud and utterly mandarin in its granite-like refusal to contemplate the meritricious or the transient (or the popular, critics of the BBC monopoly might add). Even Selwyn Lloyd applauded describing Haley as 'a public servant of outstanding distinction'.[152] Yet, as the BBC's official historian, Asa Briggs, put it: 'One thing was certain. The long-awaited Beveridge inquiry had settled nothing.'[153]

The same could be said, with the benefit of forty years of hindsight, of so many of the artefacts of the Attlee years including even the National Health Service, the showpiece of the new postwar Labour estate of the realm, at least in a form that Nye Bevan would have recognised. Yet that era deserves an appellation Asa Briggs himself designed for another earlier time. For 1945–51 was not just an age of austerity, it was, without doubt, an age of improvement as well.[154]

It's very easy as the turn of the twentieth and twenty-first century approaches to pick out the shortcomings of mid-century Britain. Time chips away at the noblest achievements. It is true that the Attlee years, building on the changes, the instruments and the experiences brought by the Second World War, were largely devoted to putting right the ills of the interwar period. In that sense his and Bevin's eyes were on the 1930s rather than the 1960s. There now seems a trace of noble naiveté about their belief that full employment, a high degree of state leverage over the strategic direction of the British economy, not least through the newly nationalised industries bestriding its 'commanding heights', plus the social infrastructure of the welfare state, would bring about a permanent change in the relationship between capital and labour and an accrual of benefits in the implications of that for wages and costs as well as social justice.

The memory of those aspirations, the decencies built into that strategy, the 'bump of social purpose', in Richard Hoggart's phrase, which showed through in the institutions, the speeches and the statutes of that high-minded era in late Forties Britain, is both poignant and searing for anyone, however slightly touched by the virtuous aspirations, who lived through the trauma of the 1970s as, seemingly one by one, the artefacts of the postwar settlement crumbled under the stress of stagflation and the economic and industrial unrest it fuelled. By the late 1970s, as Britain teetered on the brink of the Thatcher era, the inadequacies of the Beveridge Report and the Keynes-inspired full employment White Paper of 1944 stood out more than the utility of the remedies they proposed or the severity of the interwar ills they were designed to cure and, for so long, seemed to have succeeded in doing so.

Even though the Treasury, as the 1951 election campaign broke into its stride, were busily preparing papers to make the Conservatives' flesh creep should the electorate once more place them in charge of the Whitehall machine (they succeeded, as Rab Butler's memoirs show);[155] even though the Korean War was raging in the far East and Mossadegh was threatening the lubricant of the British economy in the Middle East, the domestic problem – the ancient argument about who gets what courtesy of whom at home – seemed in the autumn of 1951 to have been settled in a manner fairer, more effective, more accepted and, therefore, more enduring than could have been expected by those who had lived through the disappointments and setbacks of the 1920s and 1930s. This time a land fit for heroes *did* appear to have emerged from the rubble and smoke of war. The 'never again' impulse had, thanks to the reconstruction planning of the Coalition and Labour's creative burst of legal and institution building which both drew upon it and extended it, actually fed through into a transformation of both living standards and life chances.

Didn't the data of the Central Statistical Office prove it with that key indicator, the unemployment figures? In the first six years after the 1918 Armistice, the percentage of the labour force out of work oscillated as follows – 3.0 per cent (1919); 1.9 per cent (1920); 11.0 per cent (1921); 9.6 per cent (1922); 8.0 per cent (1923); 7.1 per cent (1924). The comparable figures for Britain post-VE Day were 1.7 per cent (1946); 1.3 per cent (1947); 1.3 per cent (1948); 1.4 per cent (1949); 1.4 per cent (1950) and 1.1 per cent (1951).[156] To the interwar generation (and that meant everyone at the top of political, public and industrial life in mid-century Britain) those statistics alone seemed miraculous. Add to them the presence of a steadily rising standard of living, for all the Crippsian austerity, and an inflation rate that never threatened to get out of control and you have what to 1930s eyes could only have seemed a virtuous cycle well established.

And did Sam Watson's proud claims at the party conference in 1950 seem that hyperbolic when Seebohm Rowntree published the following year the latest of his regular surveys of life and consumption in York? Compared to the findings of his 1936 survey, it seemed to indicate beyond doubt that the welfare state built in the interim really had cracked the problem of poverty. Chart after chart showed dramatic improvement in basic living standards by

EFFECT ON FAMILIES OF ALL THE WELFARE MEASURES TAKEN TOGETHER

Class	Actual situation in 1950		The situation in 1950 if welfare measures had been identical with those in force in 1936	
	No. of families	%	No. of families	%
'A'	81	0.41	1,197	6.62
'B'	765	4.23	3,276	18.11
'C'	3,510	19.40	2,592	14.32
'D'	3,141	17.38	2,412	13.32
'E'	10,602	58.58	8,622	47.63

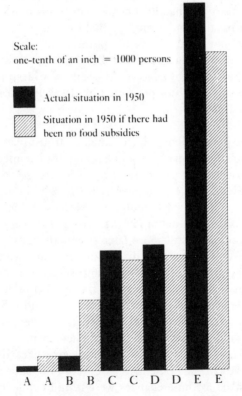

Scale:
one-tenth of an inch = 1000 persons

■ Actual situation in 1950

▨ Situation in 1950 if there had been no food subsidies

A   A   B   B   C   C   D   D   E   E

simply placing in two bars alongside each other, the numbers of people who in 1950 would have filled a certain income bracket under the welfare provisions prevailing in 1936 and the real-life figures thrown up by the Rowntree survey undertaken in September 1950.[157] Rowntree divided the citizens of York into five main bands, A to E, according to the 'available income for man, wife and three children, or its equivalent for differently constituted families'. 'A' was under 77 shillings per week (1 old shilling = 5 new pence); 'B' between 77s and 100s; 'C' between 100s and 123s; 'D' 123s and under 146s; 'E' 146s and over.[158] The table and the bar chart show the most dramatic impact of the mid-century welfare state on families on the next to lowest income band. With the 1936 safety net, over 17 per cent of the population would have been struggling to manage on it. In 1950 York, the actual figure was 2.4 per cent.[159]

The key finding of Rowntree vindicated the Attlee Government's elevation of full employment policy above all others as the 'never again' factor that mattered most. 'The disappearance of unemployment as a cause of poverty' was what had transferred York between 1936 and 1950.

No able-bodied person was found to be in poverty because of unemployment. The male householders who were unemployed despite being fit, and wishing to work, were all in classes 'C' or 'D', since each of them had a source of income other than his unemployment insurance benefit. The rates of that benefit payable under the National Insurance Act are not alone sufficient to maintain a family above the poverty line even if the other welfare measures are taken into account. It follows that large-scale unemployment, such as occurred in the 1930s, could result in widespread poverty which would be alleviated, but not prevented by the welfare legislation at present on the Statute Book.[160]

The Rowntree poverty line, which came out at just over £5 per week for a family of five (excluding rent),[161] would not exactly guarantee a life of clover for any household just above it (no more than did Beveridge's definitions in 1942). And the so-called 'rediscovery' of poverty by the Child Poverty Action Group and others in the 1960s turned round calculations and arguments about the ingredients of this difficult definition that have raged ever since.[162]

It's true, to anticipate still more later twentieth-century debates, that the Forties vision of welfare had (family allowances apart, with its philosophy of putting purchasing power in the mother's purse) scarcely a trace of a feminist perspective about it. The huge increase in the number of married women with jobs – from 16 per cent to 40 per cent between 1931 and 1951[163] – had surprisingly little impact on the shaping of welfare policy even though 'women into the factories' was one of the more celebrated phenomena of the wartime experience. Not until the end of the Fifties did sociologists like Michael Young begin to write about the changing chemistry of family life and its implications for public policy, linked as those changes were to full employment, the National Health Service and the spread of contraception.[164]

Similarly, though one or two demographers such as David Glass were predicting by the early 1950s that the economic and welfare reforms of the late 1940s were unlikely to transform the possibilities of upward social mobility for the sons and daughters of the semi- and unskilled members of the labour force,[165] only a decade or more later did the work of analysts such as Richard Titmuss and Brian Abel-Smith show just how especially beneficial the welfare changes had been to the middle classes rather than the manual workers and their families in whose name the new social infrastructure had largely been put in place.

Thirty years later, sociologists like John Goldthorpe were declaiming that the explosion in professional and service jobs since the Attlee years had transformed the occupational and class picture of Britain. But the changes were absolute rather than relative even though the postwar 'project of creating a more open society was undertaken ... in circumstances which might be regarded as highly favourable to it'.[166] The data, however, according to Professor Goldthorpe and his collaborators, leads

> clearly to the conclusion that, despite these supposedly propitious circumstances, no significant reduction in class inequalities was in fact achieved. Systematic shifts were evident in the pattern of absolute mobility rates, of a kind that would be expected from the nature of the changes occurring in the occupational structure. But relative mobility rates, which we take as our indicator of the degree of openness, remained generally unaltered, and the only trends that could arguably be discerned (apart from over the early stages of the life-cycle) were indeed ones that would point to a widening of differences in class chances.[167]

Mercifully, Jim Griffiths, Ellen Wilkinson, Nye Bevan and Attlee himself didn't live long enough to see the desiccated calculating machinery of social scientific analysis putting their dreams through such an unforgiving mangle.

Any historical assessment of an era, however, has the nature of a balance sheet. What really strikes early 1990s eyes about those brave, semi-collectivist years of mid-century Britain is the combination of hope and public purpose. That sour law of unintended consequences, of change-can-only-make-things-worse, was scarcely visible in the land. Just as later generations had too little faith in the possibilities of centrally conceived, nationally applied public policy as a bringer of beneficial change in the economic and social structure, it seems now that the people of late Forties and early Fifties Britain had too much – so much, in fact, that disillusion could only have set in. How one envies them that faith, however.

To them there was good reason to hold it. A decade of unbroken experience from 1940 on had seemed to endorse the strategy, even if regular transfusions of finance through a transatlantic life-line were needed to put the bricks and mortar where the blue prints were. But would it now appear such a mixed memory of nobility of purpose turning, at first gradually and then, by the early 1970s, very rapidly into a nightmare of frustration and disappointment (as, seemingly, all sense of social solidarity disappeared in the glare of naked trade union power, so painfully ironic given the changes in labour relations so confidently predicted by the early engineers of full employment), if the British economy had managed to grow at its late-Forties rate of just under 3 per cent for the entire postwar period? I doubt it. If that had been the record, and not economic stop/go, wouldn't the postwar settlement built on Keynesian and Beveridgite lines have held and with it the politics of the Forties, Fifties and early Sixties? Would Mrs Thatcher or Arthur Scargill have been conceivable as the main political actors of mid-Eighties Britain in the special circumstances of a bitter coal strike? And that level of economic performance, surely, was sustainable even with a late Forties union structure and labour market (and a Beveridge-style welfare state), if the load on the economic base had been eased by a reduction of costly, Great Power-driven burdens and/or a fuller participation in the postwar *European* economic miracle that earlier membership of the Community might well have brought? Such issues will be the sinewy themes of future volumes in this collection.

The Attlee years had their failures – a refusal to confront the truly harsh reality of diminished world status, a reluctance to modernise the state, a tendency to look back at the problems of the Thirties rather than forward to the needs of the Fifties. Yet Britain had never – and still hasn't – experienced a progressive phase to match 1945–51. It is largely, though not wholly, the achievement of these years – and the wartime experience, the crucial platform on which those advances were built – that 1951 Britain, certainly compared to the UK of 1931 or *any* previous decade, was a kinder, gentler and a far, far better place in which to be born, to grow up, to live, love, work and even to die. Such an epitaph cannot be placed with conviction on the plinths of any of the eras to come as Mr Attlee's Britain gave way to Mr Churchill's.

Chronology

1945

April	30	Hitler commits suicide in Berlin.

May   7   Germany surrenders at Rheims.

8   Victory in Europe Day.

23   Churchill disbands Wartime Coalition and forms a Caretaker Government pending an election.

June   4   Churchill in an election broadcast claims a Labour Government 'would have to fall back on some kind of Gestapo'.

July   5   Election day. Three-week delay in announcing result while Forces' votes are garnered and counted.

15   Blackout ends. Street lights lit in London.

17   Potsdam Conference convenes in Berlin.

26   Allies at Potsdam call on Japan to surrender.

British election results announced: Labour, 393 seats; Conservatives, 213; Liberals, 12; others, 22. Formation of first Labour Government with a majority (146 seats).

Bevin surprise appointment at the Foreign Office; Dalton to the Treasury. Attlee survives plot against his leadership.

August   6   United States Air Force drops atomic bomb on Hiroshima.

9   Atomic bomb on Nagasaki.

14   Japan surrenders.

15   Victory in Japan Day. Second World War ends.

Parliament opened by George VI. King's Speech announces nationalisation of the mines and repeal of the Trade Disputes Act.

21   Truman stops Lend-Lease.

1945 *continued*

September   2   Japan formally surrenders on board USS *Missouri* in Tokyo Bay.

              19   In a broadcast Attlee says it's time for Indians to decide their own destiny.

October   4   UK unofficial dock strike begins.

              13   Dalton's first Budget: income and purchase taxes reduced; profits tax introduced; surtax raised.

              14   Dock strike deepens. Over 40,000 men out. Six thousand troops called in to unload food.

              29   Stalin orders crash programme to develop a Soviet atomic bomb.

November   5   Dock strike ends.

               7   RAF Gloster Meteor jet sets new world air speed record flying at 606 miles per hour above Herne Bay in Kent.

December   6   US Loan Agreement signed in Washington.

              13   House of Commons votes to accept terms of the American Loan.

              16   Foreign Ministers' Conference opens in Moscow.

              27   International Monetary Fund and World Bank established in Washington.

1946

January   1   Heathrow Airport officially opened.

              27   Two thousand RAF personnel 'strike' in India, Ceylon and Singapore in protest at slow rate of demobilisation.

February   7   Rationing tightened in UK to release supplies for British Zone in Germany.

              12   Rioting in India after Navy mutiny.

March   1   Bank of England nationalised.

               5   Churchill delivers 'Iron Curtain' speech in Fulton, Missouri.

              21   Bevan unveils plans for a National Health Service in Parliament.

April   5   Grand National run at Aintree for first time since 1940.

               9   Dalton's second Budget: purchase tax reduced; income tax allowances increased.

| April | 17 | Government announces plans to nationalise iron and steel. |
| | 21 | Keynes dies. |

May	16	Attlee announces plans for a united independent India.
	22	Trade Disputes Act repealed.
	27	Government plans to double the number of British scientists.
	30	Bread rationing to be introduced.

June	5	Derby run for the first time since 1940.
	8	Victory Parade in London.
	19	Jay warns Attlee of fuel crisis next winter.

July	13	US Congress approves American loan to Britain.
	22	King David Hotel blown up in Jerusalem by Jewish terrorists.
	24	Shinwell warns of insufficient coal to get through winter.
	29	Muslim League demands separate 'Pakistan'.

| August | 19 | Hindu–Muslim riots in Calcutta. |

September	1	Football League restarts in first postwar season.
	19	Churchill calls for a 'United States of Europe' in a speech in Zurich.
	29	BBC Third Programme inaugurated.

| October | 1 | Twelve leading Nazis are sentenced to death at the end of their trials in Nuremberg. |

| November | 12 | King's Speech announces nationalisation of railways, ports, long-distance road transport and inland waterways. |
| | 22 | Ballpoint 'biros' go on sale in London. |

| December | 27 | Cotton mills shut down and Midlands plan four-day week because of coal shortages. |

1947

January	1	Coal and Cable and Wireless nationalised.
	7	Transport strike begins in London.
	8	Secret Cabinet committee authorises manufacture of a British atomic bomb.
		Steel works close down because of lack of coal.
		Troops called in to deliver London food supplies.
	16	London hauliers vote to return to work.

1947 *continued*

January	22	Meat ration reduced.
	24	Severe cold weather hits UK.
	29	Power cuts spread as temperature falls to minus 16°F.

February	6	Ellen Wilkinson dies.
	12	Heavy snowstorms exacerbate fuel crisis.
	14	Palestine problem referred to the United Nations by UK Government.
	20	Attlee announces transfer of power in India not later than June 1948. Mountbatten appointed Viceroy.

March	10	Foreign Ministers meet in Moscow to discuss future of Germany.
	12	Truman announces aid to Greece and Turkey.
	16	Widespread gales and flooding in UK.
	26	Royal Commission on the Press established.
	27	Sir Edwin Plowden appointed Chief Planning Officer.
	31	March the wettest month on record.

April	1	School-leaving age raised to fifteen.
	3	National Service reduced to one year.
	6	Troops sent in to subdue Indian riots.
	8	Snow and gales return.
	15	Dalton's third Budget: death duties, profits tax, purchase tax, stamp and tobacco duties raised.
	24	Foreign Ministers' Conference breaks up in Moscow without agreement on postwar settlement in Europe. Government bans use of coal and gas fires until September.

May	15	Bevin announces UK and US Zones to merge in Germany.
	23	Cabinet agrees to Mountbatten's proposal to partition India.

June	3	Attlee confirms partition. Power to be transferred in India on 15 August 1947.
	5	Marshall's Harvard speech on aid to Europe.
	18	Britain and France welcome Marshall speech and announce conference of European nations in Paris.
	25	Colonial Development Corporation established.
	27	Bevin, Bidault and Molotov meet in Paris to discuss Marshall proposals.
	30	Cuts in dollar imports of petrol, tobacco and newsprint. 75 per cent levy on foreign films. Meat ration to be cut from 13 July.

July	2	Molotov walks out of Paris talks and Soviet Union rejects Marshall Plan.
	4	Twenty-two European countries invited to Paris Conference on Marshall proposals.
	9	Marriage of Princess Elizabeth to Lieutenant Philip Mountbatten announced.
	12	Paris Conference opens. Sixteen nations attend. Meeting boycotted by Eastern European nations. Two British sergeants kidnapped by Jewish terrorists in Palestine.
	15	Sterling made convertible into dollars on foreign exchanges in accordance with terms of the American Loan. Parliament passes Indian Independence Bill.
	17	Treasury draws up secret 'famine food programme' for UK in case Marshall Plan discussions fail.
	18	Jewish refugees prevented from landing in Palestine from the vessel *Exodus*.
	21	Reduction in size of newspapers and periodicals.
	31	Sergeants found hanged near Haifa.
August	6	Attlee announces crisis austerity plan for British economy.
	15	British rule ends in India. First UK atomic reactor goes critical at Harwell.
	18	Financial talks open in Washington as sterling convertibility puts pound under pressure.
	21	Sterling convertibility suspended.
	24	More than 10,000 believed dead in border clashes in Punjab. First Edinburgh Festival begins.
	27	Attlee warns of 'peril and anxiety' over ability to pay for imports. Food rations cut. Basic petrol ration abolished to halt pleasure motoring.
September	7	Coal strike in South Yorkshire closes Sheffield steelworks.
	16	John Cobb establishes new land speed record of 394 mph in Utah.
	20	Denis Compton sets new record (3,816) for runs scored in an English cricket season.
	24	One thousand two hundred Muslim refugees slaughtered on train in Amritsar in worst single massacre since partition.
	26	UK announces relinquishment of Palestine Mandate.
	29	Cripps appointed Minister of Economic Affairs. Wilson becomes President of the Board of Trade at thirty-one. New Cabinet committee on economic policy created.

1947 continued

September	29	Attlee survives second plot against his leadership.

October	1	Foreign travel allowance abolished for UK citizens.
	5	Cominform created by Soviet bloc nations.
	17	Burma to be independent from January 1948.
	19	Bacon ration halved.
	21	King's Speech outlines plans for gas nationalisation, curbing of powers for the House of Lords, abolition of Poor Law and reductions in size of Armed Forces.
	23	Ban on imports of US tobacco.
	26	British troops withdraw from Iraq.
	30	Twenty-three nations sign a General Agreement on Tariffs and Trade in Geneva.

November	1	Belgium, the Netherlands and Luxembourg form customs union.
	8	Potato rationing introduced.
	10	US agrees to ending of UK Mandate in Palestine on 31 May 1948.
	12	Emergency Budget: profits tax, purchase tax and drink duties raised. (Dalton resigns following day after leaking proposals to a journalist on way into Chamber.)
	13	Cripps appointed Chancellor of the Exchequer.
	20	Princess Elizabeth weds Lieutenant Mountbatten who becomes Prince Philip, Duke of Edinburgh.
	25	Council of Foreign Ministers opens in London.
	30	UN General Assembly votes to partition Palestine.

December	1	White Paper outlines cuts in capital expenditure.
	7	British troops withdraw from Italy.
	14	Stanley Baldwin dies.
	15	Council of Foreign Ministers adjourns *sine die*.
	19	US Congress passes interim Foreign Aid Bill.

1948

January	1	Railways nationalised.
	4	Burma independent.
	7	Truman urges Congress to authorise $6,800 million in Marshall Aid.
	30	Gandhi assassinated in New Delhi.
		UK Government publishes bill to end double voting and to abolish the twelve University seats.

January	31	Rioting in India after the death of Gandhi.
February	9	Cripps' wage freeze launched in White Paper on prices, costs and incomes.
	10	Ceylon independent.
	16	Communist Peoples' Republic established in North Korea.
	27	Communist coup in Czechoslovakia.
	28	Last British troops leave India.
March	3	Final £25 million drawing exhausts the American Loan.
	10	Masaryk dies in Prague.
	14	US Senate passes Economic Co-operation Act.
	15	Purge of Communists and Fascists in sensitive Civil Service posts announced by Attlee.
	17	Brussels Treaty signed binding UK, France and Benelux in a fifty-year mutual defence pact. Truman addresses both Houses on foreign policy.
	22	Secret talks about an Atlantic Pact start in Washington involving American, British and Canadian officials.
	27	Cheese ration cut.
	31	House of Representatives passes European Co-operation Act. Russians start controlling western rail movements to Berlin after walking out of Allied Control Council on 20 March.
April	1	Electricity nationalised.
	5	Fifteen die after mid-air crash between British airliner and Soviet fighter near Berlin.
	6	Cripps' first Budget: capital levy introduced; tobacco and drink duties up; pools betting tax established; income tax relief granted.
	8	Private motorists to be restricted to 90 miles a month from 1 June.
	15	Bevan offers doctors freedom of practice within the NHS.
	16	Sixteen nations sign up for the European Recovery Programme under Marshall Aid.
	25	Milk ration raised to 3.5 pints a week.
	26	GCE to replace School and Higher School Certificates.
May	12	A.V. Alexander tells Parliament UK is to manufacture its own atomic bomb.
	14–15	British Mandate ends in Palestine.
	16	Weizmann named as first President of Israel.
	31	Dalton rejoins Cabinet as Chancellor of the Duchy.

1948 *continued*

June	18	Currency reform proclaimed in western zones of Germany. Soviets prohibit all traffic between Russian Zone and the west.
	21	*Empire Windrush* arrives in Tilbury.
	24	Soviets cut railway line between Berlin and Helmstedt.
	26	Berlin Airlift begins.
	28	State of Emergency declared as unofficial strike by 19,000 dockers paralyses 232 ships.
	30	Dockers return to work.
		Last British troops leave Palestine.
July	5	National Health Service inaugurated.
	6	Marshall protests to Soviets about Berlin blockade.
		France and Benelux join secret Atlantic Pact discussions in Washington.
	10	Berlin blockade by land and water made absolute.
	13	Cabinet's Berlin Committee approve stationing of US B29 bombers in East Anglia.
	16	Vickers Viscount makes its maiden flight.
	23	Joint Intelligence Committee tells ministers Soviet Union unlikely to have the atomic bomb before 1951 and that it will be unable to wage a global war until 1957.
	25	Bread rationing ends.
	29	Olympic Games open in London.
August	3	Government publishes report on disturbances in the Gold Coast.
	14	Don Bradman bows out with a duck at the Oval in his last test match.
September	1	West German constituent assembly meets in Bonn.
	18	Record 7,000 tons of supplies flown into Berlin in one day.
	29	Western powers refer Berlin Blockade to UN Security Council.
October	8	Belcher named in alleged corruption scandal.
	16	European Payments Agreement signed.
	26	European Co-operation Administration grants $310 million loan to Britain.
	27	Thirty-two British firms exhibit at Earls Court Motor Show.
November	2	Truman re-elected President.

November	5	Wilson announces 'bonfire of controls' on manufactured goods.
	14	Prince Charles born.
	23	George VI cancels Australian tour because of blood clot.
	26	UK Government proposes a Council of Europe.

December	1	Parliament approves extension of National Service to eighteen months.
	15	Republic of Ireland Bill passed.

1949

January	1	British Nationality Act comes into force.
	7	Ceasefire between Egypt and Israel in first Arab-Israeli war. Dean Acheson becomes US Secretary of State.
	29	UK recognises Israel *de facto*.

February	3	Belcher resigns from Board of Trade.
	8	Eire says it could not join an Atlantic Pact while Ireland is divided.
	18	Millionth ton of supplies airlifted into Berlin.

March	15	Clothes rationing ends.
	18	Eight western nations agree to form a North Atlantic Treaty Organisation.

April	1	Bill passed creating twelve National Parks.
	2	Floodlights and neon signs relit in UK after ten-year ban.
	4	NATO Treaty signed in Washington.
	6	Cripps' second Budget: income tax relief; beer and wine duties reduced; betting tax and death duties raised; food subsidies cut.
	8	US, Britain and France agree on creation of West Germany.
	18	Eire becomes a republic and leaves the Commonwealth.
	24	Chocolate and sweet rationing ends. Constitution agreed for West Germany.
	26	Soviet Union calls for four power talks to end Berlin crisis.

May	1	Gas nationalised.
	9	First launderette opens in London.
	12	Berlin blockade ends. Transport links restored between Soviet and western zones.
	13	Full diplomatic relations established between UK and Israel.

1949 *continued*

May	18	Dock strike at Avonmouth.
	23	Federal Republic of Germany comes into existence.
June	7	Troops go into Avonmouth and Liverpool docks.
	13	Cripps warns Cabinet Economic Policy Committee that if dollar drain continues at present rate position will be 'desperate'.
		Manchester University unveils its 'computing machine'.
	15	Cripps warns colleagues that currency reserves could be gone within a year, precipitating 'a complete collapse of sterling'.
	29	Royal Commission on the Press gives newspapers clean bill of health but warns journalists against taking information unquestioningly from government departments.
July	1	Cabinet's Economic Policy Committee in all-day emergency meeting on pound.
		Dock strike in London.
	7	Troops move food in London docks.
	14	Cripps announces emergency £100 million cuts in dollar imports.
	22	London dock strike ends.
	27	Comet makes maiden flight at over 500 mph.
August	8	Council of Europe meets for first time in Strasbourg.
	29	Cabinet secretly approves devaluation of sterling. Cripps and Bevin to consult on new rate in Washington.
	30	Cricket County Championship tied for first time. Title shared between Middlesex and Yorkshire.
September	4	Ill-fated Brabazon airliner makes maiden flight.
	11	Milk ration cut to 2.5 pints a week.
	12	Bevin and Cripps decide on new $2.80 rate for pound in Washington Embassy.
	18	Devaluation announced. Sterling drops from $4.03 to $2.80. Cripps apologises for 'necessary deception in a wicked world'.
	20	Adenauer forms first West German Government.
		France proposes Western European Monetary Union.
	21	Military government ends in West Germany.
		Mao proclaims a People's Republic of China.
	23	Truman announces Soviets have tested an atomic bomb.

October	1	Communist régime takes over in Peking.
	12	German Democratic Republic set up in Soviet Zone.
	24	Attlee announces cuts of £140 million in capital spending and £120 million in current expenditure; bank loan restrictions; building controls.
	26	UK recognises People's Republic of China.
November	15	Government postpones iron and steel nationalisation until 1951.
	19	New agreement between Government and trade unions on wages standstill.
December	16	Royal assent given to Parliament Bill restricting Lords' delaying powers to twelve months.

1950

January	10	Soviet Union walks out of UN Security Council in protest at refusal to seat Communist China's envoy.
	21	George Orwell dies.
	26	India declares itself a republic.
	31	Truman says US will build a hydrogen bomb.
February	3	Klaus Fuchs charged with giving atomic secrets to the Soviet Union.
	14	Seretse Khama arrives in London after refusing to resign.
	23	General Election: Labour, 315 seats; Conservatives, 298; Liberals, 9; others, 3. Labour majority of 5.
March	1	Fuchs sentenced to fourteen years.
	8	Marshall Voroshilov announces Soviet Union possesses atomic bombs.
April	18	Cripps' last Budget: income tax reduced; fuel tax and purchase tax raised.
	19	Strike in London docks.
	24	Troops move into London docks.
May	1	London dock strike ends.
	11	Schuman in London with French plan for a European Coal and Steel Community.
	26	Petrol rationing ends.
June	1	French ultimatum on Coal and Steel Community.

1950 *continued*

June	2	Cabinet rejects ultimatum.
	25	North Korean troops invade South Korea across 38th parallel.
		Cabinet formally rejects Schuman Plan.
	27	UN Security Council urges members to repel attack on South Korea.
	28	Seoul falls to the Communists.
		Attlee places Royal Navy ships in Far East under US/UN command.
July	10	Soap rationing ends.
	26	British troops to be sent to Korea.
	31	Sainsbury opens first self-service store in Croydon.
August	3	UK defence estimates trebled.
	29	British troops arrive in Korea.
September	2	Wage freeze breaks down as TUC votes against incomes policy.
	15	National Service extended to two years.
	16	UN forces land at Inchon.
	19	European Payments Union established.
	25	Seoul recaptured by UN forces.
	29	UN troops reach 38th parallel.
October	1	South Koreans cross 38th parallel.
	15	Chinese enter Korean War.
	19	Cripps resigns due to ill health. Succeeded as Chancellor of the Exchequer by Gaitskell.
November	5	MacArthur confirms Chinese forces have moved into Korea.
	27	UN forces withdraw south in Korea after huge Chinese assault.
	30	Truman statement raises fear of atomic bomb being used in Korea.
December	3	Pyongyang evacuated by UN troops.
	4	Attlee flies to Washington for meeting with Truman on atomic bomb and defence burden-sharing.
	13	Announcement that Marshall Aid to the UK will end on 1 January.
	14	Communiqué on Attlee-Truman talks published.

| December | 19 | Eisenhower appointed NATO Supreme Commander in Europe. |
| | 28 | Chinese troops cross the 38th parallel. |

1951

January	4	Seoul retaken by the Communists.
	9	Government abandons East African Ground Nuts scheme.
	17	Bevan appointed Minister of Labour; Isaacs to Pensions; Marquand Minister of Health.
	28	Meat ration reduced.
	29	Attlee announces defence spending of £4,700 million over three years; 255,000 reservists called up.

| February | 15 | Iron and steel nationalised. |

March	9	Bevin leaves Foreign Office to become Lord Privy Seal. Replaced as Foreign Secretary by Morrison.
	14	Seoul recaptured by UN and South Korean forces.
	15	Iranian Parliament nationalises Anglo-Iranian Oil Company's holdings.

April	10	Gaitskell's first Budget: income tax, purchase tax and petrol duties increased; 'initial allowances' on new plant scrapped.
	14	Bevin dies.
	15	Abadan oil refinery closes.
	21	Bevan resigns over dental and spectacle charges.
	22	Wilson resigns over defence estimates.
	24	Shawcross appointed to Board of Trade, Robens to the Ministry of Labour.
	28	Mossadegh becomes Prime Minister of Iran.

May	2	Shah signs decree approving nationalisation of Anglo-Iranian.
	3	Festival of Britain opened by George VI.
	12	US test hydrogen bomb.
	25	Burgess and Maclean disappear.

| June | 19 | Iranian Government breaks off talks with Anglo-Iranian. |
| | 26 | Soviet Union calls for Korean ceasefire. |

| July | 9 | Formal termination of state of war between UK and Germany. |

1951 *continued*

July	26	Korean ceasefire talks open.
		Restrictions on UK bank credits, dividends and prices.
	30	UK agrees to reopen talks with Iran.
August	6	UK/Iran talks open in Tehran.
	31	Deutsche Grammophon launch first 33 rpm long-playing record.
September	8	Wartime Allies (Soviet Union apart) sign peace treaty with Japan.
	19	General election called for 25 October.
	23	George VI has operation on his lungs.
	27	Iranian troops take control of Abadan oil refinery.
	28	UK refers Iranian dispute to UN Security Council.
October	3	All but eleven staff leave Abadan oil refinery.
	17	First German car (a Porsche) at UK Motor Show since before the war.
	25	General Election: Conservatives, 321 seats; Labour, 295; Liberals, 6; others, 3. Conservative majority of 17.
	26	Churchill becomes Prime Minister.

Notes

The following abbreviations are used in the notes:

AACP	Anglo-American Council on Productivity	GDP	Gross Domestic Product
ADM	Admiralty	ICBH	Institute of Contemporary British History
AIR	Air Ministry	IMF	International Monetary Fund
ARP	Air Raid Precautions	IOLR	India Office Library and Records
BMA	British Medical Association	JIC	Joint Intelligence Committee
BOT	Board of Trade	JPC	Joint Production Council
CAB	Cabinet or Cabinet Committee Papers	MO	Mass Observation
CEEC	Committee for European Economic Co-operation	MOD	Ministry of Defence
		MOH	Ministry of Health
CEPS	Central Economic Planning Staff	MOI	Ministry of Information
CO	Colonial Office	NATO	North Atlantic Treaty Organisation
CUP	Cambridge University Press	NEC	National Executive Committee of the Labour Party
ECA	Economic Co-operation Administration		
ECSC	European Coal and Steel Community	NROC	National Research and Development Corporation
ED	Board of Education		
EPC	Cabinet Committee on Economic Policy	OEEC	Organisation for European Economic Co-operation
EPU	European Payments Union		
ERP	European Recovery Programme	OUP	Oxford University Press
FO	Foreign Office	PRO	Public Records Office
FRUS	Foreign Relations of the United States	T	HM Treasury
GATT	General Agreement on Tariffs and Trade	UN	United Nations

PREFACE

1 George Steiner, *Real Presences*, Faber, 1989, p. 10.
2 Walter Bagehot, 'Matthew Arnold on the London University', *Fortnightly Review*, 1 June 1868, reprinted in Norman St John-Stevas, (ed.), *The Collected Works of Walter Bagehot, Vol. Seven, Economist*, 1974, p. 388.
3 G.R. Elton, *The History of England*, Inaugural Lecture as Regius Professor of Modern History at the University of Cambridge, 26 January 1984, CUP, 1984, pp. 15–16.
4 Enoch Powell, *Byline*, BBC 1, 3 July 1989.
5 Peter Hennessy, 'Never Again', in Harriet Jones and Brian Brivati, *What Difference Did the War Make . . . ?*, Leicester University Press, (forthcoming).
6 Peter Hennessy, unpublished diary entry for 8 July 1991.
7 Hennessy, 'Never Again'.
8 Patrick Cosgrave, *The Lives of Enoch Powell*, Bodley Head, 1989, pp. 245–55.

9　Ibid., p. 54.
10　'Never Again'.
11　Elton, *The History of England*, p. 24.

INTRODUCTION

1　George Orwell, *The Lion and the Unicorn; Socialism and the English Genius*, Secker and Warburg, 1941, pp. 11, 12.
2　J. Enoch Powell, 'Differences between history and politics', *Spectator*, 26 November 1988.
3　The phrase was first used by Philip Graham as his ambition for the magazine *Newsweek* when he bought it in 1961. David Halberstam, *The Powers That Be*, Chatto and Windus, 1979, p. 161.

CHAPTER 1

Who Do You Think You Are Kidding?

1　Bud Flanagan, theme tune of *Dad's Army*, On the Air. *60 years of BBC Theme Music*, BBC Records, 1982, originally recorded in 1969 when the programme started.
2　A.J.P. Taylor, *English History, 1914–1945*, OUP, 1965, p. 600.
3　George Orwell, *The Lion and the Unicorn; Socialism and the English Genius*, Secker and Warburg, 1941, p. 33.
4　'Mrs T's Leadership Will End in a Muddle', Lord Whitelaw in conversation with Douglas Keay, *Woman's Own*, 7 May 1988.

Part One: The Beginning, 1938–40

1　Harold Macmillan, *Winds of Change 1914–1939*, Macmillan, 1966, p. 562.
2　Quoted in Ronald Seth, *The Day War Broke Out*, Neville Spearman, 1963, pp. 59–60.
3　L.A.M. Brech quoted in Ben Wicks, *No Time to Wave Goodbye*, Bloomsbury, 1989, p. 32.
4　John Colville, *The Fringes of Power, Downing Street Diaries 1939–1955*, Hodder, 1985, p. 122.
5　Taylor, *English History*, p. 427.
6　Tom Harrisson and Charles Madge, *Britain*, Cresset Library edition, 1986, p. 88. First published as a Penguin Special in 1939.
7　Ibid.
8　Ibid., pp. 88–9.
9　Ibid., pp. 94–5.
10　Taylor, *English History 1914–1945*, p. 428.
11　For the singing sailors see Harrisson and Madge, *Britain*, p. 176. I'm grateful for his reconstruction of the Munich period in Chelsea Barracks to Sergeant Ernie Teal. Conversation with Sergeant Teal, 27 March 1989.
12　Harrisson and Madge, *Britain*, pp. 238–9.
13　John W. Wheeler-Bennett, *King George VI*, Macmillan, 1958, pp. 352–3.
14　Ronald Lewin, *Ultra Goes to War*, Hutchinson, 1978, p. 51.
15　See pp. 39–45.
16　Taylor, *English History 1914–1945*, p. 432.
17　John W. Wheeler-Bennett, *John Anderson, Viscount Waverley*, Macmillan, 1962, pp. 222–3.
18　Richard M. Titmuss, *Problems of Social Policy*, HMSO, 1950, pp. 63–6.
19　Tom Harrisson, *Living Through the Blitz*, Collins, 1976, p. 24.

20 Seth, *The Day War Broke Out*, p. 35.
21 Alan Bullock, *Hitler, A Study in Tyranny*, Odhams, 1952.
22 Peter Hennessy, 'Such a refreshing change after all those "clever" people', *The Times Higher Education Supplement*, 5 October 1973.
23 Arthur Marwick, *Britain in the Century of Total Wars: War, Peace and Social Change 1900–1967*, Bodley Head, 1968, p. 17.
24 Arthur Longmate, *How We Lived Then, A history of everyday life during the Second World War*, Arrow, 1973, p. 1.
25 Winston S. Churchill, *The Second World War, Vol. 6, War Comes to America*, Cassell, 1964, pp. 207–10.
26 Lord Butler, *The Art of the Possible*, Penguin, 1973, p. 81.
27 Ibid.
28 W.S. Hewison, *This Great Harbour Scapa Flow*, Orkney Press, 1985, pp. 255–60.
29 Conversation with Sir Frank Cooper, 5 April 1989.
30 For a comprehensive account of the evacuation see Angus Calder, *The People's War, Britain 1939–45*, Cape, 1969, pp. 35–50; for a scholarly one Titmuss, *Problems of Social Policy*, pp. 102, 137; for a moving one Wicks, *No Time to Wave Goodbye*.
31 Wicks, *No Time to Wave Goodbye*, pp. 83–4.
32 Ibid., p. 86.
33 Ibid., p. 75.
34 Conversation with Brian Cleminson, 5 April 1989.
35 Wicks, *No Time to Wave Goodbye*, pp. 207–8.
36 Sir Harold Scott, *Your Obedient Servant*, Andre Deutsch, 1959, p. 193.
37 Ibid., pp. 117–18.
38 Ibid., p. 109.
39 Ibid., p. 118.
40 An extract from the Lloyd Papers quoted in Martin Gilbert, *Winston S. Churchill, Vol. VI, Finest Hour 1939–1941*, Heinemann, 1983, p. 290.
41 For example, I felt the need to revive interest in this important and neglected topic almost fifty years after the Norway Crisis. See Peter Hennessy, 'Whitehall Watch: Troubled question of the prerogative', *Independent*, 10 April 1989.
42 Nigel Nicolson (ed.), *Harold Nicolson, Diaries and Letters, 1939–45*, Fontana, 1970, entry for 7 May 1940, p. 72.
43 For an appreciation of Murrow, his background, his singularity and his importance, see A.M. Sperber, *Murrow, His Life and Times*, Michael Joseph, 1987.
44 Edward R. Murrow, 'A Reporter Remembers', *Listener*, 28 February 1946.
45 The description is Harold Nicolson's, Nicolson (ed.), *Harold Nicolson, Diaries and Letters, 1939–45*, p. 72.
46 Ibid.
47 Ibid., pp. 72–3.
48 Wheeler-Bennett, *King George VI*, p. 439.
49 Ibid., pp. 439–40.
50 Nicolson (ed.), *Harold Nicolson, Diaries and Letters 1939–45*, diary entry for 7 May 1940, p. 72.
51 Ibid., diary entry for 8 May 1940, p. 74.
52 *Clem Attlee, The Granada Historical Records Interview*, Granada, 1967, p. 19.
53 Kenneth Harris, *Attlee*, Weidenfeld, 1982, pp. 172–3.
54 Leo Amery, *My Political Life; Vol. III, The Unforgiving Years, 1929–1940*, Hutchinson, 1953, pp. 368–9.
55 Chamberlain Diary, entry for 11 May 1940, quoted in Keith Feiling, *The Life of Neville Chamberlain*, Macmillan, 1946, p. 440.
56 For Attlee's preference for Churchill see Harris, *Attlee*, p. 174; for his characterisation of Halifax see *The Granada Historical Records Interview*, p. 20.

57 Amery delivered his judgment at a lecture organised by the Extra-Mural Department of London University. It is reprinted in J.J. Craik-Henderson (ed.), *Parliament, A Survey*, Allen and Unwin, 1952, pp. 37–71. Attlee's one-liner on Halifax can be found in *The Granada Interview*, p. 20.

58 Winston S. Churchill, *The Second World War, Vol. 2, The Twilight War*, Cassell, 1964, p. 235.

59 King George VI diary entry for 10 May 1940 quoted in Wheeler-Bennett, *King George VI*, pp. 443–4.

60 Churchill, *The Second World War, Vol. 2, The Twilight War*, pp. 237–8.

61 Ibid., pp. 238–9.

62 Taylor, *English History 1914–1945*, p. 4, footnote.

Part Two: The Shock-Absorber, 1940–41

1   James Lansdale Hodson, *Through the Dark Night*, Gollancz, 1941, p. 308.

2   Frances Faviell, *A Chelsea Concerto*, Cassell, 1959, p. 115.

3   Conversation with Squadron Leader Teddy Haslam, 22 June 1978.

4   See Angus Calder, *The People's War, Britain 1939–45*, Cape, 1969, p. 233.

5   W.H. Thompson, *Sixty Minutes with Winston Churchill*, C. Johnson, 1953, pp. 44–5.

6   Speech on the occasion of his eightieth birthday, Westminster Hall, 30 November 1954.

7   House of Commons, *Official Report*, 13 May 1940, Columns 1501–2.

8   Ronald Hyam, 'Winston Churchill before 1914', *Historical Journal, Vol. XII*, no. 1 (1969), pp. 164–73.

9   See Charles Cruikshank, 'Dad's Army had real teeth after all,' *The Times*, 2 January 1981.

10 Nigel Nicolson (ed.), *Harold Nicolson, Diaries and Letters, 1939–45*, pp. 92–3, diary entries 15 and 19 June 1940.

11 Alan Bullock, *The Life and Times of Ernest Bevin, Vol. Two, Minister of Labour 1940–1945*, Heinemann, 1967, p. 4.

12 A.J.P. Taylor, *A Personal History*, Hamish Hamilton, 1983, p. 153.

13 Conversation with Martin Gilbert, 26 May 1988.

14 Martin Gilbert, *Winston S. Churchill, Vol. VI, Finest Hour, 1939–1941*, Heinemann, 1983, p. 418.

15 Ibid.

16 Ibid., p. 419.

17 Ibid.

18 Ben Pimlott (ed.), *The Second World War Diary of Hugh Dalton, 1940–45*, Cape, 1986, diary entry for 28 May 1940, pp. 27–8.

19 Gilbert, *Winston S. Churchill, Vol. VI, Finest Hour, 1939–1941*, p. 421.

20 Ibid., pp. 610–11.

21 Calder, *The People's War*, p. 161.

22 Ibid.

23 Sir Harold Scott, *Your Obedient Servant*, Andre Deutsch, 1959, p. 124.

24 Calder, *The People's War*, p. 162.

25 Ibid.

26 For evidence of this appealingly cavalier attitude which masked both fear and serious intent see Hodson, *Through The Dark Night*, pp. 340–4.

27 Calder, *The People's War*, p. 166.

28 Ibid., p. 167.

29 Hodson, *Through the Dark Night*, p. 344.

30 Calder, *The People's War*, pp. 178–9.

31 Scott, *Your Obedient Servant*, p. 125.

32 Lady Felicity Harewood, '*Clem, Father and Politician*', The Third Attlee Memorial Lecture, The Attlee Foundation, 20 February 1985.
33 A.M. Sperber, *Murrow, His Life and Times*, Michael Joseph, 1987, pp. 165–8.
34 A.P. Herbert, *The Thames*, Weidenfeld, 1966, pp. 163–5.
35 Gilbert, *Winston S. Churchill, Finest Hour*, pp. 774–5.
36 Ibid., p. 779.
37 Winston S. Churchill, *The Second World War, Vol. 4, The Commonwealth Alone*, Cassell, 1964, p. 16.
38 Correlli Barnett, *The Audit of War, The Illusion and Reality of Britain as a Great Nation*, Macmillan, 1986, pp. 159–61.
39 Ibid., p. 157.
40 Phillip Whitehead, *The Writing on the Wall*, Michael Joseph, 1985, p. 413.
41 Tom Harrisson, *Living Through the Blitz*, Collins, 1976, p. 157.
42 Ibid., p. 154.
43 Ibid., pp. 153–4.
44 Ibid., p. 167.
45 Ibid.
46 Calder, *The People's War*, p. 243.
47 Ibid., p. 257.
48 Ibid., p. 261.
49 Richard M. Titmuss, *Problems of Social Policy*, HMSO, 1950, pp. 335–6.
50 James Lansdale Hodson, *Home Front*, Gollancz, 1944, p. 43, diary entry for 20 May 1942.
51 John Strachey, *Post D*, Gollancz, 1941, pp. 92–3.
52 Quoted in Norman Longmate, *How We Lived Then, A History of Everyday Life During the Second World War*, Arrow, 1973, p. 126.
53 John Lehmann, *I Am My Brother*, Weidenfeld, 1960, p. 79.
54 Calder, *The People's War*, p. 261.
55 Ibid., pp. 261–2.
56 Bernard Crick, *George Orwell, A Life*, Secker and Warburg, 1980, p. 273. Crick describes it as 'a neglected book whose significance is often ignored'. It has had a profound and lasting effect on me, so much so that I delivered a public lecture to mark the fiftieth anniversary of its preparation.
57 George Orwell, *The Lion and the Unicorn; Socialism and the English Genius*, Secker and Warburg, 1941, p. 9.
58 Ibid., pp. 48–50.
59 It's the thesis which underpins Arthur Marwick's *Britain in the Century of Total Wars; War, Peace and Social Change 1900–1967*, Bodley Head, 1968.
60 Orwell, *The Lion and the Unicorn*, p. 87.
61 Ibid., p. 78.
62 Ibid., pp. 75–6.
63 Ibid., p. 35.
64 Ibid., p. 55.
65 Ibid., pp. 15–16.
66 Ibid., pp. 117–18.

Part Three: The Long Haul, 1941–45

1 Quoted in A.J.P. Taylor, *English History, 1914–1945*, OUP, 1965, p. 513.
2 Alec Cairncross, *Years of Recovery: British Economic Policy 1945–51*, Methuen, 1985, pp. 7–8.
3 Sir Richard made this assessment in his Introduction to D.N. Chester (ed.), *Lessons of the British War Economy*, CUP, 1951, p. 2.

4   Dame Alix Meynell, *Public Servant, Private Woman*, Gollancz, 1988, pp. 203–4.

5   J.L. Hodson, *Home Front*, Gollancz, 1944, p. 236, diary entry for 11 November 1942.

6   W.K. Hancock, *Country and Calling*, Faber, 1954, pp. 196–7.

7   Author of, *On the Psychology of Military Incompetence*, Macdonald, 1979.

8   The occasion was the 'Strategic Leadership Course' run by Sir Douglas Hague and Norman Strauss.

9   W.K. Hancock and M.M. Gowing, *The British War Economy*, HMSO, 1949, pp. 86–7.

10 Ibid., p. xv.

11 Paul Kennedy, *The Rise and Fall of the Great Powers*, Unwin Hyman, 1988, p. xv.

12 Hancock and Gowing, *British War Economy*, pp. 101–2.

13 Ibid., p. 102.

14 Ibid., pp. 102–3.

15 F.H. Hinsley, E.E. Thomas, C.F.G. Ransom, R.C. Knight, *British Intelligence in the Second World War, Vol. 2*, HMSO, 1981, Chapter 19, pp. 163–234; Chapter 26, pp. 525–72 and F.H. Hinsley, E.E. Thomas, C.F.G. Ransom, R.C. Knight, *British Intelligence in the Second World War, Vol. 3, Part 1*, HMSO, 1984, Chapter 35, pp. 211–46.

16 Hancock and Gowing, *British War Economy*, p. 99.

17 Winston S. Churchill, *The Second World War, Vol. 2, Their Finest Hour*, Cassell, 1949, p. 501.

18 Quoted in Warren F. Kimball (ed.), *Churchill and Roosevelt: The Complete Correspondence, Vol. 1*, Princeton University Press, 1984, pp. 101–9.

19 David Dimbleby and David Reynolds, *An Ocean Apart, The Relationship between Britain and America in the Twentieth Century*, BBC Books and Hodder, 1988, p. 133 and Henry Pelling, *Britain and the Marshall Plan*, Macmillan, 1988, pp. 2–4 and 111.

20 Dimbleby and Reynolds, *An Ocean Apart*, p. 164.

21 For the bureaucratic anatomy and command structure of wartime Whitehall see J.M. Lee, *The Churchill Coalition 1940–45*, Batsford, 1980.

22 See Peter Hennessy, *Whitehall*, Secker and Warburg, 1989, Chapter 3, pp. 88–119.

23 R.J. Hammond, *Food, Vol. II, Studies in Administration and Control*, HMSO, 1956, p. 109.

24 See A.H. Halsey, 'Norman Chester and Nuffield College' in David Butler and A.H. Halsey (eds), *Policy and Politics, Essays in Honour of Norman Chester*, Macmillan, 1978.

25 Chester (ed.), *Lessons of the British War Economy*, pp. 21–3.

26 Hodson, *Home Front*, p. 45, diary entry for 23 May 1942.

27 Ibid., p. 46.

28 Hancock and Gowing, *British War Economy*, p. xiv.

29 Angus Calder, *The People's War, Britain 1939–45*, Cape, 1969, p. 353.

30 E.L. Hargreaves and M.M. Gowing, *Civil Industry and Trade*, HMSO, 1952, p. 251.

31 Hammond, *Food, Vol. II*, p. 445.

32 Lord Woolton, *Memoirs*, Cassell, 1959, Chapters 5 and 6, pp. 53–85.

33 Ibid., pp. 251–2.

34 I am grateful to Dr Kathleen Burk of Imperial College, London, for lending it to me.

35 As late as 1948 the Barnet bypass just north of London sprouted barley, a few feet from the tarmac of the A1. Illustration 274 in James Cameron, *Memory Lane, A Photographic Album of Daily Life in Britain, 1930–1953*, Dent, 1980.

36 Marion Yass, *This is Your War: Home Front Propaganda in the Second World War*, HMSO, 1983, pp. 50–1.

37 It is reproduced as illustration 194 in Cameron, *Memory Lane*.

38 Quoted in Norman Longmate, *The Home Front, An Anthology of Personal Experience, 1938–1945*, Chatto and Windus, 1981, pp. 95–6.

39 My researcher Brett Arends found the exact rations for the last week of the European War in Ministry of Food files at the Public Record Office. His note was a full one but

the file number slipped out of the sheaf and even the finest sleuths at the PRO were unable to rediscover it for me.

40 See Richard M. Titmuss, *Problems of Social Policy*, HMSO, 1950, pp. 506–38.

41 John Vaizey in the 'Introduction' to *CC41, Utility Furniture and Fashion 1941–1951*, Inner London Education Authority, 1974, p. 5.

42 *The Times*, 15 September 1941.

43 Woolton, *Memoirs*, p. 209.

44 Hennessy, *Whitehall*, p. 107.

45 *The Times*, 2 April 1985.

46 PRO, INF 1/292.

47 PRO, INF 1/284.

48 Hammond, *Food, Vol. II*, p. 753.

49 Susan Briggs, *Keep Smiling Through, The Home Front 1939–45*, Fontana, 1976, p. 148.

50 *The Autobiography of Eleanor Roosevelt*, Hutchinson, 1962, pp. 185–6.

51 It is reproduced in Peter Lewis, *A People's War*, Channel 4 and Methuen, 1986, p. 155.

52 Christopher Hibbert, *The Court at Windsor, A Domestic History*, Longman, 1964, p. 288.

53 Churchill disclosed this in the House of Commons after the King's death in 1952. Martin Gilbert, *Never Despair, Winston S. Churchill, 1945–1965*, Heinemann, 1988, p. 699.

54 Betty Spencer Shew, *Queen Elizabeth, The Queen Mother*, Macdonald, 1955, p. 76.

55 John W. Wheeler-Bennett, *King George VI*, Macmillan, 1958, p. 467.

56 Calder, *The People's War*, pp. 652–3.

57 Tom Harrisson, *Living Through the Blitz*, Collins, 1976, pp. 281–2.

58 Peter Hennessy, 'Professor Richard Titmuss', *Times Higher Education Supplement*, 20 April 1973.

59 Titmuss, *Problems of Social Policy*, p. 324.

60 Ibid.

61 He used the phrase as the title of a chapter, ibid., pp. 322–36.

62 Ibid., p. 333.

63 Ibid., p. 334.

64 Ross Wyld, *The War Over Walthamstow, the Story of Civil Defence, 1939–1945*, Walthamstow Borough Council, 1945, p. 20. I am very grateful to Lord Bottomley, Chairman of the Borough Emergency Committee 1939–41, for giving me his copy.

65 Ibid.

66 Ibid.

67 Calder, *The People's War*, p. 648.

68 Wyld, *The War Over Walthamstow*, p. 22.

CHAPTER 2

Bunting and Ballots

1 Conversation with Sergeant Teal, 27 March 1989.

2 Quoted in Martin Gilbert, *Never Despair, Winston S. Churchill, 1945–1965*, Heinemann, 1988, p. 111.

3 Quoted in Peter Hennessy, 'The Attlee Governments 1945–1951', in Peter Hennessy and Anthony Seldon (eds), *Ruling Performance, British Governments from Attlee to Thatcher*, Blackwell, 1987, p. 32. I heard the story originally from Sir Robin Day.

4 Ben Pimlott (ed.), *The Political Diary of Hugh Dalton 1918–40, 1945–60*, Cape, 1986, p. 361.

5 Quoted in Anthony Howard, 'We are the Masters Now', in Michael Sissons and Philip French (eds), *The Age of Austerity 1945–51*, Penguin, 1964, p. 16.

6 John W. Wheeler-Bennett, *King George VI*, Macmillan, 1958, p. 624.

7 Kingsley Martin, *Critic's London Diary*, Secker and Warburg, 1960, 'London Diary' for 7 April 1945, p. 119.

8 Conversation with Lord Bancroft, 18 April 1989.

9 For an account of his Civil Service career see Peter Hennessy, *Whitehall*, Secker and Warburg, 1989, pp. 150–1, 273–4, 508–10, 632–3.

10 Churchill's War Cabinet Rooms are now open for public inspection. They are entered by a staircase at the foot of the Clive Steps at the bottom of King Charles' Street in London SW1.

11 From the typescript of Captain Pim's Memoirs. Quoted in Martin Gilbert, *Winston S. Churchill, Volume VII, Road to Victory, 1941–1945*, Heinemann, 1986, p. 1336.

12 Lord Moran, *Winston Churchill: The Struggle for Survival 1940/1965*, Sphere edition, 1968, diary entry for 7 May 1945, p. 272.

13 Sir Arthur Bryant, *Triumph in the West, 1943–46: based on the diaries and autobiographical notes of Field Marshal the Viscount Alanbrooke*, Collins, 1959, diary entry for 7 May 1945, pp. 455–6.

14 Gilbert, *Road to Victory*, p. 1338.

15 Ibid.

16 I am grateful to Mr Benn for showing me his diary entry for 7 May 1945 and for giving me permission to quote from it.

17 Benn Diary, 7 May 1945.

18 Gilbert, *Road to Victory*, p. 1341.

19 *CC 41*, p. 17.

20 Wheeler-Bennett, *King George VI*, p. 625.

21 Nigel Nicolson (ed.), *Harold Nicolson, Diaries and Letters, 1939–45*, Fontana, 1970, HN to NN [Nigel Nicolson], 8 May 1945, pp. 460–1.

22 Wing-Commander Ernest Millington had just won a by-election at Chelmsford for the utopian Socialist Common Wealth Party which shone briefly in the latter years of the war as the electoral truce between the Coalition Parties created highly artificial and advantageous conditions for minority parties. 'Chips' Channon would have been especially sensitive towards Millington's behaviour as he sat for a nearby Conservative stronghold in Southend.

23 Robert Rhodes James (ed.), *Chips, the Diaries of Sir Henry Channon*, Weidenfeld, 1967, pp. 405–6.

24 Lord Ismay, *The Memoirs of Lord Ismay*, Heinemann, 1960, pp. 395–6.

25 Alan Bullock, *The Life and Times of Ernest Bevin, Vol. Two, Minister of Labour, 1940–45*, Heinemann, 1967, p. 373.

26 Gilbert, *Road to Victory*, p. 1347.

27 Letter from Kathleen Townsend, 25 September 1988.

28 James Callaghan, *Time and Chance*, Collins, 1987, p. 62.

29 Harry Hopkins, *The New Look, A Social History of the Forties and Fifties in Britain*, Secker and Warburg, 1963, p. 16.

30 See Charles Cruikshank, *The German Occupation of the Channel Islands*, Imperial War Museum, 1975.

31 W.S. Hewison, *This Great Harbour Scapa Flow*, Orkney Press, 1985, p. 263.

32 Ibid.

33 Ibid.

34 Wheeler-Bennett, *King George VI*, p. 626.

35 Private information.

36 Nicolson (ed.), *Diaries and Letters, 1939–45*, pp. 462–3, diary entry for 8 May 1945.

37 Rhodes-James (ed.), *Diaries of Sir Henry Channon*, p. 425, diary entry for 10 January 1946.

38 Ibid., p. 414.

39 Graham Payn and Sheridan Morley, *The Noel Coward Diaries*, Papermac, 1983, p. 29, diary entry for 8 May 1945.

40 Quoted in Gilbert, *Never Despair*, p. 1350.

41 Mary Soames, *Clementine Churchill*, Penguin, 1981, pp. 521–37.

42 Gilbert, *Never Despair*, p. 3.

43 Kenneth Harris, *Attlee*, Weidenfeld, 1982, p. 247.

44 Robert Rhodes James, *Anthony Eden*, Weidenfeld, 1986, p. 294.

45 Quoted in Gilbert, *Never Despair*, pp. 5–6.

46 Ibid., p. 6.

47 Wheeler-Bennett, *King George VI*, p. 638.

48 C.R. Attlee, *As it Happened*, Odhams edition, 1954, p. 171.

49 Rhodes-James (ed.), *Diaries of Sir Henry Channon*, p. 414, diary entry for 14 November 1945.

50 Henry Pelling, *Britain and the Second World War*, Fontana, 1970, p. 233.

51 David Butler, *British General Elections Since 1945*, Blackwell, 1989, p. 108.

52 Sissons and French (eds), *The Age of Austerity*, p. 16 and Ian Mikardo, *Backbencher*, Weidenfeld, 1988, p. 80.

53 Mikardo, *Backbencher*, p. 80.

54 Ibid.

55 BBC Radio 4 *Analysis*, 'The Mind Behind the Cross', 10 October 1991.

56 The occasion was a 'Witness Seminar' on the Conservative Government of 1959–64 held by the Institute of Contemporary British History and the Institute of Historical Research on 26 October 1988.

57 Bernard Donoughue, *Prime Minister. The Conduct of Policy Under Harold Wilson and James Callaghan*, Cape, 1987, p. 191.

58 Conversation with Dr David Butler, 1 November 1988. For the original use of the metaphor see L.B. Namier, *Avenues of History*, Hamish Hamilton, 1952, p. 183.

59 Walter Bagehot, *The English Constitution*, Fontana edition, 1963, pp. 72–3.

60 Conversation with Professor Peter Clarke, 28 September 1991.

61 *Social Insurance and Allied Services*, Cmd. 6404, HMSO, 1942, p. 6.

62 Quoted in Trevor Burridge, *Clement Attlee, A Political Biography*, Cape, 1985, p. 2.

63 *Clem Attlee, The Granada Historical Records Interview*, Granada, 1967, pp. 27–8.

64 Alan Bullock, *Ernest Bevin, Foreign Secretary*, Heinemann, 1983, p. 856.

65 Alan Bullock, *The Life and Times of Ernest Bevin, Vol. Two, Minister of Labour 1940–1945*, Heinemann, 1967, p. 1.

66 Ibid., p. 4.

67 Douglas Jay, *Change and Fortune, A Political Record*, Hutchinson, 1980, p. 99.

68 Francis Williams, *Ernest Bevin, Portrait of a Great Englishman*, Hutchinson, 1952, p. 217.

69 Quoted in ibid.

70 Ibid.

71 Ibid.

72 J.B. Priestley, *Postscripts*, Heinemann, 1940, p. 27.

73 Angus Calder, *The People's War, Britain 1939–45*, Cape, 1969, p. 118.

74 Richard M. Titmuss, *Problems of Social Policy*, HMSO and Longmans, Green, 1950, p. 506.

75 Ibid., pp. 507–8.

76 Paul Addison's account of this crucial transition period, 'New Deal at Dunkirk', has never been surpassed. See Addison, *The Road to 1945*, pp. 103–26.

77 José Harris, *William Beveridge, A Biography*, OUP, 1977, p. 74.

78 Ibid., p. 386.

79 Ibid., pp. 386–7.

80 Ibid., p. 420.

81 Hopkins, *The New Look*, p. 25.
82 *Social Insurance and Allied Services*, p. 6.
83 Harris, *William Beveridge*, p. 448.
84 *Social Insurance and Allied Services*, p. 164.
85 Harris, *William Beveridge*, p. 421.
86 J.L. Hodson, *Home Front*, Gollancz, 1944, p. 250, diary entry for 2 December 1942.
87 Quoted in Harris, *William Beveridge*, pp. 422–3.
88 Wheeler-Bennett, *King George VI*, p. 509.
89 Harris, *William Beveridge*, p. 426.
90 Ibid.
91 Beatrice Webb's Diary, entry for 19 December 1942, Passfield Papers in the British Library of Economic and Political Science.
92 Harris, *William Beveridge*, pp. 426–7.
93 Addison, *The Road to 1945*, p. 217.
94 Ibid.
95 *The Beveridge Report and the Public*, BIPO, 1943.
96 Tom Hopkinson (ed.), *Picture Post, 1938–1950*, Chatto and Windus, 1984, which reproduces Tom Hopkinson, 'Beveridge – The Fight is On', *Picture Post*, 6 March 1943, on pp. 135–9.
97 For a detailed portrait of Anderson see John W. Wheeler-Bennett, *John Anderson, Viscount Waverley*, Macmillan, 1962. For a shorter one see Hennessy, *Whitehall*, pp. 559–65.
98 H of C Debates, Vol. 386, 16 February 1943, col. 1678.
99 Addison, *The Road to 1945*, pp. 222–3.
100 Woolton's diary entry for 16 February 1943, quoted in Kenneth O. Morgan, *Labour in Power, 1945–51*, OUP, 1984, p. 26.
101 R.B. McCallum and Alison Readman, *The British General Election of 1945*, OUP, 1947, p. 51.
102 It is the title of Chapter VIII in Addison, *The Road to 1945*, pp. 211–28.
103 For an account of Mass Observation and its techniques see the Preface to Tom Harrisson, *Living Through the Blitz*, Collins, 1976, pp. 11–17.
104 Ibid., p. 13.
105 Ibid., pp. 314–15.
106 Ibid., p. 315.
107 Ibid.
108 Ibid.
109 Ibid., pp. 315–16.
110 Tom Harrisson, *The Mood of Britain 1938–1944*, Mass Observation, 1944. It can be consulted in the Mass Observation Archive at Sussex University.
111 Addison, *The Road to 1945*, p. 159.
112 Harrisson, *Living Through the Blitz*, p. 316.
113 McCallum and Readman, *The British General Election of 1945*, p. 4.
114 Taken from the rubric of the 1988 membership card of Enid Hennessy.
115 Mikardo, *Backbencher*, p. 74.
116 Ibid.
117 Ibid., pp. 74–5.
118 Ibid., p. 77.
119 Gilbert, *Never Despair*, p. 6.
120 Ibid., p. 20.
121 Harris, *Attlee*, p. 250.
122 Bernard Donoughue and G.W. Jones, *Herbert Morrison, Portrait of a Politician*, Weidenfeld, 1973, p. 334.
123 His close friend, Ellen Wilkinson, the Party Chairman, did the rounds at Blackpool

assiduously pressing Morrison's claims to the Leadership. Ben Pimlott (ed.), *The Second World War Diary of Hugh Dalton, 1940–45*, Cape, 1986, pp. 860–62.

124 James Stuart, Viscount Findhorn, *Within the Fringe, An Autobiography*, Bodley Head, 1967, p. 137.

125 Oliver Lyttelton, Viscount Chandos, *The Memoirs of Lord Chandos*, Bodley Head, 1964, pp. 322–3.

126 Pimlott (ed.), *The Second World War Diary of Hugh Dalton*, diary entry for 28 May 1945, p. 865.

127 Gilbert, *Never Despair*, p. 24.

128 Ibid., p. 32.

129 Harris, *Attlee*, p. 256.

130 *Clem Attlee, The Granada Historical Records Interview*, p. 29.

131 Henry Pelling, *Winston Churchill*, Macmillan, 1974, p. 552.

132 Soames, *Clementine Churchill*, p. 545.

133 John Colville, *The Fringes of Power, Downing Street Diaries 1939–1955*, Hodder, 1985, p. 606.

134 I sat beside him as he recalled the moment at a Fabian Society discussion on vol. 2 of his Diaries in the Grand Committee Room of the House of Commons on 28 November 1988.

135 Mr Powell has confirmed for me his use of the phrase, its origin being the tune 'Lilibulero' with which the Protestants whistled the Stuarts from the throne.

136 Soames, *Clementine Churchill*, p. 545.

137 Mikardo, *Backbencher*, pp. 83–4.

138 Harrisson, *Living Through the Blitz*, p. 316.

139 Morgan, *Labour in Power*, p. 43.

140 One of its prominent members was Leo Abse who later became MP for Pontypool. See Leo Abse, *Private Member*, Macdonald, 1973.

141 Conversation with Sergeant Teal, 27 March 1989.

142 *News Chronicle*, 11 June 1945.

143 McCallum and Readman, *The British General Election of 1945*, p. 150, footnote 1.

144 Ibid., p. 242.

145 Henry Pelling, *The Labour Governments, 1945–1951*, Macmillan, 1984, p. 27.

146 Wheeler-Bennett, *King George VI*, p. 635.

147 Mikardo, *Backbencher*, p. 86.

148 Lady Felicity Harewood, *Clem, Father and Politician*, The Third Attlee Memorial Lecture, The Attlee Foundation, 20 February 1985.

149 Ibid.

150 Harris, *Attlee*, p. 263.

151 Gilbert, *Never Despair*, p. 108.

CHAPTER 3

Songs in Their Hearts

1 *Clem Attlee, Granada Historical Records*, Granada, 1967, p. 29.

2 Roy Jenkins, *Gallery of 20th Century Portraits*, David and Charles, 1988, pp. 235–6.

3 Correlli Barnett, *The Audit of War, The Illusion and Reality of Britain as a Great Nation*, Macmillan, 1986, p. 304.

4 A.H. Halsey, 'A Sociologist's View of Thatcherism', in Robert Skidelsky (ed.), *Thatcherism*, Chatto and Windus, 1988, p. 186.

5 Peregrine Worsthorne, *The Politics of Manners and the Uses of Inequality*, Centre for Policy Studies, 1988, p. 5.

6 Ibid.

7   E.P. Thompson, *The Heavy Dancers*, Merlin, 1988, p. 244.

8   The system and its products are miraculously preserved in aspic in the booklet that accompanied a superb exhibition of utility items at the Geffrye Museum in Shoreditch in 1974. See *CC41*, op. cit.

9   History has immortalised Arthur Egerton-Savory as *the* demob suit man. His story is told in Paul Addison, *Now the War is Over, A Social History of Britain 1945–51*, BBC Books and Cape 1985, pp. 16, 17, 20, 23–5.

10   George Mikes, *How to Be an Alien*, Wingate, 1946, p. 44.

11   See Trevor Royle, *The Best Years of Their Lives, The National Service Experience 1945–63*, Coronet edition, 1986, pp. 25–6.

12   For his first Budget see Hugh Dalton, *High Tide and After, Memoirs 1945–1960*, Muller, 1962, pp. 24–31.

13   Quoted in W.K. Hancock and M.M. Gowing, *The British War Economy*, HMSO, 1949, pp. 546–53.

14   Dan van der Vat, *The Grand Scuttle, The Sinking of the German Fleet at Scapa Flow in 1919*, Grafton, 1988, p. 161.

15   See Fitzroy Maclean's account in his *Eastern Approaches*, Cape, 1949, pp. 505–6.

16   The cartoon is reproduced in Susan Briggs, *Keep Smiling Through, The Home Front 1939–45*, Fontana, 1976, p. 61.

17   Royle, *The Best Years of Their Lives*, p. 31.

18   Ibid., p. 32.

19   Howard K. Smith, *The State of Europe*, Cresset, 1950, p. 25.

20   Royle, *The Best Years of Their Lives*, p. 34.

21   Michael Foot, *Aneurin Bevan, Vol. One, 1871–1945*, paperback edition, Four Square, 1966, p. 438.

22   John Gallagher, *The Decline, Revival and Fall of the British Empire*, CUP, 1982, p. 74.

23   James Morris, *Farewell the Trumpets, An Imperial Retreat*, Penguin edition, 1979, pp. 459–60.

24   Macmillan's diary entry for 20 May 1943 reproduced in Harold Macmillan, *The Blast of War 1939–45*, Macmillan, 1967, p. 324.

25   Ibid.

26   Morris, *Farewell the Trumpets*, p. 460.

27   Bevin's protest was made in a letter to Attlee on 1 January 1947. See Peter Hennessy, 'Bevin plea failed to stop India "Scuttle"', *The Times*, 6 September 1980.

28   Recalled by his private secretary, Sir Nicholas Henderson, in his valedictory despatch from the Paris Embassy on 31 March 1979 and printed in *The Economist*, 2 June 1979, pp. 29–40.

29   See David Watt, 'Withdrawal from Greece' in Michael Sissons and Philip French (eds), *The Age of Austerity, 1945–51*, Penguin, 1964, pp. 106–7.

30   George F. Kennan, *Memoirs, 1925–1950*, Hutchinson, 1968, p. 359.

31   Paul Kennedy, *The Rise and Fall of the Great Powers*, Unwin Hyman, 1988, p. 367.

32   Winston S. Churchill, *The Second World War, Vol. 2, Their Finest Hour*, Cassell, 1949, p. 503.

33   David Dimbleby and David Reynolds, *An Ocean Apart, The Relationship Between Britain and America in the Twentieth Century*, BBC Books and Hodder, 1988, p. 164.

34   Cairncross, *Years of Recovery*, p. 4.

35   R.F. Harrod, *The Life of John Maynard Keynes*, Pelican, 1972, p. 704.

36   Ibid., p. 705.

37   Alan Bullock, *Ernest Bevin, Foreign Secretary, 1945–51*, Heinemann, 1983, p. 121.

38   Ben Pimlott (ed.), *The Political Diary of Hugh Dalton, 1918–40, 1945–60*, Cape, 1986, p. 362, diary entry for 17 August 1945.

39   Alec Cairncross, *Years of Recovery: British Economic Policy 1945–51*, Methuen, 1985, pp. 92–4.

40 Harrod, *The Life of John Maynard Keynes*, pp. 705–6.
41 Ibid., p. 713.
42 Douglas Jay, *Change and Fortune, A Political Record*, Hutchinson, 1980, p. 137.
43 Ibid., p. 131.
44 Cairncross, *Years of Recovery*, p. 105.
45 PRO, CAB 128/2, Cabinet Conclusions 29 November and 5 December 1945.
46 Kenneth Harris, *Attlee*, Weidenfeld, 1982, p. 275.
47 Kenneth O. Morgan, *Labour in Power, 1945–1951*, Clarendon, 1984, pp. 149–50.
48 Harris, *Attlee*, p. 275.
49 Douglas revealed this to Robert Hall, Head of the Cabinet Office's Economic section in Washington in September 1949. Alec Cairncross (ed.), *The Robert Hall Diaries, 1947–1953*, Unwin Hyman, 1989, p. 79, diary entry for 9 September 1949.
50 Lord Robbins, *Autobiography of an Economist*, Macmillan, 1971, pp. 207–8.
51 Martin Wiener, *English Culture and the Decline of the Industrial Spirit, 1850–1980*, CUP, 1981, p. 3.
52 Sidney Pollard, *The Wasting of the British Economy*, second edition, Croom Helm, 1984, p. 2.
53 Peter Pagnamenta and Richard Overy, *All Our Working Lives*, BBC Books, 1984, pp. 37–9.
54 Hancock and Gowing, *British War Economy*, p. 321.
55 Christopher Harvie, *No Gods and Precious Few Heroes, Scotland since 1914*, Edward Arnold, 1981, p. 4.
56 Pagnamenta and Overy, *All Our Working Lives*, p. 134.
57 Ronald Blythe, *The Age of Illusion*, OUP, 1984, pp. 163–5.
58 See the valedictory despatch of Bevin's former private secretary, Sir Nicholas Henderson, from the Paris Embassy dated 31 March 1979, printed in *The Economist*, 2 June 1979, pp. 29–40.
59 On the afternoon of 30 July 1947, with the Government in the throes of the Convertibility Crisis, Bevin addressed senior figures from the National Coal Board and the National Union of Mineworkers at a meeting in No. 10 and made his plea for increased production. Bullock, *Ernest Bevin, Foreign Secretary*, pp. 743–4.
60 Harold Wilson, *New Deal for Coal*, Contact, 1945, p. 1.
61 Hancock and Gowing, *British War Economy*, pp. 476–7.
62 Ibid. See the Chart on p. 479.
63 Over a thousand summonses were issued. See Alan Bullock, *The Life and Times of Ernest Bevin, Vol. Two, Minister of Labour 1940–1945*, Heinemann, 1967, pp. 267–8.
64 Hancock and Gowing, *British War Economy*, p. 477.
65 Sir Norman Chester, *The Nationalisation of British Industry 1945–51*, HMSO, 1975, pp. 11–12. The words are Sir Norman's not Sir Charles Reid's.
66 Ibid., p. 11.
67 The phrase 'blood on the coal' is attributed to the miner-author Bert Coombes in 1944. See his *These Poor Hands, The Autobiography of a Miner Working in South Wales*, Gollancz, 1939.
68 Kenneth O. Morgan, *Labour in Power*, OUP, 1984, p. 11. Tawney saw a 'liberated' and nationalised coal industry in terms of 'the provision of service' rather than 'the provision of dividends'. R.H. Tawney, *The Acquisitive Society*, first published 1921, Wheatsheaf edition, 1982, p. 111.
69 Frances Donaldson, *Edward VIII*, Weidenfeld, 1974, p. 253.
70 Pagnamenta and Overy, *All Our Working Lives*, p. 83.
71 Ibid., p. 87.
72 Hancock and Gowing, *British War Economy*, p. 520.
73 Froom Tyler, *Cripps, A Portrait and a Prospect*, Harrap, 1942, p. 12.
74 William Plowden, *The Motor Car and Politics*, Bodley Head, 1971, pp. 312–14.

75   Jonathan Woods, *Wheels of Fortune: The Rise and Fall of the British Motor Industry*, Sidgwick and Jackson, 1988, p. 130.

76   Ibid., pp. 100–1 and Pagnamenta and Overy, *All Our Working Lives*, pp. 227–8.

77   Ibid., p. 228.

78   G. Maxcy and Aubrey Silberston, *The Motor Industry*, Allen and Unwin, 1959, p. 111.

79   I am very grateful to Mr McLaughlin, my colleague at Strathclyde University, for his help with this section.

80   Quoted in Andrew McLaughlin, 'Heroic Strategies and Humdrum Problems: Governing the Car-makers 1945–1990', unpublished PhD thesis, University of Strathclyde, 1992.

81   William Horsley and Roger Buckley, *Nippon New Superpower: Japan Since 1945*, BBC Books, 1990. See Chapter 2, 36–72 and pp. 51–2 for the impact of the Korean War.

82   Quoted in McLaughlin, 'Heroic Strategies and Humdrum Problems'.

83   PRO, BOT 211/92.

84   Ibid.

85   McLaughlin, 'Heroic Strategies and Humdrum Problems'.

86   Woods, *Wheels of Fortune*, p. 99.

87   For Brabazon and the reason for his departure from the Ministry of Aircraft Production see David Egerton, *England and the Aeroplane*, Macmillan, 1991, pp. 66–7.

88   Quoted in Pagnamenta and Overy, *All Our Working Lives*, pp. 61–2.

89   Group-Captain Winterbotham's account was the first to receive a cautious tacit approval from the security and intelligence authorities in 1974. F.W. Winterbotham, *The Ultra Secret*, Weidenfeld, 1974.

90   Angus Calder, *The People's War, Britain 1939–45*, Cape, 1969, p. 530.

91   I am relying here on the scholarship of my friend Professor Sir Douglas Hague.

92   F.H. Hinsley, *British Intelligence in the Second World War, Vol. 3, Part I*, HMSO, 1984, pp. 477–8.

93   Ibid., p. 479.

94   Ibid.

95   Ibid., p. 482.

96   Stephen Lavington, *Early British Computers*, Manchester University Press, 1980, and Geoffrey Tweedale, 'Marketing in the Second Industrial Revolution: A Case Study of the Ferranti Computer Group, 1949–63', *Business History*, 34 (1992), pp. 272–303.

97   Asa Briggs, *The BBC, The First Fifty Years*, OUP, 1985, p. 243.

98   Pagnamenta and Overy, *All Our Working Lives*, p. 153.

99   Correlli Barnett, *The Collapse of British Power*, Eyre Methuen, 1972, p. 88.

100 *Report of the Committee on Land Utilisation in Rural Areas*, Cmd. 6378, HMSO, 1942.

101 Howard Newby, *The Deferential Worker, A Study of Farm Workers in East Anglia*, Penguin, 1979, p. 80.

102 Conversation with Pip Stanley, 11 August 1988.

103 T.C. Barker, *The Glassmakers, Pilkington: 1826–1976*, Weidenfeld, 1977, p. 411.

104 J.B. Priestley, *English Journey*, Heinemann, 1934, pp. 397–401.

105 Goronwy Rees, *St. Michael. A History of Marks and Spencer*, revised edition, Pan, 1985, p. 159.

106 C.I. Savage, *Inland Transport*, HMSO, 1957, p. 11.

107 Ibid., p. 31.

108 Ibid., p. 29.

109 Ibid., p. 31.

110 Ibid., p. 98.

111 James Lansdale Hodson, *The Way Things Are*, Gollancz, 1947, diary entry for 5 October 1946, p. 272.

112 Savage, *Inland Transport*, p. 634.

113 Ibid.

114   Ibid., p. 638.

115   Lord Keynes, 'Overseas Financial Policy in Stage III', 3 April 1945 circulated to the War Cabinet on 15 May by Sir John Anderson, Chancellor of the Exchequer, as WP(45)301. PRO, CAB 66/65.

116   Ibid.

CHAPTER 4

Building Jerusalem

1   H of C *Official Report*, fifth series, Vol. 418, cols. 1900–01.

2   Quoted in Peter Hennessy, 'Whitehall Watch: Welfare state founded on figures that never add up', *Independent*, 3 July 1989.

3   Peter Calvocoressi, *The British Experience, 1945–1975*, Bodley Head, 1978, pp. 35–6.

4   Gillian Reynolds addressing a Royal Society of Arts Symposium on 'The Future of UK Radio', 10 April 1989.

5   John Redcliffe-Maud, *Experiences of an Optimist*, Hamish Hamilton, 1981, p. 51.

6   Frank Prochaska, *The Voluntary Impulse, Philanthropy in Modern Britain*, Faber, 1988, p. 7.

7   Quoted in Pauline Gregg, *The Welfare State*, Harrap, 1967, p. 9.

8   David Donnison, 'Drawing Conclusions', in Paul Barker (ed.), *Founders of the Welfare State*, Heinemann Educational, 1984, p. 121 and Prochaska, *The Voluntary Impulse*, p. 43.

9   Ibid., p. 49.

10   William Temple, *Citizen and Churchman*, Eyre and Spottiswoode, 1941.

11   A.E. Zimmern, *Quo Vadimus?*, OUP, 1934.

12   Sir George Schuster, *United Empire*, XXVIII (1937), p. 518. I'm grateful to Dr Rodney Lowe of Bristol University for suggestions as to the earlier usage.

13   W.J. Braithwaite, *Lloyd George's Ambulance Wagon*, Cedric Chivers, 1970, pp. 84–5.

14   John Grigg, *Lloyd George, The People's Champion 1902–1911*, Eyre Methuen, 1978, p. 335.

15   R.H.S. Crossman, *Government and the Governed* (new edition), Christophers, 1947, p. 314.

16   Douglas E. Ashford, *The Emergence of the Welfare States*, Blackwell, 1986, pp. 241–2. I am grateful to Professor Alan Milward of the London School of Economics for making me aware of the legitimacy aspect of the push towards welfare states in postwar western Europe. Conversation with Professor Milward, 3 August 1989.

17   Ashford, *The Emergence of the Welfare States*, p. 311.

18   Ibid., pp. 297–8.

19   Harry Eckstein, *English Health Service*, Harvard, 1959, p. 2.

20   James Griffiths, *Pages from Memory*, Dent, 1969, pp. 80–1.

21   Ibid., p. 81.

22   Ibid., p. 79.

23   Quoted in Braithwaite, *Lloyd George's Ambulance Wagon*, p. 24.

24   Live from Chequers on 21 March 1943 quoted in Martin Gilbert, *Winston S. Churchill, Vol. VII, Road to Victory 1941–1945*, Heinemann, 1986, p. 367.

25   Griffiths, *Pages from Memory*, p. 89.

26   Conversation with Basil Kibbey, 12 December 1989.

27   Quoted in Gilbert, *Road to Victory*, p. 292.

28   Dr Addison made his remark during the radio discussion 'Living With . . . Winston', BBC Radio 4, 12 September 1989.

29   Gregg, *The Welfare State*, p. 4.

30 Quoted in Rudolf Klein, 'Edwin Chadwick, 1800–90', in Barker (ed.), *Founders of the Welfare State*, p. 11.

31 Ibid.

32 Gregg, *The Welfare State*, pp. 8–9.

33 The Webbs published it as a book: Sidney Webb and Beatrice Webb, *The Break Up of the Poor Law*, Longman, 1909.

34 Rodney Lowe, 'The Origins of the Welfare State in Britain', *Modern History Review*, Vol. 1, No. 1, September 1989, pp. 24–5.

35 Gregg, *The Welfare State*, p. 10.

36 Ibid., p. 11.

37 H of C, *Official Report*, 4 May 1911, vol. 25, col. 644.

38 Grigg, *Lloyd George, The People's Champion, 1902–1911*, p. 343.

39 Peter Hennessy, *Whitehall*, Secker and Warburg, 1989, pp. 57–9.

40 For its post-1919 housing powers see pp. 167–9.

41 Gregg, *The Welfare State*, pp. 14–16.

42 Lowe, 'The Origins of the Welfare State in Britain'.

43 José Harris, *William Beveridge, A Biography*, OUP, 1977, p. 417.

44 The Ministry had, in fact, been founded in 1944 and its first Minister was a Labour member of the Coalition, Sir William Jowitt, who later became Lord Chancellor in the Attlee administration.

45 Paul Addison, *The Road to 1945*, Cape, 1975, p. 247, Griffiths, *Pages from Memory*, p. 81.

46 Ibid., pp. 79–80.

47 Ibid., p. 81.

48 Ibid.

49 Kenneth O. Morgan, *Labour in Power*, OUP, 1984, pp. 172–3.

50 Ibid., p. 72.

51 Griffiths, *Pages from Memory*, p. 84.

52 Ibid., pp. 85–6.

53 Ibid., p. 86.

54 Peter Hennessy, 'Whitehall brief: Cycling to dizzy heights in the Civil Service', *The Times*, 23 June 1981.

55 Douglas Jay, *The Socialist Case*, Faber, 1937, p. 317.

56 Paul Addison, *Now the War is Over. A Social History of Britain 1945–51*, BBC Books and Cape, 1985, p. 86.

57 Rudolf Klein, *The Politics of the National Health Service*, Longman, 1983, p. 1.

58 Michael Foot, *Aneurin Bevan, A Biography, Vol. Two: 1945–1960*, Davis Poynter, 1973, p. 106.

59 Aneurin Bevan, *In Place of Fear*, 1952, Heinemann, p. 85.

60 Klein, *The Politics of the National Health Service*, p. vii.

61 Quoted in Foot, *Aneurin Bevan, Vol. Two*, p. 105.

62 Ibid.

63 In the first edition of Laski's *Parliamentary Government in England*, the word appeared as 'reform', a misprint I'm sure, when the word 'form' was intended.

64 Harold J. Laski, *Parliamentary Government in England, A commentary*, Allen and Unwin, 1938, p. 117.

65 Charles Webster, *The Health Services Since the War, Vol. 1, Problems of Health Care, The National Health Service Before 1957*, HMSO, 1988, p. 17.

66 Ibid., p. 24.

67 Ibid., p. 21.

68 Klein, *The Politics of the National Health Service*, p. 7.

69 Richard M. Titmuss, *Problems of Social Policy*, HMSO and Longmans, Green, 1950, Chapter V, pp. 54–86.

70 H of C *Official Report*, Vol. 374, cols 1116–20, 9 October 1941.
71 Ibid., vol. 386, cols 1660–3, 16 February 1943.
72 *A National Health Service*, Cmd. 6502, HMSO, 1944.
73 Webster, *The Health Services Since the War*, p. 57.
74 Klein, *The Politics of the National Health Service*, p. 14.
75 Ibid., pp. 15–16.
76 Kenneth O. Morgan, *Labour People, Leaders and Lieutenants: Hardie to Kinnock*, OUP, 1987, p. 205.
77 Ibid., p. 208.
78 Foot, *Aneurin Bevan 1945–1960*, p. 40.
79 Ibid., p. 41.
80 Letter from Pauline Trevelyan to Jennie Lee, quoted in Jennie Lee, *My Life with Nye*, Penguin, 1981, p. 183.
81 Ibid.
82 Michael Foot, *Aneurin Bevan. A Biography. Vol. One: 1879–1945*, Four Square, 1966, pp. 71–2.
83 Frank Honigsbaum, *Health, Happiness and Security. The Creation of the National Health Service*, Routledge, 1989, p. 174.
84 Foot, *Aneurin Bevan 1945–1960*, p. 131.
85 Honigsbaum, *Health, Happiness and Security*, pp. 172–4; Foot, *Aneurin Bevan 1945–1960*, p. 132.
86 Honigsbaum, *Health, Happiness and Security*, pp. 113–14.
87 Ibid., pp. 173–4.
88 Ibid., p. 174.
89 Rucker's minutes can be found at the Public Record Office in MH 80/34.
90 Sir Kenneth Stowe, *On Caring for the National Health*, Nuffield Provincial Hospitals Trust, 1989, p. 41.
91 *Working for Patients*, Cm 555, HMSO, 1989.
92 Stowe, *On Caring for the National Health*, p. 77.
93 Ibid., p. 78.
94 Honigsbaum, *Health, Happiness and Security*, p. 7.
95 Ibid., p. 48, p. 133.
96 Ibid., p. 133.
97 A copy of Sir Farquhar's statement can be found in PRO, MH 80/34.
98 PRO, CAB 129/3.
99 Ibid.
100 For Morrison's LCC years see Bernard Donoughue and G.W. Jones, *Herbert Morrison, Portrait of a Politician*, Weidenfeld, 1973, Chapter 14, pp. 189–210.
101 A 'Memorandum by the Lord President of the Council', 'The Future of the Hospital Services', PRO, CAB 129/3.
102 See Morgan, *Labour in Power*, pp. 154–6, and Honigsbaum, *Health, Happiness and Security*, pp. 176–8.
103 Morgan, *Labour in Power*, p. 155.
104 Webster, *The Health Services Since the War*, p. 133.
105 Lee, *My Life with Nye*, p. 183.
106 Peter Jenkins, 'Bevan's Fight with the BMA', in Michael Sissons and Philip French (eds), *The Age of Austerity, 1945–51*, Penguin, 1964, p. 245.
107 Ibid.
108 Quoted in Honigsbaum, *Health, Happiness and Security*, p. 146.
109 Jenkins, 'Bevan's Fight with the BMA', in Sissons and French, *Age of Austerity*, p. 247.
110 This could be seen on billboards across London in the summer of 1989.
111 *British Medical Journal*, 6 April 1946, p. 541.

112 Jenkins, 'Bevan's Fight with the BMA', in Sissons and French, *Age of Austerity*, pp. 248–9.
113 Foot, *Aneurin Bevan, 1945–1960*, pp. 164–5.
114 Ibid., p. 165.
115 Ibid.
116 Ibid., p. 173.
117 H of C, *Official Report*, Vol. 447, cols 35–160, 9 February 1948.
118 *British Medical Journal*, 21 February 1948, pp. 352–3.
119 Quoted in Brian Abel-Smith, *The Hospitals, 1800–1948*, Heinemann, 1964, p. 480.
120 Honigsbaum, *Health, Happiness and Security*, p. 116.
121 Ibid., pp. 149–50.
122 *British Medical Journal*, 8 May 1948, Supplement, pp. 119–20.
123 Honigsbaum, *Health, Happiness and Security*, p. 151.
124 Foot, *Aneurin Bevan, 1945–1960*, p. 241.
125 *Report of the NHS Management Inquiry*, Department of Health and Social Security, 1983, pp. 3–24.
126 H.C. Dent, *A New Order in English Education*, University of London Press, 1942, p. 7.
127 Lord Butler, *The Art of the Possible*, Penguin, 1973, pp. 107–8.
128 Quoted in Betty D. Vernon, *Ellen Wilkinson, 1891–1947*, Croom Helm, 1982, p. 201.
129 Fred Blackburn, *George Tomlinson*, Heinemann, 1954, p. 173.
130 Lord Butler, *The Art of Memory, Friends in Perspective*, Hodder, 1982, pp. 79–95.
131 Ibid., p. 89.
132 Ibid., p. 79.
133 Butler, *The Art of the Possible*, p. 91.
134 For Rab's early life and intellectual antecedence see Anthony Howard, *RAB, The Life of R.A. Butler*, Cape, 1987, Chapters 1–5, pp. 1–38.
135 Peter Hennessy, 'Rab: politics as a matter of heart', *Independent*, 8 May 1987.
136 S.J. Curtis, *Education in Britain since 1900*, Andrew Dakers, 1952, p. 7.
137 This useful distinction belongs to Dr Curtis. See ibid., Chapter II, 'From State Assistance to State Supervision', pp. 23–44.
138 Correlli Barnett, *The Collapse of British Power*, Eyre Methuen, 1972, pp. 94–5.
139 *Report from the Select Committee on Scientific Instruction*, House of Commons, 1868, Vol XV, p. iii.
140 W.R. Ward, *Victorian Oxford*, Frank Cass, 1965, p. 406.
141 Paul Langford, 'The Eighteenth Century', in Kenneth O. Morgan (ed.), *The Oxford Illustrated History of Britain*, OUP, 1984, p. 392.
142 Philip Magnus, *Gladstone, A Biography*, John Murray, 1964 edition, p. 117.
143 Martin Wiener, *English Culture and the Decline of the Industrial Spirit, 1850–1980*, CUP, 1981.
144 Speech to the North of England Conference, Rotherham, 9 January 1987.
145 See Hennessy, *Whitehall*, p. 42.
146 Barnett, *The Collapse of British Power*, pp. 24–5.
147 A.R. Stanley, *The Life and Correspondence of Thomas Arnold, DD*, Ward Lock, 1890, p. 498.
148 *Noel Coward At Las Vegas*, CBS Records, undated.
149 *Report of the Endowed Schools Commission*, House of Commons, 1868, Vol. XXVIII, Part 1, p. 72.
150 Ibid., p. 80.
151 Curtis, *Education in Britain since 1900*, p. 8.
152 Harry Judge, 'R.L. Morant 1863–1920' in Barker (ed.), *Founders of the Welfare State*, p. 62.
153 Barnett, *The Collapse of British Power*, p. 100.

154 *Second Report of the Royal Commissioners on Technical Instruction*, Vol. 1, C. 3981, 1884, p. 337.
155 Ibid., pp. 505–8.
156 Curtis, *Education in Britain since 1900*, p. 12.
157 John Kenyon, *The History Men, The Historical Profession in England since the Renaissance*, Weidenfeld, 1983, p. 235.
158 Curtis, *Education in Britain since 1900*, p. 13, p. 27.
159 G.A.N. Lowndes, *The Silent Social Revolution*, OUP, 1937, p. 4.
160 Ibid., p. 101.
161 Ibid., p. 4.
162 Barnett, *The Collapse of British Power*, p. 105.
163 John Carswell, *Government and the Universities in Britain*, CUP, 1985, p. 3, p. 1.
164 Lowndes, *The Silent Social Revolution*, p. 190.
165 Quoted in Curtis, *Education in Britain since 1900*, p. 55.
166 Judge, 'R.L. Morant', in Barker (ed.), *Founders of the Welfare State*, pp. 61–3.
167 Ibid., p. 64.
168 See Curtis, *Education in Britain since 1900*, Chapter 11, pp. 23–44.
169 *The Times*, 2 November 1942.
170 Butler, *The Art of Memory*, p. 159.
171 Curtis, *Education in Britain since 1900*, pp. 77–85.
172 H.A.L. Fisher, *An Unfinished Autobiography*, OUP, 1940, p. 110.
173 Ross Terrill, *R.H. Tawney and His Times, Socialism as Fellowship*, Andre Deutsch, 1974, p. 63.
174 *The Education of the Adolescent*, HMSO, 1926, pp. xxi–xxii.
175 Curtis, *Education in Britain since 1900*, p. 91.
176 Addison, *Now the War is Over*, p. 141.
177 Ibid., p. 145.
178 Butler, *The Art of the Possible*, p. 94.
179 Sir John Colville in Sir John Wheeler-Bennett (ed.), *Action This Day, Working with Churchill*, Macmillan, 1968, pp. 74–5.
180 Butler, *The Art of the Possible*, p. 95.
181 Ibid., p. 96.
182 Ibid., p. 97.
183 H.C. Dent, *Growth in English Education, 1946–1952*, Routledge, 1954, p. 79.
184 Curtis, *Education in Britain since 1900*, p. 108.
185 This highly useful concept suffuses their classic work, Ronald Robinson and John Gallagher, *Africa and the Victorians, The Official Mind of Imperialism*, Macmillan, 1901.
186 Addison, *Now the War is Over*, p. 146.
187 Quoted in ibid., pp. 146–7.
188 H.C. Dent, *Growth in English Education, 1946–1952*, p. 79.
189 Addison, *Now the War is Over*, p. 150.
190 Vernon, *Ellen Wilkinson*, p. 226.
191 *The New Secondary Education*, Pamphlet No. 9, HMSO, 1947.
192 The Wilkinson Minute is reproduced in the form of extracts in Vernon, *Ellen Wilkinson*, pp. 222–3. The original can be found in PRO, ED 136/788.
193 Addison, *Now the War is Over*, pp. 151–3.
194 See Stuart Maclure, *Educational Development and School Building: Aspects of Public Policy 1945–73*, Longman, 1984.
195 Curtis, *Education in Britain since 1900*, pp. 201–2.
196 Vernon, *Ellen Wilkinson*, p. 216.
197 Carswell, *Government and the Universities in Britain*, p. 14.
198 Ibid., p. 12.
199 Ibid., p. 14.

200   Curtis, *Education in Britain since 1900*, p. 201.
201   Morgan, *Labour in Power*, p. 175.
202   PRO, CAB 128/9.
203   Vernon, *Ellen Wilkinson*, p. 209.
204   Ibid.
205   Ibid.
206   PRO, ED 136/727.
207   Ibid.
208   Quoted in Vernon, *Ellen Wilkinson*, p. 211.
209   Ibid., p. 233.
210   Ibid.
211   Dr Maclellan as quoted in Donoughue and Jones, *Herbert Morrison*, p. 392.
212   Lord Woolton, diary entry for 1 November 1940, Woolton MS 2, Department of Western Manuscripts, Bodleian Library, Oxford.
213   Quoted in Addison, *Now the War is Over*, pp. 68–9.
214   Quoted in ibid., p. 58.
215   Quoted in Foot, *Aneurin Bevan, 1945–1960*, p. 78.
216   Quoted in ibid., p. 61.
217   Patrick Nuttgens, *The Home Front*, BBC, 1989, p. 7.
218   D.V. Donnison, *Housing Policy Since the War*, Codicote Press, 1960, p. 9.
219   Fernand Braudel, *Civilization and Capitalism, 15th–18th Century, Volume 1, The Structures of Everyday Life*, Fontana edition, 1988, p. 479.
220   H.C.G. Matthew, 'The Liberal Age (1851–1914)', in Morgan (ed.), *The Oxford Illustrated History of Britain*, p. 474.
221   The description is Eric Hobsbawm's. Conversation with Professor Eric Hobsbawm, 24 March 1992.
222   See Frederick Engels, *The Condition of the Working-Class in England in 1844*, Allen and Unwin, 1920 edition, especially chapters 1 and 2, pp. 19–74.
223   Charles Dickens, *Hard Times*, 1854 Charles Dickens Library Edition, 1944.
224   R.C.K. Ensor, *England 1870–1914*, OUP, 1936, p. 127.
225   Quoted in Nuttgens, *Home Front*, p. 21.
226   Ibid., p. 47.
227   Donnison, *Housing Policy Since the War*, p. 10.
228   For the eighteenth- and nineteenth-century philanthropists see Nuttgens, *Home Front*, Chapter Two, 'The Pursuit of Environment', pp. 21–46.
229   See Peter Hall, 'Ebenezer Howard' in Barker (ed.), *Founders of the Welfare State*, pp. 45–51.
230   Raymond Unwin, *Nothing Gained by Overcrowding*, Garden Cities and Town Planning Association, third edition, 1918.
231   Nuttgens, *Home Front*, p. 50.
232   *Report of Local Government Boards from England, Wales and Scotland, no. 391*, HMSO, 1918.
233   Nuttgens, *Home Front*, pp. 52–3.
234   For an account of his career see Kenneth and Jane Morgan, *Portrait of a Progressive: the Political Career of Christopher, Viscount Addison*, OUP, 1980.
235   Donnison, *Housing Policy Since the War*, p. 10.
236   Taylor, *English History 1914–1945*, p. 146.
237   Nuttgens, *Home Front*, p. 53.
238   Ibid., p. 56.
239   A.J.P. Taylor, *English History 1914–1945*, OUP, 1965, p. 147.
240   Ibid., p. 148.
241   Donnison, *Housing Policy Since the War*, p. 10.
242   Ibid., p. 11.

243 Ibid.
244 Ministry of Reconstruction, *Housing*, Cmd. 6609, HMSO, 1945, p. 2.
245 Donnison, *Housing Policy Since the War*, p. 12.
246 Addison, *Now the War is Over*, p. 56.
247 Ibid., p. 57.
248 Morgan, *Labour in Power*, p. 163.
249 Ibid.
250 'Ten Cooks Are Spoiling the Broth', *Picture Post*, 28 September 1946.
251 Donnison, *Housing Policy Since the War*, p. 15.
252 See Patricia Tisdall, *Agents of Change: The Development and Practice of Management Consultancy*, Heinemann, 1982, p. 36.
253 Morgan, *Labour in Power*, p. 165.
254 Ibid., p. 166 and Foot, *Aneurin Bevan, 1945–1960*, pp. 72–3.
255 Morgan, *Labour in Power*, p. 164.
256 Ibid., p. 165.
257 A.J.P. Taylor, *Beaverbrook*, Hamish Hamilton, 1972, p. 334.
258 Foot, *Aneurin Bevan, 1945–1960*, p. 78.
259 Hugh Dalton, *High Tide and After, Memoirs 1945–60*, Muller, 1962, p. 358.
260 Donnison, *Housing Policy Since the War*, p. 16; Foot, *Aneurin Bevan, 1945–1960*, p. 80.
261 Foot, *Aneurin Bevan, 1945–1960*, p. 72.
262 Ibid., p. 75 and Donnison, *Housing Policy Since the War*, p. 13.
263 Foot, *Aneurin Bevan, 1945–1960*, pp. 81–2.
264 Both kinds are visible, for example, from my house in Walthamstow filling the gap left by the bomb which fell in April 1944. The difference in height is especially striking.
265 J.H. Forshaw and Patrick Abercrombie, *County of London Plan*, Macmillan, 1943.
266 Patrick Abercrombie, *Greater London Plan 1944*, HMSO, 1944.
267 Steve Humphries and John Taylor, *The Making of Modern London, 1945–1985*, Sidgwick and Jackson, 1986, pp. 82–4.
268 Addison, *Now the War is Over*, p. 80.
269 Foot, *Aneurin Bevan, 1945–1960*, p. 84.
270 Addison, *Now the War is Over*, p. 68.
271 Quoted in ibid., p. 105.
272 Private information.
273 See Appendix 1 in Keith Jeffery and Peter Hennessy, *States of Emergency, British Governments and Strike-breaking since 1919*, Routledge, 1983, pp. 270–3.
274 Howard Levenson, *Subsidised Legal Services in Criminal Proceedings*, unpublished LLM thesis, University of Sheffield, 1971, p. 8.
275 Alan Paterson, *Legal Aid as a Social Service*, Cobden Trust, 1970, p. 9.
276 Ibid.
277 Ibid., p. 10.
278 Brian Abel-Smith and Robert Stevens, *Lawyers and the Courts*, Heinemann Educational, 1967, p. 319.
279 *Report of the Committee on Legal Aid and Legal Advice in England and Wales*, Cmd. 6641, HMSO, 1945.
280 *Law Society's Gazette*, Vol. XLII, July 1945.
281 Paterson, *Legal Aid as a Social Service*, p. 10.
282 Quoted in *The Times*, 20 March 1952.
283 H of C, *Official Report*, 5th Series, Vol. 459, 15 December 1948, col. 1221.
284 Abel-Smith and Stevens, *Lawyers and the Courts*, pp. 328–33.
285 Quoted in Alistair Buchan, *The Spare Chancellor, The Life of Walter Bagehot*, Chatto and Windus, 1959, p. 266.
286 Asa Briggs, *The BBC, The First Fifty Years*, OUP, 1985, p. 242.

287 For a gem of a profile of Haley at the height of his powers see 'The Head of His Profession' in *New Statesman Profiles*, Readers Union, 1958, pp. 35–42.

288 Ibid., p. 39.

289 A great believer in anonymity, he reviewed widely under the pen name 'Oliver Edwards'. See Oliver Edwards, *Talking of Books*, Heinemann, 1957.

290 Briggs, *The BBC, The First Fifty Years*, p. 243.

291 Ibid., p. 244.

292 Quoted in ibid., p. 241.

293 Addison, *The Road to 1945*, p. 14.

294 Basil Kibbey, 'Progress and trends of social security in the United Kingdom', paper presented to the 'Managers' Conference', organised by the Canadian Unemployment Insurance Commission, 1967, p. 5.

295 Ibid., p. 14.

296 See Hennessy, *Whitehall*, pp. 322, 326, 344 and 488.

297 This view is one of the philosophical pillars of his *The Audit of War*.

298 See Stowe, *On Caring for the National Health*, and Hennessy, 'Whitehall Watch: Welfare State founded on figures that never add up'.

299 Edward Heath's most celebrated application of this phrase was in connection with the use of offshore funds by Lonrho in 1973. But it was a deep-felt view. As his Political Secretary, Douglas Hurd, recorded in his diary for 11 May 1972, Heath had revealed it to an uncomprehending Scottish Party Conference: 'EH explodes. The ugly face of capitalism, class distinctions, the essential responsibility of management. Not very well composed, but passionate – and they don't understand a word.' Douglas Hurd, *An End to Promises, Sketch of a Government*, Collins, 1979, pp. 87–8. For the Heath quote in full see David Butler and Gareth Butler, *British Political Facts*, 1900–1985, Macmillan, 1986, p. 279.

300 Ralph Miliband, *Parliamentary Socialism, A Study in the Politics of Labour*, first published 1961, paperback edition, Merlin, 1973, p. 291.

301 Ibid., p. 286.

302 Ibid.

303 See Rodney Lowe, 'The Second World War, Consensus and the Foundation of the Welfare State', *Twentieth Century British History*, Vol. 1, No. 2, 1990, pp. 152–82.

304 T.H. Marshall, *Citizenship and Social Class*, CUP, 1950.

305 This lovely phrase belongs to Arthur Marwick, *Britain in the Century of Total War: War, Peace and Social Change 1900–1967*, Little Brown, 1968, pp. 314–23.

306 See Norman Furniss and Timothy Tilton, *The Case for the Welfare State*, Indiana University Press, 1977.

307 Lowe, The Second World War, Consensus and the Foundation of the Welfare State'.

308 Cmd. 6386.

309 *Control of Land Use*, Cmd. 6537, HMSO, 1944, p. 2.

310 Andrew Cox, *Adversary Politics and Land, The Conflict Over Land and Property Policy in Post-war Britain*, CUP, 1984, p. 98.

311 Kibbey, 'Progress and trends of social security in the United Kingdom', p. 14. The analysis to which he refers can be found in *National Insurance Bill – Report by the Government Actuary on the Financial Provisions of the Bill*, Cmd. 6730, HMSO, 1946, paragraphs 1–29.

312 See the account of my discussions with Frank Honigsbaum and Rudolf Klein in Peter Hennessy, 'Whitehall Watch: Health Ministers set to take Control', *Independent*, 18 December 1989.

313 Graham Hart, Director of Operations, NHS, 'The Challenges of Health Care', in *Customer Service in the Public Sector*, PA Consulting Group/RIPA, 1990, p. 9.

314 H.V. Rhodes, *Setting Up a New Government Department*, British Institute of Management, 1949.

315 See Hennessy, *Whitehall*, Chapter 4, 'The Missed Opportunity', pp. 120–68.
316 *Employment Policy*, Cmd. 6527, HMSO, May 1944, p. 3.
317 Lowe, 'The Second World War, Consensus and the Foundation of the Welfare State'.

CHAPTER 5

Towards the Commanding Heights

1 H of C, *Official Report*, Vol. 423, col. 1114, 28 May 1946.
2 Hugh Dalton, diary entry for 12 April 1946, British Library of Economics & Political Science.
3 Sidney Pollard, *The Wasting of the British Economy*, second edition, Croom Helm, 1984, p. 31.
4 Alec Cairncross (ed.), *The Robert Hall Diaries, 1947–1953*, Unwin Hyman, 1989, diary entry for 18 November 1948, recording a conversation with Lucius Thompson-McCausland of the Bank of England.
5 David Marquand, *The Unprincipled Society, New Demands and Old Politics*, Cape, 1988, pp. 210–11.
6 For a particularly good example, with a trio of miners erecting it, see Alan Thompson, *The Day Before Yesterday, An Illustrated History of Britain from Attlee to Macmillan*, Sidgwick and Jackson, 1971, p. 44.
7 H of C, *Official Report*, Vol. 401, cols 525–32, 23 June 1944.
8 *Plan for Britain: A Collection of Essays Prepared for the Fabian Society*, Routledge, 1943, pp. 34–50.
9 See John Campbell, *Nye Bevan and the Mirage of British Socialism*, Weidenfeld, 1987, p. 361, footnote.
10 *Labour Party Annual Conference Report, 1959*, pp. 151–2.
11 *Meet the Challenge, Make the Change*, Labour Party, 1989, p. 6.
12 Susan Howson and Donald Moggridge, *The Collected Papers of James Meade, Volume IV: The Cabinet Office Diary 1944–46*, Unwin Hyman, 1989, diary entry for 26 August 1945, pp. 114–15.
13 The phrase belongs to Sir Alec Cairncross; see his *Years of Recovery, British Economic Policy 1945–51*, Methuen, 1985, p. 15.
14 José Harris, *William Beveridge, A Biography*, OUP, 1977, pp. 435–41.
15 Woolton to Churchill, 16 May 1944, PRO, CAB 124/214. In fact the Government's White Paper beat Beveridge's *Full Employment in a Free Society*, Allen and Unwin, 1944 by five months. See Harris, *William Beveridge*, p. 438.
16 PRO, CAB 124/214.
17 Lord Kahn, 'On Re-reading Keynes', British Academy Keynes Lecture, 1974, quoted in Cairncross, *Years of Recovery*, p. 16.
18 Jewkes to Woolton, 27 March 1944, PRO, CAB 124/214.
19 For a wonderfully detailed account of *the* great set-piece of interwar economic argument see Peter Clarke, *The Keynesian Revolution in the Making, 1924–1936*, Clarendon, 1988, pp. 103–230.
20 PRO, CAB 124/214.
21 Rodney Lowe, 'The Second World War, Consensus and the Foundation of the Welfare State', *Twentieth Century British History*, Vol. I, No. 2, 1990.
22 G.C. Peden, 'Sir Richard Hopkins and the "Keynesian revolution" in employment policy making', *Economic History Review*, Vol. 36, 1983, pp. 281–96.
23 Anthony Booth, 'The "Keynesian revolution" in economic policy making', *Economic History Review*, Vol. 36, 1983, pp. 103–23.
24 Lowe, 'The Second World War, Consensus and the Foundation of the Welfare State'.
25 Ibid.

26 Richard Stone, 'The Use and Development of National Income and Expenditure Esti-
    mates' in Chester (ed.), *Lessons of the British War Economy*, CUP, 1951, p. 83 and
    pp. 97–8.
27 A.J.P. Taylor, *English History, 1914–1945*, OUP, 1965, p. 511.
28 Stone, 'The Use and Development of National Income and Expenditure Estimates' in
    Chester (ed.), *Lessons of the British War Economy*, p. 85.
29 PRO, CAB 66/65.
30 Stone, 'The Use and Development of National Income and Expenditure Estimates' in
    Chester (ed.), *Lessons of the British War Economy*, p. 94.
31 Ibid.
32 Marquand, *The Unprincipled Society*, p. 210.
33 Howson and Moggridge (eds), *The Collected Papers of James Meade, Volume IV*, diary
    entry for 27 April 1945, p. 69.
34 Ibid., p. 85, diary entry for 27 May 1945.
35 Ibid., p. 26, diary entry for 7 January 1945.
36 Quoted in David Hubback, 'Sir Richard Clarke, 1910–1975. A Most Unusual Civil
    Servant', *Public Policy and Administration*, Vol. 3, No. 1 (Spring 1988), p. 19.
37 Cairncross (ed.), *The Robert Hall Diaries*, 1947–1953, p. 105, diary entry for 15 Feb-
    ruary 1950.
38 Cairncross, *Years of Recovery*, pp. 54–5.
39 Kevin Theakston and Geoffrey K. Fry, 'Britain's Administrative Elite: Permanent
    Secretaries 1900–1986', *Public Administration*, Vol. 67, No. 2 (Summer 1989), p. 141.
40 Howson and Moggridge (eds), *The Collected Papers of James Meade, Volume IV*, p. 23,
    diary entry for 31 December 1944.
41 Ibid., pp. 23–4.
42 Ibid., p. 24.
43 Roy Jenkins, *Nine Men of Power*, Hamish Hamilton, 1974, p. 83.
44 Ibid., pp. 93–4.
45 Edwin Plowden, *An Industrialist in the Treasury, The Postwar Years*, Andre Deutsch,
    1989, p. 19.
46 Douglas Jay, *Change and Fortune, A Political Record*, Hutchinson, 1980, p. 135.
47 Kenneth Harris, *Attlee*, Weidenfeld, 1982, p. 350.
48 Harold Wilson, *A Prime Minister on Prime Ministers*, Book Club Associates, 1977,
    p. 291.
49 Jenkins, *Nine Men of Power*, p. 89.
50 Plowden, *An Industrialist in the Treasury*, p. 20.
51 Sir Stafford Cripps, *Democracy Up-To-Date*, Allen and Unwin, 1939.
52 PRO, PREM 4/63/2. Prime Minister's Minute, 27 August 1942. For a full account of
    Cripps' wartime thinking see Michael Lee, *Reviewing the Machinery of Government
    1942–52: An Essay on the Anderson Committee and its Successors*, 1977, (available from
    Professor Michael Lee, Department of Politics, University of Bristol).
53 H of C, *Official Report*, Columns 964–5, 10 March 1947.
54 Allan Beattie, 'Conservatives, Consensus and the Constitution', *LSE Quarterly*, Vol. 3,
    No. 2 (Summer 1989), p. 140 and p. 145.
55 Professor Griffith delivered himself of this judgment at the time of the Westland affair
    in 1986. See Peter Hennessy, 'Helicopter Crashes into Cabinet: Prime Minister
    and Constitution Hurt', *Journal of Law and Society*, Vol. 13, No. 3 (Autumn 1986),
    p. 423.
56 According to LSE legend Morrison delivered perhaps his most famous one-liner
    during one of Professor Robert Mackenzie's seminars in the Government Department
    in the 1950s. Conversation with Professor George Jones, 8 December 1991.
57 Cairncross, *Years of Recovery*, pp. 19–20.
58 PRO, CAB 66/65, WP(45) 301.

59 Kenneth O. Morgan, *Labour in Power*, OUP, 1984, p. 130.

60 Conversation with Lord Jay, 30 November 1989.

61 Herbert Morrison, *Socialisation and Transport*, Constable and Co., 1933, p. 149.

62 Christopher Mayhew, interviewed by George Jones and Bernard Donoughue, 3 July 1968. Morrison Archive, British Library of Political and Economic Science.

63 Ibid. Interview with Sir Alexander Johnstone, 16 September 1968.

64 Quoted in Harris, *Attlee*, p. 324.

65 For Anglo-Iranian see Henry Pelling, *Winston Churchill*, Macmillan, 1974, p. 152; for the BBC see Asa Briggs, *The BBC, The First Fifty Years*, OUP, 1985, Chapter 11, 'From Company to Corporation', pp. 35–106.

66 Bernard Donoughue and G.W. Jones, *Herbert Morrison, Portrait of a Politician*, Weidenfeld, 1973, pp. 140–50.

67 Sidney Pollard, *The Development of the British Economy, 1914–1950*, Edward Arnold, 1962, p. 157.

68 Quoted in Thompson, *The Day Before Yesterday*, p. 26.

69 Interview with Lord Attlee, 1 March 1967, Morrison Archive.

70 See Donoughue and Jones, *Herbert Morrison*, Section V, pp. 189–210.

71 Interview with James Griffiths, 12 January 1968, Morrison Archive.

72 Ibid.

73 Interview with Christopher Mayhew, Morrison Archive.

74 Conversation with Tony Benn, 29 January 1990. Mr Benn had been lunching with Morrison in January 1951 at the House of Commons. Attlee stopped by their table for a few words. Morrison mentioned a story critical of Attlee in that morning's papers, suggesting it was a scandal! 'Never read it,' said Attlee, and passed on. 'You know', said Morrison, 'I've known that man for 40 years and I still don't know whether to believe what he says.'

75 James Margach, *The Abuse of Power, The War Between Downing Street and the Media from Lloyd George to James Callaghan*, W.H. Allen, 1978, pp. 88–90.

76 Interview with Christopher Mayhew, Morrison Archive.

77 Interview with Lord Bridges, 30 April 1969, Morrison Archive.

78 Interview with James Griffiths, Morrison Archive.

79 Interview with Lord Chandos, 25 November 1969, Morrison Archive.

80 Ibid.

81 Morgan, *Labour in Power*, p. 97.

82 Interview with Lord Bridges, Morrison Archive.

83 Interview with Sir Alexander Johnstone, Morrison Archive.

84 Morgan, *Labour in Power*, p. 100.

85 Ibid.

86 *The Times*, 28 October 1946.

87 Ralph Miliband, *Parliamentary Socialism, A Study in the Politics of Labour*, first published 1961, paperback edition Merlin, 1973, p. 288.

88 *Labour Party Annual Conference Report 1945*, p. 90.

89 C.R. Attlee, *As It Happened*, Odhams edition, 1954, p. 189.

90 Ibid., p. 192.

91 Morgan, *Labour in Power*, p. 99.

92 Ben Pimlott, *Hugh Dalton*, Papermac, 1985, Chapter 1, 'The Royal Connection', pp. 3–23.

93 R.W.B. Clarke, *Diary 1946–48*, Churchill Archives Centre, Clarke Collection, Box 25, Churchill College, Cambridge. Both these gems are contained in the entry for 12 February 1946.

94 Jay, *Change and Fortune*, p. 110.

95 For Dalton's account of nationalising the Bank see *High Tide and After*, pp. 32–50.

96 Nicholas Davenport, *Memoirs of a City Radical*, Weidenfeld, 1974, p. 161.

97 Elizabeth Durbin, *New Jerusalems, The Labour Party and the Economics of Democratic Socialism*, Routledge, 1985, pp. 82–3.

98 Francis Williams, *Nothing So Strange*, Cassell, 1970, p. 112.

99 Davenport, *Memoirs of a City Radical*, p. 160.

100 Ibid.

101 Conversation with Mrs Castle, 10 November 1989.

102 Morgan, *Labour in Power*, p. 106.

103 R. Kelf-Cohen, *Twenty Years of Nationalisation, The British Experience*, Macmillan, 1969, p. 44.

104 Sir Norman Chester, *The Nationalisation of British Industry 1945–51*, HMSO, 1975, p. 1003.

105 Kelf-Cohen, *Twenty Years of Nationalisation*, p. 42.

106 Morgan, *Labour in Power*, p. 105.

107 *Report of Advisory Committee on Organisation*, National Coal Board, 1955, para. 109.

108 The Act can be conveniently scanned as Appendix 1 in Keith Jeffery and Peter Hennessy, *States of Emergency, British Governments and Strike Breaking Since 1919*, Routledge, 1983, pp. 270–2.

109 Kelf-Cohen, *Twenty Years of Nationalisation*, pp. 100–2

110 Michael Fry, *Patronage and Principle: A Political History of Modern Scotland*, Aberdeen University Press, 1981, p. 239.

111 Thomas Johnston, *Memories*, Collins, 1950, p. 150.

112 Kelf-Cohen, *Twenty Years of Nationalisation*, p. 121.

113 Henry Pelling, *The Labour Governments, 1945–1951*, Macmillan, 1984, pp. 81–2.

114 Kelf-Cohen, *Twenty Years of Nationalisation*, p. 61.

115 Quoted in ibid., p. 69.

116 T.R. Gourvish, *British Railways 1948–73, A Business History*, CUP, 1986, p. 21.

117 Jay, *Change and Fortune*, pp. 88–9.

118 Sir John Harvey-Jones, *Does Industry Matter? 1986 Richard Dimbleby Lecture*, BBC Books, 1986, p. 11.

119 Kenneth O. Morgan, *Rebirth of a Nation: Wales 1880–1980*, Clarendon Press, 1981, pp. 312–13.

120 Fry, *Patronage and Principle*, p. 192.

121 Dame Alix Meynell, *Public Servant, Private Woman*, Gollancz, 1988, p. 220.

122 See PRO, T 172/1828. 'Note to the Chancellor', 15 January 1935. Also D.W. Parsons, *The Political Economy of British Regional Policy*, Croom Helm, 1986, pp. 16–20.

123 Addison, *The Road from 1945*, p. 43. For the report itself, see *Report of the Royal Commission on the Distribution of the Industrial Population*, Cmd. 6153, HMSO, 1940.

124 Alix Meynell, 'Location of Industry', *Public Administration*, Vol. 37, (1959), p. 13.

125 Jay, *Change and Fortune*, pp. 102–3.

126 Hugh Dalton, *The Fateful Years*, Frederick Muller, 1957, p. 437.

127 Meynell, *Public Servant, Private Woman*, p. 219.

128 Ibid., pp. 219–20.

129 For a full list see Peter Hennessy, *Whitehall*, Secker and Warburg, 1989, pp. 105–6.

130 Parsons, *The Political Economy of British Regional Policy*, p. 98.

131 Ibid., p. 99. (Dalton's notes can be found in PRO, T 171/386.)

132 Ibid., p. 109.

133 Cmd. 7540.

134 Hugh Dalton, *High Tide and After, Memoirs 1945–60*, Frederick Muller, 1962, pp. 310–11.

135 Davenport, *Memoirs of a City Radical*, p. 149.

136 Ibid., p. 150.

137 *Clarke Diary*, Churchill Archives Centre.

138 Howson and Moggridge (eds), *The Collected Papers of James Meade, Volume IV*, pp. 240–1.
139 Plowden, *An Industrialist in the Treasury*, p. 4.
140 *Clarke Diary*, entry for 5 February 1946.
141 Cairncross, *Years of Recovery*, p. 19.
142 Hugh Dalton, *Principles of Public Finance*, Routledge, 1922.
143 Max Nicholson, interview, *Morrison Papers*.
144 Cairncross, *Years of Recovery*, p. 20.
145 *Clarke Diary*, entry for 3 January 1946.
146 H of C, *Official Report*, Vol. 430, col. 1425, 26 November 1946.
147 Richard N. Gardner, *Sterling-Dollar Diplomacy: The Origins and Prospects of Our International Economic Order*, McGraw Hill, 1969 edition, p. 306.
148 *The Times*, 21 October 1946.
149 The memo is quoted in Jay, *Change and Fortune*, p. 147.
150 PRO, PREM 8/195.
151 PRO, CAB 66/65.

CHAPTER 6

Jewels from the Crown

1 Quoted in Trevor Royle, *The Last Days of the Raj*, Michael Joseph, 1989, p. 3.
2 *Clem Attlee, The Granada Historical Records Interview*, Granada, 1967, pp. 42–3.
3 Quoted in Royle, *The Last Days of the Raj*, p. 176.
4 From his 1974 Oxford University Ford Lectures reprinted in the posthumously published John Gallagher, *The Decline, Revival and Fall of the British Empire*, CUP, 1982, p. 144 and p. 146.
5 Institute of Contemporary British History Witness Seminar on 'Decolonisation in Africa', 12 December 1988, held at the Institute of Commonwealth Studies, University of London.
6 Edwin Plowden, *An Industrialist in the Treasury, The Postwar Years*, Andre Deutsch, 1989, p. 109.
7 Paul Kennedy, for example, compares it to 'the shock' the Russians received in the Crimean War and the Americans to their 'global hubris' after the fall of Saigon at the end of the Vietnam War in 1975. Paul Kennedy, *The Rise and Fall of the Great Powers*, Unwin Hyman, 1988, p. 406.
8 James Morris, *Farewell the Trumpets, An Imperial Retreat*, Penguin edition, 1979, p. 129.
9 Ibid., p. 139.
10 Ibid., p. 141.
11 Ibid., pp. 141–2.
12 Robert Taylor, *Lord Salisbury*, Allen Lane, 1975, p. 191.
13 W.R. Louis, 'The Road to Singapore: British Imperialism in the Far East, 1932–1942', in W.J. Mommsen and L. Kettenacker (eds), *The Fascist Challenge and the Policy of Appeasement*, Allen and Unwin, 1983, p. 385.
14 ICBH Witness Seminar on 'Decolonisation in Africa'.
15 Royle, *The Last Days of the Raj*, p. 46.
16 Ibid.
17 Private information.
18 Patrick Gordon Walker, *The Commonwealth*, Mercury, 1965, see Chapter 11, 'The Rise of the Commonwealth Nations', pp. 25–78.
19 Ibid., p. 15.
20 Martin Gilbert, *Winston S. Churchill, Vol. VII, Road to Victory 1941–1945*, Heinemann, 1986, p. 254.

21 Kenneth Harris, *Attlee*, Weidenfeld, 1982, pp. 75–84.
22 Francis Williams, *A Prime Minister Remembers*, Heinemann, 1961, p. 206.
23 PRO, CAB 65/28, WP (42)154, 18 November 1942.
24 Max Beloff, *Dream of Commonwealth 1921–42, Vol. 2 of Imperial Sunset*, Macmillan, 1989, p. 384.
25 See PRO, CAB 134/1556, CPC (57)30 (Revise), 'Future Constitutional Development in the Colonies,' 6 September 1957.
26 T.O. Lloyd, *The British Empire, 1558–1983*, OUP, 1984, pp. 314–15.
27 Quoted in Gallagher, *The Decline, Revival and Fall of the British Empire*, p. 146.
28 Ibid., p. 147.
29 Ibid., pp. 142–3.
30 PRO, CAB 66/65, WP (45) 301.
31 Ibid.
32 Conversation with Aaron Emanuel, 17 January 1990.
33 Ibid.
34 ICBH Witness Seminar on 'Decolonisation in Africa'.
35 Ibid.
36 Colin Cross, *The Fall of the British Empire*, Book Club Associates, 1968, p. 152. Sir Ralph Furse wrote his own memoir, *Aucuparius, Recollections of a Recruiting Officer*, OUP, 1962.
37 For a vivid account of Cumming see Christopher Andrew, *Secret Service, The Making of the British Intelligence Community*, Heinemann, 1985, pp. 73–7.
38 Cross, *The Fall of the British Empire*, p. 153.
39 Ibid., p. 264.
40 For Hankey see Stephen Roskill's three volume life, *Hankey, Man of Secrets, Volume 1, 1877–1918*, Collins, 1970; *Volume II, 1919–1931*, Collins, 1972; *Volume III, 1931–1963*, Collins, 1974. For Bridges see Richard Chapman, *Ethics in the British Civil Service*, Routledge, 1988 and Peter Hennessy, *Whitehall*, Secker and Warburg, 1989, pp. 138–50. For Fisher see Eunan O'Halpin, *Head of the Civil Service, A Study of Sir Warren Fisher*, Routledge, 1989.
41 Cross, *The Fall of the British Empire*, p. 264.
42 Nanki Poo sings the line as part of his 'A Wand'ring Minstrel' in *The Mikado*, 1885.
43 Cross, *The Fall of the British Empire*, p. 263.
44 Morris, *Farewell the Trumpets*, pp. 508–10.
45 Cross, *The Fall of the British Empire*, p. 263.
46 ICBH Witness Seminar on 'Decolonisation in Africa'.
47 Ibid.
48 Ibid.
49 PRO, PREM 11/272A.
50 Ibid. Churchill to Lyttelton, Prime Minister's Personal Minute to Secretary of State for the Colonies, 30 December 1951.
51 Ibid. Minute on 'New Colonial Office' from Minister of Works to Prime Minister, 13 December 1951.
52 ICBH Witness Seminar on 'Decolonisation in Africa'.
53 Ibid.
54 Harris, *Attlee*, pp. 355–6.
55 Quoted in Philip Ziegler, *Mountbatten, The Official Biography*, Fontana, 1986, p. 315.
56 Ibid.
57 Harris, *Attlee*, p. 361.
58 H of C, *Official Report*, 20 December 1946, cols.
59 Arthur Bottomley, *Commonwealth Comrades and Friends*, Somaiya Publications, 1985, p. 58.
60 Ibid., p. 57.

61 Lord Listowel, 'With Attlee for Indian Independence', Attlee Memorial Lecture, 16 February 1988, p. 2.
62 Lord Wavell, *Other Men's Flowers*, Cape, 1952.
63 Quoted in Brian Lapping, *End of Empire*, Granada/Channel 4, 1985, p. 61.
64 Listowel, 'With Attlee for Indian Independence', p. 2.
65 *The Memoirs of Lord Ismay*, Heinemann, 1960, p. 414.
66 Royle, *The Last Days of the Raj*, p. 126.
67 Brian Lapping, *End of Empire*, Granada/Channel 4, 1985.
68 Ibid., p. 63.
69 Ibid.
70 Ibid., p. 65.
71 Ibid.
72 John W. Wheeler-Bennett, *King George VI*, Macmillan, 1958, pp. 709–10.
73 Harris, *Attlee*, p. 371.
74 Harris, *Attlee*, p. 373.
75 Listowel, 'With Attlee for Indian Independence', p. 6.
76 PRO, FO 800/470/IND/47/1.
77 PRO, FO 800/470/IND/47/2.
78 Listowel, 'With Attlee for Indian Independence', p. 3.
79 Ziegler, *Mountbatten*, p. 474.
80 Quoted in Harris, *Attlee*, p. 382.
81 David Cannadine, *The Pleasures of the Past*, Collins, 1989, pp. 65–6.
82 Hennessy, *Diary*, Entry for 1 January 1989.
83 Quoted in Lapping, *End of Empire*, p. 87.
84 Ziegler, *Mountbatten*, p. 416.
85 Lapping, *End of Empire*, p. 81.
86 Peter Hennessy, *Whitehall*, Secker and Warburg, 1989, p. 567.
87 Louis Heren, *Growing Up on The Times*, Hamish Hamilton, 1978, p. 53.
88 Quoted in Lapping, *End of Empire*, p. 92.
89 Ibid., pp. 93–4.
90 Cross, *The Fall of the British Empire*, p. 250.
91 Listowel, 'With Attlee for Indian Independence', pp. 5–6.
92 Heren, *Growing Up on The Times*, p. 34.
93 Ibid., pp. 36–7.
94 Lapping, *End of Empire*, pp. 104–5.
95 Quoted in William Roger Louis, *The British Empire in the Middle East, 1945–51*, Clarendon Press, 1984, p. 39.
96 PRO, FO 371/52509/E1413/G 1st February 1946.
97 Lapping, *End of Empire*, pp. 110–11.
98 Quoted in Harris, *Attlee*, p. 390. The source is Dalton who claimed to have heard Attlee express the same view 'several times'.
99 Lapping, *End of Empire*, p. 125.
100 Quoted in Jon and David Kimche, *Both Sides of the Hill: Britain and the Palestine War*, Secker and Warburg, 1960, pp. 21–2.
101 Ben Pimlott (ed.), *The Political Diary of Hugh Dalton, 1918–40, 1945–60*, Cape, 1986, diary entry for 20 February, 1951, p. 508. This side of Attlee came as a shock to Ian Mikardo who knew nothing of it before the Dalton diaries were published. Conversation with Ian Mikardo, 29 November 1991.
102 Douglas Jay, *Change and Fortune, A Political Record*, Hutchinson, 1980, p. 99.
103 Lapping, *End of Empire*, p. 121.
104 Harris, *Attlee*, p. 397.
105 Alan Bullock, *Ernest Bevin, Foreign Secretary, 1945–1951*, Heinemann, 1983, p. 240.

106 Pimlott (ed.), *The Political Diary of Hugh Dalton*, pp. 368–9, diary entry for 22 March 1946.

107 Meetings of the Cabinet's Defence Committee, 8 and 18 March, 1946, PRO, CAB 131/2.

108 Louis, *The British Empire in the Middle East, 1945–51*, p. 10.

109 Quoted in ibid., p. 4.

110 Ibid., pp. 10–11.

111 Quoted in Alan Bullock, *Ernest Bevin, Foreign Secretary, 1945–51*, Heinemann, 1983, p. 178.

112 Ibid.

113 Lapping, *End of Empire*, p. 134.

114 Ibid., pp. 138–9.

115 Quoted in Avi Shlaim, *Collusion Across the Jordan: King Abdullah, the Zionist Movement, and the Partition of Palestine*, Clarendon Press, 1988, p. 57.

116 Walid Khalidi (ed.), *From Haven to Conquest*, Institute for Palestine Studies, 1971, p. lxxxiii.

117 Quoted in Shlaim, *Collusion Across the Jordan*, p. 219.

118 Morris, *Farewell the Trumpets*, pp. 511–12.

119 Ibid., p. 515.

120 H.V. Hodson, *Twentieth-Century Empire*, Faber, 1948, pp. 160–1.

121 Michael Charlton, *The Price of Victory*, BBC, 1983, p. 172.

122 J.A. Hobson, *Imperialism, A Study*, first published by Allen and Unwin in 1902, is now most easily read in an Unwin Hyman edition of 1988. For an excellent survey of the economic debate about empire, see John Cunningham Wood, *British Economists and the Empire*, Croom Helm, 1983.

123 Patrick K. O'Brien, 'The Costs and Benefits of British Imperialism 1848–1914', *Past and Present*, no. 120 (August 1988), p. 165.

124 Henry Pelling, *The Labour Governments, 1945–51*, Macmillan, 1984, p. 126.

125 Enoch Powell is especially good on this. See his *Sunday Telegraph* article of 17 July 1966 as summarised in Patrick Cosgrave, *The Lives of Enoch Powell*, Bodley Head, 1989, p. 61.

CHAPTER 7

Chill from the East

1 Quoted in Alan Thompson, *The Day Before Yesterday, An Illustrated History of Britain from Attlee to Macmillan*, Sidgwick and Jackson, 1971, p. 49.

2 India Office Library Records, JIC (48)9 (0), 'Russian Interests, Intentions and Capabilities', 23 July 1948, p. 3 IOLR, L/WS/1/1173.

3 Denis Healey, 'NATO, Britain and Soviet Military Policy', *Orbis*, Vol. XIII, No. 1, Spring 1969, p. 48.

4 A BBC Home Service talk, 'A Sense of the Future', reprinted in J. Bronowski, *A Sense of the Future, Essays in Natural Philosophy*, MIT, 1977, p. 1.

5 Lord Hailsham, *The Granada Guildhall Lecture 1987*, delivered at the Guildhall in the City of London, 10 November 1987.

6 IOLR, JIC(48)9 (0), p. 2.

7 Alan Bullock, *Ernest Bevin, Foreign Secretary, 1945–1951*, Heinemann, 1983, p. 82.

8 IOLR, JIC (48)9 (0), p. 2.

9 He voiced the possibility in 'The Role of Military Intelligence since 1945', a paper delivered at the Twentieth Century British Politics and Administration Seminar at the Institute of Historical Research, London University, 24 May 1989.

10 See Peter Hennessy, 'Whitehall Watch: Trying to decode the signals from the east', *Independent*, 26 February 1990.

11 IOLR, JIC(48)9 (0), p. 2.

12 Ibid.

13 Ibid.

14 Ibid., p. 19.

15 Ibid., p. 2.

16 Ibid., pp. 2–3.

17 Ibid., p. 18.

18 Ibid., p. 3.

19 Private information.

20 IOLR, JIC(48)9 (0), p. 16.

21 Ibid., p. 30.

22 Sir Percy Sillitoe, *Cloak Without Dagger*, Quality Book Club, 1955.

23 Herman, 'The Role of Military Intelligence Since 1945', p. 6.

24 For the ups and down of interwar intelligence see Christopher Andrew, *Secret Service, The Making of the British Intelligence Community*, Heinemann, 1985, Chapters 9–13, pp. 259–411.

25 For a superb short history of SOE see M.R.D. Foot, *SOE, The Special Operations Executive, 1940–46*, BBC Books, 1988.

26 Anthony Verrier, *Through the Looking Glass, British Foreign Policy in the Age of Illusions*, Cape, 1983, p. 52.

27 Herman, 'The Role of Military Intelligence since 1945', p. 1.

28 Ibid., p. 6.

29 Ibid., p. 9.

30 Christopher Mayhew, *Time to Explain, An Autobiography*, Hutchinson, 1987, pp. 107–8.

31 Ibid., p. 110.

32 See Peter Hennessy, 'Whitehall Watch: Spy caused reappraisal of bomb policy', *Independent*, 25 September 1989.

33 Richard Aldrich and Michael Coleman, 'The Cold War, The JIC and British Signals Intelligence, 1948', *Intelligence and National Security*, Vol. 4, No. 3, July 1989, p. 114.

34 Ibid., p. 118.

35 It is reprinted in full in Appendix 2 to the Aldrich and Coleman article cited above. The original can be found in IOLR, L/WS/1/1196.

36 Bullock, *Ernest Bevin, Foreign Secretary*, p. 345.

37 Ibid.

38 I have not seen written evidence of Ismay's delivering this marvellous one-liner, but it's been Ministry of Defence folklore for generations and passed on to me by more than one very senior figure.

39 Julian Lewis, *Changing Direction, British Military Planning for Post-War Strategic Defence, 1942–47*, Sherwood Press, 1988, p. 1. The request and Ismay's comments can be found in PRO, CAB 119/64, 20 February 1942. A useful, shorter account of the vicissitudes of the postwar planners can be found in Anthony Gorst, 'Military Planning for Post-War Defence, 1943–45', in Anne Deighton (ed.), *Britain and the First Cold War*, Macmillan, 1990, pp. 91–108.

40 PRO, WP(42) 516, 27 November 1942.

41 Quoted in Lewis, *Changing Direction*, p. 36.

42 Quoted in ibid., p. 59.

43 Ibid., p. 68.

44 Ibid., p. 106.

45 Ibid., p. 132. The remark about the planners must, even now, rank as private information.

46 For an excellent summary of the cold war literature see Anne Deighton, *The Impossible*

Peace: Britain, the Division of Germany, and the Origins of the Cold War, Clarendon Press 1990, pp. 1–3.

47 William Appleman Williams, *The Tragedy of American Diplomacy*, World Publishing Company, 1959; D.F. Fleming, *The Cold War and Its Origins 1917–1950*, Doubleday, 1960; D.F. Fleming, *The Cold War and Its Origins, 1950–1960*, Doubleday, 1961.

48 Quoted in Lewis, *Changing Direction*, pp. 90–1.

49 Ibid., p. 91.

50 See Sir John Slessor, *The Central Blue*, Cassell, 1956, pp. 610–22.

51 Lewis, *Changing Direction*, p. 91.

52 Bullock, *Ernest Bevin, Foreign Secretary*, p. 65.

53 Ibid., p. 66.

54 Diary of Sir Hughe Knatchbull-Hugessen, Churchill College Archives Centre, Cambridge, entry for 15 August 1945.

55 Emrys Evans MSS., British Library, Harvey to Evans, 26th August 1945.

56 In the Kremlin on 9 October 1944, Churchill wrote down the following on a half sheet of paper:

Roumania

Russia	90%
The others	10%

Greece

Great Britain	90%
(in accord with USA)	
Russia	10%

Yugoslavia	50–50%
Hungary	50–50%

Bulgaria

Russia	75%
The others	25%

He pushed it across the table to Stalin who 'took his blue pencil and made a large tick upon it', Martin Gilbert, *Winston S. Churchill, Vol. VII, Road to Victory, 1941–1945*, Heinemann, 1986, p. 993.

57 Raymond Smith, 'Ernest Bevin, British Officials and British Soviet Policy, 1945–47', in Deighton, (ed.), *Britain and the First Cold War*, p. 35.

58 PRO, CAB 66/63, WP(45), 197, 20 March 1945, 'Future defence policy in the Suez Canal area'.

59 PRO, CAB 66/65, WP(45) Z56, 13 April 1945, 'Defence of the Middle East'.

60 T.M. Campbell and G.C. Herring (eds), *The Diaries of E.R. Stettinius Jr., 1943–1946*, New Viewpoints, 1975, pp. 417–18.

61 PRO, CAB 131/1, DO(46) 3rd meeting, 21 January 1946.

62 Diary of Admiral of the Fleet, Lord Cunningham, British Library, entry for 16 February 1946.

63 PRO, CAB 131/2, DO(46) 27, 2 March 1946, Memorandum by the Prime Minister on the 'Future of the Italian Colonies'.

64 Alanbrooke Diary, Liddell Hart Centre for Military Archives, King's College, London, 5/12, entry for 5 April 1946.

65 Ibid., diary entry for 27 July 1944.

66 Deighton, *The Impossible Peace*, p. 25.

67 Ibid.

68 Sir Charles Webster, Webster Diary, British Library of Political and Economic Science, entry for 27 February 1946.

69 The original of the Sargent memorandum can be read in full in Rohan Butler and M.E. Pelly (eds), *Documents on British Policy Overseas*, 1st series, 1, HMSO, 1984, p. 181ff.

70   Deighton, *The Impossible Peace*, pp. 25–6.

71   Mayhew, *Time to Explain*, reproduces his diary entry for 13 December 1947 on p. 107.

72   Bullock, *Ernest Bevin, Foreign Secretary*, pp. 116–17; Bradford Perkins, 'Unequal Partners: The Truman Administration and Great Britain', in W.M. Roger Louis and Hedley Bull, *The Special Relationship: Anglo-American Relations Since 1945*, OUP, 1986, pp. 47–8.

73   Bullock, *Ernest Bevin, Foreign Secretary*, pp. 115–16.

74   Mayhew, *Time to Explain*, diary entry for 13 December 1947, p. 107.

75   Smith, 'Ernest Bevin, British Officials and British Soviet Policy, 1945–47', in Deighton, (ed.), *Britain and the First Cold War*, pp. 37–8.

76   Ibid., p. 38.

77   Lord Gladwyn, *The Memoirs of Lord Gladwyn*, Weidenfeld, 1972, p. 227.

78   PRO, PO 371/71687, Warner to Jebb, 22 November 1948.

79   Ibid.

80   Maurice Hankey, Mss, HNKY 3/47, Churchill College Archives Centre, M. Hankey to H. Hankey, 1 September 1945, recording a conversation with Lord Hankey's son, Robin, a senior FO official who headed its Northern Department in the early cold war years.

81   'The more I study this the less I like it,' said Bevin. Kirkpatrick's memorandum can be found in PRO, FO 930/488 and is dated 22 May 1946. Bevin's undated comment is part of the same file.

82   PRO, FO 181/1023, Warner to Roberts, 1 May 1946.

83   Andrei Gromyko, *Memories from Stalin to Gorbachev*, Arrow, 1989, pp. 194–7.

84   Mayhew, *Time to Explain*, p. 105.

85   The very full minutes of the meeting are preserved in PRO, FO 945/16 and in PRO, FO 371/55586.

86   Ibid.

87   Deighton, *The Impossible Peace*, p. 53.

88   PRO, CAB 129/9, CP(46) 183, 3 May 1946.

89   Alan Foster, 'The British Press and the Coming of the Cold War', in Deighton (ed.), *Britain and the First Cold War*, pp. 11–31.

90   Quoted in ibid., p. 28.

91   PRO, CAB 128/7, CM 43(46) Confidential Annex, 7 May 1946.

92   John Zametica, 'British Strategic Planning for the Eastern Mediterranean and the Middle East, 1944–47'. Unpublished PhD thesis, Cambridge, 1986, pp. 131–2. On 10 May 1946 Liddel Hart sent Attlee a Paper entitled 'Africa or the Middle East', which Leslie Rowan, the PM's Principal Private Secretary, acknowledged the receipt of three days later saying Attlee had found it 'interesting'; Liddel Hart Papers, King's College Archive, LH1/28/14.

93   PRO, CAB 21/1086, COS(46) 108th meeting, 12 July 1946.

94   PRO, CAB 131/2, DO(46), 47, 2 April 1946.

95   PRO, CAB 1311/1, DO(46) 22nd meeting, 19 July 1946.

96   Ibid.

97   PRO, FO 800/475, ME/46/22, Attlee to Bevin, 1 December 1946.

98   The relevant Technical Warfare Committee file is retained by the Cabinet Office though Julian Lewis, somehow, has found a copy elsewhere in the archive – Lewis, *Changing Direction*, pp. 228–30.

99   Quoted in Peter Hennessy, *Cabinet*, Blackwell, 1986, p. 125.

100 Quoted in Margaret Gowing, *Britain and Atomic Energy, 1939–45*, Macmillan, 1964, p. 17.

101 Lewis Wolpert, 'Leo Szilard' in 'Heroes and Villains', *Independent Magazine*, 2 June 1990.

102 H.G. Wells, *The World Set Free*, Nisbet, 1914.

103 Gowing, *Britain and Atomic Energy, 1939–1945*, p. 41.
104 Sir Rudolf Peierls interviewed for *A Bloody Union Jack on Top of It: Programme 1; An 'Of Course' Decision*, BBC Radio 4, 5 May 1988.
105 Gowing, *Britain and Atomic Energy, 1939–1945*, p. 43.
106 Ronald W. Clark, *Einstein, The Life and Times*, Avon Books, 1984, pp. 674–80.
107 Margaret Gowing, *Independence and Deterrence: Britain and Atomic Energy 1945–1952, Vol. 1; Policy Making*, Macmillan, 1974, pp. 1–2.
108 Jill Edwards found the nickname in the Truman Archives in Independence, Missouri. Jill Edwards, 'Roger Makins: "Mr Atom"', in John Zametica (ed.), *British Officials and British Foreign Policy, 1945–50*, Leicester University Press, 1990, p. 33, footnote 1.
109 Lord Sherfield interviewed for BBC Radio 4's *A Bloody Union Jack on Top of It*.
110 The full text of the Quebec Agreement is reproduced as Appendix 4 in Gowing, *Britain and Atomic Energy, 1939–1945*, pp. 439–40.
111 Reproduced as Appendix 8 in ibid., p. 447.
112 Ibid., p. 372.
113 Kenneth Harris, *Attlee*, Weidenfeld, 1982, p. 285.
114 Lord Sherfield interviewed for *A Bloody Union Jack on Top of It*. (I have heard that the American copy didn't surface in the Navy Department until the early 1960s).
115 Ibid. For Attlee's 2,000 word despatch to Truman see Harris, *Attlee*, pp. 284–5.
116 Gowing, *Independence and Deterrence, Vol. 1*, pp. 107–8.
117 Lord Sherfield interviewed for BBC Radio 4's *A Bloody Union Jack on Top of It*.
118 Harris, *Attlee*, p. 285.
119 Peter Hennessy, *Whitehall*, Secker and Warburg, 1989, p. 712.
120 PRO, CAB 130/2, GEN 75, 1st Meeting, 18 December 1945.
121 Ibid.
122 Lord Sherfield interviewed for BBC Radio 4's *A Bloody Union Jack on Top of It*.
123 Sir Michael Perrin recalling the occasion on *Timewatch*, BBC2, 29 September 1982.
124 Roy Jenkins, *Nine Men of Power*, Hamish Hamilton, 1974, p. 63.
125 PRO, CAB 130/2, GEN 75, 15th Meeting, 25 October 1946.
126 PRO, CAB 21/2281 B, Prime Minister's Personal Minute, serial no. M 140c/51, 8 December 1951.
127 Bullock, *Ernest Bevin, Foreign Secretary*, p. 195.
128 Ibid., p. 311.
129 Tony Benn, otherwise an Attlee admirer, continued to upbraid him for this forty years on. Tony Benn, on 'British Politics 1945–1987' in Peter Hennessy and Anthony Seldon (eds), *Ruling Performance, British Governments from Attlee to Thatcher*, Blackwell, 1987, pp. 302–3.
130 PRO, CAB 21/2281 B.
131 John Mackintosh, *The British Cabinet*, University Paperback, 1968, p. 496.
132 PRO, CAB 130/16, 'Note by the Controller of Production of Atomic Energy', 31 December 1946; PRO, CAB 130/16, GEN 163, 1st meeting, 8 January 1947, Confidential Annex, Minute 1, 'Research in Atomic Weapons'.
133 A.V. Alexander's Parliamentary answer of 12 May 1948 and the Press coverage it received can be found in Peter Hennessy, *What the Papers Never Said*, Politics Association, 1985, pp. 17–29.
134 Conversation with Lord Penney, 19 November 1987.
135 PRO, AIR 2/59 60: 'Draft Air Staff Requirement. No. OR/230'.
136 For a history of the V-force see Robert Jackson, *V-Bombers*, Ian Allan, 1981.
137 PRO, CAB 130/16, GEN 163, 1st meeting.
138 'A fount of wisdom' Attlee called him. *Clem Attlee, the Granada Historical Records Interview*, Granada, 1967, p. 54.
139 PRO, CAB 130/16, GEN 163, 1st meeting.

140 Lord Sherfield, 'Clement Attlee and Foreign Policy', The Attlee Foundation Lecture, 1986, p. 4.
141 Ibid., p. 2.
142 Harris, *Attlee*, p. 288.
143 The phrase belongs to Smith and Zametica, 'The Cold Warrior, Clement Attlee Reconsidered, 1945–7'.
144 PRO, FO 800/476, ME/47/1, Attlee to Bevin 5 January 1947.
145 Bullock, *Ernest Bevin, Foreign Secretary*, pp. 349–50.
146 PRO, FO 800/476, ME/47/1.
147 PRO, FO 800/476, ME/47/4, Bevin to Attlee, 9 January 1947.
148 PRO, FO 800/476, ME/47/5.
149 Nigel Hamilton, *Monty, The Field Marshal 1944–1976*, Hamish Hamilton, 1986, p. 672.
150 Ibid., p. 676.
151 Quoted in ibid.
152 Field Marshal Viscount Montgomery of Alamein, *Memoirs*, Collins, 1958, p. 438.

CHAPTER 8

Ice, Dollars and New Looks

1 John W. Wheeler-Bennett, *King George VI, His Life and Reign*, Macmillan, 1958, p. 662.
2 Howard K. Smith, *The State of Europe*, Cresset, 1950, pp. 20–6.
3 PRO, T229/236, 'Marshall Proposals. Alternative action in event of breakdown', 17 July 1947.
4 E.W. Swanton, *Sort of A Cricket Person*, Fontana, 1974, p. 152.
5 Quoted in Paul Addison, *Now the War Is Over. A Social History of Britain 1945–51*, BBC Books and Cape, 1985, p. 52.
6 Wheeler-Bennett, *King George VI*, diary entry for 21 January 1946.
7 See Keith Jeffery and Peter Hennessy, *States of Emergency, British Governments and Strikebreaking Since 1919*, Routledge, 1983, pp. 169–77.
8 Wheeler-Bennett, *King George VI*, p. 652, diary entry for 27 November 1945.
9 Quoted in Addison, *Now the War is Over*, pp. 34–5.
10 Conversation with Professor Geoffrey Warner, 20 June 1990.
11 Nicholas Henderson, *The Private Office, A Personal View of Five Foreign Secretaries and of Government from the Inside*, Weidenfeld, 1984, pp. 32–4.
12 Harold Wilson, *The Making of a Prime Minister, Memoirs 1916–1964*, Weidenfeld and Michael Joseph, 1986, pp. 104–5.
13 Edwin Plowden, *An Industrialist in the Treasury, The Postwar Years*, Andre Deutsch, 1989, p. 19.
14 Sheila McNeil once told me the Attlees used the smallest sherry glasses she had ever seen.
15 Richard Hoggart, *A Sort of Clowning, Life and Times: 1940–59*, Chatto, 1990, pp. 81–2.
16 Ibid., p. 82.
17 R.J. Hammond, *Food*, Volume 3, HMSO, 1962, p. 714.
18 Henry Pelling, *The Labour Governments, 1945–51*, Macmillan, 1984, p. 70; Hugh Thomas, *John Strachey*, Eyre Methuen, 1973, pp. 235–6.
19 Lord Plowden told the story of Bevin's problems with his digestive system during a seminar at the Institute of Historical Research on 'The Central Economic Planning Staff, 1947–53', 22 February 1989.
20 James Lansdale Hodson, *The Way Things Are*, Gollancz, 1947, p. 199.
21 Addison, *Now the War Is Over*, p. 37.

22 PRO, CAB 129/17, *Report by Dr Magnus Pyke on the Nutrition of the People of Britain in March 1947*, 21 March 1947.
23 Thomas, *John Strachey*, p. 238.
24 Dalton, *High Tide and After, Memoirs 1945–60*, Frederick Muller, 1962, Chapter 22, pp. 187–92.
25 Ibid., p. 205.
26 Alan Thompson, *The Day Before Yesterday, An Illustrated History of Britain from Attlee to Macmillan*, Sidgwick and Jackson, 1971, p. 45.
27 *The British Fuel and Power Industries*, PEP, 1947, p. 328.
28 Alex. J. Robertson, *The Bleak Midwinter 1947*, Manchester University Press, 1987, pp. 45–6.
29 Shinwell quoted in the *Daily Herald*, 25 October 1946.
30 Douglas Jay, *Change and Fortune, A Political Record*, Hutchinson, 1980, Chapter 7, pp. 128–56.
31 PRO, PREM 8/440, Jay to Attlee, 19 June 1946.
32 Ibid., Attlee to Dalton, 24 July 1946.
33 Robertson, *The Bleak Midwinter*, pp. 54–60.
34 We conducted our exercise while preparing *Mr Attlee's Engine Room: Cabinet Committee Structure and the Labour Government 1945–51*, Strathclyde Papers and Politics No. 26, 1983.
35 *1947 A Year to Remember*, Parkfield Pathé Video, 1990.
36 For an evocative and fact-filled account of the 1947 winter see Robertson, *The Bleak Midwinter*, Chapter 1, pp. 1–22.
37 Lord Bancroft, 'Whitehall: Some Personal Reflections', LSE, Suntory-Toyota Lecture, 1 December 1983.
38 Hodson, *The Way Things Are*, p. 316.
39 Ibid., p. 309, diary entry for 29 January 1947.
40 Mass Observation, file report No. 2468, *Fuel Crisis*, May 1947, Mass Observation Archive, University of Sussex.
41 Payn and Morley (eds), *The Noel Coward Diaries*, p. 79, entry for 29 January 1947.
42 Louis Heren, *Memories of Times Past*, Hamish Hamilton, 1988, pp. 58–9.
43 Ibid., p. 65.
44 At this time Orwell was living at 27b, Canonbury Square in Islington, north London.
45 George Orwell, 'As I Please', *Tribune*, 28 March 1947.
46 Robertson, *The Bleak Midwinter*, p. 123.
47 For a vivid contemporary account see Dudley Barker, *Harvest Home, The Story of the Great Floods of 1947*. Originally published in 1948, it was reprinted by Providence Press in 1985.
48 Ibid., pp. 52–3.
49 Ibid., p. 88.
50 Ibid., pp. 79–82.
51 David Watt, 'Withdrawal from Greece' in Michael Sissons and Philip French (eds), *The Age of Austerity, 1945–51*, Penguin, 1964, pp. 106–7.
52 William Roger Louis, *The British Empire in the Middle East, 1945–51*, Clarendon Press, 1984, p. 99.
53 Alan Bullock, *Ernest Bevin, Foreign Secretary, 1945–51*, Heinemann, 1983, p. 369.
54 Joseph Marian Jones, *The Fifteen Weeks, An Inside Account of the Genesis of the Marshall Plan*, Harbinger, 1964, p. 39. The Monroe Doctrine declared America's right to a commercial, free trade hegemony in the western hemisphere.
55 Truman unveiled his doctrine at a joint session of both Houses of Congress on 12 March 1947.
56 Jones, *The Fifteen Weeks*, p. 4.
57 Bullock, *Ernest Bevin, Foreign Secretary*, p. 370.

58 Gladwyn, *The Memoirs of Lord Gladwyn*, p. 202.

59 Andrei Gromyko, *Memories from Stalin to Gorbachev*, Arrow, 1989, p. 66.

60 It's reproduced in Thompson, *The Day Before Yesterday*, pp. 66–7.

61 Gladwyn, *The Memoirs of Lord Gladwyn*, p. 207.

62 Quoted in Smith, *The State of Europe*, p. 97.

63 Bullock, *Ernest Bevin, Foreign Secretary*, p. 90.

64 Smith, *The State of Europe*, p. 97.

65 Ibid., p. 98.

66 William Appleman Williams, *The Tragedy of American Diplomacy*, World Publishing Company, 1959, pp. 206–7.

67 PRO, FO 1030/3, Dean to Dixon, 17 March 1947.

68 The metaphor is Howard Smith's who was reporting the Conference – Smith, *The State of Europe*, p. 116.

69 Anne Deighton, *The Impossible Peace: Britain, the Division of Germany, and the Origins of the Cold War*, Clarendon Press, 1990, p. 165.

70 Ibid., p. 166.

71 PRO, FO 800/447, Bevin to Attlee, 16 April 1947.

72 PRO, T 236/999, Hall-Patch to Sir Wilfrid Eady, 2 May 1947.

73 Quoted in Jones, *The Fifteen Weeks*, p. 27.

74 As recorded in a letter from Jebb to Dixon, 16 March 1947. See Deighton, *The Impossible Peace*, pp. 137–8.

75 The gold and dollar statistics are taken from Sir Alec Cairncross, *Years of Recovery, British Economic Policy 1945–51*, Methuen, 1985, pp. 121–2.

76 Ibid., pp. 129–30.

77 Clarke Papers, Box 25, diary entry for 20 April 1947.

78 Ibid. The survey was published as Cmd. 7046, HMSO, 1947.

79 H of C, *Official Report*, vol. 434, col. 1355, 12 March 1947.

80 *Clarke Diary*, entry for 20 April 1947.

81 Ibid.

82 Ibid.

83 Cairncross, *Years of Recovery*, p. 20.

84 Jones, *The Fifteen Weeks*, p. 34.

85 Ibid., p. 35.

86 Bullock, *Ernest Bevin, Foreign Secretary*, p. 404.

87 Leonard Miall, 'How the Marshall Plan Started', *Listener*, 4 May 1967.

88 Address to the National Press Club in Washington, 1 April 1949.

89 Bullock, *Ernest Bevin, Foreign Secretary*, p. 404.

90 PRO, T236/782.

91 The main debunker of the wireless version is Alan Milward in his *The Reconstruction of Western Europe 1945–51*, Methuen, 1984, p. 61.

92 Quoted in Henry Pelling, *Britain and the Marshall Plan*, Macmillan, 1988, p. 3.

93 *Clarke Diary*, entry for 7 April 1947.

94 David Mayers, *George Kennan and the Dilemmas of US Foreign Policy*, OUP, 1988, p. 132.

95 Martin Gilbert, *Never Despair, Winston S. Churchill, 1945–1965*, Heinemann, 1988, p. 337.

96 Kennan and Bohlen made this plain to Marshall at the end of May 1947 when he asked them what if the Soviets accept? Mayers, *George Kennan and the Dilemmas of US Foreign Policy*, pp. 140–1.

97 Ibid., pp. 125–6.

98 *Foreign Relations of the United States, 1947*, Vol. iii, U.S. Government Printing Office, 1972, p. 230.

99 Ibid., p. 228.

100   Quoted in Deighton, *The Impossible Peace*, p. 177.
101   *FRUS, 1947*, Vol. iii, p. 291.
102   Historians are largely reliant on the American record of this revealing meeting in *FRUS, 1947*, Vol. iii, pp. 268–96.
103   Bullock, *Ernest Bevin, Foreign Secretary*, p. 416.
104   Ibid., p. 415.
105   Conversation with Lord Franks, 24 January 1977.
106   Quoted in Deighton, *The Impossible Peace*, p. 186.
107   PRO, CAB 129/19, CP (47) 197, 5 July 1947; CAB 128/10, CM (47) 60, 8 July 1947.
108   John Kenneth Galbraith, *The American Left and some British Comparisons*, Fabian Tract 405, 1971, pp. 11–12.
109   Milward, *The Reconstruction of Western Europe*, p. 54.
110   Ibid., p. 502.
111   Ibid., Chapters II and III, pp. 56–125 and Alan S. Milward, 'The War, the Netherlands and the development of the European Economic Community in M.R.D. Foot (ed.), *Holland At War Against Hitler, Anglo-Dutch Relations 1940–1945*, Frank Cass, 1990, pp. 200–12.
112   PRO, T229/136.
113   Ibid.
114   Ibid.
115   Ibid. Robinson to Plowden, undated, but almost certainly 23 July 1947.
116   Letter from Lord Plowden to the author, 12 July 1979.
117   Conversation with Sir Austin Robinson, 22 June 1979.
118   Letter from Sir Frank Figgures to the author, August 1979.
119   Letter from Sir Harry Lintott to the author, 28 June 1979.
120   PRO, T229/136, R.W.B. Clarke to Sir John Henry Woods, 23 July 1947.
121   Ben Pimlott (ed.), *The Political Diary of Hugh Dalton, 1918–40, 1945–60*, Cape, 1986, p. 400, diary entry for 29 July 1947.
122   Ben Pimlott, *Hugh Dalton*, Cape, 1985, Papermac edition, 1986, p. 481.
123   Dalton, *High Tide and After*, p. 254.
124   Ibid., p. 197.
125   Ibid., p. 5.
126   Ibid., p. 254.
127   Pimlott, *Hugh Dalton*, p. 482.
128   Pimlott (ed.), *The Political Diary of Hugh Dalton*, p. 407, diary entry for 8 August 1947.
129   Lord Trend, quoted in Pimlott, *Hugh Dalton*, p. 482.
130   Ibid.
131   Pimlott (ed.), *The Political Diary of Hugh Dalton*, p. 406, diary entry for 8 August 1947.
132   Ibid., p. 405, diary entry for 30 July 1947.
133   Cairncross, *Years of Recovery*, p. 137.
134   Letter from Lord Trend to the author, 27 July 1979.
135   Bernard Donoughue and G.W. Jones, *Herbert Morrison, Portrait of a Politician*, Weidenfeld, 1973, p. 410.
136   PRO, CAB 129/26, CP (47) 233, 16 August 1947.
137   Ibid.
138   PRO, CAB 128/10, CM (47) 71st Conclusions, 17 August 1947.
139   Ibid. Pimlott (ed.), *The Political Diary of Hugh Dalton*, p. 411, diary entry for 17 August 1947.
140   Richard N. Gardner, *Sterling-Dollar Diplomacy, The Origins and Prospects of Our International Economic Orders*. McGraw Hill, 1969 edition, pp. 321–3.
141   Quoted in Pimlott, *Hugh Dalton*, p. 489.
142   Milward, *The Reconstruction of Western Europe*, p. 6.
143   Ibid., p. 464.

144 Nicholas Davenport, *Memoirs of a City Radical*, Weidenfeld, 1974, p. 173.
145 Ibid., p. 171.
146 Conversation with Lord Bancroft, 18 April 1989.
147 Neville Cardus, *Close of Play*, Collins, 1956, p. 55.
148 Quoted in Addison, *Now the War is Over*, p. 120.
149 Swanton, *Sort of A Cricket Person*, p. 152.
150 Ibid.
151 Ibid., pp. 153–4.
152 Quoted in Addison, *Now the War is Over*, p. 120.
153 Swanton, *Sort of A Cricket Person*, p. 153.
154 Letter to the author, 1 April 1989.
155 Ibid. I'm grateful to Dicky Bird for showing me his diary.
156 Hoggart, *A Sort of Clowning*, p. 192.
157 Ibid., pp. 191–2.
158 Addison, *Now the War is Over*, p. 114.
159 Ibid., p. 113.
160 Ibid.
161 Susan Cooper, 'Snoek Piquante', in Sissons and French (eds.), *Age of Austerity*, pp. 56–7.
162 Kenneth O. Morgan, *Labour in Power*, OUP, 1984, p. ix.
163 A.N. Wilson, 'Miracle-Worker in the Charm School', *Spectator*, 30 June 1990.
164 Eric White, *The Arts Council of Great Britain*, Davis-Poynter, 1975, p. 5.
165 Quoted in Roy Shaw, *The Arts and the People*, Cape, 1987, p. 41.
166 Paul Ferris, *Sir Huge, The Life of Huw Wheldon*, Michael Joseph, 1990, pp. 69–75.
167 Addison, *Now the War is Over*, p. 136.
168 PRO, CAB 134/177, Note of Home Office Meeting, 19 January 1951.
169 'Sir William Haley: The Head of His Profession', *New Statesman*, 6 February 1954.
170 Asa Briggs, *The BBC, The First Fifty Years*, OUP, 1985, p. 249.
171 Frances Donaldson, *The British Council, The First Fifty Years*, Cape, 1984, pp. 63–7, pp. 142–5.
172 Briggs, *The BBC, The First Fifty Years*, p. 250.
173 Ibid. He was contemplating moving to Ireland though he believed 'it is no country in which to bring up children'. Michael Davie (ed.), *The Diaries of Evelyn Waugh*, Weidenfeld, 1976, p. 662, diary entry for 9 November 1946.
174 Ibid., p. 650.
175 Briggs, *The BBC, The First Fifty Years*, p. 252.
176 Conversation with Richard Hoggart, 17 July 1990.
177 Sir John Seeley, *The Expansion of England*, first published by Macmillan in 1883, 1907 edition, p. 10.
178 Conversation with Richard Hoggart, 17 July 1990.
179 Neville Cardus, *Sir Thomas Beecham, A Memoir*, Collins, 1961, pp. 81–122.
180 Angus Calder, *The People's War, Britain 1939–45*, Cape, 1969, p. 415.
181 Wilfred Pickles, *Between You and Me*, Werner Laurie, 1949, p. 174.
182 Ibid., p. 192.
183 Rex North, *The Butlin Story*, Jarrolds, 1962, p. 48.
184 Ibid., p. 59.
185 Ibid., p. 75.
186 Addison, *Now the War is Over*, p. 116.
187 North, *The Butlin Story*, pp. 87–8.
188 Holidaymaker quoted in Addison, *Now the War is Over*, p. 116.
189 Ibid.
190 Ibid., p. 118.
191 Ibid., p. 114.

192 I'm indebted to Paul Addison's 'Living It Up' chapter in *Now the War is Over*, for this fusillade of statistics.

193 Quoted in Addison, *Now the War is Over*, p. 139.

194 Harry Hopkins, *The New Look, A Social History of the Forties and Fifties in Britain*, Secker and Warburg, 1963, p. 95.

195 *1947: A Year to Remember*, Parkfield Pathé Video.

196 Nigel Nicolson (ed.), *Harold Nicolson, Diaries and Letters, 1939–45*, Fontana, 1970, pp. 282–3. Letter to Benedict and Nigel Nicolson, 20 February 1943.

197 Arthur Marwick, *British Society Since 1945*, Penguin, 1990 edition, p. 79.

198 T.S. Eliot, *Notes Towards the Definition of Culture*, Faber, 1948.

199 Edward Hyams, *The New Statesman, The History of the First Fifty Years 1913–1963*, Longman, 1963, p. 227, p. 275.

200 J.B. Priestley, *New Statesman*, 2 July 1949.

201 This is extracted from Connolly's editorial in the last issue of *Horizon*, published in January 1950. Robert Hewison's *In Anger, Culture in the Cold War 1945–60*, Weidenfeld, 1981, has been invaluable for plucking these pessimistic outbursts from the turn of the decades.

202 Vincent Brome, *J.B. Priestley*, Hamish Hamilton, 1988, pp. 477–9.

203 Hewison, *In Anger*, p. 10.

204 Ibid., p. 19.

205 Geoffrey Faber, 'The Critical Moment', *Spectator*, 5 November 1948.

206 Ibid.

207 R.H.S. Crossman (ed.), *The God That Failed*, Harper and Row, 1950.

208 For the involved and protracted story of *Animal Farm* see Orwell and Angus, *The Collected Essays, Journalism and Letters of George Orwell, Volume 3, As I Please, 1943–1945*, pp. 72, 118–19, 168–9, 207, 219, 406–7, 438, 444, 454.

209 J.B. Priestley, *The Arts Under Socialism*, Turnstile Press, 1947.

210 *Listener*, 30 January 1947.

211 Hewison, *In Anger*, pp. 6–10.

212 Sir Walter Moberly, *The Crisis in the Universities*, SCM Press, 1949.

213 Michael Oakeshott, 'The Universities' was first published in the *Cambridge Journal*, ii, 1948–49. It can most conveniently be found in Timothy Fuller, (ed.), *The Voice of Liberal Learning, Michael Oakeshott on Education*, Yale, 1989. This quote comes from p. 127.

214 Ibid., p. 129.

215 Isaiah Berlin, *Concepts and Categories, Philosophical Essays*, OUP, 1978, p. viii.

216 K.R. Popper, *The Open Society and Its Enemies, Volume I, Plato; Volume 2, Hegel and Marx*, Routledge, 1945.

217 Bryan Magee, *Popper*, Fontana, 1973, p. 12.

218 Quoted in ibid., p. 8.

219 F.R. Leavis, 'Memories of Wittgenstein', *The Human World*, No. 10 February 1973, p. 72.

220 F.R. Leavis, *Education and the University*, Chatto and Windus, 1943.

221 To experience Leavis *contra mundum* one only has to read his public lectures, e.g. 'Elites, Oligarchies and an Educated Public' delivered at York University in 1971 and reproduced in *The Human World*, No. 4, August 1971, pp. 1–22.

222 J.H. Plumb, 'The Atomic Historian', *New Statesman*, 1 August 1969.

223 H.R. Trevor-Roper, *The Last Days of Hitler*, third edition, Macmillan, 1967.

224 H.R. Trevor-Roper, 'The Century 1520–1640', *Economic History Review*, 2nd series, Vol. vii, 1954. The controversy, which deeply wounded the ageing Tawney, is described in John Kenyon, *The History Men, The Historical Profession in England since the Renaissance*, Weidenfeld, 1983, pp. 246–8.

225 A.J.P. Taylor, *The Habsburg Monarchy 1809–1918, A History of the Austrian Empire and Austria-Hungary*, Hamish Hamilton, 1948.

226 J.H. Plumb, *England in the Eighteenth Century, 1714–1815*, Pelican, 1950.

227 S.T. Bindoff, *Tudor England*, Pelican, 1950.

228 David Thompson, *England in the Nineteenth Century*, Pelican, 1950.

229 For the story of this Victorian publishing phenomenon see Kenyon, *The History Men*, pp. 71–84.

230 G.M. Trevelyan, *An Autobiography and Other Essays*, Longmans, 1949, pp. 48–9.

231 See 'Hitler's Reform', in Peter Hennessy, *Whitehall*, Secker and Warburg, 1989, chapter 3, pp. 88–119.

232 Alec Cairncross (ed.), *The Robert Hall Diaries, 1947–1953*, Unwin Hyman, 1989, p. 3, diary entry for 3 September 1947.

233 *The Collected Writings of John Maynard Keynes, Volume X, Essays in Biography*, Macmillan 1972, pp. 221–3; John Vaizey, 'Keynes and Cambridge' in Robert Skidelsky, *The End of the Keynesian Era*, Macmillan, 1977, pp. 10–17; Peter Clarke, *The Keynesian Revolution in the Making, 1924–1936*, Clarendon Press 1988, pp. 18–22, 167–8, 176–7.

234 F.A. Hayek, *The Road to Serfdom*, First Popular Edition, Routledge 1944, pp. 177–8.

235 Lord Robbins, *Autobiography of an Economist*, Macmillan 1971, Chapter X, pp. 213–40.

236 Donald G. MacRae, 'The Basis of Social Cohesion' in William Robson (ed.), *Man and the Social Sciences*, LSE/Allen and Unwin, 1972, pp. 53–4.

237 Frank Field, *Losing Out, The Emergence of Britain's Underclass*, Blackwell, 1989, pp. 1–2.

238 See Lavington, *Early British Computers*, Manchester University Press, 1985.

239 Winston S. Churchill, *The Second World War: The Commonwealth Alone*, Cassell, paperback edition, 1964, p. 55.

240 Marwick, *British Society Since 1945*, p. 91.

241 This view is put with especial force by Brian Oakley who directed Britain's Alvey Programme in the 1980s. See Peter Hennessy, 'Whitehall Watch: Britain's computer hopes are left on the launch pad', *Independent*, 25 June 1990.

242 J.M. Lee, *Reviewing the Machinery of Government 1942–1952, An Essay on the Anderson Committee and its Successors*, 1977, p. 30, available from Professor Michael Lee, Department of Politics, University of Bristol.

243 Ibid., p. 77.

244 Anon, *Science in War*, Penguin Special No. 74, 1940.

245 Solly Zuckerman, *From Apes to Warlords, An Autobiography, 1904–46*, paperback edition, Collins, 1988, p. 365.

246 Zuckerman's memo, dated 16 September 1945, is reproduced as appendix seven in ibid., pp. 425–6.

247 Ibid., p. 426.

248 Lee, *Reviewing the Machinery of Government*, p. 30.

249 See Margaret Gowing, *Independence and Deterrence: Britain and Atomic Energy 1945–1952*, Vols 1 and 2, Macmillan, 1974, and Hennessy, *Whitehall*, pp. 707–17.

250 Quoted in Hewison, *In Anger*, p. 28.

251 Ibid., pp. 14–16.

252 Ibid., p. 16.

253 'T.E.B. Clarke. Scriptwriter of best Ealing Comedies', Obituaries, *The Times*, 13 February 1989.

254 A.J.P. Taylor, *Beaverbrook*, Hamish Hamilton, 1972, p. 585.

255 Stephen Koss, *The Rise and Fall of the Political Press in Britain, Vol. 2: The Twentieth Century*, Hamish Hamilton, 1984, p. 638.

256 R.B. McCallum and Alison Readman, *The British General Election of 1945*, OUP, 1947, p. 181.

257 Koss, *The Rise and Fall of the Political Press in Britain, Vol. 2*, pp. 625–6.
258 Barrington-Ward Diary quoted in Koss, *The Rise and Fall of the Political Press in Britain, Vol. 2*, p. 617.
259 Donald McLachlan, *In the Chair, Barrington-Ward of The Times, 1927–1948*, Weidenfeld, 1971, pp. 280–1.
260 *Royal Commission on the Press, 1947–49*, Col. 7700, HMSO, 1949, p. 1.
261 Taylor, *Beaverbrook*, p. 584.
262 Denis Hamilton, *Editor-in-Chief, Fleet Street Memoirs*, Hamish Hamilton, 1989, pp. 55–9.
263 Ibid., p. 67.
264 Ibid.
265 Col. 7700, paragraph 650.
266 Geoffrey Robertson, *People Against Press, the Enquiry into the Press Council*, Quartet, 1983, pp. 9–10.
267 Francis Williams, *Parliament, Press and Public*, Heinemann, 1946, p. 136.
268 Quoted in Peter Hennessy, *What the Papers Never Said*, Politics Association, 1985, p. 81.
269 See Peter Hennessy, 'The Quality of Political Journalism', *Royal Society of Arts Journal*, no. 537b, Vol. CXXXV, November 1987, pp. 926–34.
270 I wrote the Kuh and Einzig cases up in 'Tap, tap: is MI5 still there?' *The Economist*, 6 March 1982, p. 28. The story of Williams' secretary, whom Attlee had sacked on the spot, is recalled in Jay, *Change and Fortune*, p. 135.
271 For an affectionate portrait of Massingham see his successor Alan Watkins' *Brief Lives*, Hamish Hamilton, 1982, pp. 112–23.
272 James Margach, *The Anatomy of Power; An Enquiry into the Personality of Leadership*, W.H. Allen, 1979, p. 146.
273 Ibid.
274 For a polemical critique of the lobby system see Michael Cockerell, Peter Hennessy and David Walker, *Sources Close to the Prime Minister*, Macmillan, 1984, Papermac, 1985.
275 PEP, *Report on the British Press*, Political and Economic Planning, 1938.
276 See Glasgow University Media Group, *Bad News* (Vol. 1), Routledge, 1976; (Vol. 2) *More Bad News*, Routledge, 1980; *War and Peace News*, Open University Press, 1985; *Seeing and Believing, The Influence of Television*, Routledge, 1990.
277 Hewison, *In Anger*, p. 14.
278 *1945: A Year to Remember*, Parkfield Pathé video, 1990.
279 *1947: A Year to Remember.*
280 Ibid.
281 *1946: A Year to Remember*, Parkfield Pathé video, 1990.
282 *1947: A Year to Remember.*
283 Ibid.
284 *1946: A Year to Remember.*
285 Ibid.
286 Ibid.
287 *1947: A Year to Remember.*
288 Ibid.
289 Ian Mikardo, *Backbencher*, Weidenfeld, 1988, p. 100.
290 Ibid., pp. 94–5.
291 Quoted in Thompson, *The Day Before Yesterday*, p. 31.
292 Quoted in ibid., p. 32.
293 Ibid.
294 Its principal authors were Foot, Crossman and Mikardo. Mikardo, *Backbencher*, p. 110.

295 Ibid., p. 107.
296 Denis Healey, *The Time of My Life*, Michael Joseph, 1989, p. 106.
297 *Cards on the Table*, Labour Party, 1947, pp. 12–13.
298 Healey, *The Time of My Life, p. 107.*
299 PRO, FO 800/493/PLT/47/8.
300 PRO, CAB 21/1701, 'Organisation of Cabinet Committees, 1946–47', Bridges to Brook, 5 July 1946.
301 Dalton, *High Tide and After*, pp. 236–7.
302 Pimlott (ed.), *The Political Diary of Hugh Dalton*, p. 397, diary entry for 26 July 1947.
303 Jay, *Change and Fortune*, p. 135. Conversation with Lord Jay, 10 August, 1990.
304 Kenneth Harris, *Attlee*, Weidenfeld, 1982, p. 347. For the *Daily Mail* story see Pimlott, *Hugh Dalton*, p. 514.
305 Harris, *Attlee*, pp. 347–50.
306 Attlee to Morrison, 20 September 1947, quoted in Donoughue and Jones, *Herbert Morrison*, p. 421.
307 Cairncross, *Years of Recovery*, p. 51.
308 Letter from Lord Croham to the author, 27 June 1979.
309 Ralph Miliband, *Parliamentary Socialism, A Study in the Politics of Labour*, first published 1961, paperback edition Merlin, 1973, p. 300.
310 Ibid., p. 301.
311 PRO, CAB 128/10, CM (47) 42nd. Conclusions.
312 Don Cook, *Forging The Alliance, NATO 1945 to 1950*, Secker and Warburg, 1989, p. 138.
313 PRO, CAB 128/10.
314 PRO, CAB 128/10, CM (47) 64th. Conclusions,
315 PRO, CAB 128/10, CM (47) 80th. Conclusions.
316 Kenneth O. Morgan, 'Nationalisation and Privatisation', *Contemporary Record*, Vol. 2, No. 4, Winter 1988, pp. 32–3.
317 Quoted in Pimlott, *Hugh Dalton*, p. 518.
318 Pimlott (ed.), *The Political Diary of Hugh Dalton*, p. 419.
319 Ibid., pp. 419–20.
320 Pimlott, *Hugh Dalton*, pp. 425–30.
321 Ibid., pp. 540–4.
322 *Clem Attlee, Granada Historical Records Interview*, Granada, 1967, p. 45.
323 Private information.
324 Davenport, *Memoirs of a City Radical*, pp. 172–3.
325 Pimlott, *Hugh Dalton*, pp. 638–40.
326 Cairncross (ed.), *The Robert Hall Diaries, 1947–1953*, p. 19.
327 Douglas Jay, 'The Attlee Government', *Contemporary Record*, Vol. 2, No. 4, winter 1988.

CHAPTER 9

Partners, Pounds and Productivity

1 Quoted in Don Cook, *Forging the Alliance: NATO 1945 to 1950*, Secker and Warburg, 1989, p. 125.
2 Quoted in Michael Charlton, *The Price of Victory*, BBC, 1983, p. 77.
3 Quoted in Charlton, *The Price of Victory*, p. 61.
4 Quoted in Paul Addison, *Now the War is Over, A Social History of Britain 1945–51*, BBC and Cape, 1985, pp. 195–6.
5 Quoted in Charlton, *The Price of Victory*, p. 58.
6 Bevin noticed this and told Acheson about it. Cook, *Forging the Alliance*, p. 93.

7 Michael McGwire, *The Genesis of Soviet Threat Perceptions*, Brookings, 1987, pp. 33–4.

8 Ibid., p. 36.

9 Sheila Kerr, 'The Secret Hotline to Moscow: Donald Maclean and the Berlin Crisis of 1948', in Anne Deighton (ed.), *Britain and the First Cold War*, Macmillan, 1990, pp. 71–87.

10 See C.J. Morris and W.S. Lucas, 'A Very British Crusade: The Information Research Department and the Start of the Cold War', in Richard J. Aldrich (ed.), *British Intelligence Strategy and the cold war, 1945–51*, Routledge, 1992 (forthcoming).

11 John Erickson, 'Threat Identification and Strategic Appraisal by the Soviet Union 1930–41', in E.R. May (ed.), *Knowing One's Enemies: Intelligence Assessment Before the Two World Wars*, Princeton, 1986, p. 421.

12 Peter Hennessy and Kathleen Townsend, 'The Documentary Spoor of Burgess and Maclean', *Intelligence and National Security*, Vol. 2, No. 2, April 1987, pp. 291–301.

13 All I could say was, 'It's you, Roger. It's you.' Conversation with Lord Sherfield, 16 December 1987.

14 Charlton, *The Price of Victory*, p. 58.

15 Ibid.

16 Ibid., p. 59.

17 'CEEC Washington Delegation to Participating Governments', 31 October 1947, *Foreign Relations of the United States*, 1947, Vol. iii, p. 458.

18 PRO, T 236/1893, Hall-Patch to Foreign Office, 12 May 1948.

19 Henry Pelling, *Britain and the Marshall Plan*, Macmillan, 1988, p. 65.

20 PRO, FO 371/77985, FO to Washington, 10 March 1949.

21 Bevin recalled the episode in his flat for Harold Nicolson who put it in his diary. Nigel Nicolson (ed.), *Harold Nicolson, Diaries and Letters, 1945–62*, Fontana, 1971, p. 107.

22 Acheson was more sympathetic to Bevin's 'summer storm' outbursts of temper. See *Present At The Creation*, Hamish Hamilton, 1970, p. 251.

23 Cook, *Forging the Alliance*, pp. 107–8.

24 Alan Bullock, *Ernest Bevin, Foreign Secretary, 1945–1951*, Heinemann, 1983, p. 498.

25 PRO, FO 371/64250, Minutes of Bevin-Marshall meetings, 17–18 Dec. 1947.

26 Cook, *Forging the Alliance*, p. 222.

27 Ibid., p. 224.

28 Sir Nicholas Henderson, *The Birth of NATO*, Weidenfeld, 1982, pp. 10–11.

29 Alan Milward, *The Reconstruction of Western Europe, 1945–51*, Methuen, 1984, footnote 34 which traverses pp. 71–2.

30 Lucius D. Clay, *Decision in Germany*, Doubleday, 1950, pp. 354–5.

31 The telegram is preserved in the Clay Papers and quoted in Avi Shlaim, *The United States and the Berlin Blockade, 1948–49, A Study in Crisis Decision-making*, University of California, 1983, p. 106.

32 Ibid., p. 107.

33 Quoted in Stephen E. Ambrose, *Rise to Globalism, American Foreign Policy, 1938–1970*, Penguin, 1971, p. 165.

34 Nigel Hamilton, *Monty, The Field Marshal, 1944–1976*, Hamish Hamilton, 1986, pp. 725–6.

35 Ambrose, *Rise to Globalism*, p. 165.

36 Cook, *Forging the Alliance*, p. 129.

37 *Foreign Relations of the United States, 1948*, Vol. iii, pp. 32–3.

38 He peppered them with Cabinet papers in the first days of 1948, PRO, CAB 129/23; CP(48)5, 5 January 1948; CP(48)6, 4 January 1948.

39 H of C *Official Report*, 22 January 1948.

40 Charlton, *Price of Victory*, p. 54.

41 PRO, CAB 129/23.

42 Roy Jenkins, *Nine Men of Power*, Hamish Hamilton, 1974, pp. 67–8.

43 See Ann and John Tusa, *The Berlin Blockade*, Coronet, 1988, Chapter 5, 'Putting on the Squeeze', pp. 124–51.

44 Quoted in Cook, *Forging the Alliance*, p. 151.

45 Ibid., pp. 151–2.

46 Bullock, *Ernest Bevin, Foreign Secretary*, pp. 575–6.

47 Keith Jeffery and Peter Hennessy, *States of Emergency*, pp. 193–5.

48 Letter from Sir Patrick Nairne, 12 October 1990.

49 Cook, *Forging the Alliance*, pp. 119–21.

50 James Lansdale Hodson, *Thunder in the Heavens*, Wingate, 1950, p. 104.

51 Ibid., p. 139.

52 Ibid., p. 142.

53 A BBC Home Service talk, 'A Sense of the Future', reprinted in J. Bronowski, *A Sense of the Future, Essays in Natural Philosophy*, MIT, 1977.

54 *FRUS*, 1948, Vol. ii, pp. 895–6.

55 As a young philosophy student, Renford Bambrough heard Russell deliver this view in postwar Cambridge. Conversation with Renford Bambrough, 14 February 1992.

56 Kerr, 'The Secret Hotline to Moscow' in Deighton (ed.), *Britain and the First Cold War*, p. 78 and footnote 51 on p. 86.

57 Alec Cairncross (ed.), *The Robert Hall Diaries, 1947–1953*, Unwin Hyman, 1989, p. 20, diary entry for 24 March 1948.

58 Kerr, 'The Secret Hotline to Moscow' in Deighton (ed.), *Britain and the First Cold War*, p. 78.

59 PRO, CAB 16/388. British Joint Services Mission to Cabinet Office, 16 April 1948.

60 Quoted in *The World Today*, Vol. 16, August 1960, p. 320.

61 Tony Benn, *Arguments for Democracy*, Penguin, 1982, pp. 12–13.

62 Ibid., p. 13.

63 Sir Frank Cooper, 'Corridors of Power', pp. 3–4, unpublished address to the American alumni of Pembroke College, Oxford. I am grateful to Sir Frank for sending me a copy. Letter from Sir Frank Cooper, 4 July 1990. Sir Frank Cooper interviewed for the BBC Radio 4 *Analysis* programme *Moneybags and Brains*, 24 September 1990.

64 Bullock, *Ernest Bevin, Foreign Secretary*, p. 576.

65 Walter Millis (ed.), *The Forrestal Diaries, The Inner History of the Cold War*, Cassell, 1952, p. 428, diary entry for 2 July 1948.

66 Margaret Gowing, *Independence and Deterrence, Britain and Atomic Energy 1945–1952*, Vol. I, *Policy Making*, Macmillan, 1974, footnote at bottom of p. 310. Its minutes can be found at the PRO in CAB 130/88.

67 Bullock, *Ernest Bevin, Foreign Secretary*, p. 577, footnote 7.

68 PRO, CAB 21/2244, 'United States Heavy Bombers', Brook to Attlee, September 1948.

69 Gowing, *Independence and Deterrence*, Vol. 1, p. 311, footnote.

70 Lord Sherfield speaking in *A Bloody Union Jack on Top of It*, Programme 1: an 'Of Course' Decision, BBC Radio 4, 5 May 1988. For the full text of the 'modus vivendi' see Gowing, *Independence and Deterrence*, Vol. 1, pp. 266–72.

71 Ibid., pp. 311–12.

72 Ibid., p. 316.

73 Ibid., p. 413.

74 Private information.

75 PRO, FO 371/97592.

76 Henderson, *The Birth of NATO*, p. 34.

77 George Kennan, *Memoirs 1925–1950*, Hutchinson, 1968, pp. 410–11; p. 365.

78 Cook, *Forging the Alliance*, p. 207.

79 The full treaty is reproduced in Appendix B of Henderson's *The Birth of NATO*, pp. 119–22.

80   Ibid., pp. viii–ix.
81   Bullock, *Ernest Bevin, Foreign Secretary*, p. 672.
82   Ibid.
83   Cook, *Forging the Alliance*, p. 221.
84   Tusa and Tusa, *The Berlin Blockade*, p. 452.
85   Churchill to Cripps, 26 April 1948, quoted in Martin Gilbert, *Never Despair, Winston S. Churchill, 1945–1965*, Heinemann, 1988, p. 406.
86   Ibid., pp. 407–8.
87   As recalled by his private secretary, Sir Roderick Barclay, in Charlton, *The Price of Victory*, p. 75.
88   Ibid., p. 77.
89   Ibid., p. 79.
90   Eric Roll, *Crowded Hours*, Faber, 1985, p. 58.
91   Edwin Plowden, *An Industrialist in the Treasury, The Postwar Years*, Deutsch, 1989, p. 72.
92   Ibid., p. 73.
93   Lord Plowden's note of the meeting is preserved in PRO, FO 371/77933, 'Note of Four Conversations with M. Monnet between March 3rd and March 7th, 1949, at one of which was present the Chancellor of the Exchequer'.
94   Plowden, *An Industrialist in the Treasury*, pp. 73–4.
95   Quoted in Charlton, *The Price of Victory*, p. 83.
96   Richard Mayne, *The Recovery of Europe*, Weidenfeld, 1970, p. 175.
97   Cairncross (ed.), *The Robert Hall Diaries*, 1947–53, p. 57, diary entry for 26 May 1949.
98   Plowden, *An Industrialist in the Treasury*, p. 75.
99   Jean Monnet, *Memoirs*, Collins, 1978, pp. 280–1.
100 Plowden, *An Industrialist in the Treasury*, pp. 75–6.
101 Lord Plowden quoted in Charlton, *The Price of Victory*, p. 87.
102 Milward, *The Reconstruction of Western Europe 1945–51*, p. 173, footnote.
103 PRO, FO 371/62552, Hall-Patch to Bevin, 7 August 1947.
104 Ibid.
105 Lord Franks quoted in Charlton, *The Price of Victory*, p. 71.
106 Ibid., p. 70.
107 M.R.D. Foot (ed.), *Holland At War Against Hitler, Anglo–Dutch Relations 1940–1945*, Frank Cass, 1990, p. 224.
108 Dean Acheson, *Present at the Creation, My Years in the State Department*, Hamish Hamilton, 1970, pp. 385–7.
109 Monnet, *Memoirs*, p. 306.
110 Lord Plowden quoted in Charlton, *The Price of Victory*, p. 87.
111 Henry Pelling, *Winston Churchill*, Macmillan, 1974, p. 505.
112 Robert Cecil interviewed for *Moneybags and Brains*, 26 September 1990.
113 Ibid.
114 Acheson, *Present at the Creation*, p. 323.
115 Ibid., pp. 387–8.
116 Lord Hunt of Tanworth interviewed for *Moneybags and Brains*, 15 October 1990.
117 Sir Nicholas Henderson interviewed for *Moneybags and Brains*, 27 September 1990.
118 Lucius Battle interviewed for *Moneybags and Brains*, 2 October 1990.
119 Dr Henry Kissinger interviewed for *Moneybags and Brains*, 1 October 1990.
120 Private information.
121 Dr Paul Addison interviewed for *Moneybags and Brains*, 12 October 1990.
122 Cairncross (ed.), *The Robert Hall Diaries, 1947–1953*, p. 161, diary entry for 19 July 1951.
123 Lord Franks interviewed for *Moneybags and Brains*, 12 October 1990.
124 Ibid.

125 PRO, CAB 134/220, EPC(49) 24th Meeting, 1 July 1949.
126 Paul Nitze interviewed for *Moneybags and Brains*, 2 October 1990.
127 Ibid.
128 Sir Alec Cairncross, *Years of Recovery, British Economic Policy 1945–51*, Methuen, 1985, p. 165.
129 Ibid., pp. 165–6.
130 PRO, T236 (no piece numbers), Rowe-Dutton to Eady, 26 January 1948.
131 R.W.B. Clarke to Edward Playfair and Sir Henry Wilson-Smith, 5 June 1948.
132 Ibid. Note by Wilson-Smith, 17 June 1948.
133 Cairncross, *Years of Recovery*, pp. 171–2.
134 PRO, CAB 134/222, EPC(49)63, 6 June 1949, 'Report on a visit to the United States in June 1949'.
135 Ben Pimlott (ed.), *The Political Diary of Hugh Dalton, 1918–40, 1945–60*, Cape, 1986, pp. 450–1, entry for 15 June 1949.
136 PRO, CAB 21/2245, Hall to Attlee, 29 June 1949.
137 Plowden, *An Industrialist in the Treasury*, p. 57.
138 PRO, T 269/1, Eady to Bridges, 15 June 1949.
139 Ibid., Hall to Bridges, 16 June 1949.
140 Ibid., Eady to Bridges, 15 June 1949.
141 For a vivid account of the 1931 trauma, see A.J.P. Taylor, *English History, 1914–1945*, OUP, 1965, pp. 183–5.
142 PRO, CAB 134/222, EPC(49)72, 'The Dollar Situation', Memorandum by the Chancellor of the Exchequer, 28 June 1949.
143 PRO, CAB 134/220, EPC(49) 24th Meeting, 1 July 1949.
144 Ibid.
145 Cairncross (ed.), *The Robert Hall Diaries*, pp. 63–4.
146 Ibid.
147 Plowden, *An Industrialist in the Treasury*, p. 58.
148 Douglas Jay, *Change and Fortune, A Political Record*, Hutchinson, 1980, p. 187.
149 Ibid. Cairncross (ed.), *The Robert Hall Diaries*, p. 69, diary entry for 29 July 1949.
150 Ibid. and PRO, CAB 128/16, CM(49) 51st Conclusions, 29 July, 1949, Item 2.
151 The letter is quoted in Jay, *Change and Fortune*, pp. 188–9.
152 PRO, CAB 128/16, CM(49) 53rd Conclusions, 29 August 1949, Item 1.
153 Ibid.
154 PRO, PREM 8/973, 'Devaluation'.
155 Pelling, *Britain and the Marshall Plan*, p. 85.
156 Peter Hennessy and Malcolm Brown, 'Cripps and the Search for a Whiter Loaf', *The Times*, 4 January 1980.
157 Cairncross, *Years of Recovery*, p. 186.
158 Acheson, *Present at the Creation*, p. 325.
159 Cairncross, *Years of Recovery*, p. 186.
160 Peter Hennessy and Malcolm Brown, 'Deciphering the "Rose" Code', *The Times*, 3 January 1980.
161 Hennessy and Brown, 'Cripps and the Search for a Whiter Loaf'.
162 Lord Plowden, Institute of Historical Research Seminar, 22 February 1989.
163 Hennessy and Brown, 'Cripps and the Search for a Whiter Loaf'.
164 Cairncross (ed.), *The Robert Hall Diaries 1947–1953*, p. 87, diary entry for 26 September 1949.
165 Hennessy and Brown, 'Cripps and the Search for a Whiter Loaf'.
166 Kenneth O. Morgan, *Labour in Power*, OUP, 1984, pp. 362–3.
167 The text of Cripps' speech is appended to the Cabinet Minutes for the 17 September meeting. PRO, CAB 128/16, CM(49) 55th Conclusions.
168 Ibid.

169 Jim Tomlinson, *A Missed Opportunity? Labour and the Productivity Problem 1945–51*, paper presented by Dr Tomlinson to the Economic History Society Conference in April 1989, p. 10.

170 Quoted in Addison, *Now the War Is Over*, p. 195.

171 Tomlinson, *A Missed Opportunity?*, p. 11.

172 Quoted in ibid., p. 5.

173 For the construction of the CEPS see Plowden, *An Industrialist in the Treasury*, pp. 7, 12.

174 Cairncross (ed.), *The Robert Hall Diaries 1947–53*, p. 4 and p. 6.

175 Plowden, *An Industrialist in the Treasury*, p. 23.

176 For a description of Monnet's plan, his people and his methods see Monnet, *Memoirs*, Chapter 10, 'The Modernization of France', pp. 232–63.

177 Frances Lynch, 'France' in Andrew Graham with Anthony Seldon, *Government and Economies in the Postwar World*, Routledge, 1990, p. 56.

178 Ibid., p. 65.

179 Quoted in ibid., p. 62.

180 PRO, T 273/9.

181 For a full account of the 1946 debate within the permanent secretaries' 'club' see Peter Hennessy, *Whitehall*, Secker and Warburg, 1989, pp. 122–5.

182 Tony Benn, *Out of the Wilderness, Diaries 1963–67*, Hutchinson, 1987, diary entry for 28 May 1965, p. 264.

183 David Marquand, *The Unprincipled Society, New Demands and Old Politics*, Cape, 1988, pp. 102–7.

184 Martin Chick, *Investment, Rationalisation and Productivity: The Case of the Iron and Steel Industry*, p. 8, paper delivered at a Conference on Labour and Private Industry 1945–51, London School of Economics, 10 September 1990.

185 Ibid., p. 9.

186 Monnet, *Memoirs*, pp. 248–9.

187 Ibid., p. 234.

188 Ibid., p. 237.

189 H of C *Official Report*, Vol. 468, Col. 182, 28 September 1949. I am indebted on the subject of 'The Attlee Governments and Private Industry' to the paper presented to the LSE Conference on 10 September 1990 by Dr Neil Rollings.

190 Introducing her paper at the LSE Conference on Labour's 'Policy on Monopolies and Cartels'.

191 Cmd 7321, HMSO, 1948.

192 Morgan, *Labour in Power*, p. 372.

193 PRO, CAB 129/32, Part 2, CP(49)28. 'Wage Movements in 1948. Memorandum by the Minister of Labour and National Service', 15 February 1949.

194 Morgan, *Labour in Power*, p. 373.

195 Ibid., p. 379.

196 Central Intelligence Agency, *Review of the World Situation*, CIA 6-49, 15 June 1949, p. 2. Copy available in the British Library Archives, Boston Spa, Lincolnshire. I am very grateful to Michael Bilton of Yorkshire Television for bringing it to my attention.

197 Ibid., pp. 3, 4.

198 Ibid., p. 4.

199 Ibid.

200 Ibid., p. 5.

CHAPTER 10

Shot and Shell

1   Roy Hattersley, *Attlee: The Reasonable Revolutionary*, BBC2, 1983.
2   Lord Croham, interviewed for the BBC Radio 4 *Analysis* programme *Moneybags and Brains*, 10 October 1990.
3   Lord Franks, interviewed for *Moneybags and Brains*, 12 October 1990.
4   Paul Nitze, interviewed for *Moneybags and Brains*, 2 October 1990.
5   *Clem Attlee, Granada Historical Records Interview*, Granada, 1967, p. 55.
6   Quoted in Michael Foot, *Aneurin Bevan, A Biography: Vol. Two 1945–1960*, Davis Poynter, 1973, p. 335.
7   Bernard Donoughue and G.W. Jones, *Herbert Morrison, Portrait of a Politician*, Weidenfeld, 1973, p. 981.
8   Bernard Crick, *George Orwell, A Life*, Secker and Warburg, 1980, p. 404.
9   Conversation with David Astor, 23 April 1992.
10 Peter Hennessy, *The Lion and the Unicorn Repolished*, University of Reading Department of Politics, Occasional Paper No. 1, February 1990.
11 Peter Hennessy, unpublished *Diary*, entry for 18 May 1990.
12 Tony Benn, at the Institute of Historical Research, 12 December 1990.
13 Quoted in Kenneth O. Morgan, *Labour in Power*, OUP, 1984, p. 402.
14 Donoughue and Jones, *Herbert Morrison*, p. 449.
15 Lord Jay told me his 'Stafford-and-God' theory on more than one occasion. See my 'The Attlee Governments 1945–1951' in Peter Hennessy and Anthony Seldon (eds), *Ruling Performance: British Governments from Attlee to Thatcher*, Blackwell, 1987, p. 46.
16 Martin Gilbert, *Never Despair, Winston S. Churchill, 1945–1965*, Heinemann, 1988, p. 510.
17 For an excellent summary of this debate see Dennis Kavanagh and Peter Morris, *Consensus Politics from Attlee to Thatcher*, Blackwell, 1CBH, 1989.
18 David Butler, *British General Elections since 1945*, Blackwell, ICBH, 1989, pp. 10–11.
19 Kenneth Harris, *Attlee*, Weidenfeld, 1982, pp. 445–6.
20 Butler, *British General Elections since 1945*, p. 11.
21 Harris, *Attlee*, p. 412.
22 *Granada Historical Records Interview*, p. 45.
23 Harris, *Attlee*, pp. 445–6; Burridge, *Clement Attlee: A Political Biography*, Cape, 1985, pp. 293–4.
24 J.K. Galbraith, 'The death of liberalism', *Observer*, 26 March 1989.
25 *Kenneth Younger Diary*, entry for 27 February 1950. The Younger Diary is, as yet, unpublished. I am grateful to its editor, Professor Geoffrey Warner, for showing it to me.
26 Harris, *Attlee*, p. 446.
27 *Hennessy Diary*, 5 July 1991.
28 Alan Bullock, *Ernest Bevin, Foreign Secretary, 1945–1951*, Heinemann, 1983, p. 744; Dean Acheson, *Present at the Creation, My Years in the State Department*, Hamish Hamilton, 1970, p. 349.
29 Central Intelligence Agency *Review of the World Situation*, CIA 6–49, 15 June 1949, p. 8.
30 Jean Monnet, *Memoirs*, Collins, 1978, p. 293.
31 Ibid., p. 292.
32 Ibid., p. 291.
33 Ibid., p. 298.
34 Quoted in Michael Charlton, *The Price of Victory*, BBC, 1983, p. 108.
35 Ibid., p. 105.

36   Monnet, *Memoirs*, p. 311.
37   Ibid., pp. 281–2.
38   Ibid., p. 450.
39   Ibid., p. 306.
40   Charlton, *The Price of Victory*, p. 307.
41   Harold Wilson, *Memoirs, 1916–1964: The Making of a Prime Minister*, Weidenfeld and Michael Joseph, 1986, pp. 56–7.
42   Monnet, *Memoirs*, p. 308.
43   Acheson, *Present at the Creation*, pp. 382–4.
44   Kenneth Younger's Diary is especially eloquent on Bevin's greatly diminished capacities.
45   Henry Pelling, *Britain and the Marshall Plan*, Macmillan, 1988, pp. 88–91. The 'superman' jibe is contained in a telegraph from Bevin to Franks in Washington on 23 December 1949 preserved in PRO, FO 800/516.
46   Holmes to Acheson, 7 January 1950, *FRUS 1950*, iii, p. 616.
47   Ibid.
48   Acheson, *Present at the Creation*, p. 385.
49   Ibid.
50   Dean Acheson, *Sketches from Life of Men I have Known*, Hamish Hamilton, 1961, p. 44.
51   PRO, PREM 8/1428. 'Record of conversation between Mr Bevin, Mr Acheson and M. Schuman'; 11 May, 1950.
52   Ibid.
53   Acheson, *Sketches from Life*, p. 46.
54   I have been working from a copy of the first meeting of GEN 322 contained in PRO, PREM 8/1428.
55   *The Memoirs of Lord Gladwyn*, Weidenfeld, 1972, p. 176.
56   *Younger Diary*, entry for 14 May 1950.
57   Ibid.
58   Quoted in Charlton, *The Price of Victory*, pp. 120–1.
59   PRO, PREM 8/1428.
60   *Younger Diary*, entry for 12 June 1950.
61   Ibid.
62   Edwin Plowden, *An Industrialist in the Treasury, The Postwar Years*, Andre Deutsch, 1989, p. 86.
63   Alec Cairncross (ed.), *The Robert Hall Diaries, 1947–1953*, Unwin Hyman, 1989, p. 112, entry for 17 May 1950.
64   PRO, PREM 8/1428, Robert Hall, 'Franco–German Steel and Coal Authority', 11 May 1950.
65   PRO, CAB 134/228.
66   PRO, CAB 134/295, 'Notes of a meeting held at the Hyde Park Hotel SW1, on 16 May 1950, with M. Jean Monnet, Commissioner General of Planning for the French Government'.
67   Lord Sherfield, quoted in Peter Hennessy and Caroline Anstey, *Moneybags and Brains: The Anglo-American 'Special Relationship' since 1945*, Strathclyde, *Analysis* Paper No. 1, Department of Government, Strathclyde University, 1990, p. 9.
68   Plowden, *An Industrialist in the Treasury*, p. 89.
69   Cairncross (ed.), *The Diaries of Robert Hall, 1947–1953*, p. 113, entry for 17 May 1950.
70   PRO, CAB 134/293, FO(50), 2nd meeting, 17 May 1950.
71   PRO, T 229/749. 'Interim Report by Officials on Proposed Franco-German Steel Authority; 17 May 1950.'
72   Monnet, *Memoirs*, p. 308.
73   Ibid., p. 313.
74   Ibid.

75 Hennessy and Anstey, *Moneybags and Brains*, p. 8.
76 PRO, CAB 129/40, 'Integration of French and German Coal and Steel Industries, Report by Committee of Officials', 2 June 1950.
77 Plowden, *An Industrialist in the Treasury*, p. 91.
78 *Younger Diary*, entry for 12 June 1950.
79 Leslie Hunter, *The Road to Brighton Pier*, Arthur Barker, 1959, p. 13.
80 PRO, CAB 128/17, CM(50) 34th Conclusions, 2 June 1950.
81 Ibid.
82 Douglas Jay, *Change and Fortune, A Political Record*, Hutchinson, 1980, p. 199.
83 PRO, CAB 129/48, C(51)32, 29 November 1951.
84 PRO, FO 371/85847 Bevin to Franks, 5 June 1950.
85 PRO, PREM 8/1428, Attlee to Bevin, 7 June 1950.
86 Quoted in Monnet, *Memoirs*, p. 314.
87 As recalled by Etienne Hirsch in Charlton, *The Price of Victory*, p. 122. Lord Sherfield expressed his bafflement to me at the Twenty-Fifth Anniversary Dinner of the Kennedy Scholars on 29 May 1990.
88 PRO, CAB 129/40, CP(50)120, 2 June 1950.
89 Alan Milward, *The Reconstruction of Western Europe, 1945–51*, Methuen, 1984, p. 406.
90 Monnet, *Memoirs*, pp. 316–7.
91 PRO, PREM 11/2993. 'Visit of the Prime Minister and Foreign Secretary to Bonn, August 10–11, 1960'. 'Record of a Meeting at the Palais Schaumberg, 10 August 1960.
92 Ibid.
93 Max Hastings, like most scholars who have written about Korea, remains puzzled by the continuing neglect of it, certainly in the popular mind, compared to World War II which predated it and Vietnam which came after and scarred the American psyche so deeply. Max Hastings, *The Korean War*, Pan, 1988, p. xiii.
94 Anthony Farrar-Hockley, *The British Part in the Korean War*: Vol. 1; *A Distant Obligation*, HMSO, 1990, pp. 120–40.
95 PRO, PREM 8/1405/Part I, Franks to Attlee, 15 July 1950.
96 Conversation with Lord Franks, 12 October 1990 for *Moneybags and Brains*.
97 See Geoffrey Smith, *Reagan and Thatcher, The Extraordinary Story of the 'Special Relationship'*, Bodley Head, 1990.
98 Glenn Frankel, 'Britain Reclaiming Role as Top US Ally', *Washington Post*, 19 January 1991.
99 Peter Hennessy, 'Whitehall Watch: Closer links as special friends go to war again', *Independent*, 28 January 1991.
100 'Back to the bulldog stuff', *The Economist*, 19 January 1991.
101 *Hennessy Diary*, entry for 24 August 1990.
102 Quoted in Hastings, *The Korean War*, p. 261.
103 *Hennessy Diary*, entry for 27 August 1990.
104 Quoted in Farrar-Hockley, *A Distant Obligation*, p. 33.
105 Callum MacDonald, *Britain and the Korean War*, Blackwell, 1990, p. 11.
106 I.F. Stone, *The Hidden History of the Korean War*, Monthly Review reprint, 1970.
107 *Khruschev Remembers*, Andre Deutsch, 1971, pp. 367–8.
108 *Younger Diary*, entry for 6 July 1950.
109 Conversation with Lord Franks, 12 October 1990.
110 Cook, *Forging the Alliance*, pp. 250–6.
111 Sir Anthony Farrar-Hockley, letter to the author, 29 October 1990 for *Moneybags and Brains*.
112 Richard Rovere, *Senator Joe McCarthy*, Meridian, 1960.
113 Peter Hennessy and Gail Brownfeld, 'Britain's Cold War Security Purge, The Origins of Positive Vetting', *The Historical Journal*, 25, 4 (1982), pp. 969–70.

114 Ibid., p. 965.

115 PRO. CAB 21/2248, Brook to Attlee, 'Overseas Operations (Security of Forces Bill)', 15 November 1950.

116 Peter Hennessy and Geoffrey Warner, 'Donald Maclean's invaluable services to Stalin disclosed', *The Times*, 2 January 1981.

117 Peter Hennessy, 'Burgess knew US analysis of Russian aid', *The Times*, 2 February 1981.

118 Hennessy and Brownfeld, 'Britain's Cold War Security Purge', pp. 965–73.

119 Quoted in Hennessy and Anstey, *Moneybags and Brains*, p. 7.

120 Conversation with Lord Franks, 12 October 1990 for *Moneybags and Brains*.

121 Bullock, *Ernest Bevin, Foreign Secretary*, p. 895.

122 Daniel Yergin, *Shattered Peace, The Origins of the Cold War and the National Security State*, Houghton Mifflin, 1977, pp. 401–3.

123 PRO, DEFE 6/14, JP(50)90 (Final), 'The Spread of Russian Communism', 11 July 1950.

124 IOLR, JIC (48) (0).

125 PRO, DEFE 6/14, JP (50) 90.

126 Ibid.

127 Ibid.

128 Ibid.

129 Peter G. Boyle, 'Oliver Franks and the Washington Embassy, 1948–52' in Zametica (ed.), *British Officials and British Foreign Policy, 1945–51*, Leicester University Press, 1990, p. 200.

130 Conversation with Lord Franks, 12 October 1990 for *Moneybags and Brains*. The original of the Franks telegram of 23 July 1950 can be found at the PRO in FO 371/FK 1022/198.

131 Conversation with Lord Franks, 12 October 1990 for *Moneybags and Brains*.

132 Ibid.

133 Plowden, *An Industrialist in the Treasury*, Chapter twelve, pp. 125–33.

134 Richard Hoggart, *A Sort of Clowning, Life and Times: 1940–59*, Chatto, 1990, p. 198.

135 Ibid., pp. 198–9

136 Cairncross, (ed.), *The Robert Hall Diaries, 1947–1953*, pp. 114–15.

137 Ibid., p. 120. Diary entry for 28 June 1950.

138 Ibid., pp. 155–6. Diary entry for 30 April 1951.

139 Quoted in Hennessy and Anstey, *Moneybags and Brains*, p. 6.

140 Conversation with Lord Plowden, 4 March 1991.

141 Lord Graham is probably referring to the *Economic Survey for 1951* which was dominated by the Korean War rearmament. Cmd 8195, HMSO, April 1951.

142 Quoted in Hennessy and Anstey, *Moneybags and Brains*, p. 6.

143 Thelma Liesner, *One Hundred Years of Economic Statistics*, Economist Publications, 1989, p. 53.

144 Hennessy and Anstey, *Moneybags and Brains*, p. 7.

145 Quoted in Peter Hennessy, 'The economic legacy of a forgotten war', *Director*, November 1990, p. 28.

146 Ibid.

147 Private information.

148 Sidney Pollard, *The Wasting of the British Economy*, Croom Helm, 1984 edition, p. 37.

149 Plowden, *An Industrialist in the Treasury*, p. 119.

150 Charles Webster, *The Health Services Since the War*, Vol. I, HMSO, 1988, p. 134.

151 Ibid.

152 Ibid., p. 157.

153 Ibid., p. 149.

154 Michael Foot, *Aneurin Bevan, 1945–1960*. It is the title of chapter eight in volume two of his biography of Bevan.

155 Ibid., pp. 311–12.

156 Philip Williams (ed.), *The Diary of Hugh Gaitskell, 1945–1956*, Cape, 1983, p. 239, diary entry for 30 April 1951.

157 Ibid., and Foot, *Aneurin Bevan*, p. 246.

158 Foot, *Aneurin Bevan, 1945–60*, pp. 320, 329.

159 Williams (ed.), *The Diary of Hugh Gaitskell, 1945–56*, p. 248. Diary entry for 4 May 1951.

160 Ibid., p. 251. Diary entry for 4 May 1951.

161 Ibid., p. 244. Diary entry for 30 April 1951.

162 Ibid., p. 246. Diary entry for 30 April 1951.

163 Wilson, *Memoirs, 1916–1964*, p. 118.

164 Williams (ed.), *The Diary of Hugh Gaitskell, 1945–50*, pp. 252–3. Diary entry for 4 May 1951.

165 Ibid., p. 251.

166 Bullock, *Ernest Bevin, Foreign Secretary*, p. 835.

167 Quoted in Foot, *Aneurin Bevan, 1945–1960*, p. 330.

168 Ibid., p. 331.

169 Wilson, *Memoirs, 1916–1964*, p. 119.

170 'We've wasted twenty years of the fifty years since the war, fighting one another rather than the Tories . . . In both cases in opposition we stayed in opposition because we fought one another.' Denis Healey, quoted in Peter Hennessy and Caroline Anstey, *Diminished Responsibility. The Essence of Cabinet Government*, Strathclyde *Analysis* paper No. 2, 1991, pp. 8–9.

171 Williams (ed.), *The Diary of Hugh Gaitskell, 1945–1956*, p. 257. Diary entry for 4 May 1951.

172 Daniel Yergin, *The Prize: The Epic Quest for Oil, Money and Power*, Simon and Schuster, 1990, p. 462.

173 Brian Lapping, *The End of Empire*, Granada, 1985, p. 207.

174 PRO, FO 371/9145a, Shepherd to Furlonge, 5 May 1951.

175 Bullock, *Ernest Bevin, Foreign Secretary*, p. 833.

176 William Roger Louis, *The British Empire in the Middle East, 1945–1951*, Clarendon Press, 1984, pp. 642–3; p. 64.

177 Donoughue and Jones, *Herbert Morrison*, p. 510.

178 Morrison's views were expressed at various times at Cabinet level: PRO, CAB 129/46, CP (51) 212, 20 July 1951; CAB 128/20, CM (51) 60, 27 September 1951. Shinwell's flash of jingo was most vividly expressed to the Chiefs of Staff ('We must be prepared to show that our tail could not be twisted interminably and that there was a limit to our willingness to have advantage taken of our good nature'), PRO, DEFE 4/43, COS (51) 86, 23 May 1951.

179 Quoted in Yergin, *The Prize*, p. 464.

180 Lapping, *The End of Empire*, p. 206.

181 Louis, *The British Empire in the Middle East, 1945–1951*, pp. 653–4.

182 Yergin, *The Prize*, pp. 431–49.

183 Louis, *The British Empire in the Middle East, 1945–1951*, pp. 645–6.

184 Quoted in ibid., p. 650.

185 Acheson, *Present at the Creation*, p. 503.

186 Henry Longhurst, *Adventure in Oil: The Story of British Petroleum*, Sidgwick and Jackson, 1959, pp. 143–4.

187 See Kermit Roosevelt, *Countercoup: The Struggle for the Control of Iran*, McGraw Hill, 1979 and C.M. Woodhouse, *Something Ventured*, Granada, 1982.

188 Yergin, *The Prize*, pp. 475–8.

189 Louis, *The British Empire in the Middle East, 1945–1951*, pp. 676–7.
190 Ibid., p. 669.
191 Ben Pimlott (ed.), *The Political Diary of Hugh Dalton, 1918–40, 1945–60*, Cape, 1986, p. 554. Diary entry for 16 September 1951.
192 Ibid.
193 Ibid.
194 Foot, *Aneurin Bevan, 1945–1960*, p. 320.
195 Cairncross (ed.), *The Robert Hall Diaries, 1947–1953*, pp. 166–7. Diary entry for 21 September 1951; p. 174, diary entry for 24 October 1951.
196 Peter Clarke, *A Question of Leadership: Gladstone to Thatcher*, Hamish Hamilton, 1991, p. 205.
197 Harris, *Attlee*, p. 486.
198 Kenneth O. Morgan, *Labour in Power*, OUP, 1984, p. 483.
199 Williams (ed.), *The Diary of Hugh Gaitskell*, p. 293. Diary entry for 16 November 1951.
200 Cairncross (ed.), *The Robert Hall Diaries, 1947–1953*, pp. 168–9, diary entry for 15 October 1951; pp. 173–4, diary entry for 24 October 1951.
201 See Hugh Cudlipp, *Walking on the Water*, Bodley Head, 1976, p. 207.
202 Morgan, *Labour in Power*, p. 484.
203 Clarke, *A Question of Leadership*, p. 198.
204 Anthony King, 'Overload: Problems of Governing in the 1970s', *Political Studies*, xxii, 2–3 (June–September 1975), p. 163.
205 Clarke, *A Question of Leadership*, p. 209.
206 Harris, *Attlee*, p. 450.
207 Quoted in Clarke, *A Question of Leadership*, p. 208.

CHAPTER 11
Mid-century Britain

1 Jean Monnet, *Memoirs*, Collins, 1978, p. 452.
2 Conversation with Professor Eric Hobsbawm, 12 February 1991.
3 Quoted in Peter Hennessy and Caroline Anstey, *From Clogs to Clogs? Britain's Relative Economic Decline Since 1851*, Strathclyde *Analysis* Paper No. 3, Department of Government, Strathclyde University, 1991, p. 21.
4 Speaking in 'The Rewriting on the Wall', BBC Radio 4 *Analysis*, 10 May 1990.
5 Conversation with Sir Ralf Dahrendorf, 2 November 1990.
6 Ben Pimlott (ed.), *The Political Diary of Hugh Dalton, 1918–40, 1945–60*, Cape, 1986, p. 592, diary entry for 30 June 1952.
7 Quoted in Henry Pelling, *Winston Churchill*, Macmillan, 1974, pp. 633–4.
8 The Royal Society of Arts had raised the idea privately with the Government as early as 1943. Bernard Donoughue and G.W. Jones, *Herbert Morrison, Portrait of a Politician*, Weidenfeld, 1973, p. 492, footnote.
9 Ibid.
10 Ibid., p. 493.
11 Ibid., p. 491.
12 Ibid., p. 494.
13 The description is Michael Frayn's. See his 'Festival', in Michael Sissons and Philip French (eds), *The Age of Austerity, 1945–51*, Penguin, 1964, p. 348.
14 Arthur Marwick, 'Britain 1951', *History Today*, Vol. 41, April 1991, p. 8.
15 Frayn, 'Festival', p. 338.
16 Quoted in ibid., p. 334.
17 Ibid., p. 348.
18 See Jessica Mann, 'What a Swell Party it Was', *Independent on Sunday*, 31 March 1991.
19 Marwick, 'Britain 1951', p. 8.

20 Frayn, 'Festival', p. 331.
21 Paul Addison, *Now the War is Over, A Social History of Britain 1945–51*, BBC and Cape, 1985, p. 210.
22 Frayn, 'Festival', pp. 331–2.
23 Anthony Seldon, *Churchill's Indian Summer: The Conservative Government 1951–55*, Hodder, 1981, p. 169.
24 Quoted in Peter Clarke, *A Question of Leadership: Gladstone to Thatcher*, Hamish Hamilton, 1991, p. 135.
25 Conversation with Professor Keith Middlemas, 7 March 1991.
26 Anthony Sampson, *The Arms Bazaar. The Companies, The Dealers, The Bribes: From Vickers to Lockheed*, Hodder 1977, p. 40.
27 Its photograph appears in Addison's *Now the War is Over*, between p. 184 and p. 185.
28 Quoted in ibid., p. 209.
29 Ibid.
30 Lord Butler, *The Art of the Possible*, Penguin, 1973, pp. 158–9.
31 PRO, CAB 66/65, WP (45) 301.
32 Peter Pagnamenta and Richard Overy, *All Our Working Lives*, BBC Books, 1984, p. 254.
33 Ibid., pp. 62–3.
34 Ibid., p. 63.
35 Sampson, *The Arms Bazaar*, p. 104.
36 Professor Keith Middlemas quoted in Hennessy and Anstey, *From Clogs to Clogs?*, p. 18.
37 Sampson, *The Arms Bazaar*, p. 104.
38 Pagnamenta and Overy, *All Our Working Lives*, p. 63.
39 *1949: A Year to Remember* Parkfield Pathé video.
40 Pagnamenta and Overy, *All Our Working Lives*, p. 65.
41 Sampson, *The Arms Bazaar*, p. 104; Max Hastings, *The Korean War*, Pan, 1988, p. 310.
42 Philip Porter, *Jaguar. History of a Classic Marque*, Sidgwick and Jackson, 1988, pp. 58–62.
43 Hennessy and Anstey, *From Clogs to Clogs?*, p. 27.
44 Kenneth Harris, *Attlee*, Weidenfeld, 1982, p. 445.
45 Jon Turney, 'What drives the engines of innovation?' *New Scientist*, 16 November 1991.
46 Tom Wilkie, *British Science and Politics since 1945*, Blackwell, 1991, p. 47.
47 Ibid., p. 52.
48 Ibid.
49 Professor Steiner was speaking in 'Learning Curves', BBC Radio 4 *Analysis*, 31 October 1991.
50 For Sir Christopher Hinton's herculean efforts see Margaret Gowing, *Independence and Deterrence, Britain and Atomic Energy 1945–52, Vol. II*, Macmillan, 1974, Chapters 17 (pp. 154–202), 21 and 22 (pp. 339–441).
51 Frayn, 'Festival', p. 343.
52 Gowing, *Independence and Deterrence, Vol. II*, pp. 481–94.
53 Gowing, *Independence and Deterrence, Britain and Atomic energy 1945–52, Vol. I*, Macmillan, 1974, p. 230.
54 Ibid., p. 229.
55 Alan Wood, *The Groundnut Affair*, Bodley Head, 1950.
56 PRO, CO847/35, 'Native Administration Policy: Minute by F.J. Pedler', 1 November 1946. I am grateful to Mike Brown of the Sir George Monoux Sixth Form College in Walthamstow for bringing this document to my attention at the College's Post-War British History Workshop, 19 April 1991.
57 Edwin Plowden, *An Industrialist in the Treasury, The Postwar Years*, Deutsch, 1989, p. 109.

58 Hennessy and Anstey, *From Clogs to Clogs?*, p. 55.
59 Alan Bullock, *Ernest Bevin, Foreign Secretary, 1945–51*, Heinemann, 1983, p. 844.
60 Serge Bernstein and Peter Morris, *Political Consensus in France and Britain*, Studies in European Culture and Society: Paper 5, European Research Centre, Loughborough University of Technology, 1991, pp. 19–20.
61 See Peter Hennessy, *Whitehall*, Secker and Warburg, 1989, pp. 565–8 for Radcliffe as Victorian.
62 Lord Radcliffe, 'Power and the State', BBC Reith Lecture, broadcast on 2 December 1951.
63 Conversation with Wing-Commander Geoffrey Cooper, 22 May 1991.
64 Keith Middlemas, *Power, Competition and the State, Vol. I, Britain in Search of Balance 1940–61*, Macmillan, 1988, p. 117.
65 Hugh Dalton, *High Tide and After: Memoirs 1945–60*, Muller, 1962, p. 157.
66 Eric Hobsbawm, 'What difference did she make?', *London Review of Books*, 23 May 1991, p. 3.
67 Ibid.
68 Conversation with Professor Mancur Olson, 25 January 1991, as part of the preparation of Hennessy and Anstey, *From Clogs to Clogs?*
69 Ibid.
70 Arthur Marwick, *Culture in Britain since 1945*, Blackwell, 1991, pp. 25–35.
71 Harris, *Attlee*, p. 564.
72 Ibid.
73 William Temple, *The Hope of a New World*, Eyre and Spottiswoode, 1940, p. 20.
74 E.R. Norman, *Church and Society in England 1770–1970: A Historical Study*, OUP, 1976, p. 367.
75 William Temple, *Citizen and Churchman*, Eyre and Spottiswoode, 1941, p. 30.
76 Morgan, *Labour in Power*, p. 299.
77 *The Lambeth Conference, 1948 Encyclical Letter*, quoted in Norman, *Church and Society in England*, p. 376.
78 Ibid., p. 377.
79 Middlemas, *Power, Competition and the State, Vol. I*, p. 116.
80 *Faith in the City. A Call for Action by Church and Nation, The Report of the Archbishop of Canterbury's Commission on Urban Policy Areas*, Church House Publishing, 1985.
81 From *Towards the Conversion of England*, quoted in Norman, *Church and Society in England*, p. 394.
82 Denis Hamilton, *Editor-in-Chief, Fleet Street Memoirs*, Hamish Hamilton, 1989, p. 44.
83 B.G. Sandhurst, *How Heathen is Britain? Part I*, Collins, 1946, p. 27.
84 Quoted in Norman, *Church and Society in England*, p. 396.
85 Ibid., p. 314.
86 A.H. Halsey (ed.), *British Social Trends Since 1900: A Guide to the Changing Social Structure of Britain*, Macmillan, 1988, p. 524.
87 Conversation with Fraser Steel, 20 May 1991.
88 Vidal Dezanic quoted in *Forty Winters On: Memories of Britain's postwar Caribbean Immigrants*, Lambeth Council, 1988, p. 11.
89 Edward Pilkington, *Beyond the Mother Country: West Indians and the Notting Hill White Riots*, I B Taurus, 1988, p. 18.
90 Sam King quoted in *Forty Winters On*, p. 7.
91 Ibid.
92 Professor Stuart Hall, 'Introduction', *Forty Winters On*, p. 4.
93 Sam King quoted in ibid., p. 8.
94 E.C.S. Wade and G. Godfrey Phillips, *Constitutional and Administrative Law*, (ninth edition; ed. H.W. Bradley), Longman, 1977, p. 409.
95 Peter Hennessy, *What the Papers Never Said*, Politics Association, 1985, p. 102.

96   Pilkington, *Beyond the Mother Country*, p. 19.
97   Ibid., p. 103.
98   Sam King in *Forty Winters On*, p. 8.
99   'Baron Baker: The Man Who Discovered Brixton' in *Forty Winters On*, pp. 17–18.
100 Sam King in ibid., p. 8.
101 Steve Humphries and John Taylor, *The Making of Modern London, 1945–85*, Sidgwick and Jackson, 1986, p. 113.
102 Pilkington, *Beyond the Mother Country*, p. 37.
103 PRO, LAB 13/259.
104 *Forty Years On*, p. 13.
105 Hennessy, *What the Papers Never Said*, p. 107.
106 PRO, CAB 128/17, CM (50) 13th Conclusions, Item 7.
107 PRO, CAB Ibid., CM (50) 37th Conclusions, Item 2.
108 PRO, CAB 129/44 CP (51) 51. For the GEN 325 archive see CAB 130/61.
109 PRO, CAB 128/19 CM (51) 15th Conclusions, Item 4.
110 PRO, PREM 8/1308.
111 I am very grateful to Mel Risebraw for letting me see his unpublished undergraduate thesis, 'An Analysis of the Responses of British Government to Coloured Colonial Immigration during the period 1945–51' which he prepared for the University of East Anglia in 1983.
112 Lapping: *End of Empire*, pp. 366–96.
113 Patrick Nuttgens, *The Home Front: Housing the People 1840–1990*, BBC, 1989, p. 67.
114 Nicholas Wapshott and George Brock, *Thatcher: the major new biography*, Futura, 1983, p. 53.
115 Hugo Young, *One of Us: A Biography of Margaret Thatcher*, Macmillan, 1989, p. 31.
116 Robert Harris, *The Making of Neil Kinnock*, Faber, 1984, p. 30.
117 Edward Pearce, *The Quiet Rise of John Major*, Weidenfeld, 1991, pp. 3–4.
118 Colin Brown, 'Happy days are here again . . .', *Independent*, 17 December 1990.
119 *Criminal Statistics England and Wales*, Cmd. 8941, HMSO, 1952.
120 Terence Morris, *Crime and Criminal Justice since 1945*, Blackwell, 1989, p. 59.
121 Cmd. 8941.
122 Morris, *Crime and Criminal Justice since 1945*, p. 91.
123 Ibid., p. 90.
124 Ibid., pp. 89–90.
125 Michelle Perrot, 'Delinquency and the Penitentiary System in 19th Century France, in Robert Forster and Orest Ranum (eds), *Deviants and the Abandoned in French Society*, Johns Hopkins University Press, 1978, p. 219.
126 Martin J. Wiener, *Reconstructing the Criminal: Culture, Law and Policy in England, 1830–1914*, CUP, 1990, p. 11.
127 Ibid., p. 2.
128 Morris, *Crime and Criminal Justice since 1945*, p. 62.
129 Ibid., p. 96.
130 David Hughes, 'The Spivs' in Sissons and French (eds), *The Age of Austerity*, pp. 97–8.
131 Ibid., pp. 86–91.
132 Hopkins, *The New Look*, pp. 100–3.
133 Morris, *Crime and Criminal Justice since 1945*, p. 33.
134 Wiener, *Reconstructing the Criminal*, pp. 9–10.
135 Leslie T. Wilkins, *Delinquent Generations*, HMSO, 1960.
136 Morris, *Crime and Criminal Justice since 1945*, pp. 92–5.
137 For an excellent summary of the 1948 changes see ibid. pp. 75–7.
138 Carl Belz, *The Story of Rock*, Harper Colophon, second edition, 1972, pp. 17–19.
139 Humphries and Taylor, *The Making of Modern London, 1945–1985*, p. 30.

140   Hastings, *The Korean War*, p. 409.
141   Phillip Whitehead in a review of Max Hastings' *The Korean War*, in the *Listener*, 22 October 1987, pp. 22–3.
142   Asa Briggs, *The BBC, The First Fifty Years*, OUP, 1985, p. 382.
143   Ibid., pp. 247, 382.
144   Ibid., p. 295.
145   'The Goons, 23 December 1956', in Robert Low (ed.), *The Observer Book of Profiles*, W.H. Allen, 1991, p. 323.
146   Dave Gelly, 'Blown up, deaded, but not forgotten', *Observer*, 26 May 1991.
147   D.R. Thorpe, *Selwyn Lloyd*, Cape, 1989, pp. 132–41.
148   Cmd. 8116, HMSO, 1951.
149   Briggs, *The BBC: The First Fifty Years*, p. 263.
150   Cmd. 8291, HMSO, 1951.
151   Briggs, *The BBC: The First Fifty Years*, p. 260.
152   Ibid., p. 265.
153   Ibid., p. 270.
154   Lord Briggs applied it to the years 1783–1867. See his *The Age of Improvement*, Longman, 1959.
155   Butler, *Art of the Possible*, pp. 158–9.
156   Listener, *One Hundred Years of Economic Statistics*, pp. 44–5.
157   B. Seebohm Rowntree and G.R. Lavers, *Poverty and the Welfare State: A third social survey of York dealing only with economic questions*, Longmans, 1951, p. 35.
158   Ibid., p. 31.
159   Ibid., p. 39.
160   Ibid., p. 45.
161   Ibid., p. 24.
162   See David Donnison, *The Politics of Poverty*, Martin Robertson, 1982, pp. 5–8.
163   See Jane Lewis, *Women in England 1870–1950*, Wheatsheaf Books, 1984. I am grateful to Jennifer Marchbank of the Department of Government, University of Strathclyde, for bringing these figures to my attention.
164   Michael Young, *The Chipped White Cups of Dover: A discussion of the possibility of a new progressive party*, Unit 2, 1960, p. 10.
165   See D.V. Glass (ed.), *Social Mobility in Britain*, Routledge, 1954.
166   John H. Goldthorpe (in collaboration with Catriona Llewellyn and Clive Payne, *Social Mobility and Class Structure in Modern Britain*, second edition, OUP, 1987, p. 327.
167   Ibid., p. 328.

Index